This book, as always, is dedicated to our children,

Katie, Jamie, Alex and Lauren.

We love you.

To my mother, Dorothy Caroline (Schick) McEachern,

I will miss you every day of my life.

Until we meet again.

Deborah

InsidersChoice to Microsoft MCP/MCSE: Installing, Configuring, and Administering Microsoft® Windows® XP Professional, Exam 70-270 Second Edition

Deborah Timmons, MCT, MCSE
Technical Editor:
Patrick Timmons, B.Sc., MCT, MCSE+I

About the Author

Deborah Timmons is a Microsoft Certified Trainer and Microsoft Certified Systems Engineer. She came into the Microsoft technical field after six years in the adaptive technology field, providing technology and training for persons with disabilities. She is the President and co-owner of Integrator Systems Inc.

Patrick Timmons is a Microsoft Certified Systems Engineer + Internet. He has been working in the IT industry for approximately 15 years, specializing in network engineering, and has recently completed his Bachelor of Science degree, with a Major in Computer Science. Patrick is the CEO of Integrator Systems Inc., a company based in Ottawa, Ontario, Canada.

Patrick and Deborah have four children--Lauren, Alexander, James and Katherine who take up a lot of their rare spare time.

Integrator Systems Inc. designs and implements network solutions based on Microsoft and 3Com technology, produces custom applications based on customer needs, provides local and remote network troubleshooting and support, and provides courseware, training, and consultants to various horizontal and vertical markets. Integrator Systems is a Microsoft Certified Partner and 3Com Focus Partner.

About the Book

As Microsoft Certified Trainers and practicing IT professionals, we drew on our backgrounds to design this study guide specifically to help you *pass* the MCP/MCSE Certification: Installing, Configuring, and Administering Microsoft Windows XP Professional Exam 70-270.

Part of the TotalRecall IT Certification Success System, this comprehensive study manual provides detailed information for each exam topic, includes numerous practical tips, and cites a wealth of useful websites, articles and other learning aids found in no other book. Since it also offers lots of real-world material, we know you will continue to reach for this handy reference when tackling challenges on the job.

Each chapter includes a pre- and post-assessment quiz to measure your comprehension of each exam topic. Chapter summaries reinforce key points. The large glossary at the end of the book provides a review of essential exam-related terms and concepts that will prove invaluable just before taking the exam. Helpful tips and time management techniques will alleviate pre-exam jitters and put you in control. For implementing Windows XP Professional in a production environment, tips on pre-installation, workstation tuning, application tuning, registry hacks, and maintenance techniques are included.

And we offer another exclusive—a FREE download of the popular BeachFront Quizzer test engine with integrated eBook. The test engine includes practice exams drawn from a base of over 300 questions, along with detailed explanations linked to related chapters in an eBook version of this manual. Many explanations also link to additional resources, such as web sites, articles, etc. The adaptive nature of the BeachFront Quizzer software is that it keeps generating types of questions that you find difficult to answer until they are no longer hard for you. By focusing on your rough spots, we will get you certified fast—or get money back!

You can also get this same comprehensive study manual with a CD-ROM of the BeachFront Quizzer test engine, instead of an free download, in our *InsideScoop* to *MCP/MCSE Certification: Installing, Configuring, and Administering Microsoft Windows XP Professional Exam 70-270.*

If you are looking for in-depth understanding, then this comprehensive package of study manual, free test engine download, and eBook is the complete "certification success system" for you. However, if you are already networking with other professionals and don't need a thorough grounding in each exam topic, then try one of our two other guides from TotalRecall Publications. *ExamInsight for the MCP/MCSE Certification: Installing, Configuring, and Administering Microsoft Windows XP Professional Exam 70-270* is a "refresher course" with compact information and practice questions that includes a 50% discount for a BeachFront Quizzer online test engine. *ExamWise for MCP/MCSE Certification: Installing, Configuring, and Administering Microsoft Windows XP Professional Exam 70-270* is a handy Q&A workbook that uses a unique format of two questions per page, with answers and explanations on the reverse page. It also includes 30-day free access to a BeachFront Quizzer online exam.

All four books carry TotalRecall's proven guarantee—pass, or get money back! See our web site for details www.totalrecallpress.com.

See our web site for details http://www.totalrecallpress.com

A Quick overview of the book chapters:

Table of Contents

Introduction

I've realized something as I've stared at this blank page. It can be harder to write an introduction to a book than it is to write the book itself. What can I say that is new and different and exciting?

We've all seen the commercials on television for Windows XP: wonderful shadings, bodies soaring through the air, and the familiar Madonna tune. The first time I installed XP Professional, my initial reaction was, "Wow! That's colorful!" XP provided a shiny, new, slick user interface that removed some of the common irritants with previous incarnations of Windows–hundreds of desktop shortcuts cluttering up the screen, twenty copies of Internet Explorer open on the taskbar.

But having worked in the technical field for a number of years, I knew that slick and shiny wasn't going to make me want to run out and start upgrading all my systems. I needed a better reason. What's new with XP? What makes it different? Better?

As with any new technology, it took a little while to find the answers. Those answers are the ones I've tried to provide to you in this book. I've done my best to show you all the new features of Windows XP Professional, noted the differences between Professional and Home Edition, and brought you the "guts" of XP—the similarities and differences between it and the previous versions of Windows.

Hopefully, you will finish the book with a good grasp of what XP Professional really is. You should end up with the information you need to make the decisionto upgrade or not to upgrade. After all, that really is the question!

Deborah Timmons

President, Integrator Systems Inc.

How To Read This Book

The styles used in this book are listed in the following table. In the left column is the definition of what is being displayed and the right column displays the formatting used for the definition.

INTERNET ADDRESS	HTTP://WWW.INTEGRATORSYSTEMS.CA/
Command to type	**CONVERT D: /FS:NTFS**
Replacement in Commands	drive
Option to select	Clean Install
Tips, Notes:	**Remember:** **Don't run with scissors**

Chapter 1: Installing Windows XP Professional

The objective of this chapter is to provide you with an understanding of the following:

1. Perform an attended install of Windows XP Professional.
2. Perform an unattended install of Windows XP Professional using Remote Installation Services.
3. Perform an unattended install of Windows XP Professional using the System Preparation Tool.
4. Create unattended answer files by using Setup Manager to automate the installation of Windows XP Professional.
5. Upgrade from a previous version of Windows to Windows XP Professional.
6. Prepare a computer to meet upgrade requirements.
7. Migrate existing user environments to a new installation.
8. Perform post-installation updates and product activation.
9. Troubleshoot failed installations.

Getting Ready – (Questions)

1). What are the minimum processor requirements to install Windows XP Professional?

2). What are the recommended RAM requirements for a Windows XP Professional installation?

3). How can you verify that your hardware will support Windows XP Professional?

4). Can I upgrade from Windows 3.1 to Windows XP Professional?

5). If I create a dual-boot system, with both the Windows XP operating system and Windows XP Professional, will Microsoft still provide me with support?

Getting Ready – (Answers)

1). To install Windows XP Professional, you must have, at minimum, 233 MHz 5th generation or better, for example an Intel Pentium MMX or an AMD K6-2 processor.

2). While you only need 64B RAM to install Windows XP Professional, it is recommended that you have a minimum of 128MB RAM, with a 4GB recommended maximum limit.

3). You should always verify your hardware by checking the Hardware Compatibility List (HCL). If your hardware device is not listed, contact the manufacturer and check whether a Windows XP Professional compatible driver exists. You can also use the Upgrade Advisor, either online or included with XP Professional.

4). Unlike using the upgrade path to Windows NT 4.0 Workstation, you CANNOT upgrade from Windows 3.1 to Windows XP Professional. A full installation is required. There is also no upgrade path from Windows 95, Windows NT Server 3.51, 4.0 or Windows 2000 Server to Windows XP.

5). Microsoft did not support dual-boot systems between Windows 9x and Windows NT 4.0 Workstation. Microsoft will now support dual or multiple boot systems between Windows XP Professional and a number of other operating systems. Certain caution must be taken with dual or multi-boot systems.

I Introduction

Windows XP is the "latest and greatest" incarnation of the Microsoft Windows operating system. Taking the strengths of the Windows 2000 suite–reliability, strong standards-based security and manageability–and combining them with the plug-and-play and ease-of-use features of Windows ME, have resulted in an operating system that is robust enough for a professional environment and friendly enough to use at home.

eTesting Labs (Ziff Davis) was hired by Microsoft to do independent testing of XP against earlier versions of Windows, including Windows 2000. They concluded that XP was the fastest version of Windows to date, without sacrificing any of the much-needed stability and security features of Windows 2000. Full test results can be found at: http://www.etestinglabs.com/MAIN/REPORTS/MICROSOFT.ASP or

http://www.veritest.com/clients/reports/microsoft/default.asp

Windows XP was developed on Windows 2000 technology, with an "at home" version and a "Professional" version, each geared to meet the needs of the selected client base. This book is taking a look at the Professional edition of Windows XP–the version you are likely to encounter during your workday. Throughout the course of this chapter, we will examine the key issues surrounding the installation of Windows XP Professional in your work environment. As you review this material, think of these questions: Are my systems ready for Windows XP? Can I upgrade or should I do a fresh installation? What method of installation is going to be the most efficient and effective in my corporate environment? How can I quickly and effectively troubleshoot problems that may occur?

II Preparing To Install Windows XP

Well, the decision has been made. Your work environment is going to Windows XP Professional. Nevertheless, before you start upgrading your systems, a careful planning process should occur. Microsoft recommends a five-step process, as outlined in Figure 1.1 below.

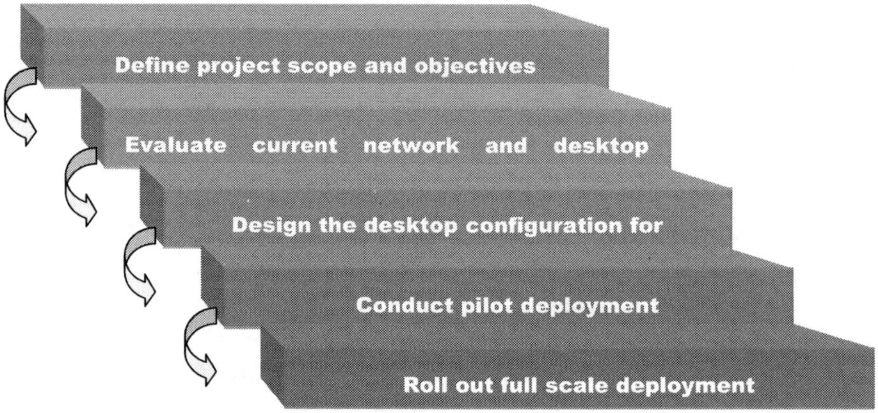

Figure 1-1: Five Principal Planning Stages

Define Project Scope and Objectives

The very first step in planning a deployment of Windows XP Professional in your workplace is to determine the project scope. Some of the factors you should consider include:

- How many computers are affected in the rollout?
- Are they in the same location or in different locations?
- What is your physical network?
- What is the scope of the rollout? Is this just a change in desktop, or are you upgrading servers at the time? Deploying Active Directory? Upgrading your hardware?
- Are you planning on standardizing the desktops? Who will be administering the network? What security needs to be in place?

Evaluate Current Network and Desktop Environments

As with most operating systems, Windows XP Professional has a minimum set of hardware requirements in order to successfully install. Table 1.1 outlines both the minimum and the recommended system requirements needed for installation.

Minimum Hardware Requirements

It is important to note that Windows XP Professional has advanced power management, as well as plug-and-play features. On some computers, the BIOS version may not be compatible with Professional. This is because it may not have a compliant ACPI BIOS. Without upgrading the BIOS, you won't be able to gain full power management functionality, which is ACPI-based. APM (Advanced Power Management), which is an older technology, is supported in an extremely limited way since it is only available for notebook computers. If the BIOS is not upgraded prior to installation, you will need to reinstall Windows XP Professional to gain full power management functionality.

Please note that XP Professional supports both single and dual CPU systems.

Before installation of Windows XP Professional, check the BIOS on the computer, both portable and desktop, to verify that the BIOS has been updated. If the system does not have ACPI functionality, the BIOS is not compatible. You will need to obtain the updated BIOS from the manufacturer. Most manufacturers carry BIOS updates on their websites.

> **Remember** Know the minimum and recommended hardware requirements for Windows XP Professional.

	MINIMUM	RECOMMENDED
PROCESSOR	233 MHz 5th generation or better Intel Pentium MMX AMD K6-2	300 MHz 6th generation or better Intel Pentium II AMD Athlon
RAM	64 MB	128 MB (4 GB maximum)
HARD DISK	2 GB with 650 MB free space (more if installing over a network)	2 GB free space
DISPLAY	VGA with compatible or higher monitor	SVGA with Plug and Play Monitor
REMOVABLE MEDIA	CD-ROM or DVD drive (required for compact disc installation).	CD-ROM or DVD drive (12x or faster)
INPUT DEVICES	Keyboard, mouse or other pointing device	Keyboard, mouse or other pointing device
NETWORK	Network adapter (required for network installation).	Network adapter

Table 1-1: Minimum/Recommended Hardware Requirements

Hardware and Software Compatibility

The Hardware Compatibility List (HCL) is nothing new to those of you who have worked with Windows NT products in the past. For those of you who have not, the HCL is a list of hardware devices that have been extensively tested for compatibility with NT-based operating systems. When Windows XP Professional is installed on a system where the hardware is not compatible, installation can fail.

Verify all hardware by checking the HCL. You can check the most up-to-date information at http://www.microsoft.com/hcl

You can also use the Upgrade Advisor, which is included with the Windows XP Installation CD. This is illustrated in Figure 1.2 below. It is also available for online use, or download, at WWW.MICROSOFT.COM/WINDOWSXP/PRO/HOWTOBUY/UPGRADING/ADVISOR.ASP

The Upgrade Advisor is a tool, supplied by Microsoft, which will check your system hardware and software to verify its readiness for upgrade to Windows XP. Running Upgrade Advisor online has one advantage. If your system needs updates that are available on the Windows Update Web site, Upgrade Advisor will find and install the updates for you.

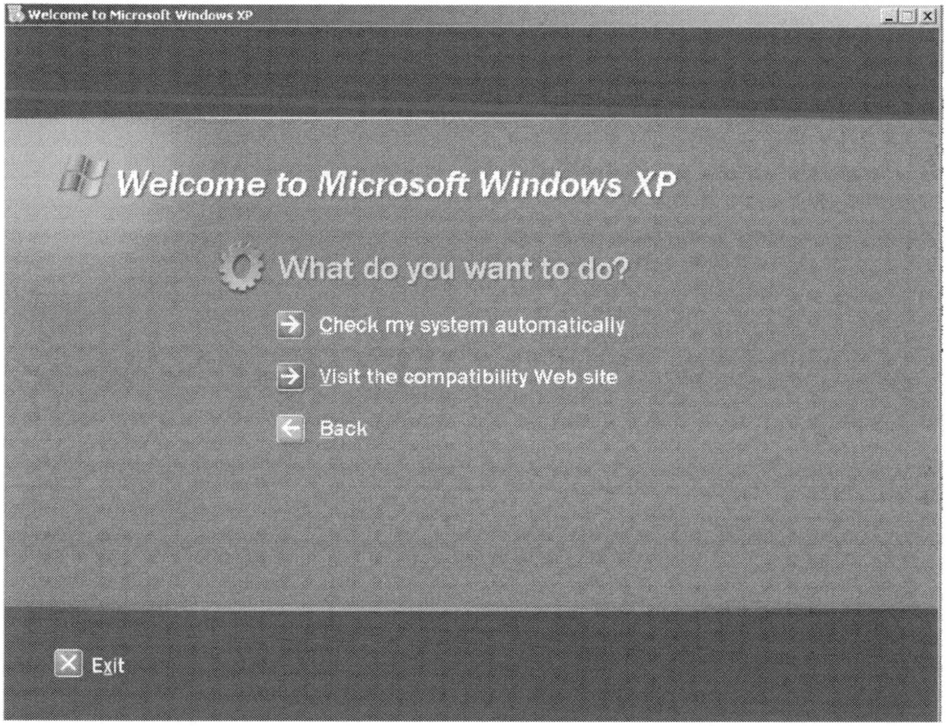

Figure 1-2: Windows XP Upgrade Advisor

If your hardware device is shown as incompatible, contact the manufacturer and check whether a Windows XP Professional compatible driver exists.

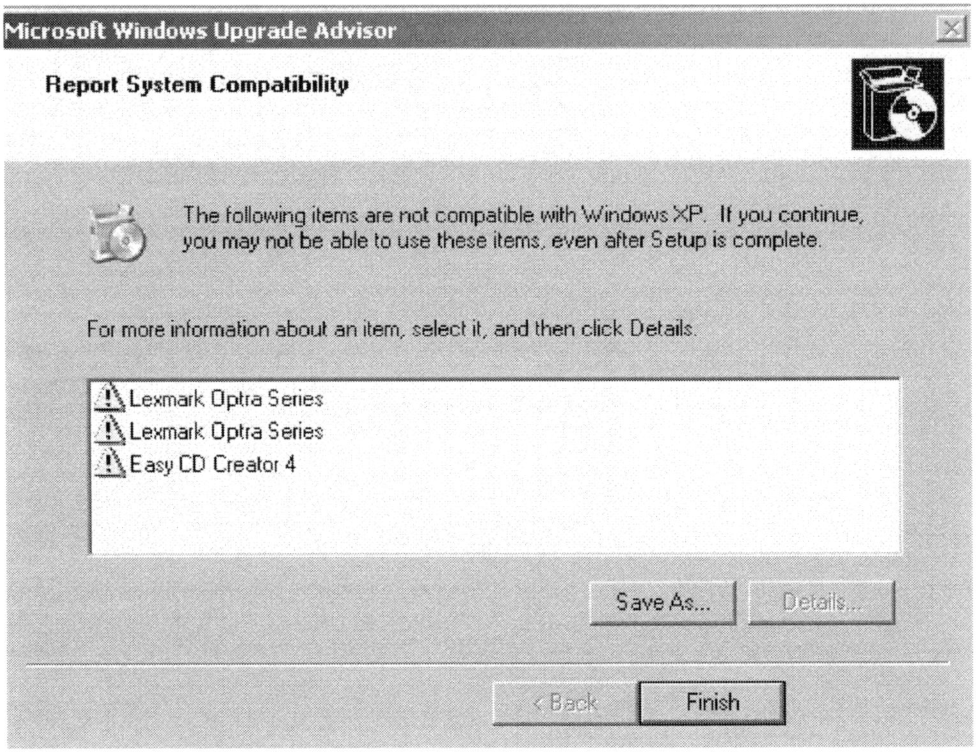

Figure 1-3: System Compatibility

It is best to test your applications for compatibility with Windows XP Professional to make sure that they work as efficiently and effectively as they did under the previous operating system. You may find that you may have to do some modifications to eliminate problems that occur–by reinstalling the application after upgrade, purchasing an XP-friendly upgrade, using migration DLLs, or using the "Run in Compatibility Mode" tool. Some system tools, such as Scan Disk, cannot be upgraded to Windows XP Professional. If your software is using 16-bit drivers, it will be necessary to upgrade these drivers to the 32-bit equivalents that are Windows XP compatible. Check with the manufacturer to see if these drivers are available.

Network Issues

As part of the evaluation of your network environment, you should ensure that a record of the current network architecture is in place. This should include its topology, current size, and the pattern of traffic. You should document which users need access to which resources (applications, data, newsgroups, printers, etc.), what level of access they currently have, and how they obtain access. Are they accessing the data through access, or are data accessed through shared folders? Do they use Internet printers? Is read-only access required?

Diagrams and checklists can assist in documenting your network in the project plan. You may wish to diagram both the physical and logical network that is currently in place. Your physical network diagram could include cables, server names, IP addresses, domain membership, and locations of printers, hubs, switches, bridges, routers, proxy servers and other network devices, as well as the WAN connections. Your logical diagram could include domain architecture, the server roles–especially primary and backup domain controllers, DHCP, DNS and WINS servers—as well as any trust relationships and policy restrictions that could affect your deployment.

Design the Desktop Configuration

To decide which features of Windows XP Professional will work best in your business environment, you need to have identified your business needs. Those business needs will determine how you want to implement features to assist the administration of both users and computers in your environment. There is one important word in all of this–standardize!

As we progress through this book, you will become more aware of the new and exiting features of Windows XP Professional. Keep a standard desktop design in mind while you explore these features. The end result should be a standardized desktop design that will meet users' needs and simplify the administration.

Conduct Pilot Deployment

Before you rollout Windows XP Professional to all users in your work environment, it is an excellent idea to "test drive" your installation plan.

A pilot deployment should be a replica of your planned final deployment, only in miniature. When creating the base for your pilot rollout, you should make sure that the systems (and persons) involved in the test are a cross-section of your current work environment, both in terms of the operating systems being upgraded, as well as the user recipients of the deployment. You don't want to test your deployment only on users that "know what they are doing." It is equally as important to understand the impact of the rollout on all users—those who are computer-proficient as well as those who will require some "hand-holding" to survive the upgrade. This is especially important if you are designing an upgrade from the Windows 9x platform (including Windows ME). The Windows 9x platform does not, of course, include such features as domain computer accounts, the need to logon locally, and NTFS file systems. These new features can cause some disruption among your users, and it is important to be able to be prepared, in advance, for increased user support demand.

With a good pilot deployment plan, you will be able to estimate the time it will take to perform the final upgrade, how many upgrades you can sustain at one time, and how much support your users will require post-install. You can also catch any errors you may have made in your installation plan, and correct them prior to a full-scale deployment.

Keeping that in mind, let's examine some of the issues regarding deployment of Windows XP Professional.

Upgrading vs. Clean Installation

As noted previously, only certain operating systems can be upgraded to Windows XP Professional. These operating systems are Windows 9x, Windows ME and Windows NT Workstation 3.51 and 4.0.

The advantage to an upgrade is that your existing user and application settings are preserved. Setup will replace only the existing Windows operating system files. The disadvantage is that some applications might not be compatible with Windows XP Professional. They may not function properly, or at all, after an upgrade.

The following table outlines which Windows operating systems can be upgraded to Windows XP Professional:

Operating System	XP Professional
Windows 3.1	No
Windows Operating Systems Evaluation Version	No
Windows Operating Systems Server Version	No
Windows 95	No
Windows 98/98 SE	Yes
Windows ME	Yes
Windows NT Workstation 3.51	No
Windows NT Workstation 4.0	Yes
Windows XP	Yes
Windows XP Home Edition	Yes

Table 1-2: Upgrading your operating system

Remember: Unlike using the upgrade path to Windows NT 4.0 Workstation, you CANNOT upgrade from Windows 3.1 to Windows XP Professional. A full installation is required. There is also no upgrade path from any version of Server, including NT 3.51, 4.0 and Windows 2000.

You may choose to do an upgrade to Windows XP Professional if:

- You are currently running Windows 98, Windows ME or Windows NT Workstation 4.0 or Windows XP, AND you wish to upgrade your existing operating system with Windows XP Professional;
- You have verified that installed applications are compatible with Windows XP Professional;
- You need to retain your existing user and application settings; and
- You wish to keep any local users or groups created under NT Workstation.

You will need to do a clean installation of Windows XP Professional if:

- You currently have no operating system on your computer;
- You are currently running an operating system that does not support upgrading to Windows XP Professional;
- Your operating system supports an upgrade, but it is not necessary to retain user and application settings; or
- You have multiple partitions and wish to retain the existing operating system to co-exist with Windows XP Professional; that is, you wish to have a dual-boot system.

Dual/Multiple Booting Systems

Microsoft did not support dual-boot systems between Windows 9x and Windows NT 4.0 Workstation. This, of course, did not mean it could not be done. It just meant that if you ran into trouble, calling Microsoft was not going to get you any sympathy.

Microsoft now acknowledges that many people like to have multi-boot systems. While they do issue some cautions on multi-boot systems, such as disk space and dynamic disk issues, they have posted an article on their site “Multibooting with Windows 2000 and Windows XP.”

The URL for this site is currently:

http://www.microsoft.com/windows2000/techninfo/administration/management/mltiboot.asp

Your first concern should be whether your current disk configuration supports multibooting. The Microsoft article mentioned above will give you further details. Keep in mind that each operating system must be installed on its own partition. Microsoft will not support multiple-boot systems where Windows XP Professional and another operating system co-exist on the same partition

DISK CONFIGURATION	CAUTIONS ON MULTIPLE BOOT SYSTEMS
Basic disk or disks	Will support multiple operating systems, from DOS on. Each operating system must reside on a separate partition or logical drive.
Single dynamic disk	Can only support one operating system.
Multiple dynamic disks	Each disk can support one installation of Windows 2000, Windows XP or "Whistler" (current name for XP Server). Dynamic disks cannot support any operating system prior to Windows 2000.

Table 1-3: Disk Configuration and Multi-booting

The following summarizes some of the key points that must be remembered when dealing with dual or multiple-boot systems in conjunction with Windows XP Professional.

- Install each operating system on a different partition and install applications used with each O/S in the partition where it resides.
- Install the latest operating system last. For example, if you are creating a machine that will dual-boot between Windows XP and Windows XP Professional, install Windows 2000 first and then Windows XP.

> **Warning:** I installed Windows XP Professional onto a system that was currently running Windows XP. XP was installed onto a separate partition, to ensure dual-boot capabilities. However, after the XP installation, no selection menu was provided, and the system booted only into Windows XP. Editing the boot.ini file eliminated that problem and the system now successfully dual-boots.

- Do not install Windows 2000 or Windows XP on a compressed drive unless the drive was compressed using the NTFS file system. The NTFS should be the version released with Service Pack 4, Windows NT 4.0.
- The primary partition on a dual-boot system for any operating system prior to Windows 95 OSR2 must be FAT. Windows 95 OSR2 and newer releases (Windows 98, ME) can have a primary partition that is FAT or FAT32. NTFS may be used on systems booting between NT 4.0 and XP, if NT 4.0 is installed on the system partition. However, if NT 4.0 is not installed on the system partition, it is recommended that the system partition be formatted with FAT.
- Each operating system will need to have its own installation of software, such as MS Office. Programs cannot be shared across operating systems.
- If you are using NTFS, and you are dual booting between Windows NT 4.0 Workstation and Windows XP Professional, the Windows NT 4.0 Workstation installation must be upgraded to Service Pack 4 or later before continuing with the Professional install. This is due to the changes in NTFS (see the Chapter 4 section on File Systems)

There are a number of other precautions to be observed on dual-boot systems beyond these main ones. Before proceeding with a multiple-boot system, make sure you do your research and check any new information or technical notes on the Microsoft website.

Backing Up Critical Files

The final consideration before implementing a clean installation of Windows XP Professional is, of course, backing up your critical files. All files will be lost upon installation of the new operating system. How you choose to perform this backup depends on the operating system currently in use, whether you are using the built-in backup utility of the operating system or a third-party application.

These are the important factors to remember:

- Data files should always be backed up, verified, and preferably given a trial restore before installation. This includes any electronic mail that is not stored on a mail server.
- Application files, operating system files, and temporary files do NOT need to be backed up. Applications will need to be reinstalled, operating system files will not be necessarily need to be reinstalled, and temp files are, well, temp files.

Pop Quiz 1.1

Pop Quiz 1.1 Questions

1. To obtain full power management functionality, what functionality should your BIOS have?
2. How can you verify that your hardware and software are compatible with Windows XP Professional before performing an upgrade installation?
3. You are currently running Windows NT 3.51 Server. Can you upgrade to Windows XP Professional?
4. You plan on running a dual-boot system, running Windows NT 4.0 Workstation and Windows XP Professional, with an NTFS file system. What additional task must you do?
5. Before implementing a clean installation of Windows XP Professional, which critical files should be backed up?

Pop Quiz 1.1 *Answers*

1. To have full power management functionality, which is ACPI-based, your system must have a compliant ACPI BIOS. APM is supported, but is limited to notebook computers.
2. Use the Upgrade Advisor. The Upgrade Advisor is a tool, supplied by Microsoft, which will check your system hardware and software to verify its readiness for upgrade to Windows XP.
3. No. You cannot upgrade from any Windows Server to Windows XP Professional. A clean installation is required.
4. You must upgrade the NT 4.0 Workstation to Service Pack 4 or later before continuing with the Professional installation. This is due to changes in NTFS that were implemented in Service Pack 4.
5. You should always back up data files, including any electronic mail that is not stored on a server. These files should also be verified and a trial restore performed before performing the installation. Application files, operating system files and temporary files do not need to be backed up.

Installation Methods

Whew! All that information and we have not even yet begun to do the installation yet! However, careful planning can lessen or totally eliminate a lot of installation headaches.

So now that we have done all that preparatory work, let's install Windows XP Professional.

You can configure your disk partitions prior to installation, or you can create the partition as part of the setup procedure. It is recommended that Windows XP Professional be installed on a 2GB partition. The following table outlines the possible installation methods for Windows XP, and what is required for each method:

	UPGRADE OR CLEAN INSTALL	HARDWARE REQUIRED	SERVER REQUIRED?	MODIFICATIONS ALLOWED?
CD-ROM	Both	CD-ROM	No	No
UNATTENDED	Both	A network boot disk if using a remote distribution share, or a CD-ROM drive and a floppy disk drive	No	Yes—must modify the Unattend.txt
SYSPREP	Clean Install	All recipient computers need similar hardware configurations	No	Yes—must update and reimage master installation
RIS	Clean Install	PXE-enabled recipient computers	Windows 2000 Server with AD	Yes—mmodify answer file.
SMS	Upgrade	Fast connection to SMS site	Windows Server with SMS, running an SMS site	Yes—create an advertising package

Table 1-4: Installation Methods

III Installation – Standalone Methods

Whew! All that information, and we have not even begun to do the installation yet! However, careful pre-planning can lessen or totally eliminate a lot of installation headaches.

Once you have selected the installation method(s) that will work best for your environment, successfully piloted the rollout to a variety of test groups, and completed troubleshooting any errors you encounter in the pilot, you are ready for full deployment. So now that we have done all that preparatory work, let's install Windows XP Professional.

You can configure your disk partitions prior to installation or you can create the partition as part of the setup procedure. It is recommended that Windows XP Professional be installed on a 2GB partition.

We will spend this section examining the different methods of installation that you may select for your XP deployment.

As mentioned in the last section, there are a number of ways you can install Windows XP Professional. Some methods will support only a clean installation, others only an upgrade installation, while still others will support both. Which method, or methods, you choose will depend on several different business factors. Some of these factors may include:

- Number of computers involved in the deployment
- Amount of user interaction you wish to allow in the installment
- Need to customize the installations
- How homogenous the hardware is
- Active Directory Service availability

We are about to look at a couple of the stand-alone methods of installation—methods used when you are either installing only one system, or are installing a system that currently does not have network connectivity.

Pop Quiz 1.1 *Answers*

1. To have full power management functionality, which is ACPI-based, your system must have a compliant ACPI BIOS. APM is supported, but is limited to notebook computers.
2. Use the Upgrade Advisor. The Upgrade Advisor is a tool, supplied by Microsoft, which will check your system hardware and software to verify its readiness for upgrade to Windows XP.
3. No. You cannot upgrade from any Windows Server to Windows XP Professional. A clean installation is required.
4. You must upgrade the NT 4.0 Workstation to Service Pack 4 or later before continuing with the Professional installation. This is due to changes in NTFS that were implemented in Service Pack 4.
5. You should always back up data files, including any electronic mail that is not stored on a server. These files should also be verified and a trial restore performed before performing the installation. Application files, operating system files and temporary files do not need to be backed up.

Installation Methods

Whew! All that information and we have not even yet begun to do the installation yet! However, careful planning can lessen or totally eliminate a lot of installation headaches.

So now that we have done all that preparatory work, let's install Windows XP Professional.

You can configure your disk partitions prior to installation, or you can create the partition as part of the setup procedure. It is recommended that Windows XP Professional be installed on a 2GB partition. The following table outlines the possible installation methods for Windows XP, and what is required for each method:

Installation Steps

No matter which method you choose, the steps for installation remain the same. When Setup begins, the Windows XP Professional Setup screen appears in text mode, as in Figure 1.4 below.

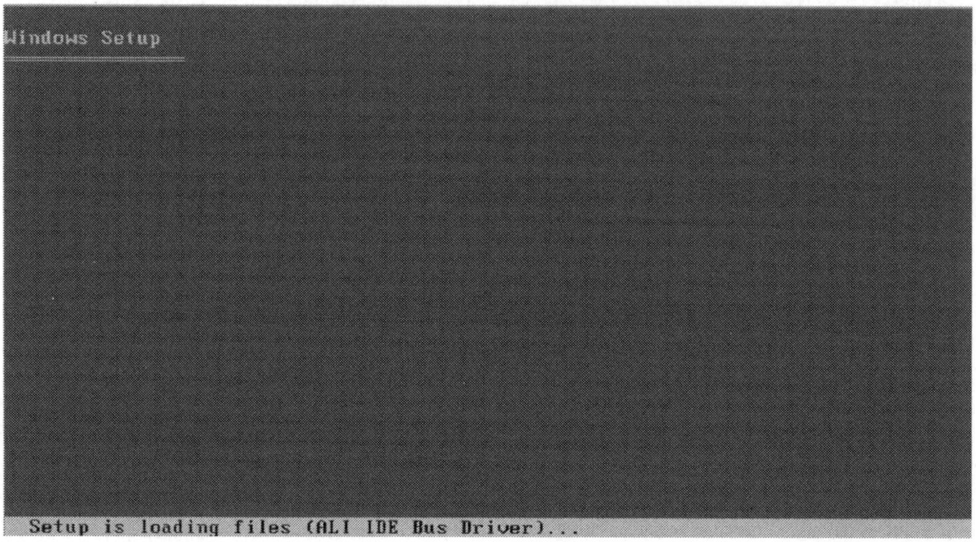

Figure 1-4: Setup Load Files

Setup inspects the computer's hardware configuration and then installs the Setup and driver files.

After all files are installed, the Welcome to Windows XP Professional Setup screen appears, still in text mode. Three choices are given for your selection (Figure 1-5):

- To setup Windows XP now, press ENTER.
- To repair a Windows XP installation using Recovery Console, press R.
- To quit Setup without installing Windows XP Professional, press F3.
- To continue with the installation, press ENTER.

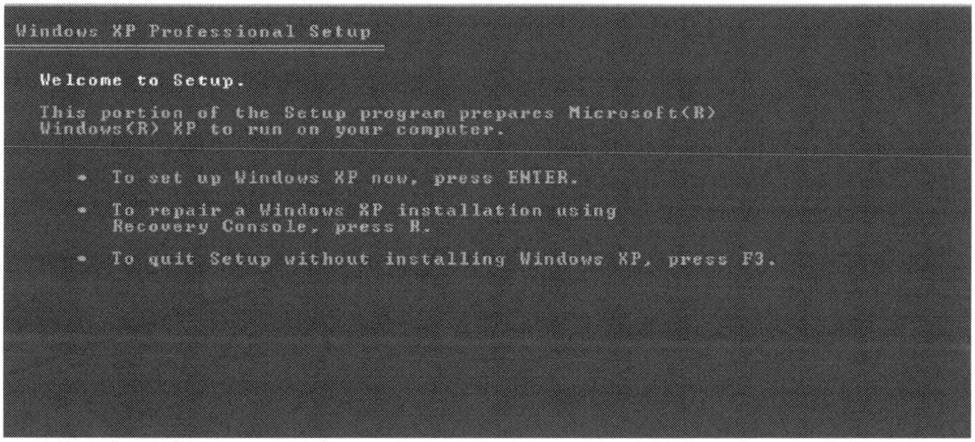

Figure 1-5: Selecting the Setup Option

The next text screen displays the license agreement. You will need to press Page Down a few times to read the entire agreement. When you have read the entire agreement, and are at the bottom of the screen, press F8 if you agree to the terms outlined and wish to continue with the installation.

The Windows XP Professional Setup screen appears, welcoming you to Setup, and then a second, text-based screen appears with the following options (Figure 1-6):

- To setup Windows 2000 on the selected partition, press ENTER.
- If you have unpartitioned space on your hard drive, Setup will ask whether you wish to create a partition. Press C to select this option.
- If you wish to create a new partition, but want to delete the existing partition first, press D.

> **NOTE:** Any new partition will need to be formatted either as FAT or NTFS.

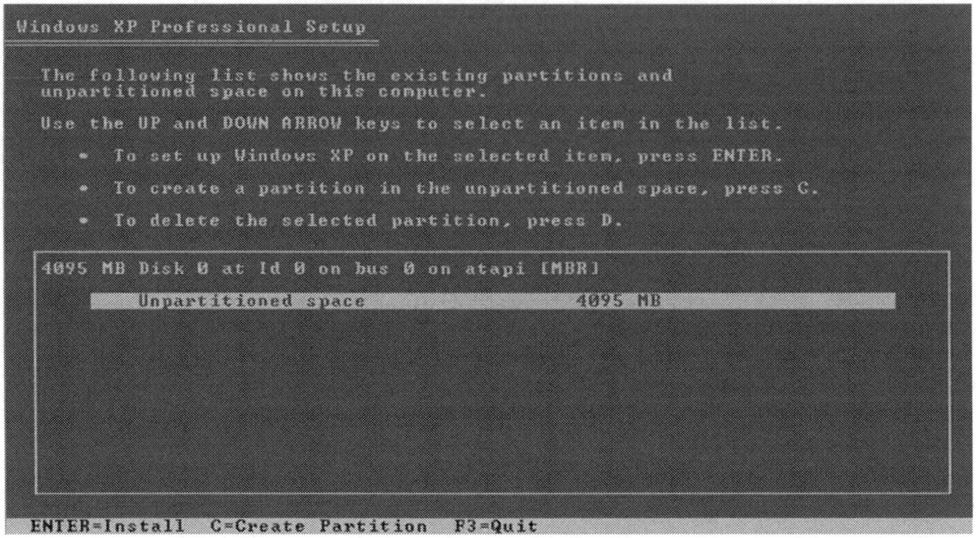

Figure 1-6: Selecting a Partition

If the partition you select for installation is a FAT partition, Windows Setup will ask if you wish to leave the current file system intact, convert the existing file system to NTFS, or format the partition using the NTFS file system. Figure 1-7 below displays the screen you will view.

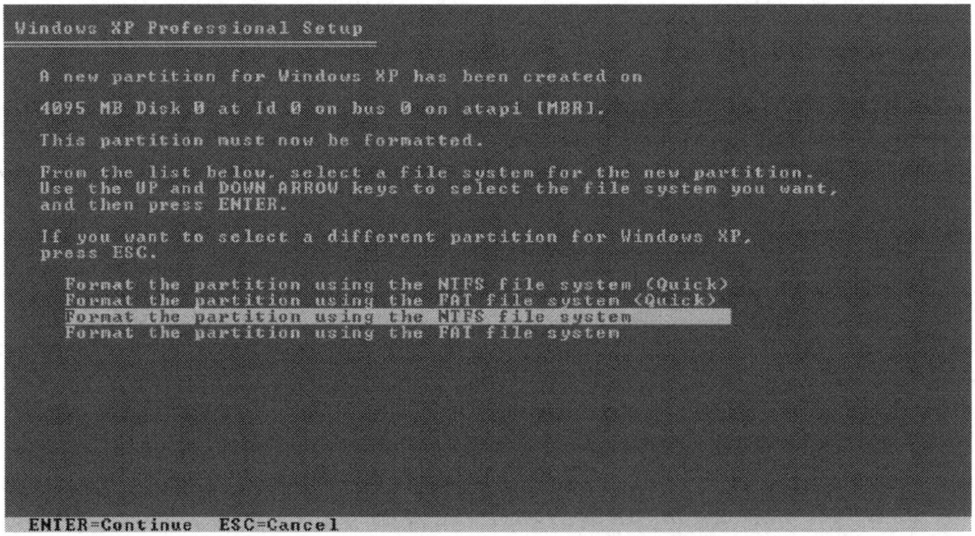

Figure 1-7: Formatting the Partition

The final step in the text-based mode is for Setup to examine the existing hard drive or drives. It then copies the files needed to complete the Windows XP Professional installation to the hard disk and reboots the computer. Upon restart, Setup enters the GUI mode. The Windows 2000 GUI mode Setup Wizard screen appears at this point. First, Setup will collect system information. It will then do Dynamic Update, if possible.

> **Remember:** Converting a partition to NTFS leaves any files that presently exist on the partition intact. Formatting will delete all files on the partition in the process.
>
> **NOTE:** Dynamic Update is a new feature of Windows XP. During the installation process, before any files are even installed, Windows XP checks the Microsoft website for critical updates. If any are available, it then downloads them so that they can be included in the installation. Windows XP gives the user the opportunity to load the most recent critical updates.

Finally, it prepares for installation, and then begins the installation process. Setup detects and installs devices, such as the mouse and the keyboard.

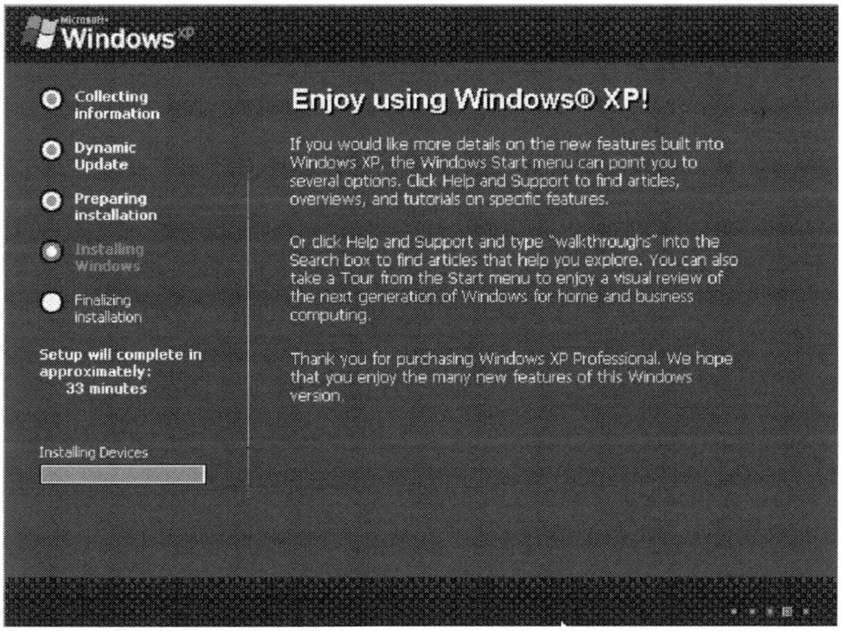

Figure 1-8: GUI Installation Screen: Installing Devices

The next screen (Figure 1.9) is the regional options dialog box where you customize Windows XP Professional to your locale, currency, or number format. You can also add additional languages, such as Spanish or French, so that your XP installation can work in more than one language, when required.

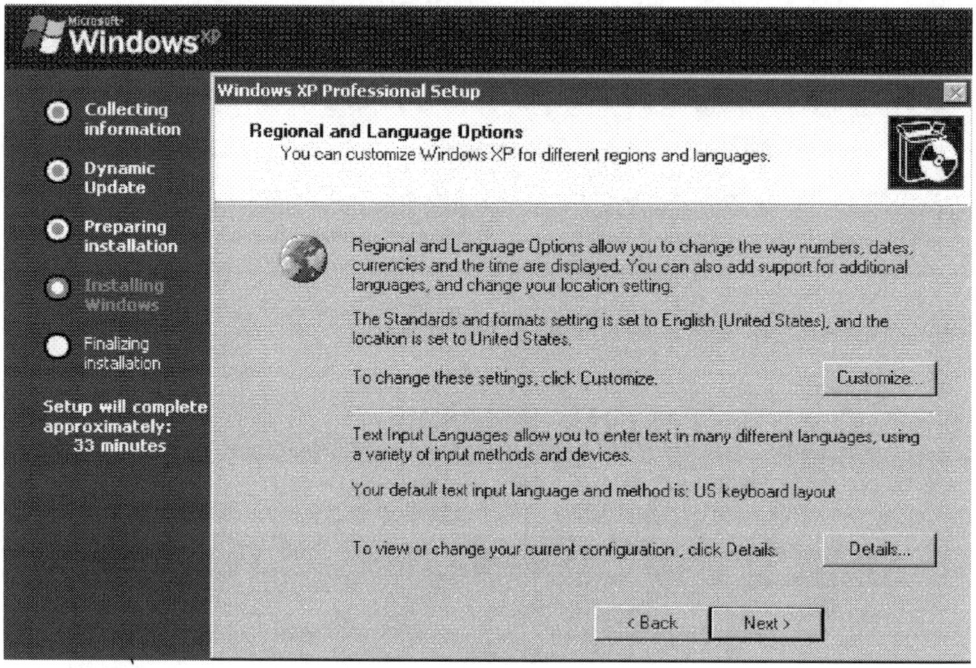

Figure 1-9: Regional and Language Options

The Personalize your Software screen is next. You are asked to type in your name and organization.

Following that is the Product ID dialog box, as displayed in Figure 1.10. You will need to enter the alphanumeric 25-character product key that is on the CD jewel case for Windows XP Professional, or which has been provided to you by a volume license agreement.

> **NOTE:** The license key displayed in Figure 1-10 is NOT a valid license key. This has been displayed for demonstration purposes only, and will not be recognized during this portion of the installation process.

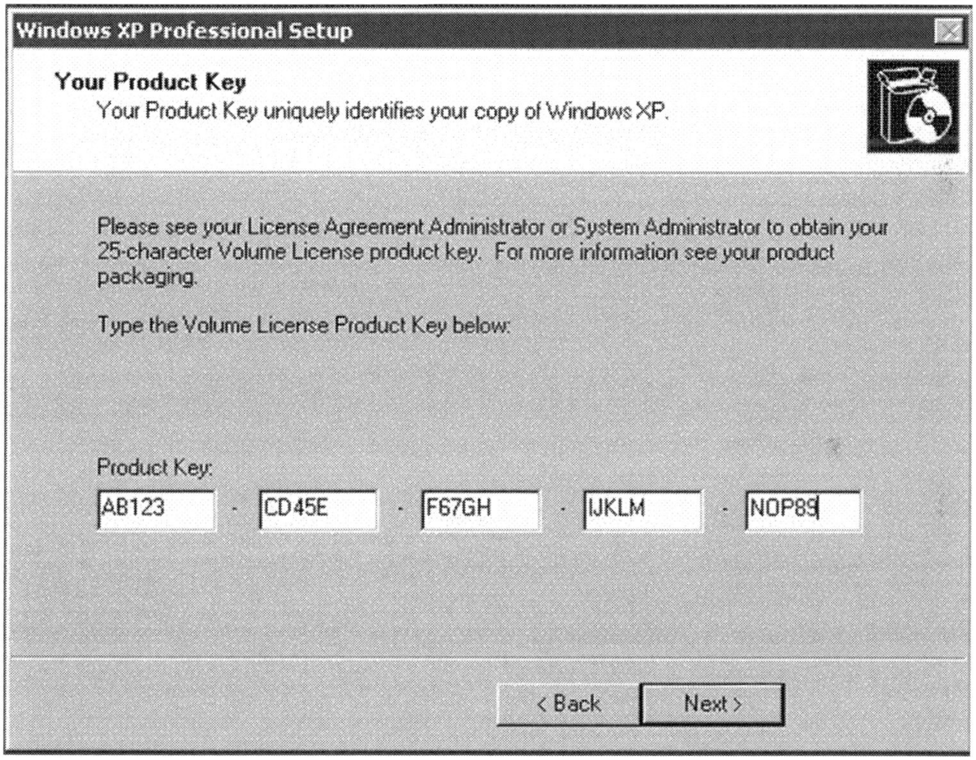

Figure 1-10: Configuring the License Key

The next screen will be the Computer Name and Password dialog box (Figure 1-11). Windows XP Professional will generate a default computer name, which you can accept, or you can change the name of the computer to meet administrative requirements. You will also be prompted for an administrator password, which will be the password for the built-in local Administrator account after installation. There is no requirement for a password and it can be left blank, but this is HIGHLY discouraged because it leaves the computer's security at extreme risk.

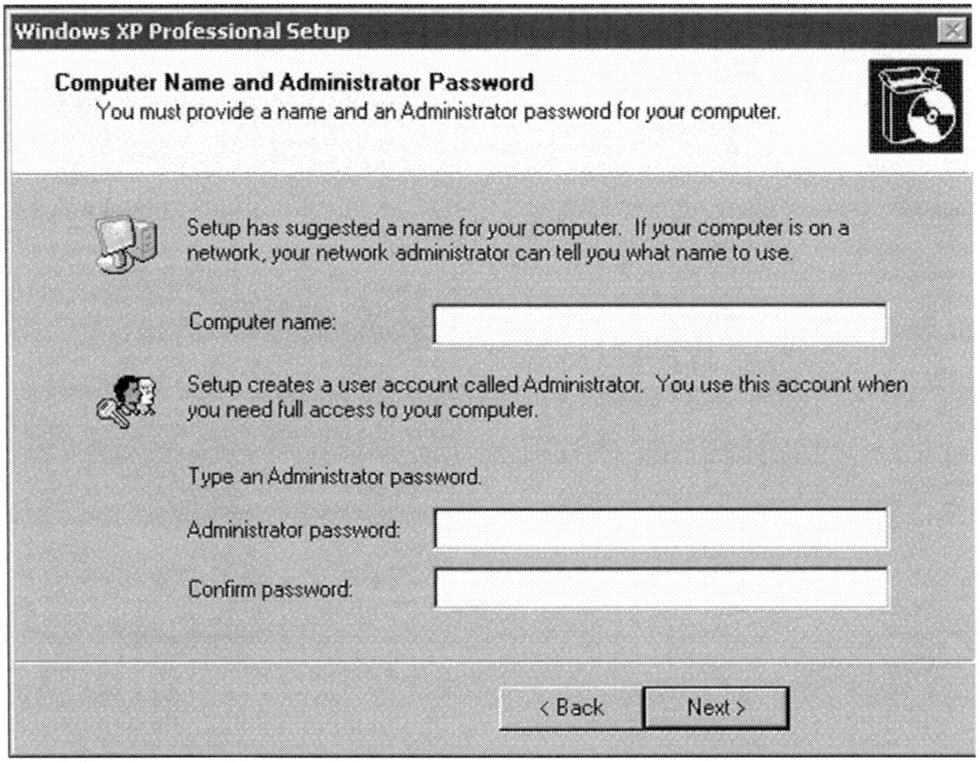

Figure 1-11: Computer Name and Administrator Password

The Date and Time settings dialog box follows (Figure 1.12). You should check the system date to make sure it is correct and select the appropriate time zone for your system. If the system is being shipped elsewhere after installation, you may wish to adjust the time zone accordingly.

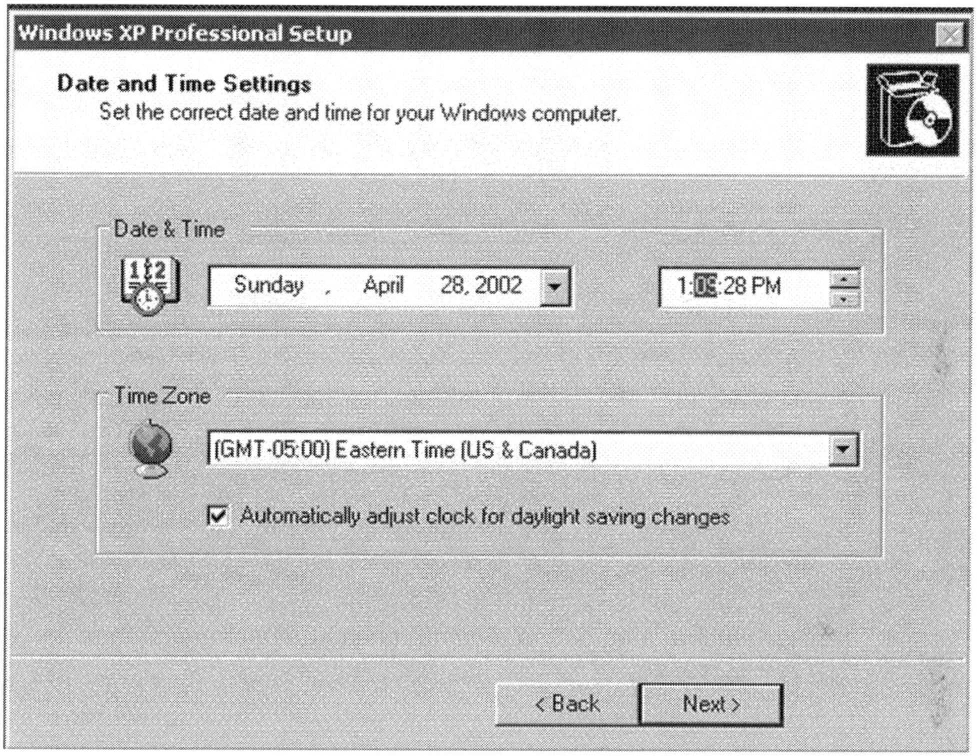

Figure 1-12: Adjusting the Date and Time for Local Settings

At this point in the setup, the network is installed (Figure 1-13). There will be no need for user interaction, and the status bar is once again displayed, with the time needed, approximately, to complete the installation.

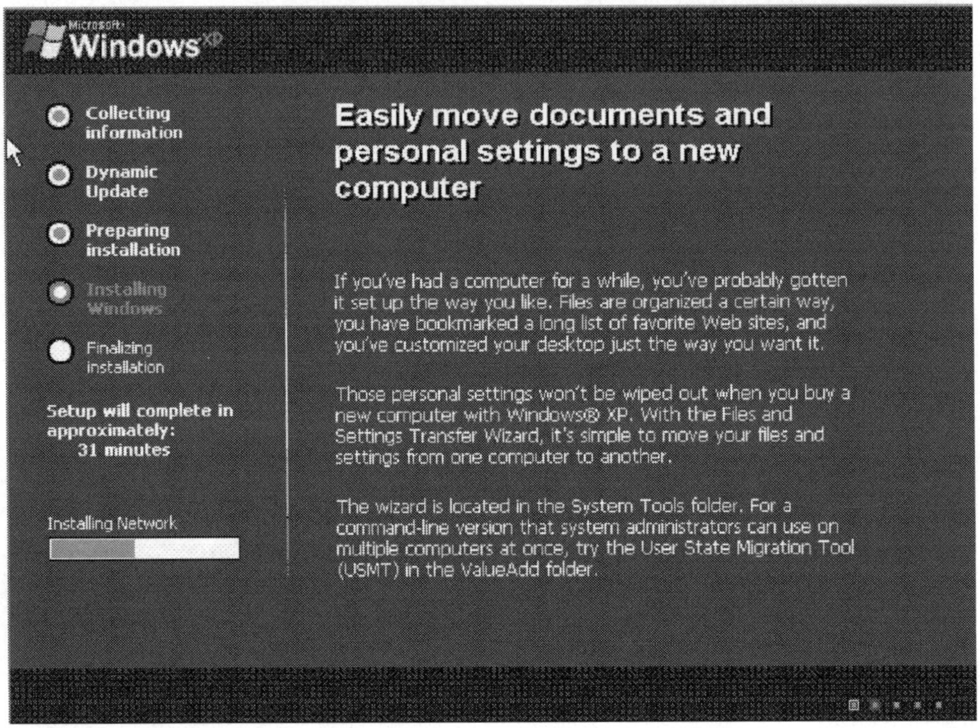

Figure 1-13: Network Installation

The Network Settings dialog box (Figure 1-14) is next. Setup will detect your network settings and then ask whether you wish to use Typical or Custom settings. Typical settings include File and Print for Microsoft Networks, TCP/IP protocol using DHCP, and Client for Microsoft Networks. If you wish to choose the network components required for your environment—for example, if your network will be using static IP addresses rather than DHCP—you should select Custom.

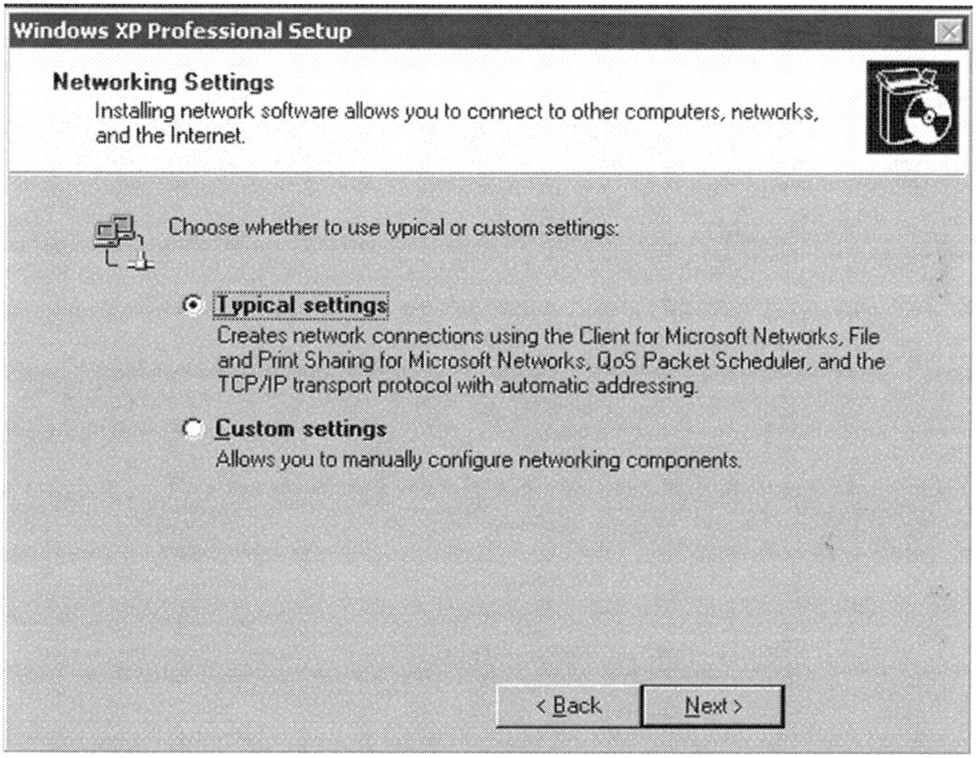

Figure 1-14: Choosing your Network Settings

Next is the Workgroup or Computer Domain dialog box (Figure 1-15). You can add your computer to a workgroup at this point, or join a domain. You must have the appropriate administrator rights to create a computer account in the domain, if you choose domain membership.

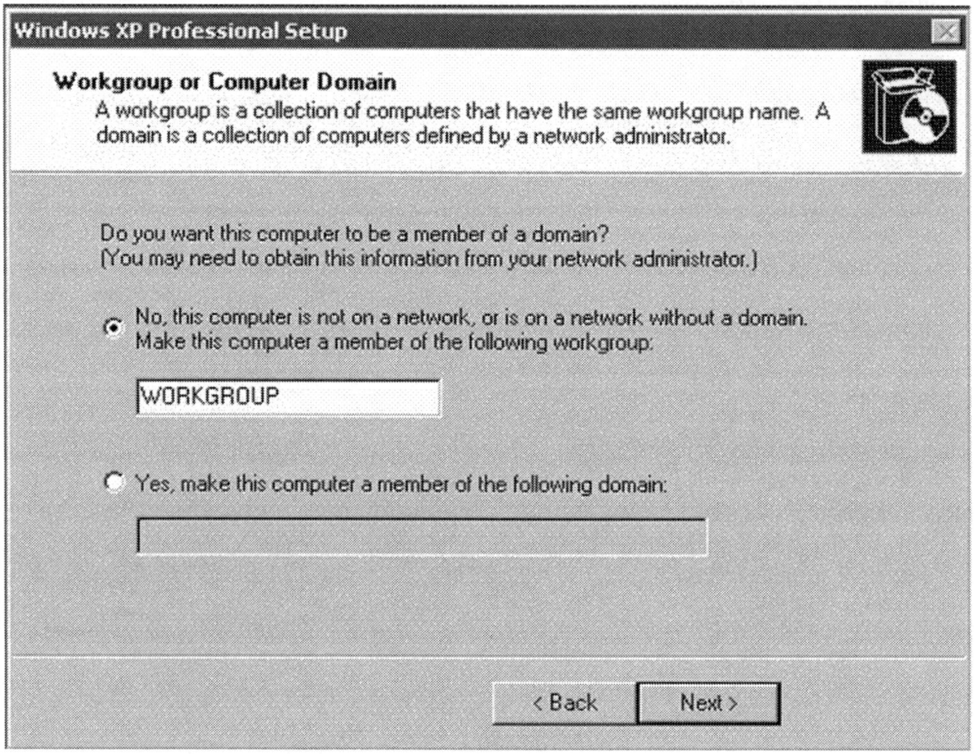

Figure 1-15: Joining a Workgroup or a Domain.

The final stage of installation takes place when Windows XP Professional Setup completes the following tasks:

- Installs the Start menu items
- Registers components
- Saves settings
- Removes temporary files

The next screen is the Finalizing Installation screen (Figure 1-16). Setup installs the operating system components at this point, which can take a few minutes.

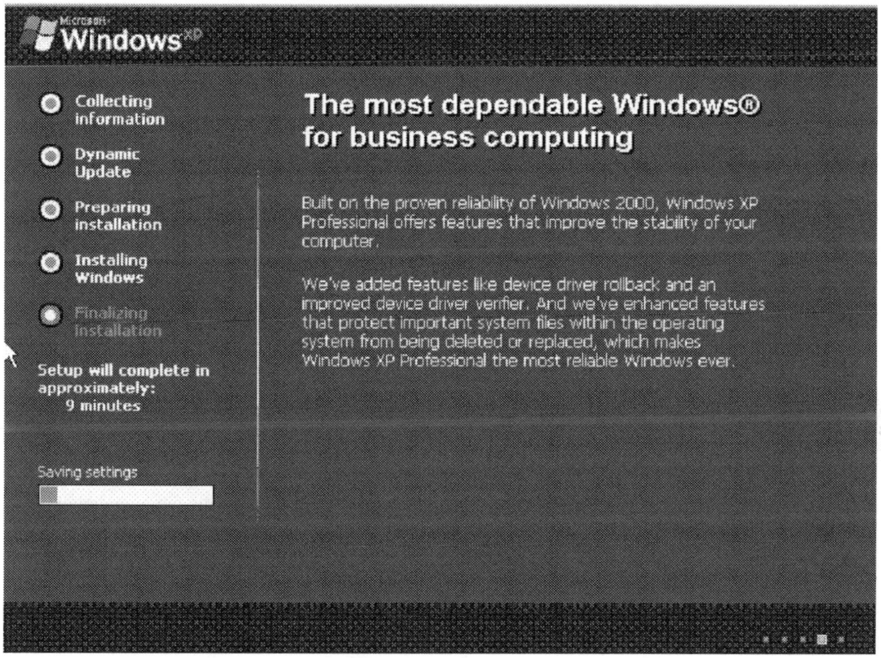

Figure 1-16: Finalizing Installation

Congratulations! The standard installation for Windows XP Professional is complete!

Pop Quiz 1.2

Pop Quiz 1.2 Questions

1. What are the two types of CD-ROM installations?
2. What is the syntax to connect to the shared network folder that contains the Setup file?
3. What are the three choices given to you when the Windows XP Professional Setup screen appears?
4. What is the difference between converting your partition to NTFS and formatting your partition as NTFS?
5. What is Dynamic Update?

Pop Quiz 1.2 *Answers*

1. The first type is standard installation, when the CD is auto-detected and the Setup Wizard starts automatically. The other type of CD-ROM installation is a bootable CD-ROM. An automated clean install can be provided for any system that does not have a network connection. An image, created with SysPrep, can be copied onto a CD-R. This type of install can be either fully automated, with a unique script for each user created on a floppy disk, or can be deployed with user interaction.

2. The command is: \\SERVERNAME\SHARENAME\I386\WINNT.EXE, where SERVERNAME is replaced with the name of your server and SHARENAME is replaced with the name of your shared directory.

3. The three choices are:

    A. To setup Windows XP now, press ENTER.

    B. To repair a Windows XP installation using Recovery Console, press R.

    C. To quit Setup without installing Windows XP Professional, press F3.

4. Converting a partition to NTFS leaves any files that presently exist on the partition intact. Formatting will delete all files on the partition in the process.

5. Dynamic Update is a new feature of Windows XP. During the installation process, before any files are even installed, Windows XP checks the Microsoft website for critical updates. If any are available, it then downloads them so that they can be included in the installation. Windows XP gives the user the opportunity to load the most recent critical updates.

IV Deployment -- Unattended Installations

Well, we now know how to install Windows XP on a single computer. It is more likely that we will have to install Windows XP Professional on 50, or 100, or even a 1,000 computers. Now you may be a patient soul who does not mind installing XP on 1,000 computers, one at a time. However, the odds are that business needs will require a faster, more efficient way of completing the task at hand. So, let us take a look at some of the choices provided by Windows XP Professional to do a large numbers of installations.

Remote Installation Services

Remote Installation Services (RIS) is used to install a copy of Windows XP on local computers from remote locations. Using this technology, a workstation can start up, contact a DHCP server to obtain an IP address of a RIS Server and then contact the RIS Server to install the operating system.

There are several advantages to using RIS for the installation of Windows XP. These include:

- Ability to remotely install Windows XP Professional
- Simplification of server management by allowing access to the Windows distribution files and using Plug-and-Play for hardware detection during the installation process
- Ability to quickly recover the operating system in the event of failure
- Retention of Windows security when you restart the destination computer

> **NOTE:** This section is not intended to be a definitive guide for using RIS technology, but rather to outline the process and the conditions for use. For detailed information on RIS, Microsoft has provided a guide "Technical Guide to Remote Installation Services – Microsoft Product Support Services White Paper," which is free for download at: http://www.microsoft.com/windows2000/techinfo/administration/management/remosadmin.asp

There are some factors of which you should be aware before you choose RIS as the method for installing Windows 2000 on your network:

- At present, only a clean install of either Windows XP or Windows XP is supported by RIS. This method cannot be used for upgrade installations, nor can it be used to install any other operating system, including Windows 2000 Server.
- You need to have a Windows 2000 Server to act as the RIS Server. This server must have at least two disk partitions, one for its operating system, and one for RIS images. The partition that holds the RIS images must be at least 2GB in size and must be formatted as NTFS. The server must also either be running the following services, or have these services be accessible to the RIS server from another network server:
    - o DHCP Server (used to assign IP addresses to RIS clients)
    - o DNS Server (used to locate Active Directory)
    - o Active Directory (used to locate RIS servers, clients, and to manage configuration settings and client installation options)

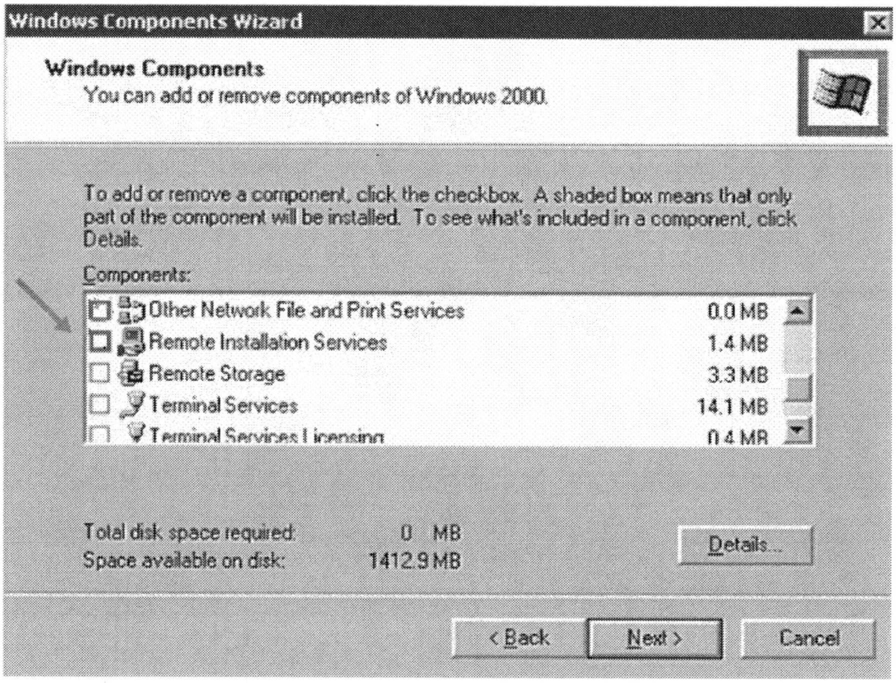

Figure 1-17: Windows Components Wizard on Windows 2000 RIS Server

The RIS Server

As part of the server installation (Figure 1.4), four services critical to the remote installation process are added to the Windows 2000 Server (Table 1-5):

Boot Information Negotiation Layer (BINL) Service	Used to respond to client requests.
Single Instance Store (SIS) Service	Used to reduce the storage requirements needed to store images by combining duplicate files.
SIS Groveler Service	Scans the SIS volume for identical files when the system is idle. It will perform a series of tests to compare files to ensure they are identical and then copy them to a volume reserved by the SIS service. A link will be provided to the original files.
Trivial File Transfer Protocol (TFTP) Service	Part of the TCP/IP suite, the file transfer protocol used to download the Client Installation Wizard from the RIS Server to the client.

Table 1-5: RIS Services

Figure 1-18: RIS Setup Wizard

After installation, configuration of the RIS server is done through the Remote Installation Services Setup Wizard (risetup.exe). This wizard (Figure 1.5) can be called in two ways. When you first start or restart the server, click **Finish Setup in the Configure Your Server** dialog box. This starts the Add/Remove Programs tool. In the Set Up Servers area, click **Configure Remote Installation Services** to run Risetup.exe. You can also initiate the Setup Wizard by using the **Start | Run** RISETUP.EXE command.

The first step will be for you to state the location of the RIS installation image files that will be used to install your clients. Although the default directory will be the first available NTFS volume that does not contain the system or boot partitions, any NTFS volume on the server can be used, with the exception of the system and boot partitions.

The next step will be to configure the RIS Server to respond to all client requests or only to those who have known client accounts (Machine Account Object) in Active Directory.

The third step requests that you specify the folder in which you want to store the files for the image that Risetup.exe copies.

The final step of the Wizard asks to you give a user-friendly name for the operating system package and associated help text. This will allow users to select the correct package for their systems.

Each RIS server must be authorized in the Active Directory tree before RIS can service or respond to client requests.

This is done through the DHCP Manager.

> Remember: **Only members of the Enterprise Administrators group have the necessary rights to authorize RIS servers. If you want to give other users or groups this ability, you must give them the permission to authorize DHCP servers in Active Directory.**

RIS Client Installation

Before you can use RIS to install to a client, certain conditions must be met for the client and for the network:

The client computer must meet the hardware requirements for the installation of XP, including a network adapter card.

The BIOS load boot order must boot the network before booting the hard disk.

Network capabilities must be available through one of the following:

- o A PXE-based boot ROM with a BIOS that supports starting the computer with that ROM; or
- o A network adapter that supports PXE and can be used with a RIS boot disk; or
- o The ability to follow the Net PC standard, which supports the ability to boot to the network, prevent users from changing hardware and o/s configuration, and manage upgrades.

The network providing RIS services must have available:

- An active DHCP Server on the network so that the client can obtain an IP address.
- A RIS Server with the appropriate images prepared

As well, users must have the right to create computer accounts on the network, or in their OU. If this right is not given, then the account must be created in Active Directory prior to RIS client installation.

What is PXE?

PXE (Pre-Boot Execution Environment) is defined on industry-standard Internet protocols and services—TCP/IP, DHCP, and TFTP. On computer startup, the client sends out a DHCP discover packet that indicates that it is using the PXE protocol. The IP address that is supplied is that of the RIS Server. The client may, but does not need to, request an IP address for itself during the same process. The client then uses TFTP to download the install package from the RIS Server.

When the system is powered on, the network boot option is selected, the MAC address of the client is displayed, and the system begins to request an IP address and locate a boot server. When a server is found, the user is told to press F12 for a network service boot.

The Client Installation Welcome screen is displayed. The user will need to press ENTER to continue. Next, the Windows 2000 Logon dialog box appears. The user needs to supply a valid username and password for the domain. The next menu will have choices for (Table 1-6):

Automatic Setup	The client is setup with default values.
Custom Setup	The user can type in a computer name and OU (if nothing is supplied, default values are used).
Restart a previous Setup attempt	If setup has failed before the GUI stage, Setup can be restarted without the user going through all the screens again.
Maintenance and Troubleshooting	Provides access to diagnostics and maintenance tools created by third-party manufacturers, such as BIOS updates.

Table 1-6: Setup Menu

> **NOTE:** The second, third and fourth options will be displayed ONLY if Group Policy allows. Otherwise, the default will be Automatic Setup.

If there is only one RIS image, it will be automatically installed; otherwise, the user will see a menu of RIS images to choose from. After selection, the remote installation process will begin. If answer files have been provided, there may be no further need for user interaction.

Creating a RIS Boot Disk

RIS Boot Disks can be created on a Windows XP workstation that is connected on the same network as the RIS Server. This is done by the **Start | Run** command line: \\RISSERVER\REMINST\ADMIN\I386\RBFG.EXE. This will call the Windows 2000 Boot Disk Generator wizard, which will allow you to create one or many RIS Boot Disks simply by clicking the Create Disk button.

System Preparation Tool

The System Preparation Tool (SysPrep) is used to prepare disk images that will be duplicated using a third-party manufacturer's imaging utility. Some examples of third-party tools that you can use to deploy the image are Symantec's Norton Ghost, Altiri's RapiDeploy, Powerquest's DriveImage Professional, and Micro House's Imagecaster. Disk imaging is an excellent choice for automatic deployment of Windows XP Professional when you have a large number of computers with similar configuration requirements. SysPrep eliminates some of the problems encountered in the past using disk imaging tools, such as duplicate Security IDs (SID).

To use the System Preparation Tool, the source and client computers must have identical Hardware Abstraction Layers (the same processor type), Advanced Configuration and Power Interface (ACPI) support, and mass storage controller devices (SCSI or IDE). The hard drive on the client computer must have the same or greater capacity as that on the source computer. Windows 2000 will detect automatically any Plug and Play devices, and SysPrep will redetect and evaluate the devices on the system when the computer is turned on. In other words, any Plug and Play devices (network cards, modems, video and sound cards) do not have to be the same on the source and client computers, as long as the drivers are available.

The first step in preparing for a disk image installation is to create a master or source computer. Windows XP Professional should be installed on this computer with the standard configuration requirements, such as browser settings, printer settings, and desktop settings. Any applications that will be standard can also be installed on the source computer, provided you have a legal license for each instance of duplication of the software.

Once the source computer is configured correctly, you are ready to run the System Preparation Tool. Start Setup Manager on the source computer to create a Sysprep.inf file. This will allow you to completely automate the installation except for the computer name. Choose the first option, **Create a New Answer File**. When prompted, choose the SysPrep Install answer file.

Okay. So where is the Setup Manager anyway?

If it has been a while since you have done remote setup, you may not remember that Setup Manager (along with other system tools) is not installed by default on a Windows XP Professional machine. You can find the setup for this (and all the other support tools) on your Windows XP CD ROM under CDROM:\SUPPORT\TOOLS. Setup manager is found in the deploy.cab file.

You can allow the user to supply the computer name when Windows XP Professional is started for the first time, or you can supply the Sysprep.inf file for each machine on a floppy disk, and include a unique computer name for each Sysprep.inf file (Figure 1-19).

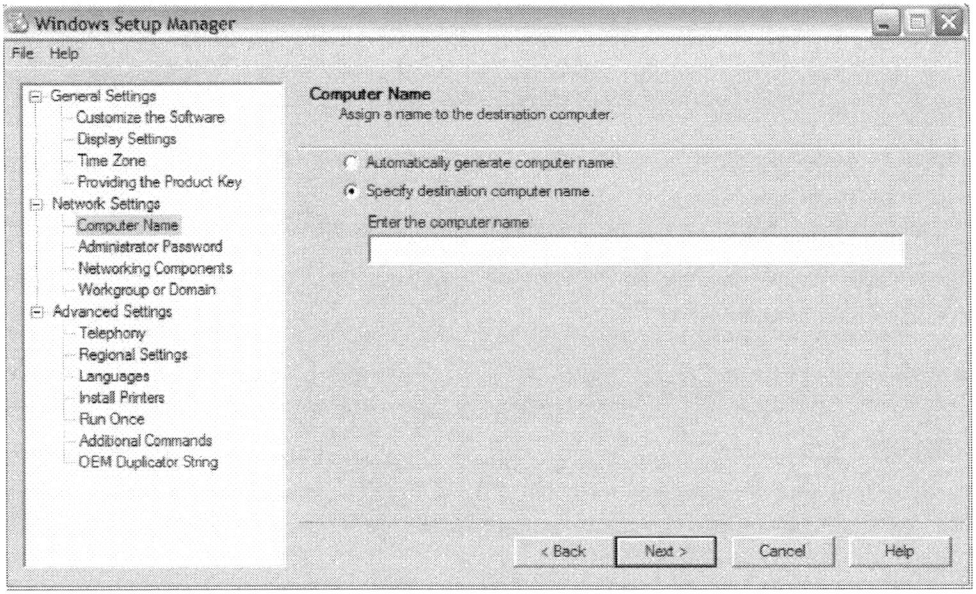

Figure 1-19: Choosing the Computer Name

You are then ready to run the setup. At the command prompt, enter:

- CD SYSPREP
- SYSPREP –REBOOT

By adding the "-reboot" switch, the source computer will automatically reboot after SysPrep has completed.

What has happened during this process is that the System Preparation tool has removed information that has to be unique on each computer running Windows XP Professional, such as the SID (security ID) and computer name.

You are now ready to use a third-party tool to create your image.

Deployment of the image can be done in a number of ways:

- Bootable CD
- Network Download (requires a boot floppy to gain access to the network)
- Hard disk replication
- Transportable media (such as ZIP)

What is the difference between SYSPREP and RIPREP?

Quite frequently, there is confusion between the two preparation formats. RIPREP (Remote Installation Preparation wizard) is a part of the Remote Installation Services that is used to create operating system images and to install them on the RIS server. SYSPREP, on the other hand, is a tool that prepares the hard disk on a source computer for duplication to target computers and then runs a non-Microsoft disk-imaging process. This method can only be used when the hard disk on the source computer is identical to those of the target computers.

Unattended Answer Files

You can create unattended answer files by using Setup Manager to automate the installation of Windows XP. If you have a large number of computers to install, and the computers are not PXE-compliant, using an unattended installation process with a distribution server may prove to be the easiest way to deploy Windows XP.

A distribution server contains all Windows XP files needed for installation. How to set up a distribution server is beyond the scope of this section, however, detailed information may be obtained at:

http://www.microsoft.com/TECHNET/WIN2000/DGUIDE/CHAPT-25.ASP

> **NOTE:** While this URL seems to specify installation for Windows XP, the same rules hold true for setting up a distribution server for Windows XP.

When using a distribution server for an unattended installation, it can be helpful to develop answer files. Answer files are installation scripts that respond to prompts that normally require user input. Setup Manager, included with the Windows 2000 Deployment Tools on the Windows XP CD, will help you create answer files so that installation can be fully automated, or "silent".

> **NOTE:** Answer files can also be used for RIS and SysPrep installations.

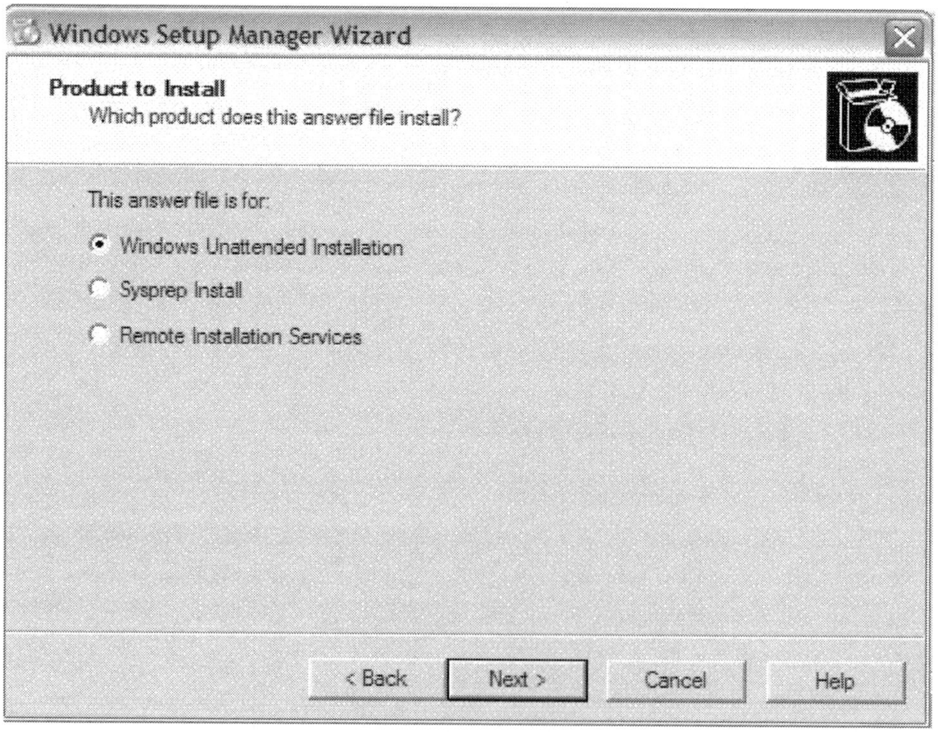

Figure 1-20: Product to Install window

On a Windows XP computer, on which you have installed the Windows 2000 deployment tools, use the Start | Run command to execute **SETUPMGR.EXE**. This starts the Setup Manager Wizard. A welcome screen appears. After the welcome screen, a dialog box appears entitled **"New or Existing Answer File."** This dialog box allows you to create a new answer file, create an answer file that will duplicate the computer on which you are running Setup Manager, or modify an existing answer file.

Presuming that we are creating a new answer file, the **Product to Install** page appears. The choices are for RIS, SysPrep, or Unattended Installation. Because we are examining answer files for unattended installations, we will follow this path (Figure 1-20). The next screen allows us to choose the **platform** to which the answer file will install. There are three choices given:

- Windows XP Home Edition
- Windows XP Professional
- Windows XP

To proceed, we will choose Windows XP Professional.

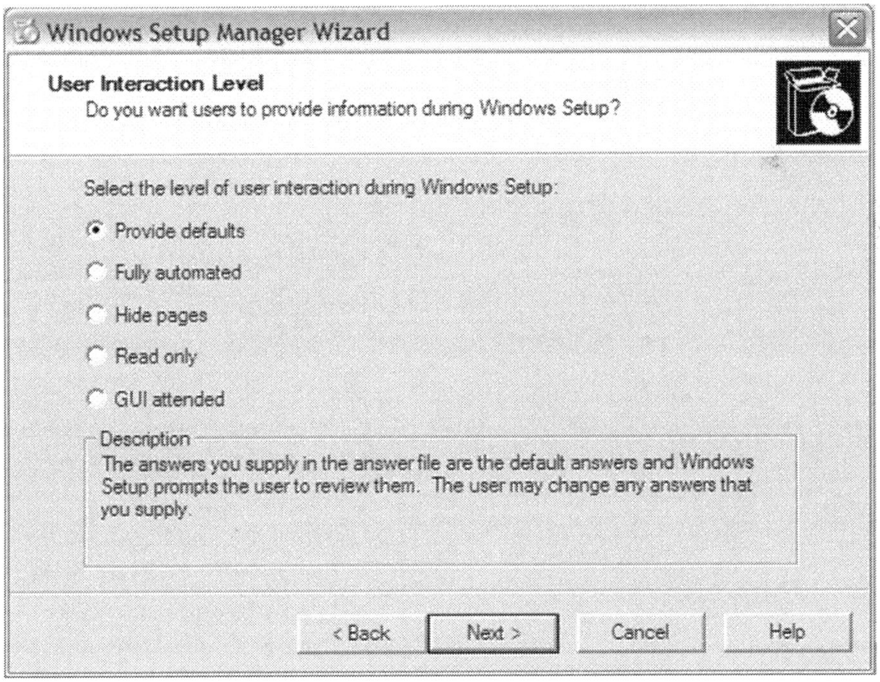

Figure 1-21: Setup Manager User Interaction Level

The User Interaction Level page follows (Figure 1-21). This page allows us to choose the amount of interaction we will allow with the user:

- Provide Defaults: This will allow you to provide default answers to the prompts. The user can choose to accept the default answer, or change it to suit their needs.
- Fully Automated: This will use all of the answers you supply in the answer file and will not prompt for any user interaction.
- Hide Pages: This will run the Wizard invisibly provided you have provided all the answers to required prompts.
- Read Only: This will display the Setup Wizard to the user, but will not allow the user to make changes.
- GUI Attended: This requires user interaction once the text-mode portion of Setup has been completed. Answers must be supplied for the text-mode portion.

Once you have chosen an installation method, you then continue through many screens:

- Distribution Folder: A distribution folder can be created on the computer, or network, with the required source files. Files, such as additional device drivers, can be added to further customize your installation.
- Set Default User Information.
- Allows you to specify a username and organization.
- Display Settings: Allows you to select display settings, such as color, screen area and refresh frequency.
- Time Zone: Allows you to select a time zone for the destination computer
- Product Key: Allows you to enter the product key, or keys, for the copies of Windows you wish to install.
- Computer Name.
- Allows you to enter multiple names, which Setup Manager will use to create the UDF (uniqueness database file) that is needed to add a unique name to each system during setup.
- Administrator Password: Allows you to prompt the user for a password, or supply the password yourself. You can also choose to have the Administrator logon automatically.
- Network Settings: Allows you to choose “Typical Settings” (TCP/IP, DHCP-enabled, Client for Microsoft Networks) or “Custom Settings” (where you can choose network settings and services).

- Workgroup or Domain: Allows you to have the destination computers participate in a Workgroup, or join a Windows Server Domain. You can also create a computer account in the domain for each computer, if you have the appropriate domain rights.
- Advanced Settings: Allows you to edit telephony settings, regional settings, languages, browser settings, the installation folder, the printer installation, and even a command, such as a program, that will run the first time a user logs on.

Figure 1-22 shows an example of a UDF (**Uniqueness Database File**) that can be created.

```
[UniqueIDs]
UserID1 = Userdata,GuiUnattended,Network
UserID2 = Userdata,GuiUnattended,Network
[UserID1:UserData]
FullName = "User ID-1"
ComputerName = "MACHINE-1"
[UserID1:GuiUnattended]
TimeZone = " (GMT-05:00) Eastern Time (US &amp; Canada)"
[UserID1:Network]
JoinDomain = "DomainEast"
[UserID2:UserData]
FullName = "User ID-2"
ComputerName = "MACHINE-2"
[UserID2:GuiUnattended]
TimeZone = "(GMT-06:00) Central Time (US &amp; Canada)"
[UserID2:Network]
JoinDomain = "DomainCentral"
```

Figure 1-22: Sample UDF (Uniqueness Database File)

Figure 1-23 is a sample answer file that was created using Setup Manager. For more explanation on available options in the setup file, See **Appendix B: Unattended Installs**.

```
;SetupMgrTag
[Data]
   AutoPartition=1
   MsDosInitiated="0"
   UnattendedInstall="Yes"
[Unattended]
   UnattendMode=ProvideDefault
   OemPreinstall=No
   TargetPath=\WINDOWS
[GuiUnattended]
   AdminPassword="password"
   EncryptedAdminPassword=NO
   AutoLogon=Yes
   AutoLogonCount=1
   OEMSkipRegional=1
   TimeZone=35
[UserData]
   ProductID=AB123-CD456-EF78G-HIJKL-MN90P
   FullName="Deborah Timmons"
   OrgName="Integrator Systems Inc."
   ComputerName=MyComputer
[TapiLocation]
   CountryCode=107
   Dialing=Tone
   AreaCode=613
[GuiRunOnce]
   Command0="rundll32 printui.dll,PrintUIEntry /in /n
\\servername\sharedprintername"
[Identification]
   JoinWorkgroup=WORKGROUP
[Networking]
   InstallDefaultComponents=Yes
```

Figure 1-23: Sample Unattend.txt

Pop Quiz 1.3

Pop Quiz 1.3 *Questions*

1. What are the advantages of using RIS?
2. What is the SysPrep tool?
3. What command starts the Setup Manager Wizard?
4. What amount of user interaction is needed when one chooses GUI Attended?
5. What is the difference between SYSPREP and RIPREP?

Pop Quiz 1.3 *Answers*

1. Some of the advantages to using RIS for the installation of Windows XP include:
ability to remotely install Windows XP Professional; simplification of server management by allowing access to the Windows distribution files and using Plug-and-Play for hardware detection during the installation process;
ability to quickly recover the operating system in the event of failure;
and retention of Windows security when you restart the destination computer
2. The System Preparation Tool (SysPrep) is used to prepare disk images that will be duplicated using a third-party manufacturer's imaging utility.
3. Use the Start | Run command to execute **SETUPMGR.EXE**.
4. GUI Attended requires user interaction once the text-mode portion of Setup has been completed. Answers must be supplied for the text-mode portion.
5. RIPREP (Remote Installation Preparation wizard) is a part of the Remote Installation Services that is used to create operating system images and to install them on the RIS server. SYSPREP, on the other hand, is a tool that prepares the hard disk on a source computer for duplication to target computers and then runs a non-Microsoft disk-imaging process. This method can only be used when the hard disk on the source computer is identical to those of the target computers.

V Upgrading To Windows XP Professional

Earlier in this chapter, we examined the differences between a clean installation of Windows XP Professional and an upgrade installation, and the reasons you may choose one method over the other.

Let's review what we have covered.

When considering an upgrade installation of Windows XP Professional, you must remember that only certain operating systems can be upgraded. These are:

- Windows 98, 98SE, Me
- Windows NT 4.0 Workstation
- Windows XP
- Windows XP Home Edition

If, for example, you were currently running Windows NT Workstation 3.51, you would need to first upgrade to Workstation 4.0 before you could successfully upgrade to Windows XP Professional.

An important benefit when choosing an upgrade installation is that an upgrade retains the existing applications, preferences and local users and group (under NT).

That being said, let's look at the upgrade path from Windows 9x to Windows XP Professional.

Preparing for Upgrade

There are some tasks you should perform prior to implementing an upgrade installation from Windows 9x, Windows NT or Windows XP to Windows XP. Table 1-7 is a checklist you should follow while preparing for your installation.

Back up all data and configuration files. Verify the backup and perform a trial restore.
Delete or uninstall any unneeded files, applications and program groups
Decompress any partitions that have been compressed with DoubleSpace, DriveSpace, or any other incompatible 3rd party product.
Verify that the hardware meets minimum requirements and is on the HCL
Obtain any device drivers that will be necessary for Windows XP Professional.
Perform a disk scan, a defragmentation, and a virus scan.
Document the current configuration, including applications, hardware, services, and policies.

Table 1-7: Upgrade Installation Checklist

Upgrading from Windows 98 or Windows ME

The process of upgrading from Windows 98/ME → Windows XP Professional is not as smooth as the Windows NT/Windows 2000 → Windows XP path. Because Windows XP Professional is based on NT Technology, there are fewer considerations when upgrading.

There are some situations (hardware or software related) under Windows 9x that are not supported under Professional, even though the operating system can be upgraded. These are:

Applications designed for Windows 9x, and not NT, that use file-system filters. Anti-virus software and some disk-quota management software fall under this category.

Custom power-management tools (Windows XP Professional provides its own!)

Custom Plug-and-Play solutions.

Applications designed for Windows 9x that support compressed drives, disk defragmenters and disk utilities.

Utilities and applications that use virtual device drivers or 386 drivers.

Applications that directly access the hardware.

Upgrading from Windows NT

As Windows XP Professional is based on NT technology, the upgrade procedure is fairly painless. The process will migrate the existing user profiles and configuration.

The following applications and features will not upgrade properly to XP Professional:

Applications that depend on file-system filters, such as antivirus software, disk tools and disk quote software. There are some third-party software packages that worked under NT that will not function with Windows XP without an upgrade patch. One example is Executive Software's Diskeeper for NT.

Custom power-management solutions and tools. Remove any custom tools before upgrading. XP Professional's support for ACPI and APM will replace them.

Disk mirrors and other fault-tolerant options

Other network clients and services

UPS

Performing the Upgrade

To perform the upgrade from Windows 98, ME, NT 4.0 or 2000 Professional from the installation source (e.g. the Windows XP Professional CD), you start the execution by running the command: *CDROM*:\I386\WINNT32.EXE. With the CD, the system may **AutoRun** this application for you, first prompting you whether or not you wish to install a new version of Windows on your computer. In either case, the Windows 2000 Setup Wizard is displayed (Figure 1-22).

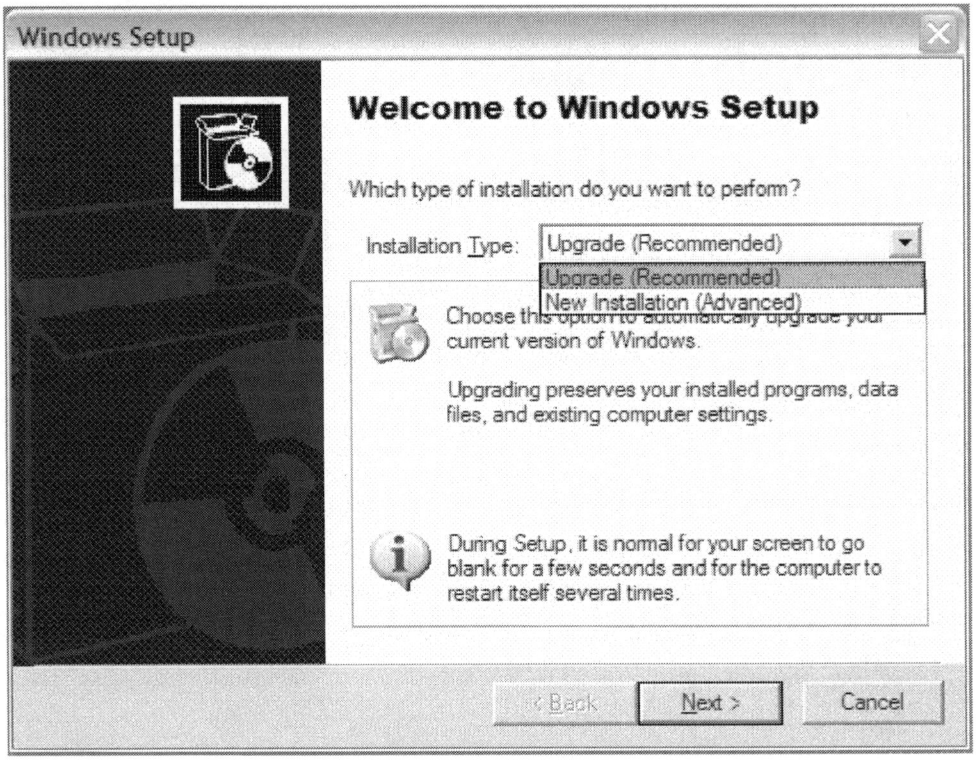

Figure 1-24: Windows Setup (Upgrade)

The first screen prompts you as to install a new copy of Windows XP, or perform an upgrade. Select **Upgrade (Recommended).**

The next step you will see is the License Agreement screen. You must accept the agreement to continue with the upgrade installation. Not accepting the agreement will abort the upgrade. At this point, the upgrade procedures diverge, depending on whether you are upgrading from Windows 98/ME, Windows NT or Windows XP.

Upgrade Path from Windows 98/Windows ME

After the License Agreement screen, you see the Windows XP Professional Upgrade Preparation screen.

The next step will be the prompt for the product key, which is on the jewel case for the Windows XP Professional CD. The product key is alphanumeric and 25 characters in length. Without a valid product key, installation cannot continue.

The next stage is the hardware detection phase of Setup. When the detection is completed, you will be prompted to provide update packs. We will be discussing update packs in detail shortly. If you need to provide update packs, selecting YES will allow you to add them at this point in the installation.

The next screen will allow you the opportunity to upgrade to the NTFS file system. This conversion upgrade is only for FAT or FAT32 drives and will only apply to the drive where the operating system files reside. Any other drives will have to be converted after installation.

> **NOTE:** It is at this point in the installation that non-compatible hardware and software can cause problems. A warning will be displayed in this case, notifying you that one or more devices or programs will be disabled if the installation proceeds.

The installer now copies the necessary files to the computer's hard drive. The computer will then restart, with a new item in the Boot Manager startup menu, and several text-mode screens.

Upgrade Path from Window NT Workstation/Windows XP

For a NT or 2000 upgrade, the next step is the request for the Product Key. After verifying the product key, Setup will run a compatibility check on devices and applications.

The next stage is where Setup begins copying installation files to the hard drive. After the installation files are copied, Setup initializes the Windows XP configuration and restarts the system. A blue text mode screen appears, and then Setup begins to load drivers, search for earlier versions of the Windows operating system, and copy the remaining Setup files to the installation folders. When this is complete, the system is again restarted.

At this point, the GUI setup process begins. This process is almost identical to the steps taken at the GUI setup process on a clean installation, with the exception that prompts will not appear for the portions of the setup where retained settings are used.

Update packs

One of the reasons you choose to do an upgrade installation is the retention of application settings. In a perfect world, all applications will function on the upgraded operating system just as smoothly as they did on the original o/s. However, the world is not a perfect one, and sometimes applications cease to operate after the upgrade. This is especially true in the case of a Windows 9x application that makes direct calls to the hardware. Windows XP Professional will not allow applications to access hardware directly. It is one of the features that provides the extra stability and security to Windows XP. In such a case, the application will have to be updated to a version that is Windows XP compliant.

What exactly are update packs? They are, essentially, migration DLLs that allow applications to function in a Windows XP Professional environment that normally would fail. The application developers or manufacturers supply these.

Pop Quiz 1.4

Pop Quiz 1.4 *Questions*

1) Which operating systems can be upgraded to Windows XP Professional?

2) Which applications are more likely to require update packs – applications designed for Windows 95 or applications designed for Windows NT Workstation?

3) You are currently running Windows NT Workstation 3.51. What must you do to upgrade to Windows XP Professional?

4) What is the first task you should perform when preparing for an upgrade?

Pop Quiz 1.4 *Answers*

1) Windows 98, 98SE, Me, Windows NT 4.0 Workstation, Windows 2000, Windows XP Home Edition can all be upgraded to Windows XP Professional.

2) Windows XP Professional is based on NT Technology, so applications designed for the NT Platform will be less likely to require update packs than those designed for the 95 Platform.

3) If you are currently running Windows NT Workstation 3.51, you will need to first upgrade to Workstation 4.0 before you could successfully upgrade to Windows XP Professional. An important benefit when choosing an upgrade installation is that an upgrade retains the existing applications, preferences and local users and group (under NT).

4) Back up all data and configuration files. Verify the backup and perform a trial restore.

VI Service Packs

Service packs are used to deliver new features to the operating system as they are developed. They are also used to correct "hidden features" – those nasty bugs and security holes that are discovered after release.

In Windows NT, service packs needed to be reapplied every time a new service was added to the operating system. For example, if you had been using a static IP address and were now moving to DHCP, after installing the DHCP Service, you would need to reapply the latest service pack. This was because parts of the service pack would be overwritten when the service was installed.

Windows XP, like Windows 2000, is using slipstream technology, which allows you to add new services without overwriting the service pack.

You can check which service pack is currently installed by using the WINVER command at the command prompt.

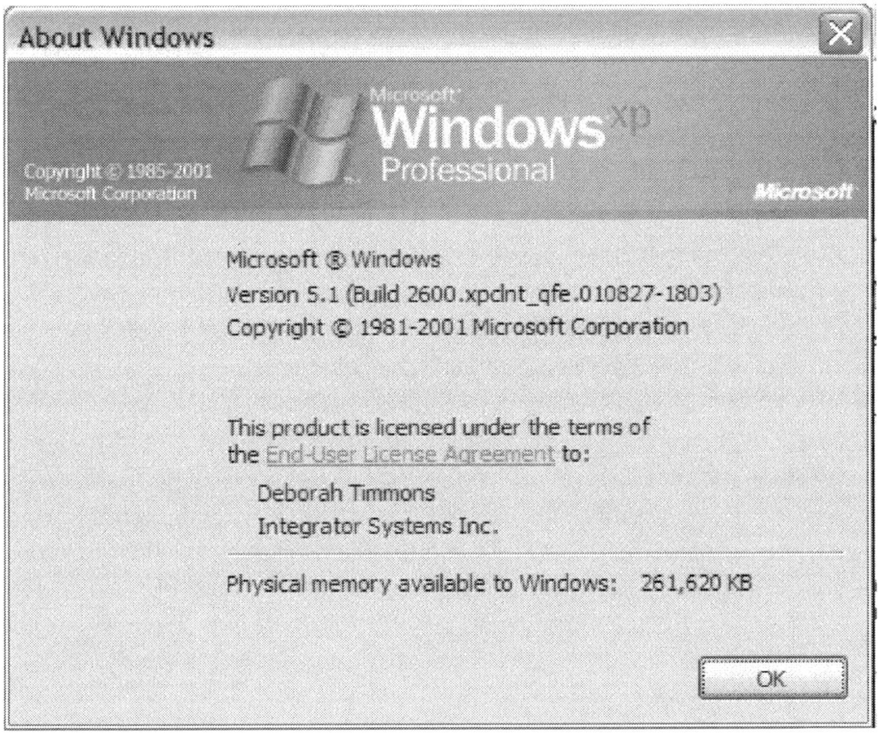

Figure 1-25: WINVER

VII Troubleshooting Failed Installations

Most installation errors occur because of hardware and driver incompatibility. By ensuring your hardware is on the HCL and all drivers are valid and present, many errors can be eliminated.

The following are a number of common errors that may occur during the installation process.

- Media Errors: Setup cannot read the CD, so it cannot proceed with the installation. Check the CD for dirt and scratches. If the CD is unreadable, a new one can be obtained from Microsoft.
- Insufficient Disk Space: Even though the minimum hard disk space requirement for Windows XP Professional is 650mb, Setup needs at least 1GB of free space to run properly.
- Not Enough Memory: Windows XP Professional needs a minimum of 64mb of RAM, and more is always better. If you have insufficient RAM, the installation may fail. There is always the possibility that installation will appear to be successful, but the system may "blue screen" after the installation has completed.
- Insufficient Processing Power: If the minimum requirements for processor are not met, the Windows XP Professional may fail, or blue screen errors will occur after installation is completed.
- Incompatible hardware: Always make sure that your hardware is on the HCL, or the device may fail to start after installation.
- No valid driver: If the hardware does not have a valid driver, Windows XP Professional will not recognize it.
- Poorly configured hardware: Windows XP Professional should configure your Plug and Play hardware correctly. However, non-Plug and Play hardware will need to be manually configured as per manufacturer's instructions.
- Incorrect CD Key: Without a valid product key, you cannot continue installation. Don't lose that CD jewel case! Remember as well that a twenty-five alphanumeric product key is prone to human error. Double check what has been typed with what is on the CD case. Also, keep in mind that typing numbers from the number pad area of the keyboard has caused some problems in the past.

Other problems that can occur during installation are directly related to network connectivity:

Failure to access TCP/IP Network Resources: On a typical Windows XP Professional installation, the client is set up to use DHCP. If no DHCP server is available, or the client cannot find the DHCP server, no IP address will be given to the client. N0 IP Address means NO network communication! Another problem that can occur is the assignment of the incorrect IP Address; refer to Chapter 6 for more information.

Failure to find a Domain Controller when joining a domain: This can be frustrating to troubleshoot because it can be a number of different things. The first thing to check is "connectivity". Simply put, is the network cable plugged into the NIC? No cable, and you won't ever find that domain controller! Verify that you have entered the correct domain name; again, bad typing can cause a failure. Make sure your network settings are correct. Is a domain controller available? If you cannot find the problem, configure the computer to join a workgroup and worry about joining the domain AFTER installation is completed.

Setup generates a number of log files during the installation process. Examining these logs may help you narrow down the reason (or reasons) that installation is failing. The Error log (setuperr.log) will include all errors that occurred during the installation, including non-fatal errors. The Action log (setupact.log) will list and describe all actions performed during the setup process.

VIII Chapter 1: Summary

We have now completed our chapter on installing Windows XP Professional. You should now feel comfortable with the following concepts:

- Performing an attended installation of Windows XP Professional.
- Performing an unattended installation of Windows XP Professional using three different methodologies.
    - Windows 2000 Server Remote Installation Services (RIS)
    - System Preparation Tool.
    - Setup Manager and unattended answer files.
- Performing and upgrading from a previous version of Windows to Windows XP Professional.
- Deployment of service packs.
- Troubleshooting of failed installations.

IX Chapter 1: Review Questions

1. John is planning to upgrade his existing Win98 system to WinXP. He is not too sure if his system can be upgraded smoothly. He does not know the components used in this computer. To spare himself unnecessary headaches, what should he do?

A. Run the command \i386\winnt32 -checkupgradeonly

B. Run the command \i386\winnt -checkupgrade

C. Contact Microsoft for a customized HCL

D. Run the command \i386\winnt32 -upgrade

E. No Answer is Correct

2. John is planning to upgrade his existing Win98 system to WinXP. He wants to sure that after the upgrade there is no need for him to additionally install a series of updates. What should he do?

A. Download the service packs and include them in the same CD, under \sp

B. Make sure an Internet connection is ready

C. Request the installation utility to retrieve dynamic updates

D. Download the service packs and include them in a separate CD, under \i386

E. No Answer is Correct

3. John is planning to upgrade his existing Win98 system to WinXP. He is not too sure if his system can be upgraded smoothly. His system has a 166MHZ processor, 128M RAM, 1.GB hard disk and a 4M SVGA adaptor. For a successful upgrade, he will have to replace or strengthen which hardware components?

A. RAM

B. Nothing has to be replaced

C. Processor

D. Display Adaptor

E. Hard disk

4. You will be installing WinXP on a computer you purchased one year ago. This computer has 256M RAM and 9GB of disk space. Five users will be sharing this computer. All of them use graphic intensive software. You need to ensure optimal performance and efficient user switching. Which of the following is a correct guideline to follow?

A. Make sure you have a 500mhz+ CPU

B. Add an additional 100MHZ for each user

C. Add an additional 64M of RAM for each user

D. Consider deploying a RAID 5 disk subsystem

E. Consider installing an OPENGL compatible video adaptor

5. You will be installing WinXP on a Compaq computer you purchased one month ago. What are the available forms of WinXP Pro installation for this computer?

A. Clean install

B. Remote install

C. Side by side

D. Diskless install

E. Upgrade over

6. Which of the following stages will be skipped if you boot your system using the WinXP installation CD for installation?

A. File copy

B. Text mode setup

C. GUI mode setup

D. Windows Welcome

E. Reboot

7. When installing WinXP, at which stage will you create the partition you want to use for the Windows XP system files?

A. File copy

B. Text mode setup

C. Windows Welcome

D. GUI mode setup

E. Reboot

8. When installing WinXP, at which stage will you activate the operating system?

A. File copy

B. System Restart

C. GUI mode setup

D. Windows Welcome

E. Text mode setup

9. As a system integrator, at which stage will you incorporate your custom registration process during WinXP installation?

A. File copy

B. Text mode setup

C. Windows Welcome

D. GUI mode setup

E. Reboot

10. You want to install WinXP on a legacy PC. This PC is equipped with enough RAM and hard drive space. However, it does not have a floppy drive. How to you ensure that a bootable CD will work properly?

A. Load smartdrv before booting

B. Disable BIOS virus scanning

C. Enable BIOS rom cacheable

D. Set the boot order in the BIOS so that the CD drive is the first boot device

E. Set the boot order in the BIOS so that the hard drive is the first boot device

X Chapter 1: Review Answers

1. John is planning to upgrade his existing Win98 system to WinXP. He is not too sure if his system can be upgraded smoothly. He does not know the components used in this computer. To spare himself unnecessary headaches, what should he do?

***A. Run the command \i386\winnt32 -checkupgradeonly**

B. Run the command \i386\winnt -checkupgrade

C. Contact Microsoft for a customized HCL

D. Run the command \i386\winnt32 -upgrade

E. No Answer is Correct

Explanation: You may run the Windows XP Upgrade Advisor before installing Windows XP on a system on which a previous version of Windows is already installed. You can start this directly from the menu that appears when you insert the Windows XP CD or when running the command: d:\i386\winnt32 -checkupgradeonly at any command prompt. This will replace D with the correct drive letter.

2. John is planning to upgrade his existing Win98 system to WinXP. He wants to sure that after the upgrade there is no need for him to additionally install a series of updates. What should he do?

A. Download the service packs and include them in the same CD, under \sp

***B. Make sure an Internet connection is ready**

***C. Request the installation utility to retrieve dynamic updates**

D. Download the service packs and include them in a separate CD, under \i386

E. No Answer is Correct

Explanation: When upgrading over an existing Windows version, Setup checks for dynamic updates. Dynamic updates include service packs, updated drivers for hardware detected on your system, and upgrade packs for programs you are currently running. This requires Internet connection to work though.

3. John is planning to upgrade his existing Win98 system to WinXP. He is not too sure if his system can be upgraded smoothly. His system has a 166MHZ processor, 128M RAM, 1.GB hard disk and a 4M SVGA adaptor. For a successful upgrade, he will have to replace or strengthen which hardware components?

A. RAM

B. Nothing has to be replaced

***C. Processor**

D. Display Adaptor

***E. Hard disk**

Explanation: You must check to confirm that your hardware satisfies the system requirements. Microsoft says the bare minimum configuration includes a 233 MHz processor; 64 MB of RAM; 1.5 GB of spare disk space; and a video adapter capable of Super VGA (800x600) resolution. The recommended configuration is at least a 300 MHz CPU with 128 MB of RAM.

4. You will be installing WinXP on a computer you purchased one year ago. This computer has 256M RAM and 9GB of disk space. Five users will be sharing this computer. All of them use graphic intensive software. You need to ensure optimal performance and efficient user switching. Which of the following is a correct guideline to follow?

A. Make sure you have a 500mhz+ CPU

B. Add an additional 100MHZ for each user

***C. Add an additional 64M of RAM for each user**

D. Consider deploying a RAID 5 disk subsystem

E. Consider installing an OPENGL compatible video adaptor

Explanation: Most of the time the speed of the CPU is probably the least critical element of an XP system. More memory will do much more to keep a system running smoothly, especially with multiple applications and multiple users. Plan to have at least 64 MB for each additional user. 128MB on a single user system is the minimum recommended setup.

5. You will be installing WinXP on a Compaq computer you purchased one month ago. What are the available forms of WinXP Pro installation for this computer?

***A. Clean install**

B. Remote install

***C. Side by side**

D. Diskless install

***E. Upgrade over**

Explanation: A clean install ensures that you are wiping out all traces of any previous Windows problems caused by installing and uninstalling programs, downloading Web-based components, and over-tweaking the computer's settings. Therefore, you will have a clean registry and a solid base of Windows system files to start with. Upgrade over or side-by-side are valid forms of upgrade, although in the real world we see many problems encountered during such upgrades.

6. Which of the following stages will be skipped if you boot your system using the WinXP installation CD for installation?

***A. File copy**

B. Text mode setup

C. GUI mode setup

D. Windows Welcome

E. Reboot

Explanation: A clean setup consists of several distinct steps. Of these steps, at the File copy step the installer copies the Windows Setup files to a folder on the partition where they can run when you restart the system. If you boot from CD, Setup skips this step and loads the files directly from the CD.

7. When installing WinXP, at which stage will you create the partition you want to use for the Windows XP system files?

A. File copy

***B. Text mode setup**

C. Windows Welcome

D. GUI mode setup

E. Reboot

Explanation: A clean setup consists of several distinct steps. Of these steps, you need have experienced the Text mode setup when you select, create and format the partition you want to use for the Windows XP system files.

8. When installing WinXP, at which stage will you activate the operating system?

A. File copy

B. System Restart

C. GUI mode setup

***D. Windows Welcome**

E. Text mode setup

Explanation: Windows Welcome is the final portion of Setup, where you have the option to create user accounts and activate Windows. You can modify these options with OEM builders to add their own logos, custom registration screens, and additional options or features.

9. As a system integrator, at which stage will you incorporate your custom registration process during WinXP installation?

A. File copy

B. Text mode setup

***C. Windows Welcome**

D. GUI mode setup

E. Reboot

Explanation: OEM System manufacturers can modify options to add their own logos, custom registration screens, and additional options or features. This is often being referred to as Out Of Box Experience, or OOBE – the experience you have when you take a new computer out of the box and set it up for the first time.

10. You want to install WinXP on a legacy PC. This PC is equipped with enough RAM and hard drive space. However, it does not have a floppy drive. How to you ensure that a bootable CD will work properly?

A. Load smartdrv before booting

B. Disable BIOS virus scanning

C. Enable BIOS rom cacheable

***D. Set the boot order in the BIOS so that the CD drive is the first boot device**

E. Set the boot order in the BIOS so that the hard drive is the first boot device

Explanation: For a bootable CD to work, you must set the boot order in the BIOS so that the CD drive is the first boot device, followed by the hard disk, floppy disk, and any other bootable devices, in whichever order you prefer. The boot options available for every computer are different. Refer to the system manual for instructions on how to access the BIOS setup program.

Chapter 2: What's New in Windows XP?

The objective of this chapter is to provide you with an understanding of the following:

1. Obtain a working knowledge the new features of Windows XP, both Professional and Home Edition, and the differences between the two versions.
2. Obtain an overview of the enhancements from Windows XP.

Getting Ready – (Questions)

1. How many versions are there of Windows XP?
2. What would make me want to switch to XP from, let's say, Windows 98SE?

Getting Ready – (Answers)

1. At the time of publication, there are five different versions of Windows XP – Home, Professional, Media Centre, Tablet PC, and 64-bit. This book focuses on Windows XP Professional and points out some of the differences between the Professional version and the Windows XP Home version.

2. Windows XP offers many improvements and enhancements that appeal to both home users and professional offices. Some of these include:

- Improved Application Compatibility
- Improved Hardware Device Compatibility
- Simplified Logon
- Fast User Switching
- Simplified User Interface and Web Views
- Enhanced Digital Media
- Software Based Firewall
- Direct X 8.0

I Introduction

In the last chapter, we looked at all the ways that Windows XP Professional could be installed. Before we delve deeply into the nuts and bolts of Windows XP, let's take a moment to look at the new and exciting features this latest product from Microsoft has to offer. Windows XP is the long-awaited single operating system that replaces both the Windows 9x (95, 98, ME) operating systems, intended for home use, and the Windows NT (3.51, 4.0, 2000) operating system, built for professional environments. XP comes in two flavors – Home Edition and Professional. While this book primarily focuses on the Professional Edition, it is certainly worthwhile to note the features both versions share, as well as the extra attributes contained in the Professional Edition.

With XP coming hot on the heels of the long-awaited Windows 2000 operating system, it is also important to note the similarities and differences between these two operating systems, and the enhancements offered in Windows XP. So keeping this in mind, let's take a look at what is new in Windows XP!

II What's New in Windows XP?

Windows XP Home Edition is particularly targeted at home users. Windows 95, 98 and Millennium (ME), while originally designed for personal, not corporate use, was frequently used by businesses as the desktop operating system for users. Windows NT 4.0 Workstation and Windows XP, which were designed for corporate use specifically because of their security and stability, were not as frequently in place as the operating system for home use.

In order to solve this challenge, with the new XP operating system, Microsoft has provided two flavors-Home Edition and Professional Edition. Both have significant enhancements over Windows XP.

Improved Application Compatibility

Microsoft has worked hard to provide fixes to hundreds of applications that simply would not work on Windows XP. As new application fixes become available, Windows Update (Figure 2.1) will provide an easy mechanism for access.

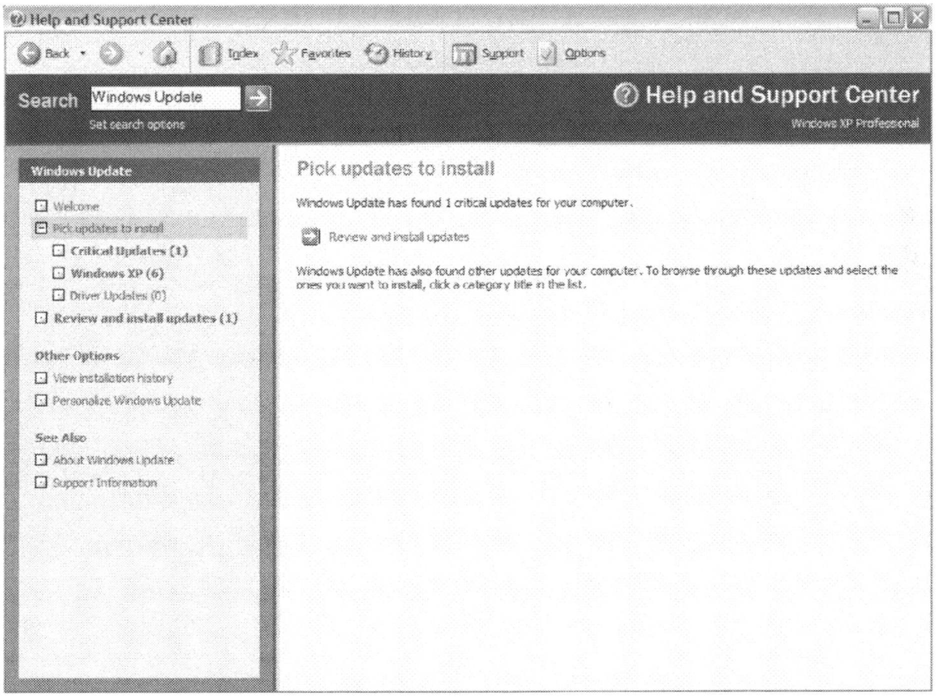

Figure 2-1: Windows Update

Windows XP has also included a Program Compatibility Wizard that allows the user to indicate whether an application was originally written to run in NT 4.0, or Windows 95/98/ME. By using the Wizard, it allows XP's system DLLs to give the appropriate responses to the application. The application is essentially "fooled" into thinking that it is running on its old platform, and will execute without a noticeable performance loss.

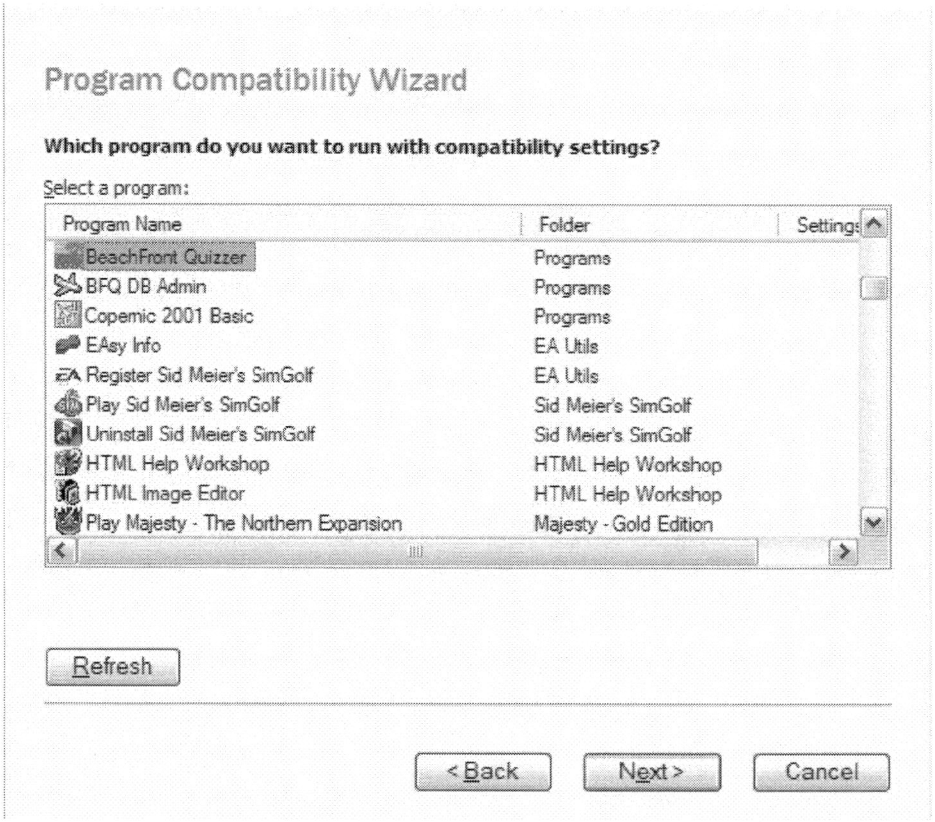

Figure 2-2: Program Compatibility Wizard

NOTE: The "Designed for Windows Logo" and listings in the Windows Catalog is by no means a complete list of programs or devices that will be compatible for Windows XP. They are, however, the ones that Microsoft has tested and guaranteed will work with XP. If you have a specific hardware device that you wish to use that is NOT listed on the Hardware Compatibility List and/or in Windows Catalog, contact the manufacturer directly to see if they have tested it against Windows XP.

Improved Hardware Device Compatibility

Windows XP has been built to support the latest hardware standards, including:

- UDF 2.01, the standard for reading DVD discs
- Formatting of DVD-RAM drives with FAT32 file system
- DirectX 8 API support
- IrDA standards (Infrared Data Association)
- USB standards (Universal Serial Bus)
- IEEE 1394 standards (high-speed bus)

As well, because it is built on the device driver verifier that exists in Windows 2000, XP continues with the tradition of rigorous stress tests for all device drivers. Any driver that passes these tests will be considered to be the most robust, stable drivers available at that time.

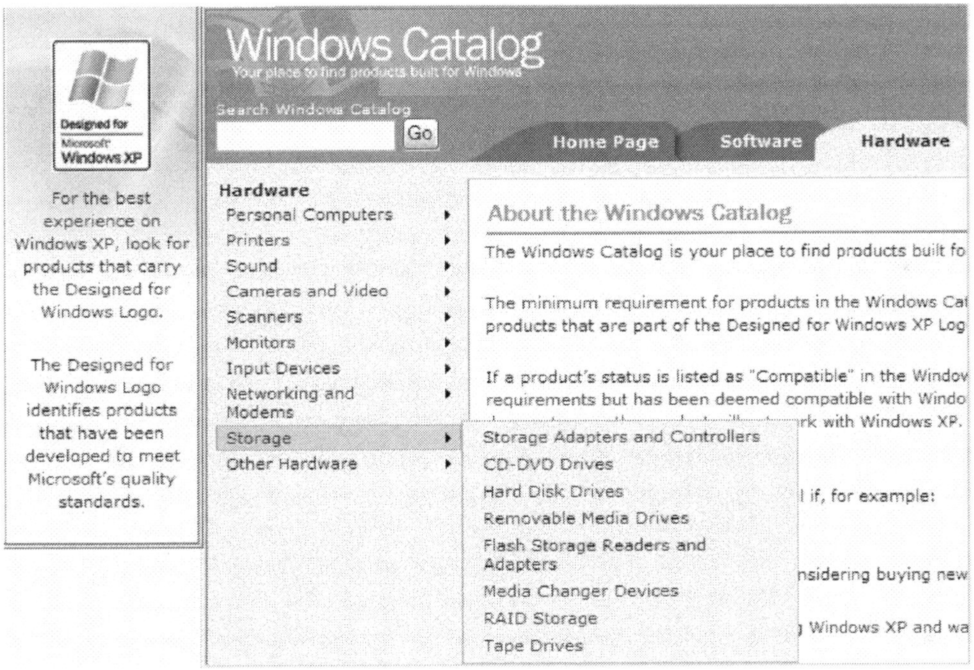

Figure 2-3: Hardware Windows Catalog

Simplified Logon

For users who are members of a domain, XP's logon stays pretty much the same as it has in the past…the familiar "username/password/domain" logon box. However, XP does include a new option that allows the administrator (or member of the domain administrators group) to require a user to press CTRL+ALT+DEL before logging on. Without selecting this option, the logon box automatically appears, without user intervention. Requiring the user to press CTRL+ALT+DEL before logging on increases security simply because it requires user interaction. This can frustrate certain Trojan horse programs.

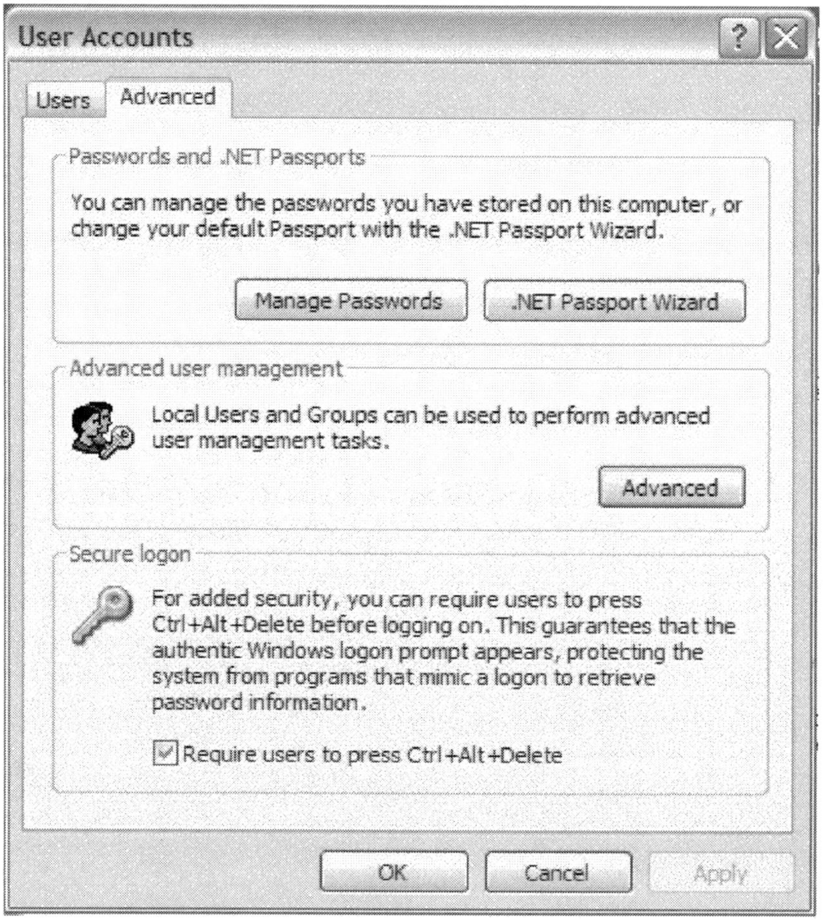

Figure 2-4: Secure Logon

Microsoft also has available on their website the new "PowerToys" for XP, the additional programs that developers work on after product release. The URL for the toys is: http://www.microsoft.com/windowsxp/pro/downloads /powertoys.asp

Included in the toys is the familiar TweakUI. TweakUI allows you to configure XP Professional to autologon…not the best for secure environments, but very handy for situations where the computer is already secure.

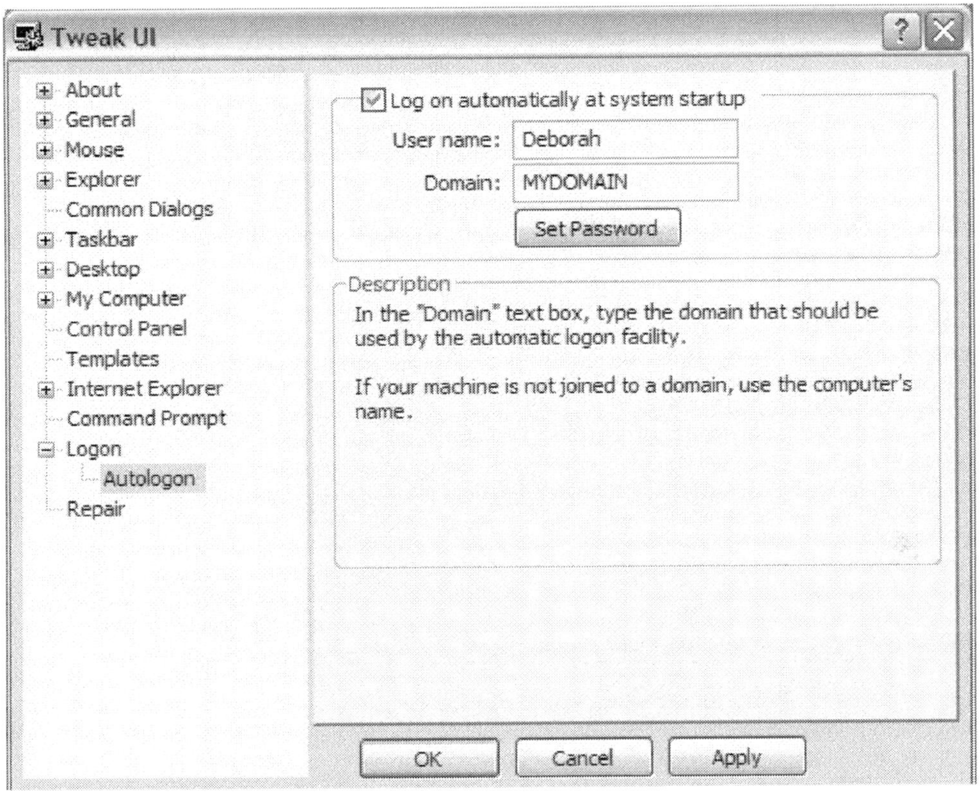

Figure 2-5: Autologon using TweakUI

However, when a user is operating in a workgroup environment, or on a stand-alone machine, the logon screen may appear to be quite different. Many people operate in an environment where more than one user interfaces with the same computer. The default Welcome screen now allows for a simple way for users to access their own desktop environment.

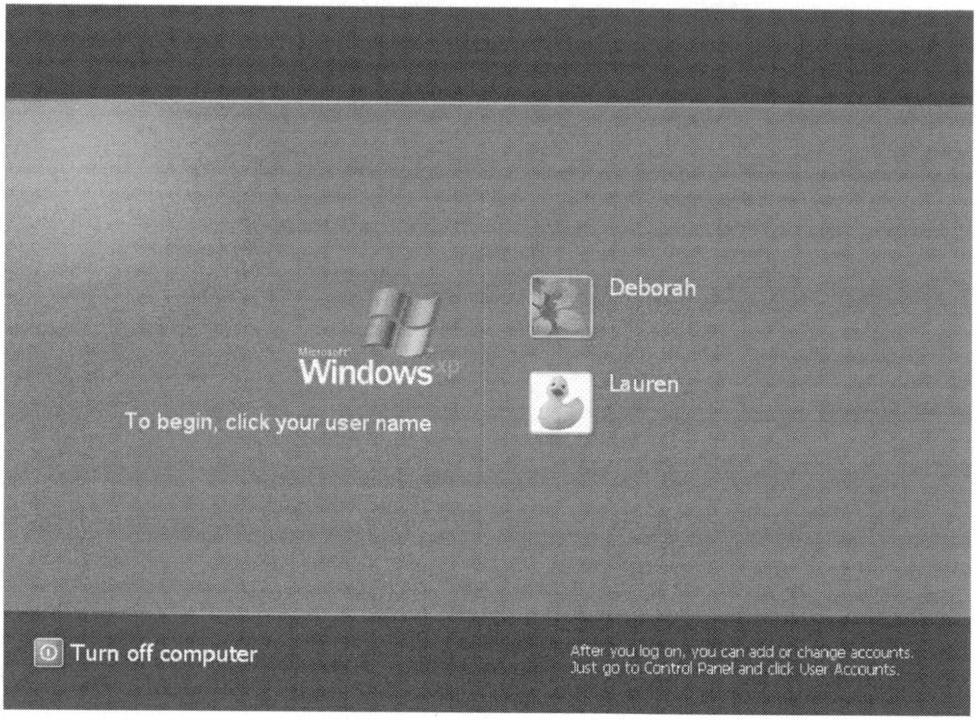

Figure 2-6: Welcome Screen

This feature is not available in domain mode.

In order to turn the Welcome screen on or off, you must have access to the computer administrator account. In Control Panel, access the User Accounts. Select **Change the way users log on or off**. If you want your users to use the Welcome Screen (Figure 2-6), then select the **Use the Welcome Screen** option. (This is selected, by default, on installation.) Using the Welcome Screen also allows for Fast User Switching, which is covered in the next section. The user simply selects their username, and if a password is assigned to the account, the user is prompted to type it.

If you wish your users to logon to the computer with the standard **Log On to Windows** dialog box, uncheck the **Use the Welcome Screen** option. The welcome screen will not longer appear, and users will have to type in their username and password, if there is one assigned to the account.

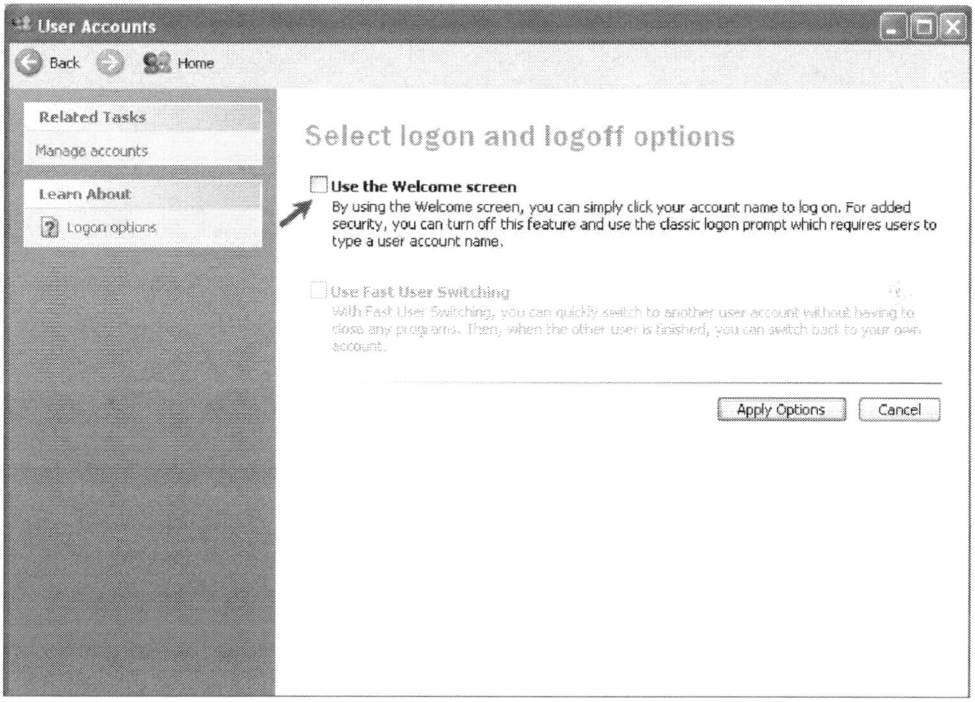

Figure 2-7: Turning On or Off the Welcome Screen

Fast User Switching

A new feature with Windows XP is Fast User Switching. Fast User Switching allows individuals to switch between users without actually logging off from the computer. Many users can use the same system, even simultaneously, switching back and forth without closing the programs that are running.

> **NOTE:** Fast user switching is available with both Professional and Home Editions of XP, but only when the computer is NOT a member of a domain – in other words, if it is a member of a workgroup or a standalone system. This feature is also only available if the Welcome Screen method of logon is being used.

To switch to another user is simple. From the Start menu, click **Log Off**. The dialog box shown in Figure 2-8 below appears. Click the **Switch User** icon and the Welcome Screen will reappear, as previously illustrated in Figure 2-6, with one difference. Under the name of each user that is currently logged onto the system, a "Logged On' line appears under their name.

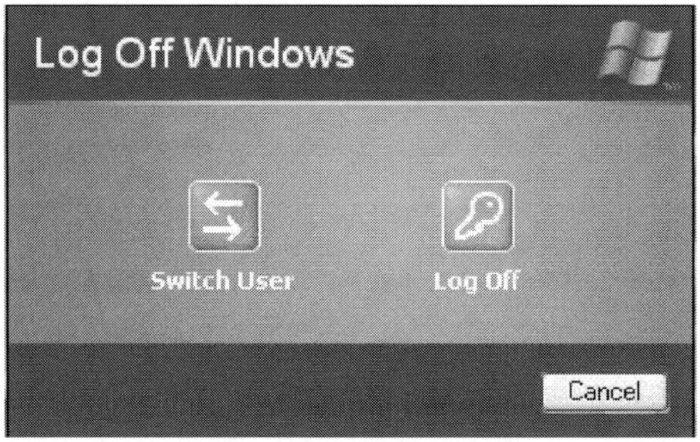

Figure 2-8: Fast User Switching

Fast user switching can be turned on and off at the same screen as changing the status of the Welcome Screen (Control Panel, Users). Deselecting the checkbox will disable fast user switching. However, this feature cannot be disabled if there are multiple users logged onto the system. All users will need to log off, with the exception of the computer administrator.

> **NOTE:** When Fast User Switching is turned on, Serial Keys will not work. Serial Keys is an accessibility feature that allows support for alternative input devices, such as puff and sip devices, for individuals who cannot access a standard keyboard or mouse.

Simplified User Interface and Web Views

Quite often, seasoned Windows users have a similar reaction when they first load XP – "Well, isn't that pretty. Why do I want it?" But XP's functionality does extend far beyond "pretty". The menus are "cleaned up" and organized (Figure 2-9).

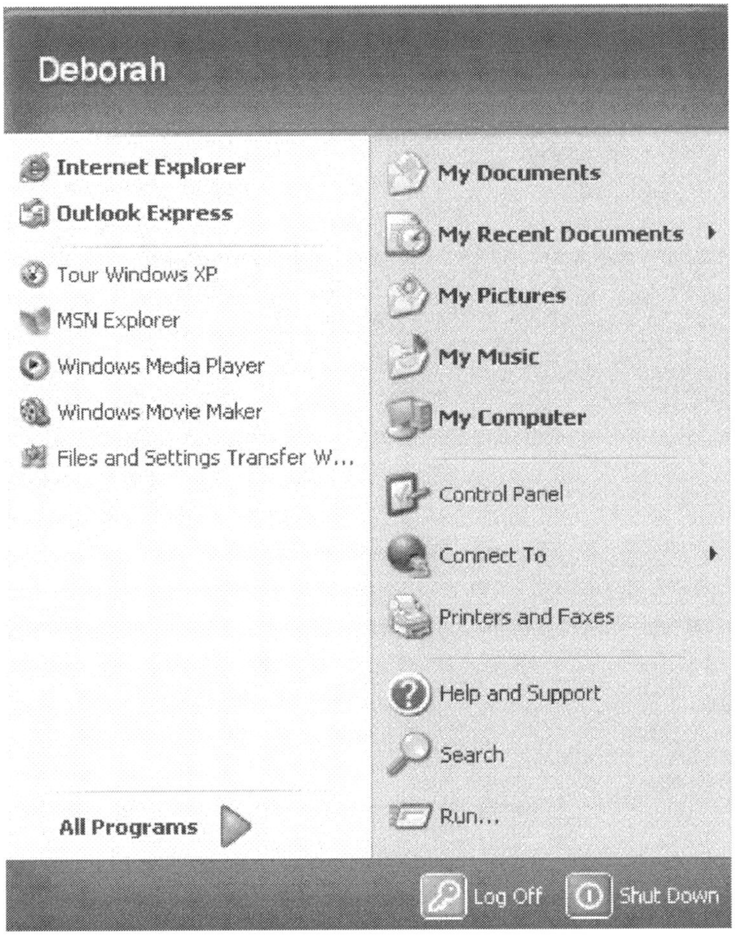

Figure 2-9: Simplified Menus

The first time you start Windows XP, you'll see only one icon—the Recycle Bin. This makes for a clean desktop (Figure 2-10).

Figure 2-10: The new XP Desktop

Familiar desktop items, such as My Computer and My Network Places can be added to the desktop by modifying its properties. Right-click the desktop, choose **Properties** from the shortcut menu, select the **Desktop** tab, and click on **Customize Desktop**. The **Desktop Items** dialog box appears (Figure 2-11), which will allow you to display My Computer, My Documents, My Network Places, and Internet Explorer shortcuts on your desktop. As well, you can opt to select the **Desktop Cleanup Wizard**, automatically every 60 days. The Cleanup Wizard will put any unused desktop icons into a folder. Just the tool needed to keep your desktop clean and uncluttered!

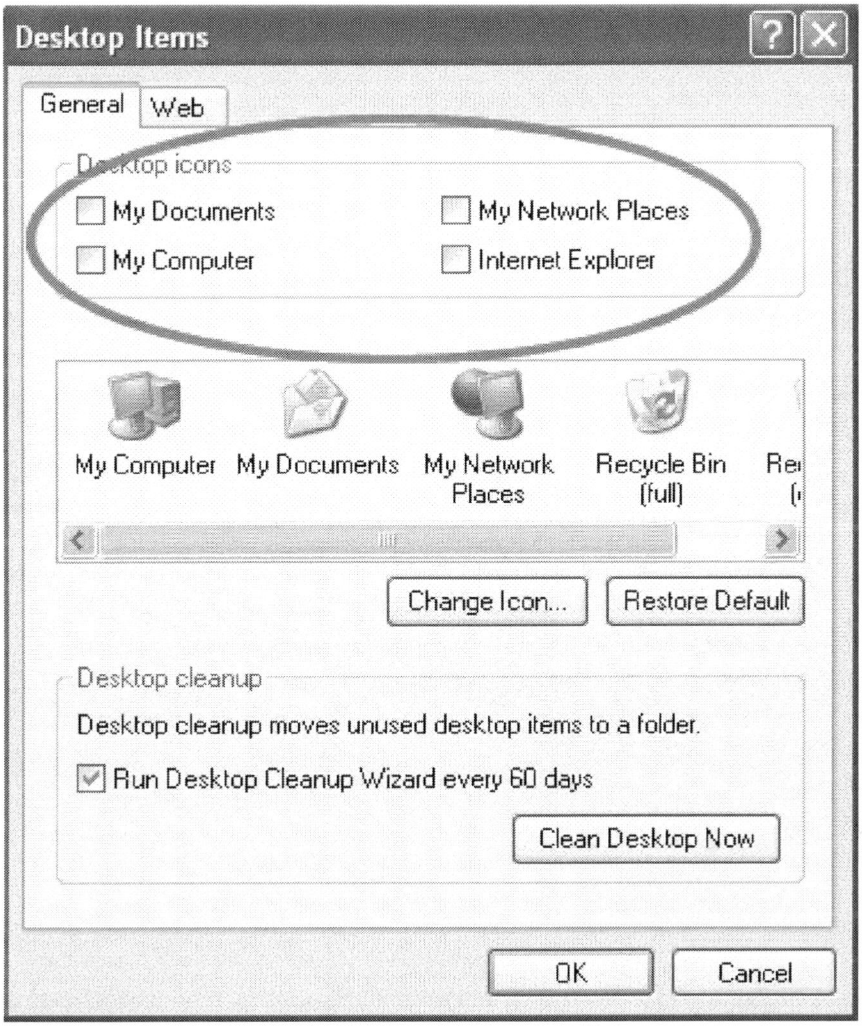

Figure 2-11: Customizing Your Desktop

There is a very different look and feel to a number of the dialog boxes. Even the Start button and other desktop items have changed look. That look is part of a new theme, and a number of the new dialog boxes have the new "web view" (Figure 2-12). While this look is designed to simplify your use of XP, unify the overall look of your working environment and, of course, clean up your desktop, you can switch back to the older, classic style.

This is done by right-clicking your desktop, selecting **Properties**, selecting the **Appearance** tab, and then choosing "Windows Classic Style" from the drop-down selection box, under the item **Windows and buttons.**

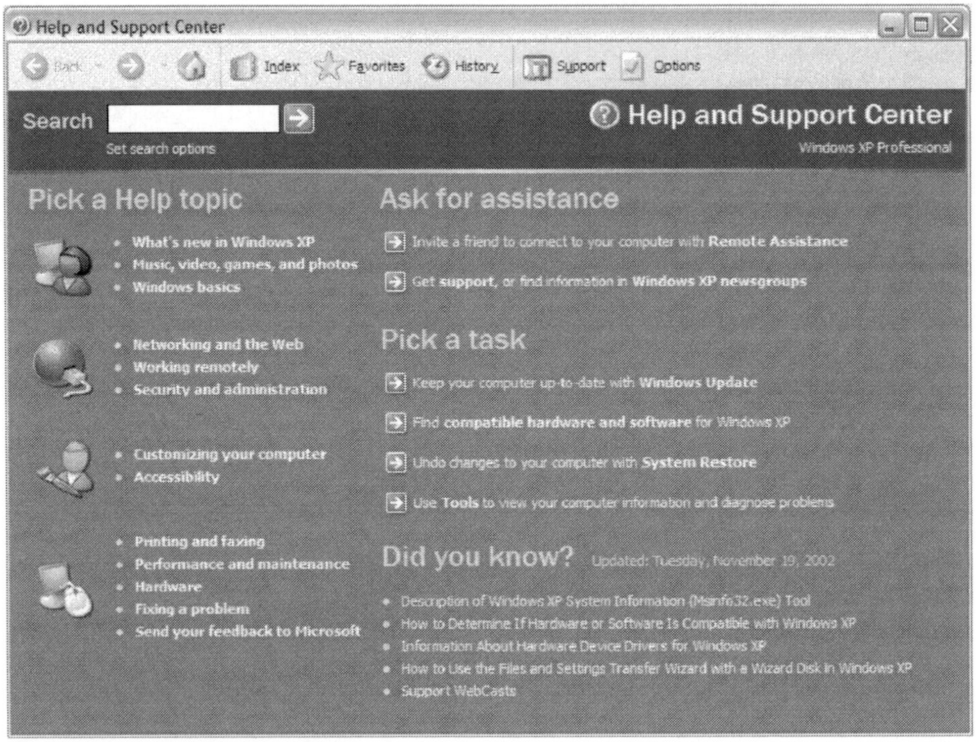

Figure 2-12: Windows XP Help: an example of new look and feel

A few of the other changes you will notice are differences in the Start Menu, the Taskbar and Control Panel. The Start menu is intuitive, showing you who is logged on and automatically moving more frequently used programs to the top-level menu. You can move any program you like to the Start Menu. My Pictures, My Documents and Control Panel are all now available from the top level menu.

The Taskbar now provides taskbar grouping, a wonderful new feature that groups like items under one taskbar button. For example, if you have a number of Internet Explorer windows open, taskbar grouping will show only one button, indicating in red the number of Internet Explorer windows you have open. Clicking on the button will provide a drop down menu from which you can choose the window that you need.

As well, notification area icons (the area by the clock) are hidden from view if you haven't used it in a while. You can click the arrow (<) next to the notification area to display all hidden icons.

Control Panel has a new view called Category View (Figure 2-13). Category View groups together similar items, while Classic View displays all items individually.

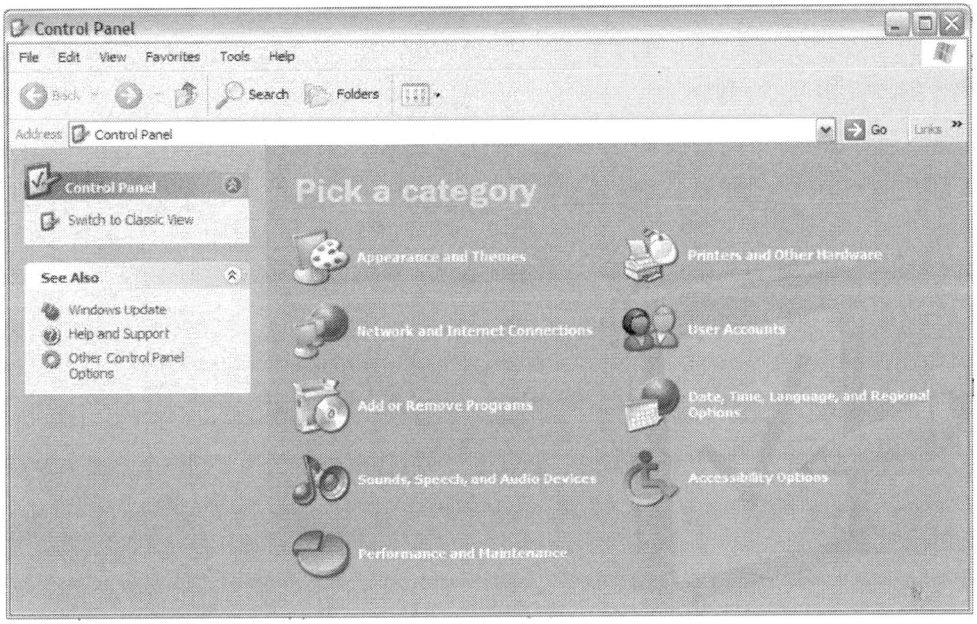

Figure 2-13: Category View Control Panel

Enhanced Digital Media

Windows Media Player (Figure 2-14) combines all of your common digital media needs into a single, easy-to-use interface. Windows Media Player allows you to do the following:

- View media-rich information. An example of this could be a virtual meetings or "just-in-time" education.
- Receive the best-possible audio and video quality. Windows Media Player adapts on-the-fly to network conditions.
- Create custom CDs, sometimes up to 700% faster than other solutions.
- View DVD movies on your PC.

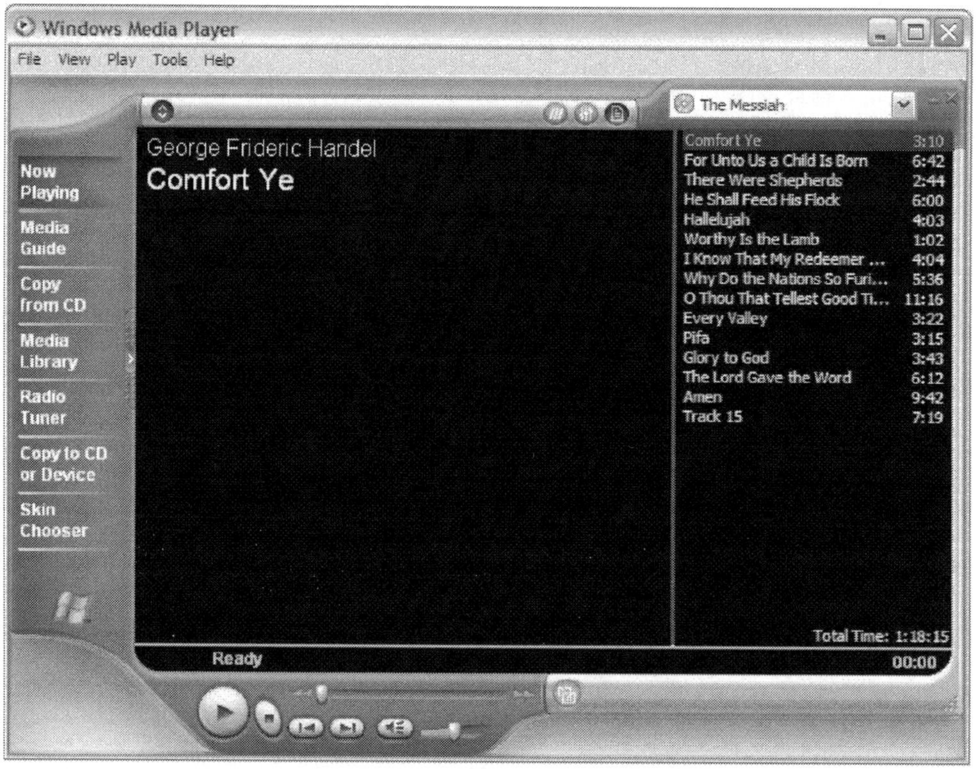

Figure 2-14: Windows Media Player

Software Based Firewall

What is a firewall? In the computer world, a firewall is a system designed to prevent unauthorized access to or from a private network. It can be either hardware and software, or a combination of both. A common use of a firewall is to prevent unauthorized Internet users from accessing information stored on a private network while they are connected to the Internet. All blocks entering or leaving the local network pass through the firewall, which examines each packet and blocks those that do not meet the specified security criteria.

Internet Connection Firewall (ICF) is firewall software that will help protect your home or network from unauthorized intrusions.

Direct X 8.0

DirectX technology helps games and other programs use the advanced multimedia capabilities of your hardware. DirectX 8.0 is the newest version of DirectX, and should help you gain a more rich multimedia experience.

Pop Quiz 2.1

Pop Quiz 2.1 *Questions*

1). What is the Program Compatibility Wizard?

2). Why might you want your users to hit CTRL-ALT-DEL to have the logon box appear?

3). Can you use Fast User Switching in a domain environment?

4). How do you get familiar desktop items, such as My Computer and My Network Places added to the desktop?

5). What is the difference between Category View and Classic View in Control Panel?

Pop Quiz 2.1 *Answers*

1. The Program Compatibility Wizard allows the user to indicate whether an application was originally written to run in NT 4.0, or Windows 95/98/ME. By using the Wizard, it allows XP's system DLLs to give the appropriate responses to the application.
2. Requiring the user to press CTRL+ALT+DEL before logging on increases security simply because it requires user interaction. This can frustrate certain Trojan horse programs.
3. Fast user switching is available with both Professional and Home Editions of XP, but only when the computer is NOT a member of a domain – in other words, if it is a member of a workgroup or a standalone system.
4. Right-click the desktop, choose Properties from the shortcut menu, select the Desktop tab, and click on Customize Desktop. The Desktop Items dialog box appears (Figure 2-11), which will allow you to display My Computer, My Documents, My Network Places, and Internet Explorer shortcuts on your desktop.
5. Category View groups together similar items, while Classic View displays all items individually.

III Comparing XP Home to XP Professional

The biggest question is often "Which version of Windows XP should I use?" Microsoft asks five questions that can help you decide which version you wish to install:.

- Do you want to remotely access your computer so you can work with all your data and applications while away from your desk?
- Do you connect to a large network?
- Do you need to protect sensitive data in files and folders that are stored on your computer?
- Do you need the ability to completely restore your system in the event of a catastrophic failure?
- Would you consider yourself a "power user"?

If you answered "yes" to any of these questions, then you will probably want to choose Windows XP Professional as your operating system. Let's look at the details for each of these questions.

Remote Desktop and Remote Assistance

One of the best things to happen to desktop computing, especially for technical support personnel, is remote assistance. While Remote Desktop and Remote Assistance rely on the same technology, and essentially the same concept, they are used for different reasons.

Remote Desktop allows you to have access to a Windows session that is running on your computer, when you are at another computer. Remote Assistance allows someone, like a Technical Support person, to use an Internet connection to access your computer to provide assistance.

Available only on Windows XP Professional, Remote Desktop allows you to:

- **Redirect the system.** Once Remote Desktop is started, any file residing on the remote computer is accessible as if it was on a network–shared drive.
- **Redirect a printer**. Let's say you are working on a work project at home one evening. Using Remote Desktop allows you to access the document on your work computer, store it on your work computer, but print it out on your printer at home.
- **Use Port redirection**. You can use the devices on your one computer and the applications on another together via Remote Desktop.
- **Use Audio**. You are attending a business presentation. Now you can run audio–enabled presentation on your office computer and hear the sound from speakers attached to the computer at your client's office.
- **Share a Clipboard**. The Remote Desktop and the client computer share a clipboard that allows data to be interchanged.
- **Feel Secure.** Remote desktop technologies used to be considered "not secure" because when you accessed your computer remotely, any person near your computer could see exactly what work you were doing. Remote Desktop locks the computer to which you connected remotely. Anyone viewing the computer will only see the logon screen.
- **Use Web Accessibility.** Without adding any client software, you can use **Remote Desktop Web Connection** to securely connect and work with the remote computer from inside Internet Explorer. Connection is made through a Web address.
- **Use Many Other Features,** such as power management, offline files and ActiveSync technology.

> **NOTE:** Remote Desktop is the way recommended by Microsoft for troubleshooting remote servers.

Remote assistance has been a lifesaver for many an IT professional. Many problems can be solved without having to be physically present at the client's workstation. Both the client and the technical assistant must be running an operating system that supports remote assistance (at this time, only Windows XP supports it). Both individuals must also be running either Windows Messenger or a MAPI-compliant email, such as Microsoft Outlook, as well as being connected to the Internet.

If there are firewalls between the computers, the firewalls must allow the traffic.

The client sends out an invitation (with a time limit) to the person providing assistance. Once the invitation is accepted, the technical assistant can see the client's computer screen, can chat with the client "real time" about what is happening, and with the client's permission can "take over" the desktop, using his or her own keyboard and mouse to control the environment.

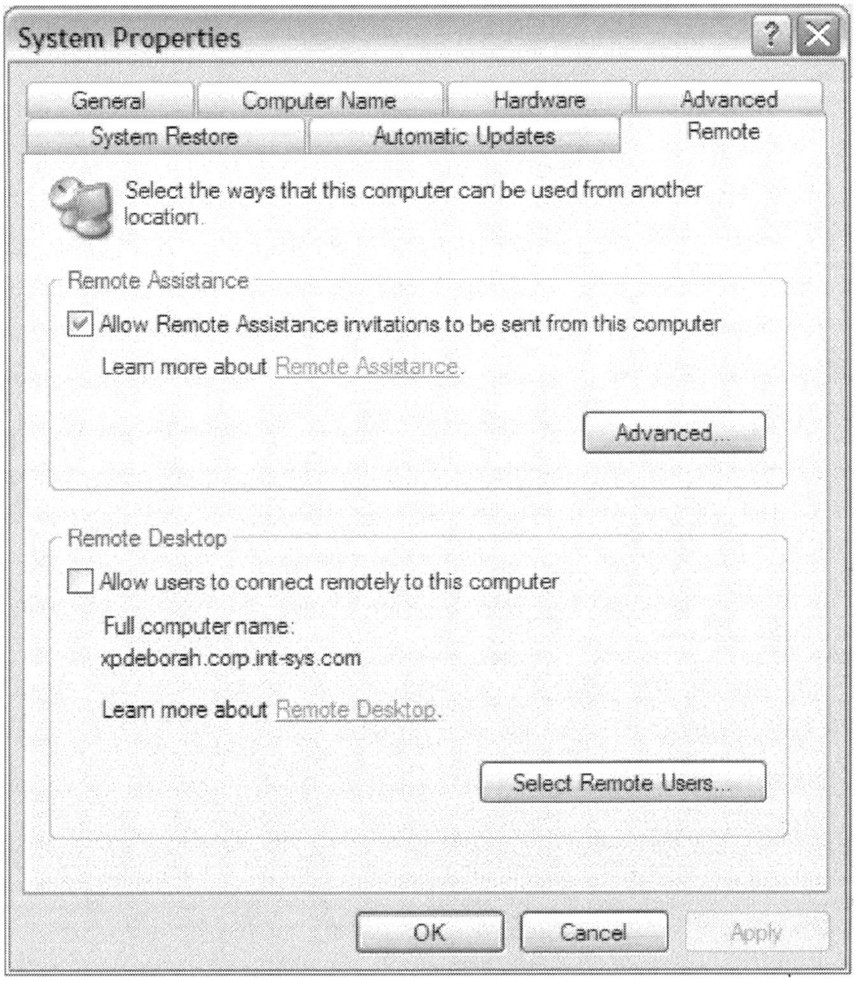

Figure 2-15: Remote Assistance and Remote Desktop

It is important to note that the remote computer must grant access before anyone can connect remotely to it. Access is granted through the **System** icon in Control Panel, on the **Remote** tab (Figure 2.15). The technical assistant must either be an administrator or a member of the local Remote Desktop Users group.

> NOTE: You must be an administrator or a member of the Administrators Group to enable the Remote Desktop feature.

You must be logged on as an administrator or a member of the Administrators group to enable the Remote Desktop feature.

Network Size

While Windows XP Home is an ideal choice for home or small networks, larger networks will benefit from XP Professional. Microsoft's recommendation is that XP Professional be used for any network that is more than five computers.

To access a domain-based network, you will require Windows XP Professional.

Security

The Encrypting File System (EFS) is found in Windows XP Professional but not Windows XP Home Edition. EFS allows an individual to encrypt files and folders for an additional level of security (especially for sensitive data) against theft or hackers. Encrypted File System (EFS) provides file encryption on an individual file basis using a public-key system. EFS encryption and NTFS file compression are mutually exclusive; you cannot compress an encrypted file. Sparse files may be encrypted.

Another feature found only in Windows XP Professional is "Restricted File Access." RFS allows you to restrict access to specific files, applications, and many other resources.

System Restore

Because it is designed for professional office use, rather than a small working environment, Windows XP Professional provides more forceful alternatives for backing up and restoring data than XP Home. An example of this is "System Restore". System Restore is essentially an "undo" command for system settings. While you are working on the system, System Restore automatically monitors and records key system changes. If you make a system setting change and then discover a problem, the change can be "rolled back" using System Restore.

Features for Power Users

If you are a user than needs "more", demands "more", wants "more" from your computer, then Windows XP Professional will be the choice for you. This operating system has a number of additional features that are covered in greater detail throughout this book. Some of the more notable features you may want to consider when making your choice include:

- Advanced networking for multiple PC environments
- Internet Information Services (IIS), a feature that lets you host and manage personal Web sites
- Support for multiple-processor systems
- Support for multiple languages

Pop Quiz 2.2

Pop Quiz 2.1 *Questions*

1. What is the difference between Remote Desktop and Remote Assistance?
2. What level of permission must you have to enable Remote Desktop?
3. When should you consider changing from Windows XP Home Edition to Professional Edition?
4. What is EFS?

Pop Quiz 2.2 *Answers*

1). Remote Desktop allows you to have access to a Windows session that is running on your computer, when you are at another computer. Remote Assistance allows someone, like a Technical Support person, to use an Internet connection to access your computer to provide assistance.

2). You must be an administrator or a member of the Administrators Group to enable the Remote Desktop feature.

3). Microsoft's recommendation is that XP Professional be used for any network that is more than five computers.

4). Encrypted File System (EFS) provides file encryption on an individual file basis using a public-key system.

IV Chapter 2: Summary

We have now completed our chapter on the new features of Windows XP. You should now feel comfortable with the following concepts:

- You should have working knowledge the new features of Windows XP, both Professional and Home Edition, and the differences between the two versions.
- You should have a general overview of the enhancements in Windows XP, which will be covered in greater detail throughout this book.

V Chapter 2: Review Questions

1. Windows XP Professional rather than purchase Windows XP Home Edition. Which additional features are available on Windows XP Professional? Choose all that apply.

A. Additional security and privacy features

B. NTFS

C. Advanced recovery options

D. Improved ability to connect to large networks

E. Disk defragmenter

2. Two years ago, John had upgraded 100 computers from NT 4.0 Workstation to Windows 2000 Professional. He just upgraded them again to Windows XP Professional. Now on all upgraded computers one legacy application has a garbled display, while all the other applications have no such display problem. What should John do?

A. Reinstall the legacy application.

B. Limit the computers to 800 by 600 pixels.

C. Limit the computers to 256 colors.

D. Limit the refresh rate to 60 MHz.

E. In the Compatibility settings for the application, select the Run in 256 colors check box.

3. Jane wants to be able to back her computer data as efficiently as possible. Which three of the following backup solutions are supported by Windows XP that were not supported by Win 9x/ME or Windows 2000 Professional?

A. CD-RW backup

B. Network backup

C. External hard drive connected via USB 2.0

D. External hard drive connected via USB Firewire (IEEE 1394)

E. Backup to DVD

4. John wants to see icons on his desktop for My Computer, My Network Places, Internet Explorer, and My Documents. In Windows XP, how does he get these icons to display?

A. In Display Properties on the Desktop tab select Customize Desktop

B. Right Click on the Start button and select Properties. On the Start Menu Tab select Customize Desktop.

C. In Control Panel, double click on System Properties. Click on the Advanced Tab and then select the Customize Desktop button.

D. In Control Panel, double click on Display Properties. Click on the Appearance Tab and then select the Advanced button.

E. Right Click on the Task Bar and select Properties. On the Advanced Tab select Customize Desktop.

5. You download Tweak UI but you don't see it on your anywhere on your Start menu. What has to be done and what will be the result? Choose two.

A. You have to double click on Tweakui.inf.

B. You have to right click on Tweakui.inf and select install.

C. You have to double click on Tweakui.exe.

D. Tweak UI will be installed into the System Tools.

E. Tweak UI will be installed into the Control Panel.

6. Other users can connect to your computer but they cannot ping it. What might be preventing this?

A. ICF

B. Group Policy

C. Local policies

D. Duplicate IP address

E. IPSEC

7. Which statement best describes how Remote Assistance and Remote Desktop differ?

A. They are the same tool but with two functions. The way that the tool is used determines its name.

B. Remote Assistance only allows viewing of your computer, while Remote Desktop allows interaction with your desktop.

C. Remote Desktop only allows viewing of your computer, while Remote Assistance allows interaction with your desktop.

D. Remote Desktop lets you view a remote desktop, but only allows you to interact with it if the remote user permits; while Remote Assistance lets you remotely connect to your computer as if you were directly connected.

E. Remote Assistance lets you view a remote desktop, but only allows you to interact with it if the remote user permits; while Remote Desktop lets you remotely connect to your computer as if you were directly connected.

8.You receive a Remote Assistance invitation to fix your boss' Windows XP computer after he returns from a meeting. Your boss reconnects to his ISP and you try to connect to his computer, but your attempt is unsuccessful. What should you do?

A. Connect to your boss' computer by his new IP address.

B. Instruct your boss to send a new invitation and then reboot his computer.

C. Instruct your boss to send a new invitation and to stay connected to his ISP.

D. Connect to your boss' computer using the connection specific DNS host name.

E. On your computer run ipconfig /flushdns.

9. You try to encrypt a file but you cannot. What might be preventing this? Choose all that apply.

A. You are not an administrator.

B. The file is compressed.

C. The file is on a FAT partition.

D. The file haves been moved from a FAT32 partition.

E. The file is a sparce file.

10. A user reports that they can't find a Word document that they just created and they have either forgotten where they saved it or deleted it. What method could **not** be used to find and retrieve it?

A. Recycle Bin

B. System Restore

C. Start > Search

D. Start > My Recent Documents

E. Start Word and look for the last documents opened.

VI Chapter 2: Review Answers

1. John is trying to decide whether he should pay the extra money for Windows XP Professional rather than purchase Windows XP Home Edition. Which additional features are available on Windows XP Professional? Choose all that apply.

***A. Additional security and privacy features**

B. NTFS

***C. Advanced recovery options**

***D. Improved ability to connect to large networks**

E. Disk defragmenter

Explanation: Enhanced Security includes the Encrypted File System. Advanced recovery options include system restore, Last Known Good Configuration, and device driver rollback. Improved ability to connect to large networks includes the ability to join and be managed by a domain, Remote Assistance, and Remote Desktop.

References:

http://www.microsoft.com/windowsxp/evaluation/default.asp,
http://www.microsoft.com/windowsxp/pro/howtobuy/choosing.asp,
http://www.microsoft.com/windowsxp/pro/evaluation/whyupgrade/featurecomp.asp

2. Two years ago, John has upgraded 100 computers from NT 4.0 Workstation to Windows 2000 Professional. He just upgraded them again to Windows XP Professional. Now on all upgraded computers one legacy application has a garbled display, while the all the other applications have no display problem. What should John do?

A. Reinstall the legacy application.

B. Limit the computers to 800 by 600 pixels.

C. Limit the computers to 256 colors.

D. Limit the refresh rate to 60 MHz.

***E. In the Compatibility settings for the application, select the Run in 256 colors check box.**

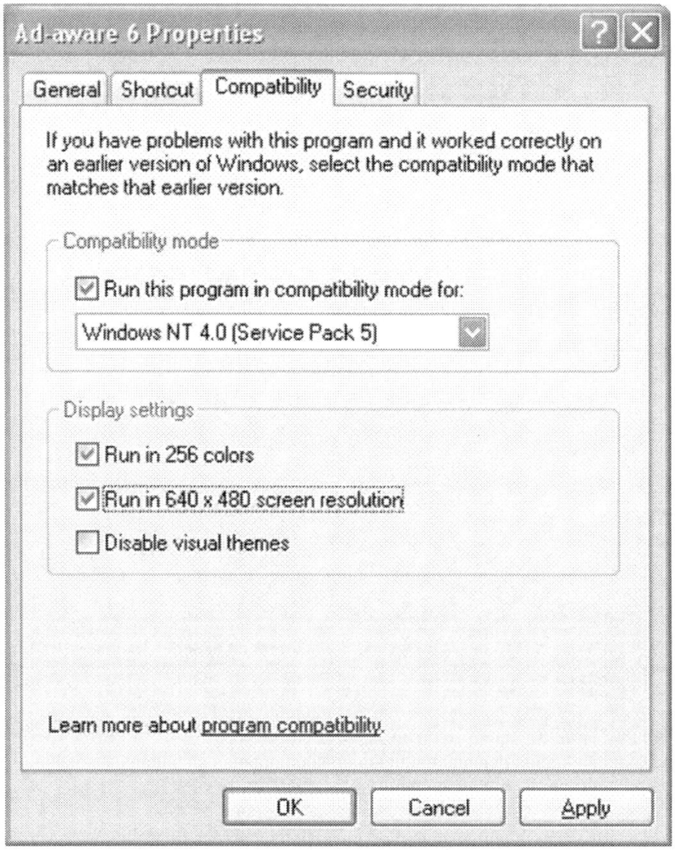

Explanation: In the Compatibility settings for the application, select the Run in 256 colors check box. This problem is specific to this application.

3. Jane wants to be able to back her computer data as efficiently as possible. Which three of the following backup solutions are supported by Windows XP that were not supported by Win 9x/ME or Windows 2000 Professional?

A. CD-RW backup

B. Network backup

***C. External hard drive connected via USB 2.0**

***D. External hard drive connected via USB Firewire (IEEE 1394)**

***E. Backup to DVD**

Explanation: Windows XP has been built to support the latest hardware standards, including:

1. UDF 2.01, the standard for reading DVD discs
2. Formatting of DVD-RAM drives with FAT32 file system
3. DirectX 8 API support
4. IrDA standards (Infrared Data Association)
5. USB 2.0 standards (Universal Serial Bus)
6. IEEE 1394 standards (high-speed bus)

4. John wants to see icons on his desktop for My Computer, My Network Places, Internet Explorer, and My Documents. In Windows XP, how does he get these icons to display?

***A. In Display Properties on the Desktop tab select Customize Desktop**

B. Right Click on the Start button and select Properties. On the Start Menu tab select Customize Desktop.

C. In Control Panel, double click on System Properties. Click on the Advanced tab and then select the Customize Desktop button.

D. In Control Panel, double click on Display Properties. Click on the Appearance tab and then select the Advanced button.

E. Right Click on the Task Bar and select Properties. On the Advanced tab select Customize Desktop.

Explanation: In Display Properties on the Desktop tab select Customize Desktop.

5. You download Tweak UI but you don't see it on your anywhere on your Start menu. What has to be done and what will be the result? Choose two.

A. You have to double click on Tweakui.inf.

***B. You have to right click on Tweakui.inf and select install.**

C. You have to double click on Tweakui.exe.

D. Tweak UI will be installed into the System Tools.

***E. Tweak UI will be installed into the Control Panel.**

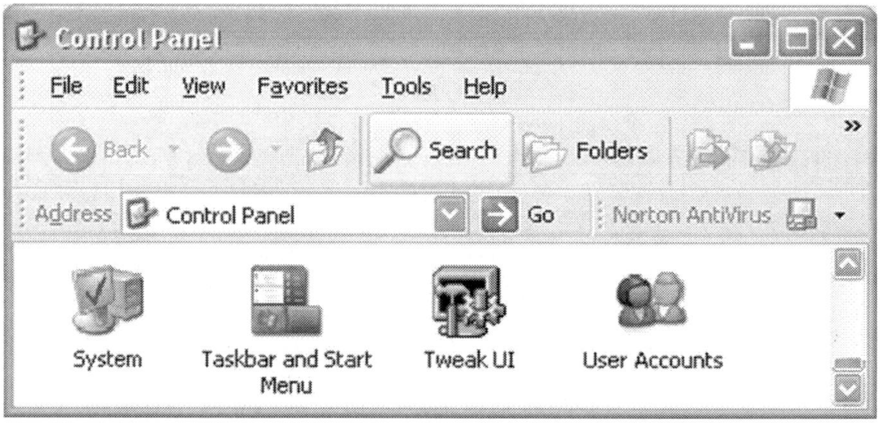

Reference:

http://www.microsoft.com/ntworkstation/downloads/PowerToys/Networking/NTTweakUI.asp

6. Other users can connect to your computer but they cannot ping it. What might be preventing this?

***A. ICF**

B. Group Policy

C. Local policies

D. Duplicate IP address

E. IPSEC

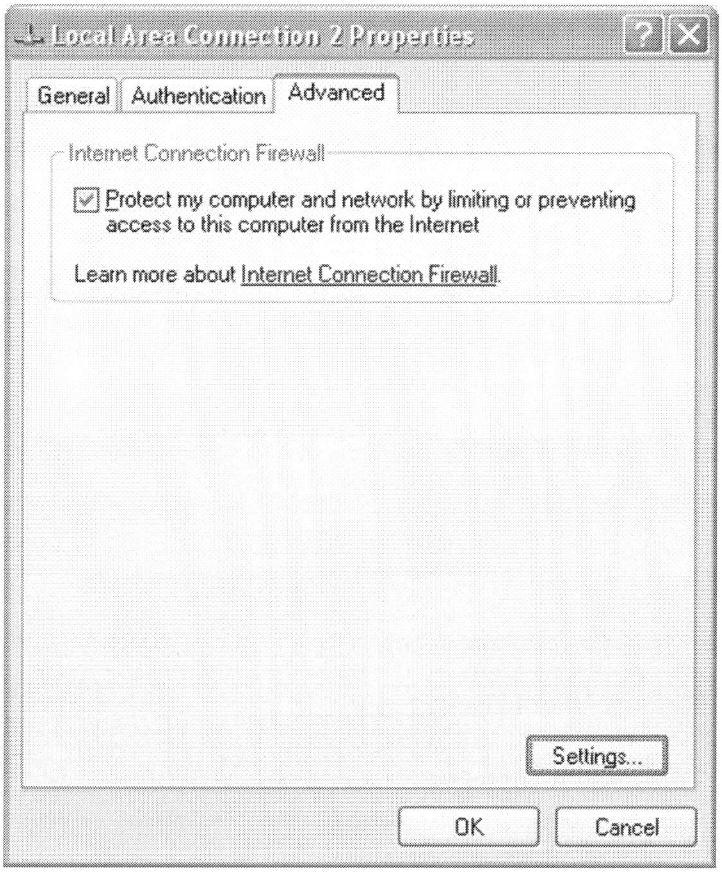

Explanation: In Display Properties on the Desktop tab select Customize Desktop. An Internet Connection Firewall can block packets based on IP address, port, or protocol.

Reference:

http://www.microsoft.com/windowsxp/pro/using/howto/networking/icf.asp

7. Which statement best describes how Remote Assistance and Remote Desktop differ?

A. They are the same tool but with two functions. The way that the tool is used determines its name.

B. Remote Assistance only allows viewing of your computer, while Remote Desktop allows interaction with your desktop.

C. Remote Desktop only allows viewing of your computer, while Remote Assistance allows interaction with your desktop.

D. Remote Desktop lets you view a remote desktop, but only allows you to interact with it if the remote user permits; while Remote Assistance lets you remotely connect to your computer as if you were directly connected.

***E. Remote Assistance lets you view a remote desktop, but only allows you to interact with it if the remote user permits; while Remote Desktop lets you remotely connect to your computer as if you were directly connected.**

Explanation: Remote Assistance lets you view a remote desktop, but only allows you to interact with it if the remote user permits; while Remote Desktop lets you remotely connect to your computer as if you were directly connected.

8.You receive a Remote Assistance invitation to fix your boss' Windows XP computer after he returns from a meeting. Your boss reconnects to his ISP and you try to connect to his computer, but your attempt is unsuccessful. What should you do?

A. Connect to your boss' computer by his new IP address.

B. Instruct your boss to send a new invitation and then reboot his computer.

***C. Instruct your boss to send a new invitation and to stay connected to his ISP.**

D. Connect to your boss' computer using the connection specific DNS host name.

E. On your computer run ipconfig /flushdns.

Explanation: Instruct your boss to send a new invitation and to stay connected to his ISP.

9. You try to encrypt a file but you cannot. What might be preventing this? Choose all that apply.

A. You are not an administrator.

***B. The file is compressed.**

***C. The file is on a FAT partition.**

D. The file haves been moved from a FAT32 partition.

E. The file is a sparce file.

Explanation: Files on NTFS partitions that have not been or do not need to remain compressed may be encrypted.

10. A user reports that they can't find a Word document that they just created and they have either forgotten where they saved it or deleted it. Which utility or method could **not** be used to find and retrieve it?

A. Recycle Bin

***B. System Restore**

C. Start > Search

D. Start > My Recent Documents

E. Start Word and look for the last documents opened.

Explanation: System Restore only acts on system files, not user files.

Reference:
http://www.microsoft.com/windowsxp/pro/using/howto/gethelp/systemrestore.asp

Chapter 3: Configuration

The objective of this chapter is to provide you with an understanding of the following:

1. Obtain a working knowledge of configuration tools used in Windows XP.
2. Configure support for multiple languages or multiple locations.
3. Configure and troubleshoot accessibility services.
4. Manage applications by using Windows Installer packages.

Getting Ready – (Questions)

1. What is the Microsoft Management Console?

2. If you needed to customize an accessibility feature for your computer, running Windows XP Professional, where would you locate the component?

3. You wish to schedule a custom program to run at a certain time on your computer. What Windows XP command can you use?

4. What TCP/IP command can you use to verify that your computer is seeing the router for your subnetwork?

5. You need to modify your local security policy. You are currently logged in under your own username, which does not have the administrative privileges. How can you perform your task without logging off, and logging on as Administrator?

Getting Ready – (Answers)

1. The Microsoft Management Console (MMC) is not an administrative tool, but rather a framework of hosted tools, called snap-ins, specifically designed for it.

2. To access a custom accessibility feature, built in to Windows XP Professional, you would locate it under the Accessibility Options icon in Control Panel.

3. One way to schedule a command or a program to run at a specific time is to use the Windows XP command "AT".

4. Using the PING command will verify a connection between computers or other systems (like routers) running TCP/IP.

5. The new service "Run As" allows you to run a program in the administrative context needed, without having to log off and log in as Administrator.

I Introduction

Windows XP offers many ways to customize the desktop to suit your needs and preferences. This can include customizing your desktop, Start Menu, taskbar, display preferences, and regional and language support.

You can also configure your computer to support more than one language or regional setting, so that you can produce bilingual documentation, or travel with your laptop and have it reflect the time zone and regional standards of the location where you are at that moment. Installer packages make it easier to install software and to customize that installation to suit your individual needs.

Microsoft has always had a strong commitment to providing accessible alternatives for persons with disabilities. Windows XP has increased that support to provide improved tools to enable access for all users.

II Tools used

There are many tools that can be used to manipulate the configuration of your system. These tools include (but are not limited to): Microsoft Management Console, Control Panel, the Command Prompt, the Registry Editor, and the Windows Script Host. As most system configuration requires administrative access, you either have to login with administrative rights, or you can use the Run As Service.

Microsoft Management Console

The Microsoft Management Console (MMC) in Windows XP presents a radical change to the administrative tools in Windows NT 4.0 or Windows 9x. The MMC is not the actual administrative tool, but a framework that can host snap-ins designed for it. The most common of these snap-ins are various administrative tools. Other items that can be added to the MMC include ActiveX controls, Web pages, and folders. Snap-ins also have the ability to load extension snap-ins that enhance its functionality. Figure 3.1 shows a newly created console. This is done buy using **Start | Run** and running the command MMC.EXE.

The left side shows two tabs: Tree and Favorites. The Tree tab provides you access to the console tree, which displays any loaded snap-in. The Favorites tab allows you to create and access shortcuts to items in the console tree. The right side provides you with a detail pane, which allows you to access and manipulate configurations for the selected snap-in.

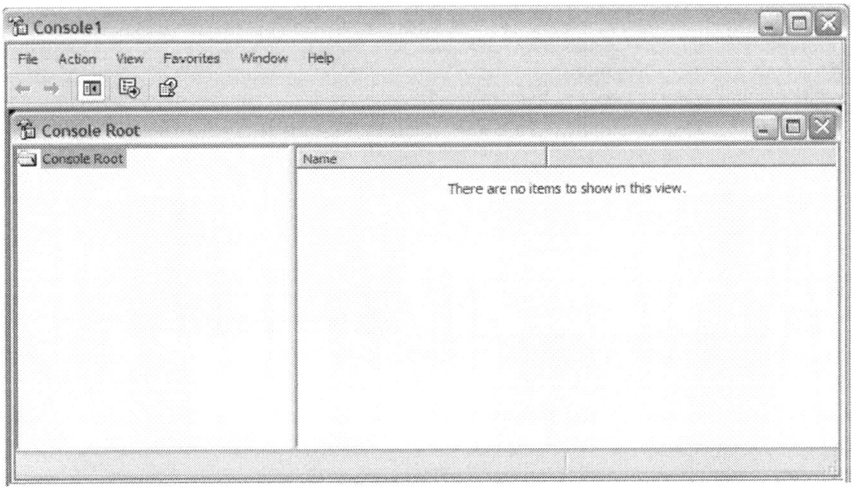

Figure 3-1: Microsoft Management Console

There is an Action menu, which will change depending on which snap-in is currently selected; likewise with the View menu.

Pre-built Consoles

Microsoft has created a number of pre-built consoles for administration of the system. Consoles you have on your system may differ depending on the options and services that were installed with Windows XP. Most of these consoles are available under Control Panel, Administrative Tools.

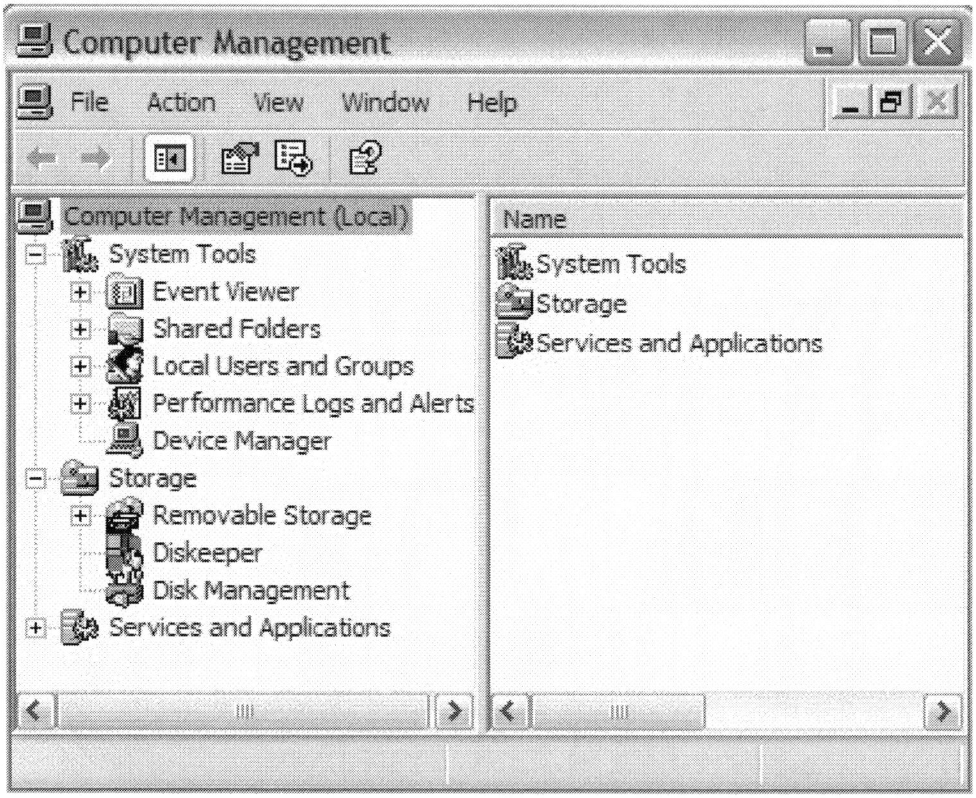

Figure 3-2: Computer Management Console using the MMC Interface

The pre-built consoles of Windows XP include:

Component services	Used to deploy and administer COM+ programs, automate administrative task using a scripting or programming language.
Computer Management	Used to facilitate quick administration of your local computer by culminating many snap-ins into one single console tree (Figure 3.2).
Device Manager	Used to provide information about the hardware installed on your computer. It allows you to views the status, change configuration, and update device drivers for you hardware.
Event Viewer	Used to view and manage various logs. These logs contain system, application and security events gathered from your computer.
Internet Services Manager	Used to configure setting used for Internet Information Server and all its services (WWW, FTP, SMTP).
Local Security Policy	Used to configure the local computer's security settings. These settings include policies for password, account lockouts, user rights, auditing, IP security, and encryption. These settings may be overridden if the computer is a member of a domain.
Performance	Used to collect and display real-time data about various aspects of your computer. These aspects range from physical devices, such as memory, disk, processor, and network, to various services running on the machine, such as IIS or Index Server.
Server Extensions Administrator	Used to configure the FrontPage 2000 Server Extensions on your Internet Information Server.
Services	Used to manage services on your computer. You can start, stop, pause or restart, disable or enable, and set recovery actions on the various services.

Table 3-1: Windows XP Pre-Built Consoles

Creating new consoles

Creating new consoles in MMC is a straightforward task. On the Console menu, select **Add/Remove Snap-in**. A dialog box will appear allowing you to add and remove the snap-ins you desire (Figure 3.3).

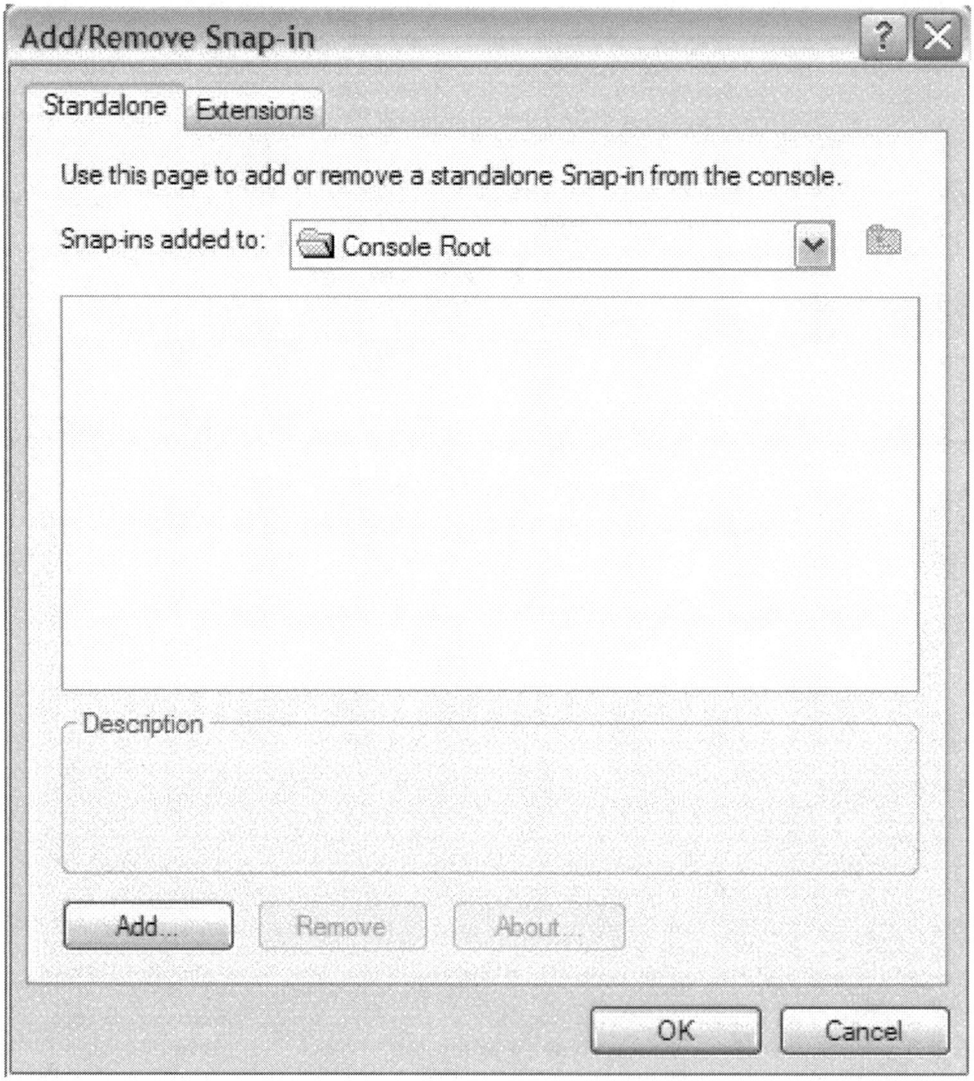

Figure 3-3: Adding a Snap-in to an MMC Console

Clicking the **Add** button displays another dialog box, showing the available snap-ins that you can add (Figure 3.4).

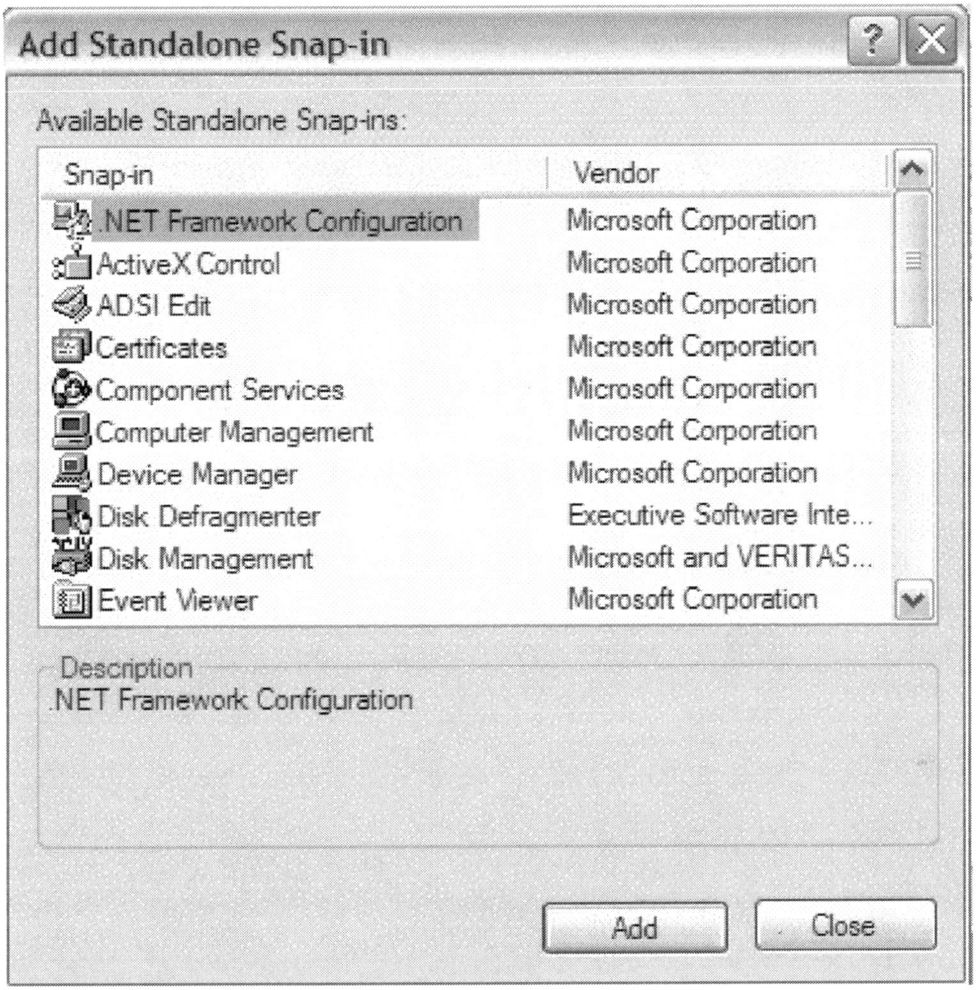

Figure 3-4: Listing the available MMC Snap-ins

To add a snap-in, just select the snap-in and click Add. Some snap-ins will further prompt you for more information. An example of this is the Computer Management snap-in, which prompts you for the computer that you wish to manage (Figure 3.5).

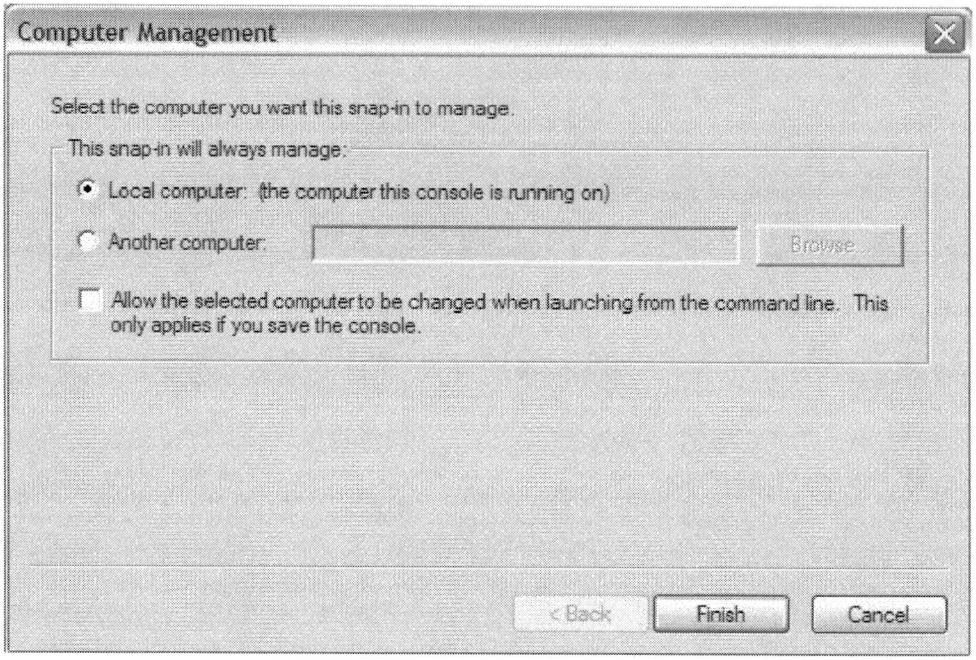

Figure 3-5: Providing information to a snap-in

Some snap-ins also provide extensions that you can add or remove from the console (Figure 3.6). This allows for further customization of the console.

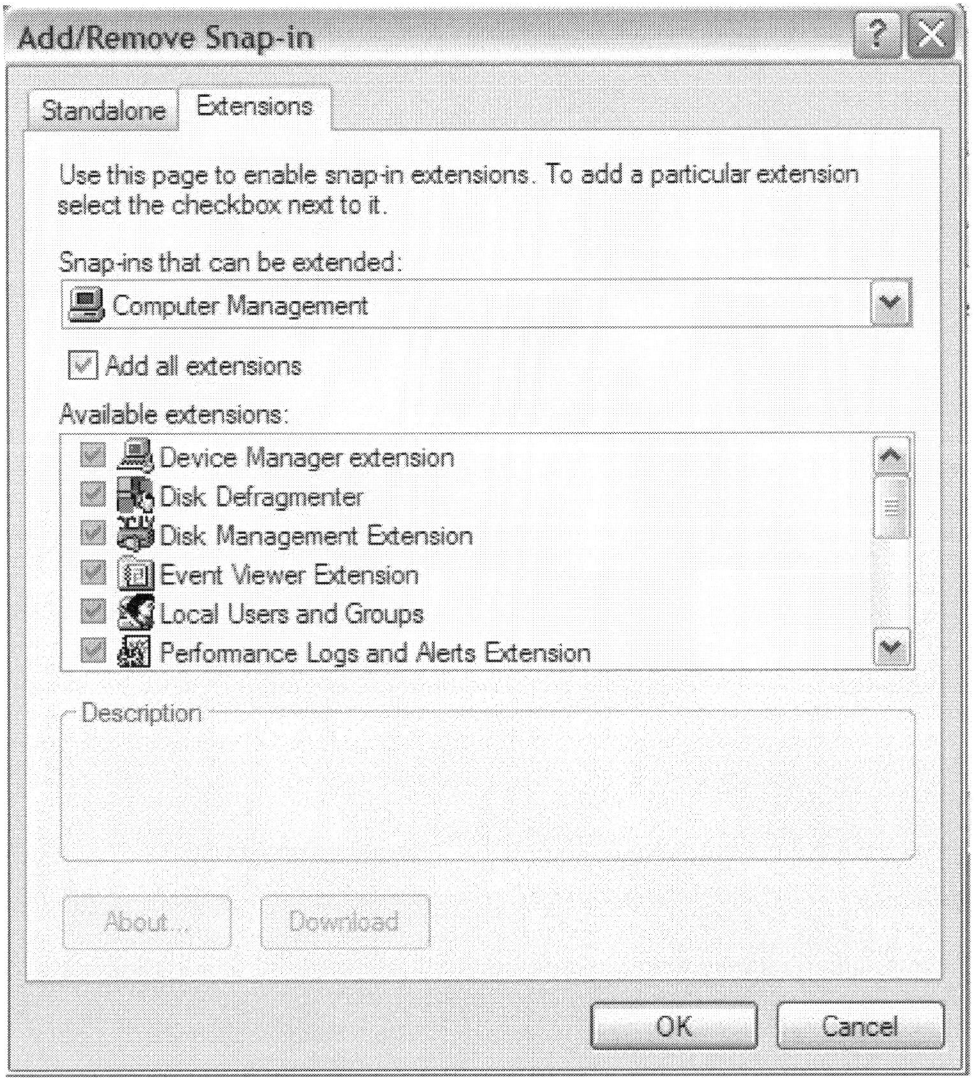

Figure 3-6: Snap-in Extensions

Once you have created your console, you can then save it as an .MSC file that you can then run at any time, from any machine.

Distributing Customized Consoles

The best feature of consoles is that they are very small files that can be distributed by many ways. You could, for example, email it to a co-worker; place it on a file share; or even a web server. Because of this versatility, the consoles can be used in many different ways.

When you use a console on another machine, there is a possibility that they may not have a particular snap-in installed. This is not a problem, as the MMC will not enable that portion of the console.

With this capability, you can create a customized console that contains connections to various services running on the network, that can be accessed from virtually any computer in the world, providing of course that the console user has the access across the network and the appropriate security access (Figure 3.7).

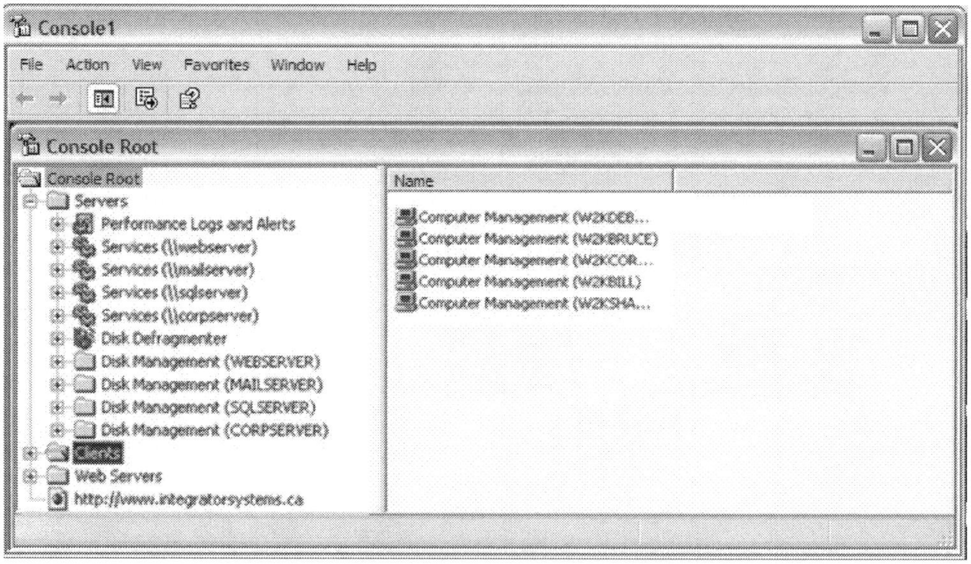

Figure 3-7: Customized Management Console

As the console author, you can specify options that restrict what modifications can be made to the console (Figure 3.8). From the Console menu, select Options. This allows you to specify an icon for the console, and to control the mode the console works in.

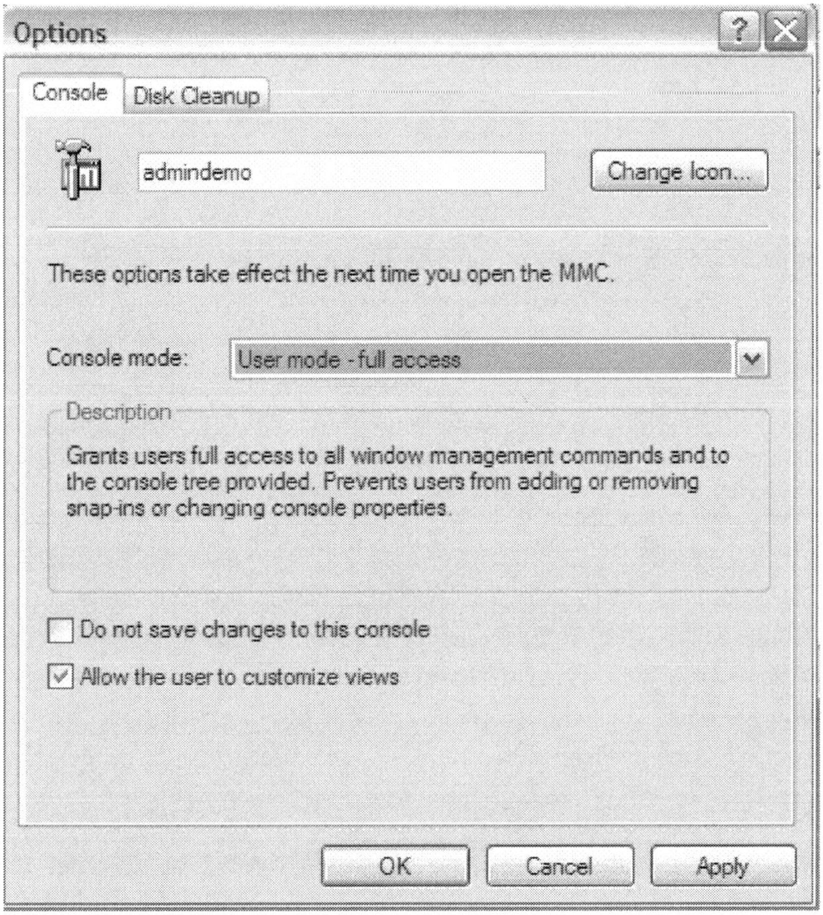

Figure 3-8: Console Modes Dialog Box

There are four settings:

Author Mode	Full access is granted to MMC, including the ability to add and remove snap-ins, create new windows and navigate the entire console tree.
User Mode – Full Access	Users are granted full access the console tree and window management functions. They cannot add or remove snap-ins or change the mode of operation. Save functionality is also removed.
User Mode – Limited Access, Multiple Window	All restrictions of Full Access are included. As well, users cannot open new windows and do not have access to parts of the console tree that were not visible when the console was saved. Multiple child windows are allowed, but they cannot be closed.
User Mode – Limited Access, Single Window	All restrictions of Multiple Window are included, with the additional restriction that there can only be one window.

Table 3-2: Console Mode Types

As well there are three checkboxes that can further restrict console settings. The option **Enable context menus on taskpads in this console** controls whether users can right-click and view commands that are available for objects on taskpads. The option **Do not save changes to this console** prevents any modifications to be retained. The option **Allow the user to customize views** controls whether users can add windows rooted on items in the console.

You can also customize the view of the console, showing and hiding particular features of the MMC, such as the toolbar (Figure 3.9). This can help eliminate the tinker factor – out of sight, out of mind!

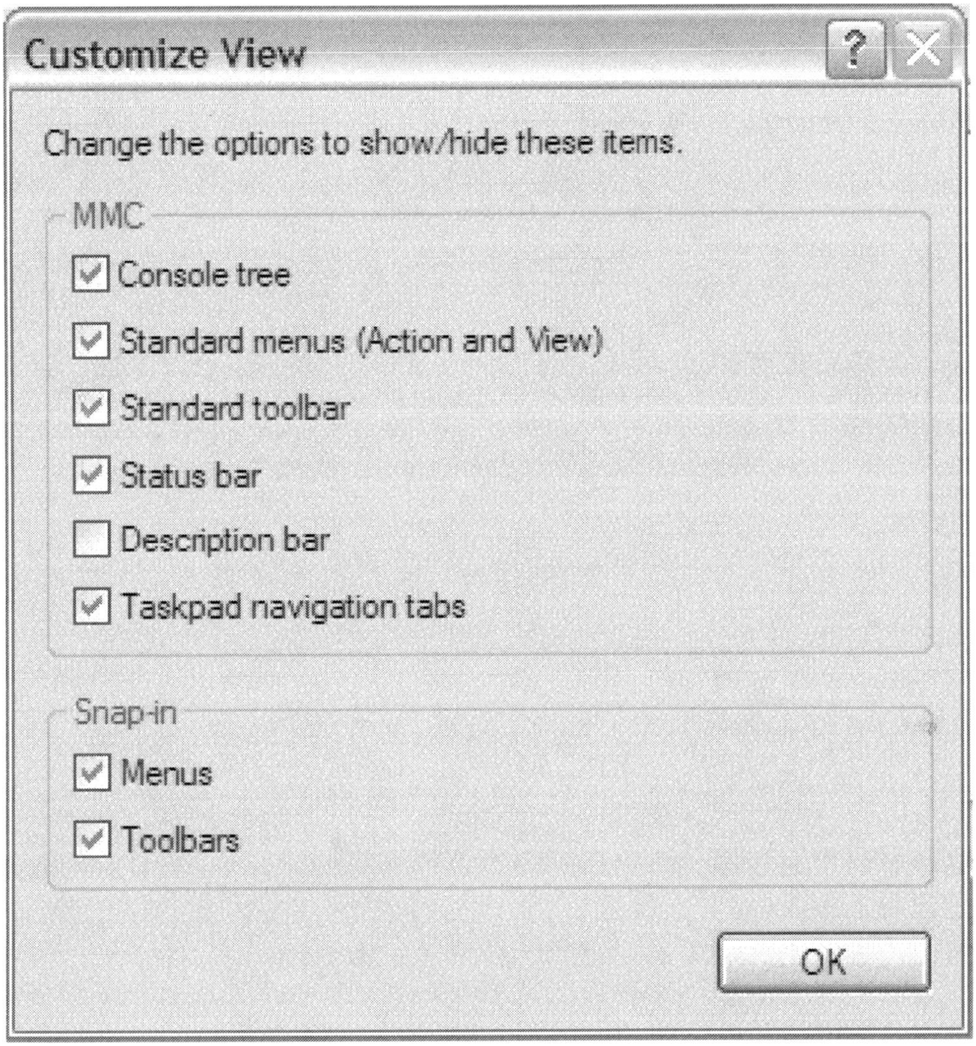

Figure 3-9: MMC Custom View

Control Panel

The Control Panel allows configuration of various hardware and software components (Figures 3.10 and 3.11). Table 3.3 shows the available Control Panel icons.

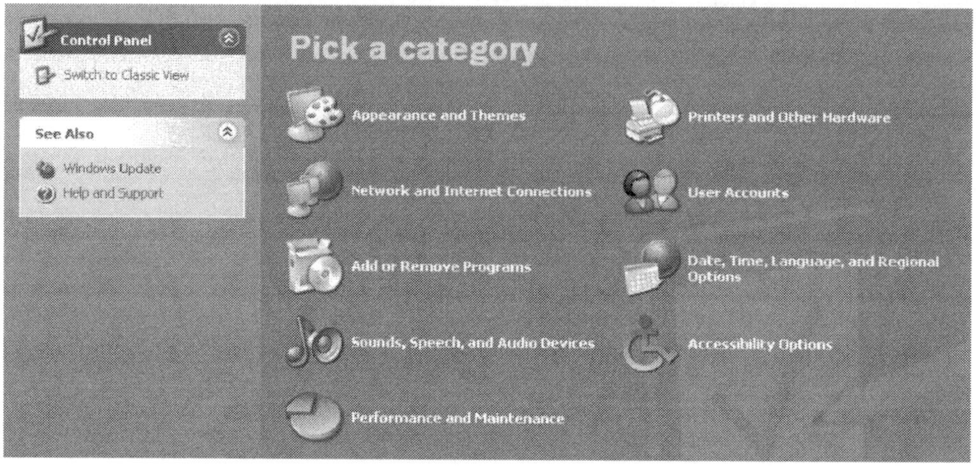

Figure 3-10 : Control Panel, Category View

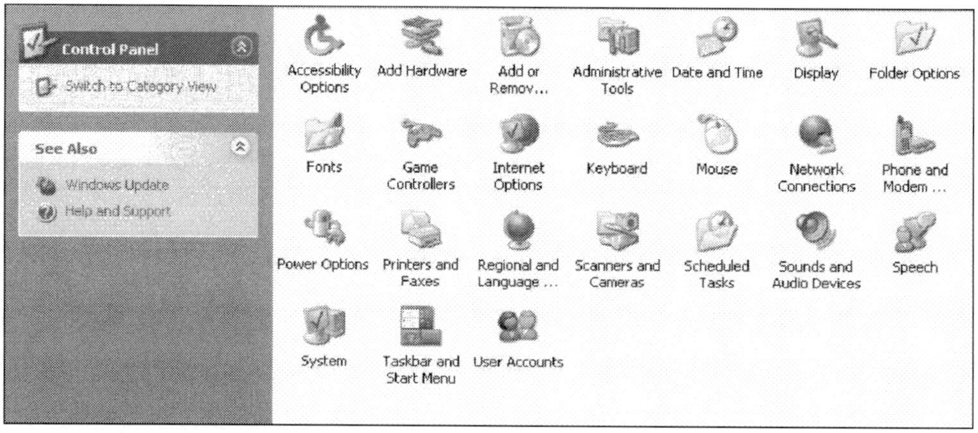

Figure 3-11: Control Panel, Classic View

CONTROL PANEL ICON	DESCRIPTION
Accessibility Options	Customizes accessibility features for your computer
Add Hardware	Installs, removes, and troubleshoots hardware
Add / Remove Programs	Installs and removes programs and Windows components
Administrative Tools	Configures administrative settings for you computer
Date and Time	Set the date, time, and time zone for your computer
Display	Customizes your desktop display and screen saver
Folder Options	Customizes the display of files and folders, changes file associations and makes network file available offline
Fonts	Displays and manages font on your computer
Game Controllers	Adds, removes, or changes settings for game controllers
Internet Options	Configures your Internet display and connection settings
Keyboard	Customizes your keyboard settings
Mouse	Customizes your mouse settings
Network Connections	Connects to other computers, networks and the Internet
Phone and Modem Options	Configures your telephone dialing rules and modem properties
Power Options	Configures energy-saving settings for your computer
Printers and Faxes	Adds, removes, and configures local and network printers and faxes
Regional and Language Options	Customizes settings for display of languages, numbers, times, and dates
Scanners and Cameras	Configures installed scanners and cameras
Scheduled Tasks	Schedules computer tasks to run automatically
Sounds and Audio Devices	Assigns sounds to events and configures sound devices
Speech	Change settings for text-to-speech and for speech recognition
System	Provides system information and changes environment settings

CONTROL PANEL ICON	DESCRIPTION
Taskbar and Start Menu	Customize the Start Menu and the taskbar, such as the types of items to be displayed and their appearance
Users and Passwords	Manages users and passwords for this computer

Table 3-3: Control Panel Item Definitions

Command Prompts

Not all commands are run within the GUI interface. The Command Prompt, which is a DOS-like environment, is where one can perform many system administration functions, file manipulations, and system or network diagnostics. It is a good idea to become familiar with the commands available to you.

Windows XP Commands

The following is a list of commands that can be used with Windows XP.

COMMAND	DESCRIPTION
ASSOC	Displays or modifies file extension associations
AT	Schedules commands and programs to run on a computer
ATTRIB	Displays or changes file attributes
BOOTCFG	Queries, configures or changes the Boot.ini file settings
BREAK	Sets or clears extended CTRL+C checking
CACLS	Displays or modifies access control lists (ACLs) of files
CHCP	Displays or sets the active code page number
CHDIR **CD**	Displays the name of or changes the current directory
CHKDSK	Checks a disk and displays a status report
CHKNTFS	Displays or modifies the checking of disk at boot time
CIPHER	Displays or alters the encryption of folders and files on NTFS volumes
CLS	Clears the screen

COMMAND	DESCRIPTION
CMD	Starts a new instance of the Windows XP command interpreter
CMSTP	Installs or removes a Connection Manager service profile
COLOR	Sets the default console foreground and background colors
COMP	Compares the contents of two files or sets of files
COMPACT	Displays or alters the compression of files on NTFS partitions
CONVERT	Converts FAT volumes to NTFS
COPY	Copies one or more files to another location
DATE	Displays or sets the date
DEFRAG	Locates and consolidates fragmented files on local volumes
DEL **ERASE**	Deletes one or more files
DIR	Displays a list of files and subdirectories in a directory
DISKCOMP	Compares the contents of two floppy disks
DISKCOPY	Copies the contents of one floppy disk to another
DISKPART	Used to manage disks, partitions or volumes by script or direct input
DISKPERF	Disk performance counters are permanently enabled on XP. This command may be used for remote Windows 2000 systems
DOSKEY	Edits command lines, recalls Windows XP commands, and creates macros
DRIVERQUERY	Displays a list of all installed device drivers and their properties
EVENTTRIGGERS	Displays and configures event triggers (local and remote machines)
EVNTCMD	Displays SNMP events
EXIT	Quits the CMD.EXE program (command interpreter)

COMMAND	DESCRIPTION
FC	Compares two files or sets of files, and displays the differences between them
FIND	Searches for a text string in a file or files
FINDSTR	Searches for strings in files
FORCEDOS	Starts the specified program in the MS-DOS subsystem. This command is necessary only for those MS-DOS programs not recognized as such by Windows 2000
FORMAT	Formats a disk for use with Windows 2000
FTYPE	Displays or modifies file types used in file extension associations
GETMAC	Returns the MAC address and associated network protocols for all network cards in each computer (local and remote)
GPRESULT	Displays Group Policy settings and RSOP (Resultant Set of Policy) for a user or computer
GPUPDATE	Refreshes local and AD-based Group Policy settings, including security settings. (Replaces secedit /refreshpolicy, now obsolete)
GRAFTABL	Enables Windows XP to display an extended character set in graphics mode
HELP	Provides Help information for Windows XP commands
HELPCTR	Starts Help and Support Center
IRFTP	Sends files over an infrared link (requires an infrared device on the computer).
LABEL	Creates, changes, or deletes the volume label of a disk
LODCTR	Registers new performance counter names and "explain" text for a service or device driver, saves and restores counter settings and "explain" text
LOGMAN	Manages and schedules performance counter and event trace log collections (local and remote)
MACFILE	Used to manage File Server for Macintosh servers, volumes, directories and files

COMMAND	DESCRIPTION
MKDIR **MD**	Creates a directory
MMC	Opens the MMC (Microsoft Management Console)
MODE	Configures a system device
MORE	Displays output one screen at a time
MOUNTVOL	Creates, deletes, or lists a volume mount point
MOVE	Moves one or more files from one directory to another directory
MSIEXEC	Used to install, modify and perform operations on the Windows Installer
MSINFO	Displays a detailed view of hardware, system components and software environment for the system
NTBACKUP	Used to perform backup operations from a command prompt or batch file
OPENFILES	Queries or displays open files. Can also disconnect files opened by network users.=
PAGEFILECONFIG[.VBS]	Display and configure a system's paging file Virtual Memory settings
PATH	Displays or sets a search path for executable files
PBADMIN	Administers phone books
PENTNT	Detects floating-point division error (if present) in the Pentium chip, disables floating point hardware, and turns on floating point emulation
PERFMON	Used to open a Windows XP performance console configured with settings files from Windows NT 4.0 version of Performance Monitor
POPD	Restores the previous value of the current directory saved by PUSHD
PRINT	Prints a text file
PROMPT	Changes the Windows XP command prompt.
PUSHD	Saves the current directory then changes it
RASDIAL	Automates the connection process for any Microsoft client

COMMAND	DESCRIPTION
RECOVER	Recovers readable information from a bad or defective disk
REG	Adds, changes and displays registry subkey information and values in registry entries
REGSVR32	Registers .dll files as command components in the registry
RELOG	Extracts performance counters from their logs into other formats
RENAME **REN**	Renames a file or files
REPLACE	Replaces files
RMDIR **RD**	Removes a directory
RSM	Manages resources using removable storage
RUNAS	Allows a user to run specific tools and programs with different permissions than the user's current logon provides
SCHTASKS	Schedules programs or commands to run at a specific time or periodically
SECEDIT	Configures and analyzes system security by comparing current configuration to at least one security template
SET	Displays, sets, or removes Windows XP environment variables
SFC	System File Checker. Scans and verifies the versions of all protected system files after system restart
SHUTDOWN	Used to shutdown or restart a computer (local or remote). Without parameters, will logoff current user.
SORT	Sorts input
START	Starts a separate window to run a specified program or command
SUBST	Associates a path with a drive letter
SYSTEMINFO	Displays detailed configuration information about a computer and its operating system

COMMAND	DESCRIPTION
TASKKILL	Ends (kills) one or more tasks or processes
TASKLIST	Displays a list of applications and services with their PID (Process ID) for all tasks currently running (local or remote)
TCMSETUP	Sets up the telephony client
TIME	Displays or sets the system time
TITLE	Sets the window title for a CMD.EXE session
TRACERPT	Processes event logs or real-time data from instrumented event trace providers, and allows generation of trace analysis reports
TREE	Graphically displays the directory structure of a drive or path
TYPE	Displays the contents of a text file
TYPEPERF	Writes performance counter data to the command window or supported log format
UNLODCTR	Removes performance counter names and "explain" text from the registry for a service or device driver
VER	Displays the Windows XP version
VERIFY	Tells Windows XP whether to verify that your files are written correctly to a disk
VOL	Displays a disk volume label and serial number
VSSADMIN	Displays current volume shadow copy backups and all installed shadow copy writers and providers in the command window
W32TM	Used to diagnose problems with Windows Time.
WINNT	Performs an installation of or upgrade to Windows 2000. (MS-DOS)
WINNT32	Sets up or upgrades to Windows 2000. (WIN32)
XCOPY	Copies files and directory trees

Table 3-4: Windows XP Command Item Definitions

Command-Line Utility

Fsutil is a command-line utility that can be used to perform many file system related tasks, for both FAT and NTFS. It is quite powerful and should be used only by administrators who have an advanced knowledge of Windows XP.

COMMAND	DESCRIPTION
Behavior	Queries, changes, enables or disables the settings for generating 8.3 character-length file names
Dirty	Queries whether volume's dirty bit is set, and sets it if it is not.
File	Locates a file by its security identifier, queries allocated ranges for a file, sets short name, valid data length or sets zero data for a file
Fsinfo	Lists all drives, queries drive type, queries volume information or file system statistics
Hardlink	Creates a hard link
ObjectID	Manages object identifiers
Quota	Manages disk quotas on NTFS volumes
Reparsepoint	Queries or deletes reparse points
Sparse	Manages sparse files
Usn	Manages the update sequence number change journal
Volume	Manages a volume

Table 3-5: Fsutil Item Definitions

Terminal Services

The following are a list of commands used with Terminal Services.

COMMAND	DESCRIPTION
CHANGE LOGON	Enables or disables logons from client sessions, or displays current logon status
change port	Lists or changes the COM port mappings. Used for compatibility with MS-DOS applications.
change user	Changes the setting for .ini file mapping
CPROFILE	Cleans specified profiles of wasted space. If user-specific file associations are disabled, it removes these associations from the registry. Profiles in use currently are not modified.
FLATTEMP	Enables or disables flat temporary files
logoff	Logs a user off a session and deletes session from server
msg	Sends a message to a user
mstsc	Creates connections to terminal servers or other remote computers, edits an existing .rdp configuration file, and migrates connections created with Client Connection Manager to new .rdp files
Query process	Displays information about processes running on a terminal server
query session	Displays information about sessions on a terminal server
query user	Displays information about user sessions on a terminal server
register	Registers a program so that it has special execution characteristics
reset session	Enables deletion of a session from a terminal server
shadow	Enables remote control on an active session of another user
tscon	Connects to another session
tsdiscon	Disconnects a session from a terminal server
tskill	Ends a process
tsprof	Copies the user configuration information from one user to another. Can also set a user's profile path.
tsshutdn	Enables an administrator to remotely shut down or reboot a terminal server

Table 3-6: Terminal Service Item Definitions

SC Commands

This executable file communicates with the Service Controller and installed services. It provides capabilities similar to what is found in the Services icon in Control Panel.

COMMAND	DESCRIPTION
sc boot	Indicates whether the last boot should be saved as **Last Known Good**
sc config	Modifies the value of a services entry in the registry and in the SCM (Service Control Manager) database
SC CONTINUE	Sends a CONTINUE control request to resume a paused service
sc control	Sends a CONTROL B to a service
sc create	Creates a subkey and entries for the service in the registry and in the SCM database
SC DELETE	Deletes a service subkey from the registry
sc description	Sets a service's description string
sc enumdepend	Lists the services that cannot run unless the specified service is running
sc failure	Specifies what action to take upon failure of the service
sc getdisplayname	Gets the display name associated with a particular service
sc getkeyname	Using the display name as input, gets the key name associated with a particular service
sc interrogate	Sends an INTERROGATE control request to a service
sc lock	Locks the SCM database
sc pause	Sends a PAUSE control request to a service
sc qc	Queries a service's configuration information for a service
sc qdescription	Displays a service's description string
sc qfailure	Displays the actions that will be performed if the specified service fails
sc query	Displays information about the specified service or type, driver or type
sc queryex	Displays extended information about the specified service or type, driver or type
sc querylock	Queries and displays the SCM database's lock status

COMMAND	DESCRIPTION
sc sdset	Sets a service's security descriptor using SDDL (Service Descriptor Definition Language)
sc sdshow	Display's a service's security descriptor using SDDL
sc start	Starts a service
sc stop	Sends a STOP control request to a service (stops a service)

Table 3-7: SC Item Definitions

Batch File Commands

These commands are only useful when writing a batch file (also referred to as a command script)

Command	DESCRIPTION
CALL	Calls one batch program from another
ECHO	Displays messages, or turns command echoing on or off
ENDLOCAL	Ends localization of environment changes in a batch file
FOR	Runs a specified command for each file in a set of files
GOTO	Directs the Windows XP command interpreter to a labeled line in a batch program
IF	Performs conditional processing in batch programs
PAUSE	Suspends processing of a batch file and displays a message
REM	Records comments (remarks) in batch files or CONFIG.SYS
SETLOCAL	Begins localization of environment changes in a batch file
SHIFT	Shifts the position of replaceable parameters in batch files
%0 → %9	Replaceable parameters (%0 and %1 to %9) that can be placed anywhere within a batch file. When the batch file is run, %0 is replaced by the name of the batch file, and the argument variables %1 to %9 are replaced by the corresponding parameters entered on the command line.

Table 3-8: Batch File Item Definitions

MS-DOS Subsystem Commands

The following commands can be used for MS-DOS compatibility. Other commands are recognized for compatibility reasons, but Windows XP does not make use of them. These commands are: fastopen, nlsfunc, and share.

> NOTE: These 16-bit MS-DOS subsystem commands are not available on the Windows XP 64-Bit Edition.

Command	**DESCRIPTION**
APPEND	Enables programs to open data files in specified folders as if these files were in the current folder
DEBUG	Starts Debug, a program you can use to test and debug MS-DOS executable files
EDIT	Starts MS-DOS Editor, which creates and changes ASCII text files
EDLIN	Starts Edlin, a line-oriented text editor with which you can create and change ASCII files
EXE2BIN	Converts .exe (executable) files to binary format. Provided as a courtesy to software developers.
FORCEDOS	Starts the specified program in the MS-DOS subsystem. This command is necessary only for those MS-DOS programs not recognized as such by Windows XP.
GRAPHICS	Loads a program into memory that allows Windows XP to print on a printer the displayed contents of the screen when you are using a color or graphics adapter
LOADFIX	Ensures that a program is loaded above the first 64KB of conventional memory, and runs the program
LOADHIGH **LH**	Loads a program into the upper memory area (UMA). Loading a program into the UMA leaves more room in conventional memory for other programs. Use the systemroot\System32\Config.nt file, or the equivalent startup file specified in a program's PIF, to specify the programs to load high.

Command	DESCRIPTION
MEM	Displays information about allocated memory areas, free memory areas, and programs that are currently loaded into memory in the MS-DOS subsystem
SETVER	Sets the MS-DOS version number that the MS-DOS subsystem reports to a program.

Table 3-9: MS DOS Subsystem Item Definitions

MS-DOS Configuration Commands

These commands are provided to configure the MS-DOS environment via the CONFIG.NT file. Other commands are recognized for compatibility reasons, but Windows XP does not make use of them. These commands are: buffers, driveparm, and lastdrive.

Command	DESCRIPTION
COUNTRY	Enables the MS-DOS subsystem to use international time, dates, currency, case conversions, and decimal separators
DEVICE	Loads into memory the device driver you specify
DEVICEHIGH **DH**	Loads device drivers into the upper memory area. This frees more bytes of conventional memory for other programs.
DOS	Specifies that the MS-DOS subsystem is to maintain a link to the upper memory area (UMA) or is to load part of itself into the high memory area (HMA)
DOSONLY	Prevents starting applications other than MS-DOS-based applications from the Command.com prompt
ECHOCONFIG	Displays messages when reading the MS-DOS subsystem Config.nt file
FCBS	Specifies the number of file control blocks (FCBs) that the MS-DOS subsystem can have open at the same time
FILES	Sets the number of files that the MS-DOS subsystem can access at one time
INSTALL	Loads a memory-resident program into memory
NTCMDPROMPT	Runs the Windows XP command interpreter, Cmd.exe, rather than Command.com after running a TSR or after starting the command prompt from within an MS-DOS application

Command	DESCRIPTION
SHELL	Specifies the name and location of an alternate command interpreter you want Windows XP to use for the MS-DOS subsystem
STACKS	Supports the dynamic use of data stacks to handle hardware interrupts
SWITCHES	Forces an enhanced keyboard to behave like a conventional keyboard

Table 3-10: MS DOS Configuration Item Definitions

TCP/IP Commands

The following commands are used to diagnose and troubleshoot the TCP/IP protocol, and to provide connectivity to various TCP/IP based services.

Command	DESCRIPTION
ARP	Displays and modifies the IP-to-Ethernet or token ring physical address translation tables used by the Address Resolution Protocol (ARP)
FINGER	Displays information about a user on a specified system running the Finger service. Output varies based on the remote system.
FTP	Transfers files to and from a computer running an FTP server service (daemon)
HOSTNAME	Prints the name of the current computer (host)
IPCONFIG	This diagnostic command displays all current TCP/IP network configuration values.
LPQ	This diagnostic utility is used to obtain status of a print queue on a computer running the LPD server.
LPR	This connectivity utility is used to print a file to a computer running an LPD server.
NBTSTAT	This diagnostic command displays protocol statistics and current TCP/IP connections using NBT (NetBIOS over TCP/IP).
NETSTAT	Displays protocol statistics and current TCP/IP network connections

Command	**DESCRIPTION**
NSLOOKUP	This diagnostic tool displays information from Domain Name System (DNS) name servers.
PATHPING	This diagnostic tool combines features of ping and tracert with additional information. Useful in determining routers or links that might be causing networks problems.
PING	Verifies connections to a remote computer or computers
RCP	Copies files between a Windows XP computer and a system running rshd (remote shell daemon), or between two rshd systems.
REXEC	Runs commands, with authentication, on remote computers running the REXEC service
ROUTE	Manipulates network routing tables
RSH	Runs commands on remote computers running the RSH service
TELNET	Allows communication with a remote computer that is using the Telnet protocol
TFTP	Transfers files to and from a remote computer running the TFTP service
TRACERT	This diagnostic utility determines the route taken to a destination by sending Internet Control Message Protocol (ICMP) echo packets with varying Time-To-Live (TTL) values to the destination.

Table 3-11: TCP/IP Command Item Definitions

Network Commands

The following commands allow diagnostics and configuration of various network related services.

Command	DESCRIPTION
ATMADM	Monitors connections and addresses registered by the ATM Call Manager on an asynchronous transfer mode (ATM) network. You can use the utility to display statistics for incoming and outgoing calls on ATM adapters.
IPXROUTE	Displays and modifies information about the routing tables used by the IPX protocol.
NET	Many Windows XP networking commands begin with the word net.
NET ACCOUNTS	Update the user accounts database and modifies password and logon requirements for all accounts. The Net Logon service must be running on the computer for which you want to change account parameters.
NET COMPUTER	Add or delete computers from a domain database. This command is available only on computers running Windows 2000 Server.
NET CONFIG	Displays the configurable services that are running, or displays and changes settings for a service (typically the Workstation and Server Services)
NET CONTINUE	Reactivates suspended services
NET FILE	Displays the names of all open shared files on a server and the number of file locks, if any, on each file. This command also closes individual shared files and removes file locks.
NET GROUP	Adds, displays, or modifies global groups on Windows 2000 Server domains. This command is available for use only on Windows 2000 Server Domain Controllers.
NET HELP	Provides a list of network commands and topics you can get help with, or provides help with a specific command or topic
NET HELPMSG	Provides help with Windows XP error messages

Command	**DESCRIPTION**
NET LOCALGROUP	Adds, displays, or modifies local groups
NET NAME	Add or delete a messaging name (sometimes called an alias), or displays the list of names the computer will accept messages for. The Messenger service must be running to use net name.
NET PAUSE	Pauses running services
NET PRINT	Displays or controls print jobs and printer queues
NET SEND	Sends messages to other users, computers, or messaging names on the network. The Messenger service must be running to receive messages.
NET SESSION	Lists or disconnects the sessions between a local computer and the clients connected to it
NET SHARE	Creates, deletes, or displays shared resources
NET START	Starts a service, or displays a list of started services.
NET STATISTICS	Displays the statistics log for the local Workstation or Server service, or the running services for which statistics are available
NET STOP	Stops a Windows XP network service
NET TIME	Synchronizes the computer's clock with that of another computer or domain. Used without the /set option, displays the time for another computer or domain.
NET USE	Connects a computer to or disconnects a computer from a shared resource, or displays information about computer connections. The command also controls persistent net connections.
NET USER	Adds or modifies user accounts or displays user account information
NET VIEW	Displays a list of domains, a list of computers, or the resources being shared by the specified computer
NETSH	Utility to display or modify the configuration of an active system. Provides a scripting feature.

Table 3-12: Network Command Item Definitions

Special Commands

The following commands provide conditional processing and redirection support. These are most useful in batch files.

Conditional Processing

<table>
<tr><td>&&</td><td>Command following this symbol runs only if the command preceding the symbol succeeds.</td></tr>
<tr><td>||</td><td>Command following this symbol runs only if the command preceding the symbol fails.</td></tr>
<tr><td>&</td><td>Separates multiple commands on the command line</td></tr>
<tr><td>( )</td><td>Groups commands</td></tr>
<tr><td>^</td><td>Escape character. Allows typing command symbols as text.</td></tr>
<tr><td>;
,</td><td>Separates parameters</td></tr>
</table>

Table 3-13: Processing Item Definitions

Redirection

<table>
<tr><td>|</td><td>Reads output from one command and writes it to input of another command (known as "pipe")</td></tr>
<tr><td>></td><td>Writes command output to a file or device (such as a printer) instead of Command Prompt window</td></tr>
<tr><td><</td><td>Reads the input needed for a command from a file rather than from the keyboard</td></tr>
<tr><td>>></td><td>Redirects and appends output from a command to the end of a file</td></tr>
<tr><td>>&</td><td>Writes output from one of the default I/O streams (stdout, stdin, stderr) into another. (stdin = 0; stdout = 1; stderr = 2)</td></tr>
<tr><td><&</td><td>Reads input from one of the default I/O streams and writes it to output of another</td></tr>
</table>

Table 3-14: Redirection Item Definitions

Registry Editor

The registry is your system's database of device and service configuration, user account settings, and software configuration. For the most part, any changes that you make in the GUI environment (such as setting up a network connection) will make changes into the registry.

The Registry Editor (REGEDT32.EXE) is an advanced administrative tool that allows you to view and change existing settings on a system, as well as add new settings. You can also place security and auditing permissions on various portions of the registry to restrict access and manipulation of it. Registry Editor can manipulate both local and remote systems. Registry Editor provides a read-only mode to prevent accidental modifications to be made.

> **EXTREMELY IMPORTANT NOTICE:** You should only manipulate your registry if it is absolutely necessary. Only advanced users who understand the registry well should use Registry Editor, as it is very easy to corrupt your system and cause your computer to cease functioning.

Depending on whether you are accessing a local or remote system, the Registry Editor will display a set of predefined keys in separate windows. The predefined keys are:

HKEY_CURRENT_USER	Contains the root of the configuration information for the user, or user's profile, who is currently logged on
HKEY_USERS	Contains the root of all user profiles on the computer. HKEY_CURRENT_USER is a subkey of HKEY_USERS.
HKEY_LOCAL_MACHINE	Contains configuration information particular to the computer
HKEY_CLASSES_ROOT	A subkey of HKEY_LOCAL_MACHINE\Software. The information stored here ensures that the correct program opens when you open a file by using Windows Explorer.
HKEY_CURRENT_CONFIG	Contains information about the hardware profile used by the local computer at system startup

When accessing a local machine, all five keys will be displayed. When accessing a remote system, only **HKEY_LOCAL_MACHINE** and **HKEY_USERS** will be displayed, but you can still access the other information.

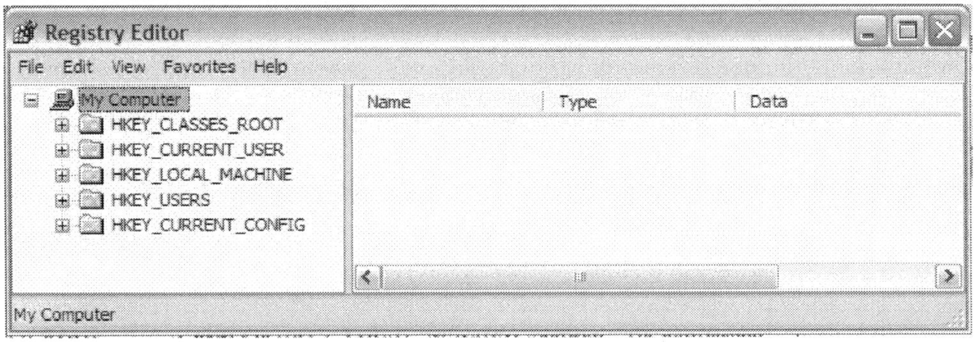

Figure 3-12: Registry Editor

Figure 3.12 shows the Registry Editor program. On the left side of each window (Navigation Pane) is a list of folders representing the various keys in the registry. On the right side (Topic Pane) are the value entries for the selected key. By double-clicking a value entry, you are then able to modify that entry. The dialog you see will depend on the data type of the entry.

Windows Script Host

The Windows Script Host (WSH) provides the ability the perform tasks in a way similar to batch files. The difference is that the WSH uses both VBScript (Visual Basic Scripting Edition) and JScript (JavaScript) to perform the tasks. This enables a user of the Windows XP system, with the appropriate security access, to perform various tasks, such as manipulating services, files, databases, Web sites, or even Active Directory, with great ease.

There are two version of WSH included with Windows 2000, a windows-based version (WScript.exe) and a command line version (CScript.exe). These two versions provide little overhead and allow both interactive and non-interactive scripts to be run. Table 3.4 shows the command line parameter for both versions. Remember to provide the options for WSH first, using the // indicator, and then the arguments for the script after.

CSCRIPT SCRIPTNAME.EXTENSION [OPTIONS] [ARGUMENTS]

WSCRIPT SCRIPTNAME.EXTENSION [OPTIONS] [ARGUMENTS]

//B	Batch or non-interactive mode
//D	Enable Active Debugging
//E:ENGINE	Use engine for executing script
//H:CSCRIPT	Changes the default script host to CScript.exe
//H:WSCRIPT	Changes the default script host to WScript.exe (default)
//I	Interactive mode (default, opposite of //B)
//JOB:XXXX	Execute a WS job
//LOGO	Display logo (default)
//NOLOGO	Prevent logo display: No banner will be shown at execution time
//S	Save current command line options for this user
//T:NN	Time out in seconds: Maximum time a script is permitted to run
//X	Execute script in debugger
//U	Use Unicode for redirected I/O from the console (CScript.exe only)

Table 3-15: WSH command line parameters

The command-line version (CSCRIPT) provides command-line options for setting script properties. This allows you to run scripts simply by entering the name of the script at the command prompt. Windows XP comes with some Visual Basic scripts built in. These, prefixed by the CSCRIPT command, are:

Command	DESCRIPTION
EVENTQUERY.VBS	Lists the events and their properties from one or more event logs
PRNCNFG.VBS	Configures or displays confirmation information about a printer
PRNDRVR.VBS	Adds, lists and deletes printer drivers
PRNJOBS.VBS	Pauses, resumes, lists and cancels print jobs
PRNPORT.VBS	Creates, lists and deletes standard TCP/IP printer ports. Also displays and changes port configuration.
PRNQCTL.VBS	Pauses or resumes a printer, clears a printer queue and prints a test page

Table 3-16: CSCRIPT Item Definitions

The windows-based version (WSCRIPT) has expanded capabilities, allowing you to provide some of these parameters automatically for a script. By accessing the properties of the script and selecting the Script tab, you can specify the time out parameter and the logo parameter (Figure 3.13).

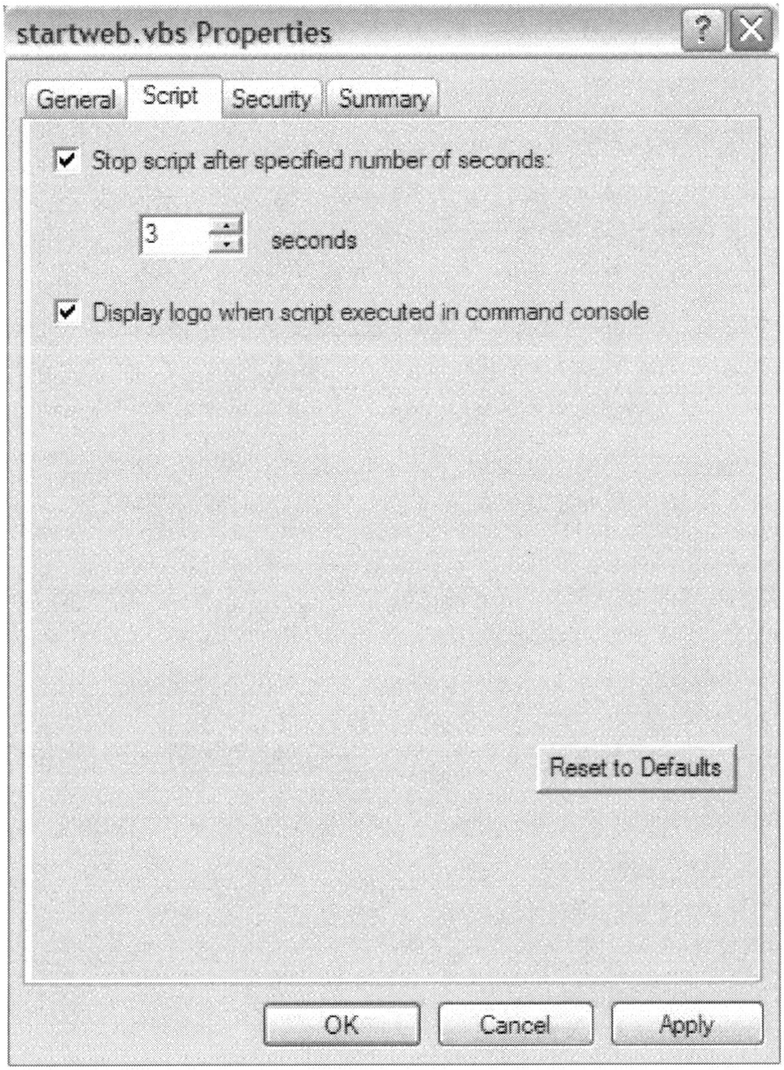

Figure 3-13: Script Properties

RunAs Command

The RunAs Service was something new to Windows 2000. In previous versions of Window NT, if you needed to perform an administrative task such as adding a new user to the computer or domain, you had to stop what you were doing, log off, and then log on with an account that had those privileges. Needless to say, there were (and still are) a number of individuals that used the Administrator account all the time, or ensured that administrator privileges were assigned to their regular account. This causes a weak point in any security infrastructure.

Using the RunAs Command, you can login with your regular account, and then, when needed, run a program in the administrative context required, without logging off the system. This provides functionality similar to the UNIX command SU.

It is important to note that the use of RunAs is not restricted to administrator accounts, although that is the most common use. Any user with multiple accounts can use RunAs to run a program, MMC console, or Control Panel item with alternate credentials.

There are three ways to run a program in another user's context. One way is to hold the shift key down and right-click the application. You then select **Run As...** and provide the credentials required (Figure 3.14).

Figure 3-14: RunAs Command

Another method is to create a shortcut to the application. You would then modify the properties of the shortcut to force the application to prompt for user credentials when run (Figure 3.15). You do this by checking the box next to **Run with different credentials**. This is located by clicking the Advanced button on the Shortcut tab of the Properties dialog box.

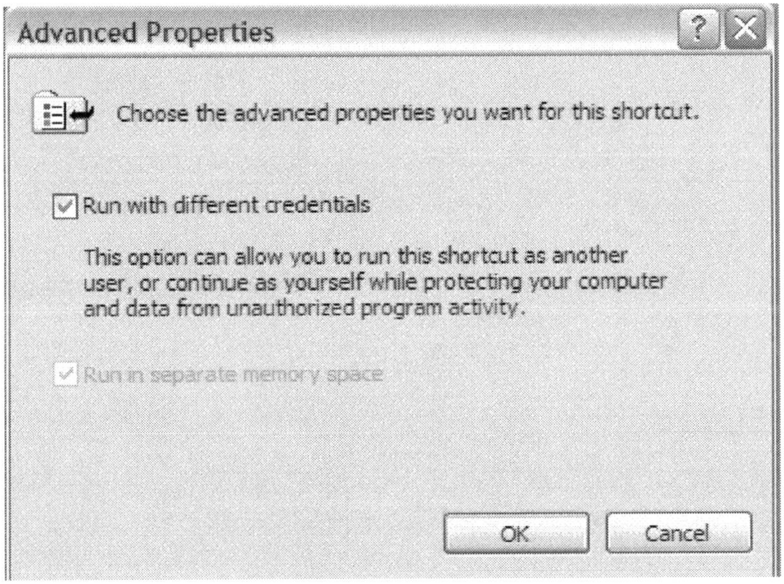

Figure 3-15: Shortcut Properties

> **NOTE:** Under Windows 2000, RunAs did not support smart card authentication, only password authentication. This has changed with Windows XP – using the toggle /smartcard will allow the credentials to be supplied from a smart card.

The final method is to run the command RUNAS from either a command prompt or from the **Start | Run** dialog. Table 3.5 shows the available command line parameters for the RUNAS command.

RUNAS [/PROFILE|/NOPROFILE] [/ENV] [/NETONLY] [/SMARTCARD] [/SHOWTRUSTLEVELS] [/TRUSTLEVEL] USER:<USERNAME> PROGRAM	
/PROFILE	Use to load the profile of USERNAME
/NOPROFILE	Do not load user profile. Can speed up load time, but may cause malfunctions in some applications.
/ENV	Use current environment instead of USERNAME
/NETONLY	Used when credentials are for remote access only
/SMARTCARD	Indicates whether a smartcard is supplying the credentials
/SHOWTRUSTLEVELS	Lists the /trustlevel options
/TRUSTLEVEL	Specifies the level of authorization at which the application is to run
/USER:*<USERNAME>*	Specifies USERNAME for security context. Must in form of USER@DOMAIN or DOMAIN\USER
PROGRAM	Command line for executable file
NOTE: ENTER USER'S PASSWORD ONLY WHEN PROMPTED	
NOTE: USER@DOMAIN IS NOT COMPATIBLE WITH /NETONLY	

Table 3-17: RUNAS command line parameters

Task Scheduler

The Task Scheduler service is started automatically, and runs in the background, every time you start Windows XP. Task Scheduler allows you to run any script or program at a time that is convenient to you. For example, you can schedule a system backup, or a disk defragmenter to run at 3:00 a.m. every morning!

You can create a new task through the **Scheduled Tasks** icon in Control Panel. By choosing **Add New Task**, a wizard will guide you through the steps of scheduling your task. This wizard is a wonderful improvement from the **AT** command process of Windows NT 4.0!

After the task has been set up, you can further configure the task through the **Properties** dialog box for the specific task. There are three tabs on the dialog box – Task, Schedule and Settings.

The "Task" and "Schedule" tabs were set up when you ran the wizard. If you wish to change the original configuration, this is where you can do it (Figure 3.16).

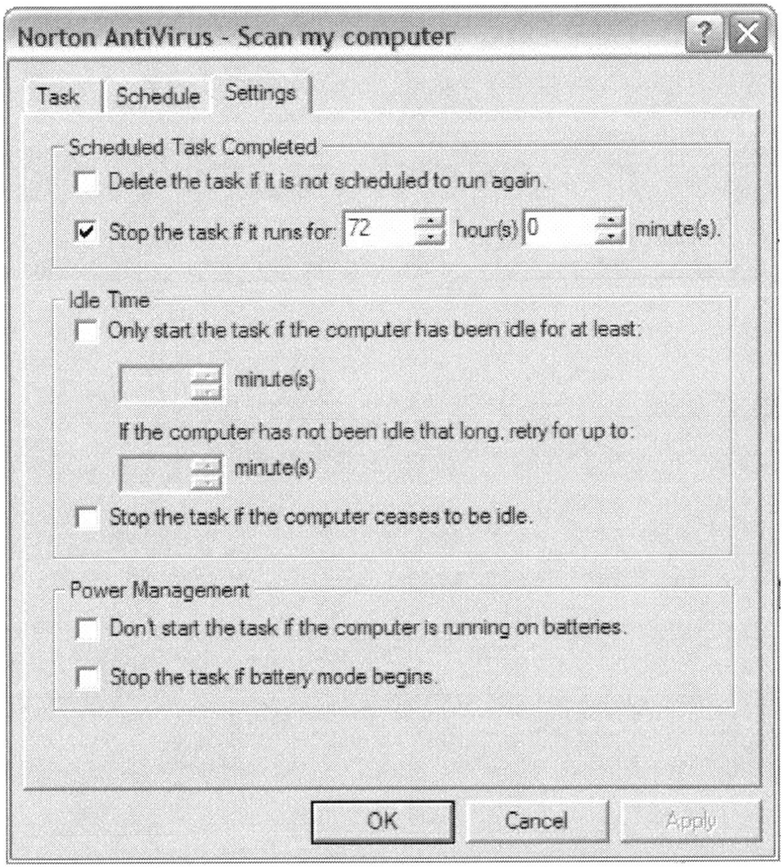

Figure 3-16: Advanced Schedule Settings

You can fine-tune your task scheduling under the **Scheduling** tab of **Properties**. Here you can stop the task if it is running for too long a period of time, make sure the system is idle for a set period of time before starting the task, and even make sure that the task doesn't run if the computer is running on battery-power.

One problem that may occur with Task Scheduler is if an incorrect username or password is used when the task is configured. The task must log on as an authorized user, and an error will cause the task not to run. Be sure to check Event Viewer if a task you have scheduled to run has failed. It should give you invaluable information as to the cause of failure.

Pop Quiz 3.1

Pop Quiz 3.1 Questions

1). What are the three ways you can run a program under administrative context using the "RUN AS" Service?
2). Which script language or languages does WSH use to perform tasks, such as manipulating services?
3). Name three of the pre-built consoles Windows XP Professional provides for use in the MMC.
4). You are distributing a customized console created for your technical staff to perform disk management. You wish them to have full access to the console tree and window management functions, but you do not want them to be able to add or remove snap-ins or change the mode of operations. As well, you want the save functionality removed. Which console mode do you select?
5) What command do you use to edit the registry in Windows XP Professional?

Pop Quiz 3.1 *Answers*

1). The three ways to run a program in another user's context are as follows:

A. Hold the SHIFT key down and right-click the application. Select Run As and provide the appropriate credentials.

B. Create a shortcut to the application and modify the properties of the shortcut by selecting the Run the program as the following user: radio button. When the program is run, the password will be request.

C. Run the command RUNAS from a command prompt or from the Start Run dialog box.

2). Windows Scripting Host (WSH) allows you to perform tasks, such as manipulating services or files in a fashion similar to batch files. It recognizes and uses both VBScript and JScript.

3). There are a number of pre-built consoles provided by Microsoft for administration of the system. These include:

A. Component Services

B. Computer Management

C. Device Manager

D. Event Viewer

E. Internet Services Manager

F. Local Security Policy

G. Performance

H. Server Extensions Administrator

I. Services

4). There are four settings you can choose to control the mode in which the console works. These are:

A. Author mode

B. User mode – full access

C. User mode – limited access, multiple windows

D. User mode – limited access, single window.

In this scenario, you will want to choose User Mode – Full Access, so that your employees have the functionality they require, and the restrictions you need.

5). The command to access the registry in Windows XP is REGEDT32.EXE. Please note that you should only manipulate the registry if it is absolutely necessary. It is very easy to corrupt your system and cause the computer to fail.

III Language Support

In many countries around the world, for example, in Canada, companies need to be able to work in more than one language. Currency, time and date format may be different from one language to another. Windows XP has addressed this need for multiple language and location support.

Enable multiple-language support

Multiple-language support consists of two separate technologies

- Multilingual editing and viewing which allows a user to compose and read documents in a bilingual (or more) format.
- Multilingual user interfaces that allow the Windows XP interface to be presented to the user in the language of their choice.

Depending on your work environment, you may choose to use either a localized or multi-language version of Windows XP. A localized version of Windows XP will support multilingual editing, viewing, and printing, but the interface is designed in the most likely language of the environment. For example, a localized version of Windows XP in Greece will support document creation in English and Greek, but the user interface will be in Greek only. Multilanguage Windows XP provides a user interface in a large number of languages. This version of Windows XP is geared to support a work environment where more than one language is used and more than one person will use the computer.

Configure multiple-language support for users

Multiple language support for users can be configured in Control Panel in the Regional and Language Options icon (Figure 3.17). Simply select the language settings that you wish to support on that computer. After the computer restarts, an icon will appear on the Taskbar that shows the current locale and keyboard inputs that are being used. Switching to another supported language is simple – just click on the icon!

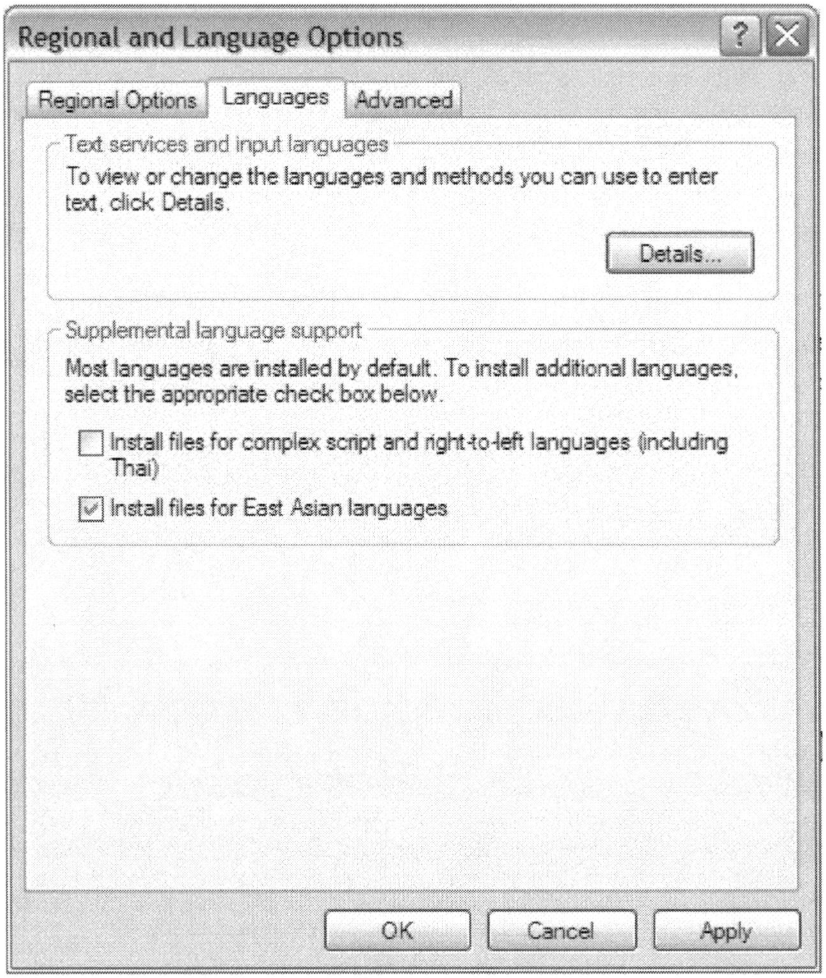

Figure 3-17: Regional Options (Languages)

Configure local settings

If you have a localized version of Windows XP, the local settings will be geared for the locale in which the version is to be distributed. For example, a Japanese localized version will support only Japanese location settings. If you have a Multilanguage version of Windows XP, you will be able to configure the numbers, currency, time, date, and keyboard (input locale) to suit the language in which you are working. This is also done through the Regional Options icon in Control Panel.

Figure 3-18: Regional Options (Location)

IV Accessibility Services

Microsoft has had an ongoing commitment to providing accessible technology to individuals with disabilities for a number of years. Working hand-in-hand with third party vendors, Windows XP has incorporated a number of built-in accessibility options to eliminate barriers to technology.

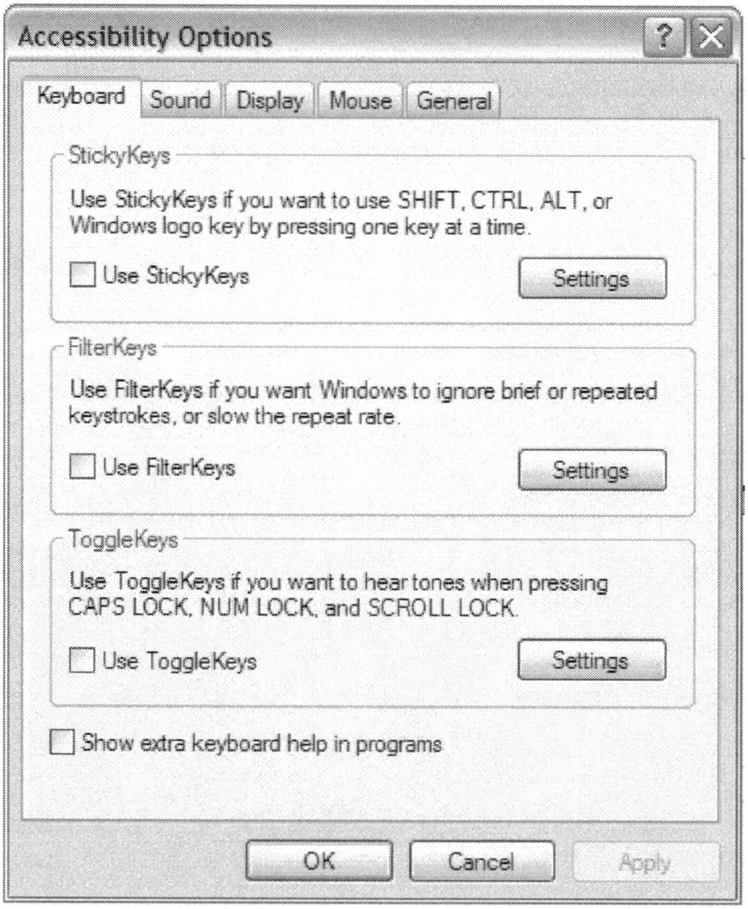

Figure 3-19: Accessibility Options

In order to configure accessibility options, you must access the dialog box under the **Accessibility** icon in Control Panel (Figure 3.19). There are five tabs in the Accessibility dialog box to help you configure the unique behavior you require from the computer to meet requirements.

The **Keyboard** tab allows you to change the behavior of the keyboard. A person with a mobility impairment may find it difficult to hold down the Ctrl-Alt-Delete key sequence at the same time. StickyKeys allows the individual to press these keys one at a time. As well, a person who lacks fine motor control may want Windows Professional to ignore brief, repeated keystrokes. The repeat rate can be slowed to accommodate this. Use FilterKeys to accomplish these requirements. ToggleKeys will sound a tone if Caps Lock, Num Lock, or Scroll Lock are pressed. There is also an option to display extra keyboard help in programs.

The **Sound** tab allows you to enable SoundSentry, an accessible feature for persons with deafness or low hearing ability. Visual warnings are generated when the computer makes a sound. ShowSounds will display captures for speech and sound on the computer.

The **Display** tab allows you to configure high-contrast settings for Windows colors and fonts. High contrast settings help persons with particular visual impairments more clearly see the taskbar, menus, etc., which are either too small, or do not have the proper contrast for their vision. There are also cursor options to allow a person to make their cursor appear wider or more narrow, as well as adjusting its blink rate.

The **Mouse** tab allows you to enable MouseKeys, which allows you to control the mouse pointer through the keyboard.

The **General** tab allows you to configure several administrative and maintenance options. You can configure SerialKey devices to provide alternate input for keyboard and mouse features. Accessibility options can be applied to the logon Desktop and as defaults for new users. Accessibility features can be turned off automatically if they have not been used for a specified amount of time and notification features notify when the features are turned on and off.

As well, Windows XP has provided the user with several accessibility wizards:

Accessibility Wizard	Configures the computer based on the user's vision, hearing, and mobility needs. The user can select the text size that is easiest to read and collects input to determine whether the user has vision, hearing, or mobility challenges.
Magnifier Utility	Creates a separate window to magnify a portion of the screen, to allow user with low vision to view sections of the screen in a large print
Narrator Utility	Provides a text-to-speech synthesizer that can read text, dialog boxes and buttons aloud. A sound output device must be installed and configured for the Narrator Utility to work.
On-Screen Keyboard	Provides a keyboard on the screen. The keyboard can be accessed through a mouse or other alternate input device, such as an Eye-Gaze system.
Utility Manager	Allows you to start and stop the accessibility features, as well as specify whether or not you want the utilities started automatically

Table 3-18: Wizards Definitions

Pop Quiz 3.2

Pop Quiz 3.2 *Questions*

1). What is the difference between localized and multi-language versions of Windows XP?

2). How can you switch between language interfaces in Windows XP?

3). Outside of the interface, what other options can you configure in the multi-language version of WinXP?

4). Normally, to activate the CTRL-ALT-DEL function, you must press all keys at the same time. If you wish to use this function, but be able to press only one key at a time, which feature should you activate in the Accessibility Options?

5). You have a user who has deafness. What feature can you activate so that sounds made by the computer are accessible to this user?

Pop Quiz 3.2 *Answers*

1). A localized version of Windows XP has its interface designed in the most likely language of the environment (for example, in Italy, the interface will appear in Italian). It will support multi-language editing, viewing and printing. A multi-language version of Windows XP will also support multi-language editing, viewing and printing, but also provides the interface in a large number of languages. For example, in Canada, the interface can appear in English or French, depending on in which language the user chooses to work.

2). Multiple language support for users is configured in Control Panel. After configuration, switching between languages is easy! Simply click on the icon in the Taskbar.

3). In the multi-language version, you are also able to configure the numbers, currency, time, date and keyboard to suit the language in which you are working.

4). The Use StickyKeys feature, under the Keyboard tab, will allow this functionality.

5). Under the Sound tab on Accessibility Options, there is a feature named Sound Sentry. It will display visual warnings when the computer makes a sound, and captures for speech and sound.

V Windows Installer packages

Windows XP has eliminated the problem of incorrect installations and accidental file loss. Windows Installer enables a "self-healing" application – if a user accidentally deletes part of an application, Windows Installer will fix it. If a newly installed application has a DLL with the same name as an existing DLL, Windows Installer will place it in a new directory.

Windows Installer packages work with applications that use one of the following file types:

- MSI (Microsoft Installer) format files – supports features such as on-demand installation of features
- Repackaged applications that use MSI files, but do not include the native Windows Installer packages. These are used to provide users with applications that are easily deployed, can self-diagnose and repair errors, and will cleanly uninstall.
- ZAP files, which are used when you do not have MSI files. They are used to install applications using their native setup program.

Packages work as published or assigned applications. A published application allows users to choose whether or not they will install the application. Installation is done through the Add/Remove Programs icon in Control Panel. Assigned applications are automatically installed on a computer when a user selects the application on the Programs menu, or if they click on a document that has the program's file extension.

To distribute applications that use the MSI standard, you will need to create a network share. The MSI file should be copied to the network share. A Group Policy Object should be created with a filter so that only authorized users will be able to install the applications. This will guarantee that you stay within your licensing restrictions. Finally, the package needs to be added to the GPO.

VI Chapter 3: Summary

Having completed the chapter on configuring and administering the desktop environment, you should now feel comfortable with how to:

- Work with the configuration tools in Windows XP
- Configure support for multiple languages or multiple locations
- Configure and troubleshoot accessibility services
- Manage applications by using Windows Installer packages

VII Chapter 3: Review Questions

1. What command is used to check your IP configuration in Windows XP?

   A. tcpipconfig

   B. winipcfg

   C. ipconfigurator

   D. ipconfig

   E. ipcfg

2. What default IP address is considered the loopback address?

   A. 224.0.0.1

   B. 254.1.1.1

   C. 127.0.0.1

   D. 10.0.0.1

   E. 192.168.0.1

3. What information is required to set up a RAS connection?

   A. IP Address of Server

   B. Username

   C. Password

   D. Ethernet

   E. Phone Number

4. What is the first step in mapping a network drive?

A. Click the Browse button

B. Right-click My Computer and select Map Network Drive.

C. Right click on the Task Bar

D. Close the Map Network Drive dialog box

E. Open up My Network Places

5. What is the first step in setting up remote access?

A. Select SetupAdmin

B. Select Setupdvr

C. Select Setupmgr

D. Select Supportmgr

E. Select RemoteAdmin

6. Your portable computer uses a dial-up connection to connect to a server at pre-scheduled times in the day. You want to set this computer up for offline files, these files include one large project file, and several small files. How can you set this up so that it does not download large files at these scheduled times?

A. Set synchronization for the personal files for only the LAN connection.

B. Configure Synchronization Settings to synchronize the project file for both the LAN connection and your dial-up connection.

C. Set synchronization for the personal files for both the LAN connection and your dial-up connection.

D. Configure Synchronization Settings to synchronize the project file only when using the LAN connection.

E. Disable synchronization while you are using the dial-up connection.

7. Your network has been assigned the IP addresses 194.134.154.10 -194.134.154.198 by a DHCP server. Your computer's IP address is 169.254.143.194, despite it being set up to use DHCP. What are the most reasonable reasons for this?

A. The DHCP server is on a different network segment

B. The DHCP server has a misconfigured scope

C. Your computer has automatically assigned itself an address from the 169.254.0.0 network

D. The DHCP server is unavailable

E. The DNS server is unavailable

8. You are troubleshooting a network that uses only TCP/IP. Computer A has the following configuration:

- IP Address: 192.168.2.234
- Default Gateway: 192.168.1.250
- WINS Server: 192.168.1.10

Computer A is unable to connect to other shared resources by using UNC names. You check the configuration settings and see that the gateway address for the subnet Computer A belongs to is 192.168.2.250. What should be done?

A. Change the IP Address

B. Configure Client2 to use a default gateway of 192.168.2.250

C. Change the WINS server address

D. Change the subnet mask

E. Change the subnet of the 2 server computers

9. You are creating Active Directory Site links so that Active Directory synchronization traffic can be optimized. You have three sites: one in Rome, Paris, and Houston.

- Houston is connected to Paris via a 256K WAN link
- Houston also has a connection to Rome via a 256K WAN link
- Paris has a connection to Rome via a 56K WAN link
- How many links should you create?

A. 2 links

B. 3 links

C. 4 links

D. 6 links

E. 1 link

10. Can a workgroup and a domain share the same name?

A. Only if it does not contain numbers

B. Not if the domain is running in mixed-mode

C. Always

D. Not if contains spaces

E. Never

11. To join a workgroup, what is required?

A. TCP/IP

B. A Username and password for the workgroup

C. A purchased workgroup name

D. IPX/SPX

E. A new or an existing workgroup name

12. To create a distribution tool and a single UNATTEND.TXT file to install pre-Windows XP computers, what tool would you select?

A. Distribution Manager

B. Computer Management

C. Add/Remove Programs Control Panel

D. Setup Manager

E. Distribution Tool

VIII Chapter 3: Review Answers

1. What command is used to check your IP configuration in Windows XP?

   A. tcpipconfig

   B. winipcfg

   C. ipconfigurator

***D. ipconfig**

   E. ipcfg

Explanation: TCP/IP Diagnostic Utilities in Windows XP

The IPCONFIG.EXE is used to check the IP configuration of a Windows XP computer you will use the command line utility IPCONFIG. The only other possible answer choice would be winipcfg, but this command is used in Windows 95 and 98.

2. What default IP address is considered the loopback address?

   A. 224.0.0.1

   B. 254.1.1.1

***C. 127.0.0.1**

   D. 10.0.0.1

   E. 192.168.0.1

Explanation: Definition of Loopback Address

If you are configuring a network application and need to specify a service running on the local machine, you can use the default loopback address (127.0.0.1) to access services on the local machine without using any network bandwidth or activity; the loopback address simply refers to the current computer.

3. What information is required to set up a RAS connection?

A. IP Address of Server

***B. Username**

***C. Password**

D. Ethernet

***E. Phone Number**

Explanation: Definition of RAS

Based on its definition, you will use a RAS connection of phone lines. Because of this, you MUST have a phone number at which you can reach the server. You will also need login information, such as a username and password.

4. What is the first step in mapping a network drive?

A. Click the Browse button

***B. Right-click My Computer and select Map Network Drive.**

C. Right click on the Task Bar

D. Close the Map Network Drive dialog box

E. Open up My Network Places

Explanation: How to Map a Network Drive

This is a navigational question. See web links for further details.

5. What is the first step in setting up remote access?

A. Select SetupAdmin

B. Select Setupdvr

***C. Select Setupmgr**

D. Select Supportmgr

E. Select RemoteAdmin

Explanation: TechNet Technology Center for RAS

Remote Access can be configured by running Setupmgr.

6. Your portable computer uses a dial-up connection to connect to a server at pre-scheduled times in the day. You want to set this computer up for offline files, these files include one large project file, and several small files. How can you set this up so that it does not download large files at these scheduled times?

A. Set synchronization for the personal files for only the LAN connection

B. Configure Synchronization Settings to synchronize the project file for both the LAN connection and your dial-up connection

***C. Set synchronization for the personal files for both the LAN connection and your dial-up connection.**

***D. Configure Synchronization Settings to synchronize the project file only when using the LAN connection.**

E. Disable synchronization while you are using the dial-up connection

Explanation: Configuring Synchronization for Offline Files

In order to synchronize your files, you should first enable synchronization for the personal files. But to prevent the large project file from being synchronized over the dial-up connection, you should configure the Synchronization Settings to only synchronize the project file when using the LAN connection.

7. Your network has been assigned the IP addresses 194.134.154.10 -194.134.154.198 by a DHCP server. Your computer's IP address is 169.254.143.194, despite it being set up to use DHCP. What are the most reasonable reasons for this?

A. The DHCP server is on a different network segment

B. The DHCP server has a misconfigured scope

***C. Your computer has automatically assigned itself an address from the 169.254.0.0 network**

***D. The DHCP server is unavailable**

E. The DNS server is unavailable

Explanation: DHCP Explanation

In the event that a computer configured to use DHCP is unable to contact the DHCP server the lease an address, it will automatically assign itself an IP address from the Autoconfiguration Range (169.254.0.0).

8. You are troubleshooting a network that uses only TCP/IP. Computer A has the following configuration:

- IP Address: 192.168.2.234
- Default Gateway: 192.168.1.250
- WINS Server: 192.168.1.10

Computer A is unable to connect to other shared resources by using UNC names. You check the configuration settings and see that the gateway address for the subnet Computer A belongs to is 192.168.2.250. What should be done?

A. Change the IP Address

***B. Configure Client2 to use a default gateway of 192.168.2.250**

C. Change the WINS server address

D. Change the subnet mask

E. Change the subnet of the 2 server computers

Explanation: Explanation of Gateway

Configure Client2 to use a default gateway of 10.10.20.1.

9. You are creating Active Directory Site links so that Active Directory synchronization traffic can be optimized. You have three sites: one in Rome, Paris, and Houston.

- Houston is connected to Paris via a 256K WAN link.
- Houston also has a connection to Rome via a 256K WAN link.
- Paris has a connection to Rome via a 56K WAN link.
- How many links should you create?

A. 2 links

***B. 3 links**

C. 4 links

D. 6 links

E. 1 link

Explanation: Active Directory Overview

Three links would be optimal in this condition because of the bandwidth limitations imposed

10. Can a workgroup and a domain share the same name?

A. Only if it does not contain numbers

B. Not if the domain is running in mixed-mode

***C. Always**

D. Not if contains spaces

E. Never

Explanation: Definition of Workgroup

A domain and a workgroup ARE able to share the same name

11. To join a workgroup, what is required?

A. TCP/IP

B. A Username and password for the workgroup

C. A purchased workgroup name

D. IPX/SPX

***E. A new or an existing workgroup name**

Explanation: How to Join a Workgroup

All that is required to join a workgroup is the workgroup name. If you specify a workgroup name that does not currently exist, it will be created. If the workgroup you specify already exists, then you will become a member of the workgroup.

12. To create a distribution tool and a single UNATTEND.TXT file to install pre-Windows XP computers, what tool would you select?

A. Distribution Manager

B. Computer Management

C. Add/Remove Programs Control Panel

***D. Setup Manager.**

E. Distribution Tool

Explanation: How to Create an Answer File

Setup Manager would be used to create a distribution tool and create a single UNATTEND.TXT file to install Windows XP computers

Chapter 4: Hardware Devices and Drivers

The objective of this chapter is to provide you with an understanding of the following:

1. Implement and manage disk devices
2. Implement and manage display devices
3. Implement and manage multimedia devices
4. Implement and manage card services
5. Implement and manage input devices
6. Implement and manage connectivity devices
7. Update drivers
8. Configure for multiple processors
9. Implement and manage hardware profiles

Getting Ready – (Questions)

1). What two types of storage does Windows XP support?

2). There are five types of dynamic volumes that can be used in Windows 2000 Server. Which three can be used with Windows XP?

3). What files systems are supported by Windows XP?

4). The Windows XP Device Manager tree is a record of the devices currently loaded, based on the configuration information in the registry. For what would you use Device Manager?

5). How many additional monitors can you configure for use on one computer under the Windows XP operating system?

Getting Ready – (Answers)

1). Windows XP supports both basic and dynamic storage.

2). Three types of dynamic volumes, Simple, Spanned, and Striped, can be used on any version of Windows 2000. The remaining two (Mirror and RAID-5) can only be created on Windows 2000 Server, but can be managed on any version of Windows 2000 or XP.

3). Windows XP is capable of using five distinct file systems: CDFS (Compact Disk File System), UDF (Universal Disk Format), FAT, FAT32, and NTFS.

4). You can use Device Manager to install or uninstall devices, troubleshoot problems, update drivers, and change the assigned device resources.

5). Windows XP allows you to configure up to nine additional monitors for use on one computer.

I Introduction

When you install Windows XP, you have to make decisions on basic disk configuration – on what partition you are going to install the operating system and how is that partition going to be formatted. After installation, you can optimize your configuration to take advantage of a number of new features available in Windows XP.

Windows XP Professional supports both basic and dynamic storage, including simple volumes, spanned volumes and striped volumes, which you can configure through Disk Management. Windows XP Home Edition, however, supports only basic storage.

Windows XP has increased Plug and Play support -- hundreds of devices not covered by Windows 2000 are now supported in Windows XP. It also has enhanced support for Universal Serial Bus (USB), IEEE 1394, Peripheral Component Interconnect (PCI), and other buses. Plug and Play itself has been improved for Windows XP, making it simpler and friendlier, as well as faster, especially in device installation. The driver models are barely modified from what exists with Windows 2000, but Windows XP has also pulled from the Windows ME models to add Windows Image Acquisition (WIA) assisting with image acquirement from devices such as scanners and digital cameras.

Plug and Play provides the following benefits:

- It will dynamically load, initialize, and unload drivers.
- It will enumerate devices and automatically allocates resources during enumeration.
- It will notify other drivers and applications when a new device is available for use.
- It provides a consistent driver and bus interface for all devices.
- It works with power management to handle insertion and removal of devices without powering down the system

When you need to install a new device, have Windows XP detect and configure it if at all possible. For Plug and Play devices, simply insert the device. For PCI and ISA Plug and Play cards, turn the computer off and then install the device. When the computer restarts, Windows XP should continue with the installation. For older legacy devices, use the Add/Remove Hardware wizard and let Windows XP detect the device.

II Disk Devices and Disk Management

Disk Management is available under the Computer Management console (Figure 3.1). Disk Management replaces the Windows NT 4.0 Disk Administrator. It offers many new features to Windows XP. These include:

- Support for basic partitions (both primary and extended with logical drives), and dynamic volumes (mirroring, extended)
- Online disk management that allows changes to be made without having to shut down the system. Most changes take place automatically.
- Local and remote administration of disks
- Shortcut menus and wizards to make the process simpler.
- The only considerations that need to be addressed are the following:
- You must be a member of the Administrators group.
- Dynamic disks and volumes are not supported on portable computers.

The console window will show you a graphical view of your system's disk configuration. To view remote systems, you must create a new console and add the Disk Management snap-in, connecting to the remote system.

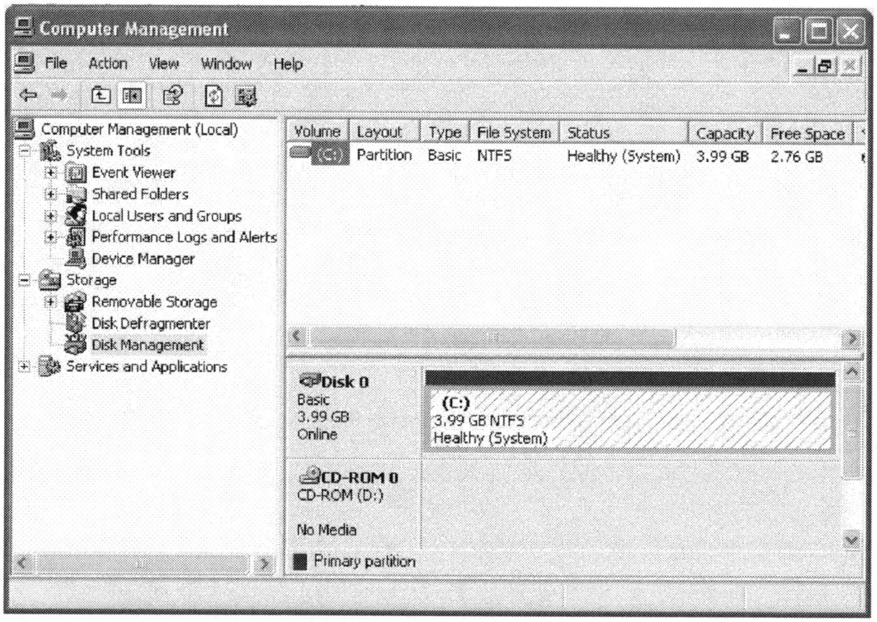

Figure 4-1: Disk Management

Configuring Disks

Windows XP supports both basic and dynamic storage. Each of these provides specific capabilities and restrictions.

Basic Storage

Basic storage consists of primary and extended partitions. Any one physical drive can have up a total of four partitions. You must have one primary partition, and you can have up to four primary partitions. You can have only one extended partition per physical hard drive. Logical drives are used to divide the extended partition into smaller chunks of workable drive space.

Using Disk Management, you can still create partitions on a basic disk, but you will not longer need to commit changes to save them, or restart your computer to implement them, as you did with Windows NT 4.0. Any changes made by Disk Management are implemented immediately. However, under Windows XP, you can no longer create volume sets or stripe sets on a basic disk, although it will support these sets if they are already in place prior to upgrading to Windows XP. You also can no longer extend volumes or volume sets on a basic disk.

The following are the tasks that can be performed on a basic disk:

- Create and delete primary and extended partitions.
- Create and delete logical drives within an extended partition.
- Format a partition.
- Mark a partition as active.
- Delete volume sets and striped sets (Windows XP upgraded from Windows NT)
- Repair and delete mirror sets and stripe sets with parity (Windows 2000 Server upgraded from Windows NT Server).

Dynamic Storage

Dynamic storage is a new feature in Windows XP. It is a physical disk that has been upgraded by and managed with Disk Management. Dynamic disks do not use partitions or logical drives, but rather dynamic volumes, which must be created by Disk Management. Only computers running a Windows XP operating system can access these dynamic volumes locally. However, any operating system (such as Windows 95 or Windows NT 3.51 Workstation) can access these volumes through a network share. Dynamic disks are not supported on portable computers or removable media.

Dynamic volumes can only be created on dynamic disks. With dynamic disks, the four-volume limitation of basic storage is removed. You can create any number of volumes on the dynamic disk; the only limit is free space.

There are five types of dynamic volumes: simple, spanned, mirrored, striped, and RAID-5. Windows XP can only use simple, spanned, and striped volumes. However, you can still create mirrored and RAID-5 volumes remotely on a Windows 2000 Server.

The following tasks can only be performed on a dynamic disk:

- Create and delete simple, spanned, and striped volumes.
- Extend a simple or spanned volume.
- Reactivate a missing or offline disk
- Create, repair, and delete mirrored and RAID-5 volumes (remotely to Windows 2000 Server).

> **NOTE:** You cannot expand the boot or system volumes. This is because neither can be on a spanned volume, and Windows XP recognizes an expanded volume as a spanned volume.

To upgrade a basic disk to a dynamic disk, select the disk (not the volumes). From there, either use the **Action Menu | All Tasks**, or right click the disk, and choose **Upgrade to Dynamic Disk**. The system will then prompt you to select which disks to upgrade, allowing you to upgrade several disks at once.

NOTE: When upgrading from basic to dynamic disk, keep in mind that the entire physical disk must be upgraded from basic to dynamic. You cannot upgrade a single partition. Upgrading is a one-way process. You can convert to dynamic disk from basic disk with no setup or data loss, but to revert back to basic disk will require the entire disk to be reformatted.

Configuring Volumes

Each of the two types of disk storage (basic and dynamic) supports their own distinct types of volumes. A basic storage disk behaves just like in Windows 95 or MS-DOS. A dynamic storage disk behaves similar to the RAID configurations of Windows NT.

Basic Volumes

Under Windows XP, basic volumes are used to provide compatibility with other operating systems (such as in a dual boot configuration). Basic volumes do not make any change to the structure and handling of drives and volumes from previous versions of Windows and Windows NT.

Basic volumes must exist on a basic disk. You are limited to 4 partitions on each drive. One of these partitions can be created as an extended partition, which can host logical drives.

When you upgrade to Windows XP, any exists partitions will change to basic volumes, including any stripe sets (striped volumes) and volume sets (spanned volumes). You cannot create new striped or spanned volumes on a basic disk, but you can repair and delete these on a basic disk.

Dynamic Volumes

There are five types of dynamic volumes that can be used in Windows XP. The first three (Simple, Spanned, and Striped) can be used on any version of Windows XP. The remaining two (Mirror and RAID-5) can only be created on Windows 2000 Server, but can be managed on any version of Windows XP.

When you upgrade from basic to dynamic disk, existing partitions and logical volumes are converted into dynamic volumes. The primary partition becomes a simple volume; the system and boot partitions become system and boot volumes; the logical drives become simple volumes; a volume set becomes a spanned volume; a stripe set becomes a stripe volume; and so on.

Volumes that have been upgraded from partitions cannot be extended. New volumes created after the conversion will be able to be extended.

> **NOTE:** An extended volume is created when free space on a single dynamic disk is combined with an existing dynamic volume on a single drive. A spanned volume is created when two or more physical disks are used.

Simple Volume

A simple dynamic volume is the same as a volume on basic storage. It contains space from a single dynamic drive. The space combined to make a dynamic volume can be contiguous or non-contiguous space, but it MUST be on a single drive.

Spanned Volume

A spanned dynamic volume follows the same rules as volume sets on basic storage. The disk space is contained on two or more dynamic drives, up to a maximum of 32 drives. Each free space section joined in a spanned volume does <u>not</u> need to be approximately the same size. Spanned volumes are used to increase the size of a volume beyond the space available on one drive. The data is written to a spanned volume sequentially – that is, from beginning to end, filling up the space on one drive before moving to the next. The main drawback to spanned volumes is that if one physical drive fails, access to the data is lost on the entire spanned volume.

Striped Volume

A striped dynamic volume is similar to a stripe set on basic storage (RAID 0). There is no fault tolerance attached to a striped volume. Data is stored in equal areas of free space between 2 to 32 dynamic drives. With a striped volume, the stripe can be extended dynamically and easily, a great improvement over stripe sets on basic storage. Striped volumes are used for two reasons – to combine equal areas of free space on several physical drives into a single volume and to increase read and write performance.

I/O performance can be improved with striped volumes, because data is written and read from several disks at the same time. The disadvantage to striped volumes is that if any drive fails in the stripe, access to the data on the entire stripe is lost.

Mirror Volume

A mirror volume an only be created on Windows 2000 Server. Mirror volumes are created to make a duplicate of another volume. A prime example of this is the system and boot volumes. To create a mirror volume requires two disks.

RAID-5 Volume

A RAID-5 Volume can only be created on Windows 2000 Server. RAID-5 volumes are used much like striped volumes, except that a portion of the space is used to write parity information. This information is calculated by 1/number of disks. This portion is spaced out across all the drives so if a failure occurs, the volume can still access information by recreating it if necessary.

File Systems

Windows XP is capable of using five distinct file systems: CDFS, UDF, FAT, FAT32, and NTFS. Each of these file systems are used to store data on different types of media. First we are going to review each file system, identifying some distinct advantages and disadvantages of each.

CDFS

Windows XP provides support for CDFS, or Compact Disc File System. CDFS is compliant to ISO 9660 standards, including Level 2 standards of long file name support.

When you are creating CD-ROMs to be used on Windows XP, you must adhere to the following standards:

- All directory and file names must be less the 32 characters
- All directory and file names must be in uppercase
- The directory tree cannot exceed 8 levels from the root
- File extensions are not mandatory

> **NOTE:** CD-ROM mastering software is not included with Windows XP.

UDF

Windows XP also provides support for UDF (Universal Disk Format), which is ISO 13346 compliant. UDF is designed for interchanging data on digital versatile disks (DVD) and CD-ROM. UDF is a cross platform solution. Windows XP reads both UDF versions 1.02 and 1.50.

> **NOTE:** UDF mastering software is not included with Windows XP

FAT File System

FAT and FAT32 are based upon an older technology originally designed for floppy disks. It has since been expanded to its furthest limitations. FAT and FAT32 partitions are used in Windows XP to facilitate dual boot configurations.

FAT partitions have a size limitation of 2GB. In today's environment where 20GB drives are common, the limitations a FAT system imposes can be easily identified. On that 20GB drive, you would have to create 10 partitions on the drive to use all the available space.

FAT (and FAT32) both use what is known as a single cluster allocation method. Cluster sizes in FAT vary depending on the size of the partition created, and are limited to 32K. The differences in the cluster size affect the amount of wasted space that can be on the drive and the size of the partition. With the FAT file system, we have the potential for a great deal of wasted space on today's larger hard drives, as well as the numerous partitions that would need to be created.

With Windows NT 4.0, Microsoft allowed the operating system to create a FAT partition with a 64K cluster size to allow a 4GB partition to be created. The only problem is that Windows NT and Windows XP are the only operating systems that can read it.

> **NOTE:** All file systems used by most operating systems (like Windows XP) organize your hard disk based upon cluster (or allocation unit) size. A cluster represents the smallest amount of disk space that can be allocated to hold a file.

As we see from Table 4.1, a partition of 2GB has the potential to waste a lot of space. Due to the single cluster allocation, even a 1K file gets 32K of space on the drive. This can lead to an enormous amount of unusable space on the drive. Now, back in 1990 this was not considered a very big problem. Drives were small in comparison to today's drives. In the mid 1990's, as drive size began to radically increase, we started to experience the limitations of the FAT file system.

Hence, FAT32 was introduced.

PARTITION SIZE	CLUSTER SIZE	EFFICIENCY
0 – 127 MB	2K	98.4%
128 – 255 MB	4K	96.6%
256 – 511 MB	8K	92.9%
512 – 1023 MB	16K	85.8%
1024 – 2048 MB	32K	73.8%
2047 – 4096 MB	64K	56.6%

Table 4-1: FAT Allocation Unit

FAT32 File System

FAT32 was a great improvement on FAT. The most obvious of the enhancements is the ability to create partitions greater that 2GB. In fact, there is a theoretical limit of 2TB (terabytes). Although the technology is close to reaching this size most people will not have the hardware to create such a large partition! Under Windows XP we can create FAT32 partitions of up to 32GB, however it will read and write larger partitions created with other operating systems (such as Windows 98) or 3rd party tools that can create larger FAT32 partitions. The only other limitation with FAT32 is that the partition has to be greater than 32MB.

In order to be able to create larger partitions, the designers of FAT32 reworked the allocation structure of the clusters so that smaller drives (less than 8GB) only used an 8K cluster. Therefore, for that 1K file, we are now only wasting 7K, as opposed to the original 31K under FAT. Table 4.2 shows the changes to the cluster size and the efficiency of each.

PARTITION SIZE	CLUSTER SIZE	EFFICIENCY
256MB – 8GB	4K	96.6%
8GB – 16GB	8K	92.9%
16GB – 32GB	16K	85.8%
32GB and up	32K	73.8%

Table 4-2: FAT32 Allocation Units

FAT32 also provides some new stability to the file system. FAT32 has the ability to relocate the root directory and use the backup copy instead of the default copy (all FAT-based file systems have 2 copies of the file allocation table).

However, FAT-based utilities, such as the MS-DOS 6.22 version of SCANDISK will corrupt the FAT32 table. This is because the program does not understand what it is trying to fix. You need to replace those tools with FAT32-aware versions.

Microsoft included FAT32 in Windows 95 OSR 2 (version 4.00.950B) and above, including Windows 98 and Windows ME. It has also added this capability to Windows XP (all versions).

NTFS File System

Microsoft realized that the FAT file system was not going to be effective in more demanding situations. FAT-based file systems did not have the reliability and security needed in those environments. When Microsoft released Windows NT 3.1, they included a new file system called NTFS (New Technology File System).

This file system broke away from the FAT file system completely. Instead of two File Allocation Tables that used single cluster allocation, it now used a single Master File Table (MFT), which works like a relational database. Where everything on the drive is an object. Another change made was the cluster allocations (Table 4.3), which were greatly improved over FAT. With this change, NTFS partitions have a theoretical limit of 16EB (exabytes), However, 2TB is the practical limit.

PARTITION SIZE	CLUSTER SIZE	
< 512MB	512 bytes	
513MB – 1024MB	1K	
1025MB – 2048MB	2K	
> 2049MB	4K	
4097MB – 8192MB	8K	Only applicable on Windows NT 3.50 and earlier, OR The command format /A:[size], OR Select a different allocation unit in the Format dialog
8193MB – 16384MB	16K	
16385MB – 32768MB	32K	
> 32768MB	64K	

Table 4-3: NTFS Allocations Units

> **NOTE:** Microsoft recommends only using NTFS on partitions greater than 400MB due to system overhead and performance.

The features that made NTFS stand out were built-in security, transactional logging, Unicode file names, long file name support, multiple data streams, and support for the POSIX subsystem. These features made NTFS a fast, secure, versatile, reliable, and recoverable file system. For example, under MS-DOS using a FAT partition, if the computer shut down in the middle of writing a file, you lost the file completely. Under Windows XP using an NTFS partition, it would recover the file after the reboot. NTFS writes everything it does into a transaction log before manipulating any data on the drive. This feature is known as lazy write.

When Microsoft released Windows NT 3.51, compression was added to NTFS. This allowed files to take up even less space on the drive, freeing up some drive space. This came in very handy when storing large files that were accessed infrequently. However, with this change came a restriction – if you wanted compression, the maximum cluster size would be 4K. This is due to the compression algorithm.

Windows XP improves on NTFS again. The following is a list of new features in NTFS version 5.0:

File encryption

File encryption provides cryptographic protection of files on NTFS volumes. Encrypted File System (EFS) provides file encryption on an individual file basis using a public-key system. EFS encryption and NTFS file compression are mutually exclusive; you cannot compress an encrypted file. Sparse files may be encrypted.

Disk quotas

A disk quota allows an administrator to control the amount of data that each user can store on an NTFS volume.

Sparse files

Normally files (typically very large) containing data that is full of zeros (or a sparse data set) occupy valuable disk space. When the sparse file facilities are used, the system does not allocate hard drive space to a file except in regions where it contains something other than zeros. The default data value of a sparse file is zero.

Distributed link tracking

Distributed link tracking enables client applications to track link sources that have been moved. As a result, clients that subscribe to the link-tracking service can maintain the integrity of their references, and the objects referenced can be moved transparently.

Reparse points

These are a collection of user-defined data, which is understood by the application that stores the data. An example of this is the Microsoft Remote Storage Server (RSS) which uses reparse points when it moves infrequently used files to a long-term storage device, but maintains a pointer in the original location.

Volume mount points

This is a directory placed on an NTFS volume that provides a transparent gateway to another volume, regardless of that volume's file system. For example, you can have a mount point defined as **C:\Mount\Data** which is actually your **D:** drive.

Change log

This is a journal that records changes made to files. This is essential to recover the file system indexing used with Windows XP. This greatly reduces the amount of time it takes to reindex the whole volume in case of failures.

Which File System to Use

The file system that is recommended by Microsoft for Windows XP partitions is NTFS. It provides the security, speed, reliability, and robustness that are needed for today's notebooks, workstations, and servers.

The more drive space you wish to partition will limit your choices. FAT is effective for small partitions (512MB and less); FAT32 is effective up until 8GB; and NTFS is good for even larger partitions. However, if any security or quota management is required, NTFS is needed, no matter what size the partition is.

This does not mean that you cannot use FAT or FAT32. In fact, there are times where it is required to use one of these other file systems. Such is the case when configuring dual-boot or multi-boot systems. A comparison of the file systems is shown in Table 4.4

FILE SYSTEM	FILE SYSTEM ACCESSIBILITY	FILE SYSTEM LIMITATIONS
NTFS	Windows 2000 has full local access to a Windows NT 4.0 or 3.51 NTFS volume Windows NT Workstation 4.0 with Service Pack 4 can access a local Windows 2000 NTFS volume Other operating systems cannot access a Windows 2000 NTFS volume in a multiple-boot configuration on the same computer	Minimum volume size is approximately 10 MB Recommended practical maximum for volumes is 2 TB (terabytes) Cannot be used on floppy disks File size limited only by size of volume
FAT32	Full local access available only through Windows 95 OSR2, Windows 98, and Windows 2000	Creates volumes up to 32GB Minimum volume size is 32 MB Maximum file size 4 GB
FAT	Full local access available through MS-DOS, all versions of Windows (including Windows NT, Windows 2000, Windows 9x, Windows ME, Windows 3.1 and 3.11 for Workstations) and OS/2	Volumes from floppy disk size up to 4 GB Maximum file size 2 GB

Table 4-4: Supported File Systems

As mentioned in Chapter 1, when you are dual booting between Windows XP and Windows NT 4.0, it is imperative to install at least Service Pack 4 on the Windows NT 4.0 machine. Without the updates that are included, the Windows NT machine will not be able to mount and access the partition. With the update, Windows NT 4.0 can access and modify data on the Windows XP NTFS partition, as long as it does not make use of any new NTFS features (reparse points, disk quotas, encryption, sparse files, or change journal)

Convert from one file system to another file system

Having now explored the differences in the various file systems supported in Windows XP, it is no wonder that Microsoft recommends using NTFS for Windows XP systems. The features in NTFS, such as disk quotas, mount points and security, make it a very rich file system.

To take advantage of all the features of Windows XP, you will find it necessary to either create new NTFS formatted partitions, or convert existing FAT and FAT32 formatted partitions to NTFS. If you were to delete your existing partition and then create a new one, you would then have to restore all your data. An easier method is to use the convert utility, which retains all of your data.

The convert utility is command line based. There is no GUI interface to perform conversions. The syntax is as follows:

```
Convert drive: /fs:ntfs
```

This will schedule a conversion to take place during system startup. You must reboot the system to allow the conversion to take place.

> **NOTE:** When you convert a FAT or FAT32 partition, it will create an NTFS partition using 512 bytes cluster allocations. This is due to the fact that FAT & FAT32 partitions are aligned on 512 byte boundaries.

> **NOTE:** The performance of NTFS converted partitions will not be as great as freshly created NTFS partitions.

Creating Mount Points

As mentioned previously, mount points are a new feature to Windows XP. Mount points provide a very nice way to handle systems with lots of data. You can present all the available data in one folder that could then be shared. This eliminates the need to have excessive amounts of shares on a system. Another use for mount points is library devices or CD-ROM changers that show as multiple drives. You can mount all the CD-ROMs into a single folder.

You can create, remove, and manage mount points in two ways. The first method is through Disk Management; the second is from a command prompt.

Using Disk Management to manage mount points

Using the Disk Management snap-in, right-click the volume that you wish to mount and select Change Drive Letter and Paths. A dialog box will appear showing you the current ways to access the volume. This dialog box also will allow you to add, remove, and modify the mount points. To add a new mount point, click Add, which will provide another dialog box (Figure 4.2).

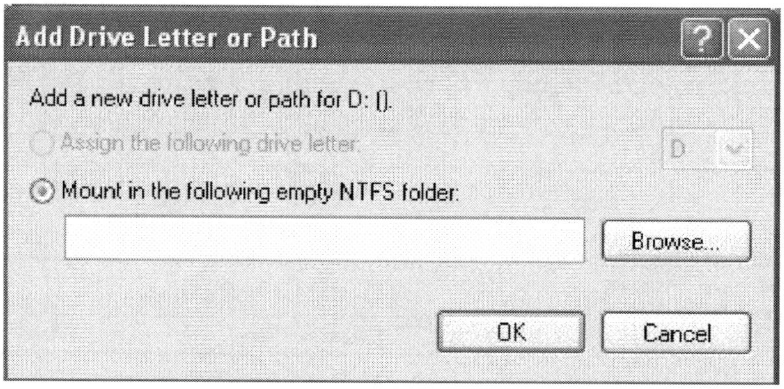

Figure 4-2: Create a New Mount Point

In this dialog box, you can then specify the NTFS folder you wish to mount the volume into. The results of this are shown in Figure 4.3.

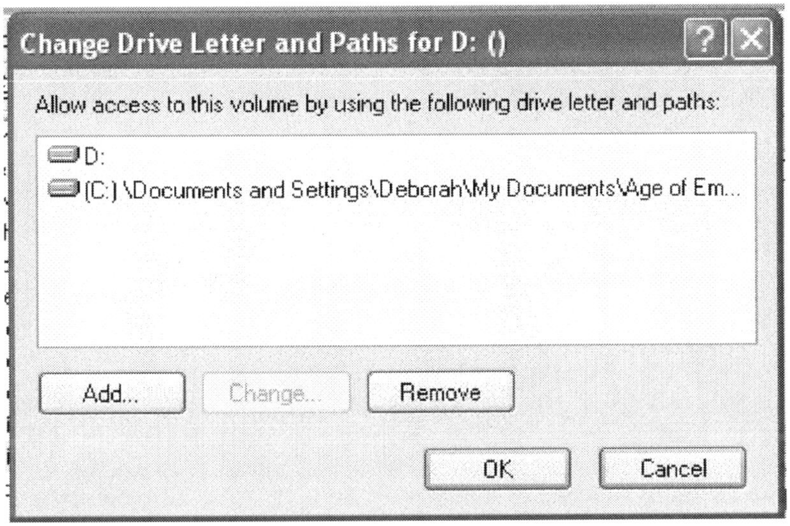

Figure 4-3: List of Mount Points

Using Command Prompt to manage mount points

From a Command Prompt, you can use the command MOUNTVOL to create, delete, or list volume mount points. Table 4.5 shows the command line parameters for the MOUNTVOL command. You can run the MOUNTVOL command with no parameters to show all mount points.

mountvol [drive:]path VolumeName

mountvol [drive:]path /d

mountvol [drive:]path /l

[DRIVE:]PATH	Specifies the NTFS directory folder to use as the mount point
VOLUMENAME	Specifies the volume name that is the target of the mount point. If not specified, it lists the volume names of all partitions
/D	Removes the volume mount point from the specified folder
/L	Lists the mounted volume name for the specified folder

Table 4-5: MOUNTVOL command line parameters

Removable Media

Removable media are devices like Zip and Jazz Drives, optical discs and tape backup systems. These are managed in the same fashion as CD-ROM devices – through Device Manager. Double-clicking on the specific removable media device will bring up a Properties box, which allows you to manage the specific device.

You can also manage removable media through the Computer Management console (on the console tree, select Removable Storage). Removable Storage allows you to track your removable storage media and to manage the hardware libraries, such as changers, that contain them. Removable Storage labels, catalogs, and tracks media; controls library drives, slots, and doors; and provides drive-cleaning operations.

Pop Quiz 4.1

Pop Quiz 4.1 Questions

1). Name four of the NTFS features supported by Windows XP?

2). What are the minimum and maximum volume size recommendations for NTFS? FAT32? FAT?

3). Under Windows XP, can you convert a drive from NTFS to FAT32 without losing any data?

4). What is a mount point?

5). On a basic disk volume, you can form volume sets. What is the similar function on a dynamic disk volume?

Pop Quiz 4.1 *Answers*

1). There are a number of new features in NTFS version 5.0. These include:

A. File encryptions

B. Disk quotas

C. Sparse files

D. Distributed link tracing

E. Reparse points

F. Volume Mount points

G. Change log.

2). NTFS has a minimum volume size of approximately 10 MB. The recommended practical maximum for volumes is 2 TB (terabytes). FAT 32 has a minimum volume size of 32 MB and can create volumes up to 32GB. FAT can create volumes from floppy disk size up to 4 GB in size.

3). No. The only way you can switch a drive from NTFS to FAT32 is by reformatting and then restoring the data from backup. You can, however, convert a drive from FAT or FAT32 to NTFS.

4). A mount point is a directory placed on an NTFS volume that provides a transparent gateway to another volume, regardless of that volume's file system. For example, you can have a mount point defined as C:\Mount\Data which is actually your D: drive.

5). A spanned dynamic volume follows the same rules as volume sets on basic storage. Spanned volumes are used to increase the size of a volume beyond the space available on one drive. The data is written to a spanned volume sequentially – that is, from beginning to end, filling up the space on one drive before moving to the next.

III Device Manager

Device Manager allows you to quickly ascertain whether or not hardware is functioning correctly, what the settings are for the device and what resources the device is using.

The Windows XP Device Manager tree is a record of the devices currently loaded, based on the configuration information in the registry. You can use Device Manager to install or uninstall devices, troubleshoot problems, update drivers, and change the assigned device resources

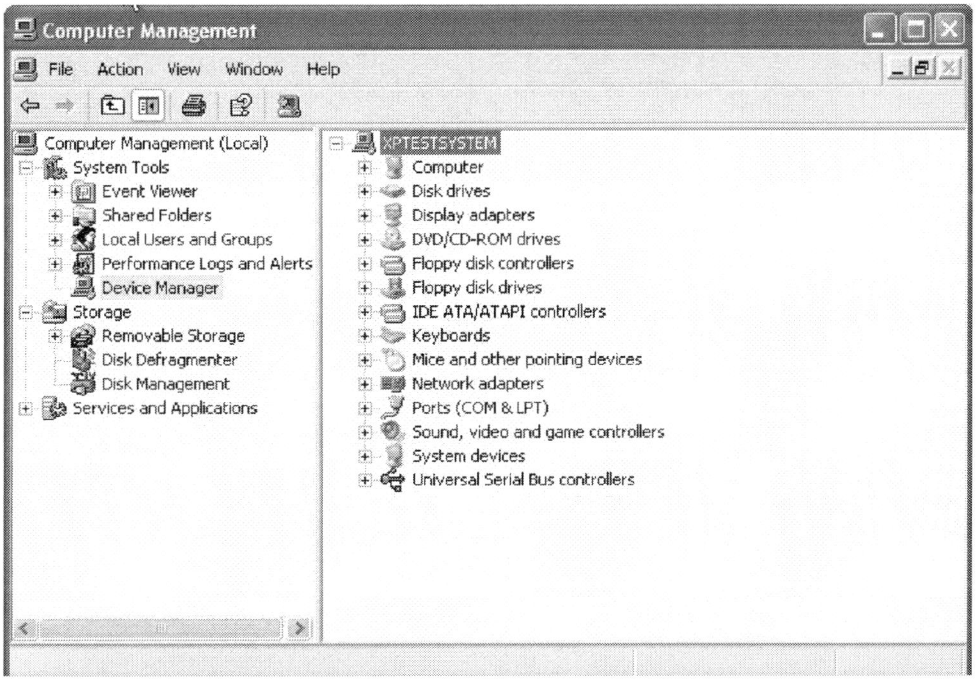

Figure 4-4: Device Manager under Computer Management

Device Manager can be run under the Computer Management Utility (a built-in MMC snap-in console) as shown in Figure 4.4. As well, it can be run as its on window by clicking Start, Control Panel. Double-click System. On the Hardware tab, click Device Manager as shown in Figure 4.5.

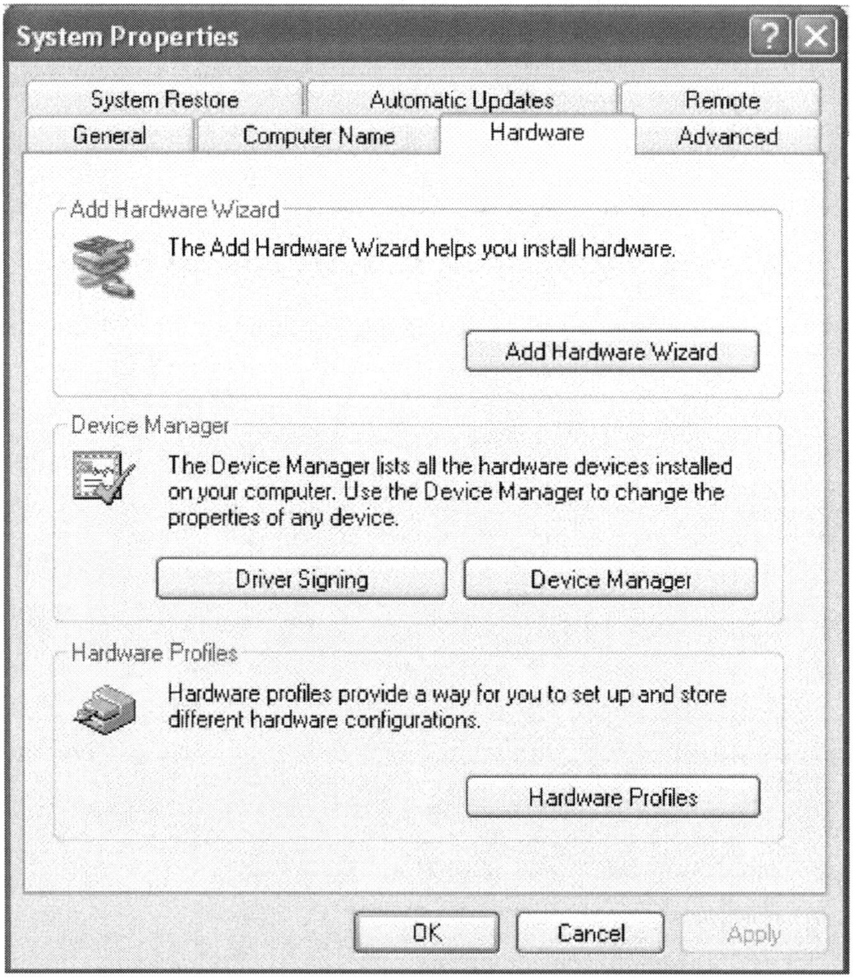

Figure 4-5: Accessing Device Manager through Control Panel

Device Manager does not display all devices by default. Non–Plug and Play devices, for example, are hidden. However, when problems occur, you may need to view these hidden devices for troubleshooting purposes. This can be done by selecting "Show Hidden Devices" under the **View** menu item. Device Manager will also not display "phantom" devices – that is, devices that are installed but not currently connected to the computer.

If you wish to display the phantom devices, before opening Device Manager, at a Command Prompt type:

set DEVMGR_SHOW_NONPRESENT_DEVICES=1.

Open Device Manager, and then at the command prompt type:

start devmgmt.msc

The phantom devices will now also appear in Device Manager.

The properties of any item listed under Device Manager will always have at least two tabs – General and Driver. Some may have more than these two (for example, the display adapter may also have a tab for Disk Properties) but these two are always present.

The General tab (Figure 4.6) shows the device type, manufacturer and location, as well as the current device status. If the device is not working properly, it should be indicated here. The "troubleshooter" button will walk you through an online help wizard to help you determine the solution to a problem.

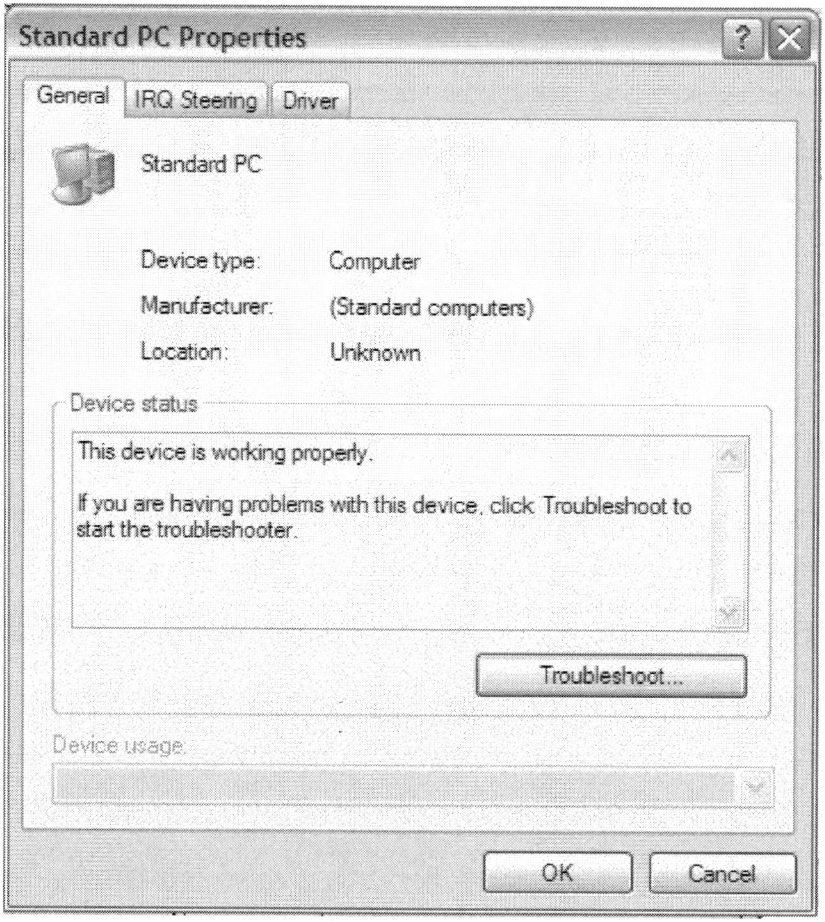

Figure 4-6: General Tab (Devices)

The Driver tab (Figure 4.7) gives current information about the driver used by device selected. The dialog box also allows you to uninstall or update the driver.

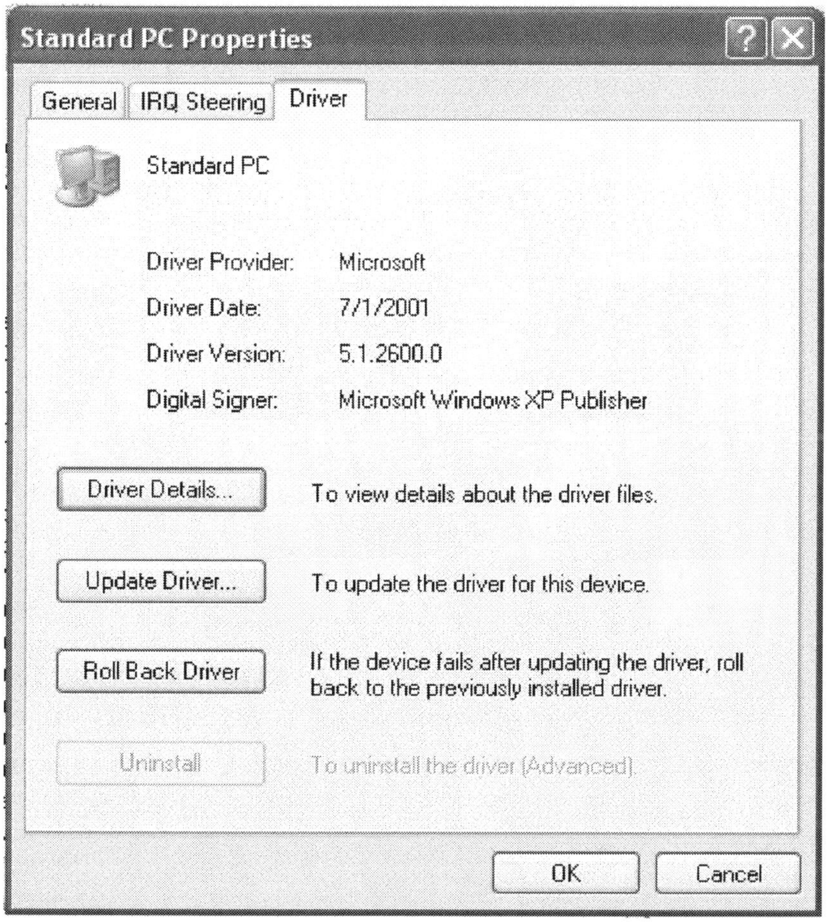

Figure 4-7: Driver Tab (Devices)

IV Display Devices

Display devices in Windows XP are obviously necessary if you wish to see what is happening on your system. Windows XP automatically provides a generic VGA adapter into all installations; however it is not going to provide you more advanced video card to perform at is greatest.

Video Adapters

In Windows XP, the Display option in Control Panel will allow you to perform the following tasks:

Change the display driver.

Change screen resolution and color depth

Change color schemes and text styles

View changes in colors, text, and display appearance before applying changes

Configure display settings for each hardware profile (frequently for docked/undocked mobile computers)

Configure multiple monitors

An incompatible device driver will not cause the operating system to crash. Windows XP ensures that, if a display driver fails to load or initialize, the generic VGA display driver will be used. In that way, Windows XP can be still started to troubleshoot a display problem.

Monitors

To gain maximum use of your system, make sure that you configure your monitor (or monitors in a multiple display environment). Ideally you should make sure that Windows XP is correctly identifying your monitor. If it is not identifying your monitor, you can choose to use a default monitor, or to select the Plug & Play monitor. You should also instruct you monitor on the proper refresh rate to use.

> **Tip:** The refresh rate helps to eliminate eye discomfort, the higher the refresh, the less flickering on your display. However, if you set a refresh rate that your monitor cannot handle, you risk damaging your monitor.

Multiple Display Support

Windows XP allows you to configure up to nine additional monitors for use on one computer. This allows the user to have different view of his or her desktop open at one time. The resolution and color depth can be adjusted for each individual display.

Hardware acceleration can be used in Windows XP to improve display performance. If hardware acceleration causes problems, it can be partially or fully disabled. It is important to note in a multiple-display situation, changing the hardware acceleration settings will affect all monitors connected to the system.

When dealing with DirectX in multiple monitor configurations, make sure that the primary monitor provides the best performance and features. Full screen DirectX applications can only run in the primary monitor. Direct 3D applications only receive full capabilities on the primary monitor.

For every monitor that you add to a system, system performance is decreased due to the increase in use of system resources. Another concern is that for VGA mode, only one card and monitor combination will receive the signal.

Portable computers can be used in a multiple display configuration, but the VGA device must be the onboard display.

To configure multiple monitors

To install additional monitors, first turn off your system and install a second video adapter into a free PCI or AGP slot. Attach a second monitor to the new video card and turn on your system. Windows XP will detect the video adapter and monitor, installing the appropriate drivers.

Open the Display icon in Control Panel, select the **Settings** tab, and click the monitor icon that represents your new addition. Select the **Extend my Windows Desktop onto this monitor** check box and click **OK**.

Common Problems

The following is a list of common problems with multiple display devices, and suggested solutions:

The system does not detect the secondary adapters

Make sure that you have the correct drivers for your monitors. Confirm that your display adapter is on the HCL

1. The primary monitor displays the startup screen and the secondary monitor is blank

   Check connectivity – is the secondary monitor plugged in? Turned on? Check the power connections and cabling. Confirm that the monitor is capable of displaying the configured mode and refresh rates. Switch the primary and secondary monitors.

2. The primary monitor displays the startup screen and the secondary monitor displays the desktop

   Shut down the computer and remove the secondary adapter. Verify that you disabled VGA on the secondary adapter display. Verify that there is no resource conflict. The display adapters may be incompatible -- install a new primary or secondary adapter.

3. After installing the secondary monitor, the system does not complete the POST routine and there is no display on either monitor

   Ensure that the primary display adapter is in PCI Slot 1. Place the secondary display adapter in a different PCI slot. Make sure that the drivers have been correctly loaded. The display adapters may be incompatible -- install a new primary or secondary adapter. If one of the displays is AGP, check in the BIOS to make sure that the Primary Video option is set correctly for the VGA-enabled device.

4. The secondary monitor performs a POST, and only the secondary monitor is listed in the Display Properties

   The secondary device completed the POST routine instead of the primary display. Because VGA is disabled on the secondary display, it prevents multiple monitor configurations. Switch PCI slots between the two adapters or set the BIOS to run POST on the display port for the VGA device.

5. After restarting, the secondary monitor has no display

   Confirm that "Extend my Windows desktop into this monitor" is selected. If two monitor icons are not displayed in the Display Properties dialog box, the display adapters may be incompatible -- install a new primary or secondary adapter.

V Multimedia Devices

Windows XP has a wide range of support for multimedia devices. These types of devices include sound cards, CD-ROM drives, and DVD drives. Windows XP also supports numerous audio and video codecs (formats) including AC3 Dolby Digital.

Sound Cards

You can install either a single sound card in Windows XP, which is the most common case, or you can install multiple sound cards -- ideal if you are a musician!

Using the Sounds and Multimedia Control Panel, you can specify your preferred device for sound playback, sound recording, and MIDI music playback (Figure 4.8).

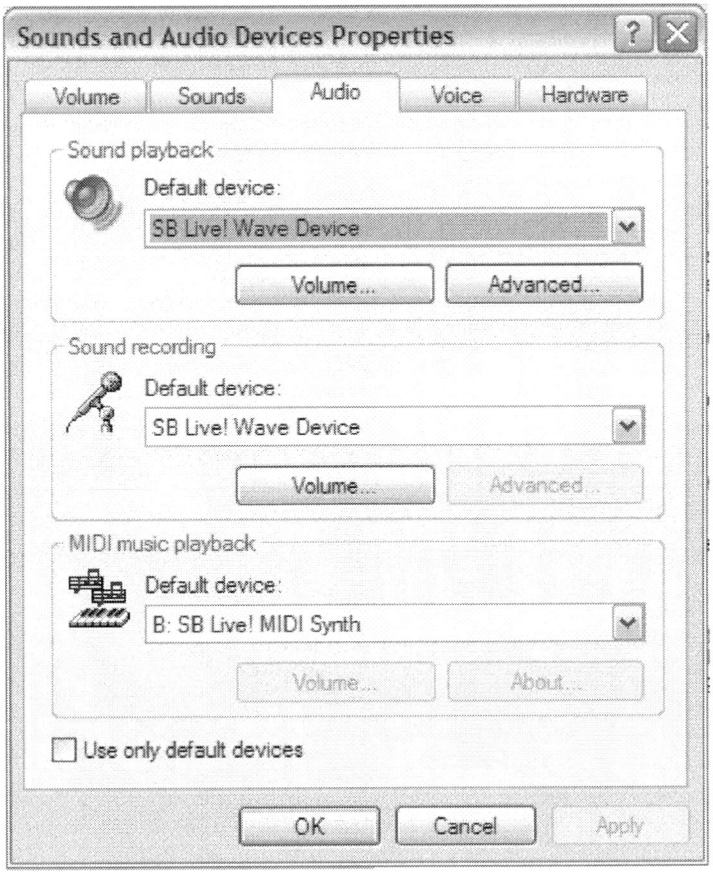

Figure 4-8: Specifying preferred sound devices

For sound playback, you can optimize your setup by choosing the speaker setup that most closely resembles your actual speaker arrangement (Figure 4.9). You can also adjust the performance of the playback -- useful when you are experiencing problems.

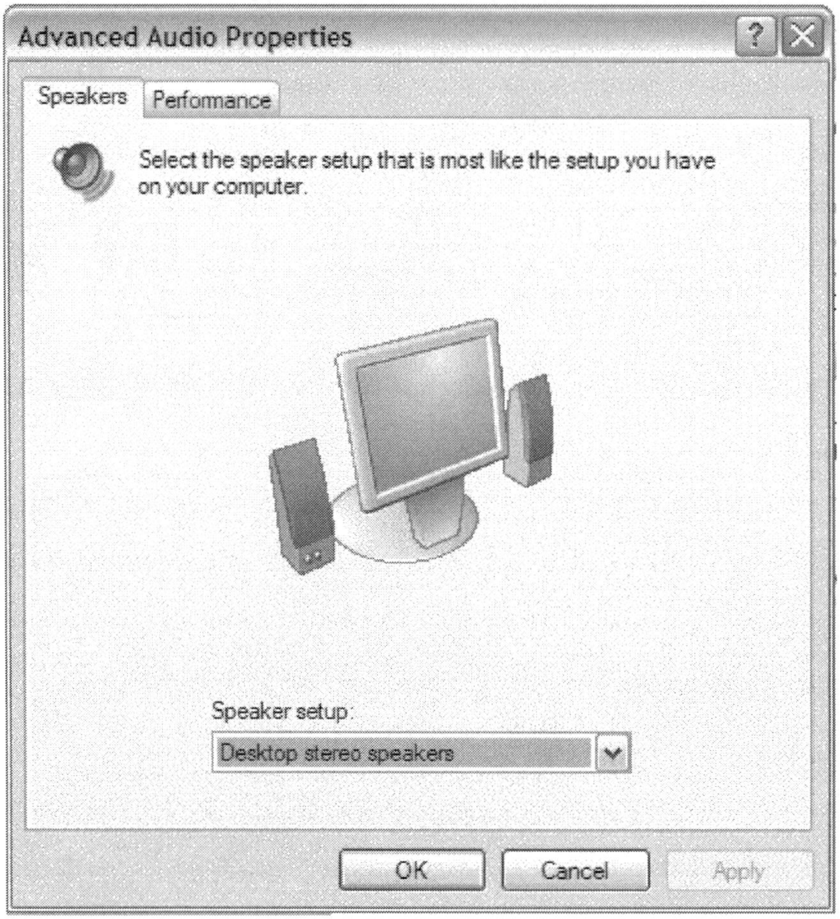

Figure 4-9: Optimizing Speaker Setup

To adjust multimedia hardware properties, you can use the Device Manager, or the Hardware tab in the Sounds and Multimedia Control Panel (Figure 4.10). One advantage of using the Hardware tab is that it allows you to conFigure the various codecs on the system.

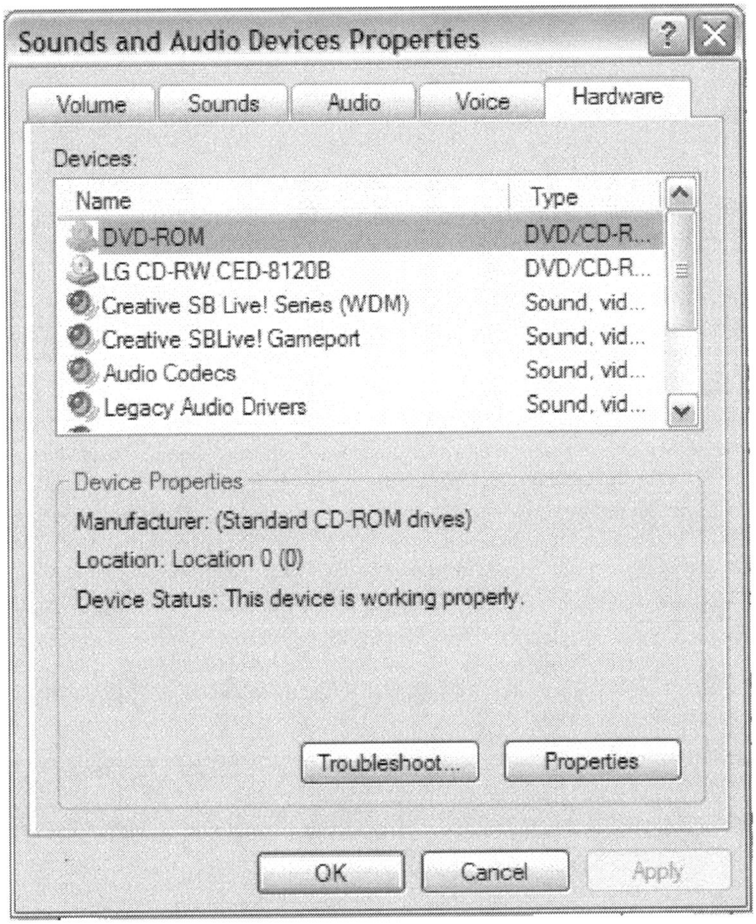

Figure 4-10: Multimedia Hardware

CDROM / DVD

CD-ROM and DVD drive properties can be accessed though Device Manager, or through the Sounds and Multimedia Control Panel on the Hardware tab. The properties of CD-ROM and DVD drives include the standard General and Drivers Tabs. The other tabs include Properties and Advanced Settings.

The Properties tab allows you to configure the volume setting for playback of CD audio, and as to use digital or analog playback (Figure 4.11). This tab is available for both CD and DVD based drives.

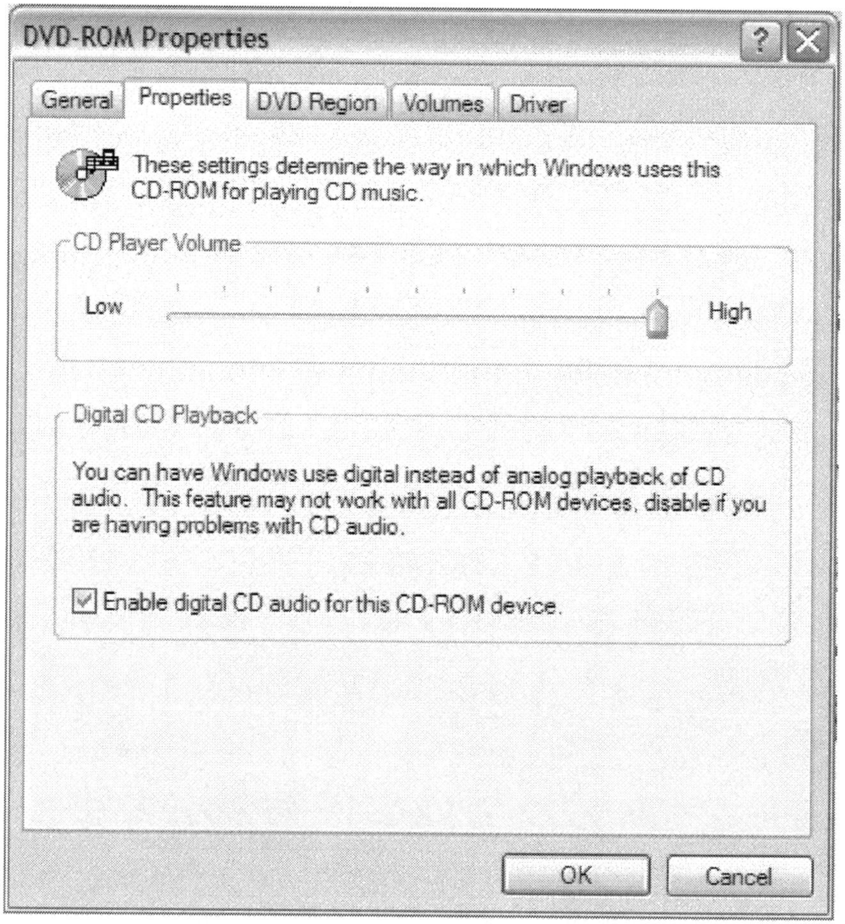

Figure 4-11: DVD / CD-ROM Properties

The DVD Region tab is only available on DVD based drives (Figure 4.12). This tab allows you to configure the region code for you DVD drive up to four times. After four times, no changes will be allowed, even if you reinstall Windows XP or move the drive to another computer. This setting is a part of the DVD drive, not of Windows XP.

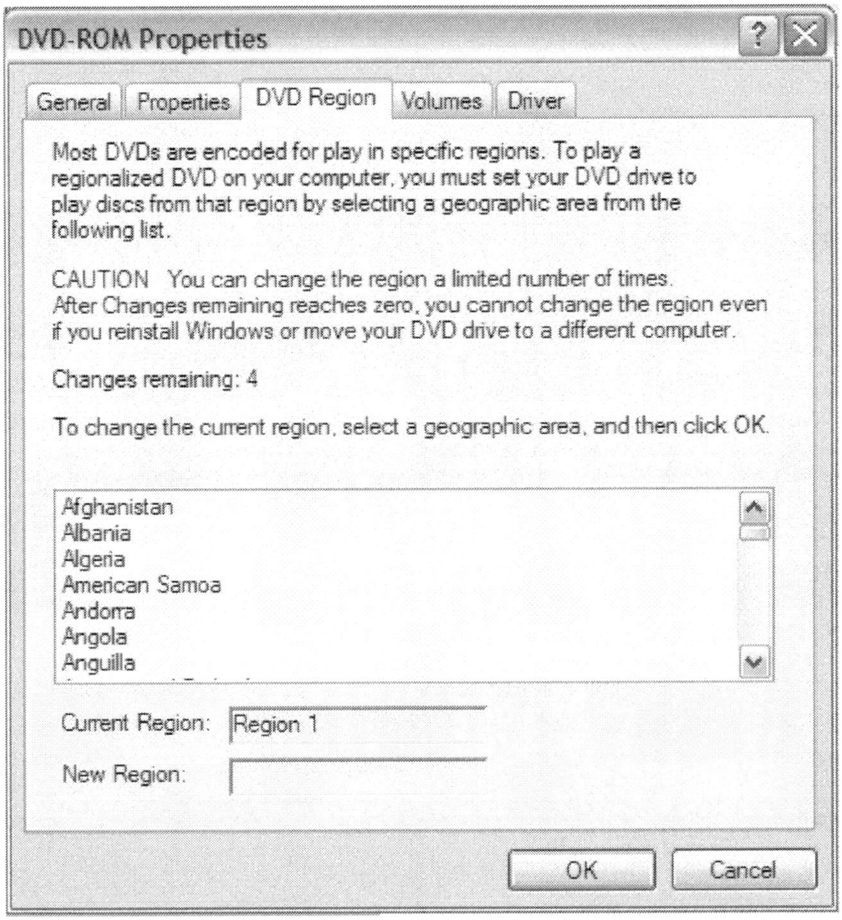

Figure 4-12: DVD Region Tab

VI Card Services (PCMCIA)

Windows XP allows you to change PCMCIA (Personal Computer Memory Card International Association) cards without powering down the system. This is called hot swapping. Make sure that the notebook or laptop you are using supports hot-swapping before you add or remove a PCMCIA card while the system is running. Even though Windows XP supports changing cards on the fly, damage can occur if the laptop itself does not.

PCMCIA cards are generally Plug-and-Play devices. Because of this, Windows XP will automatically recognize the card and install it immediately. If problems occur, the cards can be managed through Device Manager.

Pop Quiz 4.2

Pop Quiz 4.2 *Questions*

1). You need to quickly ascertain whether your DVD-ROM drive is currently functioning on your computer. What tool would you use?

2). Device Manager does not display all devices by default. Non–Plug and Play devices, for example, are hidden. As well, Device Manager will also not display devices that are installed but not currently connected to the computer, known as "phantom" devices. What steps would you perform to allow Device Manager to display all devices, including the hidden and the phantom devices?

3). You have unknowingly installed an incompatible video device driver. What will happen when you start Windows XP?

4). You have set up your computer to work with two monitors. However, on start up, the primary monitor displays the startup screen and the secondary monitor is blank. What do you do to resolve the problem?

5). Does Windows XP support "hot swapping" of PCMCIA cards?

Pop Quiz 4.2 *Answers*

1). Device Manager allows you to quickly ascertain whether or not hardware is functioning correctly as well as what the settings are for the device and what resources the device is using.

2). You can show all hidden devices by selecting "**Show Hidden Devices"** under the View menu item in Device Manager. To display phantom devices, you must, before opening Device Manager, at a Command Prompt type "SET DEVMGR_SHOW_NONPRESENT_DEVICES=1". Open Device Manager, and then at the command prompt type "START DEVMGMT.MSC".

3). An incompatible device driver will not cause the operating system to crash. If a display driver fails to load or initialize, the generic VGA display driver will be used.

4). Check your connectivity. Is the secondary monitor plugged in? Turned on? Check the power connections and cabling. Confirm that the monitor is capable of displaying the configured mode and refresh rates. Switch the primary and secondary monitors to see if this resolves the problem.

5). Windows 2000 Professional allows you to change PCMCIA cards without powering down the system (hot swapping). Make sure that the notebook or laptop you are using supports hot-swapping before you add or remove a PCMCIA card while the system is running. Even though XP supports changing cards on the fly, damage can occur if the laptop itself does not.

VII Power Management

Power management in Windows XP is has been greatly improved from Windows 9x and Windows NT 4.0. Windows XP now takes a system wide approach to power management. Most of this design is due to the ACPI (Advanced Configuration and Power Interface) and the OnNow specifications. These specifications allow a computer to converse energy while the computer is working and to place the computer in sleep mode when it is not. With these specifications in place, both workstations and notebooks can gain substantial improvements on there operations.

A workstation machine can power up in a fraction of the time it used to take under Windows NT 4.0. They can also converse less power, as devices (such as a modem) not in use can be powered down. This can also mean less noise is being produced.

For notebooks, these power conservation methods are critical, as battery life is so short. Windows XP provides longer battery life by powering down devices and the processor. It can also very quickly place a notebook in sleep mode when running on batteries.

For any of this to work, the system must be ACPI-compliant. However this does not mean you have to purchase a brand new system. Windows XP does provide support for the older APM (Advanced Power Management). With these systems, it is not Windows XP that is controlling the power management; it is the system's BIOS.

Advanced Configuration and Power Interface (ACPI) is a system interface that provides a standard method for managing both configuration of devices and power management. ACPI allows the operating system to have direct control over how the system consumes power. The devices it can control range from the processor to standard devices (hard drives, network adapters) to external devices (printers). It can also provide control for other electronic devices that may be connected to the system, such as a television or a stereo system.

In order for the system to be able to use all the features provided by OnNow, the systems BIOS, motherboard, and operating system must support ACPI. When you install Windows XP, the setup process will determine how your system handles ACPI: No support, incompatible support, or full support. To check what support you computer has, use device manager and look under the Computer node (it is visible by viewing by type or connection. Figure 4.13 shows the type of ACPI on a system, using view by connection.

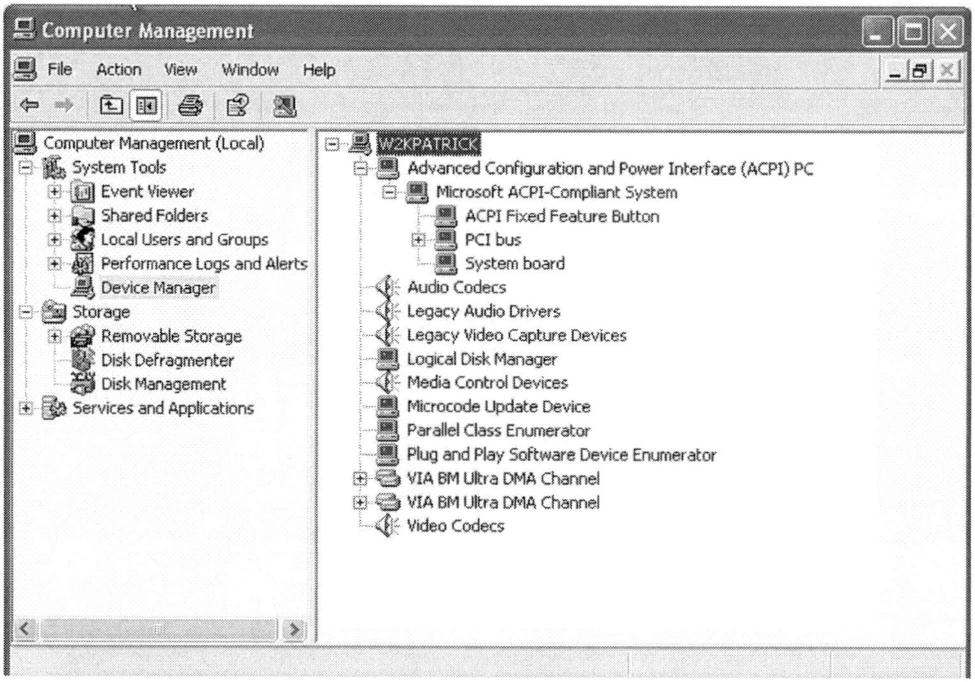

Figure 4-13: ACPI Support in Device Manager

Configuring Power Management

Power management is configured through the Power Options in Control Panel. There are three tabs (Power Schemes, Advanced, and Hibernate) that will always be available, no matter what type of system you are using.

The Power Schemes tab allows you to choose the best and most efficient power scheme for the computer. On desktop machines, you will see a display such as Figure 4.14. On notebooks, the only difference will be the addition of when the system is run on batteries. The default power schemes included in Windows XP are designed to provide a fairly decent realm of power management for your system. You can customize and create your own power schemes by changing when the monitor and/or hard drives will be automatically powered down to reserve power. This is based on a period of non-activity. You can also choose when you want the system to go on into standby mode, if at all.

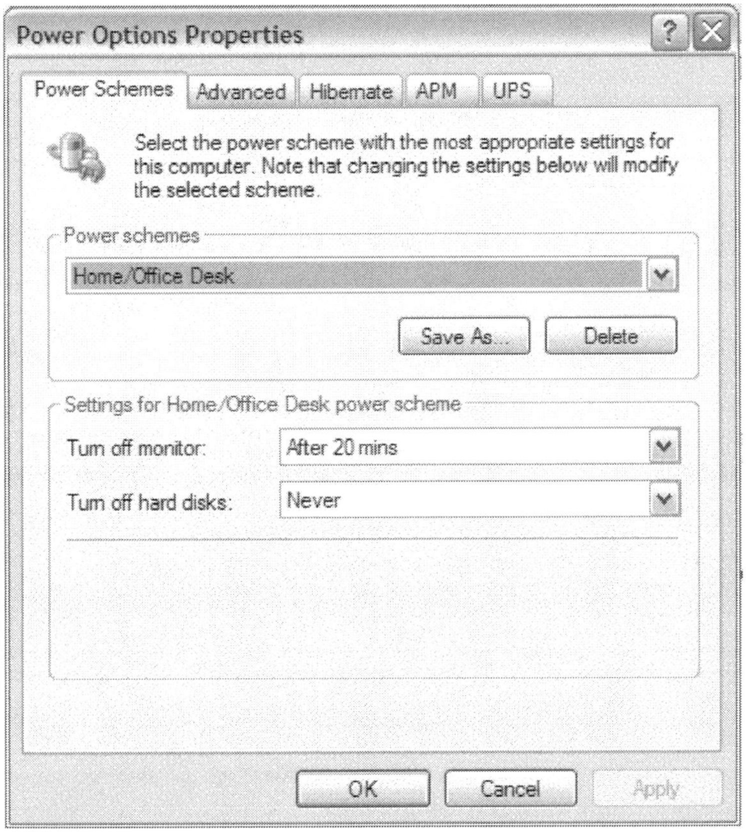

Figure 4-14: Power Schemes

The Advanced tab (Figure 4.15) always has two consistent options – whether you want the Power Options icon to be displayed on the taskbar and whether you want the user prompted for a password when the system comes off standby mode. The remaining options are dependent on the hardware configuration you are currently using on the computer.

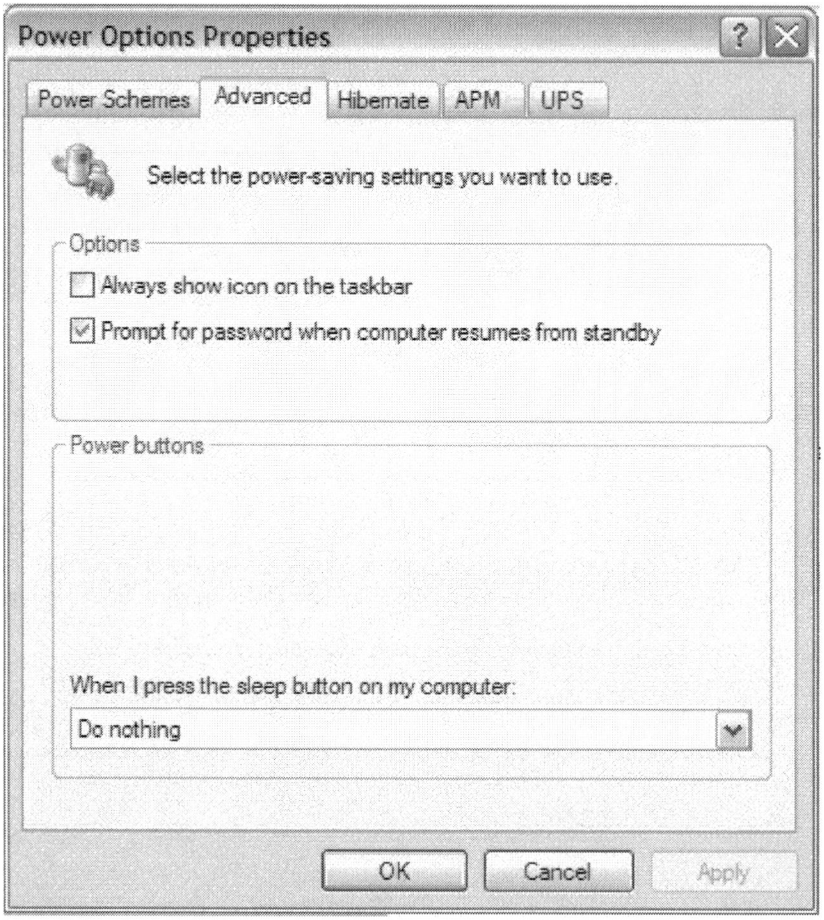

Figure 4-15: Advanced Power Options

The Hibernate tab (Figure 4.16) allows the system to store whatever information is current stored in memory on the hard drive before shutting down. When the computer is woken up, it will return to the previous state. You can choose to enable hibernation support on this tab. There is also information available to let you know whether you have enough free disk space to allow for hibernation. The free disk space required is equal to the amount of RAM you have in your system.

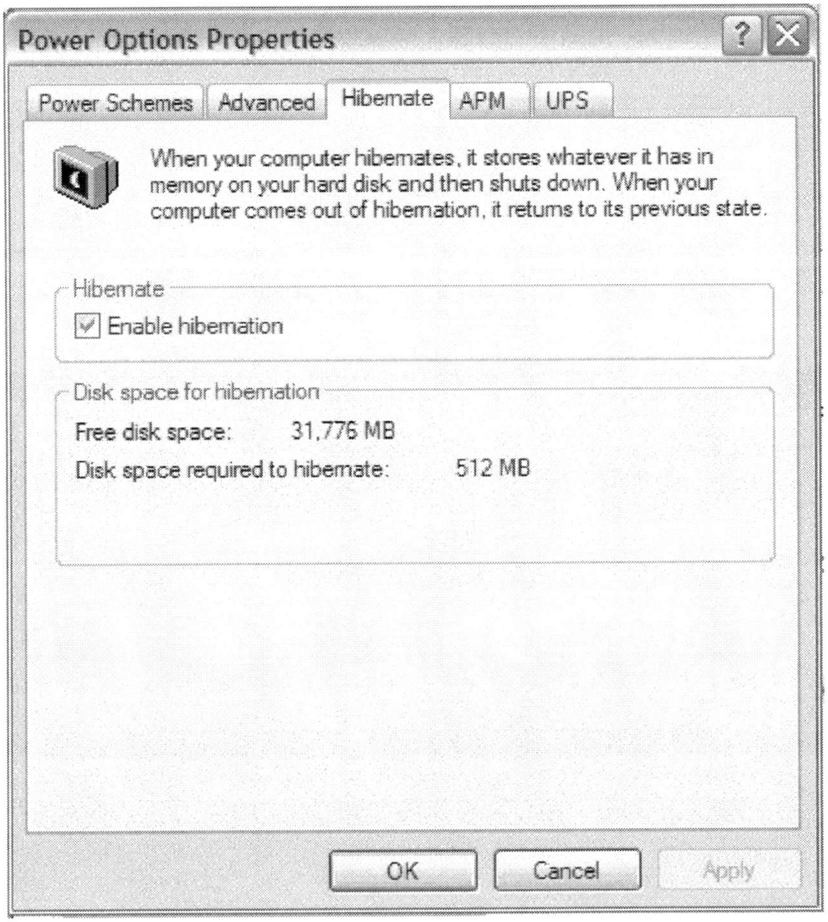

Figure 4-16: Hibernation

APM

Advanced Power Management (APM) support in Windows XP is limited. However, there is an established base of systems, specifically notebooks, which use this type of power management. In fact, APM support is only intended for notebook use, not desktop use, in Windows XP. When you install Windows XP, it goes through a number of checks to determine of which power management support your system is capable.

There are three categories under which your system may fall:

1. AutoEnable APM
   These systems require APM support. Windows XP will automatically install and enable APM.

2. Disable APM

   On these systems, APM does not work properly. Windows XP will not install APM on these machines.

3. Neutral

   APM on these systems will be installed, but not enabled. Windows XP will allow you to enable APM if you so desire (Figure 4.17).

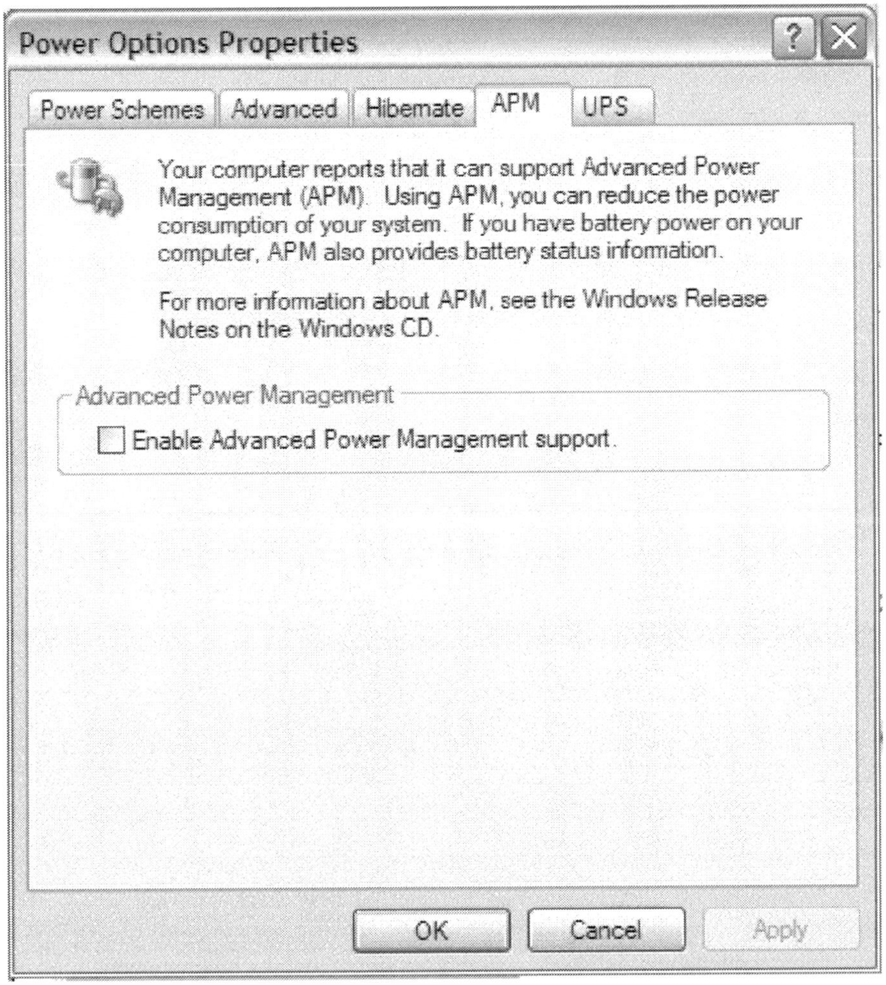

Figure 4-17: Configuring APM support

UPS

Windows XP supports Uninterruptible Power Supplies (UPS). A UPS is a device that can regulate the power your system receives. It is a known fact that brownouts and blackouts occur all the time. Unfortunately, they always seem to come at the wrong time. Currently, power problems are the largest cause of computer problems resulting in a loss of data (approximately 45%).

With a UPS, you can provide a clean consistent power source for you computer, eliminating spikes, surges, brownouts, and blackouts from destroying your data. A UPS can allow a system to write all of its data to a hard drive from its memory before shutting down the system cleanly. It is in your best to invest in a UPS no matter what type of system you are using. The UPS tab on the Power Options Control Panel (Figure 4.18) allows you to setup a UPS and then configure it to you needs.

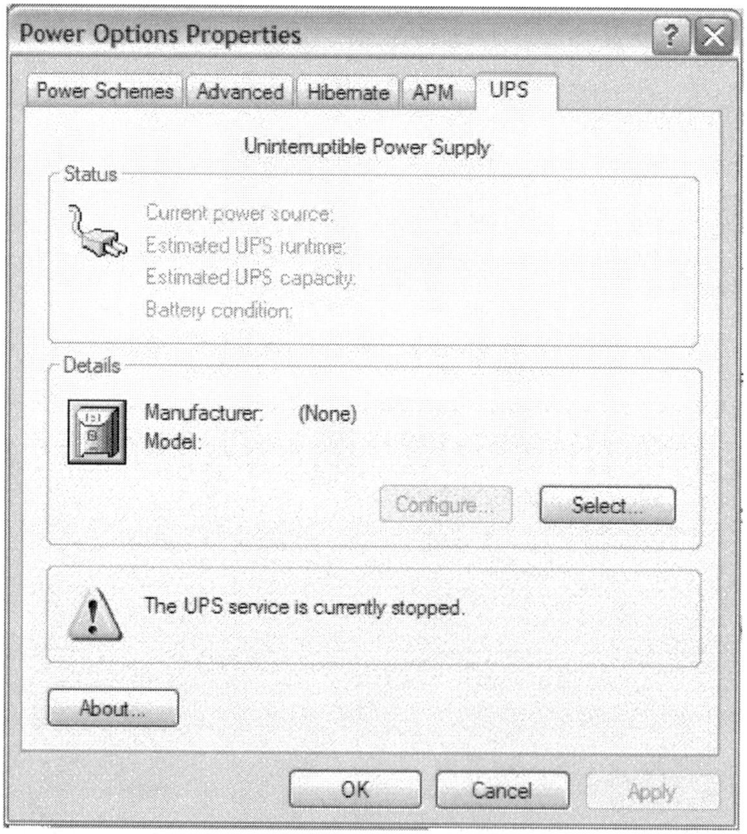

Figure 4-18: UPS Support

This configuration (Figure 4.19) allows you to set warnings and actions that will occur during power outages.

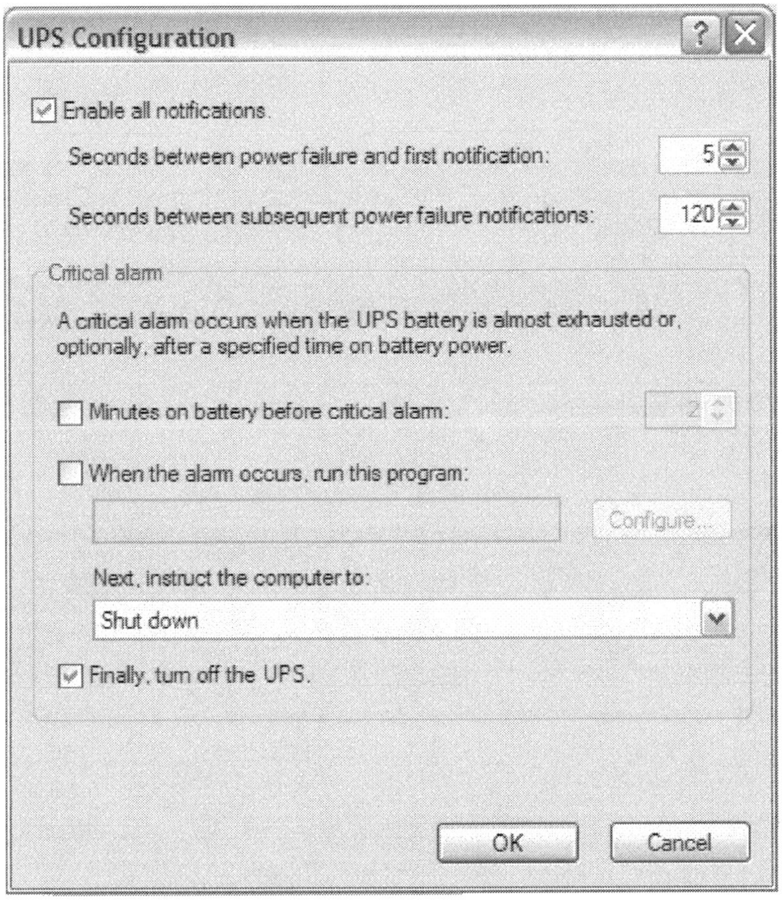

Figure 4-19: UPS Configuration

> **Tip:** Remember to test your UPS on a regular basis to provide optimal usage

VIII Input Devices

Windows XP provides support for various types of input devices. Everything from standard keyboards, USB mice, scanners, cameras, and game controllers can be used. Device compliancy can be from old standards such as PS/2 and AT connectors or serial ports, or it can be based on newer technologies such as USB or IEEE 1394 and other HID-compliant devices.

A new firmware specification called Human Interface Device (HID) provides devices with a new way to interface with the operating system. HIDs include such input devices as keyboards, mice, joysticks, and steering wheels. A HID could also be such devices as virtual reality helmets, golf clubs, treadmills, remote controls, or a space shuttle simulation device. HID-compliant devices are self-describing, plug and play, and support power management.

Windows XP provides support for HIDs through WDM (Windows Driver Model). HID support in Windows XP is primarily USB based, however support is also provided for devices connecting through older interfaces. Other interfaces, like IEEE 1394, can be implemented and supported by third party vendors.

Configuring and maintaining each of these devices is done primarily through the respective Control Panel icons.

IX Connectivity Devices

In order to make use of various services and features of Windows XP, it is required to have devices that provide some form of connectivity or the sharing of information. For example, to connect to the Internet you require a modem, a network card, or a card specific to the type of connection (i.e. ISDN). How that device is connected to your system is very important, as Windows XP can support a wide range of these devices.

Modems

Windows XP supports modems connected through the serial port, the PCI or ISA bus, the USB bus, or through Card Services. If the modem you are installing is Plug and Play-compliant, Windows XP will automatically detect and install it for you. During installation, Windows will assign a COM name according to the standard base I/O port address and IRQ of the modem, as seen in Table 4.6.

COM PORT	ADDRESS	IRQ
COM1	3F8	4
COM2	2F8	3
COM3	3E8	4
COM4	2E8	3

Table 4-6: Standard COM port Addresses

If a modem has a nonstandard base address, or if all four standard ports have been assigned to other devices, Windows XP will automatically assign the modem to COM5 or higher. You can change communications port settings by using Device Manager, as described earlier in this chapter.

> **NOTE:** Windows XP cannot detect some internal modems. In this case, you will need to manually install the device and configure it using the **Modems** option in Control Panel.

Faxes

In order for Windows XP to provide fax support, you must have a device connected to the computer that can send and receive faxes. In most cases you will find that this is a fax modem. Faxing is actually accomplished by configuring the fax device as a printer. Configuring this support is through the **Printers and Faxes** icon in Control Panel.

Each tab in the properties box will help you configure your faxes. The **User Information** tab lets you fill in the information you want to appear on your fax cover sheet. The **Cover Pages** tab allows you to create personal fax cover sheets. If corporate policy allows only a common cover page, personal pages will not be available when you send faxes. The third tab, **Status Monitor,** sends notification when a fax is sent or received. An icon can be placed on the taskbar, or a sound played when a fax is sent or received.

The fourth tab on the **Properties** dialog box is the **Advanced Options.** Advanced options include adding a fax printer. If the device that you will be using as your fax device is connected to your computer, clicking that button will add it to your system. You will receive a message that indicates that the fax printer was created successfully.

Once the fax support is configured, you will need to start the Fax Service. Like all other services, the Windows XP fax service will be started under the Services icon in Control Panel. The service can be set to Automatic or Manual start. Automatic start will happen when Windows XP is opened. Manual start requires user intervention at the time the service is to be used.

Infrared Devices

Windows XP supports the Infrared Data Association (IrDA) protocols that allow data to be transferred over infrared connections. The infrared component will be installed automatically on computers where Windows XP has detected a built-in infrared device. As well, a user can connect a serial IrDA transceiver to a serial COM. Use the **Add/Remove Hardware wizard** to install the device.

Once installed, the Wireless Link icon appears in Control Panel. When another infrared system comes in range, the Wireless Link icon appears on the desktop and on the taskbar.

A file can then be sent over the infrared connection by:

Specifying a location and one or more files using the Wireless Link dialog box.

Using drag-and-drop to move files onto the Wireless Link icon on the desktop.

By right-clicking any file or set of files on the Desktop, in Explorer, or in My Computer, and then click the Send To Infrared Recipient command.

Print to a printer configured to use an infrared port.

You can also use the Wireless Link to transfer images from a digital camera that has an infrared transmitter (Figure 4.20).

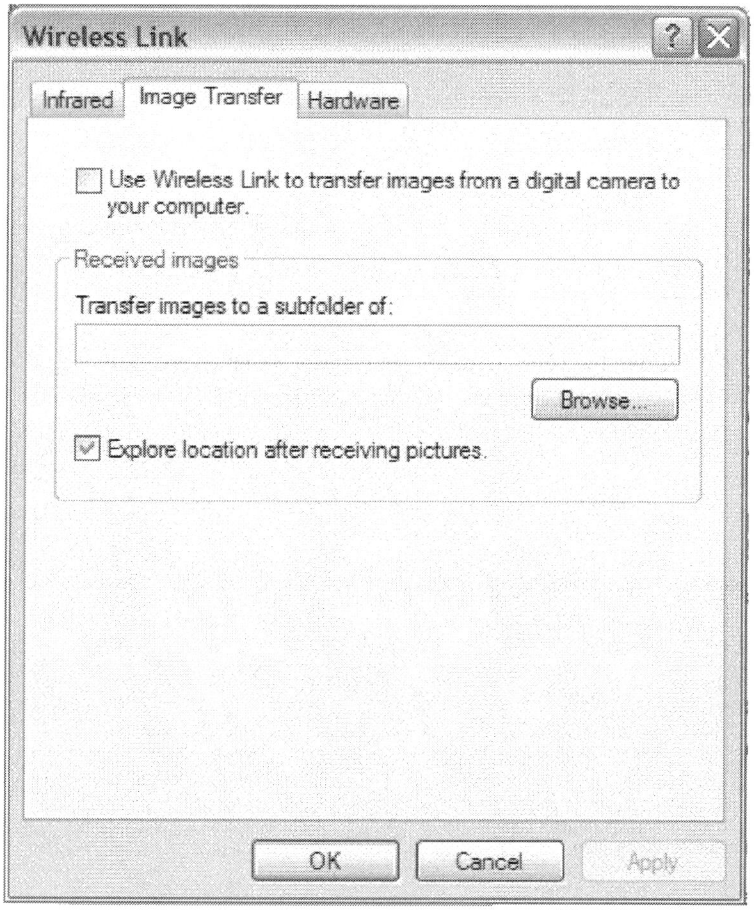

Figure 4-20: Wireless Link Image Transfer properties

Not only can you send and receive images and files, and print files, with Windows XP you are able to create a network connection between two computers by using the infrared port. You can then map shared drives between the two systems.

USB

Universal Serial Bus (USB) is a standards-based, external bus that brings the Plug and Play capability to keyboards, mice, joysticks, and hard drives by eliminating the need to install internal cards into dedicated slots. Hardware devices can be configured as soon as they are physically connected to the bus without the need to reboot the system.

USB uses a tiered topology consisting of 5 tiers. You can connect up to 127 devices to the bus. Each device can be up to five meters from its hub.

Power management capabilities in USB allow a device to be on or off, or in a suspend mode. This prevents unnecessary drainage to systems, such a notebooks running on batteries.

USB supports two data transfer modes: *isochronous* and *asynchronous*:

- Isochronous transfers require a constant bandwidth within time constraints. An example of this is a USB modem. Isochronous transfers are limited to 12 Megabits per second (Mbps), but are guaranteed.
- Asynchronous transfers are random and not guaranteed. An example of this is a USB keyboard. Asynchronous transfers are limited to 1.5 Mbps. There are three variants of asynchronous communications: interrupt (guaranteed access to transfer data at an established rate); control (transfer of specific requests such as device configuration); and bulk (transfer of large blocks of data such as in printing).

IEEE 1394

The IEEE 1394 bus (also known as FireWire and i.Link) is designed for high bandwidth devices such as digital camcorders and storage devices. The Windows XP implementation of IEEE 1394 only supports devices that are OHCI (Open Host Controller Interface) compatible. Hot plugging of IEEE 1394 devices is supported.

IEEE 1394 is a serial protocol that supports speeds ranging from 100 to 400 Mbps. You can connect up to 63 devices to a single bus and interconnect up to 1023 buses to form a large network with over 63,000 devices. Each device can have up to 256 TB of memory addressable on the bus.

IEEE 1394 supports two data transfer protocols: isochronous and asynchronous. The data transfer speeds can be S100 (98.304 Mbps), S200 (196.608 Mbps), or S400 (393.216 Mbps). Communication will automatically take place at the highest data transfer rate supported by the lowest speed device.

Network Adapters

A network adaptor (NIC) is the most common way to connect a device to the network. The network adapter contains the physical (MAC) address for the computer, and requires a driver to communicate with the Windows XP operating system. The actual network adapter can be connected to the system by means of the PCI or ISA bus, the USB bus, or through Card Services. Some network adapters are software based.

If the NIC is plug and play compliant, Windows Professional 2000 will automatically install and configure it for you. If the network adapter is not plug and play, make sure that it is on the HCL for Windows XP. If it is, you will have to manually configure the network card, either through a setup program, or manually, using the manufacturers recommended settings.

Network adapters can be installed using the **Install New Hardware** wizard, and can be configured in Control Panel through the **"Network and Dial-up Connections"** icon in Control Panel. Use the **Local Area Connection** properties.

For manual configuration, the **Resource** tab is where you will find the IRQ and I/O address setup.

The following list will outline some of the more common problems and solutions to NIC problems:

1. Network card not on the HCL

   Obtain a network adapter that is on the HCL, or alternately, contact the manufacturer to enquire whether a current driver is available for the NIC.

2. Outdated driver

   Use Windows Update to update the driver, or visit the manufacturer's website to obtain the most current driver.

3. Network adapter not recognized

   Use Device Manager to see if Professional has recognized your device. Install it manually, and verify that the resource settings do not conflict with other devices on the system.

4. Improperly configured network protocols

   Check to see that all protocols have been installed and are configured correctly. This will be discussed in Chapter 6.

Pop Quiz 4.3

Pop Quiz 4.3 *Questions*

1). You wish to configure the power management for your system. Where can you do this?

2). With Windows XP, through what can your modem be connected?

3). Once you have installed wireless services on a WinXP machine, how can you send information over the infrared connection?

4). What is USB?

Pop Quiz 4.3 *Answers*

1). Power management is configured through the Power Options in Control Panel. There are three tabs (Power Schemes, Advanced, and Hibernate) that will always be available, no matter what type of system you are using.
2). Windows 2000 Professional supports modems connected through the serial port, the PCI or ISA bus, the USB bus, or through Card Services.
3). A file can be sent over the infrared connection by:

A. specifying a location and one or more files using the Wireless Link dialog box.

B. using drag-and-drop to move files onto the Wireless Link icon on the desktop.

C. right-clicking any file or set of files on the Desktop, in Explorer, or in My Computer, and then click the Send To Infrared Recipient command.

D. printing to a printer configured to use an infrared port.

E. transferring images from a digital camera that has an infrared transmitter.

4). Universal Serial Bus (USB) is a standards-based, external bus that brings the Plug and Play capability to keyboards, mice, joysticks, and hard drives by eliminating the need to install internal cards into dedicated slots.

X Updating Drivers

Windows XP will install or update all drivers from the Windows Update website. This site contains ActiveX controls that will automatically compare the drivers currently installed on the system with the updates that are available. Newer drivers will be downloaded and installed automatically.

All drivers, including third-party drivers, will be included on the Windows Update site only if they have been digitally signed and passed the testing requirements for the Windows Logo Program.

If you need to find a driver, and it is not currently available on the Windows Update site, check the manufacturer's site for the device. Quite frequently drivers that have not yet passed Windows XP certification requirements, are placed on their site.

To upgrade to a driver that you have downloaded, first check the manufacturer's installation notes. This is important as some vendors use a setup program. For drivers that do not use setup programs, use the **Update Driver** button found in the device's properties dialog box on the Drivers tab (Figure 4.21). The Update Driver Wizard will then run; presenting a number of options you can perform.

Figure 4-21: Updating Drivers

XI Multiple Processors

For the most part, multiple processors will be found on servers. However, Windows XP supports two processors. Before you plan on installing a second processor in your system, make sure that the motherboard will support it. Follow the manufacturer's instructions for installing the second processor.

Frequently you will need to update the processor's driver to one that will support multiple processors. This can be done through the **Upgrade Device Driver** wizard. Table 4.7 provides a list of available Hardware Abstraction Layers (HALs) provided with Win XP.

TYPE	HAL
Standard	Advanced Configuration and Power Interface (ACPI) PC
	ACPI Uniprocessor PC
	ACPI Multiprocessor PC
	MPS Uniprocessor PC
	MPS Multiprocessor PC
	Standard PC
Compaq	Compaq SystemPro MultiProcessor or 100% Compatible
SGI	Silicon Graphics Visual Workstation

Table 4-7: Supported Hardware Abstraction Layers

It is vital that you select the HAL that is compatible with your system. Newer dual processor systems support the ACPI Multiprocessor PC HAL, while older systems are more likely to support the MPS (Multi-Processor Specification) Multiprocessor PC HAL.

> **NOTE:** Do not attempt to change from an ACPI HAL to a Standard HAL or from a Standard HAL to an ACPI HAL. Doing so will cause your system to either not start properly or not at all!

Verify that Windows XP has recognized the processors by checking in Task Manager. You can also use Task Manager to configure the professors. Configuration consists of associating each processor with specific processes that are running on the system. This process is called processor affinity.

Monitoring the processors is done through the System Monitor utility. Monitoring processors is covered in detail in Chapter 8.

XII Manage hardware profiles

By default, when Windows XP is installed, there is only one hardware profile (Profile 1 for desktop computers, and Docked for portable computers). The default hardware profile loads all available drivers.

Configuring new hardware profiles are especially useful for portable computers. Without a modified hardware profile, when a user logs onto a laptop that is undocked, the system will still try to find the network card and log onto the system. By creating an "undocked" profile, Windows XP will recognize that the computer is not connected to the network and load only the drivers it needs to operate.

Hardware profiles can be configured through the **System** icon in Control Panel, on the **Hardware** tab. To create a new profile, select an existing profile and click Copy (Figure 4.22).

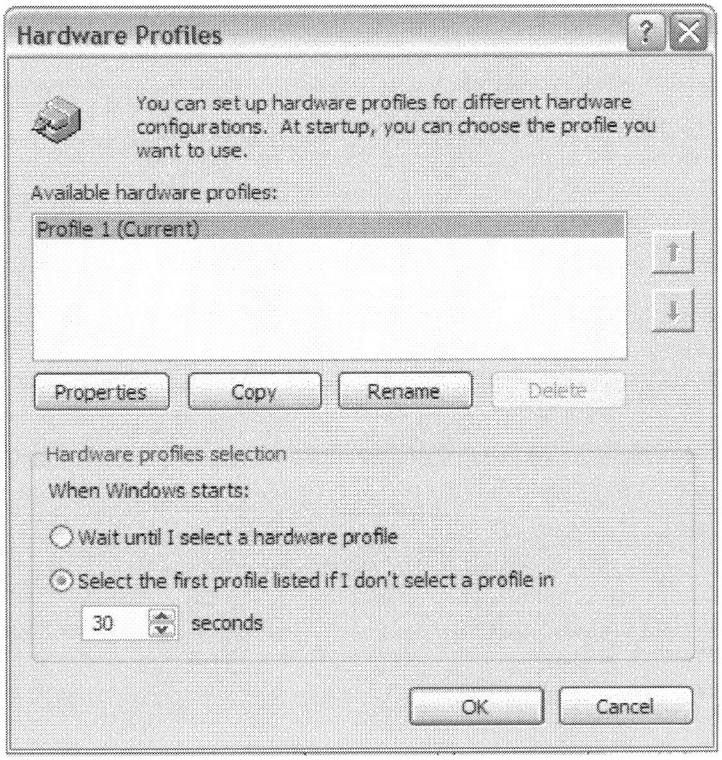

Figure 4-22: Hardware Profiles

Each of the profiles have generic settings in which can be configured (Figure 4.23). The first is whether or not it is a portable computer. If it is the profile can then be setup to be the "docked", "undocked" or "unknown" state of the computer.

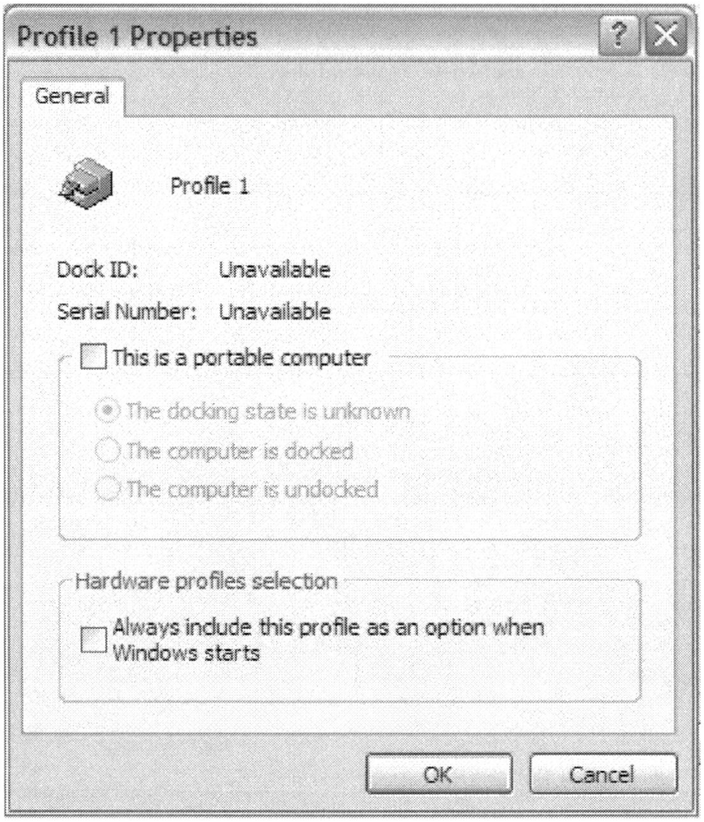

Figure 4-23: Hardware Profile Properties

Once you have created a new profile, you can then configure which devices are to be loaded in each profile. In order to do this, you must first reboot the system using the hardware profile that you wish to modify. Simply select the device and modify its device usage setting (Figure 4.24). The device usage setting has three options:

Use this device (enable)

Do not use this device in the current hardware profile (disable)

Do not use this device in any hardware profiles (disable)

Figure 4-24: Using Hardware Profiles with Devices

You can also use hardware profiles to control which services will be run in a specific configuration. To configure the service, use the Service snap-in in the MMC and change the properties of the service (Figure 4.25).

Figure 4-25: Using Hardware Profiles with Services

XIII Chapter 4: Summary

Congratulations. You have now learned the basics of implementing, administering and troubleshooting devices, and drivers in Windows XP. You should now be familiar with how to:

- Implement and manage disk devices
- Implement and manage display devices
- Implement and manage multimedia devices
- Implement and manage card services
- Implement and manage input devices
- Implement and manage connectivity devices
- Update drivers
- Configure for multiple processors
- Implement and manage hardware profiles

XIV Chapter 4: Review Questions

1. Advanced Power Management Support is most useful for which kind of computer?

   A. Any Workstation (Desktop or Tower)

   B. Server

   C. Laptop

   D. Desktop

   E. Tower

2. What control panel would you use to set Advanced Power Management?

   A. Power

   B. System

   C. Add/Remove Hardware

   D. Add/Remove Programs

   E. Power Options

3. What is the default display setting for a color video adapter and monitor?

   A. 640x480, 16 colors

   B. 800x600, 16 colors

   C. 640x480, 256 colors

   D. 800x600, 256 colors

   E. 1240x480, 256 colors

4. You have just installed an AGP Video Card in your Windows XP computer. You also installed the manufacturer's device drivers, and rebooted. The monitor went blank during the process of booting. What could you do to correct this problem?

A. Start the computer by using the Emergency Repair Disk

B. Reinstall the manufacturer's drivers

C. Enable Multi Monitor

D. Restore the original adapter driver settings

E. Reinstall windows

5. Your video driver is giving you problems. What should you do?

A. If it is an AGP card, try placing it in a PCI slot, then reboot.

B. Reinstall Windows

C. Enable Multi Monitor

D. Select Enable VGA Mode

E. Reboot the computer, and press F8 to get to the Advanced Options menu

6. Drive D of your Windows XP Professional computer is backed up everyday by Windows Backup. The drive fails on Thursday morning. You replace the failed drive with a new hard disk. You want to restore your files on drive D to the new hard disk. By viewing your backup log, you see that the backup method was incremental

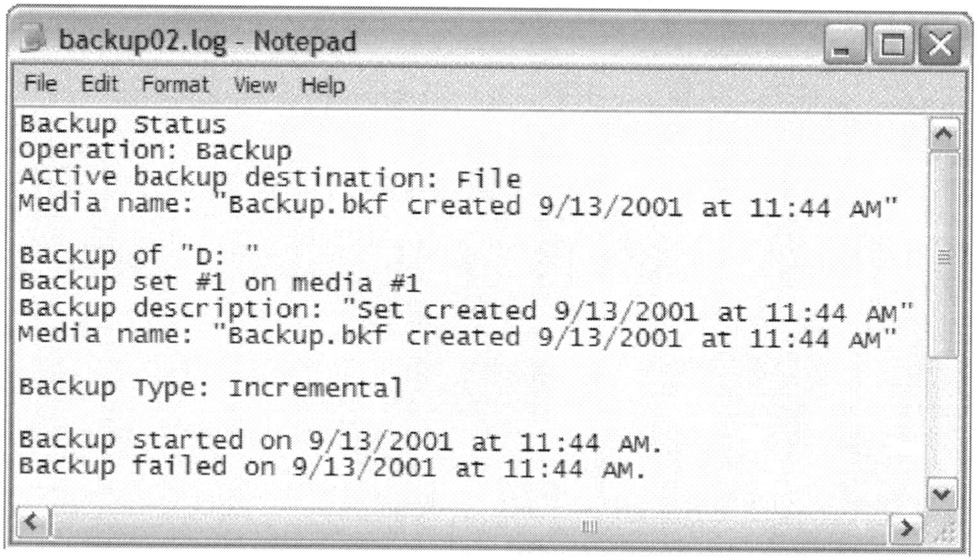


```
Backup Status
Operation: Backup
Active backup destination: File
Media name: "Backup.bkf created 9/13/2001 at 11:44 AM"

Backup of "D: "
Backup set #1 on media #1
Backup description: "Set created 9/13/2001 at 11:44 AM"
Media name: "Backup.bkf created 9/13/2001 at 11:44 AM"

Backup Type: Incremental

Backup started on 9/13/2001 at 11:44 AM.
Backup failed on 9/13/2001 at 11:44 AM.
```

What is the best order to use to restore your data?

A. Tuesday, Monday, Sunday, Saturday, Friday, Thursday, Wednesday.

Files will be current as of Wednesday.

B. Friday, Saturday, Sunday, Monday, Tuesday, Wednesday.

Files will be current as of Friday night.

C. Friday, Saturday, Sunday, Monday, Tuesday, Wednesday.

Files will be current as of Wednesday night.

D. Wednesday, Tuesday, Monday, Sunday, Saturday, Friday.

Files will be current as of Wednesday night.

E. Wednesday, Tuesday, Monday, Sunday, Saturday.

Files will be current as of Friday night.

7. You have Windows XP Professional installed on your C drive, and have a secondary drive, drive D. Your computer contains 256MB of PC100 SDRAM. Both of the drives have more over 500 MB of free disk space. You are usually running many memory intensive graphics applications at once. Drive C is much slower when you are using the graphics applications. In order to maximize performance, what can you do?

A. Reformat Drive D

B. Set the initial size of virtual memory and the maximum size of virtual memory to 256 MB

C. Move the paging file from the primary drive to the secondary drive

D. Reformat Drive C, and reinstall Windows

E. Run Checkdisk and Defragment both hard drives

8. If you cannot ping your network card's own IP address, where is the problem?

A. The router is down

B. The gateway is down

C. In the TCP/IP stack in Windows XP

D. The Network Card

E. The cable is disconnected

9. You are upgrading your computer by adding a 16-bit ISA sound card. You use the supplied manufacturer's device driver, but after you restart your computer, the system won't start correctly. You are able to boot the computer into safe mode. What should be your next step?

A. Change the IRQ of the sound card

B. Disable the sound card device driver by using Computer Management

C. Manually delete the sound card driver files

D. Install a different driver

E. Change the resource settings of the sound card

10. While installing a graphics card into a Windows XP computer, you find that the system will no longer start. What should be done first?

A. Use Safe Mode

B. Use Recovery Console

C. Use Download Manager

D. Use Boot logging

E. Use Video Manager

XV Chapter 4: Review Answers

1. Advanced Power Management Support is most useful for which kind of computer?

   A. Any Workstation (Desktop or Tower)

   B. Server

***C. Laptop**

   D. Desktop

   E. Tower

Explanation: Cut Power Use and Extend Battery Life with Standby and Hibernate

ACPI Definition

Advanced Power Management Support is a useful way to enhance the battery life of and cut power consumption of computers, especially laptops. Because of laptops' unique disposition of requiring batteries, ways have been devised to find ways to save power whenever possible. See web links for further information.

2. What control panel would you use to set Advanced Power Management?

   A. Power

   B. System

   C. Add/Remove Hardware

   D. Add/Remove Programs

***E. Power Options**

Explanation: This is a navigational question. To set Advanced Power Management options, you would use the Advanced tab in the Power Options control panel.

3. What is the default display setting for a color video adapter and monitor?

***A. 640x480, 16 colors**

B. 800x600, 16 colors

C. 640x480, 256 colors

D. 800x600, 256 colors

E. 1240x480, 256 colors

Explanation: Configuring the Display

Left unmodified, the default display settings for a color video monitor are 640x480 at 16 colors. These settings are rarely used, and are generally changed to support a larger resolution and number of colors. This video card setting is used when booting the computer in VGA mode.

4. You have just installed an AGP Video Card in your Windows XP computer. You also installed the manufacturer's device drivers, and rebooted. The monitor went blank during the process of booting. What could you do to correct this problem?

***A. Start the computer by using the Emergency Repair Disk**

B. Reinstall the manufacturer's drivers

C. Enable Multi Monitor

***D. Restore the original adapter driver settings**

E. Reinstall windows

Explanation: Installing Additional Monitors

One situation that poses a problem that cannot be "worked around" is a video adapter problem rendering a blank monitor. Usually the easiest way to correct this if you just added a new graphics card is to resume using the old adapter while you diagnose the problem with the new adapter. If this is not an option, then you could use the Emergency Boot Disk to restore the original adapter driver settings. See web links for some interesting information related to using multiple monitors.

5. Your video driver is giving you problems. What should you do?

A. If it is an AGP card, try placing it in a PCI slot, then reboot

B. Reinstall Windows

C. Enable Multi Monitor

***D. Select Enable VGA Mode**

***E. Reboot the computer, and press F8 to get to the Advanced Options menu**

Explanation: Explanation of Safe Mode

If you boot your computer, and the screen goes blank as it starts up, then you have a few options. You can attempt to reboot you computer, and when you are prompted for advanced startup options you can select F8. A menu will appear, and you will have many different boot options to choose from. If you are having a video-related problem, then select "Enable VGA Mode" to start Windows 2000 with a generic video driver. If this does not correct the problem, then you may want to consider checking for a hardware failure.

6. Drive D of your Windows XP Professional computer is backed up everyday by Windows Backup. The drive fails on Thursday morning. You replace the failed drive with a new hard disk. You want to restore your files on drive D to the new hard disk. By viewing your backup log, you see that the backup method was incremental.

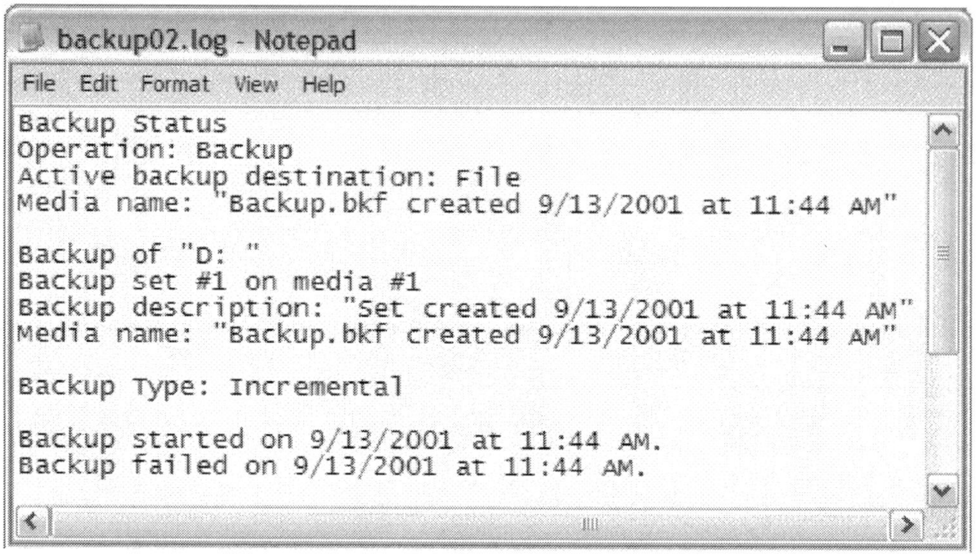


```
Backup Status
Operation: Backup
Active backup destination: File
Media name: "Backup.bkf created 9/13/2001 at 11:44 AM"

Backup of "D: "
Backup set #1 on media #1
Backup description: "Set created 9/13/2001 at 11:44 AM"
Media name: "Backup.bkf created 9/13/2001 at 11:44 AM"

Backup Type: Incremental

Backup started on 9/13/2001 at 11:44 AM.
Backup failed on 9/13/2001 at 11:44 AM.
```

What is the best order to use to restore your data?

A. Tuesday, Monday, Sunday, Saturday, Friday, Thursday, Wednesday.

Files will be current as of Wednesday.

B. Friday, Saturday, Sunday, Monday, Tuesday, Wednesday.

Files will be current as of Friday night.

***C. Friday, Saturday, Sunday, Monday, Tuesday, Wednesday.**

Files will be current as of Wednesday night.

D. Wednesday, Tuesday, Monday, Sunday, Saturday, Friday.

Files will be current as of Wednesday night.

E. Wednesday, Tuesday, Monday, Sunday, Saturday.

Files will be current as of Friday night.

Explanation: Definition of Incremental Backup

When you perform an incremental backup for the first time, all data is backed up. For every time after that, only data that has changed will be backed up. The drastically reduces the total time required for a backup procedure. When restoring data, you must do it from the least recent date to the most recent date. This ensures that the data is current as of the last day the backup was performed.

7. You have Windows XP Professional installed on your C drive, and have a secondary drive, drive D. Your computer contains 256MB of PC100 SDRAM. Both of the drives have more over 500 MB of free disk space. You are usually running many memory intensive graphics applications at once. Drive C is much slower when you are using the graphics applications. In order to maximize performance, what can you do?

A. Reformat Drive D

***B. Set the initial size of virtual memory and the maximum size of virtual memory to 256 MB**

***C. Move the paging file from the primary drive to the secondary drive.**

D. Reformat Drive C, and reinstall Windows

***E. Run Checkdisk and Defragment both hard drives**

Explanation: Definition of Virtual Memory

Definition of Paging File

Definition of Fragmentation

Because Drive C is usually the destination for the WINNT installation directory and it appears to be slower when memory intensive applications are run, it is fair to assume that is has a large demand placed upon it. To lessen this demand and more fairly distribute usage between the two drives, you could move the paging file from Drive C (the primary drive) to Drive D (the secondary drive).

Another fix you could consider would be do check the fragmentation on both drives. If they are severely fragmented, you should consider defragmenting them.

Because your computer contains 256MB of physical RAM, you should increase the maximum and initial size of your virtual memory to 256MB.

8. If you cannot ping your network card's own IP address, where is the problem?

A. The router is down

B. The gateway is down

C. In the TCP/IP stack in Windows XP

***D. The Network Card**

E. The cable is disconnected

Explanation: Definition for PING

If you are unable to ping your own IP address, check if you are using DHCP to obtain an IP. If you are, check if your current IP address is in the autoconfiguration range (169.254.x.x). If it is, then your DHCP server is probably not working. If you have a static IP address, then you should check to make sure that your network card drivers are up to date. If they are and you are still having problems, then you need to check the physical hardware itself.

9. You are upgrading your computer by adding a 16-bit ISA sound card. You use the supplied manufacturer's device driver, but after you restart your computer, the system won't start correctly. You are able to boot the computer into safe mode. What should be your next step?

A. Change the IRQ of the sound card.

***B. Disable the sound card device driver by using Computer Management.**

C. Manually delete the sound card driver files.

D. Install a different driver.

E. Change the resource settings of the sound card.

Explanation: Safe Mode Overview

When you installed the device driver and restarted, the device driver "started" as well. Since it was the device driver that caused the system to not start correctly, it should be disabled. From here, other troubleshooting steps can be taken.

10. While installing a graphics card into a Windows XP computer, you find that the system will no longer start. What should be done first?

A. Use Safe Mode

***B. Use Recovery Console**

C. Use Download Manager

D. Use Boot logging

E. Use Video Manager

Explanation: Recovery Console Tips for System Administrators

The first step in troubleshooting this problem would be to start the Recovery Console. From there you can go about correcting the problem. See the web links for further information.

Chapter 5: Network Protocols and Services

The objective of this chapter is to provide you with an understanding of the following:

1. Configure and troubleshoot the TCP/IP protocol
2. Understand the available network clients and services
3. Configure and troubleshoot NWLink, AppleTalk and DLC
4. Connect to computers by using dial-up networking
5. Connecting to networks using VPNs
6. Connect to shared resources on a Microsoft network

Getting Ready – (Questions)

1). What service do you use to allow your Windows XP Professional machine to communicate with your Novell server?

2). What network protocol is used primarily for connectivity to host machines?

3). What is the proper term for a "tunnel" through the Internet?

4). Within Windows XP Professional, what two ways are provided to allow you to connect two computers together through a serial or parallel connection?

5). What are the three typical levels of security for the connection between client and server?

Getting Ready – (Answers)

1). Client Service for Netware (CSNW) allows Windows XP Professional machines to communicate with Novell Netware servers running either Novell Directory Services (NDS) or Netware bindery-based servers.

2). The DLC (Data Link Control) protocol is a non-routable LAN protocol that is used primarily for connectivity to host machines, such as an IBM AS/400. Print servers running across the network may also use this protocol.

3). A "tunnel" through the Internet is correctly termed "Virtual Private Network" or VPN.

4). You can use Dial-up Networking or an Infrared connection to connect two computers directly using a serial or parallel connection.

5). Three typical levels of security for client/server connection are:

A. Unsecured password

B. Secured password

C. Smart card

I Introduction

When one is discussing networks today, we are referring to many ways that systems can be configured to communicate with each other. These lines of communication can take place over a network adapter, dial-up connection, the Internet, a VPN (Virtual Private Network), or over a simple direct cable connection.

The most commonly used networking protocol in the world today is TCP/IP. TCP/IP, which is actually a suite of protocols, is the language of the Internet. Most major operating systems, including UNIX, Novell, Apple and Microsoft, use TCP/IP. Other protocols that can be used with Windows XP include NWLink, AppleTalk, and DLC.

Windows XP also supports Internet Connection Sharing. A single computer can act as a gateway to the Internet for other computers in a small network.

II Network Clients

Client for Microsoft Networks

Client for Microsoft Networks allows you to access resources, such as file and print shares, running on other Windows computers. This client is installed and enabled by default on all Windows XP systems. This component is the equivalent of the Windows NT 4.0 Workstation service and the equivalent of the Windows 9x client.

There should be no need to change the configuration of this client. If you are using non-Microsoft software, such as The Open Group's DCE (Distributed Computing Environment) server or client kits or Banyan Vines networking software, then you may have need to modify the configuration.

Client Service for Netware

Client Service for Netware (CSNW) is provided to allow Windows XP machines to communicate with Novell Netware servers running either Novell Directory Services (NDS) or Netware bindery-based servers (Figure 5.1)

Figure 5-1: Client Service for Netware Configuration

CSNW, in conjunction with NWLink, is used to gain direct access to file, print and directory services running on the Netware servers. You can only connect to certain versions of Netware to gain access to the NDS and bindery (Table 5.1). If users need to connect to bindery-based resources, specify a preferred server. If users need to connect to NDS resources, specify the tree and context.

NETWARE VERSION	BINDERY	NDS
Netware 3.x	✓	
Netware 4.x	✓	✓
Netware 5.x	✓	✓

Table 5-1: Netware version support

CSNW only provides basic functionality for the connectivity, for more advanced connectivity contact Novell directly for the Novell Client for Windows XP. The differences between CSNW and Novell Client for Windows XP are show in Table 5.2.

FEATURE	MICROSOFT CLIENT SERVICE FOR NETWARE	NOVELL CLIENT FOR WINDOWS XP
Single logon and password	Yes	Yes
File and print services access	Yes	Yes
Protocols supported	NWLink	TCP/IP and IPX/SPX
NDS compatibility	Authenticates user on nonbindery mode NDS servers	Fully integrates with NDS applications
Netware/IP support	No	No
Netware administration tools	No	Yes

Table 5-2: CSNW vs. Novell Client for Windows XP

> **Warning:** Do not install both Client service for Netware and Novell Client for Windows XP on the same Windows XP machine.

III Network Services

File and Print Sharing for Microsoft Networks

File and Print Sharing for Microsoft Networks provides the ability to allow other computers to access resources, over a Microsoft network, on your system. This service is installed and enabled by default on a per connection basis. This service is the equivalent of the Windows NT 4.0 Server service.

You cannot configure this service in Windows XP.

QoS Packet Scheduler

The QoS Packet Scheduler service provides traffic control services in Quality of Service (QoS) environments. The QoS architecture in Windows XP is built from a tightly-integrated set of industry standard protocols, services, and mechanisms that control access to network resources, and either limit or guarantee network bandwidth usage. Other services necessary to control QoS are not included with Windows XP.

QoS provides the ability to deploy media-rich technologies, such as video conferencing or IP telephony, across a network environment. QoS also can improve the performance of traditional software. However, in order for QoS to have a true guarantee of service all network devices need to support one of the QoS mechanisms, such as RSVP (Resource Reservation Protocol), 802.1p, or DiffServ. If there is no support, then the traffic receives only best-effort delivery on that segment.

Remember that QoS traffic must coexist with traditional data traffic on the same network. To deploy real-time applications make sure that you have plenty of bandwidth, a minimal latency time, and minimal jitter (variations in packet arrival time).

SAP Agent

The SAP (Service Advertising Protocol) Agent provides a means for Windows XP systems to advertise their available services to computers running Netware client software and to Windows XP computers configured with just the NWLink protocol. The SAP agent is automatically installed when a service that uses SAP is installed, however you can manually install the service.

Print Services for UNIX

In order to print to a remote UNIX printer (which uses LPD – Line Printer Daemon) you must configure Windows XP to print with LPR – Line Printer. By installing Print Services for UNIX, you can install a printer in Windows XP that can use LPR as the printer port.

RIP Listener

The RIP Listener service provides a means to address routing problems in networks where more than one router is being used. RIP (Routing Information Protocol) provides dynamic configuration of routing tables across the enterprise. The RIP Listener service eavesdrops on the RIP information being transmitted on the network in order to generate the systems routing table. This process is known as *RIP listening* or *silent RIP*.

Windows XP supports both RIP version 1 and RIP version 2, as long as the RIP messages are transmitted as subnet-level broadcast. RIP v2 is not supported as the messages are sent as multicasts.

Simple TCP/IP Services

Simple TCP/IP services provide five additional services to the TCP/IP environment. These services are shown in Table 5.3.

Service	**Description**
CHARGEN	(Character generator) Sends data
Daytime	Returns messages containing the day of the week, month, day, year, current time (hh:mm:ss format) and time zone information
Discard	Discards all packets received on this port. Very useful as a TCP/IP null port
Echo	Returns the data received on this port
QUOTE	(Quote of the Day) Returns a random quotation

Table 5-3: Simple TCP/IP Services

> **NOTE:** Do not install Simple TCP/IP Services unless you specifically need this computer to support communication with other systems that use these protocol services.

SNMP

SNMP (Simple Network Management Protocol) is an industry standard network management protocol used on TCP/IP and IPX/SPX (NWLink) networks. SNMP transmits management information and commands between a management program and the network management agent running on a host. The agent send status information to one or more hosts when either a host requests it or when a significant event occurs.

The Windows XP SNMP Service provides only the agent. This agent is compliant to both SNMP versions 1 and 2C. TCP/IP or NWLink must be successfully installed before you can install SNMP.

Pop Quiz 5.1

Pop Quiz 5.1 *Questions*

1). By default, which network client is installed and enabled on Windows XP systems?

2). If you are running a Novell 5 server, and a Windows XP client running CSNW, can you connect to bindery-based resources? What about to a NDS resource?

3). What are some of the benefits of QoS?

4). What do you need to install in order to print to a remote UNIX printer?

5). SNMP transmits management information and commands between a management program and the network management agent. What does the Windows XP SNMP Service provide?

Pop Quiz 5.1 *Answers*

1). Client for Microsoft Networks, the equivalent of Windows NT 4.0 Workstation service and Windows 9x client, is installed and enabled by default on all Windows XP systems.

2). CSNW (Client Services for Netware) allows Windows XP machines to communicate with Novell Netware servers running either Novell Directory Services (NDS) or Netware bindery-based servers. If your server is Novell 5, you can connect to both bindery-based and NDS resources.

3). QoS provides the ability to deploy media-rich technologies, such as video conferencing or IP telephony, across a network environment. QoS also can improve the performance of traditional software. The QoS Packet Scheduler service provides traffic control services in Quality of Service (QoS) environments. The QoS architecture in Windows XP is built from a tightly-integrated set of industry standard protocols, services, and mechanisms that control access to network resources, and either limit or guarantee network bandwidth usage. Other services necessary to control QoS are not included with Windows XP.

4). In order to print to a remote UNIX printer (which uses LPD – Line Printer Daemon) you must configure Windows XP to print with LPR – Line Printer. By installing Print Services for UNIX, you can install a printer in Windows XP that can use LPR as the printer port.

5). The Windows XP SNMP Service provides only the agent. This agent is compliant to both SNMP versions 1 and 2C. TCP/IP or NWLink must be successfully installed before you can install SNMP.

IV Network Protocols

Microsoft allows many network protocols to be used with their OS software.

TCP/IP

Microsoft's implementation of TCP/IP is installed by default upon installation of Windows XP. TCP/IP is the most commonly used network protocol in the world today and is supported by all major operating systems. It is a scalable, routable protocol that is fault-tolerant and is able to dynamically reroute packages if network links become unavailable. There are a number of companion protocols, such as DHCP (Dynamic Host Configuration Protocol) which will automatically configure client computers with an IP address, subnet mask and default gateway, DNS (Domain Name Service) that provides host name resolution, and WINS (Window Internet Naming Service) that provides NetBIOS name resolution.

In order to run TCP/IP, you must have, at minimum, an IP address and a subnet mask. In order to communicate over a router, you must also have a default gateway address. The default gateway address is the address of the router than will route your packets out of your local subnetwork.

Your IP address uniquely identifies you on your network. If two computers have identical IP addresses, then communication will fail. In Windows XP, we are using IPv4, which is an IP address entered in decimal format in four parts (i.e.: 10.10.72.100). Each part is called an octet, because they are actually binary numbers of eight characters each. Which part of the IP address is the network address and which part is the host address primarily depends on the Class of the IP address, which is determined by the value of the first four bits of the first octet.

So why do you need a subnet mask? The subnet mask is a binary number designed to separate the network ID from the host ID on an IP address.

A Class A address has a decimal address range in the first octet of 1-126 (127 is reserved for loopback purposes). The network identifier is the first octet only, and the remaining three octets are used for unique host addresses. The default subnet mask is 255.0.0.0. 255 is 11111111 in binary, and that provides the mask for the network address.

A Class B address has a decimal range in the first octet of 128-191. The network identifier is the first two octets of the IP address, and the unique host addresses are provided from the last two octets. The default subnet mask is 255.255.0.0.

A Class C address has a decimal value range in the first octet of 192-223, with a default subnet mask of 255.255.255.0. The first three octets provide the network ID, and the last octet provides the network address.

TCP/IP decides whether an address is local (remains within the subnetwork) or remote (sends it to the default gateway for further routing) by using the subnet mask on the computer sending the information, and applying it to both the computer sending the information and the computer receiving the information.

Let's say that Computer A has an IP address of 192.168.0.22, and Computer B has an IP address of 192.168.32.11. Computer A wants to send data to Computer B. Because the IP address begins with 192, it is a Class C address. Presuming that the default subnet mask is used, IP will ascertain that the network address for Computer A is 192.168.0.x and the network address for Computer B is 192.168.32.x. The addresses are not the same so the data will be sent to the router (default gateway). If Computer B had an IP address of 192.168.0.112, the subnet mask will be applied to both IP addresses, and the result will be the same – both computers have a network address of 192.168.0.x. IP knows that the address is local and will send it out to Computer B.

> **NOTE:** This is a very elementary explanation of how subnetting works.

There is a set routine to troubleshoot communications with TCP/IP. You use two utilities, ipconfig and ping. Both these utilities are part of a standard TCP/IP suite and are used at the command prompt. Let's say you are having trouble reaching a host on a different network than you. Follow these steps to troubleshoot TCP/IP:

Run **IPCONFIG** at the command prompt. What should appear is your computer's IP address, subnet mask and default gateway. If the IP address comes back 0.0.0.0, your computer does not have an active IP address, so cannot communicate on the network. If your computer is set for automatic configuration, the problem may lie either with you or with your DHCP server. Make sure that your network card is configured correctly and that the cable is securely connected at the back of the network card. If you have a valid IP address, write down the IP address, subnet mask and default gateway for further troubleshooting purposes.

At the command prompt, ping your loopback address (Syntax: **PING 127.0.0.1**). This will check to see if the network card is responding. If successful, move on to Step 3.

At the command prompt, ping yourself by IP address. This will actually send a test packet out to the network and back. If successful, move on to step 4.

At the command prompt, ping the near side of the router – your default gateway. This will test to see that you can reach your gateway. If you cannot reach your gateway, then the problem may lie with your subnet mask, or with the router itself. If you can reach your gateway, then the problem lies either with the router, with the client on the other side, or with network traffic. Move on to Step 5.

At the command prompt, ping the far side of the router, or a different address that is not in your subnetwork. If you receive an answer, the problem is not with your system.

Sometimes the problem lies with name resolution, rather than TCP/IP configuration. If you can ping the IP address of a remote host, but you cannot ping the computer by hostname, then name resolution is the problem, not the protocol itself. Check to see if you have a DNS server configured. Try pinging another computer by hostname.

Connections that fail to resolve by name can still be made by IP address by typing \\ipaddress at the Run Command box.

NWLINK

NWLink is the Microsoft implementation of the IPX/SPX (Internetwork Packet Exchange/Sequence Packet Exchange) protocol. NWLink is a routable protocol. It can be used to connect computers running various operating systems. NetBIOS support is included in NWLink to provide additional support for Microsoft operating systems.

There are two configuration options for NWLink (Figure 5.2). The internal network number is used for internal routing options when the system is hosting IPX services. This creates an optimal path between the network and the services. In general, the internal network number does not need to be changed.

The other configuration is the frame type and external network number to use for the network connection. By default, when the system starts up, it will go through an auto-detection process on the network. This process checks for a Netware server and if a response is received, it will use the frame type and external network number of the Netware server for that segment. If a response is not received or multiple frame types are detected, Windows XP will default to a frame type of 802.2. The external network number is used for routing purposes and must be the same for all systems using the same frame type.

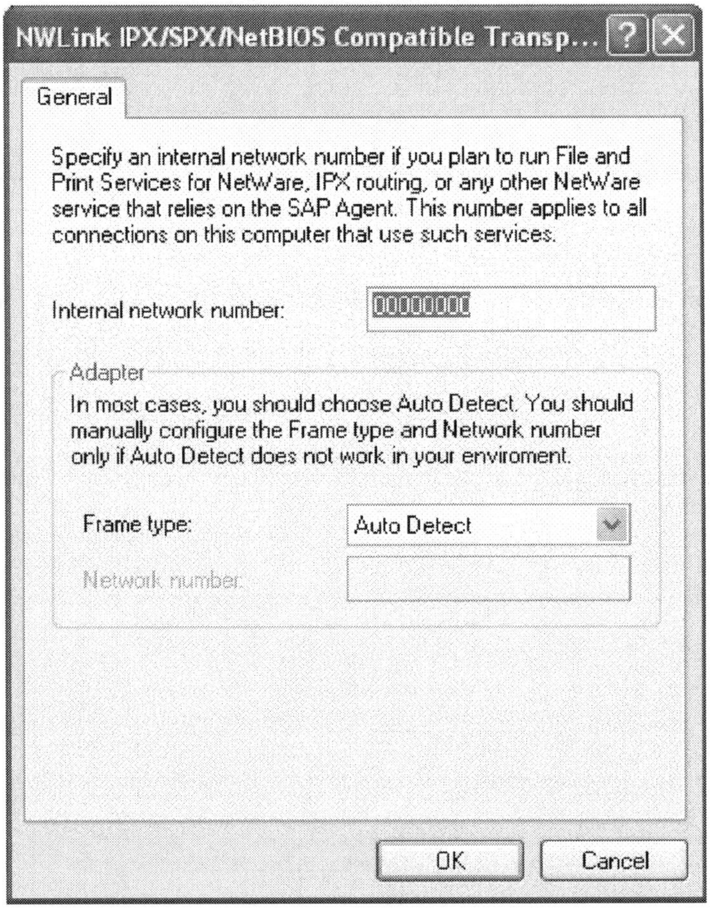

Figure 5-2: NWLink Protocol Configuration

AppleTalk

The AppleTalk protocol included with Windows XP is based upon the AppleTalk Phase 2 protocol suite designed by Apple Computer Corporation. AppleTalk can be used to communicate between Macintosh computers and Windows XP computers.

DLC

The DLC (Data Link Control) protocol is a non-routable LAN protocol that is used primarily for connectivity to host machines, such as an IBM AS/400. Print servers running across the network may also use this protocol.

> **NOTE:** You cannot use DLC as your standard network protocol; you must use TCP/IP or NWLink.

Network Monitor Driver

The Network Monitor driver provides the system the ability to communicate with the Network Monitor application (part of Windows 2000 Server and Systems Management Server). The driver allows the monitor application to receive data from the system for network analysis and performance tuning.

Pop Quiz 5.2

Pop Quiz 5.2 *Questions*

1). What decimal address range is supported in a Class A address?

2). What is a subnet mask?

3). There is a set routine to troubleshoot communications with TCP/IP) List the five basic troubleshooting steps, using IPCONFIG and PING)

4). When you are using NWLink with auto-detection, and multiple frame types are detected, what is the result?

5). When do you use the Data Link Control protocol?

Pop Quiz 5.2 *Answers*

1). The Class A address has a decimal address range from 1.x.x.x to 126.x.x.x) 127 is reserved for loopback purposes.

2). The subnet mask is a binary number designed to separate the network ID from the host ID on an IP address.

3). Run ipconfig at the command prompt. At the command prompt, ping your loopback address (Syntax: ping 127.0.0.1). At the command prompt, ping yourself by IP address. At the command prompt, ping the near side of the router – your default gateway. At the command prompt, ping the far side of the router, or a different address that is not in your subnetwork.

4). When you are using NWLink with auto-detection, and multiple frame types are detected, Windows XP will default to a frame type of 802.2. The other frame types will not be recognized.

5). The DLC (Data Link Control) protocol is a non-routable LAN protocol that is used primarily for connectivity to host machines, such as an IBM AS/400. Print servers running across the network may also use this protocol. You cannot use DLC as your main network protocol.

V Network Connections

The LAN connection is created by default when you install Windows XP and have a network card present. When you open the properties of the connection (Figure 5.3) you are then able to configure your network connection. From this dialog box, you can configure you network adapter or install, uninstall, and configure network clients, services and protocols.

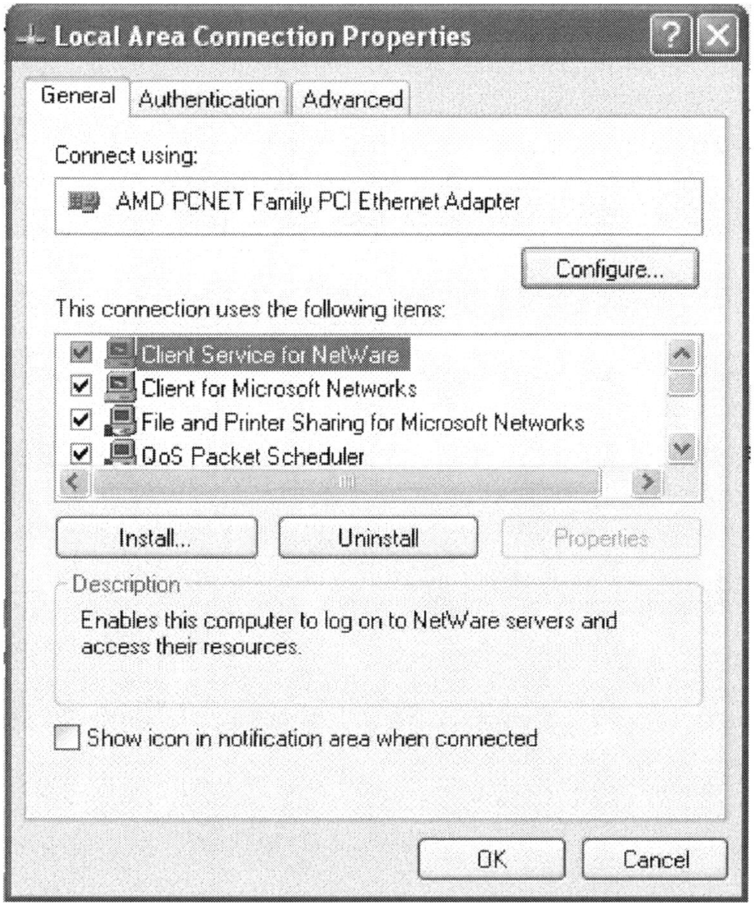

Figure 5-3: LAN Connection Properties

To configure advanced networking settings, such as the bindings, open Network Connections in Control Panel. Select **Advanced** from the menu bar at the top of the screen and choose **Advanced Settings**. From this dialog box, you select either **Adapters and Bindings** or **Provider Order**. Under **Adapters and Bindings**, you modify each connection separately, configuring the protocols and services to use on that connection. The Provider Order tab (Figure 5.4) allows you to configure the order that Windows XP attempts to access services.

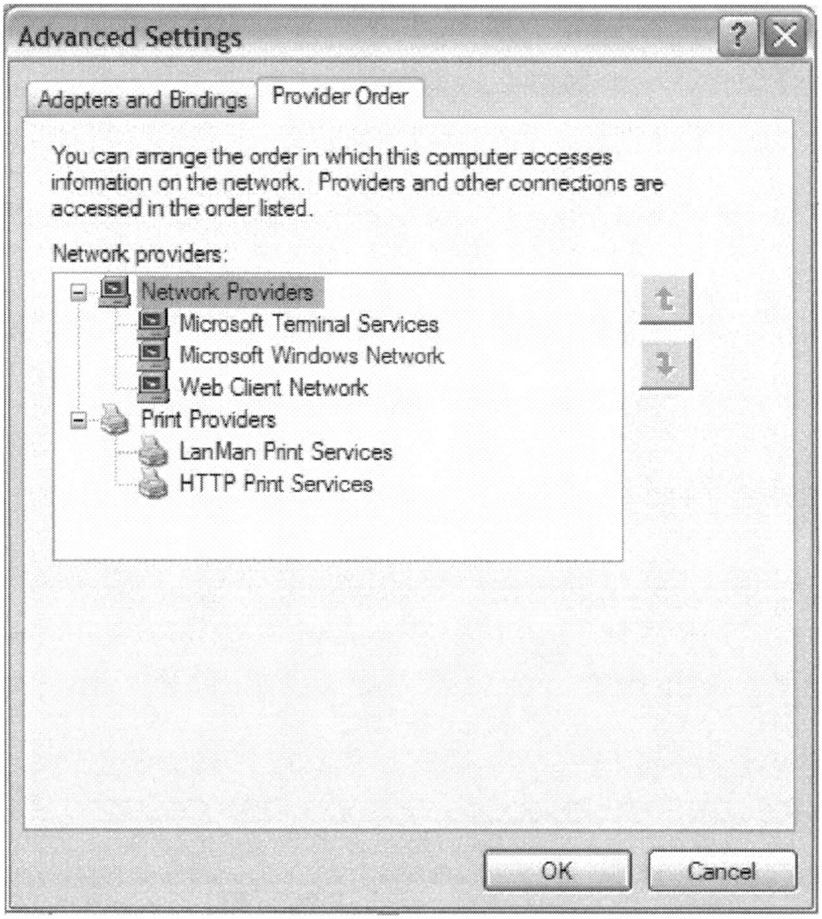

Figure 5-4: Advanced Network Settings

VI Dial-up Connections

Dial-up networking is becoming increasingly common as well as people dial up their Internet providers, telework from home, or call in from remote locations. These connections can be made through a Virtual Private Network (VPN) or through a Remote Access Server.

Dial-up networking allows remote users to connect to the corporate network, or to the Internet. You must have a modem installed and properly configured on your computer in order to set up Dial-Up Networking.

To create a dial-up connection, run the Network Connection Wizard by select **Make New Connection** in the Network and Dial-up Connection Control Panel icon (Figure 5.5).

Figure 5-5: New Connection Wizard

Connecting to Private Networks and the Internet

When you dial into a remote access server (RAS), you are making a direct connection to the server through a phone line, ISDN connection, etc. The RAS Server and the RAS client must both be using the same protocol to communicate.

Figure 5-6: RAS Connections

You create a Dial-Up Networking connection through **Network and Dial-Up Connections** in Control Panel. The **Make New Connection** icon will provide you with a wizard to walk you through the process. The wizard will what type of connection you wish to create (Figure 5.6), the phone number of the network you are connecting to, whether you wish to share this connection or keep it for your use only. The final step will be to give the new connection a name that is readily identifiable by you. For example, you could call it "Corporate Network" or "My ISP".

You will also want to set up one or more TAPI locations. TAPI (Telephone API) locations tell your system where you are calling from, whether call waiting must be disabled, whether a telephone card will be used, and any long distance prefixes that must be used. Set up a TAPI location for each place from which you will be calling.

Connecting Using a VPN to a Private Network

A virtual private network (VPN) is a process of using links across a public network, such as the Internet, to create a private connection between a server and a client. In order to have a VPN, the server must be configured to be a VPN server. Once a connection is established, authentication is required. If the client is authenticated, data is sent over the public network in an encapsulated, encrypted format. Once the VPN tunnel is established, communication can take place using any protocol, provided both the server and the client are speaking the "same language".

PPTP (Point to Point Tunneling Protocol) is frequently used in Windows XP environments to create that private tunnel through the Internet. The packets are wrapped in a TCP/IP wrapper. Anyone sniffing the packet would not realize that it was anything more than common Internet traffic. Another mechanism that could be used instead of PPTP is L2TP, a certificate based service.

The major advantage of using VPN connections is cost-savings. If you are on a business trip in Tokyo and your corporate offices are in London, dialing your network from a hotel phone line is going to be very expensive. By using VPN technology, all you need is local access to the Internet. Once connected to the Internet, you then use the Internet as a backbone to connect to your corporate offices. The only charge incurred is the cost of connecting to the Internet. There are companies, such as InterPass, that offer pay-as-you-go Internet cards and phone numbers for local Internet providers that have partnered with them. Using an ID number and password allows you to pay on a per-use basis to that Internet Provider.

Setting up a Dial-up Server

Windows XP is not designed to work as a Remote Access Server; however, it is important to note that it can act as a server to ONE connection. This is helpful if you need to dial into your own computer to access information.

Connecting Directly to Other Computers

You can use Dial-up Networking to connect two computers directly using a serial or parallel connection. You can also use Infrared connections to connect the two systems together

Pop Quiz 5.3

Pop Quiz 5.3 *Questions*

1). When you are using the Network Connection Wizard, you are given five choices on which type of network connection you wish to create? Name three.

2). What is a TAPI location?

3). Define a VPN.

4). How many remote access connections can Windows XP Professional maintain?

5). You need to connect to another computer using a serial cable. What do you use to do this?

Pop Quiz 5.3 *Answers*

1). The five types of network connection available through the Network Connection Wizard are:

A. Dial-up to a private network

B. Dial-up to the Internet

C. Connect to a private network through the Internet

D. Accept incoming connections

E. Connect directly to another computer (using serial, parallel or infrared port)

2). A TAPI (Telephone API) location will tell your system where you are calling from, whether call waiting must be disabled, whether a telephone card will be used, and any long distance prefixes that must be used. It is advisable to set up a TAPI location for each place from which you will be calling.

3). A virtual private network (VPN) is a process of using links across a public network, such as the Internet, to create a private connection between a server and a client. Once a connection is established, and the client authenticated, data is sent over the public network in an encapsulated, encrypted format, using any protocol common to both the server and client.

4). While Windows XP Professional is not designed to work as a Remote Access Server, it is important to note that it can act as a server to ONE connection. This is helpful if you need to dial into your own computer to access information.

5). You can use Dial-up Networking to connect two computers directly using a serial or parallel connection.

VII Configuring the Dial-up Connections

Once your DUN connection is created, you can manage its properties by right-clicking the new Dial-Up Connection and selecting **Properties**. There are five tabs in the Properties menu:

This tab is used to configure the connection you will use and the phone number you are dialing (Figure 5.7). You can configure additional numbers that can be used if the first number is busy or does not answer. The **Connect Using** option specifies what device you are using to make the connection (modem, ISDN adapter, etc.).

Figure 5-7: Dial-up Connection General Properties

This tab is used to configure dialing and redialing options (Figure 5.8). You can choose whether to display progress while connecting, identify that you will be prompted for authentication information (username, password, certificate), identify whether or not you need to provide a Windows logon domain, and choose to be prompted for the dial-in number. You can also specify how many redial attempts should be made, how long to wait between attempts and how long you want your system to be idle before Windows XP disconnects the session.

You can also configure terminal services for remote access under this tab, by allowing interactive logon and scripting features. This is only supported for modems and not for ISDN devices.

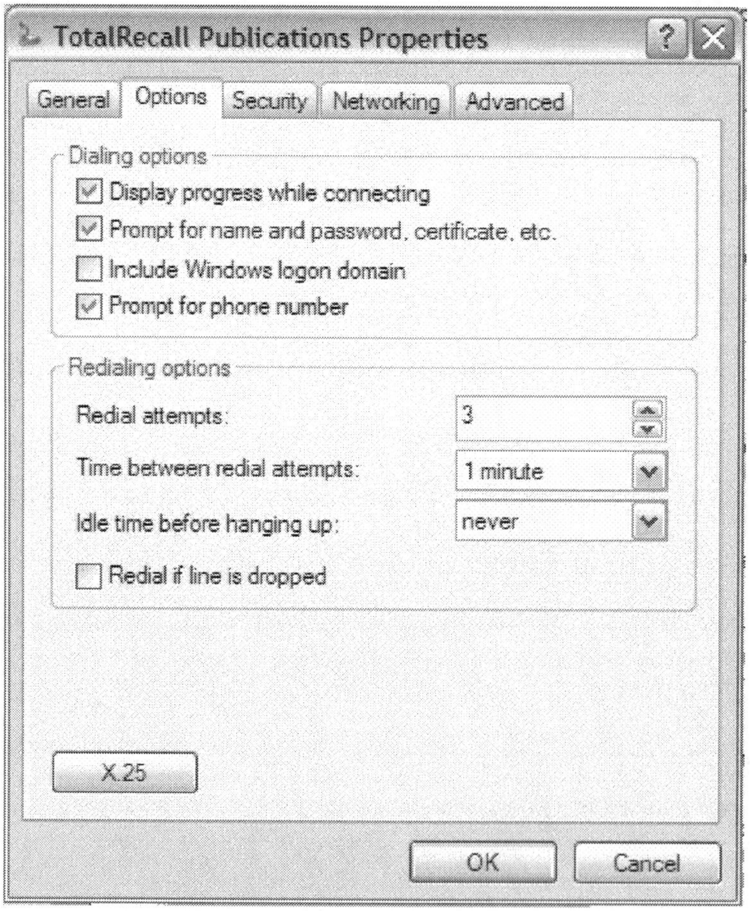

Figure 5-8: Dial-up Connection Options

This dialog box allows you to specify the level of security for the connection between client and server (Figure 5.9). The available settings for typical security are:

- **Unsecured Password** – plain text – if this is chosen, data encryption is unavailable for selection and Windows logon is unavailable under the Advanced options
- **Secured password** – encrypted password – data encryption is available and Windows logon is also available under the Advanced options.
- **Smart Card** – data encryption is available but Windows logon is not available under Advanced options.

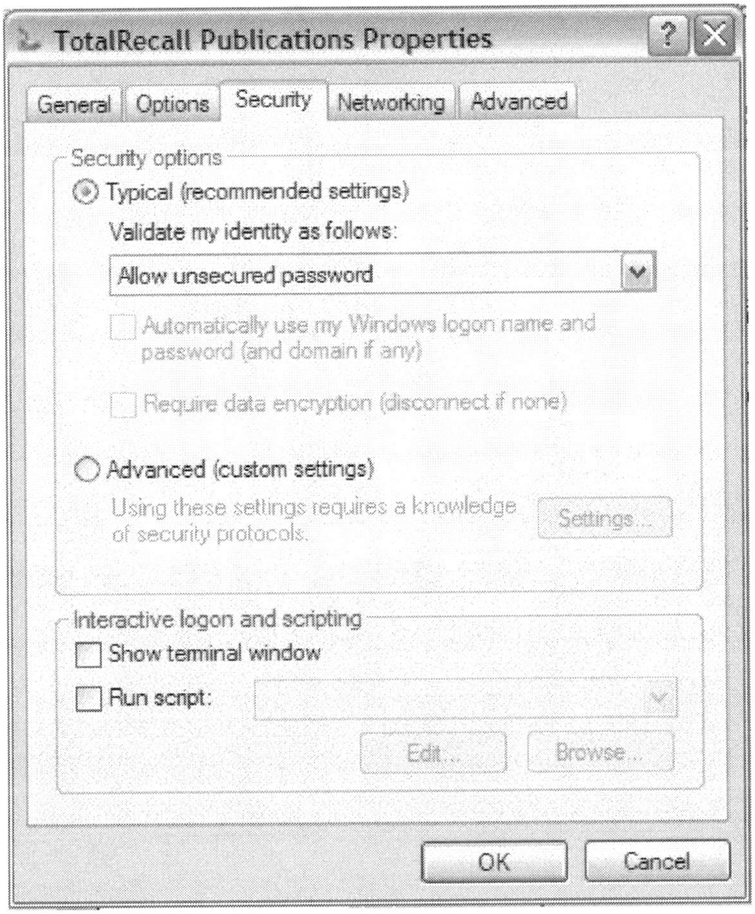

Figure 5-9: Dial-up Connection Security

Figure 5.10 illustrates the choices available under the Advanced (custom) settings. It is strongly recommended that you understand what is involved with utilizing these choices

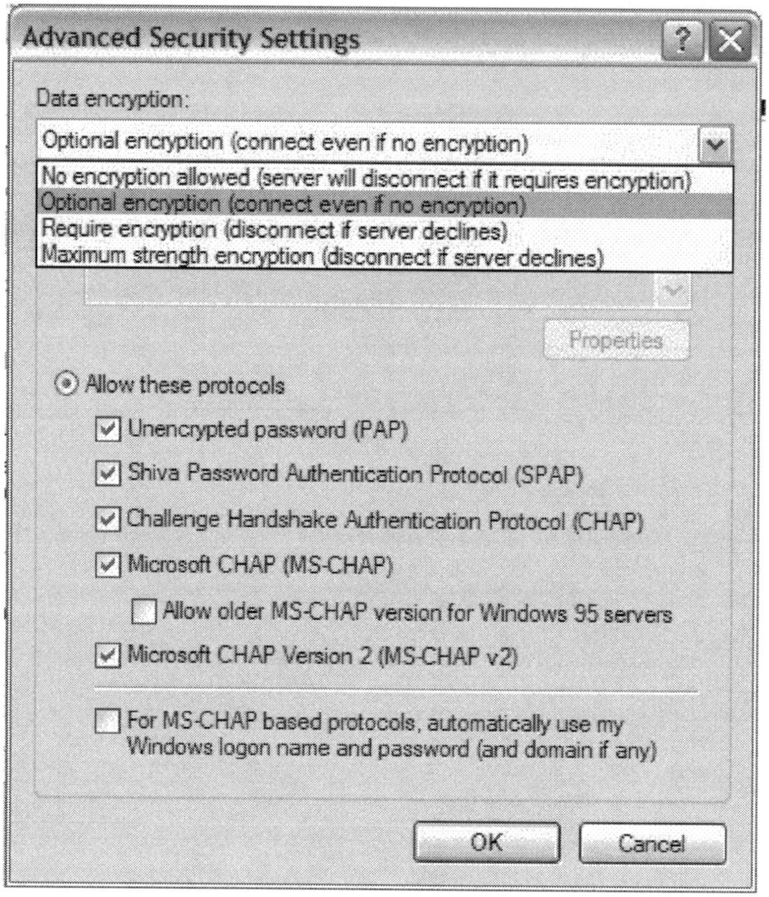

Figure 5-10: Dial-up Connection Advanced Security

Data Encryption settings include:

- **No Encryption Allowed** – the server will disconnect if encryption is required.
- **Optional Encryption** – the connection will be made whether or not encryption is enabled.
- **Require Encryption** – if the server does not support encryption, the connection will be disconnected.
- **Maximum Strength Encryption** – the server will disconnect if it is not supported.

For password authentication you can use wide range of settings. These are:

- **Unencrypted Password (PAP)** – plain text authentication scheme for authenticating remote connections, where the username and password are requested by the RAS Server and returned by the client in plain text.
- **Shiva Password Authentication Protocol (SPAP)** – A bi-directional, reversible encryption method for authenticating remote connections used specifically by Shiva remote access servers.
- **Challenge Handshake Authentication Protocol (CHAP)** – challenge-response authentication protocol for remote connections that uses MD5 unidirectional encryption to hash the response to a challenge issued by the RAS server.
- **Microsoft Challenge Handshake Authentication Protocol (MS-CHAP)** – an encrypted authentication method for remote connections similar to CHAP. The RAS Server sends a challenge to the client that consists of a session ID and an arbitrary challenge string. The client must return the username and an MD4)\ hash of the challenge string, the session ID, and the MD4-hashed password.
- **Microsoft Challenge Handshake Authentication Protocol Version 2 (MS-CHAP2)** – An encrypted authentication mechanism for remote connections that provides tighter security than CHAP and MS-CHAP by providing mutual authentication and asymmetric encryption keys.

This dialog box is used to configure networking options for dial-up connections (Figure 5.11). Connection protocols include SLIP (Serial Line Interface Protocol) for connection to older UNIX Servers, and PPP (Point to Point Protocol), which is most commonly used by Internet Servers and Microsoft servers.

This dialog box also allows you to configure the protocols to be used and any client software such as File and Print Sharing for Microsoft Networks, used by Windows XP to allow file and print capabilities on a Novell network.

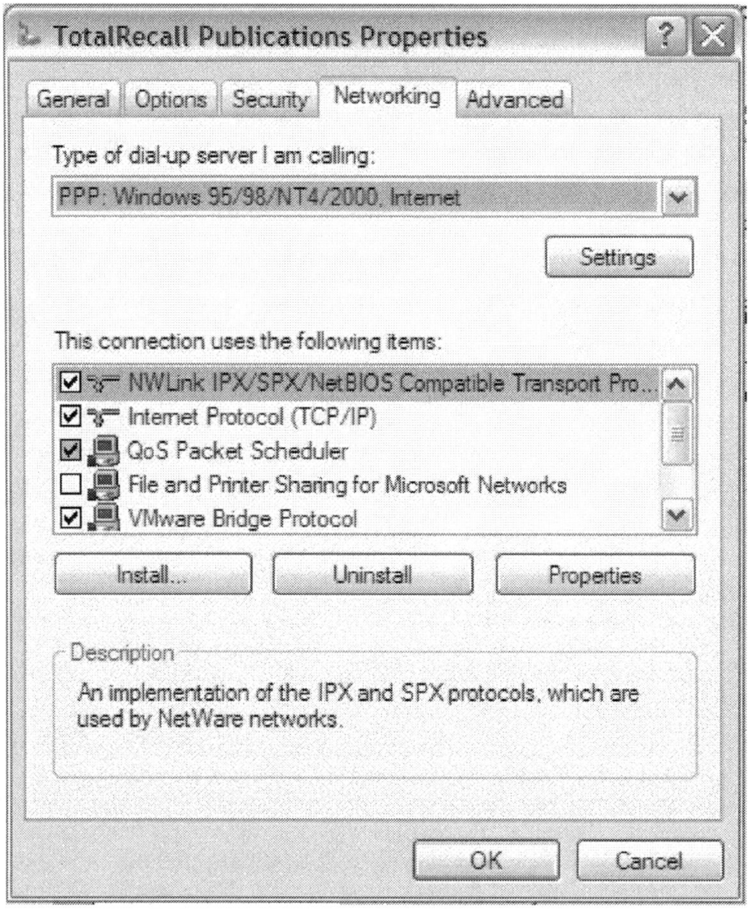

Figure 5-11: Dial-up Connection Networking Configuration

NOTE: While Windows XP can be a SLIP client, it cannot be a SLIP server.

Internet Connection Sharing allows you to connect a small network of computers to the Internet through a single connection (Figure 5.12). Essentially, one computer acts as the gateway. From the Internet, only one computer appears to be connected. That computer must provide network addressing translation, addressing and name resolution services for all the computers on the network.

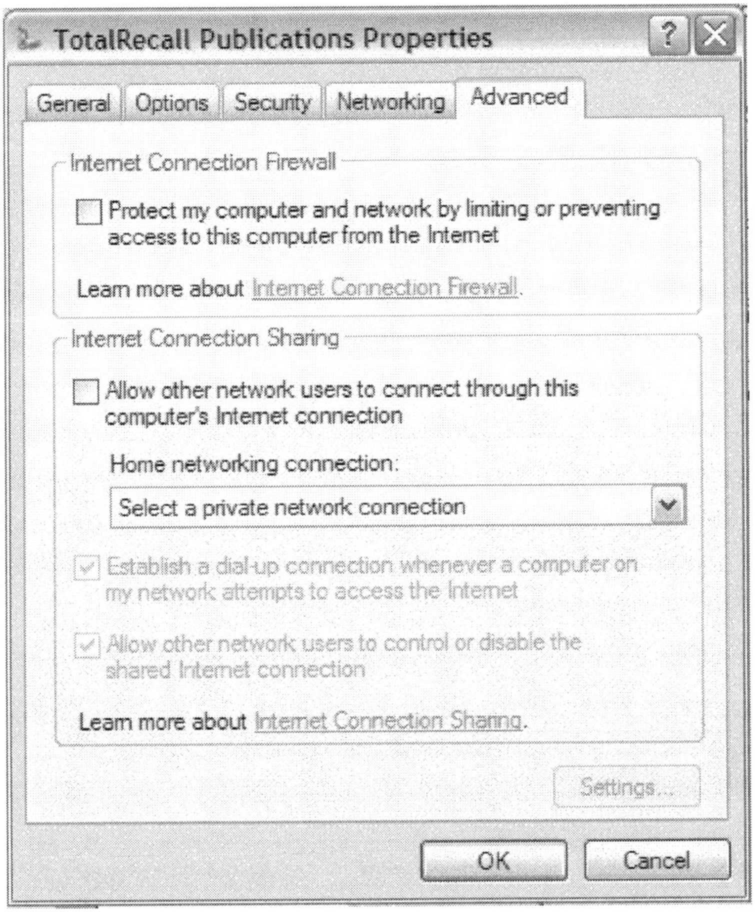

Figure 5-12: Advanced Dial-up Networking Options

By using ICS, the network of computers can use Internet applications, like Netscape and Internet Explorer, and access Internet resources.

Certain conditions must be met for ICS to be implemented:

- All network clients must be DHCP enabled—that is, set up to receive their IP addresses automatically
- The host computer must be set up to support ICS
- The client computers must be set up to use ICS

Internet Connection Firewall (ICF) is software that is used to set certain restrictions on what information is communicated from your network to the Internet, and from the Internet to your network. It acts as a firewall, or a security system that is, in essence, a protective boundary between your network to the rest of world.

If you plan on using ICS to provide Internet access to multiple computers, ICF should be enabled on the shared Internet connection. You can, however, enable both ICS and ICF separately. ICF should be enabled on the Internet connection of any computer that is connected directly to the Internet.

To enable or disable Internet Connection Firewall, under the Advanced tab, select or deselect the checkbox next to Protect my computer and network by limiting or preventing access to this computer from the Internet.

ICF should not be enabled on VPN connections or on client computers because it will interfere with both file and printer sharing. It should also not be enabled on the private connections of the ICS host.

Neither ICS nor ICF is available on the Windows XP 64-Bit Edition.

To configure ICS or ICF, you must be a member of the Administrators group.

VIII Chapter 5: Summary

We have now covered some of the basics of implementing, managing and troubleshooting network protocols and services. You should feel comfortable with how to:

- Configure and troubleshoot the TCP/IP protocol
- Understand the available network clients and services
- Configure and troubleshoot NWLink, AppleTalk and DLC
- Connect to computers by using dial-up networking
- Connecting to networks using VPNs

IX Chapter 5: Review Questions

1. You are configuring your network for Internet connections. This network is an all WinXP environment. You can only afford to buy one IP address from your ISP. What function of WinXP can you use so that every computer can access the Internet?

A. ICS

B. IIS

C. PWS

D. ISA

E. NAT

2. You are configuring your network for Internet connections. This network is a mixed network with different versions of Windows available. What is the best strategy for configuring ICS in this network?

A. Install Windows XP on the computer that is supposed to host the Internet connection. Use Windows XP Network Setup Wizard to configure other systems.

B. Run /winnt32 from a network share to set up Windows for all the clients

C. Run /winnt from a network share to set up Windows for all the clients that run the XP Home Edition. Run /winnt32 from a network share to set up Windows for all the clients that run the XP Pro

D. Configure ICS on a Windows.NET server

E. No Answer is Correct

3. You are configuring your network for Internet connections. This network is an all WinXP client environment. Your boss requests that you setup ICS on CompA. You are told that CompB is actually a server that hosts DNS and DHCP services for the network. For ICS to work smoothly, you need to:

A. Disable DHCP on CompB

B. Disable DNS on CompB

C. Disable the use of DNS on all clients

D. Disable the use of DHCP on all clients

E. Force ICS to renew leases every 10 days

4. You are managing your company network. This network runs only WinXP Pro and WinXP Home Edition PCs. What are the advantages of setting up a workgroup configuration for this setup?

A. Centralized log on management

B. Centralized audit management

C. Shared printing

D. Shared storage

E. Shared Internet access

5. You are managing your home network. This network runs only a WinXP Pro PC and a WinXP Home Edition PC. You want to have them mutually connected. You want this to be done with minimal cost. You want one of them to be connected via broadband to the Internet. You want both to be able to view web pages. How should this be done?

A. Configure ICS on the WinXP Pro computer

B. Configure the WinXP Home Ed. computer to accept dynamic IP configuration

C. Use a cross over cable to connect both computers

D. Use a hub and 2 pieces of cross over cables to connect the computers

E. Enable PWS on the WinXP Home Ed. computer

6. You are setting up your company network. This is going to be a standard Ethernet network. You plan to have all computers connected to a network hub. Which of the following are the guidelines recommended by MS?

A. Place the hub in a central location

B. The total length of all cables should not exceed 100 meters

C. The total length of all cables should not exceed 328 meters

D. Connect the server to the uplink port

E. No Answer is Correct

7. You are managing your home network. This network runs several WinXP Pro PCs and WinXP Home Edition PCs. You plan to have them connected via wireless LAN. For basic security, which of the following does Microsoft recommend?

A. WEP

B. RRAS

C. NAT

D. IP Filter

E. WAP

8. You are managing your home network. This network runs several WinXP Pro PCs and WinXP Home Edition PCs. You plan to have them connected via wireless LAN. The wireless devices require special manual configuration works to be done. How do you disable automatic wireless configuration?

A. Open Control Panel – Network Connections. Right-click the Wireless Network Connection icon and choose Properties. On the Wireless Networks tab, clear the Use Windows To Configure My Wireless Network Settings check box.

B. Open Control Panel – Wireless Properties. Right-click the Wireless Network Connection icon and choose Advanced Properties. On the Wireless Networks tab, clear the Use Windows To Configure My Wireless Network Settings check box.

C. Open Control Panel – Network Connections. Right-click the Wireless Network Connection icon and choose Wireless Configuration. On the Networks Configuration tab, clear the Use Windows To Configure My Wireless Network Settings check box.

D. Edit the corresponding registry entry using regedit

E. Configure a GPO and have it applied at the local level

9. You are managing your home network. This network runs only a WinXP Pro PC and a WinXP Home Edition PC. You want to have them connected without cables. You want to save the cost of an access point. What wireless mode should you use to connect them?

A. The ad hoc mode

B. The default mode

C. The infrastructure mode

D. The instant mode

E. The point-to-point mode

10. You are setting up your company network. This is going to be a standard Ethernet network. After you've successfully installed all the required hardware, what should you do to set the proper permissions on the shared folders and add the required keys to the registry?

A. Open Control Panel and double-click Network Connections. Click the Set Up A Home Or Small Office Network link under Network Tasks.

B. From the All Programs menu, choose Accessories, Communications, Network Setup Wizard

C. Run dcpromo

D. Refresh the system policy and then restart the computer

E. From Control Panel, choose Internet, Advanced Settings, Network Setup Wizard

X Chapter 5: Review Answers

1. You are configuring your network for Internet connections. This network is an all WinXP environment. You can only afford to buy one IP address from your ISP. What function of WinXP can you use so that every computer can access the Internet?

***A. ICS**

B. IIS

C. PWS

D. ISA

E. NAT

Explanation: With Internet Connection Sharing, you can set up Internet access on a single computer and allow every computer on the network to share that connection. This capability is most useful for Internet connection using cable or DSL modem. A large enterprise does not rely on it, as it causes conflicts with the existing DNS and DHCP services.

2. You are configuring your network for Internet connections. This network is a mixed network with different versions of Windows available. What is the best strategy for configuring ICS in this network?

***A. Install Windows XP on the computer that is supposed to host the Internet connection. Use Windows XP Network Setup Wizard to configure other systems.**

B. Run /winnt32 from a network share to set up Windows for all the clients

C. Run /winnt from a network share to set up Windows for all the clients that run the XP Home Edition. Run /winnt32 from a network share to set up Windows for all the clients that run the XP Pro.

D. Configure ICS on a Windows.NET server

Explanation: Different versions of Windows can coexist quite peacefully on a network if it is planned carefully. To use Internet Connection Sharing, you can use the Windows XP Network Setup Wizard to configure other systems running Windows XP, Windows 2000, Windows Me, or Windows 98.

3. You are configuring your network for Internet connections. This network is an all WinXP client environment. Your boss requests that you setup ICS on CompA. You are told that CompB is actually a server that hosts DNS and DHCP services for the network. For ICS to work smoothly, you need to:

***A. Disable DHCP on CompB**

***B. Disable DNS on CompB**

C. Disable the use of DNS on all clients

D. Disable the use of DHCP on all clients

E. Force ICS to renew leases every 10 days

Explanation: With Internet Connection Sharing, you can set up Internet access on a single computer and allow every computer on the network to share that connection. This capability is most useful for Internet connection using cable or DSL modem. A large enterprise does not rely on it, as it causes conflicts with the existing DNS and DHCP services.

4. You are managing your company network. This network runs only WinXP Pro and WinXP Home Edition PCs. What are the advantages of setting up a workgroup configuration for this setup?

A. Centralized log on management

B. Centralized audit management

***C. Shared printing**

***D. Shared storage**

***E. Shared Internet access**

Explanation: With a minimal cost you can connect two or more computers into a simple peer-to-peer network. This setup does not allow you to manage users and shared resources centrally; instead, each computer contains its own database of authorized user accounts and shared resources.

5. You are managing your home network. This network runs only a WinXP Pro PC and a WinXP Home Edition PC. You want to have them mutually connected. You want this to be done with minimal cost. You want one of them to be connected via broadband to the Internet. You want both to be able to view web pages. How should this be done?

***A. Configure ICS on the WinXP Pro computer**

***B. Configure the WinXP Home Ed. computer to accept dynamic IP configuration**

***C. Use a cross over cable to connect both computers**

D. Use a hub and 2 pieces of cross over cables to connect the computers

E. Enable PWS on the WinXP Home Ed. computer

Explanation: If your home network consists of two computers, you can use a crossover cable instead of buying a hub. A crossover cable is identical to a standard patch cable, except that two wires are reversed, simulating the connection that would take place if the wires were plugged into a hub. Using a crossover cable is an acceptable solution when you want to connect ONLY two computers directly without the need to house an extra server.

6. You are setting up your company network. This is going to be a standard Ethernet network. You plan to have all computers connected to a network hub. Which of the following are the guidelines recommended by MS?

***A. Place the hub in a central location**

***B. The total length of all cables should not exceed 100 meters**

C. The total length of all cables should not exceed 328 meters

D. Connect the server to the uplink port

E. No Answer is Correct

Explanation: On a standard Ethernet network, all computers must be connected to a network hub. The hub has a row of ports that accept RJ-45 connectors. To connect your network to a hub, you

Place the hub in a central location and ensure that the total length of all cables used on the network should not exceed 100 meters. Uplink ports are only used to connect two hubs or a hub to a router.

7. You are managing your home network. This network runs several WinXP Pro PCs and WinXP Home Edition PCs. You plan to have them connected via wireless LAN. For basic security, which of the following does Microsoft recommend?

***A. WEP**

B. RRAS

C. NAT

D. IP Filter

E. WAP

Explanation: To add basic security to your wireless system, you can configure Wireless Equivalent Privacy (WEP) to your network. WEP protects authorized users of a wireless network from eavesdroppers by encrypting the data flow between the networked computer and the access point.

8. You are managing your home network. This network runs several WinXP Pro PCs and WinXP Home Edition PCs. You plan to have them connected via wireless LAN. The wireless devices require special manual configuration works to be done. How do you disable automatic wireless configuration?

***A. Open Control Panel – Network Connections. Right-click the Wireless Network Connection icon and choose Properties. On the Wireless Networks tab, clear the Use Windows To Configure My Wireless Network Settings check box.**

B. Open Control Panel – Wireless Properties. Right-click the Wireless Network Connection icon and choose Advanced Properties. On the Wireless Networks tab, clear the Use Windows To Configure My Wireless Network Settings check box.

C. Open Control Panel – Network Connections. Right-click the Wireless Network Connection icon and choose Wireless Configuration. On the Networks Configuration tab, clear the Use Windows To Configure My Wireless Network Settings check box.

D. Edit the corresponding registry entry using regedit.

E. Configure a GPO and have it applied at the local level

Explanation: To set advanced options for a wireless network, you should open Control Panel, Network Connections. Right-click the Wireless Network Connection icon and choose Properties.

On the Wireless Networks tab, perform the necessary configuration.

9. You are managing your home network. This network runs only a WinXP Pro PC and a WinXP Home Edition PC. You want to have them connected without cables. You want to save the cost of an access point. What wireless mode should you use to connect them?

***A. The ad hoc mode**

B. The default mode

C. The infrastructure mode

D. The instant mode

E. The point-to-point mode

Explanation: By using ad hoc mode and not the default infrastructure mode, you can connect your wireless system directly to other computers on the network, as long as each one is equipped with a compatible wireless adapter. In fact, a Wi-Fi network running in ad hoc mode is the equivalent of a peer-to-peer network. Wireless access points add the capability to share an Internet connection, assign IP addresses, and enforce security. etc.

10. You are setting up your company network. This is going to be a standard Ethernet network. After you've successfully installed all the required hardware, what should you do to set the proper permissions on the shared folders and add the required keys to the registry?

***A. Open Control Panel and double-click Network Connections. Click the Set Up A Home Or Small Office Network link under Network Tasks**

***B. From the All Programs menu, choose Accessories, Communications, Network Setup Wizard**

C. Run dcpromo

D. Refresh the system policy and then restart the computer

E. From Control Panel, choose Internet, Advanced Settings, Network Setup Wizard

Explanation: After you have successfully installed all the required hardware for your network, you should run the Network Setup Wizard to set the proper permissions on shared folders, adds required keys to the registry, configures protocols and binds them to network cards, enables or disables the Internet Connection Firewall, and adjusts system policies...etc.

Chapter 6: User Management

The objective of this chapter is to provide you with an understanding of the following:

1. Identify Windows 2000 Professional built-in users
2. Identify Windows 2000 Professional built-in groups
3. Identify Windows 2000 Professional built-in system groups
4. Identify the user management tools
5. Implement, configure, and manage local user and group accounts
6. Configure and manage user profiles

Getting Ready – (Questions)

1). What three built-in accounts exist after Windows XP Professional has been installed?

2). I have been told that there is an account for Initial User. Why can I not find that account on my system?

3). One of your users needs you to change his password. How is this done?

4). Who are the default members of the Replicator built-in group?

Getting Ready – (Answers)

1). There are three built-in accounts existing after a successful installation of Windows XP Professional. These are:

A. Administrator

B. Guest

C. Initial User

2). Initial User is not an actual account name. The initial user account, a built-in account, is an account created in the name of the registered user. It is enabled by default and can be deleted.

3). Unlike NT 4.0 Workstation, you no longer have to open a user's account to change his or her password. As a matter of fact, you cannot do it in that fashion anymore. Using the Computer Management snap-in, under Local Users and Groups Users, you right-click the username and use the "Set Password" command.

4). By default, there are NO members of the Replicator group.

I Introduction

In order to provide the security and auditing functions of Windows XP, user accounts and groups must be created. No individual can use a computer running Windows XP Professional without a valid user account that has the right to logon to that machine.

Some users and groups already exist on your system immediately after installation.

II Built-In Users

Three built-in accounts exist after a successful installation of Windows XP Professional:

Administrator:

Administrator is a special account that has full control over the computer. During installation, you were asked to assign a password for this account. By default, this account is enabled and it cannot be deleted.

Guest:

Guest is a special account that allows users access to the computer, even if they don't have a unique username and password. This account is disabled by default, and it cannot be deleted. If the account is enabled, make sure that its permissions are limited.

Initial User:

You will not see an account called "**Initial User**". What you will see is an account created in the name of the registered user. This account is created when the computer is installed as a member of a workgroup, and by default it is a member of the Administrators group. It is enabled by default, and it can be deleted.

III Built-In Groups

There are six built-in local groups installed with Windows XP Professional:

Administrators:

This group has full permissions and privileges. They are also assigned the most user rights. Any rights and permissions they haven't been granted by default, they have the ability to grant themselves. By default, the built-in accounts Administrator and Initial User are members of this group. Membership should be limited to highly trusted users.

Backup Operators Group

The members of this group have the right to backup and restore the file system, even if they do not have permission to access the files through NTFS. They can only access the files through the Backup utility. There are no default members to this group.

Guests:

The Guests group has limited access to the computer. The group was provided so that people who are not regular users, and for whom you do not wish to create a user account, can have access specific resources. By default, the Guest user account is a member of the Guest group.

Users:

Everyone who has a user account on Windows XP Professional is a member of the Users group. However, people who are members only of the Users group have limited system rights to prevent system corruption or compromise.

Power Users:

This group lies somewhere in between the Administrators group and Users group. They have enough user rights to help in administration, but not the full-blown rights of Administrators. They can create, manage and delete local printers, modify the system clock, stop or start manual services and modify the Program Files directory. By default, this group has no members.

Replicator:

This group is designed to support directory replication, which is a feature used by domain servers. By default, there are no members.

IV Built-In System Groups

There are some special system groups that are installed with Windows XP Professional. Membership into these groups is dynamic, depending on what action is taking place at the time.

Creator/Owner:

When you create a document, you become a member of the Creator/Owner group. You created the document, so therefore you own it, and you have full power to manage the permissions to that document. Every object (files, folders, printers, etc.) has an owner.

Creator:

The group, rather than the user, that took ownership of the document. For example, if the administrator needs to take ownership of a folder, because the original creator/owner has left the company, the entire Administrators group becomes a member of the Creator group.

Everyone:

Everyone means precisely what it says – EVERYONE! Any person, who could possibly access the computer, including the Guest account, is a member of Everyone. As discussed, by default the Everyone Group has Full Control on shared files. Because of the lack of control the administrator has with membership in this group, it is always a good idea to remove the Everyone Group and assign permissions according to groups that you have designed. The Everyone Group comes in very handy, however, for auditing purposes. When you are auditing, you definitely want to audit Everyone!

Interactive:

When you log onto the computer, you become a member of the Interactive group. When you log off, your membership ceases.

Network:

When you connect to a share across the network, you become a member of the Network group. When the share is disconnected, you lose membership.

V User Accounts Control Panel

The User Accounts Control Panel icon provides you with the ability to add domain members or other workstation users to your system and to modify existing users (Figure 6.1). It does not allow you to create new users and groups in the local system. To do that, you need to use the Local Users and Groups console.

Figure 6-1: User Accounts

From this dialog box, you are able to add or remove users, change properties, and set the password for each of the users listed.

To add a new user to your system, click the Add button, which launches the Add New User wizard. The first page (Figure 6.2) prompts you provide an existing user name and their domain (or workstation).

Figure 6-2: Add New User Wizard (dialog box 1)

If you are unaware of the particulars for a domain user, you can browse the Active Directory. The second page (Figure 6.3) prompts you to select the user's access level. The access level is tied to a group membership.

Figure 6-3: Add User Permissions

A user's access level can be a Standard User (Power Users Group), a Restricted User (Users Group), or an Other Group (Administrators, Backup Operators, Guests, Power Users, Replicator, Users, or any previously created group).

Once a user is listed, you can then modify their properties. Specifically you can modify their User name, Full name, Description (Figure 6.4).

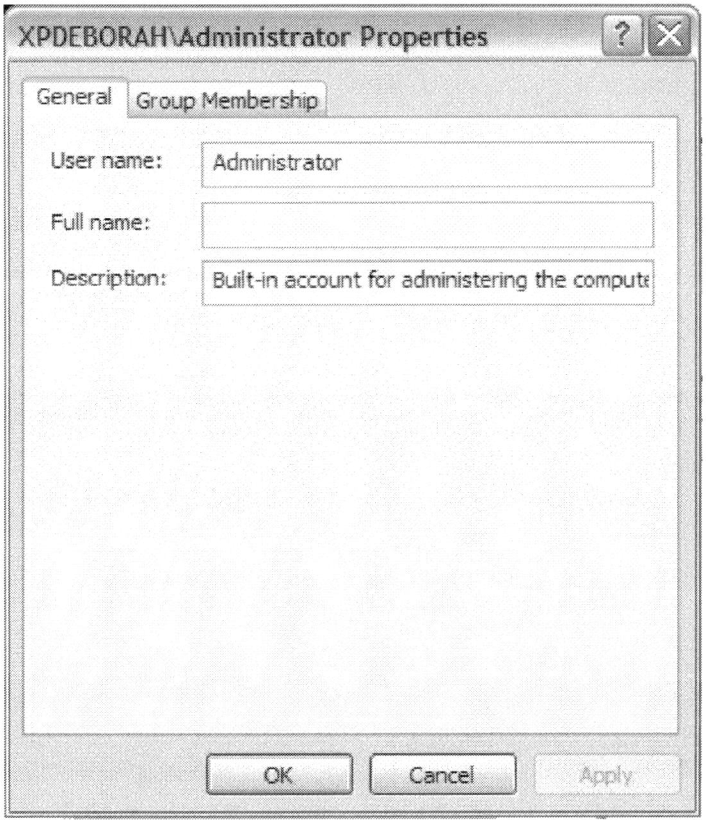

Figure 6-4: User Properties

The Users and Passwords dialog box also allows modification to some advanced properties (Figure 6.5). You can manage passwords, launch the .NET Passport Wizard and the Local Users and Groups console, and modify the secure logon settings.

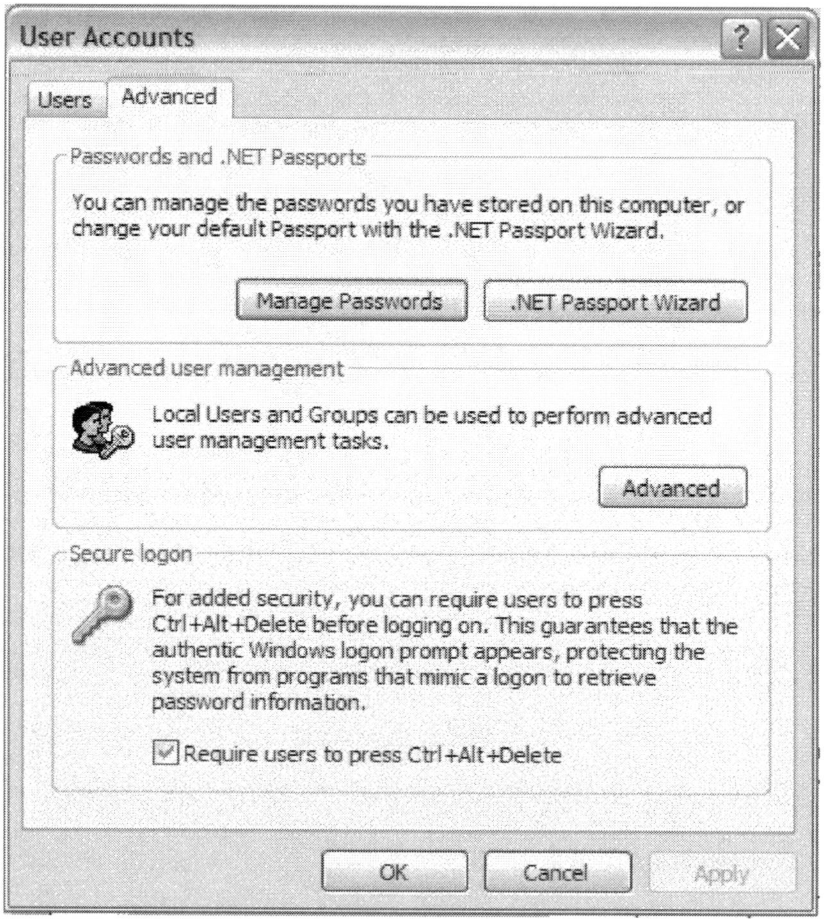

Figure 6-5: Advanced User Properties

Pop Quiz 6.1

Pop Quiz 6.1 *Questions*

1). System groups have a dynamic membership, solely dependant on the action that is taking place. Name the five built-in system groups.

2). Who are the default members of the built-in local group, Administrators?

3). You have an employee who is assigned to the Backup Operators Group. You want him to backup all user data on all servers, but your servers are formatted with the NTFS file formatting system, and he does not have permission to access the files through NTFS. What must you do to allow your employee to perform his backup duties?

4). You are creating a user account for a new employee. You want the employee to be able to operate the computer and save documents, but not to be able to install new programs. What type of user account do you create, using the Add New User wizard?

Pop Quiz 6.1 Answers

1). The five built-in system groups are:

1. Creator/Owner
2. Creator
3. Everyone
4. Interactive
5. Network

2). By default, the built-in accounts "Administrator" and the name assigned to the built-in Initial User are members of the Administrator group.

3). Absolutely nothing. The members of the Backup Operators group have the right to backup and restore the file system, even if they do not have permission to access the files through NTFS. They can, however, only access the files through the Backup utility.

4). You select "Restricted User", which assigns the account to the Users group, not the Power Users group (Standard User).

VI Local Users and Groups console

The Local Users and Groups console (Figure 6.6) provides advanced administration of users and groups. This console is the only way to add a new local user or local group to a Windows XP Professional machine.

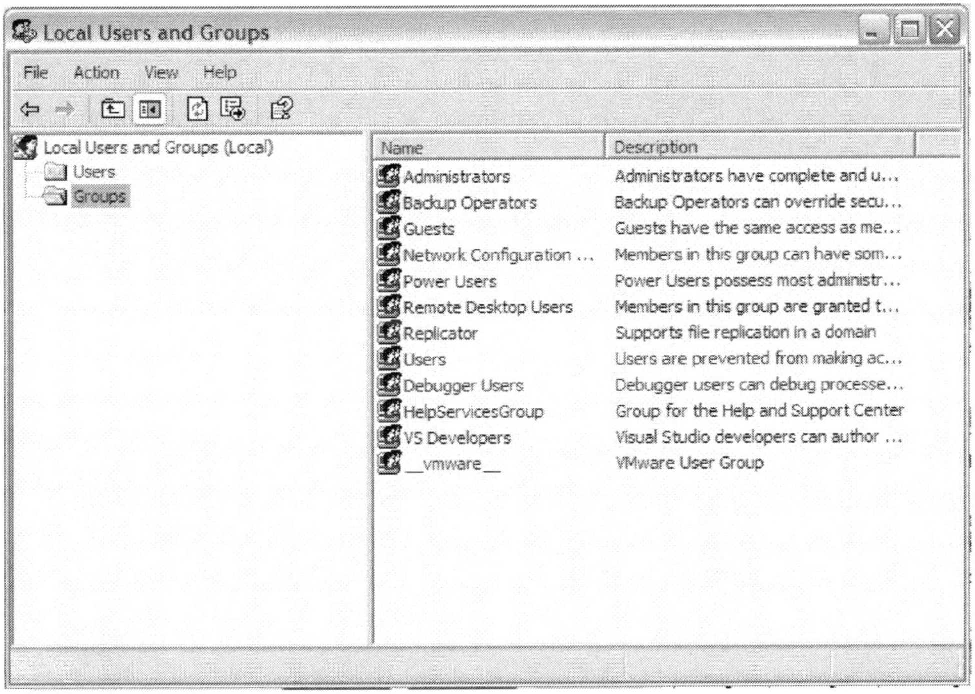

Figure 6-6: Local Users and Groups Console

Creating Users

Using the Local User and Groups console creates new users for the Windows XP Professional system. To create a new user, select the Users folder, right-clicking the folder or detail pane, or using the Action menu, and select **New User**. A dialog box then appears (Figure 6.7)

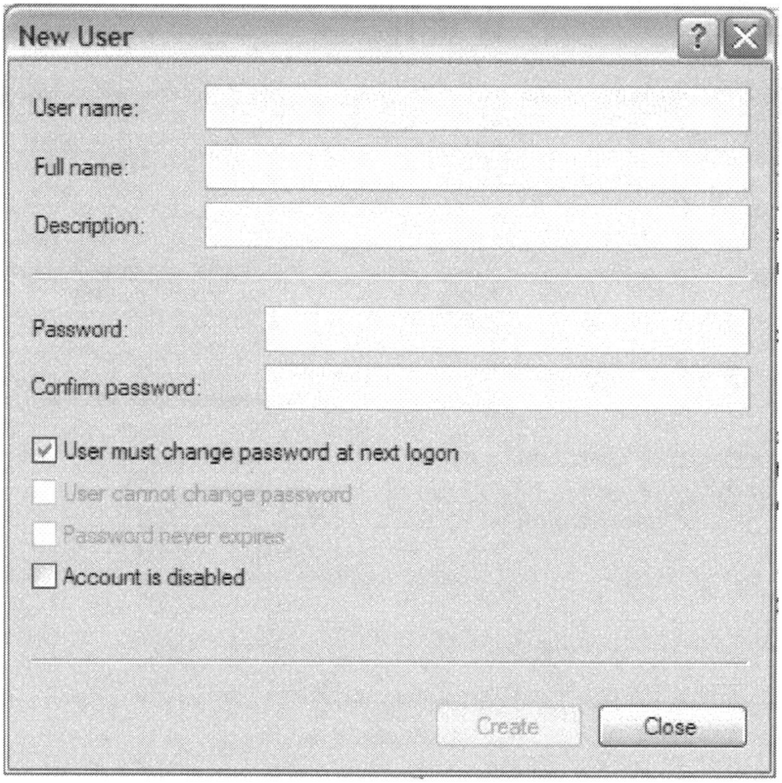

Figure 6-7: Adding a New User

Each user must have a unique username on the local system. By default, **User must change password at next logon** is selected, so that the user can assign themselves a private password. In some environments, the administrator likes to have control of the passwords. In that situation, you would select **User cannot change password**. You can also set it up so that the password never expires. As well, you can disable the account. Disabling the account is <u>not</u> the same as having the account locked out. The operating system, based on policy, will lock the account out after a certain number of incorrect password entries.

The Administrator can disable the account if, for example, someone is going on maternity leave. By disabling temporarily inactive accounts, security is tightened.

There are some restrictions and guidelines when creating new users:

Username must be unique.

Usernames are not case sensitive, but passwords are.

When creating usernames, try to follow a standard naming convention.

Usernames must be between 1-20 characters, cannot use certain reserved characters (" / \ [ ] : ; | = , + * ? < >) and cannot consist of all periods or spaces.

Passwords can be up to 127 characters, however if Windows 9x systems are running on the network, they only use up to 14 characters

Creating Groups

Groups exist to ease the management of assigning rights and permissions to users. When there are only five user accounts, it is quite simple to simply assign rights and privileges to the individual accounts. However, when you have 10,000 user accounts can turns into a lesson in futility.

Groups are usually designed to sort user accounts into categories, usually by job function or location. By assigning permissions to groups, rather than users, you only need to perform the task once.

It is considered good practice to always assign permissions to groups rather than users. This way, as people come and go, get promoted, leave the company, etc., it is easy to manage.

Think of it this way. If you have fifty sales people, all who need permission to access the Sales folder, it is much simpler to assign these people to a Sales group, and then grant access permission to the group. Even if twenty people leave, and twenty more are hired, it is simply a case of renaming the user accounts to reflect the new username. All rights and permissions assigned to the group remain the same.

New groups can only be created by using the Local Users and Group console. Select the groups folder and right-click either the folder or the details pane. From this menu, you then select **New Group**. (This command is also available from the Action menu.) To create the new group, give the group a unique, and identifiable, name and add the appropriate user accounts (Figure 6.8)

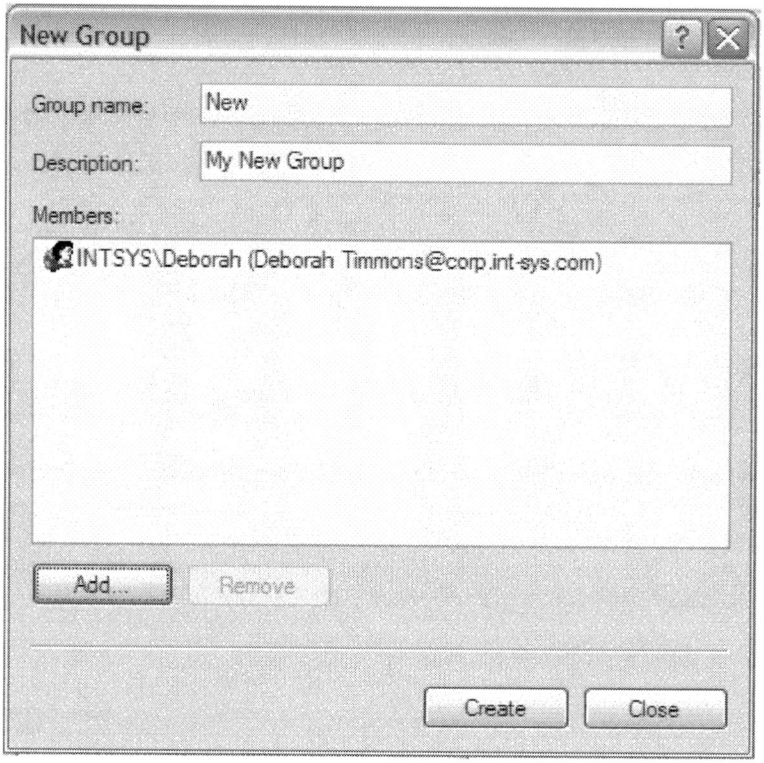

Figure 6-8: Creating a New Group

Remember, a user can belong to more than one group. If, for example, you have a group for Senior Executives, and another for IT, the Vice President of IT would belong to both groups.

There are some restrictions and guidelines when creating new groups:

- Group names must be unique.
- When creating groups, try to follow a standard naming convention.
- Group names can be up to 256 characters, cannot use certain reserved characters (" / \ [ ] : ; | = + * ? < >) and cannot consist of all periods or spaces.

VII Configure and manage user profiles

User profiles store many of the individual configuration settings for Windows XP Professional. When many people are using the same computer, user profiles allow that each person receives the configuration settings of their choice. Font size, wallpaper, shortcuts, and even things like mouse speed and button settings are all part of user profiles.

Types of user profiles include:

Local user profile:

The local user profile is created the first time a user logs on to a computer. It is stored on the local hard drive. Any changes made to the profile will be specific to that computer.

Roaming user profile:

This profile is created by the administrator and is stored on a server so that it is available any time the user logs onto the network, and is applied to any computer on the network. Any changes made to the roaming profile will be updated on the server.

Mandatory user profile:

A roaming profile that has settings that cannot be changed by the user is called a mandatory profile. It can be applied to a single user, a group of users, or all users in a corporate environment. Changes made to the profile by an individual user will not be saved, and the user will receive the original settings at the next logon. The administrator can only change these profiles.

Profiles can be administered through the **System** icon in Control Panel (Figure 6.9). You will need to select the **Advanced** tab, then the **Settings** button under User Profiles.

With a slow network connection, you may choose to avoid downloading the roaming profile. This is particularly true for remote users logging onto the network. This can be done by selecting the "**Use cached profile on slow connections**" check box after you select Roaming profile. If a roaming profile is used on more than one computer at the same time, and the profile is not a mandatory profile, the settings will be preserved from the last computer that logs off.

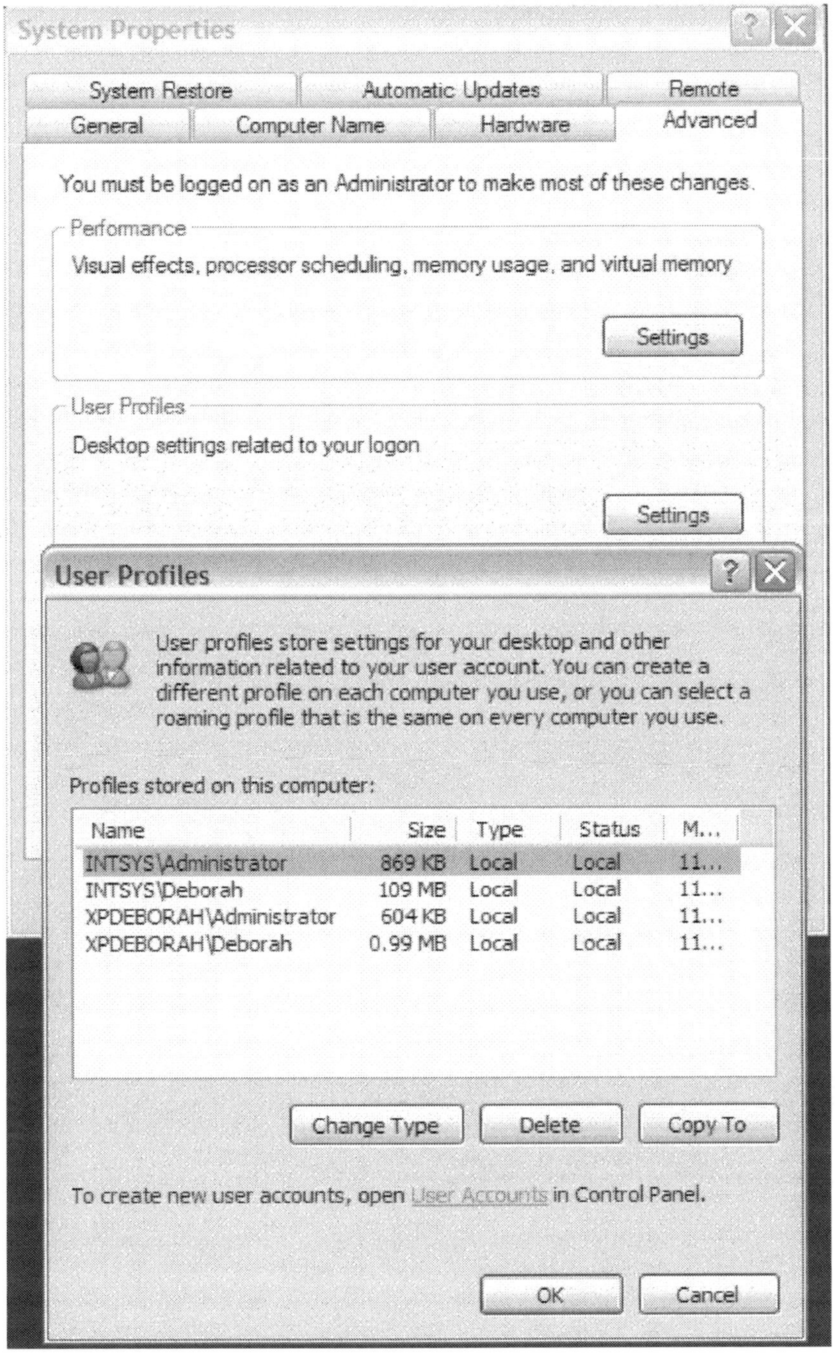

Figure 6-9: Managing User Profiles

VIII Chapter 6: Summary

We have now covered some of the basics of implementing, managing and troubleshooting network protocols, and services.

You should feel comfortable with how to:

- Identify Windows XP Professional built-in users
- Identify Windows XP Professional built-in groups
- Identify Windows XP Professional built-in system groups
- Identify the user management tools
- Implement, configure, and manage local user and group accounts
- Configure and manage user profiles

IX Chapter 6: Review Questions

1. On your WinXP computer you found that all user's profiles except the administrators' are corrupted. You know that another user named Mary has manually copy all the profile data to a separate partition as backup. To restore these data, you should copy the backed up files back to which location?

A. %SystemDrive%\Documents And Settings

B. %SystemDrive%\Documents\Profiles

C. %SystemDrive%\Documents And Settings\Identity

D. %SystemDrive%\Documents And Settings\Microsoft

E. %SystemDrive%\User Profiles\

2. You are using WinXP as your desktop. You need to share the files in your \SALES folder to your peers. However, you are getting confused about all the different setting options. Susan as the administrator can help you by:

A. Opening the Folder Options from Control Panel's Appearance And Themes category and enable the use of Simple File Sharing in the Advanced Settings box under the View tab.

B. Granting you the Power Users rights

C. Opening the Folder Options from Control Panel's Permissions category and enable the use of Simple File Sharing in the Advanced Settings box under the Security tab.

D. Opening the Security Options from Control Panel's Appearance And Themes category and enable the use of Simple File Sharing in the Security Settings box under the View tab.

E. Opening the Folder Options from Control Panel's System Security category and enable the use of Simple File Sharing in the Permissions Settings box under the Advanced tab.

3. Your XP computer is currently being used by 5 different individuals. These users complain that they do not like the pictures that represent their accounts. One user goes into the corresponding directory and modifies many of the default pictures. One of the modified pictures contains sexually harassing graphics. From where can you modify this picture and remove the harassing part?

A. AllUsersProfile%\ Application Data\Microsoft\User Account Pictures\Default Pictures

B. AllUsersProfile%\ Application Data\Microsoft\Identities\Default Pictures

C. AllUsersProfile%\ Application Data\Microsoft\Desktop\Default Pictures

D. AllUsersProfile%\ Application Data\Microsoft\User Account Pictures\Desktop Pictures

E. AllUsersProfile%\Microsoft\User Account Pictures\Default Pictures

4. You are deleting Mary's account from your XP computer. You fail. You log off and log in again as administrator, and the deletion still fails. What is the likely cause?

A. Mary is the last user account on this computer

B. Mary is an administrator

C. Mary is logged on

D. EFS has been activated, and some files belong to Mary

E. WinXP is busy updating its user database, that you should wait until it finishes before retrying.

5. You are the WinXP administrator of your company. You are specialized in user profile management. As far as you know, what is the most likely cause of the creation of convoluted folder name for user profile on a WinXP computer?

A. A user account of the same name has been deleted with a tool other than User Accounts

B. A user account of the same name has been created with a tool other than User Accounts

C. Deletion of an user account which is of the same name had failed before

D. Creation of an user account which is of the same name had failed before

E. A user of the same name has logged on from another computer remotely

6. On your XP computer you delete Mary's account because you think that she is fired. However, later on you discover that it is Marc who got fired. You need to restore Mary's account and her permissions as fast as possible. What should you do?

A. Recreate her account with the exact same information

B. Re-establish all her permissions

C. Look for her SID and assign it to the recreated account

D. Rename Marc's account to Mary. Manually modify the SID.

E. No Answer is Correct.

7. On your XP computer you have deleted Mary's account with a tool other than User Accounts. Susan advises you that Mary's account profile continues to occupy space in the Documents And Settings folder. How do you reclaim the space?

A. Right-click My Computer and choose Properties – Advanced tab – User Profiles – Settings. Delete the account named Account Unknown.

B. Right-click My Computer and choose Properties – Advanced tab – User Profiles – Documents. Delete the account named Mary.

C. Right-click the C drive and choose Properties – Advanced tab. Reclaim the wasted space.

D. Defrag the drive that contains all the user profiles.

E. Do nothing. The space will be reclaimed by XP automatically.

8. You are administering a WinXP Pro system. You found that the name of the last user who logged on is shown in the Log On To Windows dialog box of the welcome screen. For security reasons, you want to disable this. How should you do this?

A. Configure the Local Security Settings of the computer to disable the corresponding feature

B. Configure the default User Profile of the computer to disable the corresponding feature

C. Configure the User Profile for each user of the computer to disable the corresponding feature

D. Configure the registry to disable the use of keyword tracking

E. No Answer is Correct.

9. You are administering a WinXP Pro system. You are the only user of the system. You found it very annoying to enter the name every time you log on. How do you configure the system to make it convenient to logon?

A. Type secpol.msc at a command prompt. Open the Local Policies\Security Options. Disable the policy named Interactive Logon: Do Not Display Last User Name.

B. Type secpol.msc at a command prompt. Open the Local Policies\Security Options. Enable the policy named Interactive Logon: Do Not Display Last User Name.

C. Type secpol.msc at a command prompt. Open the Local Policies\Security Options. Enable the policy named Interactive Logon: Display Last User Name.

D. Type regedit secpol.msc at a command prompt. Open the Local Policies\Security Options. Disable the policy named Logon: Do Not Display Last User Name.

E. Type regedit32 at a command prompt. Open the Local Policies\Security Options. Disable the policy named Interactive Logon: Do Not Display User Name.

10. Mary is the user of a WinXP computer. She wants to work with the user profiles on her system. What are the restrictions applied towards her?

A. She can't see other user profiles

B. She can't delete her own profile

C. She can't copy her own profile

D. She can't change her own profile

E. No Answer is Correct.

IX Chapter 6: Review Answer

1. On your WinXP computer you found that all user's profiles except the administrators' are corrupted. You know that another user named Mary has manually copy all the profile data to a separate partition as backup. To restore these data, you should copy the backed up files back to which location?

***A. %SystemDrive%\Documents And Settings**

B. %SystemDrive%\Documents\Profiles

C. %SystemDrive%\Documents And Settings\Identity

D. %SystemDrive%\Documents And Settings\Microsoft

E. %SystemDrive%\User Profiles\

Explanation: By default, each user who logs on to a computer has a local user profile, which is created when the user logs on for the first time. Local user profiles are stored in %SystemDrive%\Documents And Settings. Each user's profile is stored in a subfolder with the user name as the folder name.

2. You are using WinXP as your desktop. You need to share the files in your \SALES folder to your peers. However, you are getting confused about all the different setting options. Susan as the administrator can help you by:

***A. Opening the Folder Options from Control Panel's Appearance And Themes category and enable the use of Simple File Sharing in the Advanced Settings box under the View tab.**

B. Granting you the Power Users rights

C. Opening the Folder Options from Control Panel's Permissions category and enable the use of Simple File Sharing in the Advanced Settings box under the Security tab.

D. Opening the Security Options from Control Panel's Appearance And Themes category and enable the use of Simple File Sharing in the Security Settings box under the View tab.

E. Opening the Folder Options from Control Panel's System Security category and enable the use of Simple File Sharing in the Permissions Settings box under the Advanced tab.

Explanation: If you use Windows XP Professional, you can choose to use Simple File Sharing or the classic sharing and security interface. You can switch between them. Note that Use Simple File Sharing is recommended by Microsoft.

3. Your XP computer is currently being used by 5 different individuals. These users complain that they do not like the pictures that represent their accounts. One user goes into the corresponding directory and modifies many of the default pictures. One of the modified pictures contains sexually harassing graphics. From where can you modify this picture and remove the harassing part?

***A. AllUsersProfile%\ Application Data\Microsoft\User Account Pictures\Default Pictures**

B. AllUsersProfile%\ Application Data\Microsoft\Identities\Default Pictures

C. AllUsersProfile%\ Application Data\Microsoft\Desktop\Default Pictures

D. AllUsersProfile%\ Application Data\Microsoft\User Account Pictures\Desktop Pictures

E. AllUsersProfile%\Microsoft\User Account Pictures\Default Pictures

Explanation: You can change the picture associated with the account name at the top of the Start menu and in User Accounts. By clicking the change-picture link, you can take a look at all the pictures stored in AllUsersProfile%\ Application Data\Microsoft\User Account Pictures\Default Pictures. You can also click Browse For More Pictures.

4. You are deleting Mary's account from your XP computer. You fail. You log off and log in again as administrator, and the deletion still fails. What is the likely cause?

***A. Mary is the last user account on this computer**

B. Mary is an administrator

***C. Mary is logged on**

D. EFS has been activated, and some files belong to Mary

E. WinXP is busy updating its user database, that you should wait until it finishes before retrying.

Explanation: User Accounts won't let you delete the last account on the computer even if you're logged on as Administrator. This limitation is deliberate. It helps to enforce the sound security practice of using an account other than Administrator for daily computing.

5. You are the WinXP administrator of your company. You are specialized in user profile management. As far as you know, what is the most likely cause of the creation of convoluted folder name for user profile on a WinXP computer?

***A. A user account of the same name has been deleted with a tool other than User Accounts**

B. A user account of the same name has been created with a tool other than User Accounts

C. Deletion of an user account which is of the same name had failed before

D. Creation of an user account which is of the same name had failed before

E. A user of the same name has logged on from another computer remotely

Explanation: If you use a tool other than User Accounts to delete the account, the user's original profile remains in the Documents And Settings folder. If you later create a new account with the same name, Windows creates a new profile folder, but because a folder already exists with that user's name, it appends the computer name to the user name to create a convoluted folder name. The extra folder leads to confusion about which is the correct profile folder.

6. On your XP computer you delete Mary's account because you think that she is fired. However, later on you discover that it is Marc who got fired. You need to restore Mary's account and her permissions as fast as possible. What should you do?

***A. Recreate her account with the exact same information**

***B. Re-establish all her permissions**

C. Look for her SID and assign it to the recreated account

D. Rename Marc's account to Mary. Manually modify the SID.

E. No Answer is Correct.

Explanation: You cannot restore access to resources that currently list the user in their access control lists simply by re-creating the deleted account. This includes files to which the user has permission and the user's encrypted files, personal certificates, and stored passwords for Web sites and network resources. That's because those permissions are linked to the user's original SID but not the user name.

7. On your XP computer you have deleted Mary's account with a tool other than User Accounts. Susan advises you that Mary's account profile continues to occupy space in the Documents And Settings folder. How do you reclaim the space?

***A. Right-click My Computer and choose Properties – Advanced tab – User Profiles – Settings. Delete the account named Account Unknown.**

B. Right-click My Computer and choose Properties – Advanced tab – User Profiles – Documents. Delete the account named Mary.

C. Right-click the C drive and choose Properties – Advanced tab. Reclaim the wasted space.

D. Defrag the drive that contains all the user profiles.

E. Do nothing. The space will be reclaimed by XP automatically.

Explanation: If you delete an account with a tool other than User Accounts, the account's profile continues to occupy space in the Documents And Settings folder and in the registry. To delete it, you should right-click My Computer and choose Properties. Click the Advanced tab and then click Settings under User Profiles. Select the account named Account Unknown and click Delete.

8. You are administering a WinXP Pro system. You found that the name of the last user who logged on is shown in the Log On To Windows dialog box of the welcome screen. For security reasons, you want to disable this. How should you do this?

***A. Configure the Local Security Settings of the computer to disable the corresponding feature**

B. Configure the default User Profile of the computer to disable the corresponding feature

C. Configure the User Profile for each user of the computer to disable the corresponding feature

D. Configure the registry to disable the use of keyword tracking

Explanation: Ordinarily, the name of the last user who logged on appears in the Log On To Windows dialog box. It can be a security hole as anyone can learn a valid user name just by looking at this dialog box. To prevent this you may type secpol.msc at a command prompt to open Local Security Settings and enable the policy named Interactive Logon: Do Not Display Last User Name.

9. You are administering a WinXP Pro system. You are the only user of the system. You found it very annoying to enter the name every time you log on. How do you configure the system to make it convenient to logon?

A. Type secpol.msc at a command prompt. Open the Local Policies\Security Options. Disable the policy named Interactive Logon: Do Not Display Last User Name.

B. Type secpol.msc at a command prompt. Open the Local Policies\Security Options. Enable the policy named Interactive Logon: Do Not Display Last User Name.

C. Type secpol.msc at a command prompt. Open the Local Policies\Security Options. Enable the policy named Interactive Logon: Display Last User Name.

D. Type regedit secpol.msc at a command prompt. Open the Local Policies\Security Options. Disable the policy named Logon: Do Not Display Last User Name.

E. Type regedit32 at a command prompt. Open the Local Policies\Security Options. Disable the policy named Interactive Logon: Do Not Display User Name.

Explanation: Ordinarily, the name of the last user who logged on appears in the Log On To Windows dialog box. It can be a security hole as anyone can learn a valid user name just by looking at this dialog box. To prevent this you may type secpol.msc at a command prompt to open Local Security Settings and enable the policy named Interactive Logon: Do Not Display Last User Name.

10. Mary is the user of a WinXP computer. She wants to work with the user profiles on her system. What are the restrictions applied towards her?

***A. She cannot see other user profiles**

***B. She cannot delete her own profile**

***C. She cannot copy her own profile**

***D. She cannot change her own profile**

E. She cannot view her own profile

Explanation: Users who are not members of the Administrators group cannot see other user profiles in the User Profiles dialog box. They cannot delete, copy, nor change their own profile as well.

Chapter 7: Administration of Resources

The objective of this chapter is to provide you with an understanding of the following:

1. Manage file and folder compression
2. Manage NTFS permissions on files and folders
3. Optimize file and folder access
4. Implement and manage disk quotas
5. Implement and manage shared resources
6. Implement and manage offline folders
7. Implement and manage local and network print devices
8. Implement and manage web server resources

Getting Ready – (Questions)

1). What two ways can you manipulate the compression of a file or folder on an NTFS partition?

2). When you move a file within an NTFS partition, what happens with the permission and compression attributes?

3). By default, a file inherits the permissions of its parent folder. What can you do to prevent this from happening?

4). What is the major difference between effective permissions in Windows NT 4.0 and Windows XP?

5). By default, IIS 5.0 is not installed on Windows XP Professional. What is the default if you are upgrading to Windows XP Professional and had an installation of PWS?

Getting Ready – (Answers)

1). You can manipulate the compression of a file using Windows Explorer or with the command line utility COMPACT.EXE.

2). When you move a file within a partition, essentially what you are doing is changing the pointer to the file. Nothing happens physically to the data. For that reason, when you move a file within the same NTFS volume, the compression and permission attributes of the file remain the same.

3). You can stop the inheritance of permissions from occurring by deselecting the check box next to **Allow inheritable permissions from parent to propagate to this object.**

4). Windows NT 4.0 had cumulative permissions. The total of the permissions granted the user account, by itself or by group membership was the effective permission, unless the user or group had **No Access** permission applied. Windows XP has **Allow, Deny,** and **Unset** permissions. If permission has not been specified for either the username or group, it will not be added to the allowed permissions list. If it has been allowed for one group, and not specified for another, and the user is a member of both groups, then the user will have that permission, as it has not been explicitly denied. If one group has a **Deny** permission, then the **Allow** permission is removed for the user.

5). On an upgrade to Windows XP Professional, IIS 5.0 will be installed by default, IF PWS was already installed on your previous version of Windows.

I Introduction

On a daily basis, a network administrator will spend great deal of time managing the minutiae of his or her clients. "I can't print!" a user will say, or "I printed my document an hour ago, and it still hasn't come out of the printer!" Someone can't get to a file that they needed access to "yesterday". A client shared his or her "C:" drive to give a co-worker access to a file and now is upset because that co-worker can see their personal information that is sitting in another folder on the hard drive.

Such is the day-to-day lot of network support. Windows XP offers some valuable solutions to some of the challenges that widespread access to information can supply. You can keep track of who has access to what and when. You can limit, or deny access altogether, to sensitive files and folders. Best of all, when difficulties arise, as they will, there can be quick and effective resolution.

We are going to spend this chapter looking at the "how to" of managing and troubleshooting the information items which include files, file systems, folders, printers and other devices.

II Managing Files and Folders

File Compression Methods

One thing in life these days is certain, at least in the world of the computer. There is NEVER enough hard drive space. These days there is more drive space than ever, and at a low cost, but the more space you have, the more you will need! Fortunately, Windows XP comes with some great tools that will help you manage the drive space you have to make more out of less.

There are two different methods to compress files in Windows XP. The first method is a part of NTFS; the other is a utility such as WinZip.

Compact

The compact utility is an extension of the NTFS system, and as such can only be used on NTFS partitions. The nicest thing about this compression method is that it is dynamic. Once a file is compressed, it will automatically decompress for you to use the file, and then recompress when you are finished. You can manipulate the compression of a file using Windows Explorer or with the command line utility compact.exe**.** In fact, both of these methods rely on the same information and DLL's in order to work.

With Windows Explorer, to compress a file, folder, or volume, all you need to do is to change the attribute on the object (Figure 7.1).

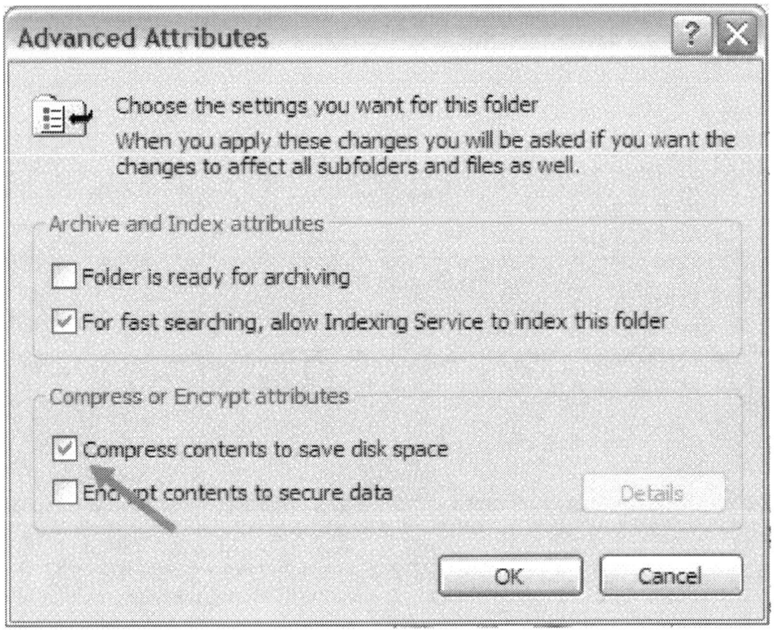

Figure 7-1: Compressing a Folder in Windows Explorer

The attribute that you want to select is **Compress contents to save disk space**. After pressing **OK**, if the object is a folder, you are then prompted on whether or not to apply this setting to all subfolder and files (Figure 7.2).

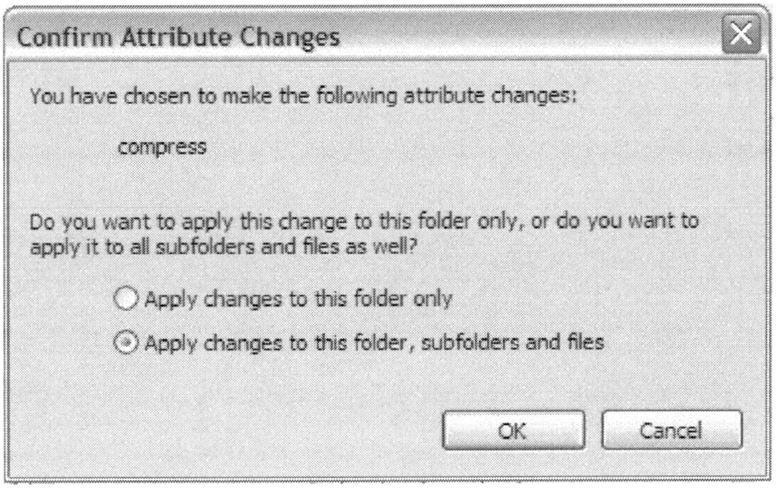

Figure 7-2: Confirming Compression Changes

At a Command Prompt, you can run the utility compact.exe. This utility, run without parameters, will display the compression state of the current directory and any files contained within (Figure 7.3).

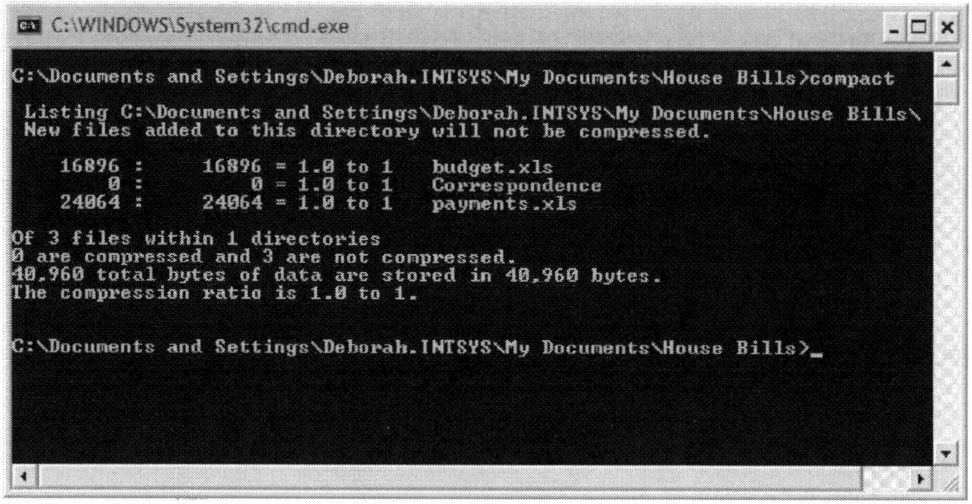

Figure 7-3: Compression Using the Compact Utility

With parameters (Table 7.1), this utility can enable or disable compression on the files and folders.

COMPACT [/C|/U] [/S[:dir]] [/A] [/I] [/F] [/Q] [filename [...]]	
/C	Compresses the specified files. Directories will be marked so that files added afterward will be compressed.
/U	Uncompresses the specified files. Directories will be marked so that files added afterward will not be compressed
/S	Performs the specified operation on files in the given directory and all subdirectories. Default "dir" is the current directory.
/A	Displays files with the hidden or system attributes. These files are omitted by default.
/I	Continues performing the specified operation even after errors have occurred. By default, COMPACT stops when an error is encountered.
/F	Forces the compress operation on all specified files, even those that are already compressed. Already compressed files are skipped by default.
/Q	Reports only the most essential information.
FILENAME	Specifies a pattern, file, or directory.

Table 7-1: Compact.exe Command Line Parameters

Compress and Expand

> **NOTE:** Compress.exe is available in the Windows XP Resource Kit

This utility can only be used at a command line. It is used to create compressed copies of one or more files, such as the 3rd party utility WinZip does. In order to use a file on which you have used compress.exe (Table 7.2), you need to use expand.exe (Table 7.3).

These commands should not be regularly used on NTFS volumes, but should be reserved for FAT-based volumes (which have no internal compression mechanism). However, there are times where the use of these tools can be useful, such as distributing files (like a company bitmap used for the desktop) inside an unattended setup.

COMPRESS [-r] [-d] [-z | -ZX | -ZQ[n]] Source Destination
COMPRESS -r [-d] [-z | -ZX | -ZQ[n]] Source [Destination]

-R	Rename compressed files
-D	Update compressed files only if out of date
-Z	MS-ZIP compression
-ZX	LZX compression
-ZQ[N]	Quantum compression and optional level N (in range 1-7, default is 4)
SOURCE	Source file specification. Wildcards may be used
DESTINATION	Destination file or path specification Destination may be a directory If Source is multiple files and -R is not specified, Destination must be a directory

Table 7-2: Compress.exe Command Line Parameters

EXPAND [-r] Source Destination	
EXPAND -r Source [Destination]	
EXPAND -D Source.cab [-F:Files]	
EXPAND Source.cab -F:Files Destination	
-R	Rename expanded files
-D	Display list of files in source
SOURCE	Source file specification. Wildcards may be used
DESTINATIO N	Destination file or path specification Destination may be a directory If Source is multiple files and -R is not specified, Destination must be a directory

Table 7-3: Expand.exe Command Line Parameters

Moving and Copying Compressed Files

For purposes of this section, when discussing compressed files, we are talking about files that have been compressed using compact.exe or have their compression attribute enabled.

Moving a file or folder within the same NTFS volume

When you move a file within a partition, essentially what you are doing is changing the pointer to the file. Nothing happens physically to the data. For that reason, when you move a file within the same NTFS volume, the compression attribute of the file remains the same. If you move an uncompressed file into a folder that is compressed, the file remains uncompressed. In the same vein, if you move a compressed file into an uncompressed folder, the file will stay compressed.

- Copying a file within the same NTFS volume, or between NTFS volumes

When you copy a file, you are actually creating a new file with the same data as the original. The compression attribute of the new file will be the same as the target folder. A copy created in an uncompressed folder will be uncompressed, whether or not the original was uncompressed, and vice versa. It does not matter whether the copy takes place within the same volume or between NTFS volumes.

- Moving a file between NTFS volumes, or from a FAT/FAT32 volume to an NTFS volume.

When you move a file between volumes, what is actually happening is that Windows 2000 is copying the file onto the target volume and then the original is deleted. Therefore the same rule applies when moving a file between NTFS volumes as when you copy a file – the file takes on the compression attribute of the target folder. If you move a file from an NTFS volume to a FAT or FAT32 volume, it will lose its compression attribute. Dynamic compression works only on NTFS volumes.

> **NOTE:** Any file compressed with the compress.exe utility will remain compressed whether or not it is copied, moved within or between volumes. The only way to uncompress these files is with the expand.exe utility.

Troubleshooting

- Adding files to an almost full NTFS volume

When writing a file to a compressed folder, NTFS reserves enough space for the uncompressed file. It will reclaim the space after the write has taken place. For that reason, when copying or saving a file to a compressed folder on an NTFS volume that is almost full, you may get an error message stating that there is not enough disk space, even if there is enough for the compressed file. You may also get read errors when you open a compressed file on an almost-full volume. This is because the file is dynamically uncompressed when opened, and there is not enough space on the volume for the file in its uncompressed state.

Regain space by deleting unnecessary files, or save the files to a different volume. You can have compression handle the data more efficiently by recopying all files back into the folder, copying the largest files or the files that compress well (such as bitmaps) first.

- Some files are uncompressed even though the parent folder is compressed.

Remember that files that are copied or moved between NTFS partitions will inherit the compression attribute of the parent folder, but files moved within the same partition won't. Compress individual files through the properties window in Explorer, or uncompress and recompress the entire folder. Make sure to select "Compress this folder, subfolders and files", as shown in Figure 7.4.

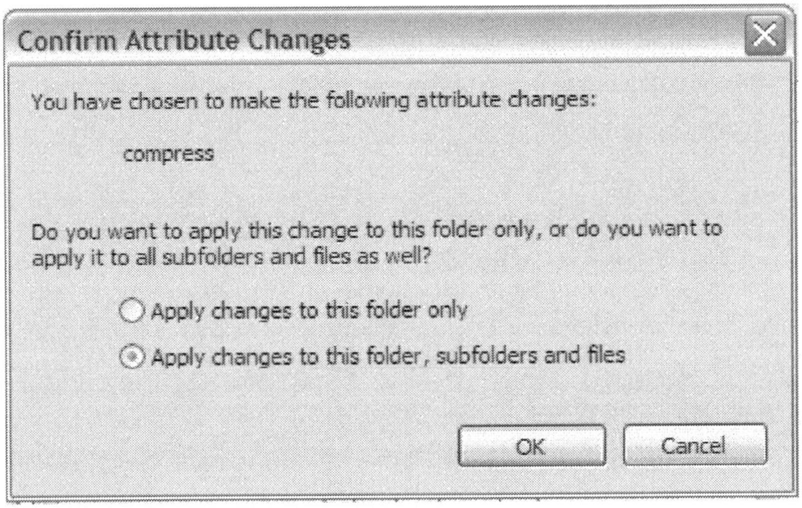

Figure 7-4: Compress folders, subfolders and files

- Performance degradation

The current implementation of NTFS compression works more efficiently on Windows XP than on Windows 2000 Server. However, you may notice a slight degradation in performance because a compression file will always be first decompressed before any action is taken on it, including copying or transfers, and then recompressed on completion of the action. Compression performance is measured by size reduction and speed of transfer. Performance monitoring of your network will enable you to decide whether the gain in disk space is greater than the effect on bandwidth when a file is transferred on the network. Comparing the file and folder sizes before and after compression will tell you how well those particular files and folders are being handled by compression.

- Compression and encryption

We will be discussing encryption in detail in Chapter 8; for the moment, it is important to note that you cannot have a file or folder that is both compressed and encrypted.

Control access with NTFS permissions

NTFS permissions are vital in an organization to protect and control access to files to prevent unauthorized access, tampering, or theft of documents and information. It is imperative to know that NTFS permissions are applied both locally (at the same computer) and over the network (on the corporate LAN or the Internet).

NTFS permissions are handled similarly to the way they were in Windows NT 4.0. However, Windows XP allows a finer degree of granularity for greater control. There are five basic NTFS permissions on a file: Full Control, Read, Write, Modify, and Read & Execute. Folders have six permissions, the same five as on files with an additional one: List Folder Contents. Each of these permissions can be allowed or denied on an individual or group basis.

By default, files and child folders inherit the permissions of the parent folder. First level folders inherit the permissions of the NTFS volume. Let's walk through how these permissions can be changed to allow for more controlled access to folders and files. Let's create a new NTFS volume, and assign it drive letter "F". By default, the volume assigns the **Everyone** group full permissions (Figure 7.5).

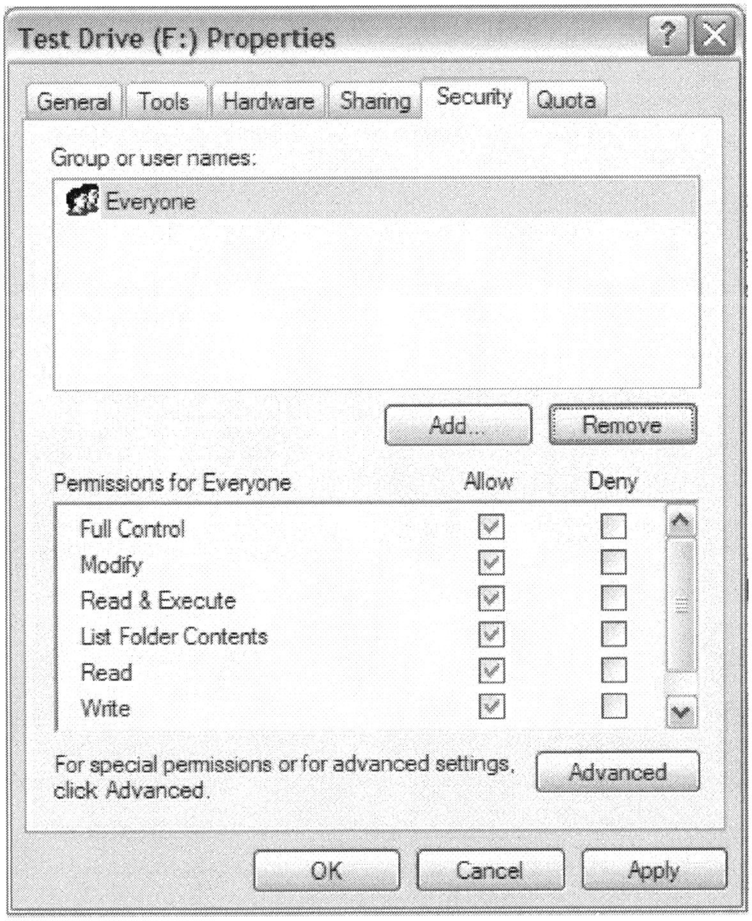

Figure 7-5: Default permissions on new NTFS volume

We will now create a new folder in this volume, named Test. The permissions for the Test folder are inherited from the volume as indicated by the checkbox "Allow inheritable permissions from parent to propagate to this object". The permission checkboxes are also faded out, indicated the inherited permissions. These faded checkboxes cannot be changed (Figure 7.6).

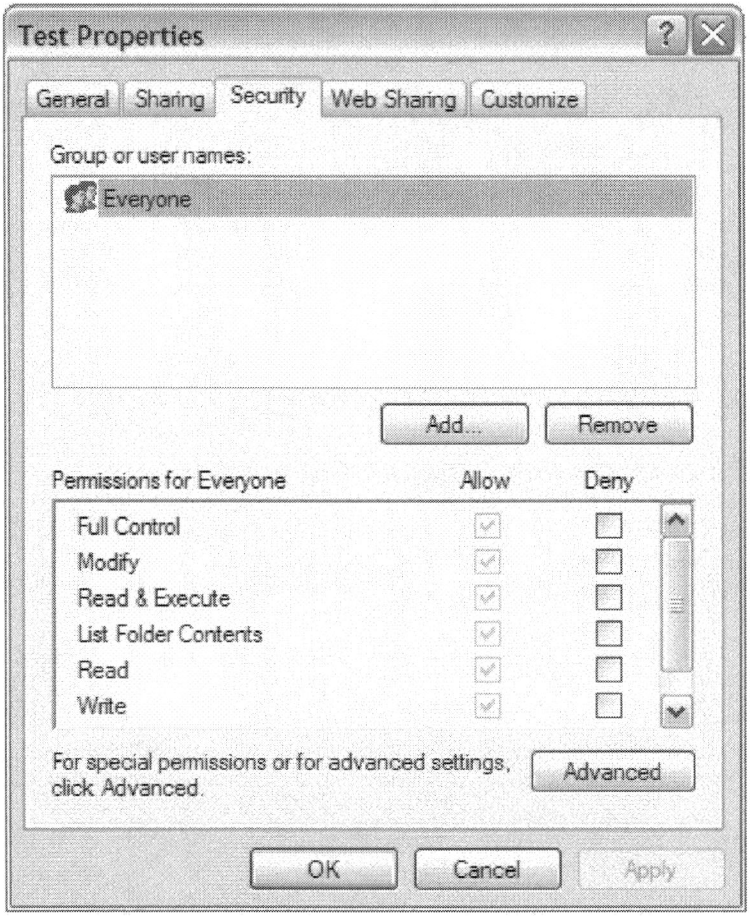

Figure 7-6: Default permissions on new NTFS folder

However, you can still specify permissions on the folder to explicitly deny access to a specific inherited permission, or to grant (or deny) access to a user or group.

A file created in this new folder will also, by default, inherit these permissions, with the exception of "List Folder Contents", which is reserved for folders only.

> **NOTE:** While the Windows XP online help seems to indicate that the Everyone system group from Windows NT 4.0 has been replaced by the Authenticated Users system group, this is not the case. By default, the Everyone group is still given full access to NTFS volumes. Because the Everyone group includes not only authenticated users, but the Guest account as well, this default permission should be changed for security reasons.

There are times when the inherited permissions will not apply to a specific folder (or even file). When situations like this arise, you can effectively stop the inheritance from occurring by deselecting the check box next to **Inherit from parent the permission entries that apply to child objects. Include these with entries explicitly defined here**.

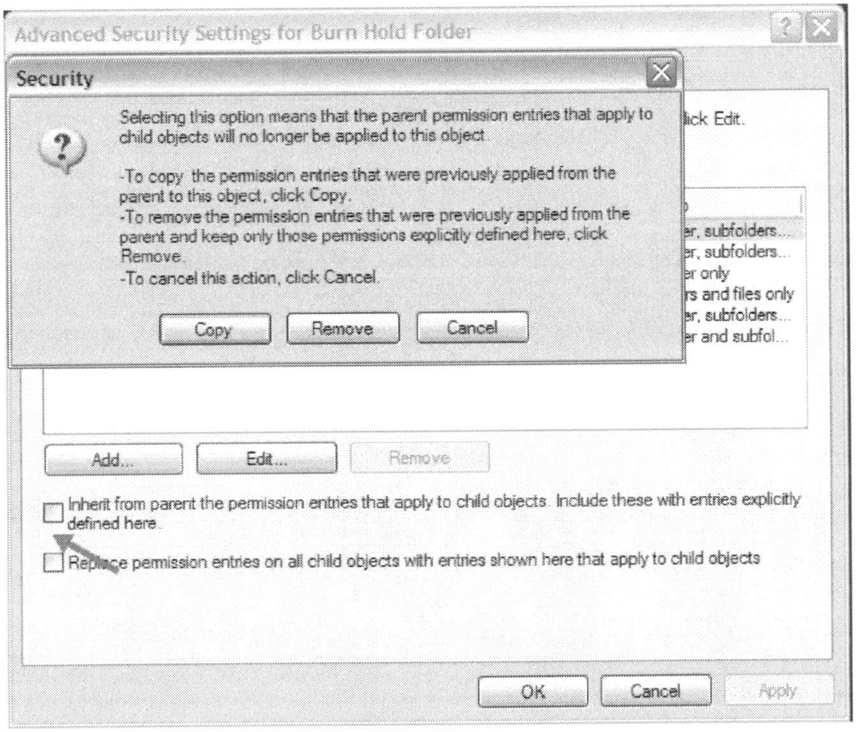

Figure 7-7: Removing inheritance from files and folders

A security dialog box will appear (Figure 7.7) which gives you three options:

- Copy

This will copy the inherited permission to the object, and will allow you to select or deselect checkboxes (they will no longer be shaded).

- Remove

This will remove all inherited permissions, leaving only those that have been explicitly assigned. New permissions will have to be assigned on a user and group basis, by clicking the "Add" button.

- Cancel

This will cancel the operation leaving the permissions as they were.

Each of the basic NTFS permissions is a generic permission that modifies a collection of advanced permissions. Table 7.4 shows the correlation between the basic NTFS permissions and the advanced NTFS permissions.

Permission	Applies to	FULL CONTROL	MODIFY	READ AND EXECUTE	LIST FOLDER CONTENTS	READ	WRITE
Traverse Folder	Folder	✓	✓	✓	✓		
Execute File	File	✓	✓	✓			
List Folder	Folder	✓	✓	✓	✓	✓	
Read Data	File	✓	✓	✓		✓	
Read Attributes	Both	✓	✓	✓	✓	✓	
Read Extended Attributes		✓	✓	✓	✓	✓	
Create Files	Folder	✓	✓				✓
Write Data	File	✓	✓				✓
Create Folders	Folders	✓	✓				✓
Append Data	File	✓	✓				✓
Write Attributes	Both	✓	✓				✓
Write Extended Attributes		✓	✓				✓
Delete	Both	✓	✓				
Delete Subfolders and Files	Both	✓					
Read Permissions	Both	✓	✓	✓	✓	✓	✓
Change Permissions	Both	✓					
Take Ownership	Both	✓					
Synchronize		✓	✓				

Table 7-4: NTFS Permissions

Each of these advanced permissions grant a user or group the ability to perform a specific task on the file or folder. Here is an explanation of each permission.

- **Traverse Folder**

Traverse Folder allows moving through folders to reach other files or folders, even if the user has no permissions for those folders (applies only to folders). Setting the Traverse Folder permission on a folder does not automatically set the Execute File permission on all files within that folder.

- **Execute File**

Execute File allows running program files (applies to files only). Setting the Traverse Folder permission on a folder does not automatically set the Execute File permission on all files within that folder.

- **List Folder**

List Folder allows viewing file names and subfolder names within the folder (applies to folders only).

- **Read Data**

Read Data allows viewing data in files (applies to files only).

- **Read Attributes**

Allows the attributes of a file or folder, such as read-only or hidden, to be viewed. Attributes are determined by NTFS and can be changed.

- **Read Extended Attributes**

Extended attributes are defined by programs, and can vary from program to program. This permission allows those extended attributes to be viewed.

- **Create Files**

Create Files allows the creation of files within the folder (applies to folders only).

- **Write Data**

Create Files allows the creation of files within the folder (applies to folders only).

- **Create Folders**

With Create Folders, the user can create folders within the folder (applies to folders only).

- **Append Data**

Append Data allows the user to make changes to the end of the file but not change, delete, or overwrite existing data (applies to files only).

- **Write Attributes**

The user can change the attributes of the file or folder, as defined by NTFS.

- **Write Extended Attributes**

The user can change the extended attributes, as defined by the program

- **Delete**

The user can delete the file or folder

- **Delete Subfolders and Files**

The user can delete the file or subfolder EVEN IF delete permission has not be granted on that specific file or folder.

- **Read Permissions**

The user can view the permissions (such as Full Control) on the file or folder

- **Change Permissions**

The user can change the permissions on the file or folder

- **Take Ownership**

The user can become Creator/Owner of the file or folder. The Creator/Owner of a file or folder can always change its permission, regardless of whether the "Change Permission" permission has been granted.

- **Synchronize**

This permission applies to only to multithreaded, multiprocessing programs, and not users. It is, however, part of the Full Control permission.

Therefore, what happens if you want a user, or group of users, to have Full Control on a folder, except for the permission to "Take Ownership"? That is where the "Advanced" permissions come in. If a user is allowed all advanced permissions, he or she has "Full Control".

However, as illustrated in Figure 7.8, these can be altered to deny any (or all) of the specified permissions. By denying "Take Ownership", the user can have full control of this particular folder, except that he or she cannot become Creator/Owner of the folder.

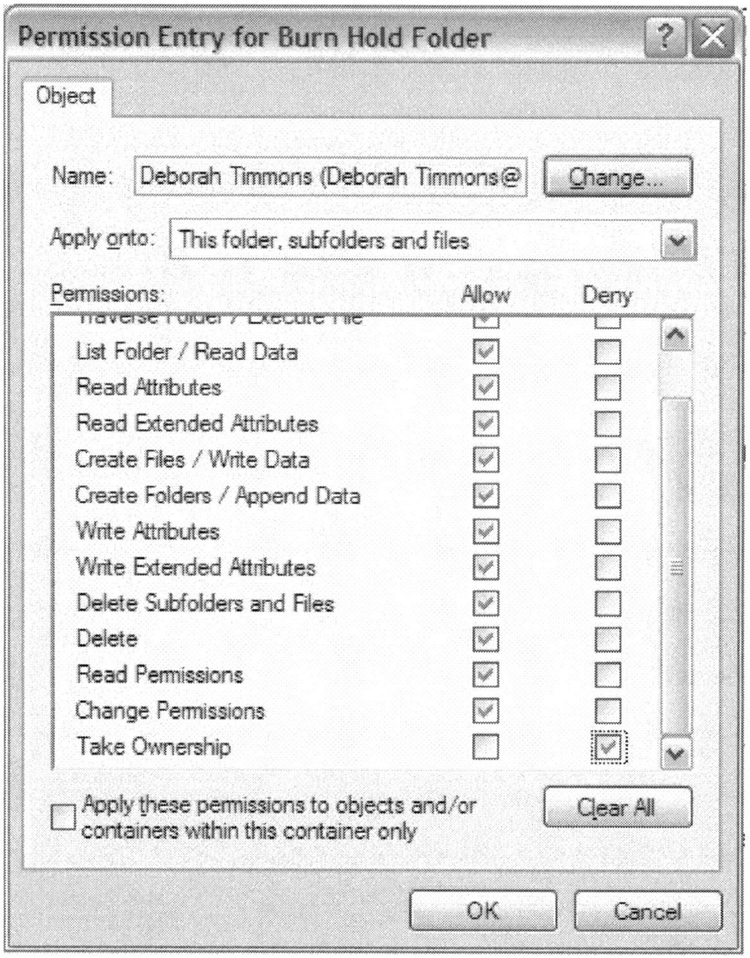

Figure 7-8: Altering Permissions

Determining a user's effective permissions

To determine a user's permissions to a specific file or folder, you add up all the allowed permissions for the username and for all groups in which the user is a member, and then subtract the permissions that have been explicitly denied for both the username and groups. If permission has not been specified for either the username or group, it will not be added to the *allowed* permissions list. If it has been allowed for one group, and not specified for another, and the user is a member of both groups, then the user will have that permission, as it has not been explicitly denied.

Allow, Deny, or Unset?

An **Allow** selection is a definite yes. It can be overturned by a **Deny** selection, which is a definite no. A permission that has not been specified just "goes along with the crowd". If another group allows a permission, then that's okay. If another group denies a permission, that's okay too. If a permission is not specified for a username, or for any groups in which that user is a member, then that permission will not be granted.

In Figure 7.9, we can see that the Everyone group has been allowed some permissions, and denied others. The allowed permissions include: Traverse Folder / Execute File, List Folder / Read Data, and Write Extended Attributes. The denied permissions include: Create Folders / Append Data, Write Attributes, Delete Subfolders and Files, and Take Ownership. The unselected permissions include: Read Attributes, Read Extended Attributes, Create Files / Write Data, Delete, Read Permissions, and Change Permissions.

So from this we can summarize that every user accessing this folder will have both *allow* and *deny* permissions set. If permissions are granted to a user (or to a group he is a member of) explicitly, the user will also have those permissions. It is just a matter of summarizing all the permissions together.

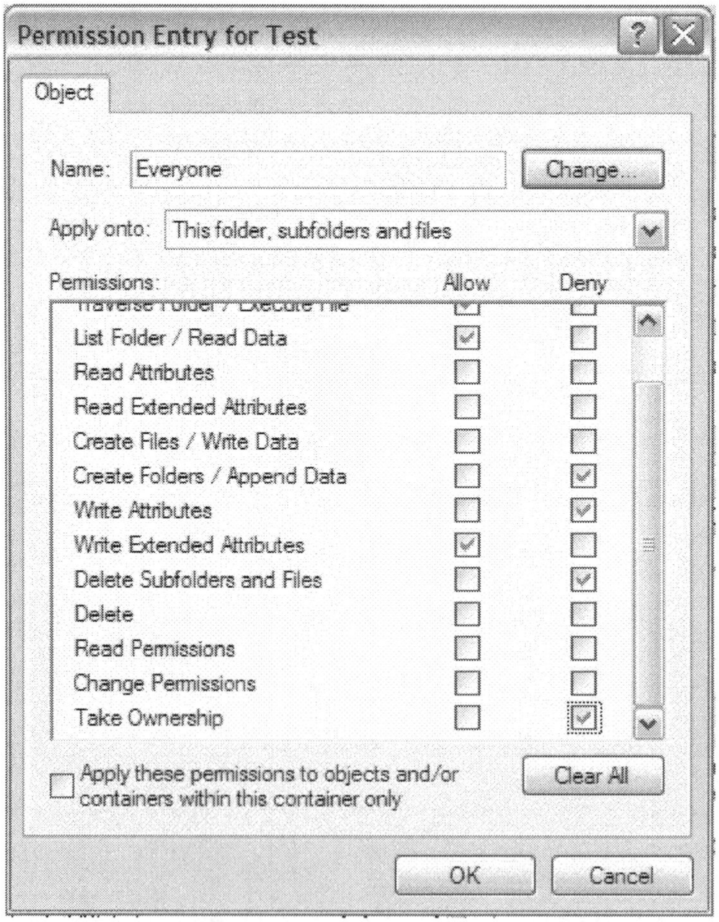

Figure 7-9: Everyone Permissions

Let's put this into action. We have a user, George, who is a member of two groups – the Sales group and the Marketing group. George, as an individual, has neither been allowed nor denied Read permission on the Information folder. The Sales Group has no specified Read permission, but the Marketing group does.

USER/GROUP	PERMISSIONS ON FOLDER
George	Not specified
Sales	Not specified
Marketing	Read (allow)

Table 7-5: Permissions Single Group

George, as a member of the Marketing group, has Read permission on the Information Folder.

Let's change the scenario a bit. George still has no specified permission on his individual user account. The Marketing group still has a specified Read permission on the folder. The Sales group, however, has had Read permission denied.

USER/GROUP	PERMISSIONS ON FOLDER
George	Not specified
Sales	Read (deny)
Marketing	Read (allow)

Table 7-6: Permissions Multiple Groups

George will NOT have Read permission to the folder. Although his user account did not specifically deny Read permission, and his membership in Marketing allowed it, the Sales group was denied Read permission, which removed it from George.

If George, Marketing and Sales all have the Read permission not specified, then the Read permission was never specifically allowed, so no Read permission will be granted.

Optimize access to files and folders

There is a rule when organizing files and folders so that they can be accessed easily – keep it simple. Give your files names that will be recognizable by users. Document1.doc is not going to be very helpful to other people who need to access your data. It won't even help you a week down the road, when you can't remember what it is! Organize your files by placing them in folders, and give the folders user-friendly names as well.

Make sure that the permissions you have given to the groups and users that will access your information work together. Deny access only when it is imperative that users or groups DO NOT have access to the information, such as financial data or human resource information.

Indexing Service

A great way to optimize access to files and folders is to use the Indexing Service to index your folders. This was a new feature in Windows 2000 Professional and has been extended to Windows XP. It works similar to the Office Fast Find service and the Index Server that came with the Windows NT 4.0 Option Pack. This feature will index the files on your volumes and network shares, and provide you with a quick retrieval of that file. You can perform searches against the index from the Search function, the Indexing Service query form, or from a Web browser.

The Indexing Service is available under the Computer Management console (Figure 7.10). This service, by default, is set to not start with Windows XP. You must start the service in order to use it.

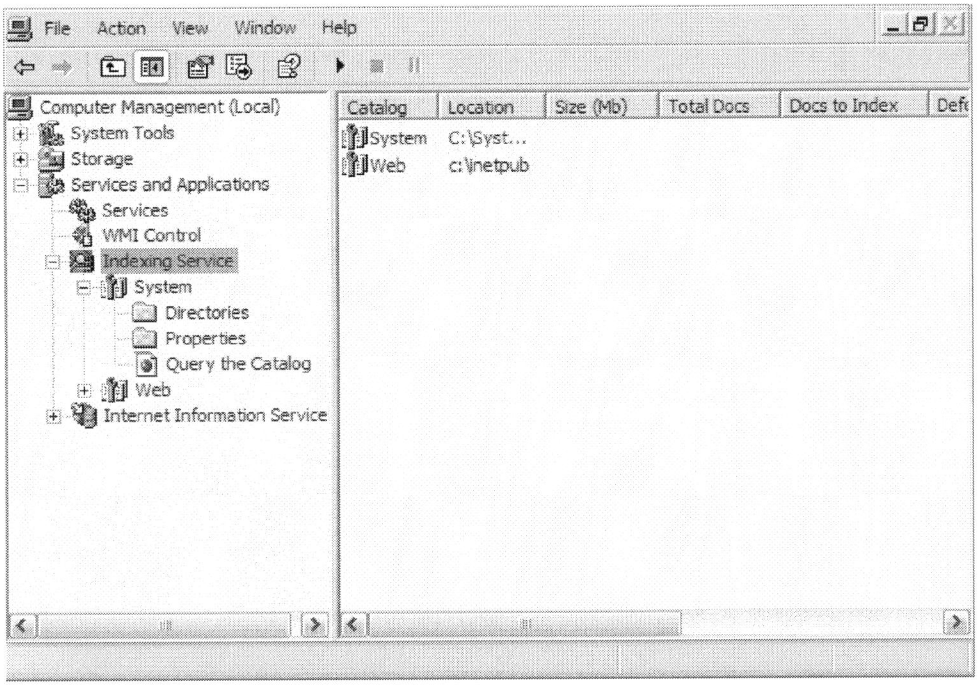

Figure 7-10: Indexing Service

Once the Indexing Service has started, it will populate its default catalog. The default catalog (System) includes the Documents and Settings directory and the boot partition, and does not include the Default User's Application Data, Local Settings, and Temporary Internet Files directories.

With the populated catalog, you can then perform a search on the catalog. This will allow you to locate any file that, for example, contains the words "Windows XP" (Figure 7.11).

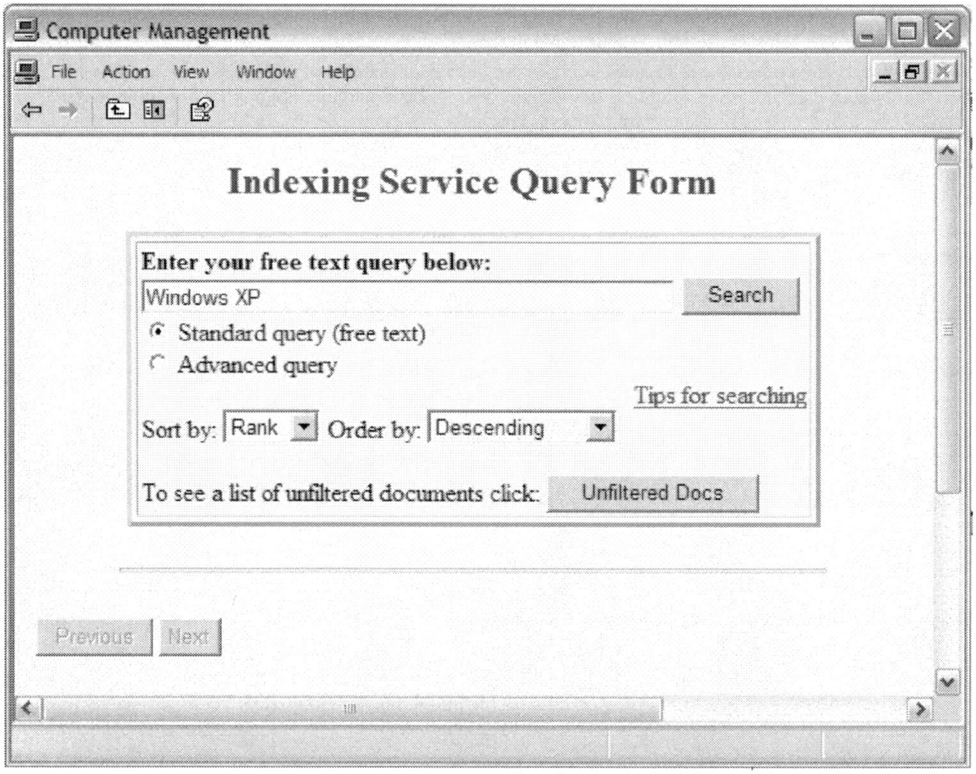

Figure 7-11: Indexing Query

The initial setup of the Indexing Service is not optimal, but functional. You can add folders to include or exclude in the catalog. This is done in three ways. The first method is to modify the catalog's directories (Figure 7.12).

Figure 7-12: Adding a Directory to the Index

The second is to modify the folder's advanced attributes to permit or deny the Indexing Service to index the folder (Figure 7.13).

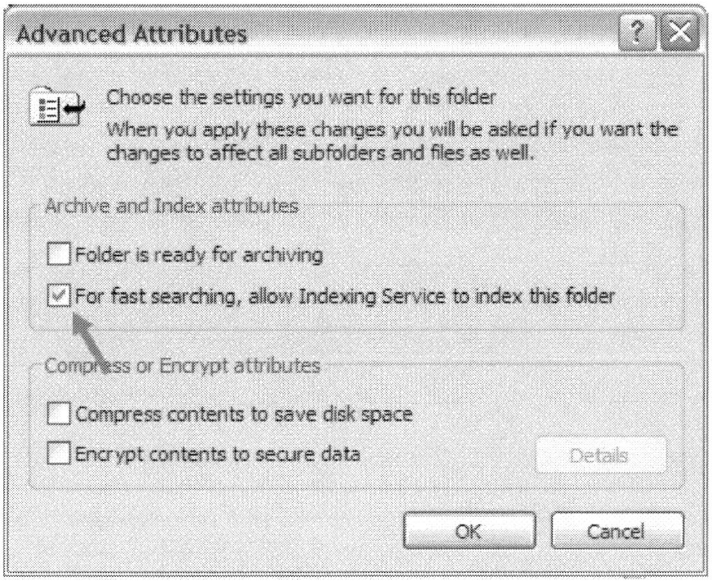

Figure 7-13: Modifying the folder attribute for the Indexing Service

The third is used for network share (Figure 7.14).

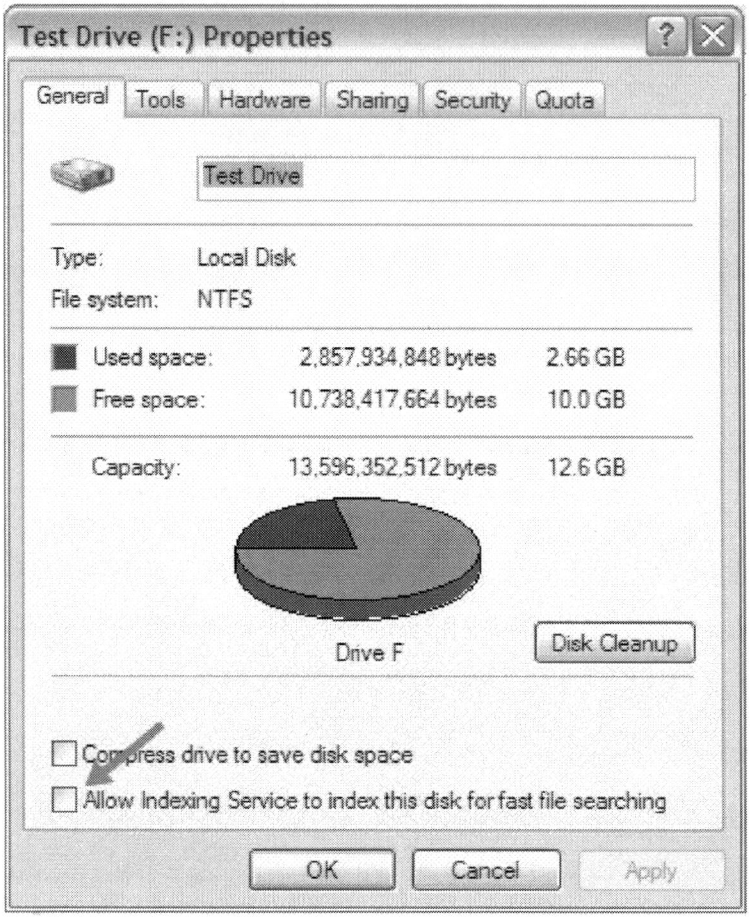

Figure 7-14: Network Share

Disk Quotas

Another new feature in Windows XP is disk quotas. Disk quotas are used to specify exactly how much disk space each user is allowed on an NTFS volume. They cannot be used on FAT or FAT32 volumes. You can create a specific quota that applies to all users on your network or you can create individual disk quotas on the user-by-user basis. The exception to this is the built in Administrator account, to which quotas cannot be applied.

There are some things of which you should be aware before you implement disk quotas. As previously mentioned, disk quotas are available only on NTFS volumes. Quotas are applied on a volume basis. Even if you have three volumes on one physical hard drive, the quotas must be set up on each volume individually. The usage of disk space is calculated on file and folder ownership and actual file size. When a user takes ownership of a folder, the uncompressed size of that folder is added to the total disk usage for that individual, even if the folder is compressed. As well, if the user decides to install an application on a volume were quotas have been implemented, the application will calculate the available free space based on the quota for that user rather than the actual free space available on that drive.

Disk quotas must be configured on a per volume basis. To enable the quota, access the Quota tab on the volume's property page (Figure 7.14). On this tab, you can then specify the parameters to be used for that volume. Here is the list of each of these options:

- **Enable quota management**

When this option is selected, quota management is enabled for about NTFS volume.

- **Deny disk space to users exceeding quota limit**

When this option is selected, users will receive an "out of disk space" error when they exceed their quota.

- **Do not limited disk usage / limit disk space**

Either disk space will not be limited or disk space will be limited to the amount specified in the "limit disk space to" text box. This amount can be specified in kilobytes, megabytes, gigabytes, terabytes, petabytes, and exabytes.

- **Set warning level to**

Users will receive a warning when they approach their limit of disk space.

- **Select the quota logging options for this volume**

You can choose to log events related to disk quotas, specifically, logging when user exceeds their quota limited, or warning level.

By following what is set in (Figure 7.15), a quota of 500 KB will apply to all new users for the volume F. They will be warned at 400 KB that they are approaching their quota limit. Unfortunately, these settings may not be optimal for some users, such as graphic artists who could fill that space in seconds.

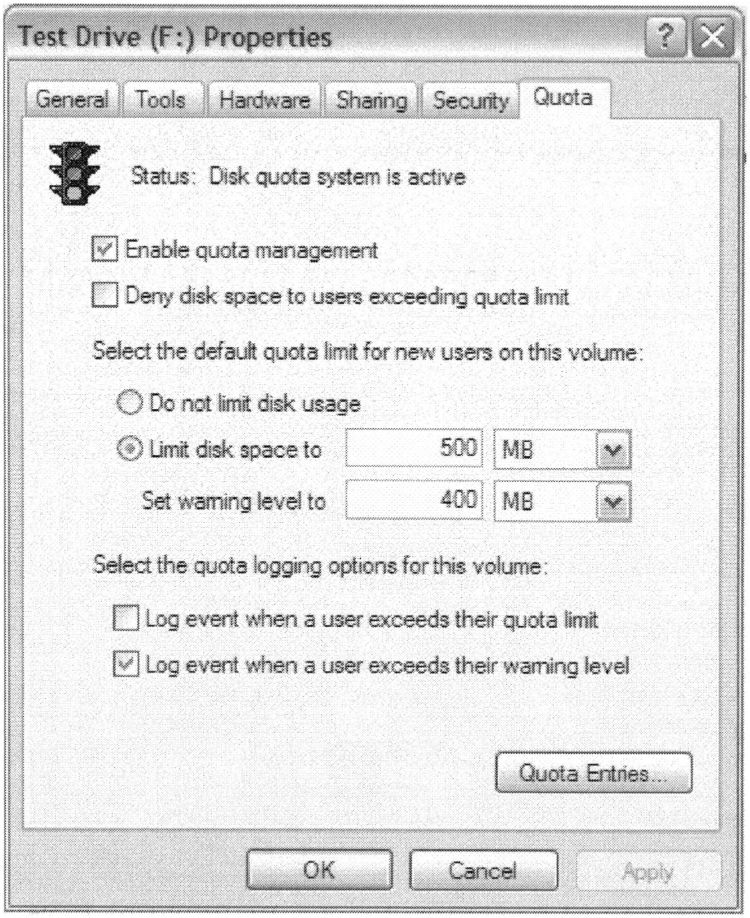

Figure 7-15: Quota Management

> **NOTE:** If you are going to restrict disk usage and deny space to users exceeding their limit, it is highly recommended that you set a warning level lower than the disk limit.

You can view current entries and grant users and groups different quota levels through the Quota Entries button (Figure 7.16).

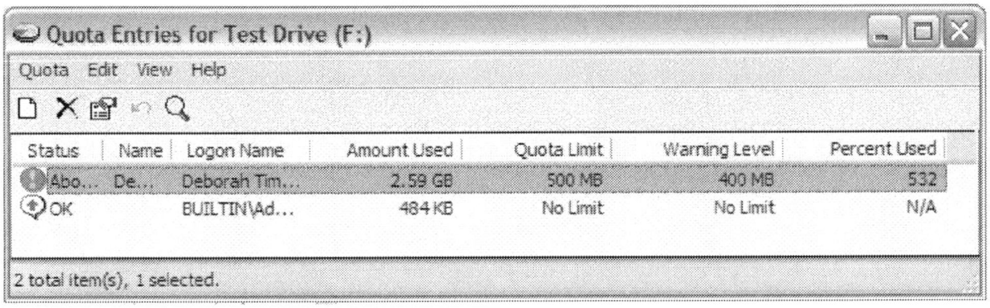

Figure 7-16: Quota Entries

Pop Quiz 7.1

Pop Quiz 7.1 *Questions*

1). What command line utility do you use to compress files or folders on an NTFS partition?

2). What command line utility can you use on a FAT partition to compress files?

3). When you copy a file from a compressed folder to an uncompressed folder within the same NTFS partition, what happens with the file's compression attributes?

4). How can you determine a user's effective permissions to a specific file or folder?

5). What is the default setting for the Indexing Service under Windows XP Professional?

Pop Quiz 7.1 *Answers*

1). The compression utility, done through Windows Explorer or through the command line utility "compact.exe", is an extension of the NTFS system, and as such can only be used on NTFS partitions. This compression method is dynamic; once a file is compressed, it will automatically decompress for you to use the file, and then recompress when you are finished.

2). "Compress.exe", a command line utility, is used to create compressed copies of one or more files, in the same fashion WinZip does. In order to use a file on which you have used COMPRESS.EXE, you will need to use EXPAND.EXE, another command line utility available from the resource kit.

3). When you copy a file, you are actually creating a new file with the same data as the original. The compression attribute of the new file will be the same as the target folder. In the scenario mentioned above, the new file would be uncompressed.

4). To determine a user's permissions to a specific file or folder, you add up all the allowed permissions for the username and for all groups in which the user is a member, and then subtract the permissions that have been explicitly denied for both the username and groups.

5). The Indexing Service, available under the Computer Management console, by default is set to not start with Windows XP Professional. You must start the service in order to use it.

III Sharing Resources

In the olden days, the 1980s in PC years, computers were stand-alone. There was only one way to share information, and that was to copy it from one computer to floppy disk, and then copy the information from the floppy disk onto another computer. Keeping information synchronous on all computers was difficult.

Networking changed all of that. By being able to share the information stored on one computer, corruption of data was lessened and the information disseminated was uniform.

Creating Folders

Folders can be shared on any volume, whether they are partitioned as FAT, FAT32, or NTFS. It is quite simple to share a folder. In Windows Explorer, right click the folder you wish to share. From the shortcut menu, select **Sharing and Security…**. A dialog box will appear (Figure 7.17).

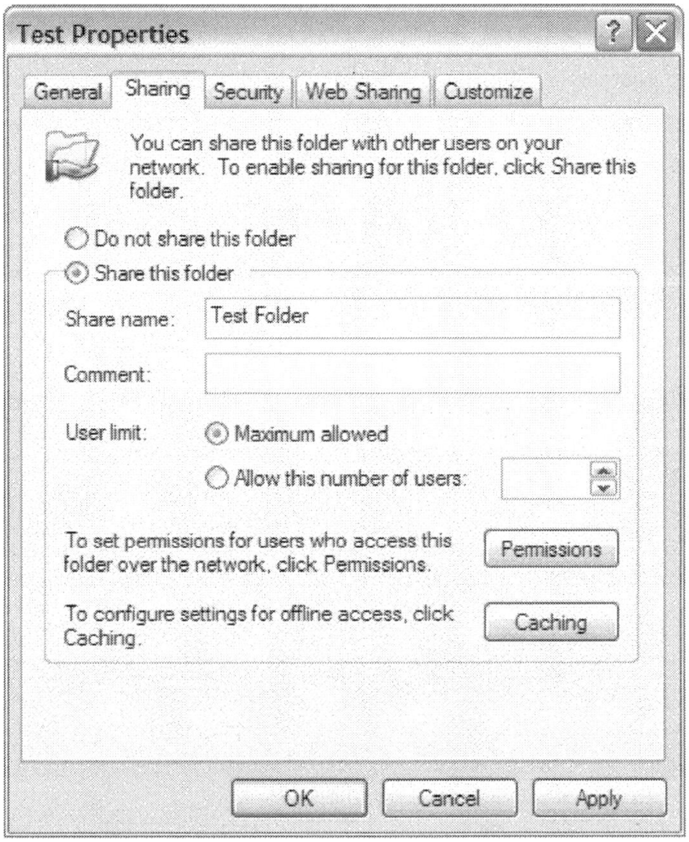

Figure 7-17: Sharing a folder

NOTE: If the volume is FAT or FAT32, the Security tab will not exist.

Select the radio button **Share this folder**. You will be prompted for a name for the share. Choose a name that is user-friendly, one that clearly identifies the contents. It is also considered good convention to keep the share name to eight characters or less, in case some of the systems that will be accessing your share cannot read long filenames. You can allow unlimited access to your shared folder, or you can limit the number of users who can access the folder at one time.

Once you have created the share and applied it, you can share the same folder again using a different share name. For example, you can share the folder in the English and French variations of the share name.

With Windows XP, there is another way to create shares, within the Computer Management console. Using Shared Folders, you can view the connections and resource usage for the local machine as well as remote resources (Figure 7.18). Shared Folders replaces the resource-related components found in Server in Control Panel in Windows NT 4.0.

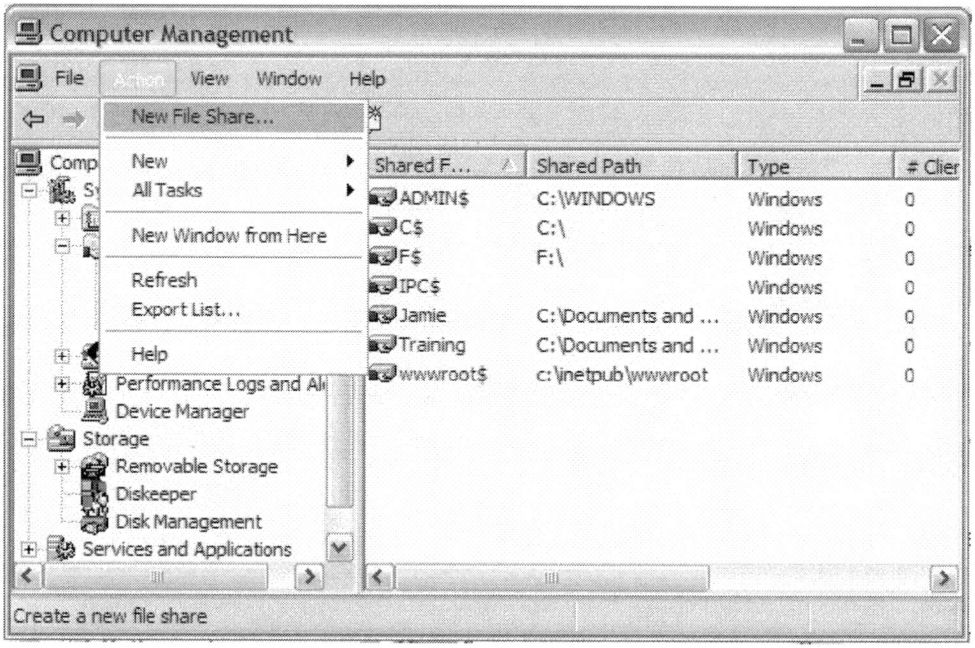

Figure 7-18: Creating a New Share using Computer Management Console

Control access with permissions

By default, the Everyone group has full control on a shared folder. What that means is that any authenticated user can read, modify, delete, or change permissions on a folder accessed remotely from the network. By controlling access through permissions, you can restrict who can read or change the documents you share.

On a FAT or FAT32 volume, share security is the only security available for the folder. You cannot put local security, that is, restrictions on who can access information when they are seated at your computer, on a FAT volume.

There are three levels of security on a shared folder – Read, Change, and Full Control. All files in the folder have the same permission as the parent folder – you cannot secure a share down to the file level. Any subfolders or files beneath the root share will all hold the same permissions. Read permission allows a user to view the contents of the folder and to read any document in the folder, as well as execute a program (RX). Change permission has the full Read permission with the additional permission to write to the file/folder or delete the folder or any file in the folder (RWXD). Full control allows the user Read, Write, Execute and Delete permissions, as well as the ability to change the permission on the folder.

By default, when you share a folder, the permissions are such the Everyone group has read access to the share (Figure 7.19).

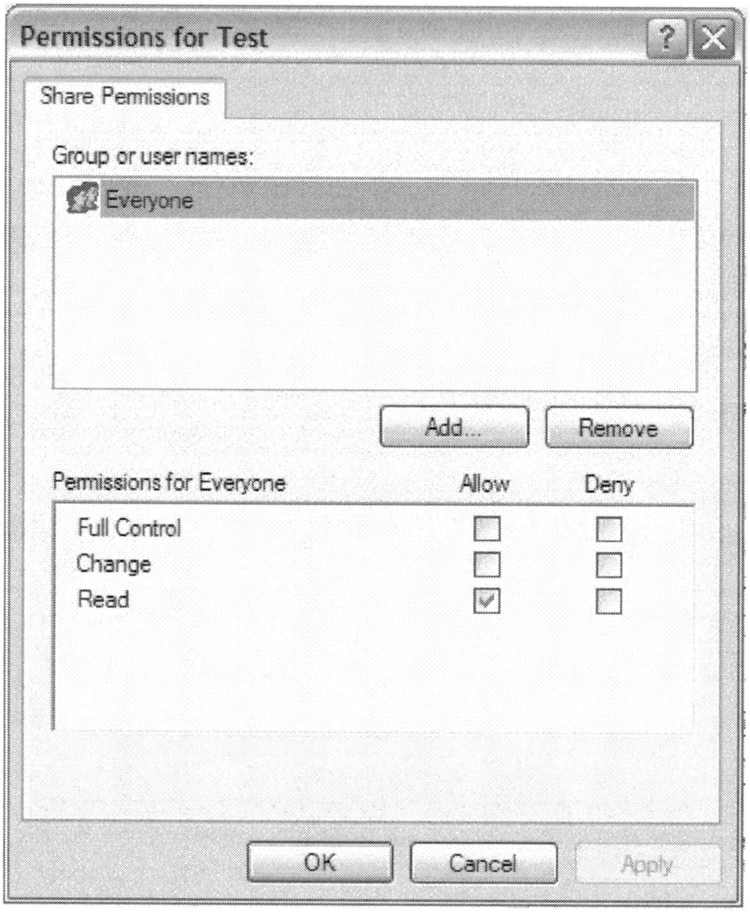

Figure 7-19: Share Permissions

Allowing or denying these three permissions can implement security. As with NTFS, you can also not specify an "allow" or "deny" for any permission. An individual's permission is calculated in the same fashion as well. All specified allow permissions for the username and groups in which the user is a member of are totaled, and then the deny permissions are removed. If a user has Change permission by virtue of membership in one group, but has Read permission denied by membership in another group, this user is going to be in the interesting position of being able to write to a folder and delete items in a folder, but be unable to read the contents of the folder or execute a program. That's a very good reason why you should plan carefully before implementing permissions.

Because NTFS permissions are also applicable on remote connection, that is, when accessing data stored on an NTFS volume through a shared folder, you may find yourself combining both types of permissions. Keep in mind how permissions are handled. All explicitly allowed permissions are tallied and then the permissions explicitly denied permissions are removed.

Combining the security of NTFS with the ability to share the data across the network gives you an ability to tightly control access to data.

Let's go back to George, who is a member of the Marketing and Sales group. We'll list his access permissions to the Information folder and calculate his effective permission.

USER/GROUP	NTFS PERMISSION	SHARE PERMISSION
George	Not specified	Not specified
Marketing Group	Read (allow) Write (allow)	Change (RWXD)
Sales Group	Modify	Change (RWXD)

Table 7-7: Effective Permission

Given this bit of information, can find that George has Change access through the share, and Modify access through the NTFS partition. With this, George can perform the same tasks both locally and remotely.

Let's change the permissions on the share.

USER/GROUP	NTFS PERMISSION	SHARE PERMISSION
George	Not specified	Not specified
Marketing Group	Read (allow) Write (allow)	Read (RX)
Sales Group	Modify	Read (RX)

Table 7-8: Share Permissions

Now, George's NTFS permissions have remained the same, granting him Modify access. However, the share permissions have changed, granting him only Read permission. With this setup, George would have Read permission over the network, and Modify access locally.

Connecting to Shared Resources

In the previous section, we discussed the ability to share information across the network. This section will show you the various methods on gaining access to those shared resources.

- **Map a Network Drive**

You can connect to a shared resource by mapping the network drive to a logical drive letter. The shared resource can then be accessed as if it were a local drive. Mapping a network drive can be done in Windows Explorer by locating the shared resource and right clicking it in the tree pane. A shortcut menu appears with the choice **Map Network Drive**. You can also map a network drive by right-clicking **My Network Places** and accessing a similar shortcut menu that allows network drive mapping.

- **My Network Places**

You can also access a shared resource by browsing through My Network Places. The advantage of doing this is when you wish to access a resource, but do not want to establish a mapping.

- **Start | Run**

The **Start | Run** command can be used to access shared resources. The syntax is: \\Computername\sharename (e.g. \\myComputer\testshare).

If you are having trouble finding the computer, you can replace the computer name with its IP address. The syntax is: \\IPAddress\Sharename (e.g. \\192.168.17.22\testshare).

- **NET USE**

The NET USE command utility dates back to the days of DOS. At the command prompt, type NET USE x: \\computername\sharename to connect to the resource (e.g.: NET USE G: **\\JOHNSCOMPUTER\JOHNSSHARE**).

IV Offline Folders

An exciting functionality has been carried over from Windows 2000, which you can use with Windows XP shared folders – offline caching. With the workforce being as mobile as it is these days, this innovation eliminates the need for duplicate and triplicate copies of documents.

Let's say that you have to do a presentation in Tokyo. You arrive at your hotel and realize that you left your hard copy on the airplane. You have brought your laptop from work, but the presentation was saved to a network drive. If you have set up automatic caching on the folder, you don't even have to be connected to the network! You would connect to the folder through Network Neighborhood, and the cached folder would be available for you.

Offline files and folders can also increase network performance even when the user is connected to the network, because a local copy can be accessed rather than using the original network copy.

Two computers, at minimum, must be used to configure offline files and folders – the computer acting as the file server and the computer acting as the client that will access offline data. The file server does not need to be running Windows 2000, but it does need to use SMB (server message blocks) as its file and print sharing protocols. All Microsoft operating system use SMB, but other systems, such as Novell, do not.

When you setup up the share on the server, there are three methods of caching you can use, depending on what type of information is to be stored in that folder. These choices are:

- **Automatic Caching for Documents**

This method is recommended for folders containing user documents. When a user opens a file, a copy is automatically downloaded. If an older copy exists, it is deleted and replaced with the updated file. The file will be made available when the person who connected to the share and opened the file is working offline, or if you are offline when the user wants to access the file again. When the user reconnects to the share online, the documents are synchronized.

- **Manual Caching for Documents**

In the instance, the user must manually specify the files or folders they wish to have available offline. This is done by right clicking on the file in the share folder, and choosing “Make Available Offline”. If a folder is chosen, the user will be presented with two options -- only the folder, or the folder and all its subfolders. Synchronization can be done manually as well. This is the default setting.

- **Automatic Caching for Programs**

This is recommended for folders with read-only data, or for applications that are run from the network. File sharing is not ensured.

To use a file or folder offline, you must be able to connect to the computer acting as the file server. In other words, the folder must be shared and you must have the appropriate permissions to access the file. You must configure your computer to use offline files through the **Tools** menu of Windows Explorer, under **Folder Options, Offline Files** tab (Figure 7.20).

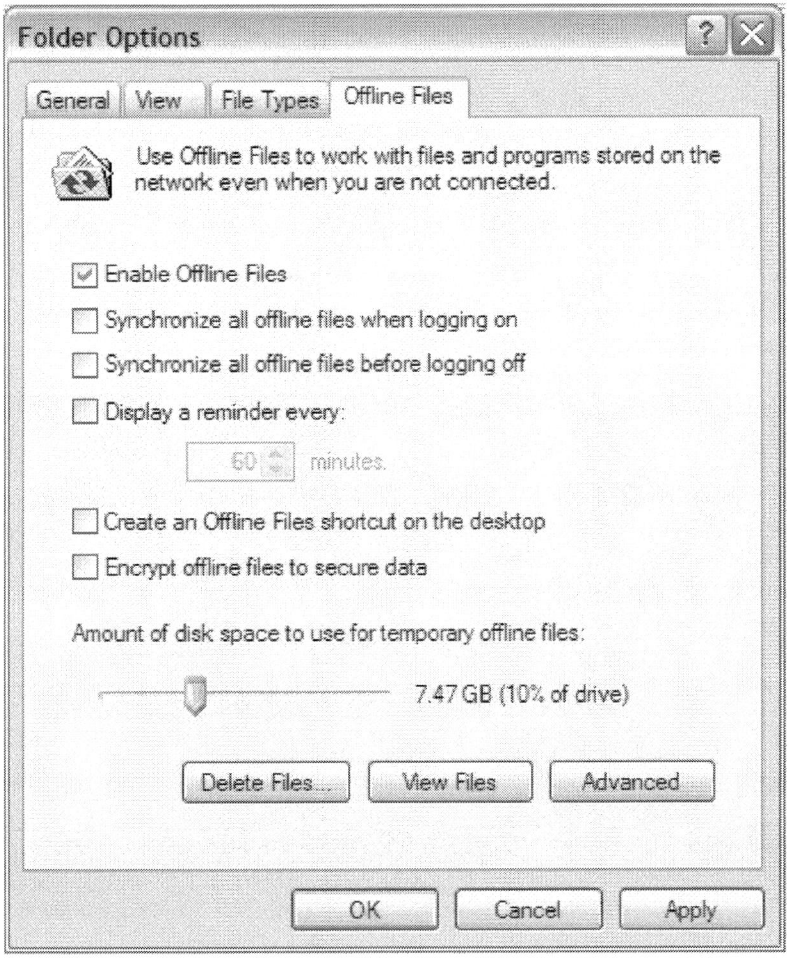

Figure 7-20: Enabling Offline Files

Leaving the default value of **Enable Offline Files** and adding **Synchronize all offline files before logging off** options will eliminate the need to manually synchronize the files and folders. Once you have completed this task, it is simple to set up the files you need to have available offline. Connect to the shares you wish to make available through **My Network Places**. When you right click on a particular share, a shortcut menu appears. Select **Make Available Offline**. The first time you do this, a wizard (Figure 7-21) will guide you through the steps of making particular setting choices.

Figure 7-21: Offline Files Wizard

After the first time, a synchronization box appears, and that is all there is to it! A small icon at the bottom of the shares (Figure 7.22) will indicate to you which files are set up for offline use.

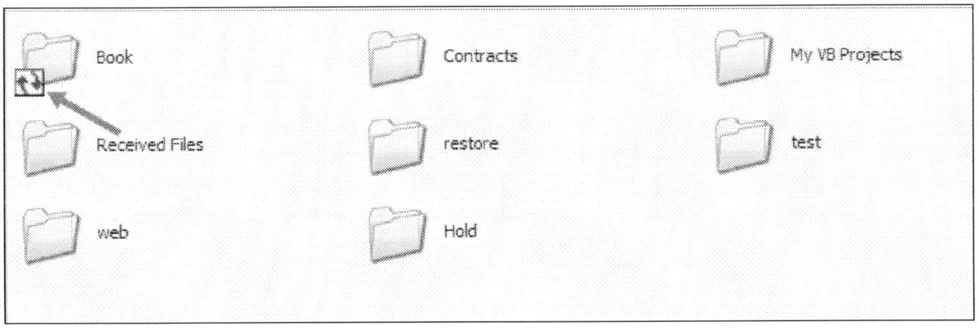

Figure 7-22: Offline Files Icon

V Local and Network Print Devices

Normally, when we're talking about printers, we mean the piece of hardware that produces printed copy. In the Windows world, the printer is a software interface between the physical printing device and the Windows XP operating system. Therefore, before you can access your physical print device, you must first configure a printer.

You can access your printer configuration by using Control Panel, or by going **Start | Printers and Faxes**. You must be a member of the Administrators or Power Users group to create a printer in Windows XP.

Connect to a local print device

When you run the Add Printer Wizard (Figure 7.22), and create the printer, the computer on which the printer has been created becomes the print server for that print device. If the printer is going to be shared on the network, make sure that the computer has enough processing power to handle the printing requests and enough free disk space to queue the print jobs.

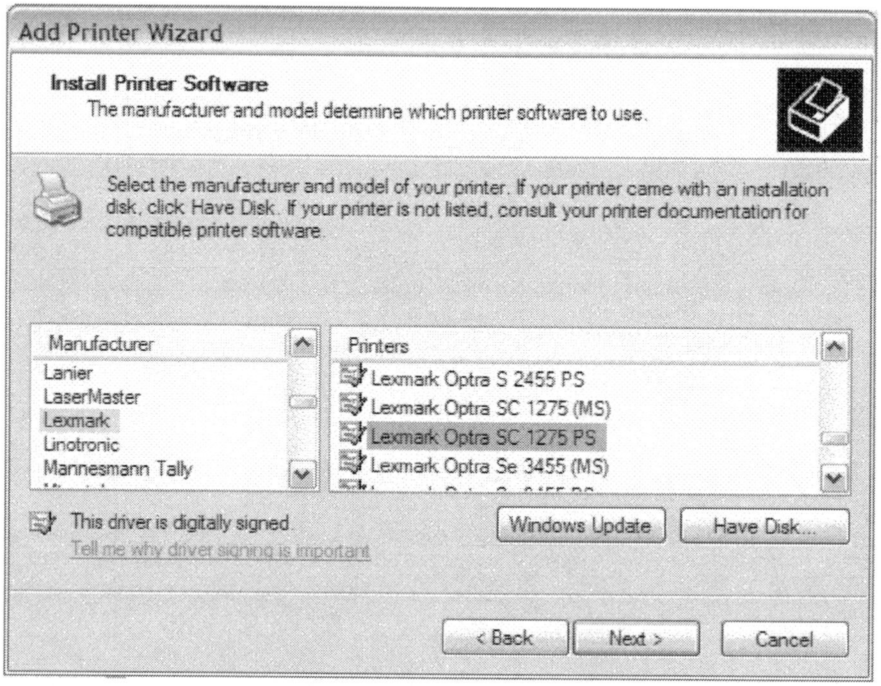

Figure 7-23: Add Printer Wizard

In order to use the printer, all clients will have to have the appropriate driver installed on their system. Most Microsoft client operating systems, including Windows 9x, Windows ME, Windows NT 3.51 and 4.0, as well as Windows 2000 and XP, will automatically download the driver from the print server the first time the client connects to the printer. If the driver is updated on the server, it will also be automatically updated on Windows NT, 2000 and XP clients the next time it connects to the print server. One word of caution – Windows 95 and 98 clients will download the driver the first time they connect to the print server. If you update the driver on the print server, you will have to manually install the updated drivers on the clients.

Other operating systems may require a specific protocol or service to be running on the print server in order to use the shared printer.

Manage printers and print jobs

You manage the printer properties by right clicking on the printer and selecting Properties. The Properties' dialog box has a number of different tabs.

Let's look at some of them. The General Tab (Figure 7.24) has the basic information and features of the installed printer, including its model name, the optional location and comment provided at the time of installation, and the features available with the printer.

Figure 7-24: Printer Properties General Tab

It also allows you to configure printing preferences, such as the layout of the paper, the page order, and the paper source. You can also print a test page from the General tab of Properties.

Printing a test page is frequently used for troubleshooting. You may choose to print a test page when you have installed an updated driver for your printer and want to verify that it is working. If a Windows XP driver is not available for the printer, and you wish to try a compatible print driver, you may wish to test the driver by printing a test page.

The Sharing tab (Figure 7.25) in Properties allows you to start or stop sharing the printer with the network. It provides a checkbox if you wish to have the printer listed in the network's Active Directory. The Additional Drivers button allows you to add drivers onto the print server for older versions of NT (3.1, 3.51 and 4.0), and for those versions of NT that ran on a MIPS or Alpha processor.

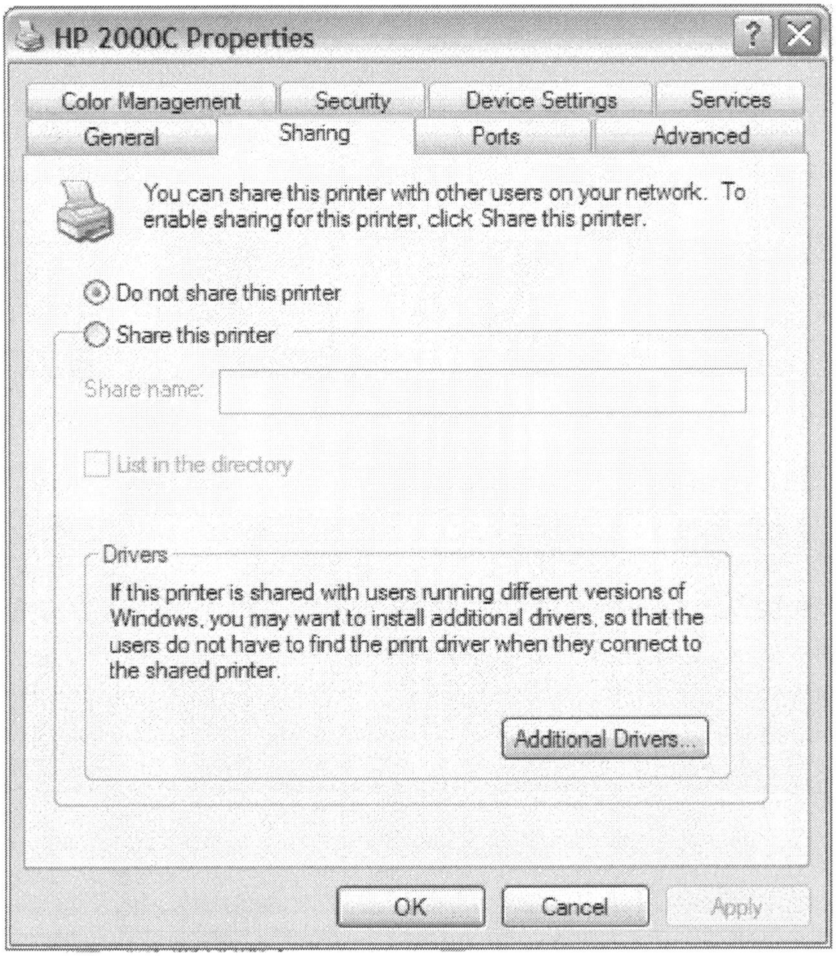

Figure 7-25: Printer Properties Sharing Tab

Windows XP supports both physical printing ports (LPT and COM) as well as logical (TCP/IP) ports. A physical (local) port is used when the print device is connected physically to the computer. A logical port is used when the print device has its own network card and IP address, and the computer will be acting as the print server for the network enabled print device.

The Ports tab (Figure 7.26) allows you to add, configure, and delete ports for the printer. It also allows you to set up printer pooling. Printer pooling is when multiple print devices are acting as one printer. The jobs sent to the printer are shared among the print devices. It should go without saying that if you create a printer pool with multiple print devices, the print devices should be located in the same physical workspace. Print devices in a printer pool MUST use the same print driver.

Figure 7-26: Printer Properties Ports Tab

If your printer device fails, the Ports tab enables you to redirect scheduled print jobs to another print device, provided that print device can use the same driver as the failed print device. To redirect a print job, click the Add Port button, select New Port, and choose New Port time. You should use the UNC naming convention to name the printer, that is, \\servername\sharename, where servername is the name of the computer acting as the print server for the new print device and sharename is the name given to the shared printer.

There are a number of options available under the Advanced Properties tab (Figure 7.27). The first item on the dialog box allows you to schedule times when the printer is available. There can be a number of reasons why you might choose to do this.

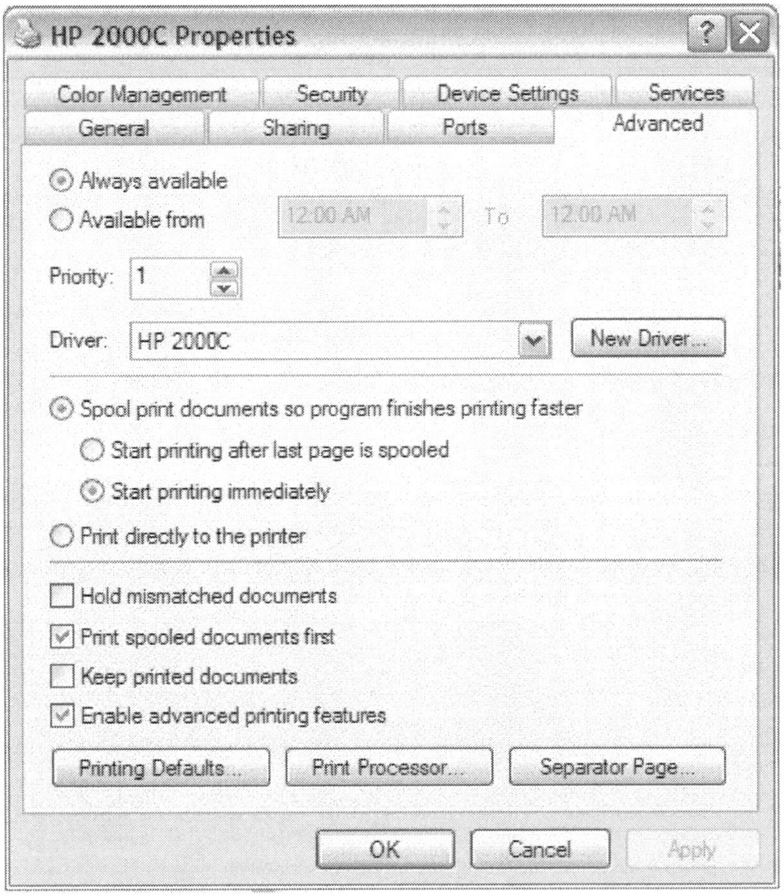

Figure 7-27: Printer Properties Advanced Tab

Let's say that the print device is in a secure area that is locked at 6:00 p.m. If a user is working late, he or she wouldn't be too happy if they printed out an important job and then discovered that they can't get to it. By scheduling the printer to not be available after 6:00 p.m., this situation can be avoided.

Keep in mind, though, that a printer is NOT a print device. You can create two printers for one physical print device. You could name one "Daytime Printer" and have it scheduled from 7:00 a.m. to 6:00 p.m. You could then create a second printer "Overnight Printer" and have it scheduled from 6:00 p.m. to 7:00 a.m. Large jobs, or jobs that are heavy in graphics that might take a long time to print, can be sent to the "Overnight" printer. Both printers work on the same print device. By default, when a printer is created, it is always available.

The next item on the Advanced Properties dialog box is Priority. This is used to ensure that urgent print jobs are produced before less urgent ones. The lowest priority is "1" and the highest priority is "99". You would create two printers for the same print device, and give each a different priority. Make sure that the share names reflect the priority of the printer. Jobs sent to the printer with the higher priority will print first on the print device.

Spooling is the next selection on the Advanced tab. You can choose to have jobs spooled or print directly to the printer. If you choose not to have the job spooled, the application doing the printing will not be free until the job is completed. Printing directly to the printer can be helpful in troubleshooting printer problems. If you can print directly to the printer, but printing fails when you try to print through the spooler, you know that the problem lies with the spooler, not the print device.

Spooling, the normal choice in a multi-user environment, allows jobs to be queued for the printer. The spooler acts as traffic lights – all the jobs do not try to print at the same time.

There are four print options available:

- **Hold Mismatched Documents**

Used when there are multiple forms associated with the printer. If, for example, you have one paper type, and need to print on both plain paper and a sales form, enabling the "Hold Mismatched Documents" feature will allow all jobs that need to be printed on the special form to be printed first, and then all the documents that need plain paper. By default, this feature is disabled.

- **Print Spooled Documents Firs/Start Printing Immediately**

A set of radio buttons, the first of which instructs the spooler to print jobs that have completed spooling before printer larger jobs that are still spooling, even if the larger job has a high priority. This option is enabled, by default, because it increases printer efficiency. If Start Printing Immediately is selected, the first job in the queue is printed, whether or not it has completed spooling. A long document will need to complete spooling and printing before a second, shorter document will begin to print.

- **Keep Printed Documents**

By default, this option is disabled, because it takes up a lot of hard disk space on the print server. When selected, jobs are kept in the spooler even after printing is completed.

- **Enable Advanced Printing Features**

Enabled by default, this option specifies that features such as Page Order and Pages Per Sheet, which are supported by your printer, can be used. If problems occur with special features, this option can be disabled.

At the bottom of the dialog box are three buttons – Printing Defaults, Print Processor, and Separator Pages. Printing Defaults opens the Print Preferences dialog box, the same one as on the General tab. The Print Processor tab is used when Windows XP needs to do additional processing to print jobs. Unless specified otherwise by the print device manufacturer, it is best to leave this at the default setting.

Separator pages are used to identify the owner of the print job. To save paper, this is normally disabled; however, when a large number of users share one printer, it can be handy. Windows XP comes with four separator page files.

SEPARATOR PAGE	DESCRIPTION
PCL.SEP	Used with HP Printers that have dual printer language capabilities, it sends a separator page when the printer has switched from PostScript to PCL.
PSCRIPT.SEP	Used to switch the print server to PostScript printing mode (does not send a separator page)
SYSPRINT.SEP	Used by PostScript printers to send a separator page
SYSPRINTJ.SEP	Used by PostScript printers to send a separator page, but also has support for Japanese characters.

Table 7-9: Separator Page

Another tab on the Properties dialog box is Color Management (Figure 7.28).

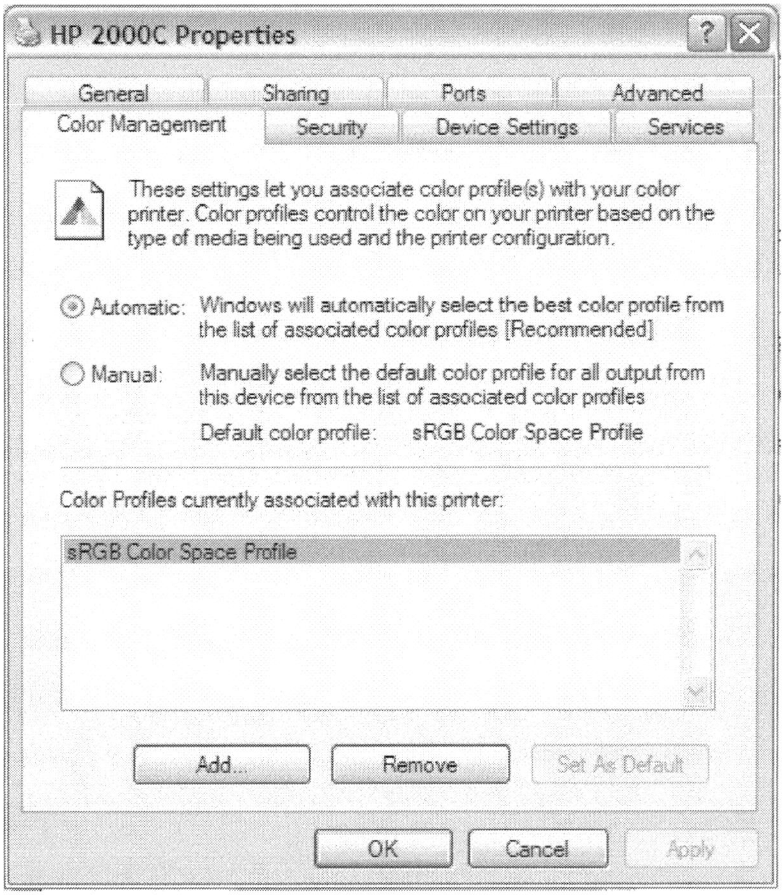

Figure 7-28: Printer Properties Color Management Tab

This tab with appear only when a color print device has been installed. The Color Management tab allows you to assign a color profile to the printer depending on what medium is being used and how the printer is configured. You can select **Automatic**, which allows Windows XP to select the color profile from the associated list. This option is selected by default. You can also choose to select **Manual**, which allows you to select which color profile will be used by default. You can also add and remove color profiles.

If you have permission to modify printer access and permissions, the security tab will appear (Figure 7-29). These permissions are covered in detail in the next section. For now, let's just take a look at the tab.

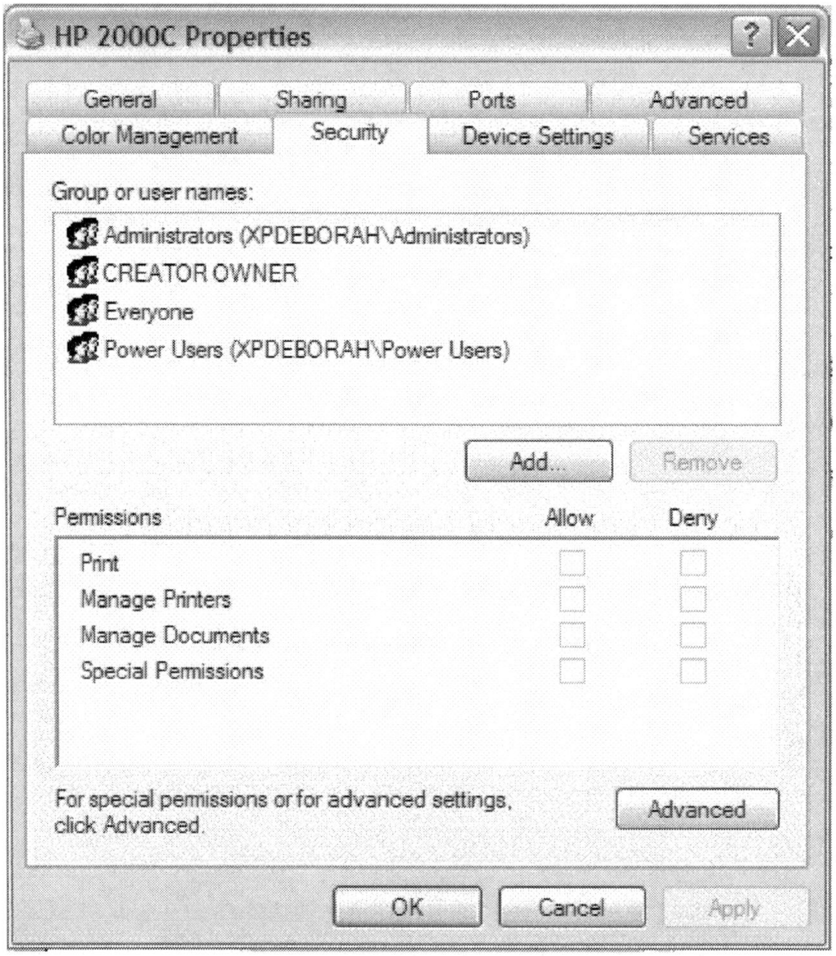

Figure 7-29: Printer Properties Security Tab

Another tab on the Properties dialog box is the Device Settings tab (Figure 7.30). The properties that are displayed are dependent upon the printer and driver installed on the print server. This tab useful if, for example, you want to assign different forms to different trays.

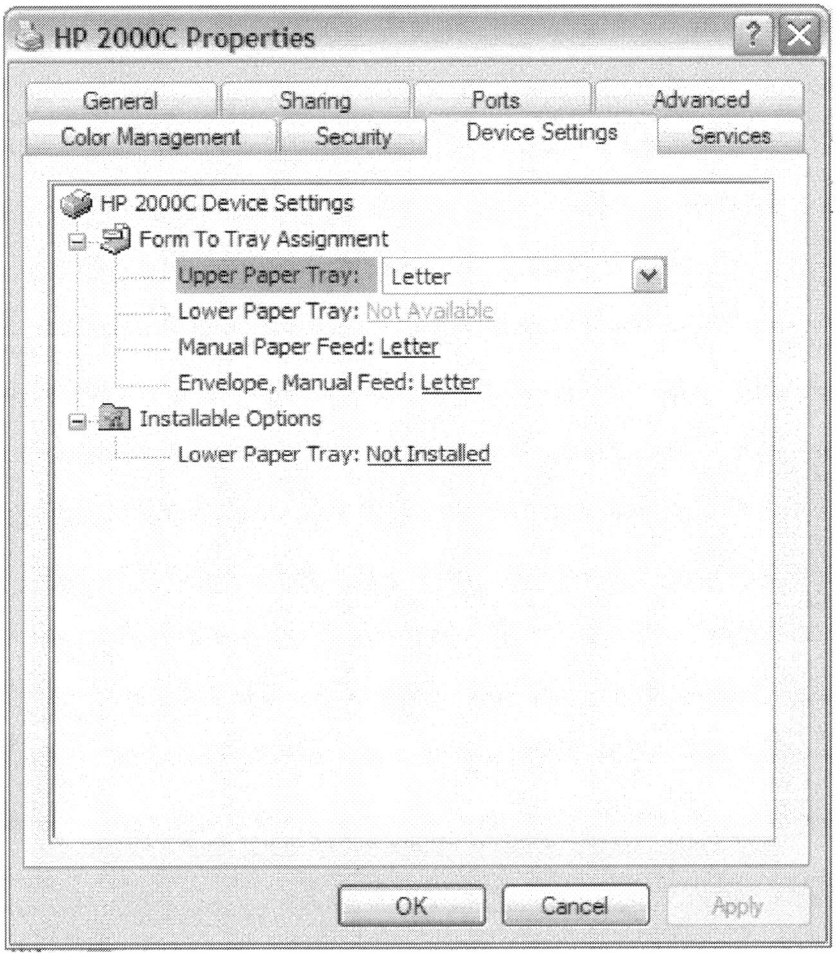

Figure 7-30: Printer Properties Device Settings Tab

Other tabs may appear with different printers. Our example printer shows a tab called Services, which allows you to do certain maintenance tasks, such as aligning or cleaning the print cartridges, or printing an ink-level page.

Other printers may have an "About" tab.

Control access with permissions

Assigning permissions to users and groups can control access to printers. Access can mean the ability to use the print device, to delete jobs, change permissions, pause, or restart the printer. As with shared folders, shared printers have different levels of access. The three levels of basic printer permissions are:

- Print

Print permission allows the user, or group, to connect to the printer and to send print jobs to the print device. A user with print permission can pause and restart his or her own print job, or delete that job from the queue. The user cannot perform any action on any other print job.

- Manage Printers

Manage Printers permission is a permission you granted to a user or group that needs to have administrative control of the printer. A user with his permission can pause and restart the printer and the spooler, change spooler settings, share the printer, as well as change printer permissions and manage properties.

- Manage Documents

Manage Documents permission is granted to user group to troubleshoot the day-to-day problems that can occur with printers. A user with this permission can pause, restart, and delete queued documents; but cannot control the printer status.

There is now a new permission, **Special Permissions** (Figure 7.31). This allows:

Read Permissions

The individual can see what permissions are effective, but cannot make changes to them.

Change Permissions

The individual can alter permissions.

Take Ownership

The individual can become the Creator/Owner.

It should be noted that permission can be changed for that printer only, the documents only, or both the printer and the documents.

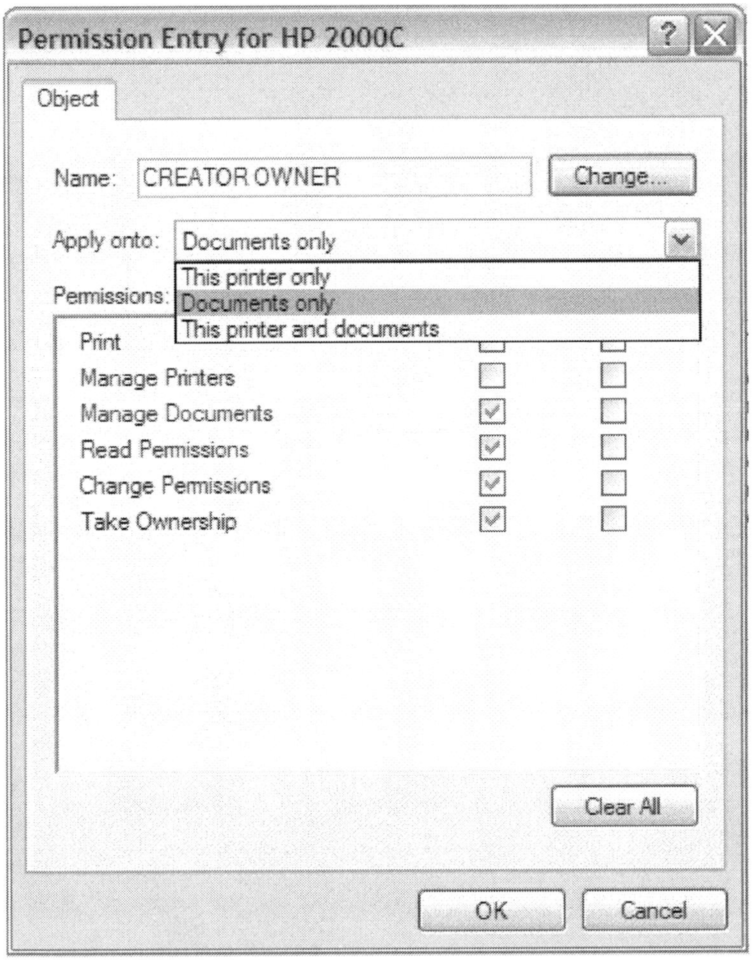

Figure 7-31: Editing Special Permissions

There are also Advanced Security Settings as shown in (Figure 7-32). This dialog box allows the management of permissions, the management of auditing, changing the Creator/Owner, and managing the permissions for that printer.

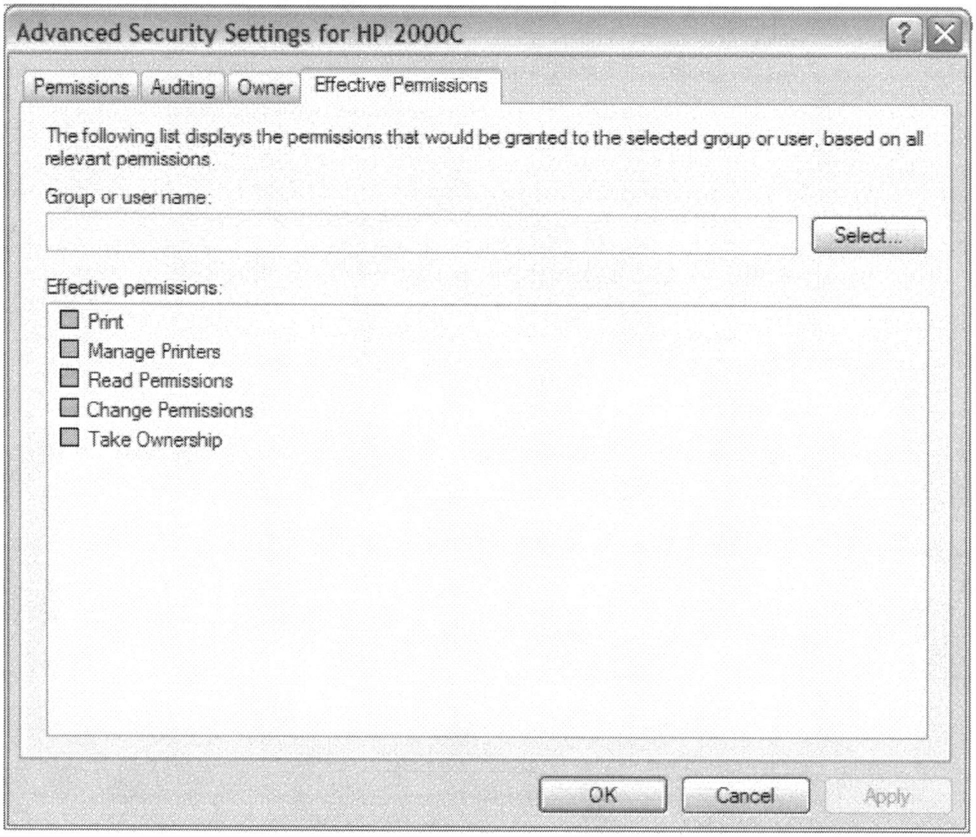

Figure 7-32: Advanced Security Settings

Printers and documents are managed from the Printers folder. The printer administrator (the user with Manage Printers permission) right clicks the printer to be managed. A shortcut menu appears with the following management choices on a local printer:

- Open
- Set as Default Printer
- Printing Preferences…
- Pause Printing
- Sharing
- Use Printer Offline
- Create Shortcut
- Delete
- Rename (Printer)
- Properties

Managing documents is done from within the print queue. Double-click the printer that contains the documents that need to be managed. By choosing Document from the menu bar, the following options are available:

- Pause
- Resume
- Restart
- Cancel
- Properties

Back on (Figure 7.28) it shows the Security tab for the printer. As with share permissions, printer permissions can be explicitly allowed, denied, or not specified. The effective permission for any user account is determined in the same fashion as share permissions.

Connect to an Internet printer

Internet printing was a feature first introduced in Windows 2000. Using Internet Print Protocol (IPP), a user can print directly to a URL.

IIS must be running for Windows XP to process print jobs that use URLs. While Internet Explorer 5 supports CHAP and Kerberos version 5, not all browsers support high levels of authentication. If all browsers are to be supported, basic authentication must be used.

To add an Internet printer, you will still use the Add Printers Wizard. When you reach the "Locate Your Printer" screen, you will choose "Connect to the printer on the Internet or on your intranet" and supply the URL of the printer (Figure 7.33). The syntax for this URL is http://computername/printers/sharename/.printer

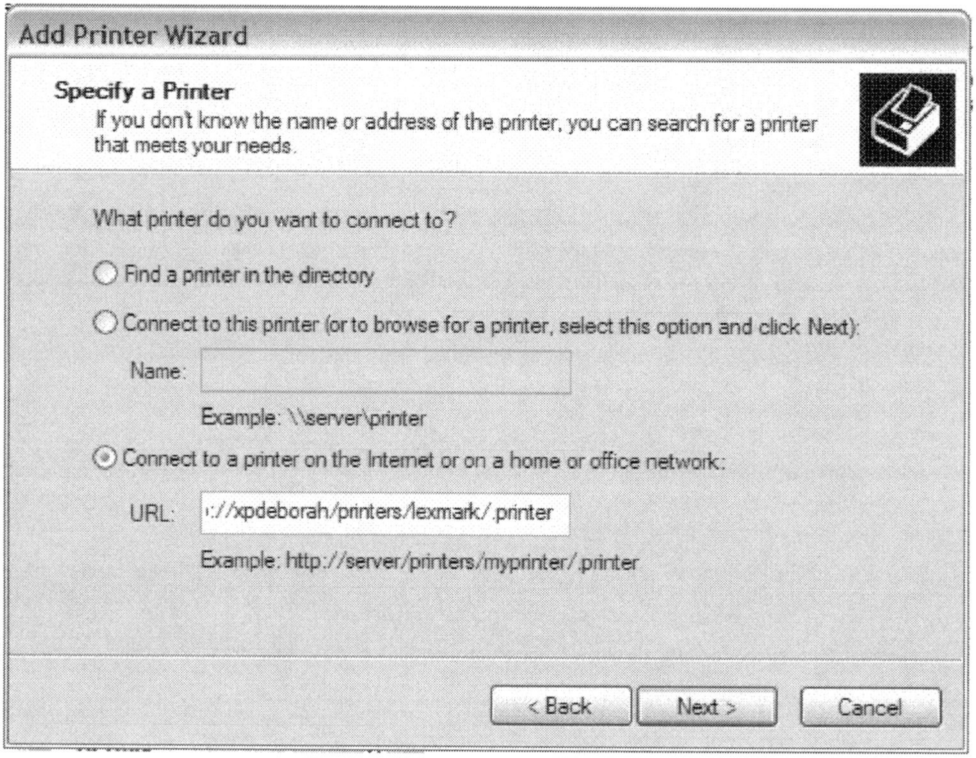

Figure 7-33: Setting up an Internet Printer

You must use Internet Explorer 4, or equivalent, to print using a browser. The browser must support frames. In the address bar, enter http://printerserver/printers, and then select the link to the printer to which you wish to connect. If the authentication has been set higher than basic, you may need to enter your username and password. Under Printer Actions, click **Connect**.

Pop Quiz 7.2

Pop Quiz 7.2 *Questions*

1). What four ways can you connect to a shared resource?

2). What is the minimum number of computers that must be used in order to configure offline files and folders?

3). When assigning a priority to a printer, what is the highest priority assignment that can be given?

4). What service must be running for Windows XP Professional to use an Internet printer?

5). What is the correct syntax for a URL of an Internet printer?

Pop Quiz 7.2 *Answers*

1). The four methods used to connect to a shared resource under Windows XP Professional are:

A. Map Network Drive

B. My Network Places

C. Start Run

D. Net use

2). Two computers, at minimum, must be used to configure offline files and folders – the computer acting as the file server and the computer acting as the client that will access offline data. The file server does not need to be running Windows XP, but it does need to use SMB (server message blocks) as its file and print sharing protocols. All Microsoft operating system use SMB, but other systems, such as Novell, do not.

3). The lowest priority for a printer is "1" and the highest priority is "99".

4). IIS must be running for Windows XP Professional to process print jobs that use Internet printing.

5). The correct syntax for the URL syntax for this URL is HTTP:**//COMPUTERNAME/PRINTERS/SHARENAME/ .PRINTER.** Do NOT forget the "." before the printer name.

VI Manage and troubleshoot Web server resources

Internet Information Services 5.1 has replaced Peer Web Services/Personal Web Server (PWS) in Windows XP. IIS 5.0 is not installed on Professional by default. You can install it, or add additional components, by using the Add/Remove Programs application in Control Panel. You must have TCP/IP installed in order to run IIS.

> **NOTE:** If you upgraded to Windows XP, IIS 5.0 will be installed by default if PWS was installed on your previous version of Windows.

The version of IIS that comes with Windows XP carries most of the same functionality as the version that comes with Windows 2000 Server; however, it is not optimized to be a full-scale web server. It has been designed to be used as a staging site, or for single site hosting. It has three services, FTP, WWW, and SMTP. It does not have an NNTP (Network News Transfer Protocol) service, however IIS 5.1 on Windows 2000 Server does. Each service is outlined below.

Service	Function
FTP	The File Transfer Protocol is used to transfer files between hosts.
WWW	The World Wide Web service is used to host a web site and transfer files using the HTTP protocol
SMTP	The Simple Mail Transfer Protocol is used to transfer mail between two SMTP mail systems.

Table 7-10: Transfer Protocol Service

You will need to use the Internet Services Manager (Figure 7.33). This is found under Accessories, as Internet Information Services. This tool allows full management of the FTP, Web, and SMTP sites. You can create virtual directories for your web site, stop and start services, assign network permissions, block IP addresses and a lot more.

IIS is a full product by itself, and it is not possible to cover all the functionality covered in the ISM in this chapter. It is important to be familiar with the ISM because it will be one of the most helpful tools for troubleshooting problems if they occur.

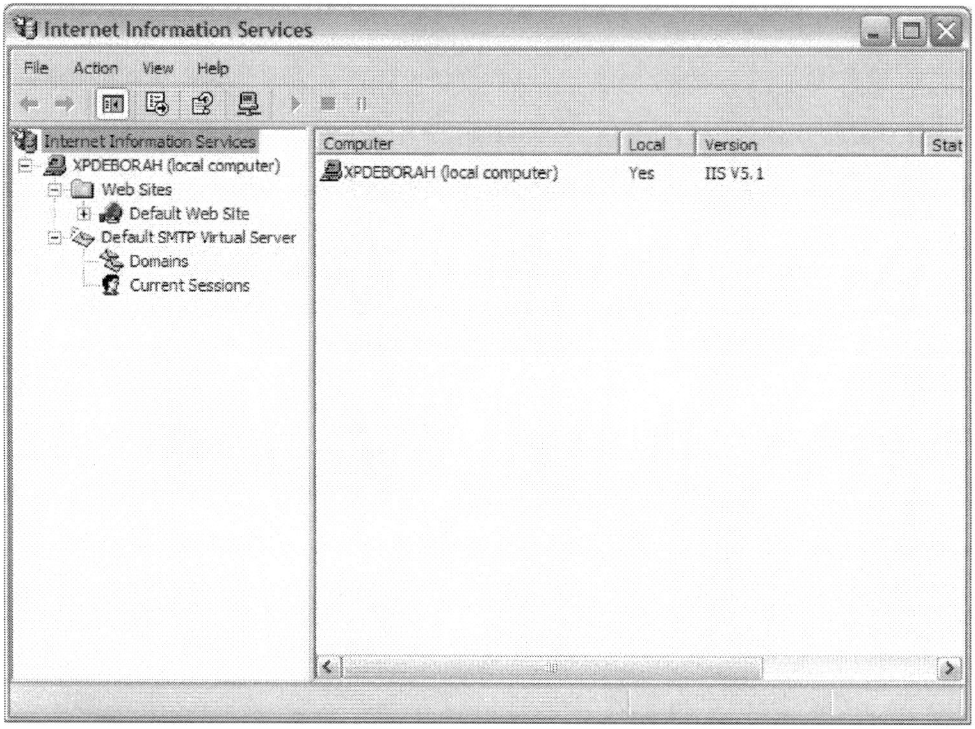

Figure 7-34: Internet Information Services

VII Chapter 7: Summary

We have now completed our chapter on implementing and administering resources on Windows XP. You should now feel comfortable with the following concepts:

- Manage file and folder compression
- Manage NTFS permissions on files and folders
- Optimize file and folder access
- Implement and manage disk quotas
- Implement and manage shared resources
- Implement and manage offline folders
- Implement and manage local and network print devices
- Implement and manage web server resources

VIII Chapter 7: Review Questions

1. Windows XP supports what file systems?

    A. HPFS

    B. FAT

    C. FAT32

    D. HFS+

    E. NTFS

2. What is the path to get to the Video Adapter properties?

    A. Display Properties --> Adapter

    B. Display Properties --> Settings --> Adapter

    C. Display Properties --> Settings --> Advanced --> Adapter

    D. Display Properties --> Settings --> Hardware --> Adapter

    E. Display Properties --> Advanced --> Monitor

3. Scheduled Tasks is capable of the following:

    A. Running a task on both a weekly and a monthly schedule

    B. Running a task on a monthly schedule

    C. Deleting a task once it has completed

    D. Running a task on a weekly schedule

    E. Running a task one time only

4. Can you save an Event Viewer log to a file?

A. Only for the Application Log

B. Only for the System Log

C. Yes

D. Only for the Security Log

5. Where can you create a Group Policy Console?

A. in Windows Explorer

B. in the Command Prompt

C. in the MMC

D. in My Computer

E. in the Users and Passwords Control Panel

6. When moving an uncompressed file within a NTFS partition into a compressed folder in Windows XP, what compression attribute does it have?

A. The file remains uncompressed

B. The file will be compressed

C. All of the files in the folder will be uncompressed

D. Other files in the folder will be unchanged

E. All of the files in the folder will be compressed

7. Your Windows XP Professional computer runs on a single disk, single NTFS partition hard drive. You need to move the Accounting folder to be under a folder named Corp on your computer. The files are currently compressed, and you want the files to remain compressed after you move the folder. Files that already exist in the Corp folder need to remain uncompressed. You also must make sure the files are recoverable in the event of disk problems. How would you accomplish this with the least amount of administrative effort?

A. Simply move the Accounting folder to the Corp folder

B. Back up the Accounting folder, copy the Accounting folder to the Corp folder, then delete the original Accounting folder

C. Back up the Accounting folder, move the Accounting folder to the Corp folder

D. Back up the Accounting folder, move the Accounting folder to the Corp folder, then compress the Accounting Folder

E. Compress the Corp folder, Move the Accounting Folder into the Corp folder, then Uncompress the other files in the Corp folder

8. A shared printer named Printer1 will print, despite it having numerous jobs in the queue. You want to send jobs to print to an identical print device, shared as Printer2 on Computer2. Without reconfiguring the default printer, how can you allow users that are currently connected to Printer1 to automatically use Printer2?

A. Enable printer duplexing

B. This cannot be done without reconfiguring the default printer

C. Configure Printer1 to add a port and set the port to \\Computer2\\Printer2

D. Cut and Paste the print jobs from Printer1 to Printer2

E. Rename Printer2 to Printer1

9. Windows XP contains a feature that allows an Administrator to enforce desktop settings for users. What is this feature?

A. Group Policy

***B. Local Policies**

***C. Roaming Profiles**

***D. Mandatory Profiles**

E. User Profiles

10. The MMC console has the following modes: (select all that apply)

A. Delegated, Multiple Window

B. Full Access

C. Delegated, Single Window

D. Basic

E. None of the above

11. You install Windows XP Professional on your portable computer. You have an external CD-ROM drive that is connected to the parallel port, but Windows 2000 Professional cannot see the CD-ROM drive. Computer Management unsuccessfully scans for the CD-ROM. You want to enable Windows 2000 Professional to detect the CD-ROM drive. What should you do?

A. Configure the parallel port to enable legacy Plug and Play detection

B. Delete the CD-ROM Drivers

C. Reinstall the CD-ROM Driver

D. The CD-ROM is too old.

E. None of the above will work

12. A computer workstation that is running Windows XP Professional is already shared by 6 users. You are also adding two new users, User7 and User8 to the computer. User7 reports that when they log onto the computer, they receive the error message: "Windows cannot copy file C:\Documents and Settings\default user\ to location C:\Documents and Settings\User7". User8 receives a similar message. What should you do? (Choose two)

A. Add the Everyone group to the DACL for the C:\Documents and Settings\default user folder.

B. Log on by using the local Administrator account and create a new folder for the default user.

C. Add the Everyone group to the DACL for the C:\Documents and Settings\User7 and User8 folders.

D. Log on by using the local Administrator account and create new folders for User7 and User8 in the c:\Documents and Settings folder.

E. Delete and re-create the User7 and User8 accounts.

IX Chapter 7: Review Answers

1. Windows XP supports what file systems?

A. HPFS

***B. FAT**

***C. FAT32**

D. NIDE

***E. NTFS**

Explanation: Definition of NTFS
Definition of FAT
Definition of FAT32
Choosing Between File Systems
The file systems that Windows 2000 supports include NTFS (can be used only for Windows NT/2000), FAT (can only be used for hard drives less than 2.1GB, is compatible with Windows 95, 98, and 2000), and FAT32 (can be used for any size hard drive up to 2TB, is compatible with Windows 95 OSR2, Windows 98, and Windows 2000).

2. What is the path to get to the Video Adapter properties?

A. Display Properties --> Adapter

B. Display Properties --> Settings --> Adapter

***C. Display Properties --> Settings --> Advanced --> Adapter**

D. Display Properties --> Settings --> Hardware --> Adapter

E. Display Properties --> Advanced --> Monitor

Explanation: This is a navigational question.

3. Scheduled Tasks is capable of the following:

***A. Running a task on both a weekly and a monthly schedule**

***B. Running a task on a monthly schedule**

***C. Deleting a task once it has completed**

***D. Running a task on a weekly schedule**

***E. Running a task one time only**

Explanation: Using Task Scheduler
Scheduled Tasks can be set to automatically run at nearly any conceivable series of times you can think of.

4. Can you save an Event Viewer log to a file?

A. Only for the Application Log

B. Only for the System Log

***C. Yes**

D. Only for the Security Log

Explanation: Event Viewer Explanation
Event log files can be saved. This is often useful because you may find it necessary to refer back to these archived logs when diagnosing future problems.

5. Where can you create a Group Policy Console?

A. in Windows Explorer

B. in the Command Prompt

C. in the MMC

D. in My Computer

E. in the Users and Passwords Control Panel

Explanation: Explanation of Group Policy
Group Policy Consoles are created and maintained using the MMC (Microsoft Management Console).

6. When moving an uncompressed file within a NTFS partition into a compressed folder in Windows XP, what compression attribute does it have?

***A. The file remains uncompressed**

B. The file will be compressed

C. All of the files in the folder will be uncompressed

***D. Other files in the folder will be unchanged**

E. All of the files in the folder will be compressed

Explanation: Explanation of NTFS Compression
The compression attribute is maintained when moving a file from an uncompressed folder to a compressed folder. Additionally, the compression attribute of other files in the folder will remain unchanged by performing the copy operation addressed in this question.

7. Your Windows XP Professional computer runs on a single disk, single NTFS partition hard drive. You need to move the Accounting folder to be under a folder named Corp on your computer. The files are currently compressed, and you want the files to remain compressed after you move the folder. Files that already exist in the Corp folder need to remain uncompressed. You also must make sure the files are recoverable in the event of disk problems. How would you accomplish this with the least amount of administrative effort?

A. Simply move the Accounting folder to the Corp folder.

B. Back up the Accounting folder, copy the Accounting folder to the Corp folder, then delete the original Accounting folder.

***C. Back up the Accounting folder, move the Accounting folder to the Corp folder.**

D. Back up the Accounting folder, move the Accounting folder to the Corp folder, then compress the Accounting Folder.

E. Compress the Corp folder, Move the Accounting Folder into the Corp folder, then Uncompress the other files in the Corp folder.

Explanation: Compresses and Decompresses NTFS Files and Folders
To ensure that files will be accessible in the event of an emergency, you should backup the Accounting folder. Then moving the Accounting folder to the Corp folder will cause the files to remain uncompressed.

8. A shared printer named Printer1 will print, despite it having numerous jobs in the queue. You want to send jobs to print to an identical print device, shared as Printer2 on Computer2. Without reconfiguring the default printer, how can you allow users that are currently connected to Printer1 to automatically use Printer2?

A. Enable printer duplexing

B. This cannot be done without reconfiguring the default printer

***C. Configure Printer1 to add a port and set the port to \\\\Computer2\\\\Printer2**

D. Cut and Paste the print jobs from Printer1 to Printer2

E. Rename Printer2 to Printer1

Explanation: Choosing and Configuring a Printer Port
Because both print devices are identical, all that must be done is reassign the location of the printer. This can be done by creating a port on Printer1 that is mapped to \\\\Computer2\\\\Printer2.

9. Windows XP contains a feature that allows an Administrator to enforce desktop settings for users. What is this feature?

***A. Group Policy**

B. Local Policies

C. Roaming Profiles

D. Mandatory Profiles

E. User Profiles

Explanation: Choosing and Configuring a Printer Port
Because both print devices are identical, all that must be done is reassign the location of the printer. This can be done by creating a port on Printer1 that is mapped to \\\\Computer2\\\\Printer2.

10. The MMC console has the following modes: (select all that apply)

***A. Delegated, Multiple Window**

***B. Full Access**

***C. Delegated, Single Window**

D. Basic

E. None of the above

Explanation: MMC Explanation
The following are the various modes that the MMC can be started in: Delegated, Multiple Window; Delegated, Single Window;
Full Access

11. You install Windows XP Professional on your portable computer. You have an external CD-ROM drive that is connected to the parallel port, but Windows 2000 Professional cannot see the CD-ROM drive. Computer Management unsuccessfully scans for the CD-ROM. You want to enable Windows 2000 Professional to detect the CD-ROM drive. What should you do?

***A. Configure the parallel port to enable legacy Plug and Play detection**

B. Delete the CD-ROM Drivers

C. Reinstall the CD-ROM Driver

D. The CD-ROM is too old.

E. None of the above will work

Explanation: Configuring Device Settings
In this case, the CD-ROM drive is considered to be a "legacy device". Because of this, you will need to enable the parallel port to detect Plug and Play devices connected to it.

12. A computer workstation that is running Windows XP Professional is already shared by 6 users. You are also adding two new users, User7 and User8 to the computer. User7 reports that when they log onto the computer, they receive the error message: "Windows cannot copy file C:\Documents and Settings\default user\ to location C:\Documents and Settings\User7". User8 receives a similar message. What should you do? (Choose two)

***A. Add the Everyone group to the DACL for the C:\Documents and Settings\default user folder.**

B. Log on by using the local Administrator account and create a new folder for the default user.

C. Add the Everyone group to the DACL for the C:\Documents and Settings\User7 and User8 folders.

***D. Log on by using the local Administrator account and create new folders for User7 and User8 in the c:\Documents and Settings folder.**

E. Delete and re-create the User7 and User8 accounts.

Explanation: Using Access Control inheritance
These errors were reported because of security problems. The users did not have read access to the "C:\Documents and Settings\default user" folder. The users were also unable to create folders in the "C:\Documents and Settings" folder due to security restrictions.

Chapter 8: Implementing Security

The objective of this chapter is to provide you with an understanding of the following:

1. Implement and manage data encryption with EFS
2. Implement and manage local group policy
3. Implement and manage user rights
4. Implement and manage auditing
5. Implement and manage account policy
6. Implement Internet protocol security
7. Implement smart cards

Getting Ready – (Questions)

1). What file systems support EFS?

2). What will using CIPHER without parameters achieve?

3). What are the two types of Local Group Policy?

4). After installation, what is the default setting of auditing?

5). Which mechanism, included in Windows XP Professional, is used to encrypt data as it travels on a network?

Getting Ready – (Answers)

1). EFS is supported only for NTFS on Windows 2000 and Windows XP. It will not work with any other file system, including previous versions of NTFS.

2). Used without parameters, CIPHER displays the encryption state of the current directory as well as any files contained in it.

3). The two types of Local Group Policy are computer configuration policies that relate to all users of that computer, and user configuration policies that relate options specific to users and groups.

4). By default, auditing is not enabled, so you will need to manually configure it.

5). IPSec (Internet Protocol Security) is a mechanism designed to protect communications between systems. IPSec, which is included with Windows XP Professional, encrypts data as it travels between systems on a network.

I Introduction

Security, Security, Security! Is there anything else in this IT industry that people want and never seem to have enough of? The damage that can be done by a breach in security can bring down a network.

Windows XP addresses some of those security needs through EFS data encryption, security policies, secure network access, resource access restrictions, and secure user authentication.

As this is a course on Windows XP, and not Windows 2000 Server or the upcoming .NET Server, the information in this section is heavily weighted towards a small peer-to-peer network. Much of this knowledge is transferable to a larger scale network.

Encrypting File System

Encrypting File System (EFS) is an exciting feature in Microsoft Windows XP. It was first introduction with Windows 2000. EFS adds an extra layer of protection to data in files that are stored on an NTFS disk. It uses symmetric key encryption with public key technology to provide a high level of security for files.

Because EFS runs a system service, it makes it very easy to manage, but very difficult to attack. Best of all, it is transparent to the user of the file and to applications that need to access the file.

The owner of a protected file can open it and work with it, without any extra handling, as if it were a regular file. EFS decrypts the file in the background and provides the user's application with a plain text copy. Anyone else trying to access the document is denied access.

Designated recovery administrators have the ability to recover protected files if necessary. In addition, the administrator has the ability to access a user's folder and decrypt it, if necessary. This could be rather important if someone who won the lottery, and called from a tropical island to resign from his or her position owns a critical document!

Low-level disk tools that attempt to bypass EFS will be frustrated in their attempts. EFS-protected files are bulk-encrypted and cannot be attacked in this fashion.

A file is never encrypted on its own, but should be saved in designated EFS-encrypted folders. The logic behind this is because a lot of applications auto-save a background copy of an open document. Without the safety of an encrypted folder, an application could inadvertently save this background copy in plain text, leaving sensitive data open to intrusion.

EFS is supported only for NTFS on Windows 2000 and Windows XP. It will not work with any other file system, including previous version of NTFS.

CIPHER [/E | /D] [/S:DIR] [/A] [/I] [/F] [/Q] [/H] [/K] [PATHNAME [...]]	
/E	Encrypts the specified directories. Directories will be marked so that files added afterward will be encrypted.
/D	Decrypts the specified directories. Directories will be marked so that files added afterward will not be encrypted.
/S:DIR	Performs the specified operation on directories in the given directory and all subdirectories.
/A	Operation for files as well as directories. The encrypted file could become decrypted when it is modified if the parent directory is not encrypted. It is recommended that you encrypt the file and the parent directory.
/I	Continues performing the specified operation even after errors have occurred. By default, CIPHER stops when an error is encountered.
/F	Forces the encryption operation on all specified objects, even those that are already encrypted. Already-encrypted objects are skipped by default.
/Q	Reports only the most essential information.
/H	Displays files with the hidden or system attributes. These files are omitted by default.
/K	Create new file encryption key for the user running CIPHER. If this option is chosen, all the other options will be ignored.
PATHNAME	Specifies a pattern, file, or directory.

Table 8-1: Switches for cipher.exe

CIPHER is a command-line utility that allows you, as administrator, to encrypt and decrypt files on NTFS volumes. See Table 8.1 for the available command line parameters.

Used without parameters, CIPHER displays the encryption state of the current directory and any files it contains. You may use multiple directory names and wildcards. You must put spaces between multiple parameters.

III Local Group Policy

Group policies are normally implemented on a network (domain) level, and can be used to manage everything from users' desktops to IP security.

In the Windows 2000 Active Directory environment, group policies can be inherited from site to domain to organizational unit (OU). This allows a great deal of granular control to the enterprise administrator, because the group policy object (GPO) of the OU contains the final group policy settings. Users and groups that belong to that OU will receive the settings the administrator wants them to have. Active Directory GPOs take precedence over the local GPO.

However, in using local group policies, as implemented in Windows XP, there is only one GPO. All users, including the local Administrator, will be affected by that group policy.

Group Policy under Windows XP must, therefore, be handled with great care.

There are two types of Local Group Policy:

- Computer configuration policies, that relate to all users of that computer
- User configuration policies, that relate to options specific to users and groups.

Computer Configuration Policy

Figures 8.1 and 8.2 outline all of the settings to which group policy can be assigned under computer configuration.

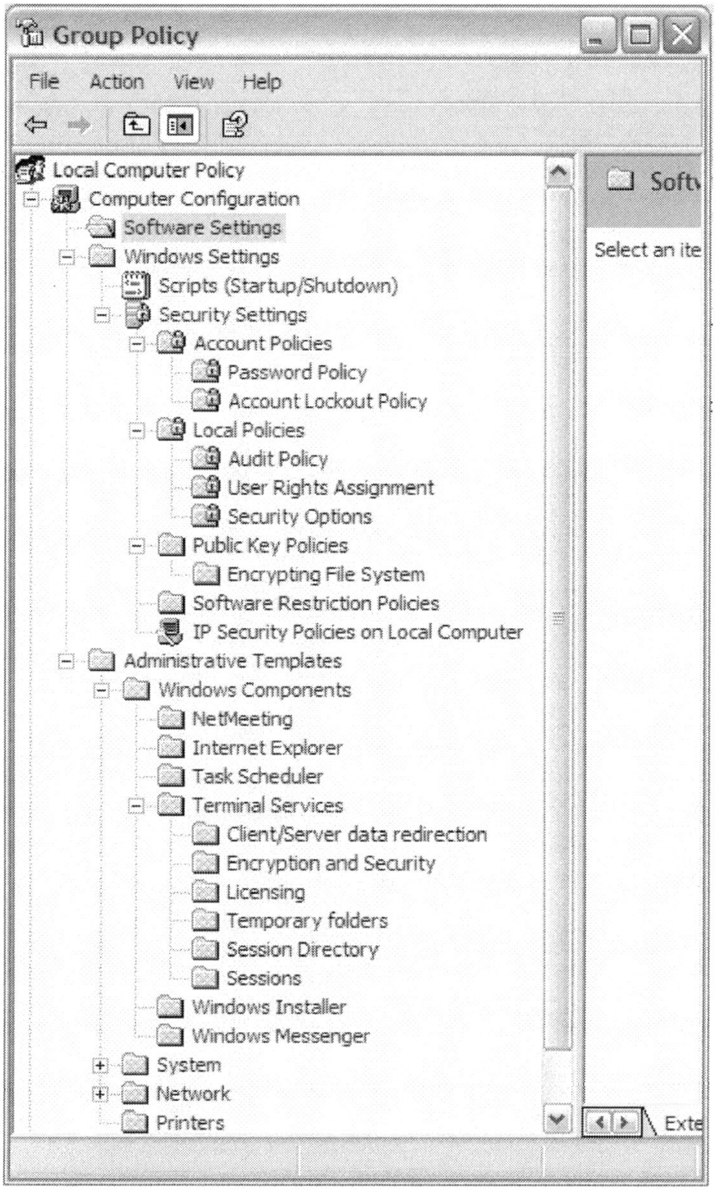

Figure 8-1: Computer Local Group Policy (Part 1)

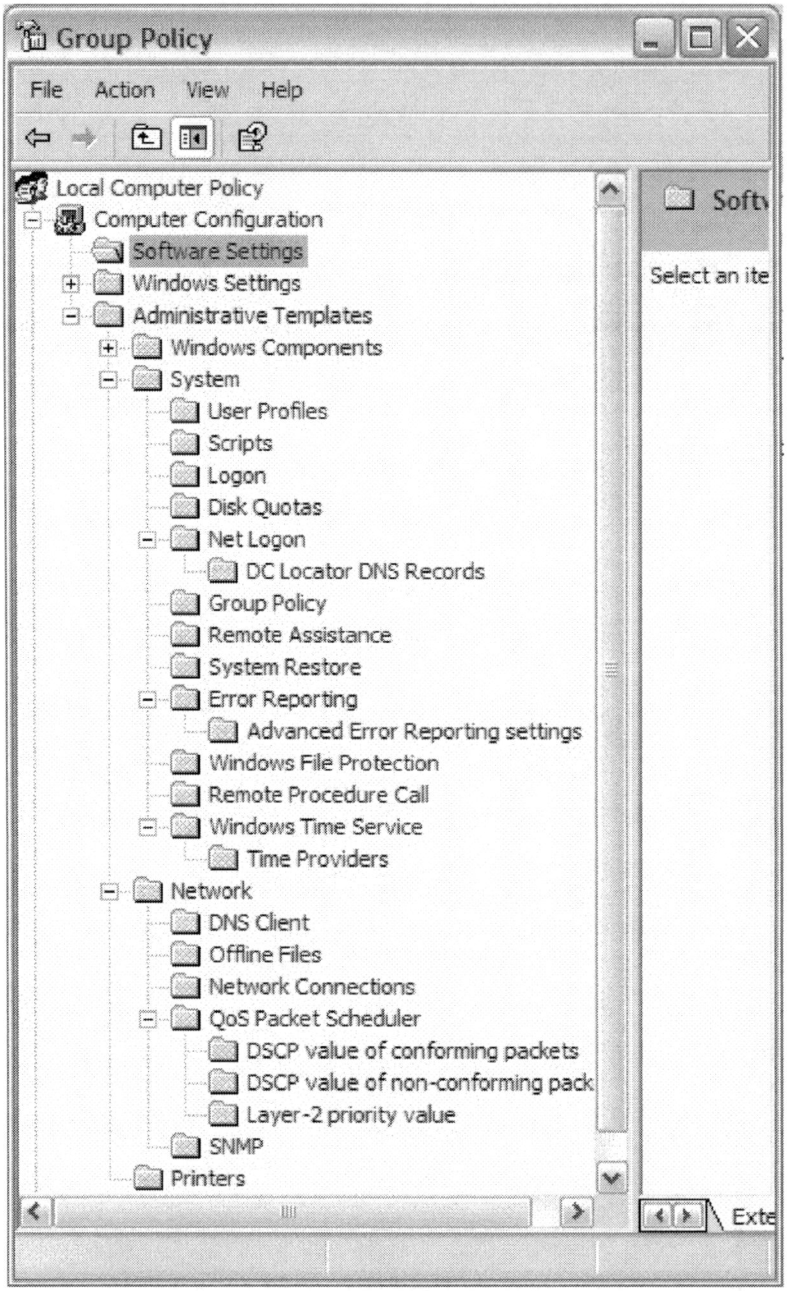

Figure 8-2: Computer Local Group Policy (Part 2)

The following tables (Table 8.2 and 8.3) outline some of the computer configuration group policy settings and their defaults.

POLICY	DEFAULT SETTING	AVAILABLE SETTINGS
Enforce password history	1 passwords remembered	Between 0 and 24 (passwords)
Maximum password age	42 days	Between 1 and 999 (in days)
Minimum password age	0 days	Between 1 and 999 (in days)
Minimum password length	0 characters	Between 0 and 14 (in characters)
Passwords must meet complexity requirements	Disabled	Disabled or Enabled (See Note)
Store password using reversible encryption for all users in the domain	Disabled	Disabled or Enabled

Table 8-2: Password Policy

NOTE: The default password filter (passfilt.dll) included with Windows XP requires that a password:

1. Does not contain all or part of the account name.
2. Is at least six characters in length.
3. Contains characters from three of four categories:
   - → English upper case characters (A...Z)
   - → English lower case characters (a...z)
   - → Base 10 digits (0...9)
   - → Non alphanumeric (For example, !,$#,%)

3. Complexity requirements are enforced upon password change or creation.

POLICY	DEFAULT SETTING	AVAILABLE SETTINGS
Account lockout duration	Not defined	Between 0 to 99999 (in minutes)
Account lockout threshold	0 invalid logon attempts	Between 0 and 999 (failed logon attempts)
Reset account lockout counter after	Not defined	Between 1 to 99999 (in minutes)

Table 8-3: Account Lockout Policy

As you can see, these are just the tip of the iceberg! It is worth the time to walk through each setting in Group Policy just to get an overview of what can be configured for computer settings.

It should also serve as a caveat. Without handling Group Policy with care and planning, it would be quite easy to make a critical error. Remember, Local Group Policy applies to everyone who logs onto the computer, even the Administrator.

User Configuration Policies

The User Configuration Policy tree is even larger than the Computer Configuration Policy tree. Figure 8.2 illustrates the Administrative Templates section of the User Configuration Policy in the MMC.

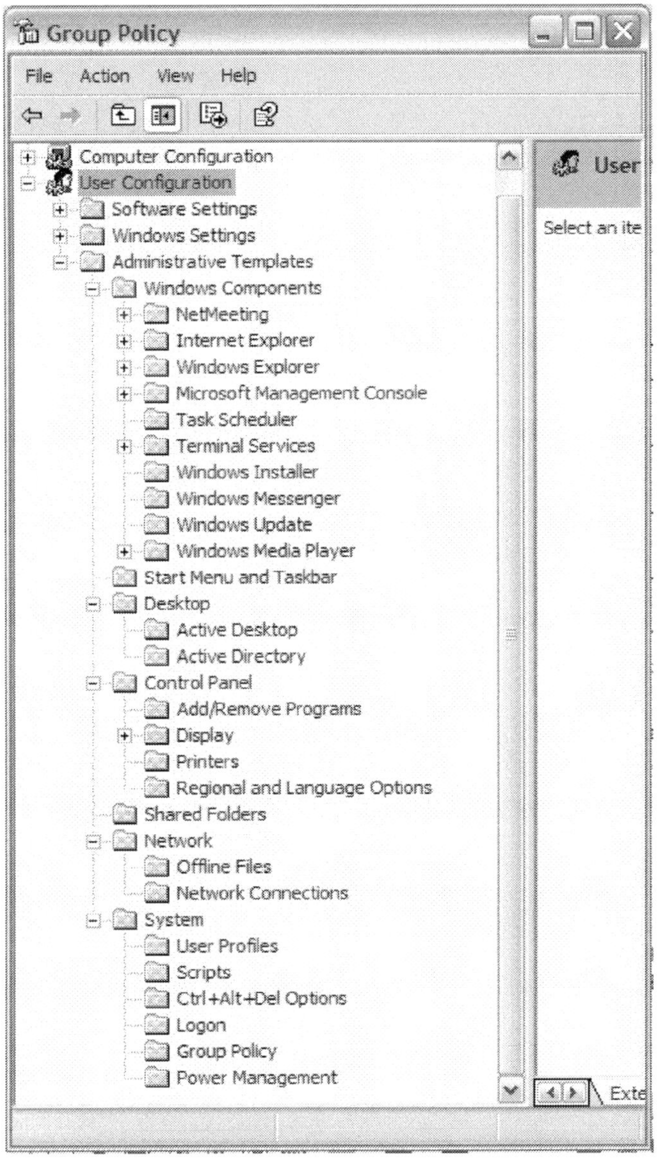

Figure 8-3: Administrative Template, User Configuration, Local Group Policy

It would take an entire book to break down every part of the User Configuration Policy in Windows XP. It has been greatly expanded since the days of NT 4.0. It is again worth your while to explore each option individually, and document your planned implementation before making any changes to policy.

A good example of how badly a mismanaged User Configuration Policy can affect you is this – one setting in User Configuration | Windows Components is Microsoft Management Console. One setting that can be disabled is the Group Policy snap-in. Oops! You would find yourself knee-deep in the registry trying to fix that one!

To fix the previously mentioned problem, modify the value to 0 (zero) at the following location: `HKCU\Software\Policies\Microsoft\MMC\{8FC0B734-A0E1-11D1-A7D3-0000F87571E3}\Restrict_Run`

IV User Authentication and Auditing

Some of the common problems you will face when dealing with user accounts are:

- Forgotten passwords
- Locked-out accounts
- Incorrect or insufficient permissions
- Conflicting permissions due to group membership

Resetting a password simply requires you to open the existing user account through the Computer Management console, entering and confirming a new password, and then setting the switch "User must change password at next logon".

When permissions are involved, take a careful look at membership. As well, check whether the permission is simply not specified, or explicitly denied.

Permissions are assigned at logon. If you assign a user a new permission, or permission level, the user must log off and log back on before the permission takes effect.

User Rights

The following table (Table 8.4) outlines the default user rights and settings with Windows XP:

POLICY	LOCAL SETTING	EFFECTIVE SETTING
Access this computer from the network	Everyone, Users, Power Users, Backup Operators, Administrators	Everyone, Users, Power Users, Backup Operators, Administrators
Act as part of the operating system		
Add workstations to domain		
Back up files and directories	Backup Operators, Administrators	Backup Operators, Administrators
Bypass traverse checking	Everyone, Users, Power Users, Backup Operators, Administrators	Everyone, Users, Power Users, Backup Operators, Administrators
Change the system time	Power Users, Administrators	Power Users, Administrators
Create a pagefile	Administrators	Administrators

POLICY	LOCAL SETTING	EFFECTIVE SETTING
Debug programs	Administrators	Administrators
Deny access to this computer from the network		
Deny logon as a batch job		
Deny logon as a service		
Deny logon locally		
Enable computer and user accounts to be trusted for delegation		
Force shutdown from a remote system	Administrators	Administrators
Generate security audits		
Increase quotas	Administrators	Administrators
Increase scheduling priority	Administrators	Administrators
Load and unload device drivers	Administrators	Administrators
Log on as a batch job		
Log on as a service		
Log on locally	Administrators, Backup Operators, Power Users, Users	Administrators, Backup Operators, Power Users, Users
Manage auditing and security log	Administrators	Administrators
Modify firmware environment values	Administrators	Administrators
Profile single process	Power Users, Administrators	Power Users, Administrators
Profile system performance	Administrators	Administrators
Remove computer from docking station	Users, Power Users, Administrators	Users, Power Users, Administrators

POLICY	LOCAL SETTING	EFFECTIVE SETTING
Restore files and directories	Backup Operators, Administrators	Backup Operators, Administrators
Shut down the system	Users, Power Users, Backup Operators, Administrators	Users, Power Users, Backup Operators, Administrators
Take ownership of files or other objects	Administrators	Administrators

Table 8-4: User Rights

That's quite a list!

What often confuses people about user rights is that they have nothing to do with permissions. Permissions are something that are assigned for accessing resources (files, printers, etc.). Rights are actions that users can take – for example, taking ownership of a document, or forcing shutdown remotely.

Rights should be assigned with a great deal of caution. Never give a user more rights than they need to do their assigned tasks.

Account Policy

Account settings refer to the password and account lockout policies that you set in Group Policy. Tables 8.2 and 8.3 outlined all the settings that can be configured and managed through Group Policy.

What you want to look at are things like minimum and maximum password age, and how they relate to the password history.

People hate changing their passwords. They will go to amazing lengths to keep the same password, for the simple reason that people tend to forget them. If you set a maximum password age of 60 days, after that period of time, the user will need to change the password. If you set a password history of six, the user will be unable to reuse the same password until he or she has used six other passwords. You would think, then, that you might have prevented the user from reusing the same password.

If you don't set the minimum password age, however, they just might. They can logon; change their password; then logoff. Then they can log back on, change their password again, and logoff. Do that a few more times, and guess what? The original password has moved off the history list and can be used again! Always remember to look at both "minimums" and "maximums" when configuring account settings.

Another setting you will want to look at is lockout policy. An effective lockout policy, combined with a lengthy duration of lockout time can frustrate someone trying to crack your security database. A good rule of thumb is a lockout policy of three bad attempts in a 24-48 hour period. You would have to be a very patient hacker to attempt three passwords, wait 48 hours, and attempt another three passwords.

Pop Quiz 8.1

Pop Quiz 8.1 *Questions*

1). Passfilt.dll, the default password filter sets certain requirements for a password. Name these three requirements.

2). What built-in group has a default user right to "deny access to this computer from the network"?

3). How do you enable auditing?

4). Name the four built-in groups that have the right to "Shut down the system" by default in Windows XP Professional.

5). How many GPOs (Group Policy Objects) are there in Windows XP Professional when it is set up as a stand-alone system?

Pop Quiz 8.1 *Answers*

1). The default filter requires that a password does not contain part or all of the account name, is at least six characters in length, and contains characters from three of these four categories – English uppercase characters, English lower case characters, Base 10 digits, and non alphanumeric characters, such as ! or $.

2). By default, no built-in group has this user right. This right should only be assigned to a built-in group, like Administrators, if is needed to do their assigned tasks.

3). You enable auditing by manually configuring it through the Group Policy snap-in.

4). By default, Users, Power Users, Backup Operators and Administrators have the right to "shut down the system".

5). In local group policies, as implemented in Windows XP Professional, there is only one GPO. All users, including the local Administrator, will be affected by that group policy.

V IP Security

Windows XP includes IPSec (Internet Protocol Security), which is a mechanism to protect communication between systems. Most networks have in place means of preventing attacks from outside the organization, but little protection inside the organization. Any system on the network, for example a visitor's notebook, can capture unprotected data and analysis it later at their convenience. Firewalls have no way of protecting such threats to your data.

IPSec is designed to encrypt data as it travels across the network between two systems. Because of this encryption, data is now protected from modification and eavesdropping. As it requires no changes to any existing applications or protocols, deployment of IPSec on a network is an effortless task.

You can also use IPSec for VPN connections that use the L2TP protocol. In this case, the IPSec tunnel is created before the L2TP connection is established, ensuring that both data and passwords are encrypted.

In order to use IPSec, an administrator must first define how the two systems will trust each other. This configuration is done using the IP Security Policy snap-in (Figure 8.4). Windows XP comes with three policies pre-configured. These are general use policies.

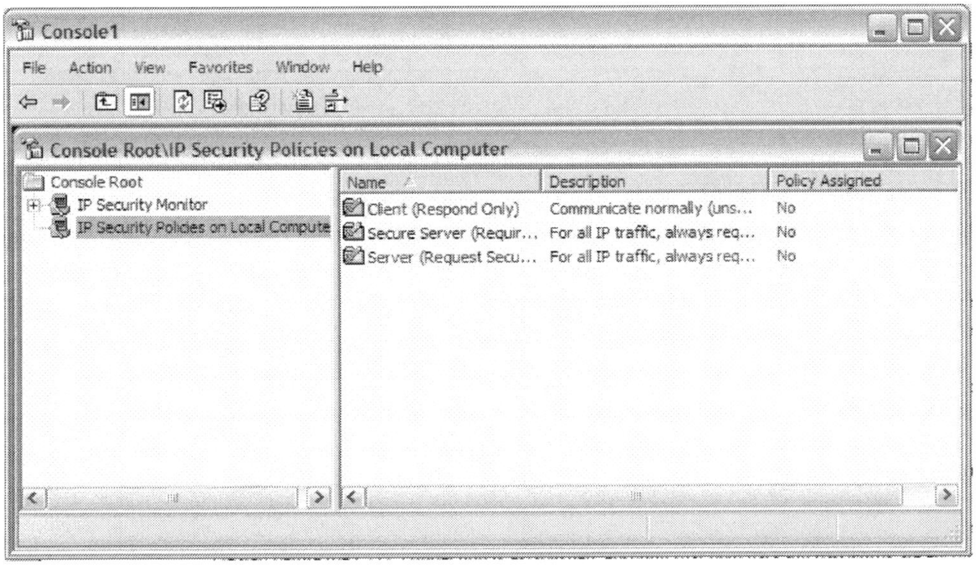

Figure 8-4: IP Security Policies

Once you have determined your policy requirement, you will have to assign the IPSec policy. To do this on a local computer, in IP Security Policies, click IP Security on Local Computer. Right-click the policy you want to assign and then select **Assign** (Figure 8-5).

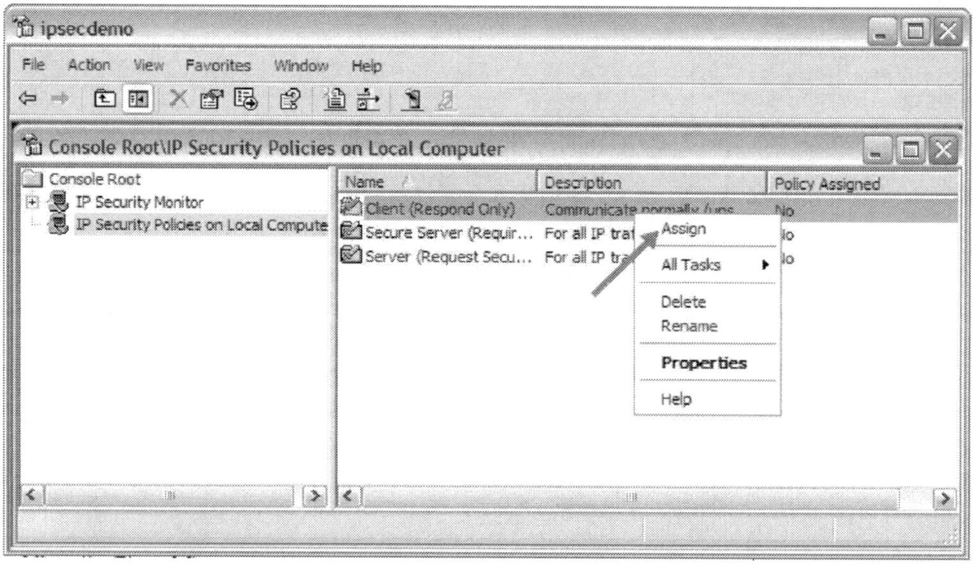

Figure 8-5: IPSec on Local Computer

> NOTE: If the computer is a member of a Windows 2000 domain and IPSec policy is assigned at the domain level, then the local computer policy will not be not used.

VI Smart Cards

A smart card is a small electronic device, about the size of a bankcard that contains an integrated circuit. It is used to store public and private keys, passwords, and other personal information in a secure fashion. Smart Card technology is fully integrated into Windows XP for authentication of users.

Windows XP will automatically detects and install Plug and Play-compliant smart card readers. Once the reader is installed, you will need to configure a dial-up network connection to use a pre-configured smart card. In the **Security** tab of the connection **Properties** box, select **Use smart card** in the **Validate my identity as follows** list (Figure 8.6).

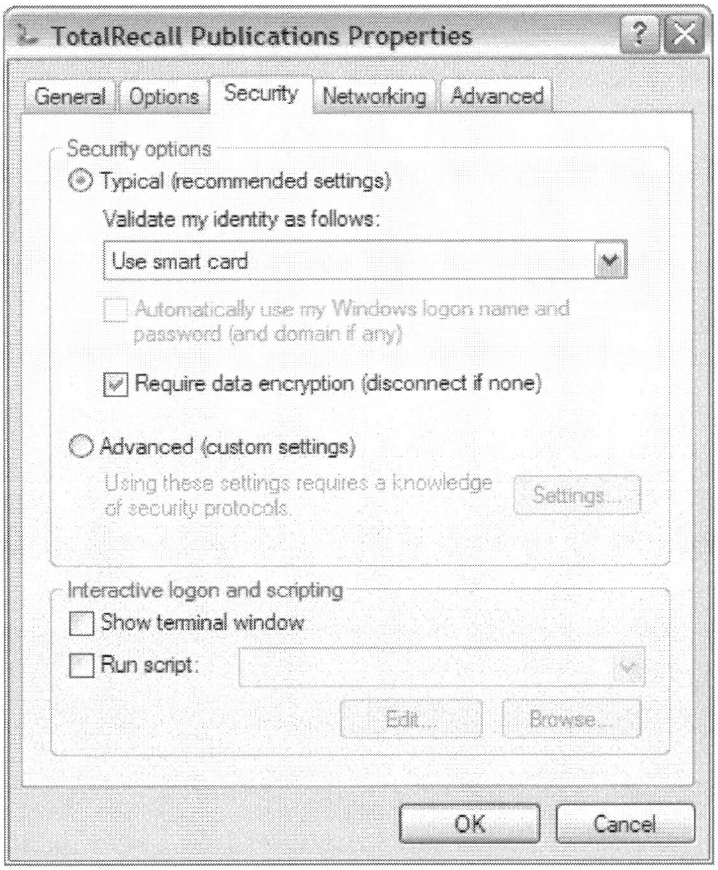

Figure 8-6: Using a smart card for authentication

VII Chapter 8: Summary

You have now completed the final chapter, Implementing, Monitoring, and Troubleshooting Security. You should now feel comfortable on how to:

- Implement and manage data encryption with EFS
- Implement and manage local group policy
- Implement and manage user rights
- Implement and manage auditing
- Implement and manage account policy
- Implement Internet protocol security
- Implement smart cards

VIII Chapter 8: Review Questions

CASE STUDY 1: You are a Network Consultant with specialized skills in designing Windows based network services. You are recently requested by the Supreme Manufacturing Company to design the Windows XP network for the company's 5 remote factories. Currently, only the head office has a LAN running Windows 2000 Active Directory. It does not YET have dedicated connection to the factories. The factories are using Win95 as dial up clients to connect to the head office server running RAS. In the coming months 256K dedicated connection will be installed.

Currently, within all locations there are already 100MBPS LANs running smoothly.

The president recognizes the importance of IT, and is planning to spend 30% of its last year revenue on the complete re-design of the IT infrastructure. Because of the growing importance of IT, the head office will house a new IT department. This department is further broken down into 4 smaller departments, including:

1. LAN 2. WAN 3. Server 4. Workstation

The staff at the factories complain that their Win95 systems are slow and unreliable. The IT director expects that you devise a plan for upgrading all the Win95 clients to WinXP Pro. However, there is no plan for installing Windows 2000 Server or Windows.NET Server in the factories.

In addition to the system upgrades, the IT director also likes you to devise a security plan to ensure that even in the factories, network security can be properly implemented without compromising the ability of the peers to share resources.

1. CASE STUDY 1: In last December, the factory in Mexico had upgraded 20% of their PCs to WinME. The result was not satisfactory. Today, you direct the staff over there to upgrade the WinME computers to WinXP Pro. At the end of the upgrade process, Windows display a dialog box, which offers to help the staff make their files and folders private. One of the staff complains that he does not receive such help. What is the likely cause?

A. He does not have admin rights

B. His partition has not been formatted as NTFS

C. He does not enable EFS

D. He did not logon as Power Users

E. No Answer is Correct.

2. CASE STUDY 1: Your assistant, along the course of system upgrade, suggest that you instruct all the staff who perform the upgrade to make their local folders "private". What can be achieved by doing so, and what are the drawbacks?

A. Other users will not be able to access the My Documents folder that belongs to "private" user profile

B. Other users who attempt to access a user's profile by opening the Documents And Settings folder will receive an "access denied" error message

C. Local file security to a certain extent can be achieved

D. System performance will be impaired

E. There will be potential conflicts with the local GPO policy settings

3. CASE STUDY 1: Your assistant Jeanie suggests that, after the computers are upgraded to WinXP, all the local drives should be converted to NTFS, and that Simple File Sharing should be disabled. By doing so, what benefits can be achieved?

A. Control access to the files on the NTFS-formatted drive

B. Control access to the folders on the NTFS-formatted drive

C. Allow different types of access for different users locally

D. Control access to the files on the NTFS-formatted drive

E. Allow different types of access for different users remotely

F. Fine-tune permissions on specific shared folders

CASE STUDY 2: You are a Network Consultant with specialized skills in designing Windows based network services. You are recently requested by the Supreme Manufacturing Company to design the Windows XP network for the company's 5 remote factories.

Currently, only the head office has a LAN running Windows 2000 Active Directory. It does not YET have dedicated connection to the factories. The factories are using Win95 as dial up clients to connect to the head office server running RAS. In the coming months 256K dedicated connection will be installed. Currently, within all locations there are already 100MBPS LANs running smoothly.

The president recognizes the importance of IT, and is planning to spend 30% of its last year revenue on the complete re-design of the IT infrastructure.

Because of the growing importance of IT, the head office will house a new IT department. This department is further broken down into 4 smaller departments, including:

1. LAN 2. WAN 3. Server 4. Workstation

The staff at the factories complain that their Win95 systems are slow and unreliable. The IT director expects that you devise a plan for upgrading all the Win95 clients to WinXP Pro. However, there is no plan for installing Windows 2000 Server or Windows.NET Server in the factories. In addition to the system upgrades, the IT director also likes you to devise a security plan to ensure that even in the factories, network security can be properly implemented without compromising the ability of the peers to share resources.

4. CASE STUDY 2: Your assistant Mary has just upgraded one of the Mexico Factory Win95 PC to WinXP. The local drive has been converted to NTFS. For some reasons she receives a message warning her that she is about to deny all access to all files on the drive by all users. What causes this message to be displayed?

A. She removed the Everyone group from the root of the C drive

B. She denied Full Control of the Everyone group for the root of the C drive

C. She enabled Full Control of the Everyone group for the root of the C drive

D. She was trying to remove entries that involve the guest group

E. She was trying to remove entries that involve the power user group

5. CASE STUDY 2: In your security plan you want to specify a tool for viewing and editing permissions on the WinXP systems. You want this tool to be executable from the command line. What tool can you use?

A. cacls

B. rplmon

C. net user

D. permset

E. preview

6. CASE STUDY 2: Your assistant Mary has upgraded the SF factory PCs to WinXP. She has configured a series of permissions, both at the share level and at the file system level, on these computers, making things very complicated. How do you tell the effective permissions of a file named fileX assigned to an individual user account Kitty on a workstation named XP3?

A. On XP3, open the properties dialog box for fileX, and choose Properties. On the Security tab, click the Advanced button and then click the Effective Permissions tab. Click the Select button to open the Select User or Group dialog box. Enter the name of Kitty, and then click OK.

B. On XP3, open the properties dialog box for fileX, and choose Properties. On the Advanced tab, click the Security button and then click the Permissions tab. Click the Select button to open the Select User or Group dialog box. Enter the name of Kitty, and then click OK.

C. On XP3, open the properties dialog box for fileX, and choose Security Properties. On the Settings tab, click the Modify button and then click the Effective Permissions tab. Click the Change button to open the Select User or Group dialog box. Enter the name of Kitty, and then click OK.

D. On XP3, open the properties dialog box for the folder that holds fileX, and choose Settings. On the Modify tab, click the Permissions button and then click the Effective Settings tab. Click the Select button to open the Select User or Group dialog box. Enter the name of Kitty, and then click OK.

E. No Answer is Correct.

CASE STUDY 2: You are a Network Consultant with specialized skills in designing Windows based network services. You are recently requested by the Supreme Manufacturing Company to design the Windows XP network for the company's 5 remote factories.

Currently, only the head office has a LAN running Windows 2000 Active Directory. It does not YET have dedicated connection to the factories. The factories are using Win95 as dial up clients to connect to the head office server running RAS. In the coming months 256K dedicated connection will be installed. Currently, within all locations there are already 100MBPS LANs running smoothly.

The president recognizes the importance of IT, and is planning to spend 30% of its last year revenue on the complete re-design of the IT infrastructure.

Because of the growing importance of IT, the head office will house a new IT department. This department is further broken down into 4 smaller departments, including:

1. LAN 2. WAN 3. Server 4. Workstation

The staff at the factories complain that their Win95 systems are slow and unreliable. The IT director expects that you devise a plan for upgrading all the Win95 clients to WinXP Pro. However, there is no plan for installing Windows 2000 Server or Windows.NET Server in the factories. In addition to the system upgrades, the IT director also likes you to devise a security plan to ensure that even in the factories, network security can be properly implemented without compromising the ability of the peers to share resources.

7. CASE STUDY 2: In your security plan you need to specify a tool for viewing and editing permissions on the WinXP systems. Mary suggests that you use the Cacls.exe utility. With this utility, what switches are available?

A. F

B. C

C. R

D. W

E. P

8. CASE STUDY 2: In your security plan you need to address the issue of security exposure caused by the paging file left on the computer's hard drive. What should you do to ensure that the paging file won't become a security hole itself?

A. Use a registry editor. Open the registry. Navigate to the KLM\System\CurrentControlSet\Control\Session Manager\Memory Management key. Set the value of ClearPageFileAtShutdown to 1.

B. Use a registry editor. Open the registry. Navigate to the KLM\System\CurrentControlSet\Control\Session Manager\Memory Management key. Set the value of ClearPageFileAtShutdown to 0.

C. Use a registry editor. Open the registry. Navigate to the KLM\System\ControlSet\Control\Session\Memory Management key. Set the value of ClearPageFileAtShutdown to 2.

D. Use the System Policy Editor. Enable the option "Clear the Paging File During Startup". Restart the system immediately.

E. No Answer is Correct

9. CASE STUDY 2: In January, there was an incident where two PCs, together with some confidential data, were stolen from the Tokyo factory. What will you include in your security plan to address such issue?

A. Deploy EFS on the local drives

B. Deploy client certificates on the local computers

C. Deploy Smart Card logon facilities on the local computers

D. Deploy SSL on the local computers

E. No Answer is Correct

CASE STUDY 2: You are a Network Consultant with specialized skills in designing Windows based network services. You are recently requested by the Supreme Manufacturing Company to design the Windows XP network for the company's 5 remote factories.

Currently, only the head office has a LAN running Windows 2000 Active Directory. It does not YET have dedicated connection to the factories. The factories are using Win95 as dial up clients to connect to the head office server running RAS. In the coming months 256K dedicated connection will be installed. Currently, within all locations there are already 100MBPS LANs running smoothly.

The president recognizes the importance of IT, and is planning to spend 30% of its last year revenue on the complete re-design of the IT infrastructure.

Because of the growing importance of IT, the head office will house a new IT department. This department is further broken down into 4 smaller departments, including:

1. LAN 2. WAN 3. Server 4. Workstation

The staff at the factories complain that their Win95 systems are slow and unreliable. The IT director expects that you devise a plan for upgrading all the Win95 clients to WinXP Pro. However, there is no plan for installing Windows 2000 Server or Windows.NET Server in the factories. In addition to the system upgrades, the IT director also likes you to devise a security plan to ensure that even in the factories, network security can be properly implemented without compromising the ability of the peers to share resources.

10. CASE STUDY 2: In your plan you mention the use of EFS for protecting local data. Janice mentions the need for fall back just in case the users lose their original certificates due to a hard disk failure. What should you request the users to do before enabling EFS?

A. Back up their personal encryption certificates with the associated private keys to a secure location

B. Back up the recovery agent certificates to a secure location

C. Defrag and compress the drives

D. Run scandisk /F on the drives

E. Backup the operating system to a tape and keep the tape in a secure location

IX Chapter 8: Review Answers

CASE STUDY 1: You are a Network Consultant with specialized skills in designing Windows based network services. You are recently requested by the Supreme Manufacturing Company to design the Windows XP network for the company's 5 remote factories. Currently, only the head office has a LAN running Windows 2000 Active Directory. It does not YET have dedicated connection to the factories. The factories are using Win95 as dial up clients to connect to the head office server running RAS. In the coming months 256K dedicated connection will be installed.

Currently, within all locations there are already 100MBPS LANs running smoothly.

The president recognizes the importance of IT, and is planning to spend 30% of its last year revenue on the complete re-design of the IT infrastructure. Because of the growing importance of IT, the head office will house a new IT department. This department is further broken down into 4 smaller departments, including:

1. LAN 2. WAN 3. Server 4. Workstation

The staff at the factories complain that their Win95 systems are slow and unreliable. The IT director expects that you devise a plan for upgrading all the Win95 clients to WinXP Pro. However, there is no plan for installing Windows 2000 Server or Windows.NET Server in the factories.

In addition to the system upgrades, the IT director also likes you to devise a security plan to ensure that even in the factories, network security can be properly implemented without compromising the ability of the peers to share resources.

1. CASE STUDY 1: In last December, the factory in Mexico had upgraded 20% of their PCs to WinME. The result was not satisfactory. Today, you direct the staff over there to upgrade the WinME computers to WinXP Pro. At the end of the upgrade process, Windows display a dialog box, which offers to help the staff make their files and folders private. One of the staff complains that he does not receive such help. What is the likely cause?

A. He does not have admin rights

***B. His partition has not been formatted as NTFS**

C. He does not enable EFS

D. He did not logon as Power Users

E. No Answer is Correct

Explanation: If you create a new account during setup, or if the Windows Setup program automatically creates your user account when you upgrade from Windows 98 or Windows Me, your account starts out with no password. When you add a password to your own account, Windows offers to help you make your files and folders private. This is possible only if NTFS is used.

2. CASE STUDY 1: Your assistant, along the course of system upgrade, suggest that you instruct all the staff who perform the upgrade to make their local folders "private". What can be achieved by doing so, and what are the drawbacks?

***A. Other users will not be able to access the My Documents folder that belongs to "private" user profile**

***B. Other users who attempt to access a user's profile by opening the Documents And Settings folder will receive an "access denied" error message**

***C. Local file security to a certain extent can be achieved**

D. System performance will be impaired

E. There will be potential conflicts with the local GPO policy settings

3. CASE STUDY 1: Your assistant Jeanie suggests that, after the computers are upgraded to WinXP, all the local drives should be converted to NTFS, and that Simple File Sharing should be disabled. By doing so, what benefits can be achieved?

***A. Control access to the files on the NTFS-formatted drive**
***B. Control access to the folders on the NTFS-formatted drive**
***C. Allow different types of access for different users locally**
***D. Control access to the files on the NTFS-formatted drive**
***E. Allow different types of access for different users remotely**
***F. Fine-tune permissions on specific shared folders**

Explanation: By disabling Simple File Sharing and using the full range of NTFS access controls, you can control access to any file or folder on any NTFS-formatted drive, allow different types of access for different users or groups of users, and fine-tune permissions on specific files or folders. Simple File Sharing is a novice user feature only.

CASE STUDY 2: You are a Network Consultant with specialized skills in designing Windows based network services. You are recently requested by the Supreme Manufacturing Company to design the Windows XP network for the company's 5 remote factories.

Currently, only the head office has a LAN running Windows 2000 Active Directory. It does not YET have dedicated connection to the factories. The factories are using Win95 as dial up clients to connect to the head office server running RAS. In the coming months 256K dedicated connection will be installed. Currently, within all locations there are already 100MBPS LANs running smoothly.

The president recognizes the importance of IT, and is planning to spend 30% of its last year revenue on the complete re-design of the IT infrastructure.

Because of the growing importance of IT, the head office will house a new IT department. This department is further broken down into 4 smaller departments, including:

1. LAN 2. WAN 3. Server 4. Workstation

The staff at the factories complain that their Win95 systems are slow and unreliable. The IT director expects that you devise a plan for upgrading all the Win95 clients to WinXP Pro. However, there is no plan for installing Windows 2000 Server or Windows.NET Server in the factories. In addition to the system upgrades, the IT director also likes you to devise a security plan to ensure that even in the factories, network security can be properly implemented without compromising the ability of the peers to share resources.

4. CASE STUDY 2: Your assistant Mary has just upgraded one of the Mexico Factory Win95 PC to WinXP. The local drive has been converted to NTFS. For some reasons she receives a message warning her that she is about to deny all access to all files on the drive by all users. What causes this message to be displayed?

***A. She removed the Everyone group from the root of the C drive**

***B. She denied Full Control of the Everyone group for the root of the C drive**

C. She enabled Full Control of the Everyone group for the root of the C drive

D. She was trying to remove entries that involve the guest group

E. She was trying to remove entries that involve the power user group

Explanation: One of the most common mistakes made by users who are inexperienced with NTFS permissions is to remove the Everyone group from the root of a drive, or select the Deny box next to Full Control for this group. These drastic measures, when detected in Windows XP Professional, will produce warning to the users.

5. CASE STUDY 2: In your security plan you want to specify a tool for viewing and editing permissions on the WinXP systems. You want this tool to be executable from the command line. What tool can you use?

***A. cacls**

B. rplmon

C. net user

D. permset

E. preview

Explanation: Cacls.exe is a command-line utility available in both Windows XP Professional and Home Edition. It provides another way to view and edit permissions. With Cacls, you can view existing permissions by typing cacls filename at a command prompt, replacing filename with the name of the file or folder you are interested in.

6. CASE STUDY 2: Your assistant Mary has upgraded the SF factory PCs to WinXP. She has configured a series of permissions, both at the share level and at the file system level, on these computers, making things very complicated. How do you tell the effective permissions of a file named fileX assigned to an individual user account Kitty on a workstation named XP3?

***A. On XP3, open the properties dialog box for fileX, and choose Properties. On the Security tab, click the Advanced button and then click the Effective Permissions tab. Click the Select button to open the Select User or Group dialog box. Enter the name of Kitty, and then click OK.**

B. On XP3, open the properties dialog box for fileX, and choose Properties. On the Advanced tab, click the Security button and then click the Permissions tab. Click the Select button to open the Select User or Group dialog box. Enter the name of Kitty, and then click OK.

C. On XP3, open the properties dialog box for fileX, and choose Security Properties. On the Settings tab, click the Modify button and then click the Effective Permissions tab. Click the Change button to open the Select User or Group dialog box. Enter the name of Kitty, and then click OK.

D. On XP3, open the properties dialog box for the folder that holds fileX, and choose Settings. On the Modify tab, click the Permissions button and then click the Effective Settings tab. Click the Select button to open the Select User or Group dialog box. Enter the name of Kitty, and then click OK.

E. No Answer is Correct.

Explanation: Remember, you can always figure out effective permissions by combining all the NTFS permissions assigned to an individual user account and to all of the groups to which that user belongs. In the past you must do this calculation yourself. With XP, the effective permission tab tells everything.

7. CASE STUDY 2: In your security plan you need to specify a tool for viewing and editing permissions on the WinXP systems. Mary suggests that you use the Cacls.exe utility. With this utility, what switches are available?

***A. F**

***B. C**

***C. R**

***D. W**

***E. P**

Explanation: With Cacls, you can view existing permissions by typing cacls filename at a command prompt, replacing filename with the name of the file or folder you are interested in. The Command-line Switches for Cacls.exe include:

F (for full control)
C (for change)
R (for read)
W (for write)

8. CASE STUDY 2: In your security plan you need to address the issue of security exposure caused by the paging file left on the computer's hard drive. What should you do to ensure that the paging file won't become a security hole itself?

***A. Use a registry editor. Open the registry. Navigate to the KLM\System\CurrentControlSet\Control\Session Manager\Memory Management key. Set the value of ClearPageFileAtShutdown to 1.**

B. Use a registry editor. Open the registry. Navigate to the KLM\System\CurrentControlSet\Control\Session Manager\Memory Management key. Set the value of ClearPageFileAtShutdown to 0.

C. Use a registry editor. Open the registry. Navigate to the KLM\System\ControlSet\Control\Session\Memory Management key. Set the value of ClearPageFileAtShutdown to 2.

D. Use the System Policy Editor. Enable the option "Clear the Paging File During Startup". Restart the system immediately.

E. No Answer is Correct.

Explanation: For local security, do not leave any tracks in the paging file. By default, the paging file remains intact when your system shuts down. You can change this behavior by changing a registry entry in HKLM\System\CurrentControlSet\Control\Session Manager\Memory Management key and set the value of ClearPageFileAtShutdown to 1. With this set, Windows fills inactive pages in the paging file with zeros whenever the system shuts down.

9. CASE STUDY 2: In January, there was an incident where two PCs, together with some confidential data, were stolen from the Tokyo factory. What will you include in your security plan to address such issue?

***A. Deploy EFS on the local drives**

B. Deploy client certificates on the local computers

C. Deploy Smart Card logon facilities on the local computers

D. Deploy SSL on the local computers

E. No Answer is Correct

Explanation: EFS provides a secure way to store your sensitive data. It uses your public key to create a randomly generated file encryption key. Windows automatically encrypts the data using this FEK as data is written to disk. The data can be decrypted only with your certificate and its associated private key. EFS is good for local system security.

10. CASE STUDY 2: In your plan you mention the use of EFS for protecting local data. Janice mentions the need for fall back just in case the users lose their original certificates due to a hard disk failure. What should you request the users to do before enabling EFS?

***A. Back up their personal encryption certificates with the associated private keys to a secure location**

***B. Back up the recovery agent certificates to a secure location**

C. Defrag and compress the drives

D. Run scandisk /F on the drives

E. Backup the operating system to a tape and keep the tape in a secure location

Explanation: Before you encrypt anything important, back up your personal encryption certificate and the recovery agent certificate. If you lose your original certificate, you can restore the backup copy and regain access to your files. But if you lose all copies of your certificate, no one can help.

Chapter 9: Optimizing System Performance

The objective of this chapter is to provide you with an understanding of the following:

1. Identify system performance tools
2. Optimize general system performance
3. Identify system performance analysis tools
4. Analyze system performance with System Monitor

Getting Ready – (Questions)

1). The Event Viewer console uses event logs to gather hardware and software information, system problems, and security events. Name the three logs that store these events.

2). You are monitoring memory performance using the counter "Memory>Pages/Sec". What will this counter tell you?

3). You are monitoring your processor using the counter "Processor>Interrupts/Sec" and the resulting number is very low. What is your best course of action?

4). What will using the Performance Logs and Alerts allow you to create?

5). You must be a member of one of two built-in groups to change process' priority. Name them.

Getting Ready – (Answers)

1). Events will be stored in one of three logs: Application, System, and Security.

2). This counter monitors the number of times the requested information had to be retrieved from the page file on the hard disk – optimal performance should be around 4.

3). Do nothing. "Processor>Interrupts/Sec" shows the number of hardware interrupts the processor receives each second. Lower is better.

4). Using the Performance Logs and Alerts will allow you to create counter and trace logs, as well as define alerts.

5). You must be an administrator or a member of the Power User group to change a process' priority.

I Introduction

Windows XP has already been industry-proven to be a sturdy and reliable operating system. However, optimizing your system to meet user requirements and network demands will only increase the performance of this hardy operating system.

II General System Performance

The Event Log service provides the capabilities for applications and services to log their respective events. These events will be stored in one of three logs: Application, System, and Security.

Event Viewer

The Event Viewer console (Figure 9.1) uses event logs to gather hardware and software information, system problems, and security events (auditing).

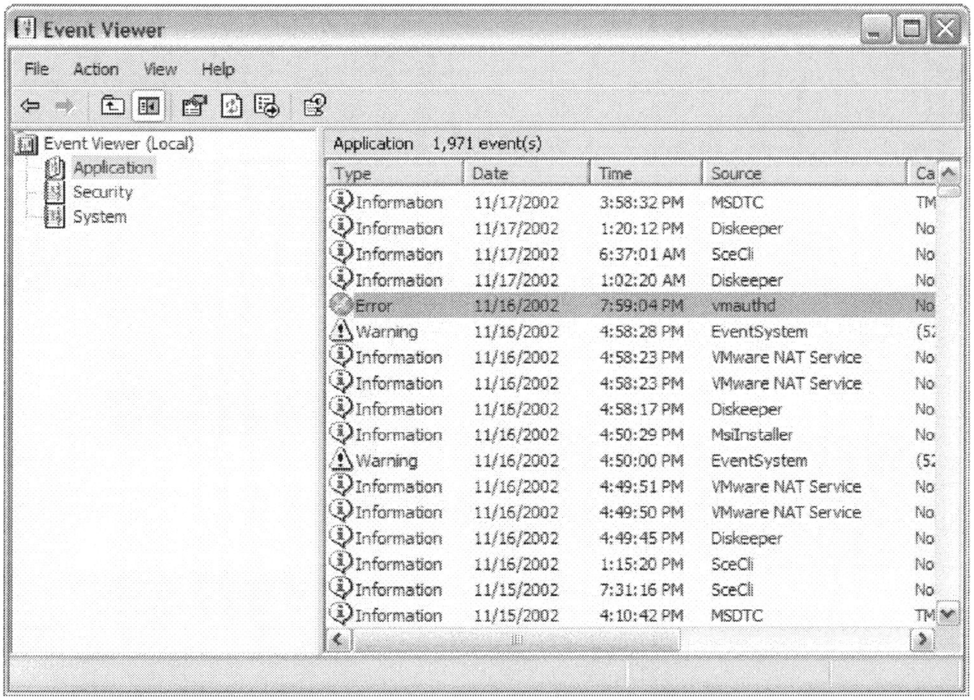

Figure 9-1: Event Viewer

The Application log contains the events logged by user applications. These events are determined by the developer of the application as to what events to produce and to what degree of verbosity to implore.

The System log contains those events generated by Windows XP system components. Microsoft predetermines these events.

The Security log records security related events such as logon validation and resource use. These events are controlled by the auditing functions of the various resources and subsystems. By default, these events are not recorded. Security logs are only viewable by administrators.

Both the Application log and the System log can show three different types of events: Error, Warning, and Information. Each of these event types shows a degree of severity for the event, with Error being the most critical.

The Security log produces two events. The first is the Success Audit, which indicates a successful security access. The second is the Failure Audit, which indicates a failed security access.

For each log you can quickly view the events in the console window. There are eight columns showing information about the event. These columns are Type, Date, Time, Source, Category, Event, User, and Computer.

With each event in Windows XP, you can show the properties of the event by simply double-clicking upon them. This presents dialog box (Figure 9.2), which provides more detailed information about the event.

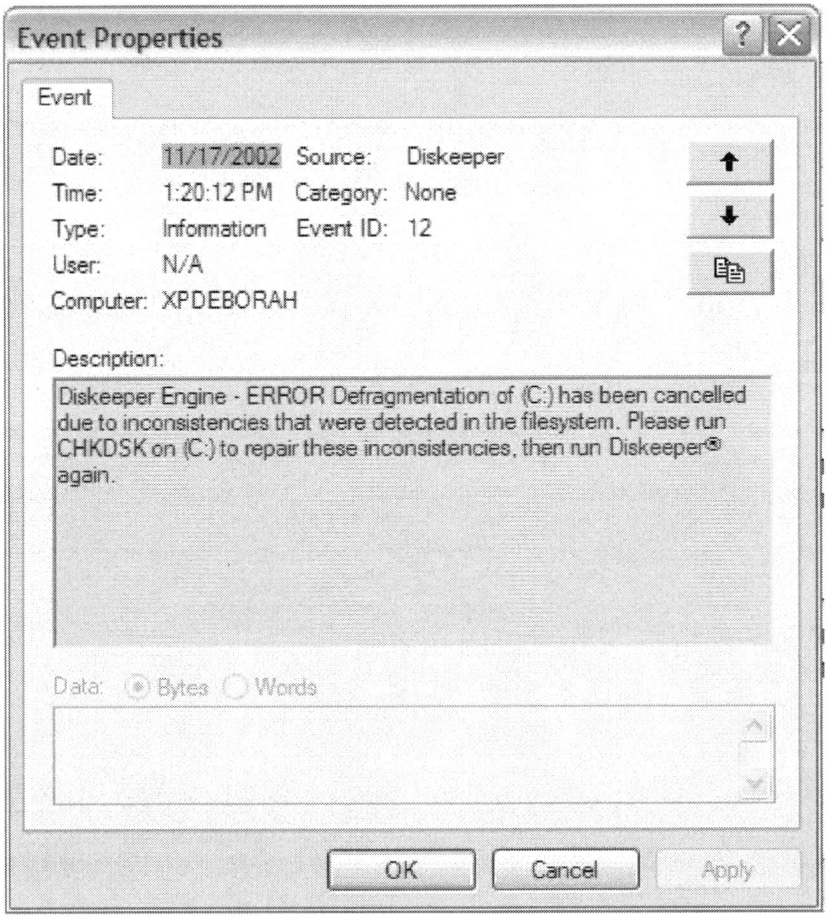

Figure 9-2: Event Viewer: Event Details

Event Viewer provides great functionality for any type of user. Not only can you view events for your own computer, but also you can view events for other remote computers. Another feature is the ability to filter the events that are displayed to identify any problem areas quickly (Figure 9.3). The filters are applied on a per log basis.

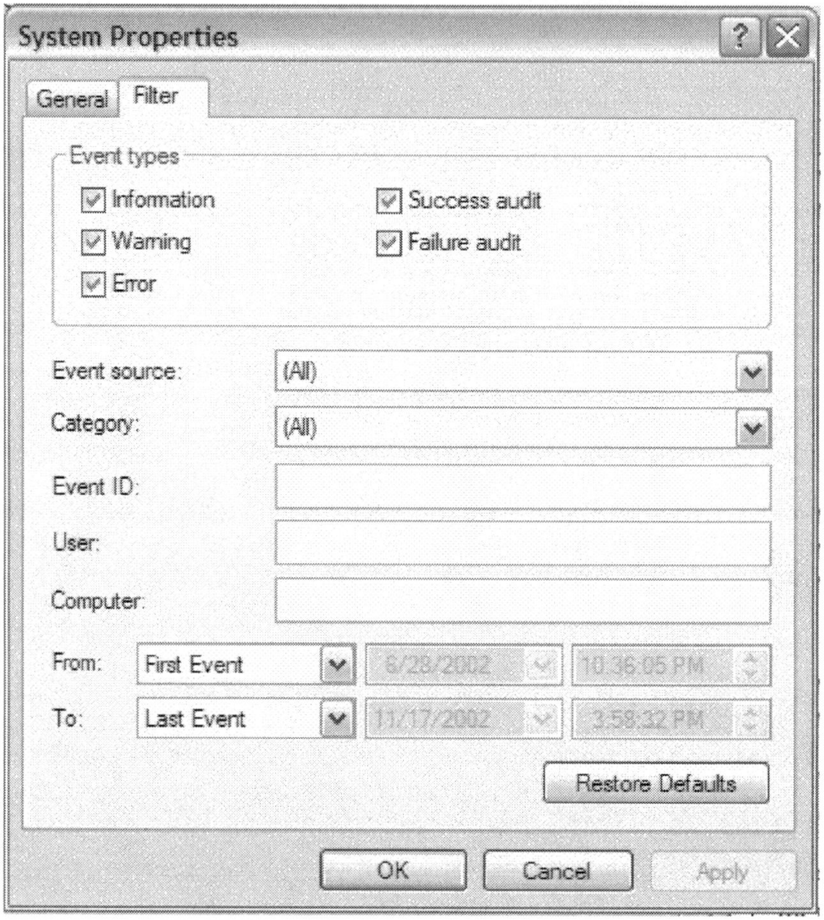

Figure 9-3: Event Viewer Filter

Check Disk

The Check Disk tool scans a specific drive for various types of damage, such as cross-linked files and incorrect file sizes. You can access this tool from the drives properties and selecting **Check Now** in the Error-checking section of the Tools tab (Figure 9.4).

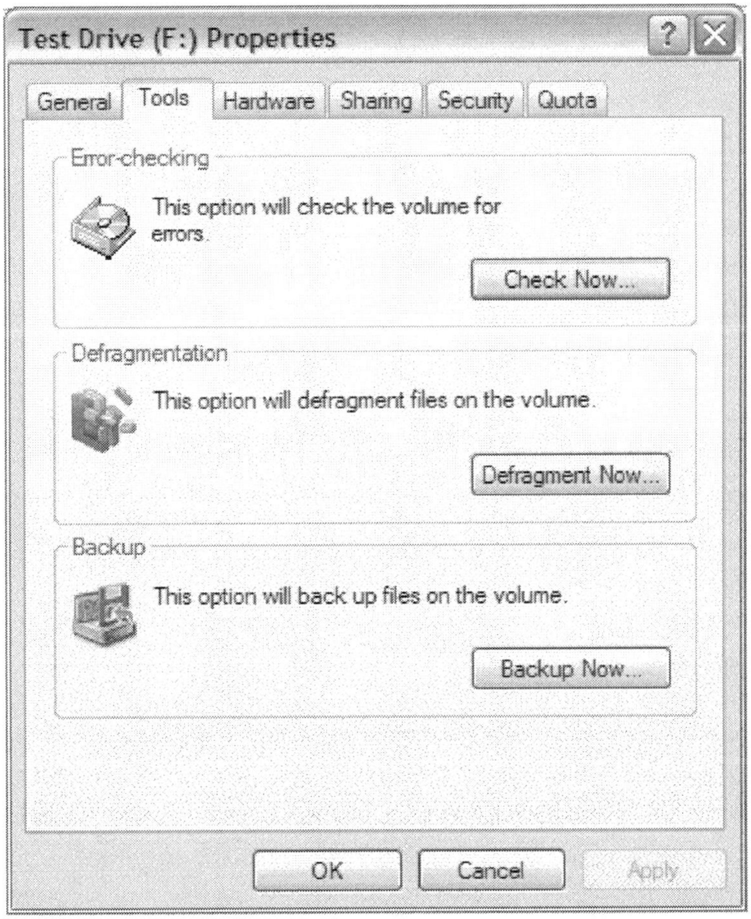

Figure 9-4: Tools: Error Checking

This will then present the Check Disk dialog box (Figure 9.5).

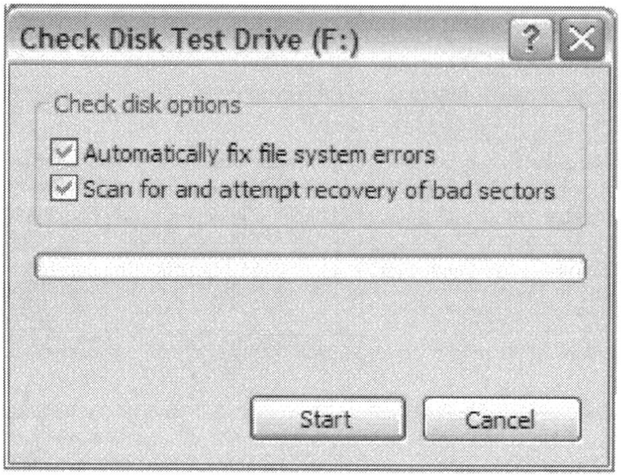

Figure 9-5: Check Disk Options

> **NOTE:** During the disk scan, the disk will be unavailable for use. Disk scanning can take a long time, especially with disks containing a large number of files.

If you run the Check Disk tool without selecting any options, it performs a basic scan of the drive. As the tool encounters errors, it will prompt you for further instructions. If you want the tool to perform these actions automatically, select the check box **Automatically fix file system errors**.

To perform a more thorough scan, select the check box **Scan for and attempt recovery of bad sectors**. This will instruct the tool to look at every sector on the disk and determine the validity of the data. If an error is detected, the tool will attempt to move the data to a free sector on the disk. This option includes the Automatically fix file system errors option.

> **NOTE:** If any files are in use on the system, the Check Disk tool will ask if you would like to schedule the disk check during the next system restart.

You can also use the command line utility CHKDSK.exe to perform these same functions. Table 9.1 provides the command line parameters available for the chkdsk command.

CHKDSK [volume[[path]filename]]] [/f] [/v] [/r] [/x] [/i] [/c] [/l[:size]]

VOLUME	Specifies the drive letter (followed by a colon), mount point, or volume name
PATH	FAT only: Specifies the path for the files to check for fragmentation
FILENAME	FAT only: Specifies the files to check for fragmentation
/F	Fixes errors on the disk
/V	On FAT/FAT32: Displays the full path and name of every file on the disk. On NTFS: Displays cleanup messages if any
/R	Locates bad sectors and recovers readable information (implies /F)
/X	Forces the volume to dismount first if necessary. All opened handles to the volume would then be invalid (implies /F)
/I	NTFS only: Performs a less vigorous check of index entries
/C	NTFS only: Skips checking of cycles within the folder structure
/L[:SIZE]	NTFS only: Changes the log file size to the specified number of kilobytes. If size is not specified, displays current size

THE /I OR /C SWITCH REDUCES THE AMOUNT OF TIME REQUIRED BY SKIPPING CERTAIN CHECKS OF THE VOLUME.

Table 9-1: Chkdsk.exe Command Line Parameters

Disk Defragmenter

Disk fragmentation occurs during normal use of the system. As you add and remove files and folders from any file system (FAT, FAT32, and NTFS), holes are left scattered about the drive. As this situation grows, the holes become even more scattered, or fragmented, causing Windows XP to place files in various locations on the drive, causing both a slowdown in the writing and reading of the data.

You use Disk Defragmenter to move these scattered pieces of files and folders so that each occupies a single, contiguous space on the drive. This results in your system being able to read the files quickly. The defragmentation of the drive also consolidates the free space on the drive, making new write requests less susceptible to fragmentation.

The Disk Defragmenter console tool can be accessed from the Computer Management console, or from the drive's property page (Figure 9.6). You have the ability to analyze and defragment one drive at a time.

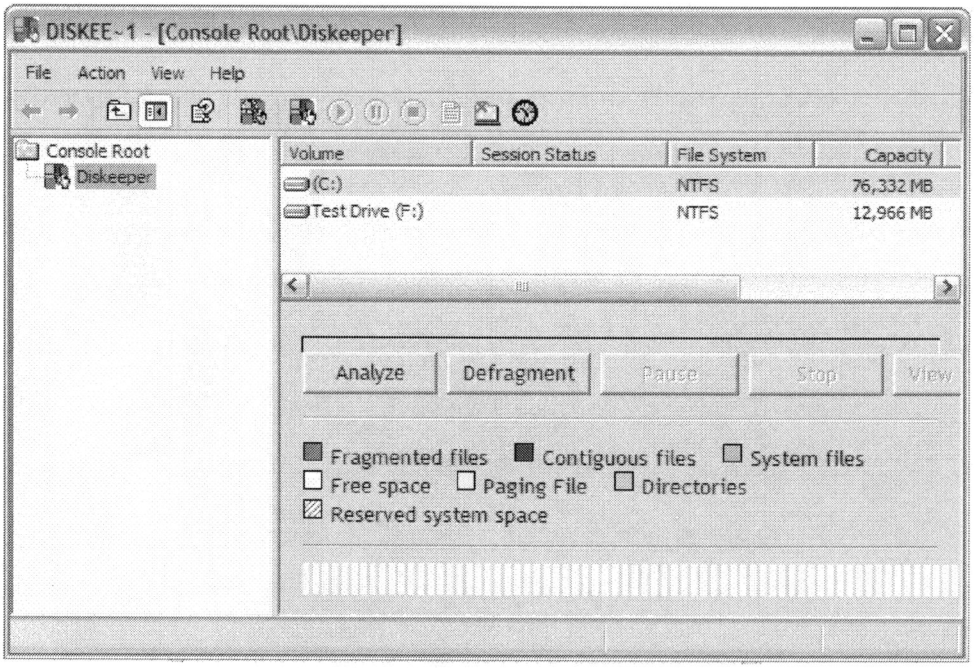

Figure 9-6: Defragmenting Hard Drives

To check the status of the drive, choose the **Analyze** button. This will scan the drive and then prompt you depending on the condition of the drive. If there is a need to defragment the drive, you will see Figure 9.7, if not, then you will see Figure 9.8.

If you select **Close**, you are then returned to Disk Defragmenter, and will see a display similar to Figure 9.6.

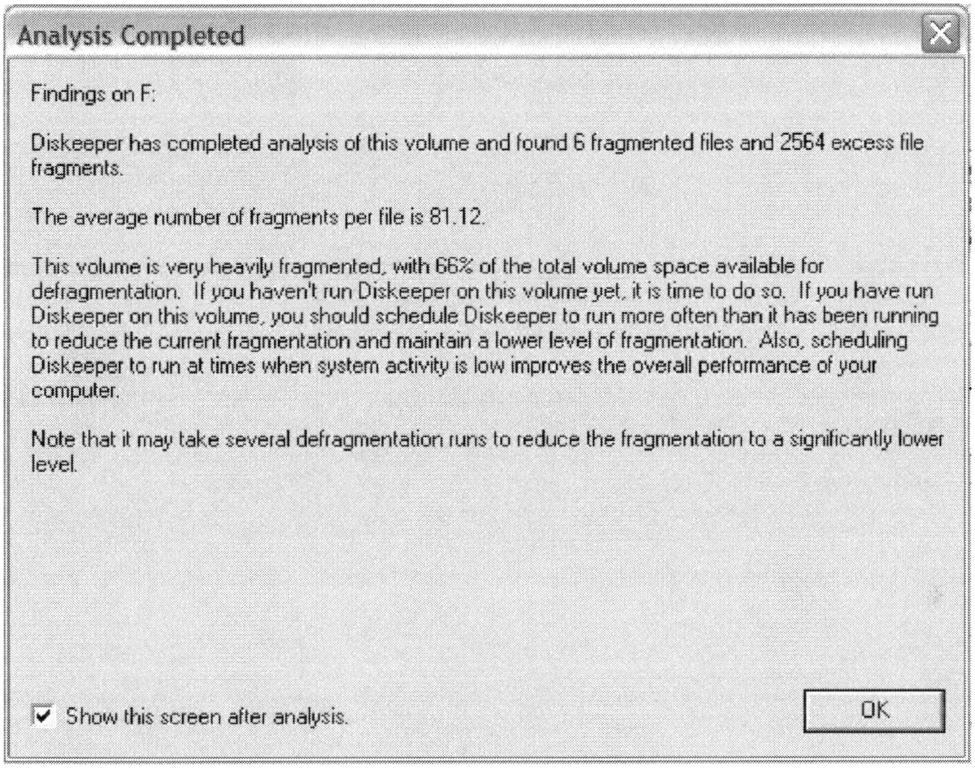

Figure 9-7: Fragmented Drive

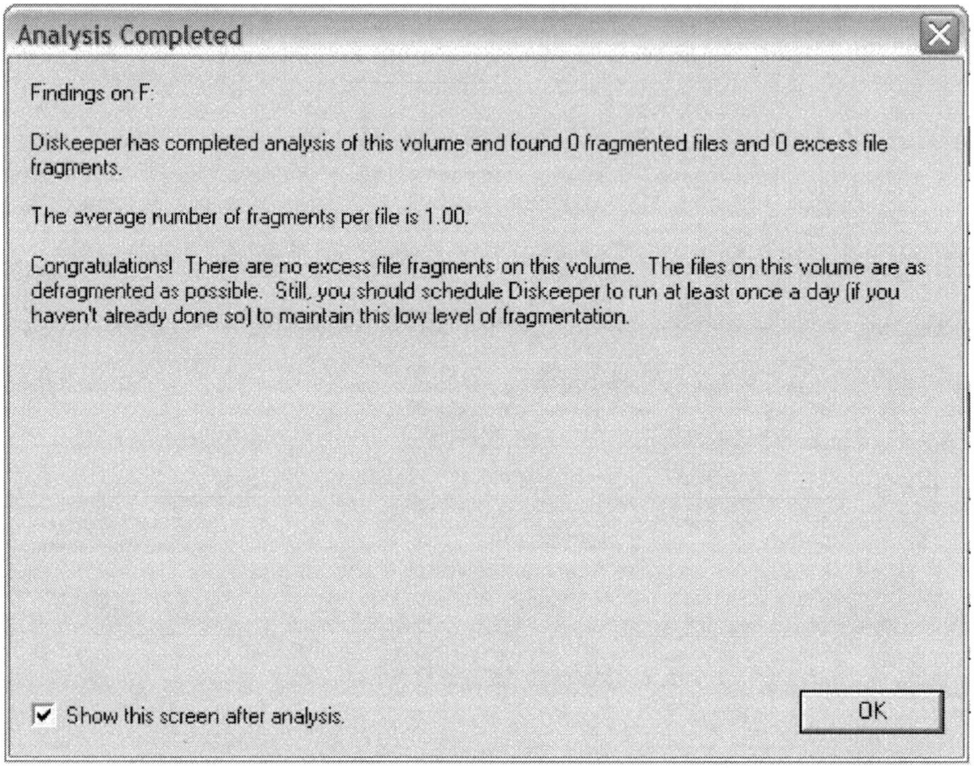

Figure 9-8: Non-Fragmented Drive

If you select the View Report button, you are then shown the Analysis Report (Figure 9.9). This report shows you the information for the drive, including the amount of free space and fragmentation.

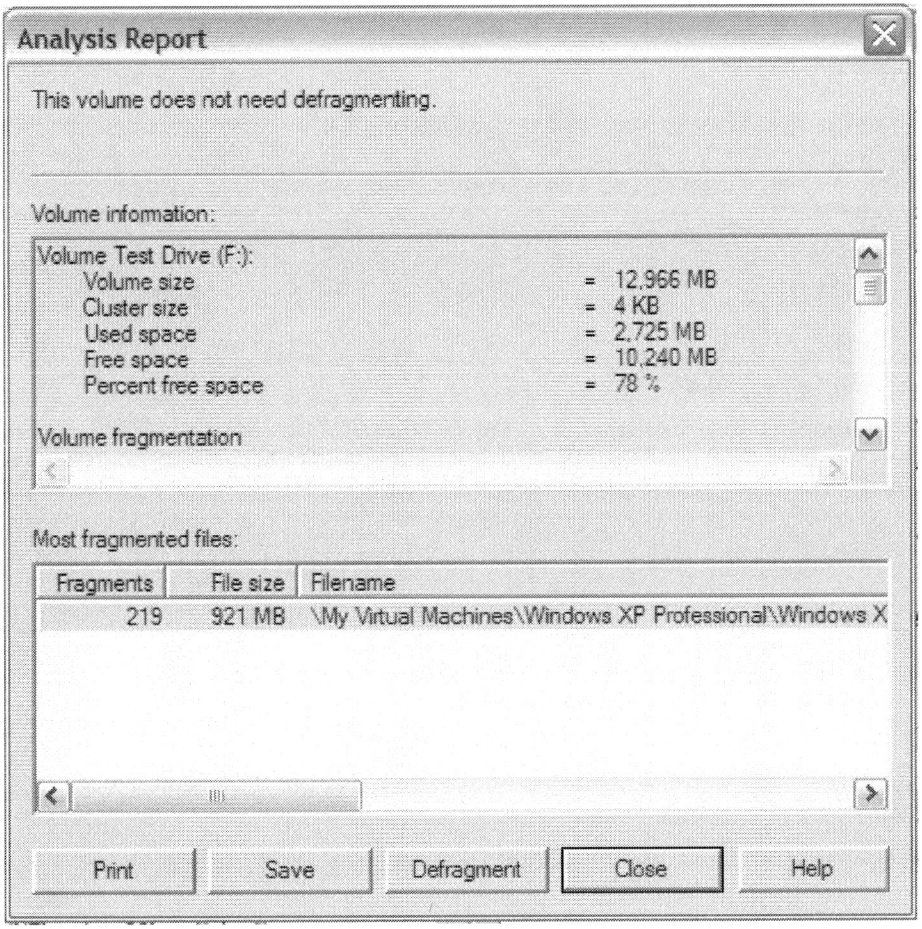

Figure 9-9: Analysis Report

You can also print and save this report for record keeping purposes, if so desired. Saving the report is a good idea as you can then refer to the information before and after a defragmentation has occurred. Figure 9.10 shows a sample of this report.

Volume WIN2K (F:):

Volume		size	=	72,332	MB
Cluster		size	=	4	KB
Used		space	=	45,593	MB
Free		space	=	30,738	MB
Percent	free	space	=	40	%

Volume fragmentation

Total		fragmentation	=	5	%
File		fragmentation	=	0	%
Free	space	fragmentation	=		13%

File fragmentation

Total		files	=		122,987
Average	file	size	=	498	KB
Total	fragmented	files	=		1,004
Total	excess	fragments	=		7,600
Average fragments per file			=		1.06

Pagefile fragmentation

Pagefile		size	=	384	MB
Total		fragments	=		1

Directory fragmentation

Total		directories	=		7,474
Fragmented		directories	=		16
Excess	directory	fragments	=		51

Master File Table (MFT) fragmentation

Total MFT size	=	128	MB	
MFT record count	=		131,268	
Percent MFT in use	=	99	%	
Total MFT fragments	= 14			

Fragments	File Size	Most fragmented files
55	296 KB	\WINNT\system32
40	184 KB	\WINNT\inf
68	364 KB	\WINNT\system32\dllcache
441	2,732 KB	\WINNT\system32\config\system
532	9,576 KB	\WINNT\system32\config\software
33	136 KB	\WINNT\system32\config\userdiff
32	8 KB	\WINNT\system32\config\software.LOG
548	2,732 KB	\WINNT\system32\config\SYSTEM.ALT
104	442 KB	\WINNT\setupapi.log
90	616 KB	\Documents and Settings\Patrick\NTUSER.DAT
37	156 KB	\WINNT\Help\iisHelp\iis\htm\asp
67	80 KB	\WINNT\$NtServicePackUninstall$

Figure 9-10: Printed Analysis Report

As we can see from the report, there are many types of fragmentation that can occur, especially on an NTFS partition. On FAT and FAT32 partitions, the information is the same, sans the MFT fragmentation section.

Once you have analyzed the drive, and it is determined that a defragmentation is necessary, simply click on a **Defragment** button. This will perform another analysis on the drive (to gather up to date information) and then defragment the drive. Once the defragmentation is complete, you are then able to see a report of the completed defragmentation. This report contains the same type of information as before.

As we see from Figure 9.11, the defragmentation was fairly successful. There are some things to be aware of with Disk Defragmenter:

- You cannot defragment open files
- You cannot perform a directory consolidation
- You cannot defragment the Master File Table (MFT)
- You cannot defragment the page file (it is also open)
- You cannot defragment system files (they are also open)
- You cannot defragment remote systems
- You cannot schedule the defragmentation (there is no command line utility)
- You can only run one Disk Defragmentation console
- You require administrative privileges

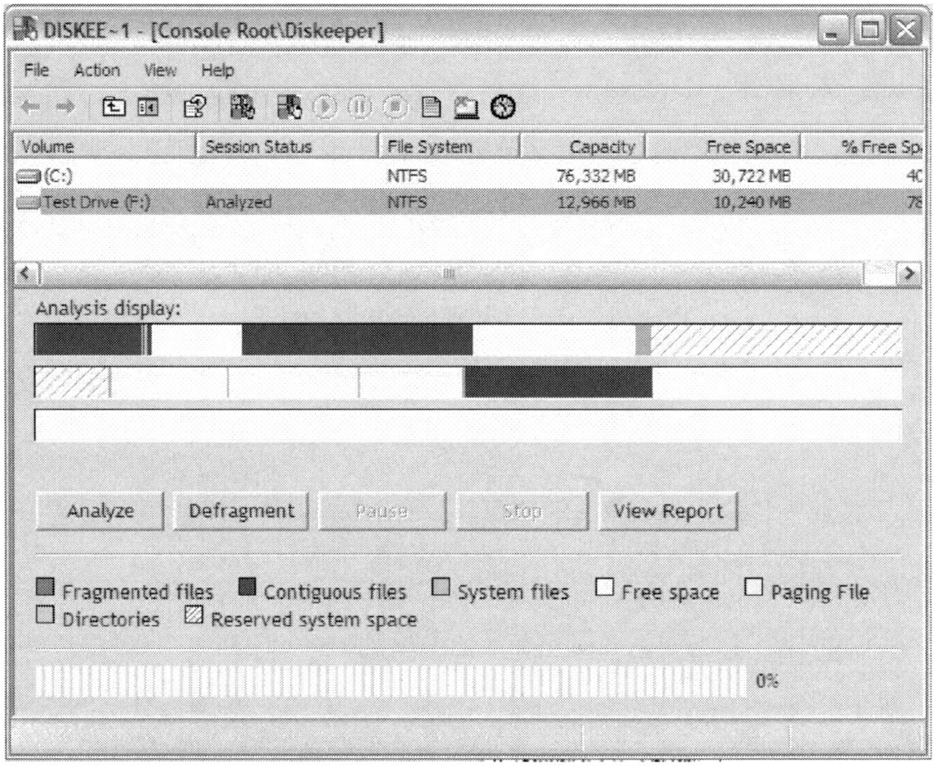

Figure 9-11: Completed Disk Defragmentation

> **NOTE:** To perform a number of these functions, you need to purchase a 3rd party utility. Once such utility is Executive Software's Diskeeper (Disk Defragmenter is a subset of this).

Task Manager

Task Manager will allow you to view the applications and processes that are currently running on your system. When you view the Applications Tab, you will see the applications that are running and their status (running, not responding, stopped) (Figure 9.12). On this tab you can end a task, switch to a task, or start a new task.

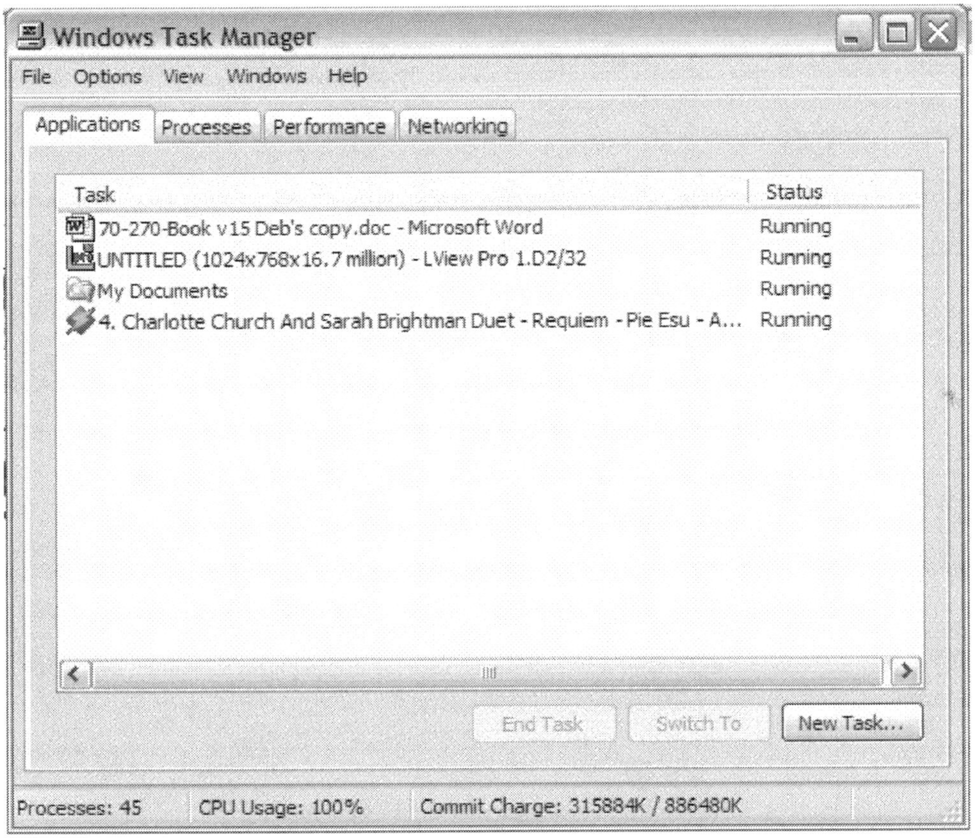

Figure 9-12: Task Manager (Applications view)

The Processes tab will show you all the processes currently running on your system, including processes used by the operating system (Figure 9.13). This tab allows you to end a process that has ceased to function or is causing system instability. If you right-click a process, a menu is displayed allowing you to end the process, end the process tree, debug (if a debugger is registered on the system), set the affinity (on multiprocessor systems) or change the priority of the process.

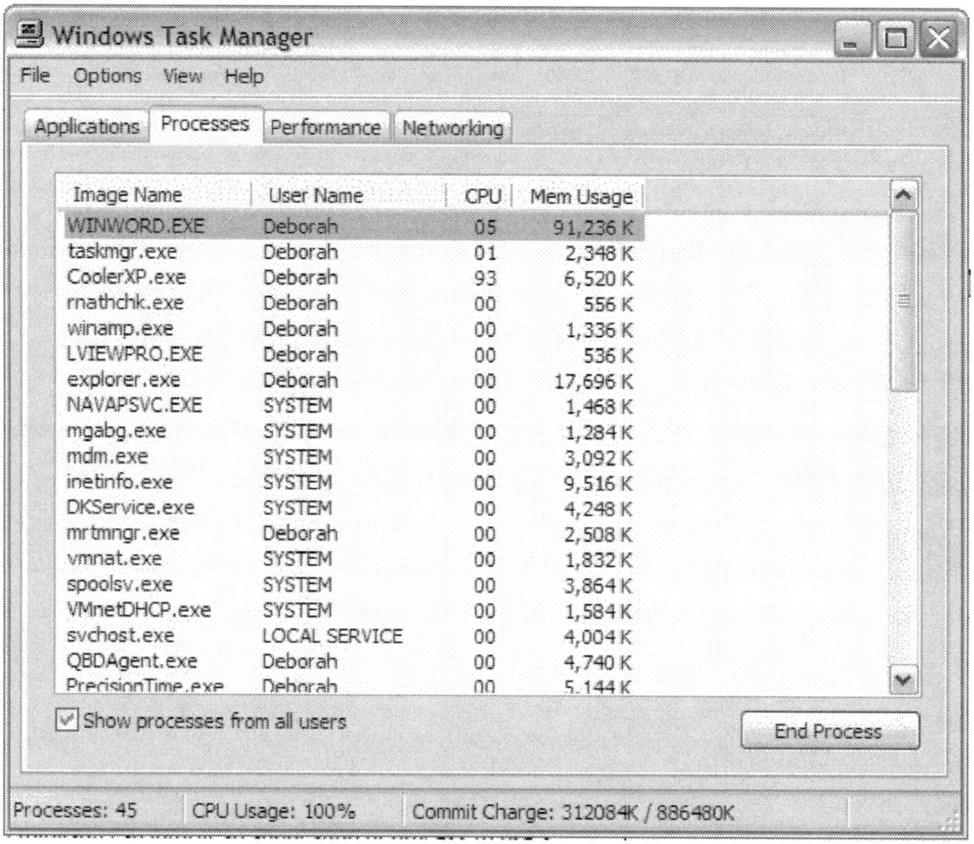

Figure 9-13: Task Manager Processes View

On multiprocessor systems, the **Set Affinity** command can inform an application or process to use a specific processor or processors. The effect of this can be a double-edged sword. You are essentially removing the ability of the process to benefit from the asymmetrical processing capabilities of Windows XP. On the other hand, certain applications can gain substantial benefits from it, specifically if they do not use threading.

By changing the priority of a process, you can optimize it to use a specific amount of processor time. This can adversely affect the overall performance of not only the process itself, but of all other processes as well. By raising the priority, you grant the process more processing time, making it run faster. Inversely, by lowering the priority, you limit the amount of processing time, making it run slower.

In order for Windows XP to guarantee that every process will get a chance for processing time, a mechanism for scheduling threads is used. This mechanism is the basis for the preemptive multitasking strategy in Windows XP. Each and every thread and process are assigned a priority, which then determines the order in which they are granted processing time. A thread's priority is based on the priority class of its parent process. There are four process priority classes:

- Idle – used for processes (such as screen savers) that periodically update the display
- Normal – the default priority class for a process
- High – these processes receive the majority of processor time
- Real Time – used mostly by kernel-mode processes (such as mouse and keyboard input)

Each of these priority classes set a range of priority values between 0 and 31. Priority 0 is reserved for system use. Priorities between 1 and 31 have increasingly higher priorities (with 1 being the lowest). Idle, Normal, and High priorities range between 1 and 15, Real Time priorities range between 16 and 31. For processes that are Real Time, the thread's priority cannot change while the thread is running. For all other priorities, the threads are considered variable (they can change thread priority while running). For threads running in the Normal or High priority classes, the thread's priority can be raised or lowered by up to a value of 2, but cannot fall below its original, program-defined base priority. The resulting value of changing the base priority for optimized thread scheduling is called the thread's dynamic priority. A listing of all Windows XP process priorities is listed in Table 9.2.

> **NOTE:** If you have at least one priority 31 thread running, other threads cannot run.

	Process Priority Classes			
Thread Priorities	Real Time	High	Normal	Idle
Time Critical	31	15	15	15
Highest	26	15	10	6
Above Normal	25	14	9	5
Normal	24	13	8	4
Below Normal	23	12	7	3
Lowest	22	11	6	2
Idle	16	1	1	1

Table 9-2: NTFS Permission Comparison

With Task Manger, you can change the base priority of a process to one of the following:

- Real-time (Time Critical)
- High (Highest)
- AboveNormal
- Normal
- BelowNormal
- Low (Lowest)

Remember that you cannot change the Process Priority Class, just the thread priority. Changes made to the base priority of the process are not permanent; they are effective only as long as the process runs.

> **NOTE:** You must be an administrator or a member of the Power User group to change a process' priority.

The information on the Processes tab can be modified to gain even more information. By choosing **Select Columns**… on the View menu will display Figure 9.14.

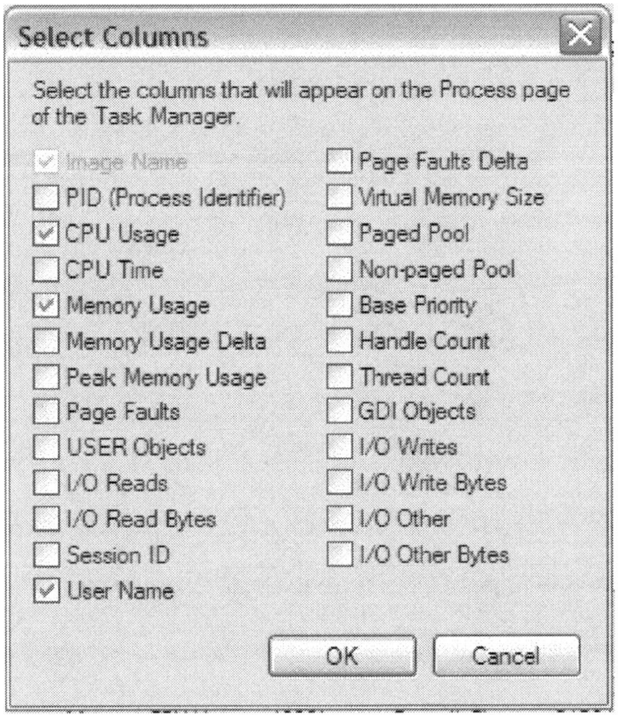

Figure 9-14: Task Manager Processes

Each of the above options are explained in Table 9.3.

COLUMN	DESCRIPTION
Base Priority	A precedence ranking that determines the order in which the threads of a process are scheduled for the processor
CPU Time	The total processor time, in seconds, used by a process since it started
CPU Usage	The percentage of time that a process used the CPU since the last update
GDI Objects	The number of Graphics Device Interface (GDI) objects currently used by a process
Handle Count	The number of object handles in a process's object table
Image Name	The name of a process
I/O Other	The number of input/output operations generated by a process that are neither a read nor a write, including file, network, and device I/Os
I/O Other Bytes	The number of bytes transferred in input/output operations generated by a process that are neither a read nor a write, including file, network, and device I/Os
I/O Reads	The number of read input/output operations generated by a process, including file, network, and device I/O's. I/O Reads directed to CONSOLE (console input object) handles are not counted.
I/O Read Bytes	The number of bytes read in input/output operations generated by a process, including file, network, and device I/Os. I/O Read Bytes directed to CONSOLE (console input object) handles are not counted.
I/O Writes	The number of write input/output operations generated by a process, including file, network, and device I/Os. I/O Writes directed to CONSOLE (console input object) handles are not counted.
I/O Write Bytes	The number of bytes written in input/output operations generated by a process, including file, network, and device I/Os. I/O Write Bytes directed to CONSOLE (console input object) handles are not counted.

COLUMN	DESCRIPTION
Memory Usage	The current working set of a process, in kilobytes. The current working set is the number of pages currently resident in memory.
Memory Usage Delta	The change in memory, in kilobytes, used since the last update
Non-paged Pool	The amount of memory used by a process, in kilobytes, that is not paged to disk
Page Faults	The number of times data has to be retrieved from disk for a process because it was not found in memory. The page fault value accumulates from the time the process started.
Page Faults Delta	The change in the number of page faults since the last update
Paged Pool	The amount of system allocated virtual memory, in kilobytes, used by a process
Peak Memory Usage	The peak amount of physical memory resident in a process since it started
PID (Process Identifier)	A numerical identifier that uniquely distinguishes a process while it runs
Thread Count	The number of threads running in a process
USER Objects	The number of USER objects (windows, menus, cursors, icons, etc) currently being used by a process
Virtual Memory Size	The amount of virtual memory, or address space, committed to a process
Session ID (Terminal Services Only)	The Terminal Services session ID that owns the process
User Name (Terminal Services Only)	The name of the user whose Terminal Services session owns the process

Table 9-3: Process Definitions

The Performance Tab will give you a quick glance at CPU and memory usage (Figure 9.15). This tab provides you with a quick version of the System Monitor tool.

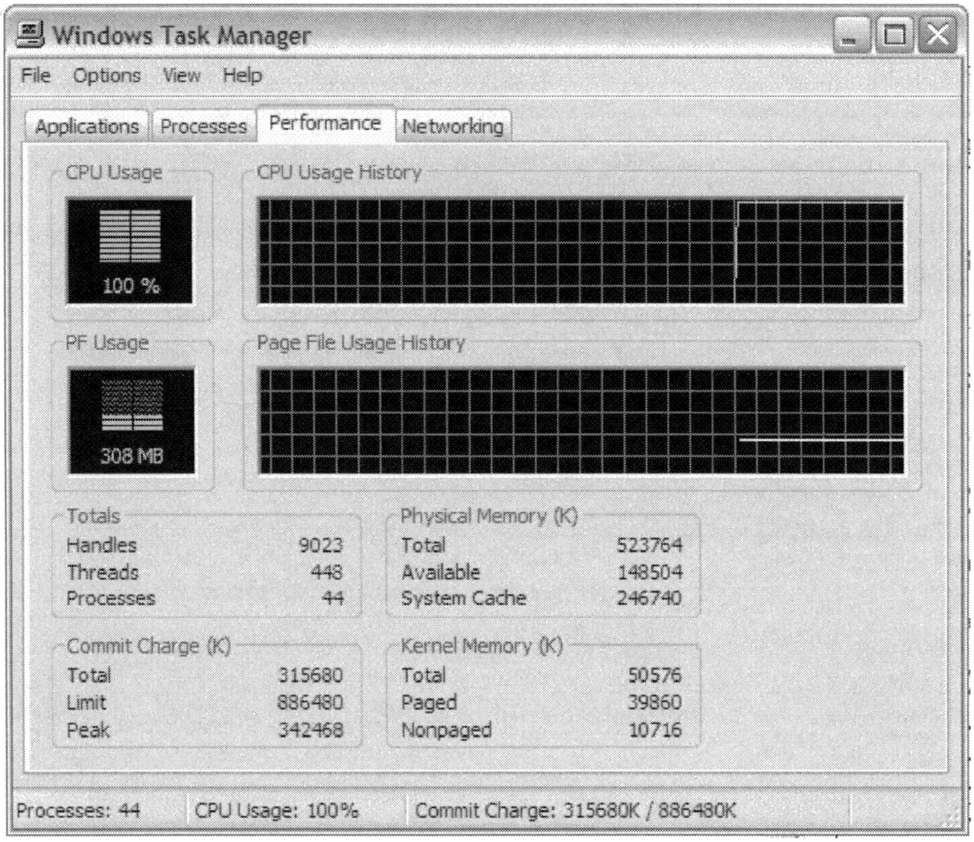

Figure 9-15: Task Manager Performance View

By clicking **Show Kernel Times** on the **View** menu, red lines are added to the CPU Usage gauge (Figure 9.16) and CPU Usage History graph. These red lines indicate the percentage of processor time consumed in privileged or kernel mode.

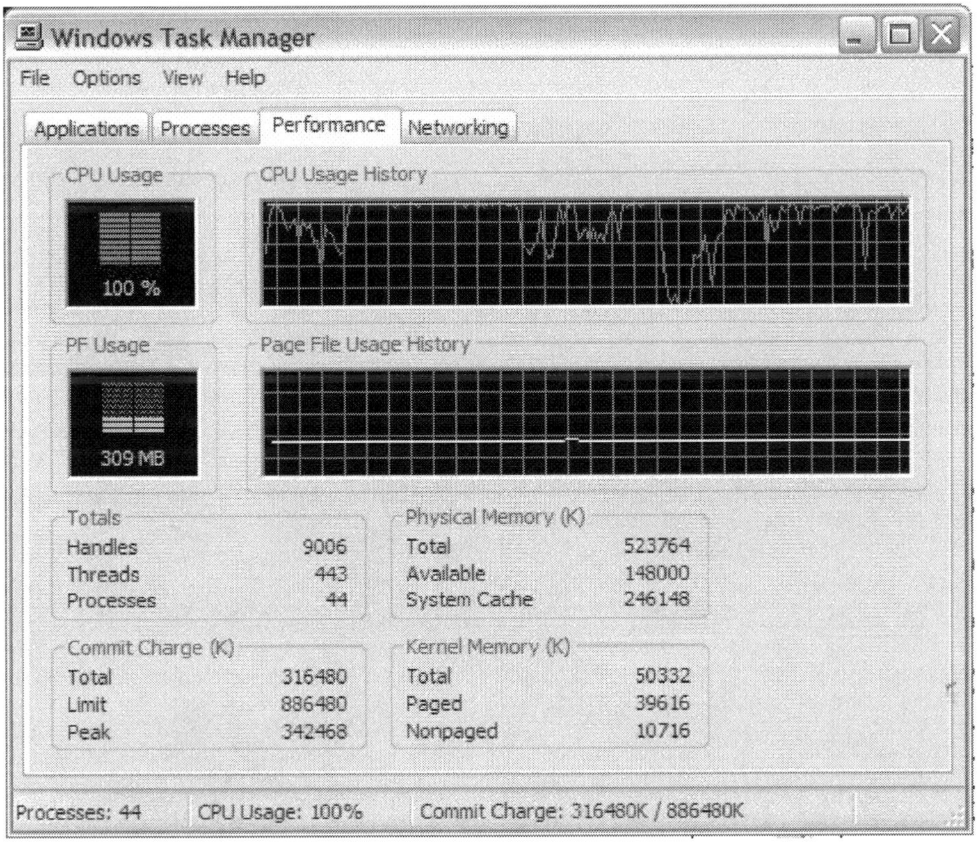

Figure 9-16: Performance View with Kernel Times

On multiprocessor systems, you can change the graph to display each processor in a single graph, or in separate graphs. Clicking CPU History on the View Menu achieves this functionality.

With Windows XP, there is also a Networking Tab (Figure 9.17). With this view, you can see bytes sent, received, and total. While it is only visible if there is a network card available, the Networking tab provides a quick indication of the network traffic on the computer. A quick reference for determining the amount of network bandwidth being consumed, when there are multiple network connections, it allows easy comparison of the traffic for each connection.

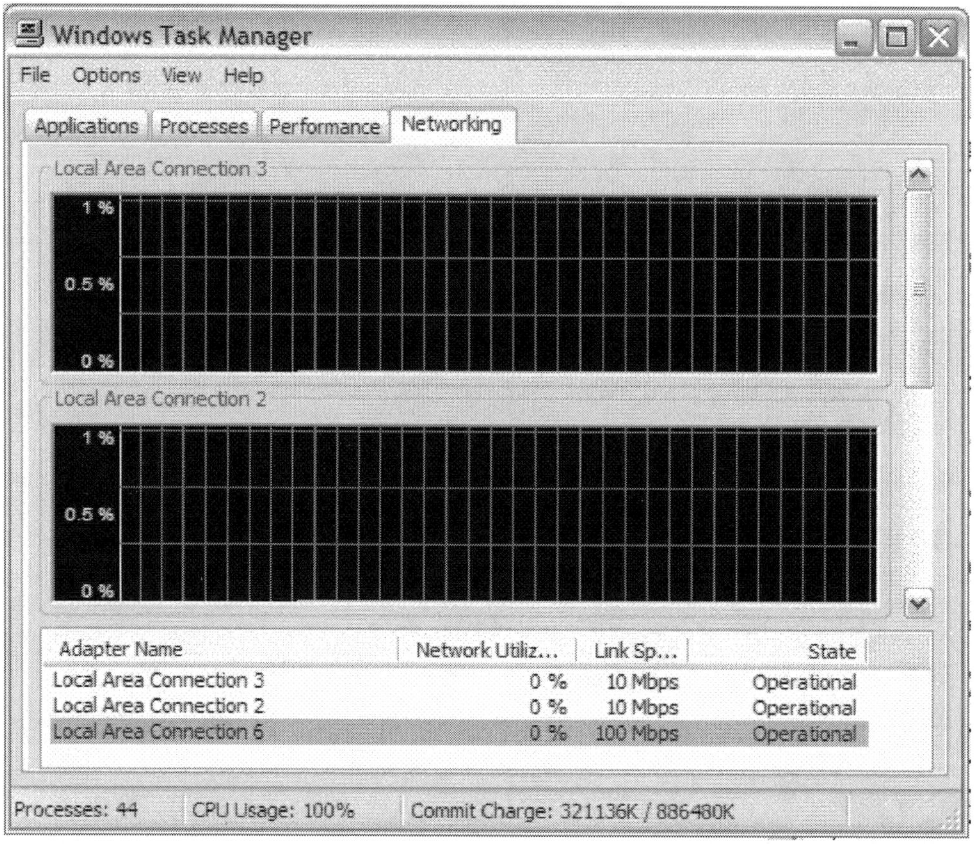

Figure 9-17: Task Manager Networking View

III System Performance Analysis Tools

Monitoring and optimizing Windows XP can be a book all by itself. Please keep in mind while reviewing this section that this will provide you with the basic knowledge to optimize your system. Detailed information can be obtained through the Microsoft Windows XP Resource kit.

Before you can optimize your system, you will need to monitor all the critical subsystems, such as memory, processor, disk, and network, to see if anything needs to be changed or upgraded on your system. Windows XP comes with two tools: **System Monitor** and **Performance Logs and Alerts.** These can be found in the **Performance** console, under Administrative Tools in Control Panel.

These system tools will allow you to create a baseline, identify system bottlenecks, and determine trends.

A baseline is a snapshot of how your system is performing. It is a good idea to take a baseline report at the same time every day for a set period of time. This will allow you to get a real feel for how your system is reacting to different requests.

A bottleneck is a system resource that is causing slowdowns because of inefficient performance. By setting counters (which we will review a little later in this chapter), you will be able to ascertain which, if any, of your systems may be causing degraded performance.

Determining trends, on the other hand, is a proactive approach to optimization. If you monitor your system on a regular basis, you may notice that your page file usage is increasing slowly but steadily. This will indicate that you will need to upgrade the amount of RAM in your system in the future. Determining trends allows you to predict what upgrades your system may need in the future so that you can plan accordingly.

System Monitor

System Monitor allows you to view real time performance of your system. You can capture this data in a log as well, so that you can view it at a later time. When you first open System Monitor, you will notice that nothing is being tracked. This is because you must first set counters to monitor the particular process in which you are interested. These counters will be displayed on the screen (Figure 9.18).

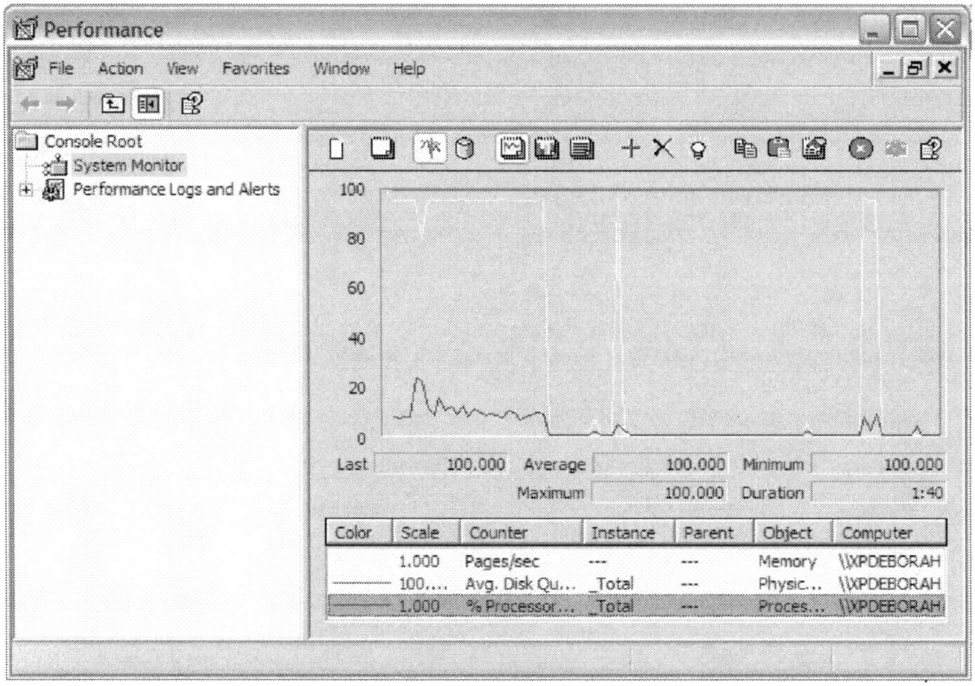

Figure 9-18: System Monitor

There are three views available to you in System Monitor:

- **Chart**

  (The default view) allows you to view a small number of counters over a set period of time
- **Histogram**

  (Bar chart) allows you to view a large number of counters as a snapshot
- **Report**

  Allows you to view the counters in text format in real time

Performance Logs and Alerts

Using the Performance Logs and Alerts will allow you to create counter and trace logs, as well as define alerts (Figure 9.19). Counter logs record data about hardware usage and activity on a system. You can configure logging to occur on a regular basis, or on-demand. Trace logs measure data on a continuous basis. Alerts are messages that are sent to the system administrator when a specific counter exceeds, or falls below, a predetermined setting.

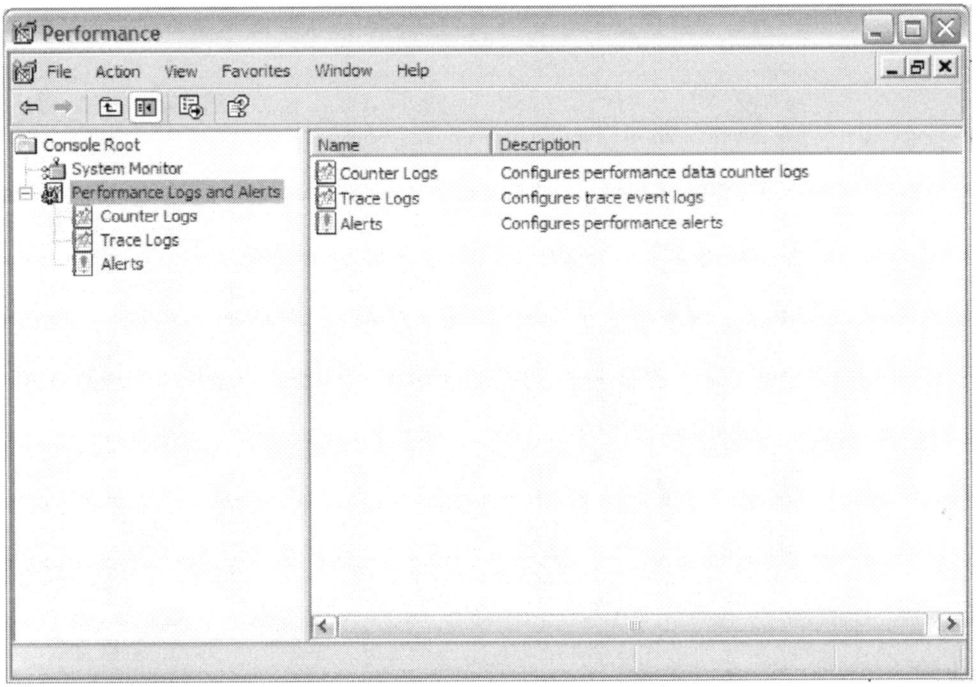

Figure 9-19: Performance Logs and Alerts

IV System Performance Analysis

Memory Performance

There was a running joke among IT Professionals using Windows NT. The solution to every performance problem is “Add RAM”. Just like NT, Windows XP loves RAM. The more RAM available to the system, the less paging (use of virtual memory) has to occur. No matter how fast your hard drive's performance, it is still going to be substantially (up to 1,000 times slower) than RAM.

Some counters that you will want to use to monitor memory usage are:

- Memory >Available Mbytes

The amount of physical memory available to run processes – the more, the better!

- Memory>Pages/Sec

The number of times the requested information had to be retrieved from the page file on the hard disk – optimal performance should be around 4.

- Paging File>% Usage

Indicates how much of the page file is currently being used – the lower, the better!

Processor Performance

Unless you are running processor intensive programs, the odds are that your processor is not the cause of your bottleneck. However, you will want to monitor the processor to make sure that it is running efficiently. Otherwise, you may want to upgrade your processor, or, if your system supports it, add another processor.

The counters you may wish to monitor are:

- Processor>%Processor Time

The amount of time the processor spends responding to system requests. Optimally, this will not be above 80%.

- Processor>Interrupts/Sec

Shows the number of hardware interrupts the processor receives each second. Lower is better.

- Disk Performance

Disk access can be improved by using faster disks and faster disk controllers. As mentioned earlier in the book, using disk striping and volume striping will also improve I/O performance. Adding another disk controller will help with load balancing as well.

There are two important counters for disk performance:

- PhysicalDisk>%Disk Time

The amount of time that the disk is busy processing read and write requests. It is preferable that this counter be below 90%. Keep in mind that paging also takes place on the hard disk; so adding RAM may also help performance in this area.

- PhysicalDisk>Current Disk Queue Length

Indicates the number of disk requests waiting to be processed. You do not want this value above 2.

Network Performance

Windows XP does not have a built-in tool for monitoring network performance. This monitoring is usually done on the server-side. However, you can optimize performance on the network card by monitoring the traffic generated on your NIC and by monitoring the network protocols you are using.

To optimize network traffic, use only the network protocols you need. There is no need to install NetBEUI, for example, if you never need to use it. If you do use multiple protocols, place the most commonly used protocols at the top of the binding order. Use faster network cards, and ones that take full advantage of the bus width.

Two counters that are useful for monitoring the network are:

- Network Interface>Bytes Total/Sec

Measures the total number of bytes sent and received by the NIC. This includes traffic from all protocols.

- TCP>Segments/Sec

Measures the number of bytes that are sent or received by the NIC by the TCP protocol only.

Application Performance

The benefit of any Windows operating system is that you can operate a number of applications at the same time. By default, the foreground application (active window) is given a higher priority than any background application. The Performance Options dialog box (Figure 9.20), through the System Icon, Advanced Tab, will allow you to configure your system so that performance is optimized for either the background applications or for the foreground applications. (By default, the Programs radio button is selected, to give priority to foreground applications.)

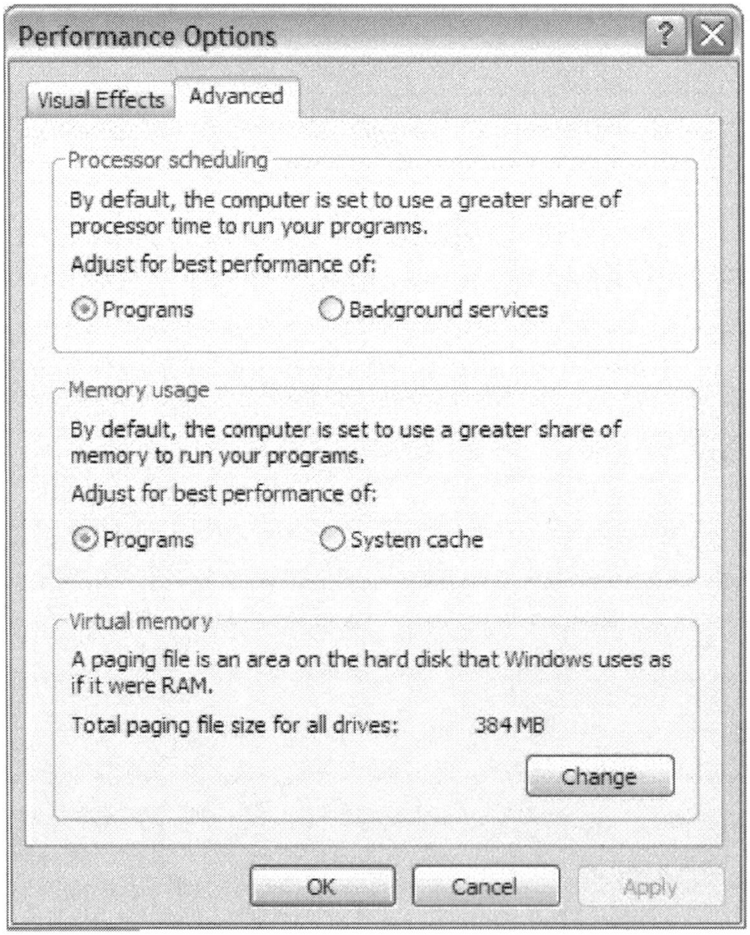

Figure 9-20: Performance Options

V Chapter 9: Summary

You have now completed the chapter on monitoring and optimizing your system performance and reliability for Windows XP. You should now feel comfortable with:

- Identifying system performance tools
- Optimizing general system performance
- Identifying system performance analysis tools
- Analyzing system performance with System Monitor, in regards to:
    - Memory subsystem
    - Processor subsystem
    - Disk subsystem
    - Network subsystem
    - Applications

VI Chapter 9: Review Questions

1. You are administering a WinXP computer. In an effort to monitor the system performance, you invoke the Task Manager. You want to have Task Manager updates its data more frequently. How can this be done?

A. In Task Manager, choose View, Update Speed and then change the frequency from Normal to High.

B. In Task Manager, choose View, Speed and then change the frequency from High to Real-time.

C. In Task Manager, choose Update, Speed and then change the frequency from Normal to High.

D. In Task Manager, choose View, Set Speed and then change the frequency from Normal to Fast.

E. No Answer is Correct.

2. You are administering a WinXP computer. In an effort to monitor the system performance, you plan to use Task Manager. How do you invoke the Task Manager from within XP?

A. Press Ctrl+Alt+Delete

B. Press Ctrl+Shift+Esc

C. Choose Start – Programs – Task Management

D. Choose Start – Programs – System Tools – Task Management Suite

E. From the command line run "taskmon"

3. You are administering a WinXP computer. In an effort to monitor the system performance, you plan to use Task Manager. You especially concern about the memory usage, as it seems like the hard drive is busy swapping all the time. Which field in Task Manager can provide you with relevant information in this regard?

A. Commit Charge

B. Commit RAM – Physical

C. Commit RAM – Logical

D. Page Size

E. RAM Bytes Occupied

4. You are monitoring the performance of your XP system. You found that Total Commit Charge is higher than Total Physical Memory. What does it indicate?

A. Paging occurs

B. Performance can be increased if more RAM is added

C. The physical memory is enough for current use

D. The system is slowed down by the disk subsystem

E. No Answer is Correct

5. You are the administrator of a XP workstation. This workstation runs applications that routinely load and reload extremely large 3D graphics data files. You are asked to plan for a system upgrade. Which component will you consider to upgrade first?

A. RAM

B. Disk subsystem

C. CPU

D. Video Adaptor

E. Motherboard

6. You are the administrator of a XP workstation. This workstation runs multiple applications. In response to a user's request for memory upgrade, you want to first identify the application that consumes the most memory. What should you do?

A. Open Windows Task Manager, click the Processes tab, and click the Mem Usage column heading twice to sort the list in descending order.

B. Open Windows Task Manager, click the Memory tab, and click the % Usage column heading twice to sort the list in descending order.

C. Open Windows Task Manager, click the Applications tab, and click the App Usage column heading twice to sort the list in descending order.

D. Open Windows Task Manager, click the Processes tab, and click the % Usage Over Time column heading twice to sort the list in descending order.

E. No Answer is Correct.

7. You are the senior system officer of your company. You are monitoring the performance of your XP system via the Task Manager. Your system currently has no application running. However, for some reasons you do not see the System Idle Process available. You suspect there is a problem with your system. What is the likely cause?

A. This is not a problem. You can find the System Idle Process by selecting the Show Processes From All Users box in the bottom left corner of the Processes tab.

B. This is not a problem. You can find the System Idle Process by selecting the Show System Processes box in the bottom right corner of the Processes tab.

C. In this case nothing can be done except for rebooting the system

D. A virus is probably eating up system resources at the background.

E. No Answer is Correct.

8. You are the senior system officer of your company. You installed WinXP on a brand new HP PC. You used only the default settings. This PC has a 400MHZ CPU, 256M RAM and 5GB hard disk. You quickly fill up 4 GB of your drive with the XP system itself and the applications. What should you do to free more space and avoid system crashes, if you do not yet have the money to buy a new hard drive, and that the current hard drive is not to be converted to NTFS?

A. Reconfigure the size of the paging file

B. Run scandisk on the drive

C. Run defrag on the drive

D. Uninstall the WinXP Program files

E. No Answer is Correct

9. You are the senior system officer of your company. You have installed WinXP on a brand new HP PC. You used only the default settings. Your tech support associate subsequently installed an additional piece of RAM to the system, making it a total of 256MB. You want to modify the size of the paging file. Under what condition can such modification be completed without the need to restart your system?

A. Decrease the size of the minimum page file settings

B. Decrease the size of the maximum page file settings

C. Create a new page file on another partition

D. Increase the size of the page file

E. No Answer is Correct

10. You are the senior system architect of your company. You are responsible for tuning the performance of your in-house systems. You are using Perfmon to monitor the performance of your XP system. In the console, which of the following are available for adding into the view for tracking different elements of the system?

A. Object

B. Counter

C. Thread

D. Application

E. Process

11. You are the senior system architect of your company. You are responsible for tuning the performance of your in-house systems. You are using Perfmon to monitor the performance of your XP system. What view under Perfmon will plot all counters against a single vertical axis scaled by a default scaling from 0 to 100?

A. Chart

B. Histogram

C. Line

D. Pie

E. Bar

12. You are the senior system architect of your company. You are tuning the performance of your XP Pro system. You find that there are 5 instances of Svchost.exe appearing in Task Manager. You suspect that this is the cause of performance degradation. What should you do?

A. Do nothing. This is normal

B. Shut down 4 of them

C. Keep the number of instances to 3 all the time

D. Keep the number of instances to 1 per processor all the time

E. No Answer is Correct

VII Chapter 9: Review Answers

1. You are administering a WinXP computer. In an effort to monitor the system performance, you invoke the Task Manager. You want to have Task Manager updates its data more frequently. How can this be done?

***A. In Task Manager, choose View, Update Speed and then change the frequency from Normal to High.**

B. In Task Manager, choose View, Speed and then change the frequency from High to Real-time.

C. In Task Manager, choose Update, Speed and then change the frequency from Normal to High.

D. In Task Manager, choose View, Set Speed and then change the frequency from Normal to Fast.

E. No Answer is Correct.

Explanation: By default, Windows Task Manager updates its data once every two seconds. To increase the frequency, choose View, Update Speed and then change the frequency setting. To study the graph of the most recent history, stop all updates by choosing View, Update Speed, Paused, then request update at anytime you like.

2. You are administering a WinXP computer. In an effort to monitor the system performance, you plan to use Task Manager. How do you invoke the Task Manager from within XP?

***A. Press Ctrl+Alt+Delete**

***B. Press Ctrl+Shift+Esc.**

C. Choose Start – Programs – Task Management

D. Choose Start – Programs – System Tools – Task Management Suite

E. From the command line run "taskmon"

Explanation: If you arousing the Welcome screen to log on to Windows, you can open the Windows Task Manager at any time by pressing Ctrl+Alt+Delete. If you aren't using the Welcome screen or you rejoined to a Windows domain, press Ctrl+Alt+Delete and then click the Task Manager button in the Windows Security dialog box.

3. You are administering a WinXP computer. In an effort to monitor the system performance, you plan to use Task Manager. You especially concern about the memory usage, as it seems like the hard drive is busy swapping all the time. Which field in Task Manager can provide you with relevant information in this regard?

***A. Commit Charge**

B. Commit RAM – Physical

C. Commit RAM – Logical

D. Page Size

E. RAM Bytes Occupied

Explanation: Commit Charge lists two numbers: The first number (the numerator) represents your current total commit charge the total amount of physical and virtual memory in use by all running processes. The denominator represents your total available memory, physical and virtual. By itself, this number will only tell you whether you are about to run completely out of memory.

4. You are monitoring the performance of your XP system. You found that Total Commit Charge is higher than Total Physical Memory. What does it indicate?

***A. Paging occurs**

***B. Performance can be increased if more RAM is added**

C. The physical memory is enough for current use

***D. The system is slowed down by the disk subsystem**

E. No Answer is Correct

Explanation: If Total Commit Charge is higher than Total Physical Memory, Windows must swap pages between fast RAM chips and the much slower virtual memory in the page file, causing the system to slow down. This is the MOST typical cause of system slow down. More RAM can resolve the problem.

5. You are the administrator of a XP workstation. This workstation runs applications that routinely load and reload extremely large 3D graphics data files. You are asked to plan for a system upgrade. Which component will you consider to upgrade first?

***A. RAM**

B. Disk subsystem

C. CPU

D. Video Adaptor

E. Motherboard

Explanation: If you use applications that routinely load and reload extremely large data files, Windows file cache is essential. For caching to run effectively, you need more RAM. RAM is always the issue when dealing with applications using large files.

6. You are the administrator of a XP workstation. This workstation runs multiple applications. In response to a user's request for memory upgrade, you want to first identify the application that consumes the most memory. What should you do?

***A. Open Windows Task Manager, click the Processes tab, and click the Mem Usage column heading twice to sort the list in descending order.**

B. Open Windows Task Manager, click the Memory tab, and click the % Usage column heading twice to sort the list in descending order.

C. Open Windows Task Manager, click the Applications tab, and click the App Usage column heading twice to sort the list in descending order.

D. Open Windows Task Manager, click the Processes tab, and click the % Usage Over Time column heading twice to sort the list in descending order.

E. No Answer is Correct.

Explanation: The best cure for memory-related performance problems is to add more RAM. Apart from this, you can shut down unneeded programs and services to free up memory. To identify the programs that are using up memory, open Windows Task Manager, click the Processes tab, and click on the Mem Usage column heading.

7. You are the senior system officer of your company. You are monitoring the performance of your XP system via the Task Manager. Your system currently has no application running. However, for some reasons you do not see the System Idle Process available. You suspect there is a problem with your system. What is the likely cause?

***A. This is not a problem. You can find the System Idle Process by selecting the Show Processes From All Users box in the bottom left corner of the Processes tab.**

B. This is not a problem. You can find the System Idle Process by selecting the Show System Processes box in the bottom right corner of the Processes tab.

C. In this case nothing can be done except for rebooting the system.

D. A virus is probably eating up system resources at the background.

E. No Answer is Correct.

Explanation: Windows XP uses a "placeholder" process called System Idle Process that indicates when the CPU is not handling other threads. If this value is not visible, select the Show Processes From All Users box in the bottom left corner of the Processes tab. The key is; the total value always has to add up to 100.

8. You are the senior system officer of your company. You installed WinXP on a brand new HP PC. You used only the default settings. This PC has a 400MHZ CPU, 256M RAM and 5GB hard disk. You quickly fill up 4 GB of your drive with the XP system itself and the applications. What should you do to free more space and avoid system crashes, if you do not yet have the money to buy a new hard drive, and that the current hard drive is not to be converted to NTFS?

***A. Reconfigure the size of the paging file**

B. Run scandisk on the drive

C. Run defrag on the drive

D. Uninstall the WinXP Program files

E. No Answer is Correct

Explanation: In a default Windows XP installation, Windows creates the page file in the root folder on the same drive that holds the Windows system files. The size of the page file is determined by the amount of RAM in your system. The default minimum size is 1.5 times the amount of physical RAM, while the maximum is 3 times that value.

9. You are the senior system officer of your company. You have installed WinXP on a brand new HP PC. You used only the default settings. Your tech support associate subsequently installed an additional piece of RAM to the system, making it a total of 256MB. You want to modify the size of the paging file. Under what condition can such modification be completed without the need to restart your system?

***A. Decrease the size of the minimum page file settings**
***B. Decrease the size of the maximum page file settings**
***C. Create a new page file on another partition**
***D. Increase the size of the page file**
E. No Answer is Correct

Explanation: If you decrease the size of either the minimum or maximum page file settings, or if you create a new page file on a drive, you must restart your computer to make the change effective. In fact, as long as you need to change the size of a page file, you will need to restart your computer.

10. You are the senior system architect of your company. You are responsible for tuning the performance of your in-house systems. You are using Perfmon to monitor the performance of your XP system. In the console, which of the following are available for adding into the view for tracking different elements of the system?

***A. Object**
***B. Counter**
C. Thread
D. Application
E. Process

Explanation: The Performance console can track everything in the form of an object and a counter:
Object - any portion of a computer's resources that can be assigned characteristics and manipulated.
Counter - types of information about the objects to which they are assigned.

11. You are the senior system architect of your company. You are responsible for tuning the performance of your in-house systems. You are using Perfmon to monitor the performance of your XP system. What view under Perfmon will plot all counters against a single vertical axis scaled by a default scaling from 0 to 100?

***A. Chart**

***B. Histogram**

C. Line

D. Pie

E. Bar

Explanation: System Monitor's Chart and Histogram views plot all counters against a single vertical axis scaled, by default, from 0 to 100. A default scaling factor is applied to each counter so that counters with large values can coexist meaningfully in a chart with low-value counters.

12. You are the senior system architect of your company. You are tuning the performance of your XP Pro system. You find that there are 5 instances of Svchost.exe appearing in Task Manager. You suspect that this is the cause of performance degradation. What should you do?

***A. Do nothing. This is normal.**

B. Shut down 4 of them.

C. Keep the number of instances to 3 all the time.

D. Keep the number of instances to 1 per processor all the time

E. No Answer is Correct.

Explanation: Multiple instances of Svchost.exe appear in Task Manager is perfectly normal, as Svchost.exe is a core piece of Windows XP code that collects a number of lower-level system-critical services and runs them in a common environment. By gathering multiple functions together, this arrangement reduces boot time and system overhead and eliminates the need to run many of the low-level services.

Chapter 10: Troubleshooting and Recovery

The objective of this chapter is to provide you with an understanding of the following:

1. Implement system and data protection
2. Implement system and data recovery
3. Creation of Emergency Repair Disks
4. Troubleshooting systems using the built-in troubleshooters
5. Troubleshooting systems using Safe mode
6. Troubleshooting systems using Last Known Good
7. Manage Driver Signing
8. Troubleshooting systems using the Recovery Console
9. Troubleshooting systems using Dr. Watson
10. Troubleshooting STOP errors

Getting Ready – (Questions)

1). In Windows XP Professional, to what media can the Backup utility store backup data?

2). The Client Services for Netware troubleshooter will help you troubleshoot what type of problem?

3). What are the three Safe mode options?

4). When do you use "Last Known Good"?

5). You are given three options with Driver Signing when a driver is downloaded and is not signed. Which option will prevent all unsigned drivers from being installed?

Getting Ready – (Answers)

1). Windows XP Professional provides a tool called "Backup" that can back up data to tape, a compressed file, or a network share.

2). The Client Service for NetWare troubleshooter will assist you with problems with CSNW, including accessing NetWare servers and Novell Directory Services (NDS) objects, printing to NetWare printers, using NetWare login scripts, and logging onto an NDS tree.

3). There are three Safe Mode options: Safe Mode, Safe Mode with Networking and Safe Mode with Command Prompt.

4). Usage of Last Known Good is for situations that require the systems registry information to be replaced with a previous version.

5). Warn, the default setting, notifies you that f the driver has not been signed and provides you with the choice whether or not to install it. Block prevents all unsigned drivers from being installed. Ignore allows all drivers to be installed, even if they have not been signed.

I Introduction

Inevitably it will happen. Guaranteed. It's a law. (Ever heard of Murphy?) Systems will crash and fail. Hard drives will grind to a halt. Some freak electrical storm will toast motherboards.

Even with Windows XP's enhancements to make it a much more reliable operating system, it is still important to take a proactive stance towards the safekeeping of your data, and to understand what is causing you system to fail.

Ensuring that verified drivers are installed on the system can prevent unexpected crashes and knowing how to recover quickly in the case of failure can all add up to a stable work environment.

II Protecting Systems and Data

The first line of defense against data loss is always a good backup. A good backup consists of a few important things:

- Critical data is backed-up on a daily basis
- A secondary backup exists in case of media failure
- Trial restores are performed on a regular basis to ensure that data is being backed up correctly

Windows XP provides a tool called "Backup" (Figure 10.1) that can back up data to tape, a compressed file, or a network share. A wizard is built into this utility to make it easy for you to configure your backup needs, and a scheduler is included.

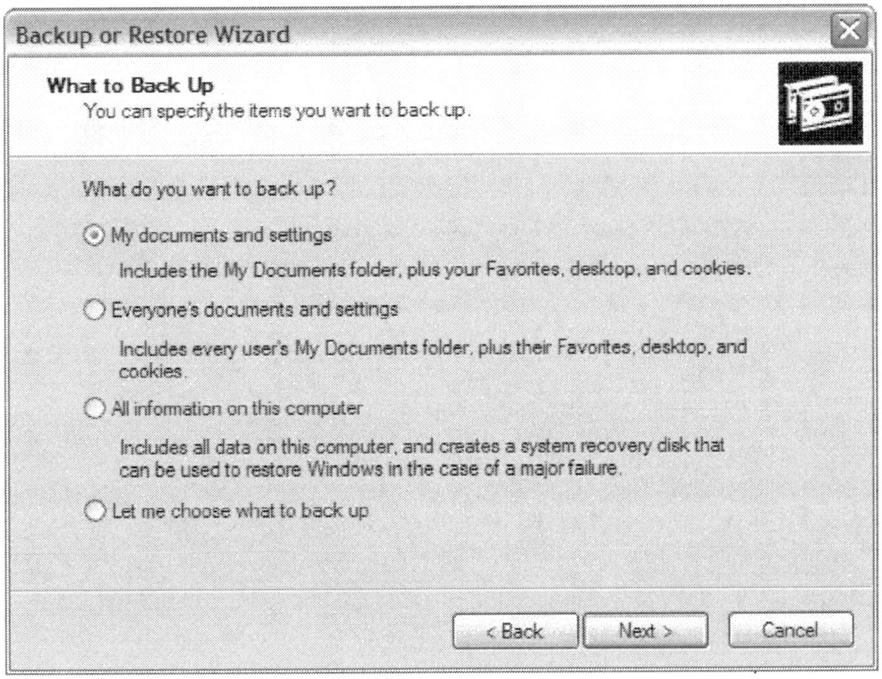

Figure 10-1: Backup Wizard

Backup Operations

You can backup your system and registry, or even just a single file to a floppy diskette(s), another volume (i.e. a Zip disk), or to a tape storage device.

There are five types of backup that Windows Backup can perform:

- **Normal**

Copies all selected files and marks each as having been backed up. Normal backups take the longest to perform because every file selected is backed-up whether or not changes have occurred since the last backup. They are the easiest to restore because you will only need the most recent backup to restore the critical data.

- **Incremental**

Backs up only those files that have been created or changed since the last normal or incremental backup and marks files as having been backed up. You should make sure that you have a normal backup of your system, and then run incremental backups for critical data recovery. Incremental backups are very useful when you need to reduce the amount of time the system uses for backups. Restoring can take a little longer than normal, because you will have to restore the last normal backup, and then each incremental backup since the normal backup, to obtain all the changes in the data.

- **Differential**

Copies files that have been created or changed since the last time the files were marked as "backed up" and does NOT set a marker. Differential backups should be done in conjunction with normal backups. They can take a little longer than incremental backups, because they will continue to backup files that have been changed since the last marker was set, whether or not Differential has backed it up before. It will increase the speed at which a system can be restored, though, because only the last normal backup and the last differential backup will be needed to restore the system to its working state.

- **Copy**

All selected files, but it does not mark each file as having been backed up. Copying is useful to maintain extra copies between normal and incremental backups because it does not affect other backup operations.

- **Daily**

Copies all selected files that have been modified on the day that the daily backup is performed. The backed up files are not marked as having been backed up.

> **NOTE:** "Normal" will take the longest amount of time to perform the backup and be the simplest to restore, because only one backup is performed, but all files are backed-up. Combining normal backups with incremental backups will save storage space and provide the quickest backup on a daily basis. Combining normal backups with differential backups will provide a quicker backup than a normal backup on a daily basis, and will provide a quicker restore than normal/incremental combinations.

It is important to remember to make sure that all files are closed before performing a backup. Open files cannot be backed-up using Windows Backup. Backups do not protect against viruses, so it is important to scan your system regularly, and make sure that your backup is free from unwanted virus infection.

Restore Operations

Once you have a backup created, you can then restore files from it (Figure 10.2). This allows you to restore your complete system or just to replace specific files.

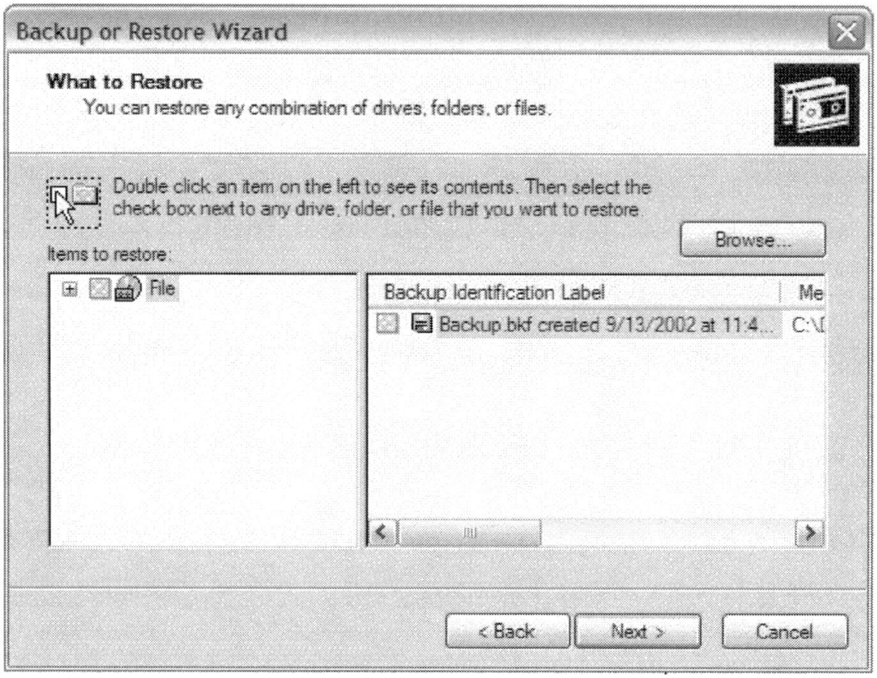

Figure 10-2: Restore Wizard

Emergency Repair Disk

The Emergency Repair Disk (ERD) option is now located in the Backup program. To create an ERD, select **Automated System Recovery Wizard** from the dialog box shown in Figure 10.3.

When you create an ERD, you are creating a non-bootable diskette that can be used with the Recovery Service. This information is taken start from the registry. You can also inform the Backup program to copy this information to the *systemroot*\repair directory.

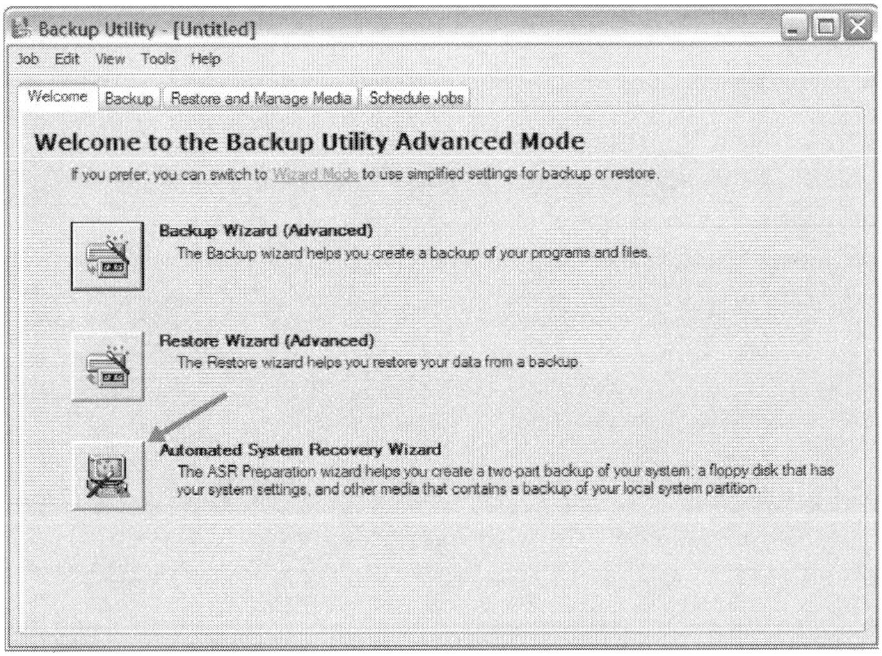

Figure 10-3: Automated System Recovery Wizard

Pop Quiz 10.1

Pop Quiz 10.1 *Questions*

1). Name the five types of backup that can be performed by Windows XP Backup utility.

2). You perform a full backup on your network data every Saturday. You wish to ensure the fastest restore time if you suffer a critical failure on Friday morning, without having to perform a complete backup every evening. What type of backup should you perform during the week?

3). Which types of backup will set a marker on files that have been backed up?

4). Where is the option located to create an Emergency Repair Disk?

5). Once you have opened the program that will allow you create an ERD, what two places allow you this option?

Pop Quiz 10.1 *Answers*

1). The five backup types that can be performed by the Backup utility are Normal, Differential, Incremental, Copy and Daily.

2). Performing a differential backup every evening, in combination with a full (normal) backup once a week, will provide the fastest restore time in the event of a critical failure.

3). Only Normal and Incremental backup types set a time and date marker on files after backup has been performed.

4). The Emergency Repair Disk (ERD) option is now located in the Backup program.

5). To create an ERD either click the Emergency Repair Disk button on the Welcome page or from the Tools menu, select Create an Emergency Repair Disk.

III Troubleshooting Systems

Troubleshooting systems is not an exact science; it is more of an art form. A fix for one machine may not necessary be the fix for another, even if they show the same symptoms on the same hardware. Finding the cause of a problem is only the beginning. You then have to test your solutions and document the outcome.

> **Tip:** Document any changes you make to the system. If you have to call Microsoft Product Support, or the manufacturer of your computer, having this information will greatly reduce the amount of time it takes to diagnose the system.

Built-In Troubleshooters

Included with the Windows XP Help System, there is a set of built-in troubleshooters that can guide you through some specific, however rather generic, problems that can occur. Table 10.1 shows the list of troubleshooters included and their related problems.

TROUBLESHOOTER	RELATED PROBLEMS
Client Service for NetWare	Client Service for NetWare, including accessing NetWare servers and Novell Directory Services (NDS) objects, printing to NetWare printers, using NetWare login scripts, and logging onto an NDS tree.
Display	Video cards and display adapters, including monitors (single and multiple), outdated or incompatible video drivers, and incorrect settings for your video hardware.
Hardware	Cameras, CD-ROM drives, game controllers, hard drives, keyboards, mouse devices, network adapter cards, and scanners. This tool is also helpful with sound cards, modem, and display adapters.
Internet connections (ISP)	Connecting and logging on to your Internet service provider (ISP)
Modem	Modem connections, setup, configuration, and detection
MS-DOS programs	Running MS-DOS programs on Windows 2000
Multimedia and games	Installing and configuring DirectX drivers and games

TROUBLESHOOTER	RELATED PROBLEMS
Networking (TCP/IP)	Internet and intranet connections that use TCP/IP on a computer running Windows XP
Print	Network or local printers and plotters, including outdated or corrupted printer drivers, network and local printer connections, and printer configuration
Remote access	Network and dial-up connections that use a telephone to connect your computer to another computer
Sound	Sound cards and speakers
System setup	Installing and setting up Windows 2000
Windows 3.x programs	Running 16-bit Windows programs on Windows 2000

Table 10-1: Built-In Troubleshooters

Safe Mode

Sometimes, after making device or driver changes, your system won't start normally. You may still be able to start your computer in Safe Mode, a diagnostic mode that loads only minimal services and base drivers. Safe Mode creates a boot log file that you can review to determine why your system is failing to start.

There are three Safe Mode options:

- **Safe Mode**

Starts Windows XP using only basic files and drivers for the mouse, monitor, keyboard, base video and default system services with no network support

- **Safe Mode with Networking**

Starts Windows XP using only basic files and drivers, with basic network support (no PCMCIA devices).

- **Safe Mode with Command Prompt**

Starts Windows XP using only basic files and drivers, but rather than loading the GUI interface of Windows 2000, after user logon, the command prompt appears.

Safe Mode will allow you to determine what changes caused the load failure and will give you the opportunity to make system changes so that a successful load occurs. To start Safe Mode after a reboot, when you see the prompt "Please select the operating system to start", press F8.

Last Known Good

Usage of Last Known Good is for situations that require the systems registry information to be replaced with a previous version. A prime example of this is the installation of a new driver, which, when the system restarts, causes a malfunction, such as a Stop error, to occur. By using the Last Known Good, you can then restore the registry information that does not contain any information about the newly installed driver.

The Last Known Good is the last process completed during the system startup process. A successful startup includes a local user logon, after which the Last Known Good is created.

> **Warning:** Using the Last Known Good configuration will result in the loss of any changes made to the system since the last successful logon.

The Last Known Good configuration will not help in situations where a Stop error or other malfunction occurs after the user has logged on to the system, or where the information is not stored in the registry.

Driver Signing

Driver Signing is included in Windows XP to ensure that only drivers that have passed strict quality tests will be installed on a Windows XP system. The digital signature associated with the driver is recognized by Windows XP and lets you know if the driver file has been changed or modified since it was included on the HCL.

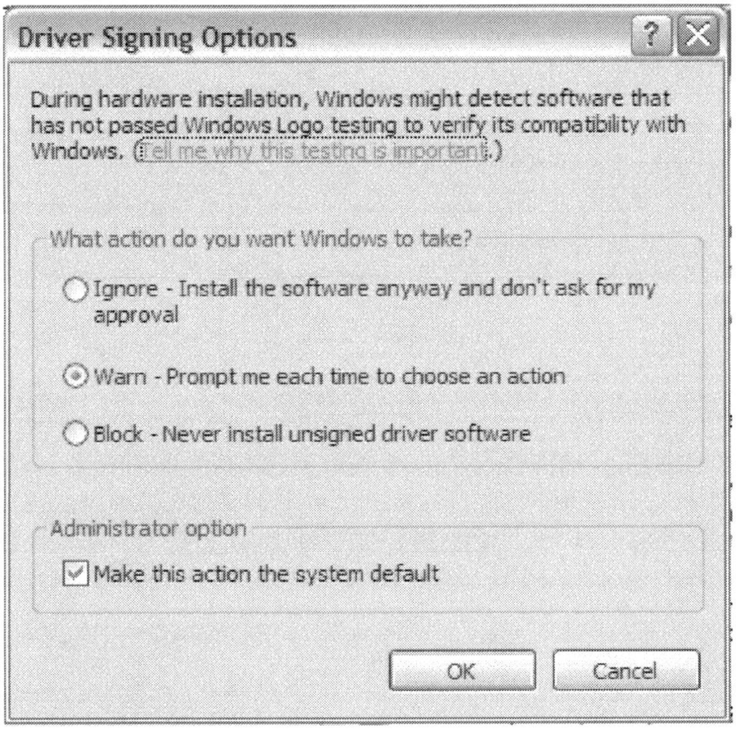

Figure 10-4: Driver Signing Options

You are given three options with Driver Signing when a driver is downloaded and is not signed (Figure 10.4). **Warn,** the default setting, notifies you that f the driver has not been signed and provides you with the choice whether or not to install it. **Block** prevents all unsigned drivers from being installed. **Ignore** allows all drivers to be installed, even if they have not been signed.

The default setting can be changed under the **System** icon of Control Panel, under the **Hardware** tab.

NOTE: You must be a member of the Administrators group to change the default settings for Driver Signing. It is NOT recommended that the setting be set to **Ignore**, as that will allow potentially unsafe drivers to be installed on the system.

Recovery Console

Recovery Console is a powerful tool that should be used only by experienced, advanced users. Improper use of Recovery Console can cause further damage to your system. It is strongly recommended that you make sure your information is backed-up before using this too, as your hard drive may be formatted as part of the recovery.

There are two ways to start the Recovery Console. If you cannot start your computer, Recovery Console can be run from the Windows XP setup disks or from a bootable CDROM. You can also be proactive and install Recovery Console on your computer, so that if something does happen that stops you from starting Windows XP, you can choose Recovery Console as an option from the boot menu. To install the Recovery Console, insert the Windows XP installation CD and run the command d:\i386\winnt32 /cmdcons, where d: represents your CDROM drive.

Recovery Console provides a command line utility during the startup process. You can use this utility to make system changes when Windows XP doesn't start. Many different tasks can be performed using Recovery Console without even starting Windows XP. A list of all commands that can be performed is shown in Table 10.2.

COMMAND	EXPLANATION AND SYNTAX
Attrib	Changes the attributes of a file or folder. At least one attribute must be set or cleared. You can set multiple attributes simultaneously.
Batch	Carries out commands specified in a text file. If no output file is specified, the command output is displayed on the screen. Batch cannot be one of the commands included in the input file.
ChDir CD	Displays the current volume and directory or changes to the folder specified

COMMAND	EXPLANATION AND SYNTAX
Chkdsk	Checks a disk and, if needed, repairs or recovers the volume. Chkdsk requires that Autochk.exe be installed in the System32 folder or be available from the Windows XPoperating system CD.
Cls	Clears the screen
Copy	Copies a single file to a specified location. Compressed files from the Windows XPoperating system CD are automatically decompressed as they are copied. The use of wildcard characters (* and ?) is not permitted.
Delete Del	Deletes one file. The use of wildcard characters (* and ?) in file names is not permitted.
Dir	Displays a list of files and folders within a folder
Disable	Disables a Windows XPsystem service or driver
Diskpart	Manages the partitions on your hard disk Warning This command can damage your partition table if the disk has been upgraded to dynamic disk. Do not modify the structure of dynamic disks unless you are using the Disk Management tool.
Enable	Enables a Windows XP system service or driver
Exit	Quits the Recovery Console and restarts your computer
Expand	Expands a compressed file stored on the Windows XP operating system CD or from within a CAB file on the Windows XP operating system CD and copies it to a specified destination
Fixboot	Rewrites the boot sector code on the hard disk. This is useful for repairing corrupted boot sectors.

COMMAND	EXPLANATION AND SYNTAX
fixmbr	Rewrites the master boot code of the master boot record (MBR) of the startup hard disk. This command is useful for repairing corrupted MBRs. Warning This command can damage your partition table if a virus is present, if you have a third-party operating system installed, if you have a non-standard MBR, or if a hardware problem exists and causes volumes to become inaccessible. It is recommended that you run antivirus software before using this command. Important Running fixmbr overwrites only the master boot code, leaving the existing partition table intact. If corruption in the MBR affects the partition table, running fixmbr might not resolve the problem.
Format	Formats the specified volume to the specified file system. If no file system is specified, NTFS is used by default. Choosing FAT formats a volume as FAT16.
Help	Shows help display for commands within the Recovery Console.
listsvc	Lists all available services, drivers, and their START_TYPES for the current Windows XP installation. The information listed by this command is extracted from the registry file System in the folder *%systemroot%\System32\Config*. If System is damaged or missing, results can be unpredictable.
logon	Lists all detected installations of Windows XP and Windows NT, and then requests the local administrator password. If more than three attempts to log on fail, the Recovery Console quits, and the computer restarts.
map	Lists all drive letters, file system types, volume sizes, and mappings to physical devices that are currently active. Important The map command might not work correctly with systems using dynamic disk.

COMMAND	EXPLANATION AND SYNTAX
Mkdir MD	Creates a directory. Wildcard characters (* and ?) are not allowed. <u>Important</u> This command might not display all of the volumes on disk or the correct volume sizes if the disk has been upgraded to dynamic disk.
More Type	Displays a text file on the screen.
Rmdir RD	Deletes a directory. Wildcard characters (* and ?) are not supported.
Rename Ren	Renames a file or directory. You cannot specify a new volume or path for your target file. Wildcard characters (* and ?) are not supported.
set	Displays and sets Recovery Console environment variables.
systemroot	Sets the current directory to the *%systemroot%* directory of the Windows XP installation with which you are currently working.

Table 10-2: Recovery Console Commands

Three commands (Enable, Disable, and listsvc) work in conjunction with each other. Both Enable and Disable are able to modify services that are listed with listsvc. Before modifying any service with these commands, they will display the current START_TYPE. Make a note of it for future reference.

These services can have one of five different START_TYPE values:

- SERVICE_DISABLED
- SERVICE_BOOT_START
- SERVICE_SYSTEM_START
- SERVICE_AUTO_START
- SERVICE_DEMAND_START

The set command allows the configuration of the Recovery Console to extend its functionality. You must use the Group Policy snap-in to enable this command. There are four environment variables that can be set:

- **AllowWildCards** – Enable wildcard support for some commands that do not otherwise support them, such as DEL
- **AllowAllPaths** – Allows access to all files and folders on the computer
- **AllowRemovableMedia** – Allows files to be copied to removable media, such as floppy disks
- **NoCopyPrompt** – Do not prompt when overwriting file

One can quickly see the potential for data theft or destruction with recovery console if the **SET** command is enabled. Use it with great caution.

Dr. Watson

The Doctor is in! Dr. Watson is known as a program error debugger. When an application that is running generates an error (or crashes), Dr. Watson can be configured to take a snapshot of the system at the time of the failure. This information can then be passed on to support personal to identify the problem. You do not have to worry about running Dr. Watson every time you start your computer as the program is automatically run when an error is detected.

To view errors that Dr. Watson has collected, run the command DRWTSN32.EXE. This launches the Dr. Watson program (Figure 10.5).

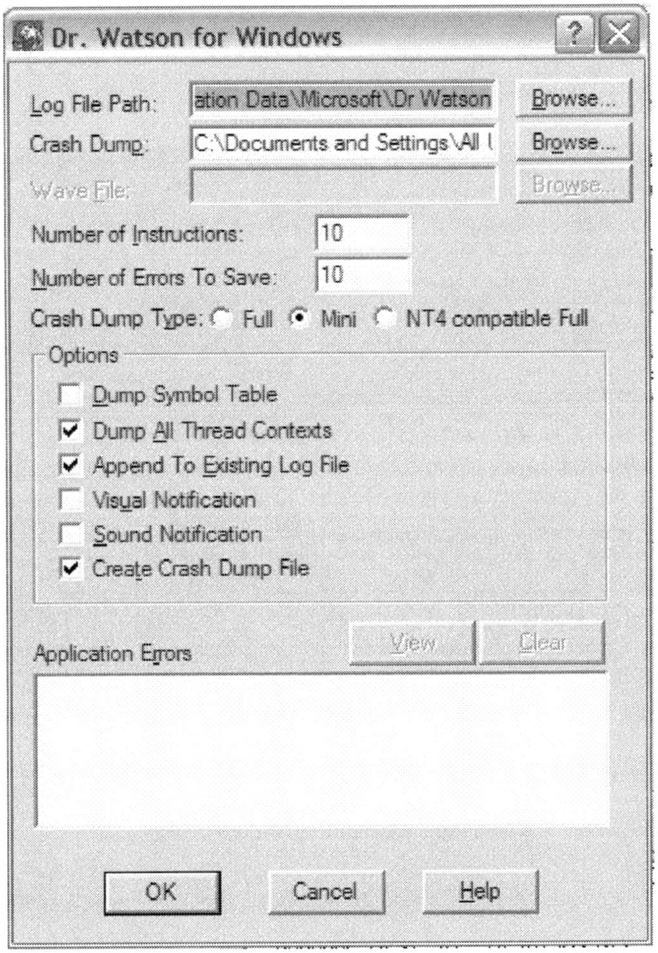

Figure 10-5: Dr. Watson

Stop Errors

When an error condition in Windows XP in which the system cannot recover from, it generates a variety of system messages. Because we are dealing with the system itself, and not the applications that are run on it, the system, in order to maintain system reliability will generate a Stop message (Figure 10.6).

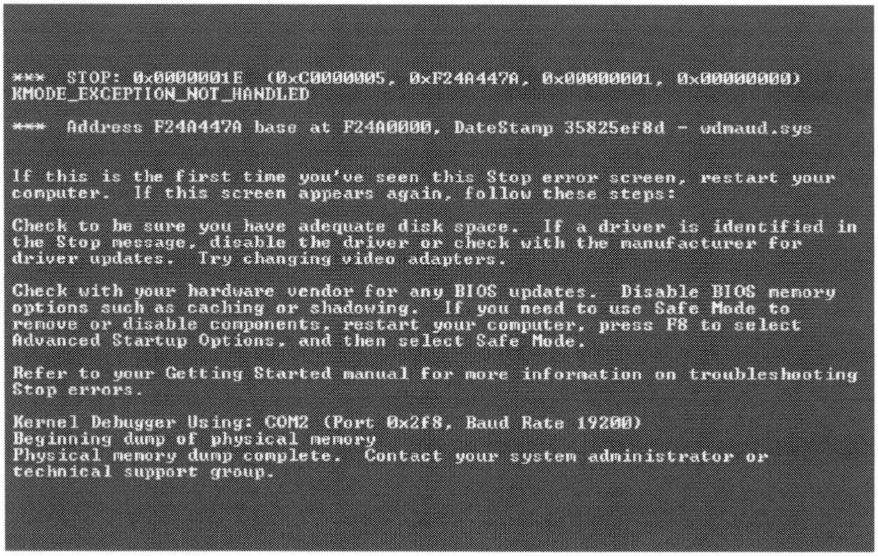

Figure 10-6: Stop Message

The ability to interpret the Stop message and take the appropriate action to resolve the cause of the message is vital to any production environment.

A Stop Message contains three distinct sections. The first section is Bugcheck Information (Figure 10.7).

Figure 10-7: Stop Message: Bugcheck Information

This area contains the Stop error code and symbolic name (description) that has occurred, parameters for the Stop code, and possibly the hexadecimal memory address and the name of the driver or file of the problem's source. Under some conditions you may only see the first line of the Stop message. In these circumstances, a vital service needed for the display has been affected (and quite possibly the cause).

In Figure 10.7, the Stop error is 0x0000001E, the symbolic name is KMODE_EXCEPTION_NOT_HANDLED, the parameters are (0xC0000005, 0xF24A447A, 0x00000001, 0x00000000), and the address is F24A447A with is running the WDMAUD.SYS file. This actually tells an individual a lot about what has gone one. The Stop error in question here is actually a fairly generic "catch-all" stop code, but at least there is one!

Next is the Recommended User Action section (Figure 10.8). This area provides a list of suggestions to attempt to recover from the error. In most cases, a simple restart of the system will rectify the situation. In other cases, such as a corrupted system driver, the reboot may not be successful and you could be looking at the same screen again.

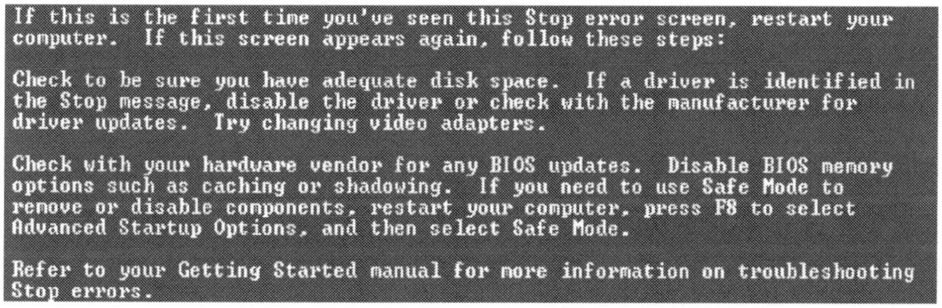

Figure 10-8: Stop Message: Recommended User Action

Tip: A generic list of troubleshooting tips is displayed when no specific information is available for a Stop message.

The final section is referred to as Debug Port Information (Figure 10.9). This provides information and confirmation of the communication used by the kernel debugger, if it is enabled and configured. This section will also display the status of the memory dump file creation, if enabled.

```
Kernel Debugger Using: COM2 (Port 0x2f8, Baud Rate 19200)
Beginning dump of physical memory
Physical memory dump complete.  Contact your system administrator or
technical support group.
```

Figure 10-9: Stop Message: Debug Port Information

Pop Quiz 10.2

Pop Quiz 10.2 *Questions*

1). Included with the Windows XP Help System, there is a set of built-in troubleshooters that can guide you through some problems that can occur. Can you name six of them?

2). What is the result of loading "Safe Mode with Command Prompt"?

3). You have started your system and logged onto Windows XP Professional. As you go to access Word, a system stop error occurs. Will Last Known Good help you in this situation?

4). By default, you do not want unsigned drivers being installed on any Windows XP Professional machine on your network. However, the programmers in the Testing Division need to use some beta drivers they have downloaded from the manufacturer's website. What setting should be set on their Professional machines to allow this testing?

5). Name two ways you can start Recovery Console.

Pop Quiz 10.2 *Answers*

1). The eight built-in troubleshooters included with the Windows 2000 Help System are: Client Service for NetWare, Display, Hardware, Internet Connections, Modem, MS-DOS Programs, Multimedia and Games, Networking (TCP/IP), Print, Remote Access, Sound, System Setup, and Windows 3.x Programs. Each will assist you in troubleshooting specific, though somewhat generic, problems associated with their assigned area.
2). Loading "Safe Mode with Command Prompt" starts Windows 2000 Professional using only basic files and drivers, but rather than loading the GUI interface of Windows 2000, after user logon, the command prompt appears.
3). No. The Last Known Good configuration will not help in situations where a Stop error or other malfunction occurs after the user has logged on to the system, or where the information is not stored in the registry.
4). Driver Signing is included in Windows 2000 Professional to ensure that only drivers that have passed strict quality tests will be installed on a Windows Professional system. The digital signature associated with the driver is recognized by Windows 2000 and lets you know if the driver file has been changed or modified since it was included on the HCL. Warn, the default setting, notifies you if the driver has not been signed and provides you with the choice whether or not to install it. Block prevents all unsigned drivers from being installed. While Block may be the default on your network, setting the Testing machines to Warn will allow the individuals to install beta drivers, while still cautioning them that the drivers may not be compatible with Professional.
5). If you cannot start your computer, Recovery Console can be run from the Windows 2000 Professional setup disks or from a bootable CDROM. You can also be proactive and install Recovery Console on your computer, so that if something does happen that stops you from starting Windows 2000 Professional, you can choose Recovery Console as an option from the boot menu.

IV Chapter 10: Summary

You have now completed the chapter on troubleshooting Windows XP. You should now feel comfortable with how to:

- Implement system and data protection
- Implement system and data recovery
- Creation of Emergency Repair Disks
- Troubleshooting systems using the built-in troubleshooters
- Troubleshooting systems using Safe mode
- Troubleshooting systems using Last Known Good
- Manage Driver Signing
- Troubleshooting systems using the Recovery Console
- Troubleshooting systems using Dr. Watson
- Troubleshooting STOP errors

V Chapter 10: Review Questions

1. You are an expert in WinXP resources administration. What predefined group in WinXP is used by the computer manufacturers to providing you with Remote Assistance?

A. Administrators

B. TechServicesGroup

C. ServiceSupportGroup

D. HelpServicesGroup

E. Support Operators

2. You are the administrator of a WinXP Pro system. You are requested to disable a particular hardware device, which is built into the motherboard. Which of the following are the valid ways to do so?

A. Right-click the My Computer icon on the desktop, choose Properties, and then select Device Management

B. From a command prompt, enter ilocaldev.msc

C. Right-click the My Computer icon on the desktop, choose Manage, and then select Device Manager

D. From a command prompt, enter devmgmt.msc

E. No Answer is Correct

3. You are troubleshooting your WinXP system. You want to invoke the Help And Support Center, and you fail. For the Help And Support Center to function, which of the following services must be running?

A. Svrhelp.exe

B. Helpsvc.exe

C. Inisvc.exe

D. Helpctr.exe

E. None of the choices

4. You are a Help Desk professional. You are requested to provide troubleshooting assistance to a user in the remote office. You want to avoid traveling to the remote office, as it will take 2 hours of driving. What feature or function of XP can help in this regard?

A. Terminal Service Admin mode

B. W2K Administrator Studio

***C. Remote Assistance**

D. Terminal Service Application mode

E. No Answer is Correct

5. You are the senior system officer of your company. You are managing a dual-CPU system running Windows XP Professional. A large number of programs are running at the same time. You are quite concerned about the performance impact introduced by 3rd party software services. How do you clearly identify these non-MS native services out of all the programs, for the purpose of troubleshooting?

A. In Task Manager Utility, sort all the processes in descending order

B. In Task Manager Utility, enable the Hide All Non Native Services check box at the bottom of the Services tab

C. In System Configuration Utility, sort all the processes in ascending order

D. In System Configuration Utility, enable the Hide All Microsoft Services check box at the bottom of the Services tab

E. No Answer is Correct

6. You are the administrator of your network. You are responsible for the planning and implementation of all the in-house PCs. After careful consideration, you decided to have hibernation enabled in all of your systems. You found that one of your APM systems has been shutting down instead of hibernating. How should you troubleshoot this problem?

A. Run Devmgmt.msc. Choose View - Show Hidden Devices. Open NT Apm/Legacy Support. Check and ensure that the NT Apm/Legacy Interface Node device is not enabled.

B. Run Devmgmt.msc. Choose View - Show Hidden Devices. Open NT Apm/Legacy Support. Check and ensure that the NT Apm/Legacy Interface Node device is enabled.

C. Run Adsmgmt.msc. Choose View - Show Hidden Devices. Open XP Apm Legacy Support. Check and ensure that the Apm/Legacy Interface Node device is not selected.

D. Run Adsmgmt.msc. Choose View - Show All Devices. Open XP Apm Legacy Support. Check and ensure that the Apm/Legacy Interface Node device is selected, and its properties states clearly as "ON.".

7. On your WinXP network you have an external cable modem connected to an ICS host. All other computers on your network connect to the ICS host via the hub. Mary is using one of those computers. How does Mary check and see if Internet connectivity is now available to her?

A. She should ping the local host

B. She should ping a neighboring computer

C. She should run tracert

D. She should ping an Internet site

E. She should ping the ICS host

8. You are the administrator of your network. This network is purely IP based. You are troubleshooting some IP connectivity issues. You are using some of the command line utilities on a connected WinXP PC. Refer to the exhibit. What command can you use to display such result?

```
        Connection-specific DNS Suffix  . : hkcable.com.hk
        Description . . . . . . . . . . . : DAVICOM 9102-Based PCI Fast Ethernet
Adapter
        Physical Address. . . . . . . . . : 00-D0-09-2C-CC-AF
        Dhcp Enabled. . . . . . . . . . . : Yes
        Autoconfiguration Enabled . . . . : Yes
        IP Address. . . . . . . . . . . . : 192.168.0.80
        Subnet Mask . . . . . . . . . . . : 255.255.255.0
        Default Gateway . . . . . . . . . : 192.168.0.1
        DHCP Server . . . . . . . . . . . : 192.168.0.1
        DNS Servers . . . . . . . . . . . : 192.168.0.1
```

A. ping local host

B. tracert local

C. ipconfig -p

D. ipstat

E. ipconfig /all

Answer Questions 9 and 10 using this Case Study Information:

You are a Network Consultant with specialized skills in managing Windows based network. You have recently been hired by Joe's Canoe Company to administer the network of the entire company. Joe's Canoe Company is a company that produces canoes of different kinds. Most of its customers are in the Vancouver area. So far there is only one office location for Joe's Canoe. There are 4 different departments. Each department has its own management team. The team leaders need to report to the CEO directly. Currently there are about 180 staffs. Of this amount, most of them need to use computers in their daily operations.

The network is purely IP based. On this network the configurations were as follow:

Number of subnets - 5, including:

Subnet A

Subnet B

Subnet C

Subnet D

Subnet E

Number of W2K Domain Controllers - 1 per subnet

Number of NT4 Domain Controllers - 0

Number of W2K DNS Servers - 2, all resides in subnet A

Number of W2K DHCP Servers - 1 per subnet

Number of W2K WINS Servers - 0

Number of W2k Pro PCs - 120, with half of them residing in subnet C

Number of Internet Connections - 1: T1

You have been requested by your boss to upgrade all the W2K PCs to WinXP Pro. After the upgrade, you need to check and ensure that all PCs are connecting to the network as expected.

9. Today, for some reasons, the DNS services on both DNS servers are not functioning. You stop the DNS services entirely. On the client PCs of subnet B, what should you use as a temporary replacement to the DNS service?

A. HelpServicesGroup

B. WINS

C. NetBIOS

D. Active Directory

E. hosts file

10. Today, you are inspecting the network health. On a WinXP PC that resides in subnet D you invoke the command prompt and run a command as shown in the exhibit. What does this command achieve?

```
C:\Documents and Settings\ycthk>ipconfig /flushdns
```

A. It clears the DNS cache to increase bandwidth efficiency

B. It clears the DNS cache in the case that you are having troubles reaching on or two particular Internet sites

C. It clears the DNS cache in the case that you are having troubles reaching the Internet

D. It clears the DNS cache to increase name resolution performance

E. No Answer is Correct

VI Chapter 10: Review Answers

1. You are an expert in WinXP resources administration. As far as you know, what predefined group in WinXP is used by the computer manufacturers to providing you with Remote Assistance?

A. Administrators

B. TechServicesGroup

C. ServiceSupportGroup

***D. HelpServicesGroup**

E. Support Operators

Explanation: Microsoft and computer manufacturers use HelpServicesGroup for Remote Assistance. With this group, technical support personnel can connect to your computer for troubleshooting.

2. You are the administrator of a WinXP Pro system. You are requested to disable a particular hardware device, which is built into the motherboard. Which of the following are the valid ways to do so?

A. Right-click the My Computer icon on the desktop, choose Properties, and then select Device Management

B. From a command prompt, enter ilocaldev.msc

***C. Right-click the My Computer icon on the desktop, choose Manage, and then select Device Manager**

***D. From a command prompt, enter devmgmt.msc**

E. No Answer is Correct

Explanation: In every case of hardware troubleshooting, your starting point is Device Manager, which provides detailed information about all installed hardware, along with controls that you can use to configure devices, assign resources, and set advanced options. To run it, from a command prompt enter devmgmt.msc.

3. You are troubleshooting your WinXP system. You want to invoke the Help And Support Center, and you fail. For the Help And Support Center to function, which of the following services must be running?

A. Svrhelp.exe

***B. Helpsvc.exe**

C. Inisvc.exe

***D. Helpctr.exe**

E. None of the choices

Explanation: The Help And Support Center uses the Microsoft Help Center Service (Helpsvc.exe) and the Help And Support Center executable (Helpctr.exe). If you look in the Windows Task Manager, you will see that both modules are running.

4. You are a Help Desk professional. You are requested to provide troubleshooting assistance to a user in the remote office. You want to avoid traveling to the remote office, as it will take 2 hours of driving. What feature or function of XP can help in this regard?

A. Terminal Service Admin mode

B. W2K Administrator Studio

***C. Remote Assistance**

D. Terminal Service Application mode

E. No Answer is Correct

Explanation: With Windows XP, Remote Assistance lets you open a direct connection between two machines over the Internet or over a local area network. Even if you are hundreds or thousands of miles away, you can watch as the user demonstrates the problem and take control of the screen to make repairs quickly and accurately. You can investigate Control Panel settings, run diagnostic tools, install updates, and even edit the registry of the problem-plagued PC.

5. You are the senior system officer of your company. You are managing a dual-CPU system running Windows XP Professional. A large number of programs are running at the same time. You are quite concerned about the performance impact introduced by 3rd party software services. How do you clearly identify these non-MS native services out of all the programs, for the purpose of troubleshooting?

A. In Task Manager Utility, sort all the processes in descending order

B. In Task Manager Utility, enable the Hide All Non Native Services check box at the bottom of the Services tab

C. In System Configuration Utility, sort all the processes in ascending order

***D. In System Configuration Utility, enable the Hide All Microsoft Services check box at the bottom of the Services tab**

E. No Answer is Correct

Explanation: The Hide All Microsoft Services check box serves an important function by highlighting added services that are not part of the Windows operating system. If you're experiencing performance or stability problems, choose this option to see the short list of third-party services. By temporarily disabling some of these services, you can identify the cause of a problem quickly.

6. You are the administrator of your network. You are responsible for the planning and implementation of all the in-house PCs. After careful consideration, you decided to have hibernation enabled in all of your systems. You found that one of your APM systems has been shutting down instead of hibernating. How should you troubleshoot this problem?

A. Run Devmgmt.msc. Choose View - Show Hidden Devices. Open NT Apm/Legacy Support. Check and ensure that the NT Apm/Legacy Interface Node device is not enabled.

***B. Run Devmgmt.msc. Choose View - Show Hidden Devices. Open NT Apm/Legacy Support. Check and ensure that the NT Apm/Legacy Interface Node device is enabled.**

C. Run Adsmgmt.msc. Choose View - Show Hidden Devices. Open XP Apm Legacy Support. Check and ensure that the Apm/Legacy Interface Node device is not selected.

D. Run Adsmgmt.msc. Choose View - Show All Devices. Open XP Apm Legacy Support. Check and ensure that the Apm/Legacy Interface Node device is selected, and its properties states clearly as "ON."

Explanation: A faulty device driver can cause a blue-screen error during the hibernation process. To find out, open the System Properties dialog box and click the Advanced tab. Under Startup And Recovery, click Settings. In the Startup And Recovery dialog box, select the Write An Event To The System Log check box and clear Automatically Restart. Close the dialog boxes and try to hibernate again. In any case, make sure that NT Apm/Legacy Interface Node device is enabled.

7. On your WinXP network you have an external cable modem connected to an ICS host. All other computers on your network connect to the ICS host via the hub. Mary is using one of those computers. How does Mary check and see if Internet connectivity is now available to her?

A. She should ping the local host

B. She should ping a neighboring computer

C. She should run tracert

***D. She should ping an Internet site**

E. She should ping the ICS host

Explanation: Your first troubleshooting step should always be to check for problems with the physical connection between the local computer and the rest of the network. If the TCP/IP protocol is in use, you may use the Ping utility. Ping allows Windows to send four echo datagrams, small Internet Control Message Protocol packets, to the target address you specify. If the target machine replies, you know that the network connection is alive.

8. You are the administrator of your network. This network is purely IP based. You are troubleshooting some IP connectivity issues. You are using some of the command line utilities on a connected WinXP PC. Refer to the exhibit. What command can you use to display such result?

```
        Connection-specific DNS Suffix  . : hkcable.com.hk
        Description . . . . . . . . . . . : DAVICOM 9102-Based PCI Fast Ethernet
Adapter
        Physical Address. . . . . . . . . : 00-D0-09-2C-CC-AF
        Dhcp Enabled. . . . . . . . . . . : Yes
        Autoconfiguration Enabled . . . . : Yes
        IP Address. . . . . . . . . . . . : 192.168.0.80
        Subnet Mask . . . . . . . . . . . : 255.255.255.0
        Default Gateway . . . . . . . . . : 192.168.0.1
        DHCP Server . . . . . . . . . . . : 192.168.0.1
        DNS Servers . . . . . . . . . . . : 192.168.0.1
```

A. ping local host

B. tracert local

C. ipconfig -p

D. ipstat

***E. ipconfig /all**

Explanation: To perform IP repairs, you may run Ipconfig.exe from the command line. The command displays the DNS suffix, IP address, subnet mask, and default gateway of your primary network connection. To see details about every available network connection, use ipconfig /all.

Answer Questions 9 and 10 using this Case Study Information:

You are a Network Consultant with specialized skills in managing Windows based network. You have recently been hired by Joe's Canoe Company to administer the network of the entire company. Joe's Canoe Company is a company that produces canoes of different kinds. Most of its customers are in the Vancouver area. So far there is only one office location for Joe's Canoe. There are 4 different departments. Each department has its own management team. The team leaders need to report to the CEO directly. Currently there are about 180 staffs. Of this amount, most of them need to use computers in their daily operations.

The network is purely IP based. On this network the configurations were as follow:

Number of subnets - 5, including:

Subnet A

Subnet B

Subnet C

Subnet D

Subnet E

Number of W2K Domain Controllers - 1 per subnet

Number of NT4 Domain Controllers - 0

Number of W2K DNS Servers - 2, all resides in subnet A

Number of W2K DHCP Servers - 1 per subnet

Number of W2K WINS Servers - 0

Number of W2k Pro PCs - 120, with half of them residing in subnet C

Number of Internet Connections - 1: T1

You have been requested by your boss to upgrade all the W2K PCs to WinXP Pro. After the upgrade, you need to check and ensure that all PCs are connecting to the network as expected.

9. Today, for some reasons, the DNS services on both DNS servers are not functioning. You stop the DNS services entirely. On the client PCs of subnet B, what should you use as a temporary replacement to the DNS service?

A. HelpServicesGroup

B. WINS

C. NetBIOS

D. Active Directory

***E. hosts file**

Explanation: A Hosts file can be useful on a mid-size network where all computers have static IP addresses. By entering computer names and IP addresses in a Hosts file, broadcast messages are eliminated. Windows finds the machine name and matching IP address in the Hosts file and access the correct address directly. You may edit the Hosts file using Notepad or another text editor.

10. Today, you are inspecting the network health. On a WinXP PC that resides in subnet D you invoke the command prompt and run a command as shown in the exhibit. What does this command achieve?

```
C:\Documents and Settings\ycthk>ipconfig /flushdns
```

A. It clears the DNS cache to increase bandwidth efficiency

***B. It clears the DNS cache in the case that you are having troubles reaching on or two particular Internet sites**

C. It clears the DNS cache in the case that you are having troubles reaching the Internet

D. It clears the DNS cache to increase name resolution performance

E. No Answer is Correct.

Explanation: Temporary DNS problems can be caused by the DNS cache, which Windows XP maintains for performance reasons. If you suddenly have trouble reaching a single site on the Internet, use the ipconfig command to clear the DNS cache with the /flushdns switch.

Appendix A: Unattended Installations

```
; Microsoft Windows XP
; © 1994–1999 Microsoft Corporation. All rights reserved.
;
; Sample Answer File for Unattended Setup
;
; This file contains information about how to automate the
; installation or upgrade of Windows XP so that
; the Setup program runs without requiring user input.
;

[Data]
; This section is required when you perform an unattended
; installation by starting Setup directly from the Windows XP
; installation CD-ROM.
Unattended install = Yes
; If you are running Unattended Setup from the CD-ROM, you must
; set the Msdosinitiated key to 0.
Msdosinitiated = "0"
; AutoPartition allows Windows XP Unattended Setup to choose a
; partition to install to.
AutoPartition = 1

[Unattended]
UnattendMode = FullUnattended
; The OemPreinstall key tells Unattended Setup that the
; installation is being performed from distribution shares if the
; value is set to Yes.
OemPreinstall = Yes
TargetPath = Winpro
FileSystem = LeaveAlone
; If the OemSkipEula key is set to Yes, it informs
Unattended
; Setup that the user should not be prompted to accept the
End
```

```
; User License Agreement (EULA). A value of Yes signifies
; agreement to the EULA and should be used in conjunction
with
; the terms of your license agreement.
OemSkipEula = Yes

[GuiUnattended]
; Sets the TimeZone. For example, to set the TimeZone for
the
; Pacific Northwest, use a value of "004." Be sure to use
the
; numeric value that represents your own time zone. To look
up
; a numeric value, see the Unattend.doc file on the Windows
XP CD.
TimeZone = "YourTimeZone"
; It is recommended that you change the administrator
password
; before the computer is placed at its final destination.
AdminPassword = AdminPassword
; Tells Unattended Setup to turn AutoLogon on and log on
once.
AutoLogon = Yes
AutoLogonCount = 1
; The OemSkipWelcome key specifies whether the welcome page
in
; the wizard phase of Setup should be skipped. A value of 1
; causes the page to be skipped.
OemSkipWelcome = 1
; The OemSkipRegional key allows Unattended Setup to skip
; RegionalSettings when the final location of the computer
is
; unknown.
OemSkipRegional = 1
```

```
[UserData]
FullName = "Your user name"
OrgName = "Your organization name"
; It is recommended that you avoid using spaces in the
; ComputerName value.
ComputerName = "YourComputer_name"
; To ensure a fully unattended installation, you must
provide a
; value for the ProductID key.
ProductID = "Your product ID"

[Display]
BitsPerPel = 8
XResolution = 800
YResolution = 600
VRefresh = 60

[Networking]
; When you set the value of the InstallDefaultComponents key
; to Yes, Setup will install default networking components.
; The components to be set are TCP/IP, File and Print
Sharing,
; and Client for Microsoft Networks.
InstallDefaultComponents = Yes
```

Appendix B: ARC Naming Conventions

Partition Numbering

There is a simple rule-of-thumb applied here -- primary partitions (on an individual hard disk) are always numbered before extended partitions.

Partition numbering begins at "1" and you can have up to four primary partitions or three primary partitions with one extended partition. The extended partition can be segmented into logical drives, each with its own partition number. Examine the following drive:

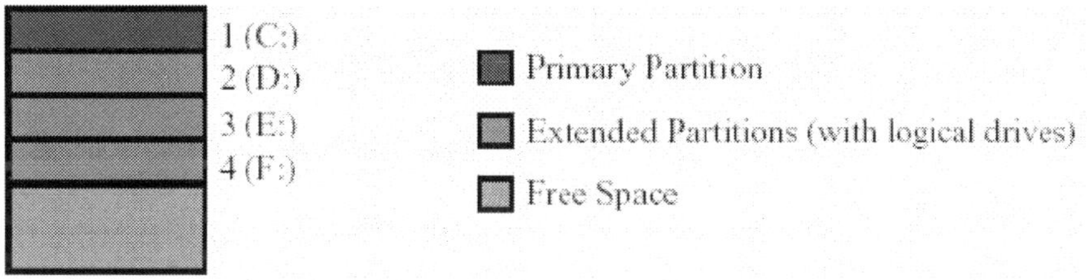

The primary partition is numbered first (1), and then the extended partition with logical drives. But what would happen if you added another primary partition?

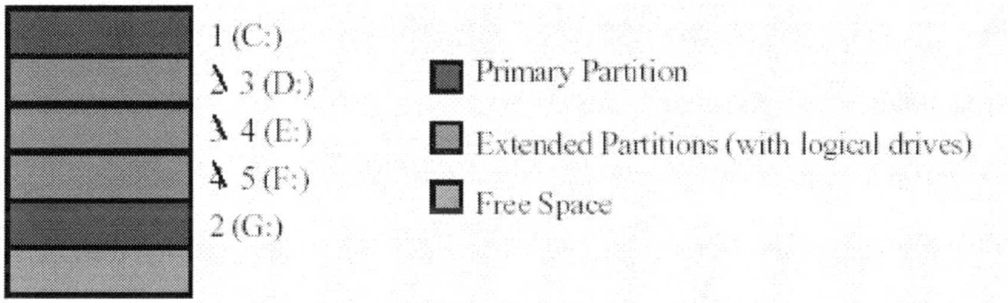

The original primary partition retains its number. The new primary partition takes the highest number not being used by a primary partition. In this instance, that number is 2. The logical drives are all renumbered, starting with the first number not being used by ANY primary partition (in this case, 3).

The way partitions are numbered affect the ARC paths in the "boot.ini" file with Microsoft Windows XP on a machine with an “x86” processor or in the list of "Boot Selections" on a RISC system.

Understanding Arc Naming Convention

An ARC path was the way that NT had to communicate with a RISC system. The RISC processor needed two distinct disk partitions for NT. The firmware started up and looked at the system partition for the operating system initialize (kernel). The system partition then called up the boot partition (the NT files). The firmware authors the boot selections menu. Boot selections were stored as hardware environmental variables in NVRAM.

In an x86 system, it works the same way, except that an x86 processor does not need two distinct partitions for XP. Frequently, both the system and boot partitions are on the same disk partition. The partition numbering is stored in ARC paths in the "boot.ini" file.

It is important to remember on an x86 system that the system partition contains what we perceive as the "boot files". The system partition calls up the boot partition, which contains the operating system files. The ARC paths in the Boot.ini point to the "boot partition", or the separate operating system files.

An ARC path in the Boot.ini file is always written one of two ways:

multi(x) disk(x) rdisk(x) partition(x)

/or/

scsi(x) disk(x) rdisk(x) partition(x)

"Multi" means that the disk is attached to either an IDE controller or a SCSI adapter with the BIOS enabled. "SCSI" means that the disk is attached to a SCSI adapter with the BIOS not enabled. If there is only one controller (or adapter) on the motherboard, the number contained in the parentheses is "0". Each subsequent controller/adapter is incremented by one. Therefore, the second controller would be multi/scsi (1), etc.

"Disk" relates to the SCSI bus number on an adapter where the BIOS is not enabled. Bus numbering starts at "0"; the first bus is "0", the second, "1", and so on. For "multi", this number is ALWAYS "0", because this section of the ARC path is not valid.

"Rdisk" refers to the ordinal number of the hard disk on an IDE controller or a SCSI adapter with the BIOS enabled. The first hard disk is numbered "0", the second "1", and so forth. For "scsi", this number is ALWAYS "0", because this section of the ARC path is not valid.

"Partition" refers to the partition referenced on the disk. Partition numbering starts at "1". As previously mentioned, primary partitions always are numbered first, with the extended partition (containing logical

drives) following.

Consider again the first diagram:

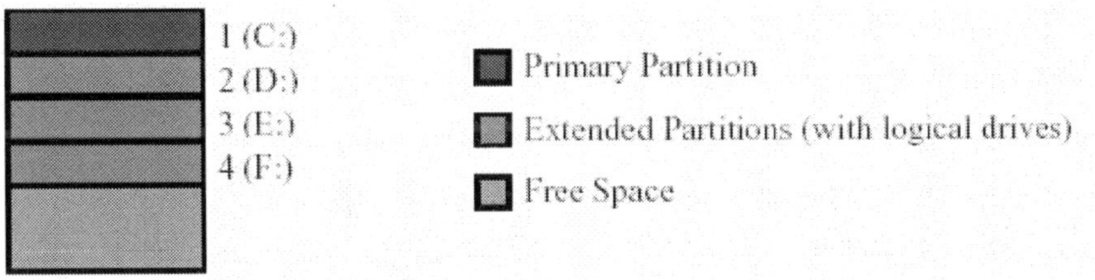

In this case, the System partition is on the primary partition, and the Boot partition is located on the extended partition, on the first logical drive. If this were the first hard drive connected to the only IDE controller, the ARC path in the Boot.ini would be:

multi(0) disk(0) rdisk(0) partition(2)

If you break it down:

multi(0) – it is an IDE controller [multi] and it is the only controller [number starts at 0]

disk(0) – because it is an IDE controller, this is null

rdisk(0) – it is the first hard drive connected [numbering starts at 0]

partition(2) – the boot partition [operating system files] are on the second partition [the extended partition, first logical drive]. Numbering begins at "1", and the primary partition is counted first.

Now examine the second diagram, when another primary partition is added:

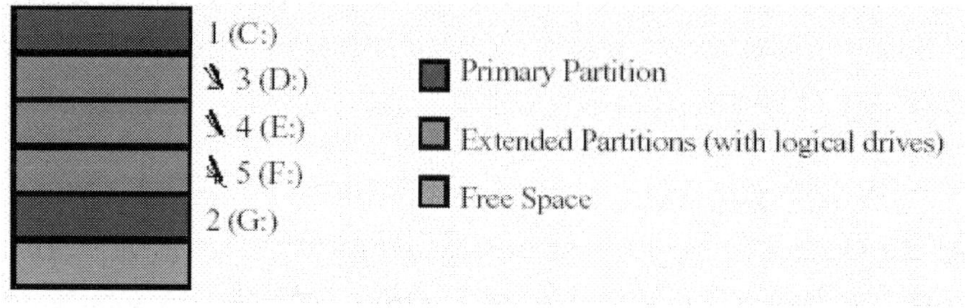

The ARC path would now read:

multi(0) disk(0) rdisk(0) partition(3)

The original primary partition retained its number (1), the new primary partition received the next highest number (2), and the logical drives were all renumbered. The boot partition was on the extended partition. The Boot.ini file should be edited and the ARC path modified to read as above.

Appendix C: List of Figures and Tables

I Listing of all Figures

II Listing of all Tables

Glossary

A

AC-3

The coding system used by Dolby Digital. A standard for high quality digital audio that is used for the sound portion of video stored in digital format.

Accelerated Graphics Port (AGP)

A type of expansion slot that is solely for video cards. Designed by Intel and supported by Windows 2000, AGP is a dedicated bus that provides fast, high-quality video and graphics performance.

Access control entry (ACE)

An entry in an access control list (ACL) containing the security ID (SID) for a user or group and an access mask that specifies which operations by the user or group are allowed, denied, or audited.

See also *access control list*; *access mask*; *security descriptor*.

Access control list (ACL)

A list of security protections that apply to an entire object, a set of the object's properties, or an individual property of an object. There are two types of access control lists: discretionary and system.

See also *access control entry*; *discretionary access control list*; *security descriptor*; *system access control list*.

Access mask

A 32-bit value that specifies the rights that are allowed or denied in an access control entry (ACE) of an access control list (ACL). An access mask is also used to request access rights when an object is opened.

See also *access control entry*.

Access token

A data structure containing security information that identifies a user to the security subsystem on a computer running Windows 2000 or Windows NT. An access token contains a user's security ID, the security IDs for groups that the user belongs to, and a list of the user's privileges on the local computer.

See also *privilege*; *security ID*.

Accessibility

The quality of a system incorporating hardware or software to engage a flexible, customizable user interface, alternative input and output methods, and greater exposure of screen elements to make the computer usable by people with cognitive, hearing, physical, or visual disabilities.

Accessibility status indicators

Icons on the system status area of the taskbar of the Windows desktop that let the user know which accessibility features are activated.

Accessibility Wizard

An interactive tool that makes it easier to set up commonly used accessibility features by specifying options by type of disability, rather than by numeric value changes.

ACPI

See *Advanced Configuration and Power Interface*.

Active Accessibility

A core component in the Windows operating system that is built on COM and defines how applications can exchange information about user interface elements.

Active Directory

The directory service included with Windows 2000 Server. It stores information about objects on a network and makes this information available to users and network administrators. Active Directory gives network users access to permitted resources anywhere on the network using a single logon process. It provides network administrators with an intuitive hierarchical view of the network and a single point of administration for all network objects.

See also *directory*; *directory service*.

ActiveX

A set of technologies that enable software components to interact with one another in a networked environment, regardless of the language in which the components were created.

Administrator

See *system administrator*.

Advanced Configuration and Power Interface (ACPI)

An open industry specification that defines power management on a wide range of mobile, desktop, and server computers and peripherals. ACPI is the foundation for the OnNow industry initiative that allows system manufacturers to deliver computers that will start at the touch of a keyboard. ACPI design is essential to take full advantage of power management and Plug and Play in Windows 2000. Check the manufacturer's documentation to verify that a computer is ACPI-compliant.
See also *Plug and Play*.

Advanced Power Management (APM)

A software interface (designed by Microsoft and Intel) between hardware-specific power management software (such as that located in a system BIOS) and an operating system power management driver.

Advertisement

In Windows 2000, the Software Installation snap-in generates an application advertisement script and stores this script in the appropriate locations in Active Directory and the Group Policy object.

Allocation unit

In file systems an allocation unit is the smallest amount of disk space that can be allocated to hold a file. All file systems used by Windows 2000 organize hard disks based on allocation units. The smaller the allocation unit size, the more efficiently a disk stores information. If no allocation unit size is specified during formatting, Windows 2000 chooses default sizes based on the size of the volume and the file system used. These defaults are selected to reduce the amount of space lost and the amount of fragmentation on the volume. Also called cluster.

American Standard Code for Information Interchange (ASCII)

A standard single byte character-encoding scheme used for text-based data. ASCII uses designated 7-bit or 8-bit number combinations to represent either 128 or 256 possible characters. Standard ASCII uses 7 bits to represent all uppercase and lowercase letters, the numbers 0 through 9, punctuation marks, and special control characters used in U.S. English. Most current x86 systems support the use of extended (or "high") ASCII. Extended ASCII allows the eighth bit of each character to identify an additional 128 special symbol characters, foreign-language letters, and graphic symbols.

See also *Unicode*.

Answer file

A text file that you can use to provide automated input for unattended installation of Windows 2000. This input includes parameters to answer the questions required by Setup for specific installations. In some cases, you can use this text file to provide input to wizards, such as the Active Directory Installation wizard, which is used to add Active Directory to Windows 2000 Server through Setup. The default answer file for Setup is known as Unattend.txt.

API

See *application programming interface*.

APM

See *Advanced Power Management*.

Application media pool

A data repository that determines which media can be accessed by which applications and that sets the policies for that media. There can be any number of application media pools in a Removable Storage system. Applications create application media pools.

Application programming interface (API)

A set of routines that an application uses to request and carry out lower-level services performed by a computer's operating system. These routines usually carry out maintenance tasks such as managing files and displaying information.

Assistive technology

System extensions, programs, devices, and utilities added to a computer to make it more accessible to users with disabilities.

Asynchronous communication

A form of data transmission in which information is sent and received at irregular intervals, one character at a time. Because data is received at irregular intervals, the receiving modem must be signaled to inform it when the data bits of a character begin and end. This is done by means of start and stop bits.

Asynchronous Transfer Mode (ATM)

A high-speed connection-oriented protocol used to transport many different types of network traffic.

ATM

See *Asynchronous Transfer Mode*.

Attribute (object)

In Active Directory, an attribute describes characteristics of an object and the type of information an object can hold. For each object class, the schema defines what attributes an instance of the class must have and what additional attributes it might have.

Auditing

To track the activities of users by recording selected types of events in the security log of a server or a workstation.

Authentication

A basic security function of cryptography. Authentication verifies the identity of the entities that communicate over the network. For example, the process that verifies the identity of a user who logs on to a computer either locally, at a computer's keyboard, or remotely, through a network connection.

See also *cryptography*; *confidentiality*; *integrity*; *Kerberos authentication protocol*; *nonrepudiation*; *NTLM authentication protocol*.

Authentication Header (AH)

A header that provides integrity, authentication, and anti-replay for the entire packet (both the IP header and the data payload carried in the packet).

Authoritative

In the Domain Name System (DNS), the use of zones by DNS servers to register and resolve a DNS domain name. When a DNS server is configured to host a zone, it is authoritative for names within that zone. DNS servers are granted authority based on information stored in the zone.

See also *zone*.

Automated installation

An unattended setup using one or more of several methods such as Remote Installation Services, bootable CD, and SysPrep.

Automatic caching

A method of automatically storing network files on a user's hard disk drive whenever a file is open so the files can be accessed when the user is not connected to the network.

Automatic Private IP Addressing (APIPA)

A feature of Windows 2000 TCP/IP that automatically configures a unique IP address from the range 169.254.0.1 to 169.254.255.254 and a subnet mask of 255.255.0.0 when the TCP/IP protocol is configured for dynamic addressing and a Dynamic Host Configuration Protocol (DHCP) Server is not available.

Available state

A state in which media can be allocated for use by applications.

Averaging counter

A type of counter that measures a value over time and displays the average of the last two measurements over some other factor (for example, PhysicalDisk\Avg. Disk Bytes/Transfer).

B

Backup

A duplicate copy of a program, a disk, or data, made either for archiving purposes or for safeguarding valuable files from loss should the active copy be damaged or destroyed. Some application programs automatically make backup copies of data files, maintaining both the current version and the preceding version.

Backup operator

A type of local or global group that contains the user rights needed to back up and restore files and folders. Members of the Backup Operators group can back up and restore files and folders regardless of ownership, access permissions, encryption, or auditing settings.

See also *auditing*; *global group*; *local group*; *user rights*.

Backup types

A type that determines which data is backed up and how it is backed up. There are five backup types: copy, daily, differential, incremental, and normal.

See also *copy backup*; *daily backup*; *differential backup*; *incremental backup*; *normal backup*.

Bad block

A disk sector that can no longer be used for data storage, usually due to media damage or imperfections.

Bandwidth

In analog communications, the difference between the highest and lowest frequencies in a given range. For example, a telephone line accommodates a bandwidth of 3,000 Hz, the difference between the lowest (300 Hz) and highest (3,300 Hz) frequencies it can carry. In digital communications, the rate at which information is sent expressed in bits per second (bps).

Barcode

A machine-readable label that identifies an object, such as physical media.

Base file record

The first file record in the master file table (MFT) for a file that has multiple file records. The base file record is the record to which the file's file reference corresponds.

Baseline

A range of measurements derived from performance monitoring that represents acceptable performance under typical operating conditions.

Basic disk

A physical disk that contains primary partitions or extended partitions with logical drives used by Windows 2000 and all versions of Windows NT. Basic disks can also contain volume, striped, mirror, or RAID-5 sets that were created using Windows NT 4.0 or earlier. As long as a compatible file format is used, MS-DOS, Windows 95, Windows 98, and all versions of Windows NT can access basic disks.

Basic input/output system (BIOS)

The set of essential software routines that tests hardware at startup, assists with starting the operating system, and supports the transfer of data among hardware devices. The BIOS is stored in read-only memory (ROM) so that it can be executed when the computer is turned on. Although critical to performance, the BIOS is usually invisible to computer users.

Basic volume

A volume on a basic disk. Basic volumes include primary partitions, logical drives within extended partitions, as well as volume, striped, mirror, or RAID-5 sets that were created using Windows NT 4.0 or earlier. Only basic disks can contain basic volumes. Basic and dynamic volumes cannot exist on the same disk.

Batch program

An ASCII (unformatted text) file containing one or more Windows NT or Windows 2000 commands. A batch program's filename has a .BAT extension. When you type the filename at the command prompt, the commands are processed sequentially. "Script" is often used interchangeably with "batch program" in the Windows NT and Windows 2000 environment.

Bi-directional communication

Communication that occurs in two directions simultaneously. Bi-directional communication is useful in printing where jobs can be sent and printer status can be returned at the same time.

Binding

A process by which software components and layers are linked together. When a network component is installed, the binding relationships and dependencies for the components are established. Binding allows components to communicate with each other.

Binding order

The sequence in which software components, network protocols and network adapters are linked together. When a network component is installed, the binding relationships and dependencies for the components are established.

BIOS

See *basic input/output system*.

BIOS parameter block (BPB)

A series of fields containing data on disk size, geometry variables, and the physical parameters of the volume. The BPB is located within the boot sector.

Boot sector

A critical disk structure for starting your computer, located at sector 1 of each volume or floppy disk. It contains executable code and data that is required by the code, including information used by the file system to access the volume. The boot sector is created when you format the volume.

Bootable CD

An automated installation method that runs Setup from a CD-ROM. This method is useful for computers at remote sites with slow links and no local IT department.
See also *automated installation*.

Bottleneck

A condition, usually involving a hardware resource, which causes the entire system to perform poorly.

BounceKeys

A keyboard filter that assists users whose fingers bounce on the keys when pressing or releasing them.

Bound trap

In programming, a problem in which a set of conditions exceeds a permitted range of values that causes the microprocessor to stop what it is doing and handle the situation in a separate routine.

Browsing

The process of creating and maintaining an up-to-date list of computers and resources on a network or part of a network by one or more designated computers running the Computer Browser service.

See also *Computer Browser service.*

Bulk encryption

A process in which large amounts of data, such as files, e-mail messages, or online communications sessions, are encrypted for confidentiality. It is usually done with a symmetric key algorithm.

See also *encryption*; *symmetric key encryption.*

C

Cable modem

A modem that provides broadband Internet access in the range of 10 to 30 Mbps.

Cache

For DNS and WINS, a local information store of resource records for recently resolved names of remote hosts. Typically, the cache is built dynamically as the computer queries and resolves names; it helps optimize the time required to resolve queried names.

See also *cache file*; *naming service*; *resource record.*

Cache file

A file used by the Domain Name System (DNS) server to preload its names cache when service is started. Also known as the "root hints" file because resource records stored in this file are used by the DNS service to help locate root servers that provide referral to authoritative servers for remote names. For Windows DNS servers, the cache file is named Cache.dns and is located in the %SystemRoot%\System32\Dns folder.

See also *authoritative*; *cache*; *systemroot.*

Caching

The process of storing recently-used data values in a special pool in memory where they are temporarily held for quicker subsequent accesses. For DNS, the ability of DNS servers to store information about the domain namespace learned during the processing and resolution of name queries. In Windows 2000, caching is also available through the DNS client service (resolve) as a way for DNS clients to keep a cache of name information learned during recent queries.

See also *caching resolve.*

Caching resolve

For Windows 2000, a client-side Domain Name System (DNS) name resolution service that performs caching of recently learned DNS domain name information. The caching resolve service provides system-wide access to DNS-aware programs for resource records obtained from DNS servers during the processing of name queries. Data placed in the cache is used for a limited period of time and aged according to the active Time To Live (TTL) value. You can set the TTL either individually for each resource record (RR) or default to the minimum TTL set in the start of authority RR for the zone.

See also *cache*; *caching*; *expire interval*; *minimum TTL*; *resolve*; *resource record*; *Time To Live (TTL).*

Callback number

The number that a RAS server uses to call back a user. This number can be preset by the administrator or specified by the user at the time of each call, depending on how the administrator configures the user's callback status. The callback number should be the number of the phone line to which the user's modem is connected.

Card Bus

A 32-bit PC Card.

Cartridge

A unit of media of a certain type, such as 8mm tape, magnetic disk, optical disk, or CD-ROM, used by Removable Storage.

Central Processing Unit (CPU)

The part of a computer that has the ability to retrieve, interpret, and execute instructions and to transfer information to and from other resources over the computer's main data-transfer path, the bus. By definition, the CPU is the chip that functions as the "brain" of a computer.

Certificate

A digital document that is commonly used for authentication and secure exchange of information on open networks, such as the Internet, extranets, and intranets. A certificate securely binds a public key to the entity that holds the corresponding private key. Certificates are digitally signed by the issuing certification authority and can be issued for a user, a computer, or a service. The most widely accepted format for certificates is defined by the ITU-T X.509 version 3 international standard.

See also *certification authority*; *private key*; *public key*.

Certificate Services

The Windows 2000 service that issues certificates for a particular CA. It provides customizable services for issuing and managing certificates for the enterprise.

See also *certificate*; *certification authority*.

Certification authority (CA)

An entity responsible for establishing and vouching for the authenticity of public keys belonging to users (end entities) or other certification authorities. Activities of a certification authority can include binding public keys to distinguished names through signed certificates, managing certificate serial numbers, and certificate revocation.

See also *certificate*; *public key*.

Certified-for-Windows Logo

A specification that addresses the requirements of computer users with disabilities to ensure quality and consistency in assertive devices.

Challenge Handshake Authentication Protocol (CHAP)

A challenge-response authentication protocol for PPP connections documented in RFC 1994 that uses the industry-standard Message Digest 5 (MD5) one-way encryption scheme to hash the response to a challenge issued by the remote access server.

Change journal

A feature new to Windows 2000 that tracks changes to NTFS volumes, including additions, deletions, and modifications. The change journal exists on the volume as a sparse file.

Changer

The robotic element of an online library unit.

CHAP

See *Challenge Handshake Authentication Protocol.*

Child object

An object that is the immediate subordinate of another object in a hierarchy. A child object can have only one immediate superior, or parent, object. In Active Directory, the schema determines what classes of objects can be child objects of what other classes of objects. Depending on its class, a child object can also be the parent of other objects.

See also *object*; *parent object.*

CIM (COM Information Model) Object Manager (CIMOM)

A system service that handles interaction between network management applications and providers of local or remote data or system events.

Cipher text

Text that has been encrypted using an encryption key. Cipher text is meaningless to anyone who does not have the decryption key.

See also *decryption*; *encryption*; *encryption key*; *plaintext.*

Client

Any computer or program connecting to, or requesting services of, another computer or program.

See also *server.*

Cluster

A group of independent computer systems known as nodes or hosts, that work together as a single system to ensure that mission-critical applications and resources remain available to clients. A server cluster is the type of cluster that the Cluster service implements. Network Load Balancing provides a software solution for clustering multiple computers running Windows 2000 Server that provides networked services over the Internet and private intranets.

In file systems a cluster is the smallest amount of disk space that can be allocated to hold a file. All file systems used by Windows 2000 organize hard disks based on clusters. The smaller the cluster size, the more efficiently a disk stores information. If no cluster size is specified during formatting, Windows 2000 chooses default sizes based on the size of the volume and the file system used. These defaults are selected to reduce the amount of space lost and the amount of fragmentation on the volume. Also called allocation units.

Cluster recapping

A recovery technique used when Windows 2000 returns a bad sector error to NTFS. NTFS dynamically replaces the cluster containing the bad sector and allocates a new cluster for the data. If the error occurs during a read, NTFS returns a read error to the calling program, and the data is lost. If the error occurs during a write, NTFS writes the data to the new cluster, and no data is lost.

Code page

A page that maps character codes to individual characters. Different code pages include different special characters, typically customized for a language or a group of languages. The system uses code pages to translate keyboard input into character values for non-Unicode based applications, and to translate character values into characters for non-Unicode based output displays.

COM

See *Component Object Model.*

COM port

Short for communications port, the logical address assigned by MS-DOS (versions 3.3 and higher) and Microsoft Windows (including Windows 95, Windows 98, Windows NT and Windows 2000) to each of the four serial ports on an IBM Personal Computer or a PC compatible. COM ports are also known as the actual serial ports on a PC where peripherals, such as printers, scanners, and external modems, are plugged in.

Commit a transaction

To record in the log file the fact that a transaction is complete and has been recorded in the cache.

Common Internet File System (CIFS)

A protocol and a corresponding API used by application programs to request higher level application services. CIFS was formerly known as SMB (Server Message Block).

Compact Disc File System (CDFS)

A 32-bit protected-mode file system that controls access to the contents of CD-ROM drives in Windows 2000.

Compact disc-record able (CD-R)

A type of CD-ROM that can be written once on a CD recorder and read on a CD-ROM drive.

Compact disc-rewritable (CD-RW)

A type of CD-ROM that can be written many times on a CD recorder and read on a CD-ROM drive.

Complementary metal-oxide semiconductor (CMOS)

The battery-packed memory that stores information, such as disk types and amount of memory, used to start the computer.

Component Object Model (COM)

An object-based programming model designed to promote software interoperability; it allows two or more applications or components to easily cooperate with one another, even if they were written by different vendors, at different times, in different programming languages, or if they are running on different computers running different operating systems. COM is the foundation technology upon which broader technologies can be built. Object linking and embedding (OLE) technology and ActiveX are both built on top of COM.

Computer Browser service

A service that maintains an up-to-date list of computers and provides the list to applications when requested. The Computer Browser service provides the computer lists displayed in the My Network Places, Select Computer, and Select Domain dialog boxes and (for Windows 2000 Server only) in the Server Manager window.

Confidentiality

A basic security function of cryptography. Confidentiality provides assurance that only authorized users can read or use confidential or secret information. Without confidentiality, anyone with network access can use readily available tools to eavesdrop on network traffic and intercept valuable proprietary information. For example, an Internet Protocol security service that ensures a message is disclosed only to intended recipients by encrypting the data.

See also *cryptography*; *authentication*; *integrity*; *nonrepudiation*.

Console tree

The tree view pane in a Microsoft Management Console (MMC) that displays the hierarchical namespace. By default it is the left pane of the console window, but it can be hidden. The items in the console tree (for example, Web pages, folders, and controls) and their hierarchical organization determine the management capabilities of a console.

See also *Microsoft Management Console (MMC)*; *namespace*.

Container object

An object that can logically contain other objects. For example, a folder is a container object.

See also *no container object*; *object*.

Copy backup

A backup that copies all selected files but does not mark each file as having been backed up (that is, the archive bit is not set). A copy backup is useful between normal and incremental backups because copying does not affect these other backup operations.

See also *daily backup*; *differential backup*; *incremental backup*; *normal backup*.

CPU

See *Central Processing Unit*.

Cryptography

The art and science of information security. It provides four basic information security functions: confidentiality, integrity, authentication, and no repudiation.

See also *confidentiality*; *integrity*; *authentication*; *no repudiation*.

D

Daily backup

A backup that copies all selected files that have been modified the day the daily backup is performed. The backed-up files are not marked as having been backed up (that is, the archive bit is not set).

See also *copy backup*; *differential backup*; *incremental backup*; *normal backup*.

Data confidentiality

A service provided by cryptographic technology to assure that data can be read only by authorized users or programs. In a network, data confidentiality ensures that intruders cannot read data. Windows 2000 uses access control mechanisms and encryption, such as DES, 3DES and RSA encryption algorithms, to ensure data confidentiality.

Data Encryption Standard (DES)

An encryption algorithm that uses a 56-bit key, and maps a 64-bit input block to a 64-bit output block. The key appears to be a 64-bit key, but one bit in each of the 8 bytes is used for odd parity, resulting in 56 bits of usable key.

Data integrity

A service provided by cryptographic technology that ensures data has not been modified. In a network environment, data integrity allows the receiver of a message to verify that data has not been modified in transit. Windows 2000 uses access control mechanisms and cryptography, such as RSA public-key signing and shared symmetric key one way hash algorithms, to ensure data integrity.

Data Link Control (DLC)

A protocol used primarily for IBM mainframe computers and printer connectivity.

Data packet

A unit of information transmitted as a whole from one device to another on a network.

Deallocate

To return media to the available state after they have been used by an application.

Decommissioned state

A state that indicates that media have reached their allocation maximum.

Decryption

The process of making encrypted data readable again by converting ciphertext to plaintext.

See also *ciphertext*; *encryption*; *plaintext*.

Default gateway

A configuration item for the TCP/IP protocol that is the IP address of a directly reachable IP router. Configuring a default gateway creates a default route in the IP routing table.

Defragmentation

The process of rewriting parts of a file to contiguous sectors on a hard disk to increase the speed of access and retrieval. When files are updated, the computer tends to save these updates on the largest continuous space on the hard disk, which is often on a different sector than the other parts of the file. When files are thus fragmented, the computer must search the hard disk each time the file is opened to find all of the parts of the file, which slows down response time. In Active Directory, defragmentation rearranges how the data is written in the directory database file to compact it.

See also *fragmentation*.

Desktop

The on-screen work area in which windows, icons, menus, and dialog boxes appear.

Destination directory

The directory (or folder) to which files are copied or moved.

See also *source directory*.

Device driver

A program that allows a specific device, such as a modem, network adapter, or printer, to communicate with Windows 2000. Although a device can be installed on a system, Windows 2000 cannot use the device until the appropriate driver has been installed and configured. If a device is listed in the Hardware Compatibility List (HCL), a driver is usually included with Windows 2000. Device drivers load (for all enabled devices) when a computer is started, and thereafter run invisibly.

See also *Hardware Compatibility List (HCL)*.

Device Manager

An administrative tool that can be used to manage the devices on your computer. Use Device Manager to view and change device properties, update device drivers, configure device settings, and remove devices.

Device Tree

A hierarchical tree that contains the devices configured on the computer.

Differential backup

A backup that copies files created or changed since the last normal or incremental backup. It does not mark files as having been backed up (that is, the archive bit is not set). If you are performing a combination of normal and differential backups, restoring files and folders requires that you have the last normal as well as the last differential backup.

See also *copy backup*; *daily backup*; *incremental backup*; *normal backup*.

Digital audio tape (DAT)

A magnetic medium for recording and storing digital audio data.

Digital certificate

See *certificate*.

Digital linear tape (DLT)

A magnetic medium for backing up data. DLT can transfer data faster than many other types of tape media.

Digital signature

A means for originators of a message, file, or other digitally encoded information to bind their identity to the information. The process of digitally signing information entails transforming the information, as well as some secret information held by the sender, into a tag called a signature. Digital signatures are used in public key environments and they provide no repudiation and integrity services.

See also *public key cryptography*.

Digital subscriber line (DSL)

A special communication line that uses modulation technology to maximize the amount of data that can be sent over copper wires. DSL is used for connections from telephone switching stations to a subscriber rather than between switching stations.

Direct hosting

A feature that allows Windows 2000 computers using Microsoft file and print sharing to communicate over a communications protocol, such as TCP or IPX, bypassing the NetBIOS layer.

Direct memory access (DMA)

Memory access that does not involve the microprocessor. DMA is frequently used for data transfer directly between memory and a peripheral device, such as a disk drive.

Directory

An information source that contains information about computer files or other objects. In a file system, a directory stores information about files. In a distributed computing environment (such as a Windows 2000 domain), the directory stores information about objects such as printers, applications, databases, and users.

Directory service

Both the directory information source and the service that make the information available and usable. A directory service enables the user to find an object given any one of its attributes.

See also *Active Directory*; *directory*.

Disable

To make a device nonfunctional. For example, if a device in a hardware profile is disabled, the device cannot be used while using that hardware profile. Disabling a device frees the resources that were allocated to the device.

Discretionary access control list (DACL)

The part of an object's security descriptor that grants or denies specific users and groups permission to access the object. Only the owner of an object can change permissions granted or denied in a DACL; thus access to the object is at the owner's discretion.

See also *access control entry*; *object*; *security descriptor*; *system access control list*.

Disk bottleneck

A condition that occurs when disk performance is reduced to the extent that overall system performance is affected.

Disk quota

The maximum amount of disk space available to a user.

Dismount

To remove a removable tape or disc from a drive.

See also *library*.

Distinguished name

A name that uniquely identifies an object by using the relative distinguished name for the object, plus the names of container objects and domains that contain the object. The distinguished name identifies the object as well as its location in a tree. Every object in Active Directory has a distinguished name. An example of a distinguished name is CN=MyName,CN=Users,DC=Reskit,DC=Com. This distinguished name identifies the "MyName" user object in the reskit.com domain.

Distributed file system (DFS)

A Windows 2000 service consisting of software residing on network servers and clients that transparently links shared folders located on different file servers into a single namespace for improved load sharing and data availability.

Distribution folder

The folder created on the Windows 2000 distribution server to contain the Setup files.

DMA

See *direct memory access*.

DNS

See *Domain Name System*.

DNS server

A computer that runs DNS server programs containing name-to-IP address mappings, IP address-to-name mappings, information about the domain tree structure, and other information. DNS servers also attempt to resolve client queries.

DNS zone

In a DNS database, a zone is a contiguous portion of the DNS tree that is administered as a single separate entity, by a DNS server. The zone contains resource records for all the names within the zone.

Domain

In Windows 2000 and Active Directory, a collection of computers defined by the administrator of a Windows 2000 Server network that share a common directory database. A domain has a unique name and provides access to the centralized user accounts and group accounts maintained by the domain administrator. Each domain has its own security policies and security relationships with other domains and represents a single security boundary of a Windows 2000 computer network. Active Directory is made up of one or more domains, each of which can span more than one physical location. For DNS, a domain is any tree or sub tree within the DNS namespace. Although the names for DNS domains often correspond to Active Directory domains, DNS domains should not be confused with Windows 2000 and Active Directory networking domain.

Domain controller

For a Windows NT Server or Windows 2000 Server domain, the server that authenticates domain logons and maintains the security policy and the security accounts master database for a domain. Domain controllers manage user access to a network, which includes logging on, authentication, and access to the directory and shared resources.

Domain local group

A Windows 2000 group only available in native mode domains that can contain members from anywhere in the forest, in trusted forests, or in a trusted pre-Windows 2000 domain. Domain local groups can only grant permissions to resources within the domain in which they exist. Typically, domain local groups are used to gather security principals from across the forest to control access to resources within the domain.

Domain name

In Windows 2000 and Active Directory, the name given by an administrator to a collection of networked computers that share a common directory. For DNS, domain names are specific node names in the DNS namespace tree. DNS domain names use singular node names, known as "labels," joined together by periods (.) that indicate each node level in the namespace.

See also *Domain Name System (DNS)*; *namespace*.

Domain Name System (DNS)

A hierarchical naming system used for locating domain names on the Internet and on private TCP/IP networks. DNS provides a service for mapping DNS domain names to IP addresses, and vice versa. This allows users, computers, and applications to query the DNS to specify remote systems by fully qualified domain names rather than by IP addresses.

See also *domain*; *Ping*.

Domain tree

In DNS, the inverted hierarchical tree structure that is used to index domain names. Domain trees are similar in purpose and concept to the directory trees used by computer filing systems for disk storage.

See also *domain name*; *namespace*.

DOT4

See *IEEE 1284.4*

DSL

See *digital subscriber line*.

Dual boot

A computer configuration that can start two different operating systems.

See also *multiple boot*.

DVD decoder

A hardware or software component that allows a digital video disc (DVD) drive to display movies on your computer screen.

See also *DVD disc*; *DVD drive*.

DVD disc

A type of optical disc storage technology. A digital video disc (DVD) looks like a CD-ROM disc, but it can store greater amounts of data. DVD discs are often used to store full-length movies and other multimedia content that requires large amounts of storage space.

See also *DVD decoder*; *DVD drive*.

DVD drive

A disk storage device that uses digital video disc (DVD) technology. A DVD drive reads both CD-ROM and DVD discs; however, a DVD decoder is necessary to display DVD movies on your computer screen.

See also *DVD decoder*; *DVD disc*.

Dvorak keyboard

An alternative keyboard with a layout that makes the most frequently typed characters more accessible to people who have difficulty typing on the standard QWERTY layout.

Dynamic disk

A physical disk that is managed by Disk Management. Dynamic disks can contain only dynamic volumes (that is, volumes created by using Disk Management). Dynamic disks cannot contain partitions or logical drives, nor can MS-DOS access them.

See also *dynamic volume*; *partition*.

Dynamic Host Configuration Protocol (DHCP)

A networking protocol that provides safe, reliable, and simple TCP/IP network configuration and offers dynamic configuration of Internet Protocol (IP) addresses for computers. DHCP ensures that address conflicts do not occur and helps conserve the use of IP addresses through centralized management of address allocation.

Dynamic priority

The priority value to which a thread's base priority is adjusted to optimize scheduling.

Dynamic volume

A logical volume that is created using Disk Management. Dynamic volumes include simple, spanned, striped, mirrored, and RAID-5 volumes. Dynamic volumes must be created on dynamic disks.

See also *dynamic disk*; *volume*.

Dynamic-link library (DLL)

A feature of the Microsoft Windows family of operating systems and the OS/2 operating system. DLLs allow executable routines, generally serving a specific function or set of functions, to be stored separately as files with .dll extensions, and to be loaded only when needed by the program that calls them.

E

EAP

See *Extensible Authentication Protocol*

EIDE

See *Enhanced Integrated Drive Electronics*

Embedded object

Information created in another application that has been pasted inside a document. When information is embedded, you can edit it in the new document by using toolbars and menus from the original program. When you double-click the embedded icon, the toolbars and menus from the program used to create the information appear. Embedded information is not linked to the original file. If you change information in one place, it is not updated in the other.

See also *linked object.*

Emergency repair disk (ERD)

A disk, created by the Backup utility, that contains copies of three of the files stored in the %SystemRoot%/Repair folder, including Setup. log that contains a list of system files installed on the computer. This disk can be used during the Emergency Repair Process to repair your computer if it will not start or if your system files are damaged or erased.

Encapsulating security payload (ESP)

An IPSec protocol that provides confidentiality, in addition to authentication, integrity, and anti-replay. ESP can be used alone, in combination with AH, or nested with the Layer Two Tunneling Protocol (L2TP). ESP does not normally sign the entire packet unless it is being tunneled. Ordinarily, just the data payload is protected, not the IP header.

Encrypting File System (EFS)

A new feature in Windows 2000 that protects sensitive data in files that is stored on disk using the NTFS file system. It uses symmetric key encryption in conjunction with public key technology to provide confidentiality for files. It runs as an integrated system service, which makes EFS easy to manage, difficult to attack, and transparent to the file owner and to applications.

Encryption

The process of disguising a message or data in such a way as to hide its substance.

Encryption key

A bit string that is used in conjunction with an encryption algorithm to encrypt and decrypt data.

See also *public key*; *private key*; *symmetric key*.

Enhanced Integrated Drive Electronics (EIDE)

An extension of the IDE standard, EIDE is a hardware interface standard for disk drive designs that houses control circuits in the drives themselves. It allows for standardized interfaces to the system bus, while providing for advanced features, such as burst data transfers and direct data access.

Enterprise Resource Planning (ERP)

A software system designed to support and automate the processes of an organization, including manufacturing and distribution, accounting, project management and personnel functions.

Environment variable

A string consisting of environment information, such as a drive, path, or filename, associated with a symbolic name that can be used by Windows NT and Windows 2000. Use the System option in Control Panel or the set command from the command prompt to define environment variables.

ERD

See *emergency repair disk.*

Ethernet

An IEEE 802.3 standard for contention networks. Ethernet uses a bus or star topology and relies on the form of access known as Carrier Sense Multiple Access with Collision Detection (CSMA/DC) to regulate communication line traffic. Network nodes are linked by coaxial cable, fiber-optic cable, or by twisted-pair wiring. Data is transmitted in variable-length frames containing delivery and control information and up to 1,500 bytes of data. The Ethernet standard provides for base band transmission at 10 megabits (10 million bits) per second.

Exabytes

Approximately one quintillion bytes, or one billion billion bytes.

Expire interval

For DNS, the number of seconds that DNS servers operating as secondary masters for a zone use to determine if zone data should be expired when the zone is not refreshed and renewed.

See also *zone*.

Explicit trust relationship

A trust relationship from Windows NT in which an explicit link is made in one direction only. Explicit trusts can also exist between Windows NT domains and Windows 2000 domains, and between forests.

Export

In NFS, to make a file system available by a server to a client for mounting.

Extended Industry Standard Architecture (EISA)

A 32-bit bus standard introduced in 1988 by a consortium of nine computer-industry companies. EISA maintains compatibility with the earlier Industry Standard Architecture (ISA) but provides for additional features.

Extended partition

A portion of a basic disk that can contain logical drives. To have more than four volumes on your basic disk, you need to use an extended partition. Only one of the four partitions allowed per physical disk can be an extended partition, and no primary partition needs to be present to create an extended partition. You can create extended partitions only on basic disks.

See also *basic disk*; *logical drive*; *partition*; *primary partition*; *unallocated space*.

Extensible Authentication Protocol (EAP)

An extension to PPP that allows for arbitrary authentication mechanisms to be employed for the validation of a PPP connection.

Extensible Markup Language (XML)

A meta-markup language that provides a format for describing structured data. This facilitates more precise declarations of content and more meaningful search results across multiple platforms. In addition, XML will enable a new generation of Web-based data viewing and manipulation applications.

F

FAT32

A derivative of the file allocation table file system. FAT32 supports smaller cluster sizes than FAT in the same given disk space, which results in more efficient space allocation on FAT32 drives.

See also *file allocation table*; *NTFS file system*.

Fault tolerance

The assurance of data integrity when hardware failures occur. On the Windows NT and Windows 2000 platforms, fault tolerance is provided by the Ftdisk.sys driver.

Fiber Distributed Data Interface (FDDI)

A type of network media designed to be used with fiber-optic cabling.

See also LocalTalk; Token Ring.

File allocation table (FAT)

A file system based on a file allocation table (FAT) maintained by some operating systems, including Windows NT and Windows 2000, to keep track of the status of various segments of disk space used for file storage.

File record

The row in the master file table (MFT) that corresponds to a particular disk file. The file record is identified by its file reference.

File system

In an operating system, the overall structure in which files are named, stored, and organized. NTFS, FAT, and FAT32 are types of file systems.

File system cache

An area of physical memory that holds frequently used pages. It allows applications and services to locate pages rapidly and reduces disk activity.

File Transfer Protocol (FTP)

A protocol that defines how to transfer files from one computer to another over the Internet. FTP is also a client/server application that moves files using this protocol.

Filter

In IPSec, a rule that provides the ability to trigger security negotiations for a communication based on the source, destination, and type of IP traffic.

See also search filter.

FilterKeys

A Windows 2000 accessibility feature that allows people with physical disabilities to adjust keyboard response time.

See also *BounceKeys*; *RepeatKeys*; *SlowKeys*.

Firewall

A combination of hardware and software that provides a security system, usually to prevent unauthorized access from outside to an internal network or intranet. A firewall prevents direct communication between network and external computers by routing communication through a proxy server outside of the network. The proxy server determines whether it is safe to let a file pass through to the network. A firewall is also called a security-edge gateway.

Folder redirection

A Group Policy option that allows you to redirect designated folders to the network.

Foreground boost

A mechanism that increases the priority of a foreground application.

Forest

A collection of one or more Windows 2000 Active Directory trees, organized as peers and connected by two-way transitive trust relationships between the root domains of each tree. All trees in a forest share a common schema, configuration, and Global Catalog. When a forest contains multiple trees, the trees do not form a contiguous namespace.

Fragmentation

The scattering of parts of the same disk file over different areas of the disk. Fragmentation occurs as files on a disk are deleted and new files are added. It slows disk access and degrades the overall performance of disk operations, although usually not severely.

See also *defragmentation*.

Free media pool

A logical collection of unused data-storage media that can be used by applications or other media pools. When media are no longer needed by an application, they are returned to a free media pool so that they can be used again.

See also *media pool*; *Removable Storage*.

G

Gatekeeper

A server that uses a directory to perform name-to-IP address translation, admission control and call management services in H.323 conferencing.

Gateway

A device connected to multiple physical TCP/IP networks, capable of routing or delivering IP packets between them. A gateway translates between different transport protocols or data formats (for example, IPX and IP) and is generally added to a network primarily for its translation ability.

See also *IP address*; *IP router*.

Global Catalog

A domain controller that contains a partial replica of every domain directory partition in the forest as well as a full replica of its own domain directory partition and the schema and configuration directory partitions. The Global Catalog holds a replica of every object in Active Directory, but each object includes a limited number of its attributes. The attributes in the Global Catalog are those most frequently used in search operations (such as a user's first and last names) and those attributes that are required to locate a full replica of the object. The Global Catalog enables users and applications to find objects in Active Directory given one or more attributes of the target object, without knowing what domain holds the object. The Active Directory replication system builds the Global Catalog automatically. The attributes replicated into the Global Catalog include a base set defined by Microsoft. Administrators can specify additional properties to meet the needs of their installation.

Global group

For Windows 2000 Server, a group that can be used in its own domain, in member servers and in workstations of the domain, and in trusting domains. In all those places a global group can be granted rights and permissions and can become a member of local groups. However, a global group can contain user accounts only from its own domain.

See also *group*; *local group*.

Globally unique identifier (GUID)

A 16-byte value generated from the unique identifier on a device, the current date and time, and a sequence number. A GUID is used to identify a particular device or component.

Graphical Identification and Authentication (GINA)

A DLL loaded during the Windows 2000 Winlogon process, which displays the standard logon dialog box, collects, and processes user logon data for verification.

Graphical user interface (GUI)

A display format, like that of Windows, which represents a program's functions with graphic images such as buttons and icons. GUIs allow a user to perform operations and make choices by pointing and clicking with a mouse.

Group

A collection of users, computers, contacts, and other groups. Groups can be used as security or as e-mail distribution collections. Distribution groups are used only for e-mail. Security groups are used both to grant access to resources and as e-mail distribution lists. In a server cluster, a group is a collection of resources, and the basic unit of failover.

See also *domain local group*; *global group*; *native mode*; *universal group*.

Group Identification (GID)

A group identifier that uniquely identifies a group of users. UNIX uses the GID to identify the group ownership of a file, and to determine access permissions.

Group memberships

The groups to which a user account belongs. Permissions and rights granted to a group are also provided to its members. In most cases, the actions a user can perform in Windows 2000 are determined by the group memberships of the user account to which the user is logged on.

See also *group*.

Group Policy

An administrator's tool for defining and controlling how programs, network resources, and the operating system operate for users and computers in an organization. In an Active Directory environment, Group Policy is applied to users or computers on the basis of their membership in sites, domains, or organizational units.

Group Policy object

A collection of Group Policy settings. Group Policy objects are the documents created by the Group Policy snap-in. Group Policy objects are stored at the domain level, and they affect users and computers contained in sites, domains, and organizational units. Each Windows 2000-based computer has exactly one group of settings stored locally, called the local Group Policy object.

H

H.323

The ITU-T standard for multimedia communications over networks that do not provide a guaranteed quality of service. This standard provides specifications for workstations, devices, and services to carry real-time video, audio, and data or any combination of these elements.

See also *QoS*.

Hardware abstraction layer (HAL)

A thin layer of software provided by the hardware manufacturer that hides, or abstracts, hardware differences from higher layers of the operating system. Through the filter provided by the HAL, different types of hardware all look alike to the rest of the operating system. This allows Windows NT and Windows 2000 to be portable from one hardware platform to another. The HAL also provides routines that allow a single device driver to support the same device on all platforms. The HAL works closely with the kernel.

Hardware Compatibility List (HCL)

A list of the devices supported by Windows 2000, available from the Microsoft Web site.

Hardware malfunction message

A character-based, full-screen error message displayed on a blue background. It indicates the microprocessor detected a hardware error condition from which the system cannot recover.

Hardware profile

A set of changes to the standard configuration of devices and services (including drivers and Win32 services) loaded by Windows 2000 when the system starts. For example, a hardware profile can include an instruction to disable (that is, not load) a driver, or an instruction not to connect an undocked laptop computer to the network. Because of the instructions in this subkey, users can modify the service configuration for a particular use while preserving the standard configuration unchanged for more general uses.

Hardware type

A classification for similar devices. For example, Imaging Device is a hardware type for digital cameras and scanners.

Heartbeat thread

A thread initiated by the Windows NT Virtual DOS Machine (NTVDM) process that interrupts every 55 milliseconds to simulate a timer interrupt.

Hop

In data communications, one segment of the path between routers on a geographically dispersed network. A hop is comparable to one "leg" of a journey that includes intervening stops between the starting point and the destination. The distance between each of those stops (routers) is a communications hop.

Hosts

A local text file in the same format as the 4.3 Berkeley Software Distribution (BSD) UNIX/etc/hosts file. This file maps host names to IP addresses. In Windows 2000, this file is stored in the \%SystemRoot%\System32\Drivers\Etc folder.

Hot keys

A Windows feature that allows quick activation of specified accessibility features through a combination of keys pressed in unison.

HTML

See *Hypertext Markup Language*.

HTML+Time

A new feature in Microsoft Internet Explorer 5 that adds timing and media synchronization support to HTML pages. Using a few Extensible Markup Language (XML)-based elements and attributes, you can add images, video, and sounds to an HTML page, and synchronize them with HTML text elements over a specified amount of time. In short, you can use HTML+TIME technology to quickly and easily create multimedia-rich, interactive presentations, with little or no scripting.

HTTP

See *Hypertext Transfer Protocol.*

Human Interface Device (HID)

A firmware specification that is a new standard for input and output devices such as drawing tablets, keyboards, USB speakers, and other specialized devices designed to improve accessibility.

Hypertext Markup Language (HTML)

A simple markup language used to create hypertext documents that are portable from one platform to another. HTML files are simple ASCII text files with embedded codes (indicated by markup tags) to indicate formatting and hypertext links. HTML is used for formatting documents on the World Wide Web.

Hypertext Transfer Protocol (HTTP)

The protocol used to transfer information on the World Wide Web. An HTTP address (one kind of Uniform Resource Locator [URL]) takes the form: http://www.microsoft.com.

I

I/O request packet (IRP)

Data structures that drivers use to communicate with each other.

ICM

See *Image Color Management.*

IDE

See *integrated device electronics.*

IEEE 1284.4

An IEEE specification, also called DOT4, for supporting multi-function peripherals (MFPs). Windows 2000 has a driver called DOT4 that creates different port settings for each function of an MFP, enabling Windows 2000 print servers to simultaneously send data to multiple parts of an MFP.

IEEE 1394 (Firewire)

A standard for high-speed serial devices such as digital video and digital audio editing equipment.

IIS

See *Internet Information Services.*

ILS

See *Internet locator service.*

Image Color Management (ICM)

The process of image output correction. ICM attempts to make the output more closely match the colors that are input or scanned.

Impersonation

A circumstance that occurs when Windows NT or Windows 2000 allows one process to take on the security attributes of another.

Import media pool

A repository where Removable Storage puts media when it recognizes the on-media identifier (OMID), but does not have the media cataloged in the current Removable Storage database.

Incremental backup

A backup that copies only those files created or changed since the last normal or incremental backup. It marks files as having been backed up (that is, the archive bit is set). If a combination of normal and incremental backups is used to restore your data, you need to have the last normal backup and all subsequent incremental backup sets.

See also *copy backup*; *daily backup*; *differential backup*; *normal backup*.

Independent software vendors (ISVs)

A third-party software developer; an individual or an organization that independently creates computer software.

Industry Standard Architecture (ISA)

A bus design specification that allows components to be added as cards plugged into standard expansion slots in IBM Personal Computers and IBM compatible computers. Originally introduced in the IBM PC/XT with an 8-bit data path, ISA was expanded in 1984, when IBM introduced the PC/AT, to permit a 16-bit data path. A 16-bit ISA slot consists of two separate 8-bit slots mounted end-to-end so that a single 16-bit card plugs into both slots. An 8-bit expansion card can be inserted and used in a 16-bit slot (it occupies only one of the two slots), but a 16-bit expansion card cannot be used in an 8-bit slot.

See also *Extended Industry Standard Architecture*.

Infrared (IR)

Light that is beyond red in the color spectrum. While the light is not visible to the human eye, infrared transmitters and receivers can send and receive infrared signals.

See also *Infrared Data Association*; *infrared device*; *infrared port*.

Infrared Data Association (IrDA)

A networking protocol used to transmit data created by infrared devices. Infrared Data Association is also the name of the industry organization of computer, component, and telecommunications vendors who establish the standards for infrared communication between computers and peripheral devices, such as printers.

See also *infrared*; *infrared device*; *infrared port*.

Infrared device

A computer, or a computer peripheral such as a printer, that can communicate using infrared light.

See also *infrared.*

Infrared port

An optical port on a computer that enables communication with other computers or devices by using infrared light, without cables. Infrared ports can be found on some portable computers, printers, and cameras.

See also *infrared device.*

Input/Output (I/O) port

A channel through which data is transferred between a device and the microprocessor. The port appears to the microprocessor as one or more memory addresses that it can use to send or receive data.

Insert/Eject (IE) port

IE ports, also called "mailslots," offer limited access to the cartridges in a library managed by Removable Storage. When an administrator adds cartridges to a library through an IE port, the cartridges are placed in the IE port and then the library uses the transport to move the cartridges from the IE port to a slot. Some libraries have no IE ports; others have several. Some IE ports handle only one cartridge at a time; others can handle several at one time.

Instantaneous counter

A type of counter that displays the most recent measurement taken by the Performance console.

Institute of Electrical and Electronics Engineers (IEEE)

An organization of engineering and electronics professionals that are notable for developing standards for hardware and software.

Integrated device electronics (IDE)

A type of disk-drive interface in which the controller electronics reside on the drive itself, eliminating the need for a separate adapter card. IDE offers advantages such as look-ahead caching to increase overall performance.

Integrated Services Digital Network (ISDN)

A type of phone line used to enhance WAN speeds. ISDN lines can transmit at speeds of 64 or 128 kilobits per second, as opposed to standard phone lines, which typically transmit at 28.8 kilobits per second. The phone company must install an ISDN line at both the server site and the remote site.

See also *wide area network*.

Integrity

A basic security function of cryptography. Integrity provides verification that the original contents of information have not been altered or corrupted. Without integrity, someone might alter information or the information might become corrupted, but the alteration can go undetected. For example, an Internet Protocol security property that protects data from unauthorized modification in transit, ensuring that the data received is exactly the same as the data sent. Hash functions sign each packet with a cryptographic checksum, which the receiving computer checks before opening the packet. If the packet-and therefore signature-has changed, the packet is discarded.

See also *cryptography*; *authentication*; *confidentiality*; *no repudiation*.

IntelliMirror

A set of Windows 2000 features used for desktop change and configuration management. When IntelliMirror is used in both the server and client, the users' data, applications, and settings follow them when they move to another computer.

Interactive logon

A network logon from a computer keyboard, when the user types information in the Logon Information dialog box displayed by the computer's operating system.

Internet

A worldwide public TCP/IP internetwork consisting of thousands of networks, connecting research facilities, universities, libraries, and private companies.

Internet Control Message Protocol (ICMP)

A required maintenance protocol in the TCP/IP suite that reports errors and allows simple connectivity. The Ping tool uses ICMP to perform TCP/IP troubleshooting.

Internet Information Services (IIS)

Software services that support Web site creation, configuration, and management, along with other Internet functions. Internet Information Services include Network News Transfer Protocol (NNTP), File Transfer Protocol (FTP), and Simple Mail Transfer Protocol (SMTP).

See also *File Transfer Protocol*; *Network News Transfer Protocol*; *Simple Mail Transfer Protocol.*

Internet Key Exchange (IKE)

A protocol that establishes the security association and shared keys necessary for two parties to communicate with Internet Protocol security.

Internet locator service (ILS)

An optional component of Microsoft Site Server that creates a dynamic directory of videoconferencing users.

Internet Printing Protocol (IPP)

The protocol that uses the Hypertext Transfer Protocol (HTTP) to send print jobs to printers throughout the world. Windows 2000 supports Internet Printing Protocol (IPP) version 1.0.

Internet Protocol (IP)

A routable protocol in the TCP/IP protocol suite that is responsible for IP addressing, routing, and the fragmentation and reassembly of IP packets.

Internet Protocol security (IPSec)

A set of industry-standard, cryptography-based protection services and protocols. IPSec protects all protocols in the TCP/IP protocol suite and Internet communications using L2TP.

See also *Layer Two Tunneling Protocol.*

Internet service provider (ISP)

A company that provides individuals or companies access to the Internet and the World Wide Web. An ISP provides a telephone number, a user name, a password, and other connection information so users can connect their computers to the ISP's computers. An ISP typically charges a monthly and/or hourly connection fee.

Internetwork Packet Exchange (IPX)

A network protocol native to NetWare that controls addressing and routing of packets within and between LANs. IPX does not guarantee that a message will be complete (no lost packets).

See also *Internetwork Packet Exchange / Sequenced Packet Exchange.*

Internetwork Packet Exchange / Sequenced Packet Exchange (IPX/SPX)

Transport protocols used in Novell NetWare and other networks.

Interrupt

A request for attention from the processor. When the processor receives an interrupt, it suspends its current operations, saves the status of its work, and transfers control to a special routine known as an interrupt handler, which contains the instructions for dealing with the particular situation that caused the interrupt.

Interrupt request (IRQ)

A signal sent by a device to get the attention of the processor when the device is ready to accept or send information. Each device sends its interrupt requests over a specific hardware line, numbered from 0 to 15. Each device must be assigned a unique IRQ number.

Intranet

A network within an organization that uses Internet technologies and protocols but is available only to certain people, such as employees of a company. An intranet is also called a private network.

IP

See *Internet Protocol.*

IP address

A 32-bit address used to identify a node on an IP internetwork. Each node on the IP internetwork must be assigned a unique IP address, which is made up of the network ID, plus a unique host ID. This address is typically represented with the decimal value of each octet separated by a period (for example, 192.168.7.27). In Windows 2000, the IP address can be configured manually or dynamically through DHCP.

See also *Dynamic Host Configuration Protocol*; *node.*

IP router

A system connected to multiple physical TCP/IP networks that can route or deliver IP packets between the networks.

See also *packet*; *router*; *routing*; *Transmission Control Protocol/Internet Protocol.*

IPP

See *Internet Printing Protocol.*

IPSec

See *Internet Protocol security.*

IPSec driver

A driver that uses the IP Filter List from the active IPSec policy to watch for outbound IP packets that must be secured and inbound IP packets that need to be verified and decrypted.

IPSec filter

A part of IPSec security rules that make up an IPSec security policy. IPSec filters determine whether a data packet needs an IPSec action and what the IPSec action is, such as permit, block, or secure. Filters can classify traffic by criteria including source IP address, source subnet mask, destination IP address, IP protocol type, source port, and destination port. Filters are not specific to a network interface.

See also *IPSec security rules.*

IPSec security rules

Rules contained in the IPSec policy that govern how and when an IPSec is invoked. A rule triggers and controls secure communication when a particular source, destination, or traffic type is found. Each IPSec policy may contain one or many rules; any of which may apply to a particular packet. Default rules are provided which encompass a variety of clients and server-based communications or rules can be modified to meet custom requirements.

IPX

See *Internetwork Packet Exchange.*

IrDA

See *Infrared Data Association.*

IRP

See *I/O request packet.*

IRQ

See *Interrupt Request.*

Outran-p

A protocol that transfers images from cameras to Windows 2000 computers using infrared transmissions, making a physical cable connection unnecessary.

Isochronous

Time dependent. Refers to processes where data must be delivered within certain time constraints. Multimedia streams require an isochronous transport mechanism to ensure that data is delivered as fast as it is displayed, and to ensure that the audio is synchronized with the video.

J

Job object

A feature in the Win32 API set that makes it possible for groups of processes to be managed with respect to their processor usage and other factors.

K

Kerberos authentication protocol

An authentication mechanism used to verify user or host identity. The Kerberos v5 authentication protocol is the default authentication service for Windows 2000. Internet Protocol security and the QoS Admission Control Service use the Kerberos protocol for authentication.

See also *Internet Protocol security*; *NTLM authentication protocol*; *QoS Admission Control Service*.

Kernel

The core of layered architecture that manages the most basic operations of the operating system and the computer's processor for Windows NT and Windows 2000. The kernel schedules different blocks of executing code, called threads, for the processor to keep it as busy as possible and coordinates multiple processors to optimize performance. The kernel also synchronizes activities among Executive-level subcomponents, such as I/O Manager and Process Manager, and handles hardware exceptions and other hardware-dependent functions. The kernel works closely with the hardware abstraction layer.

Key

A secret code or number required to read, modify, or verify secured data. Keys are used in conjunction with algorithms to secure data. Windows 2000 automatically handles key generation. For the registry, a key is an entry in the registry that can contain both subkeys and entries. In the registry structure, keys are analogous to folders, and entries are analogous to files. In the Registry Editor window, a key appears as a file folder in the left pane. In an answer file, keys are character strings that specify parameters from which Setup obtains the needed data for unattended installation of the operating system.

Keyboard filters

Special timing and other devices that compensate for erratic motion tremors, slow response time, and other mobility impairments.

L

L2TP

See *Layer Two Tunneling Protocol.*

LAN

See *local area network.*

Last Known Good Configuration

A hardware configuration available by pressing F8 during startup. If the current hardware settings prevent the computer from starting, the Last Known Good Configuration can allow the computer to be started and the configuration to be examined. When the Last Known Good Configuration is used, later configuration changes are lost.

Layer 2 forwarding (L2F)

Permits the tunneling of the link layer of higher-level protocols. Using these tunnels, it is possible to separate the location of the initial dial-up server from the physical location at which the dial-up protocol connection is terminated and access to the network is provided.

See also *Layer Two Tunneling Protocol*; *tunnel.*

Layer two Tunneling Protocol (L2TP)

A tunneling protocol that encapsulates PPP frames to be sent over IP, X.25, Frame Relay, or ATM networks. L2TP is a combination of the Point-to-Point Tunneling Protocol (PPTP) and Layer 2 Forwarding (L2F), a technology proposed by Cisco Systems, Inc.

Legend

The area of the System Monitor graph or histogram display that shows computer name, object name, counter name, instances, and other information as a reference to the lines in the graph or the bars in the histogram.

Library

A data-storage system, usually managed by Removable Storage. A library consists of removable media (such as tapes or discs) and a hardware device that can read from or write to the media. There are two major types of libraries: robotic libraries (automated multiple-media, mutative devices) and stand-alone drive libraries (manually operated, single-drive devices). A robotic library is also called a jukebox or changer.

See also *Removable Storage.*

Library request

A request for an online library or stand-alone drive to perform a task. This request can be issued by an application or by Removable Storage.

Lightweight Directory Access Protocol (LDAP)

A directory service protocol that runs directly over TCP/IP and the primary access protocol for Active Directory. LDAP version 3 is defined by a set of Proposed Standard documents in Internet Engineering Task Force (IETF) RFC 2251.

See also *Lightweight Directory Access Protocol application programming interface.*

Lightweight Directory Access Protocol application programming interface (LDAP API)

An API for experienced programmers who want to enable new or existing applications to connect to, search, and update LDAP servers. You can use the LDAP API to write directory-enabled applications that allow LDAP client applications to search for and retrieve information from an LDAP server. LDAP API enables the modification of directory objects, where such modifications are permitted. There are also functions that provide access control for servers, by allowing clients to authenticate themselves.

Line Printer

A connectivity tool that runs on client systems and is used to print files to a computer running an LPD server.

See also *Line Printer Daemon.*

Line Printer Daemon (LPD)

A service on the print server that receives documents (print jobs) from line printer remote (LPR) tools running on client systems.

See also *Line Printer.*

Line Printer Port Monitor

A port monitor that is used to send jobs over TCP/IP from the client running Lprmon.dll to a print server running an LPD (Line Printer Daemon) service. Line Printer Port Monitor can be used to enable Internet printing, UNIX print servers, or Windows 2000 print servers over a TCP/IP network.

Line Printer Remote (LPR)

See *Line Printer.*

Linked object

An object that is inserted into a document but still exists in the source file. When information is linked, the new document is updated automatically if the information in the original document changes.
See also *embedded object*.

Local area network (LAN)

A communications network connecting a group of computers, printers, and other devices located within a relatively limited area (for example, a building). A LAN allows any connected device to interact with any other on the network.
See also *wide area network*.

Local computer

A computer that can be accessed directly without using a communications line or a communications device, such as a network adapter or a modem. Similarly, running a local program means running the program on your computer, as opposed to running it from a server.

Local group

For computers running Windows 2000 Professional and member servers, a group that is granted permissions and rights from its own computer to only those resources on its own computer on which the group resides.
See also *global group*.

Local Security Authority (LSA)

A protected subsystem that authenticates and logs users onto the local system. In addition, the LSA maintains information about all aspects of local security on a system (collectively known as the local security policy), and provides various services for translation between names and identifiers.

Local user profile

A computer-based record maintained about an authorized user that is created automatically on the computer the first time a user logs on to a computer running Windows 2000.

Localmon.dll

The standard print monitor for use with printers connected directly to your computer. If you add a printer to your computer using a serial or parallel port (such as COM1 or LPT1), this is the monitor that is used.

LocalTalk

The Apple networking hardware built into every Macintosh computer. LocalTalk includes the cables and connector boxes to connect components and network devices that are part of the AppleTalk network system. LocalTalk was formerly known as the AppleTalk Personal Network.

Locator service

In a distributed system, a feature that allows a client to find a shared resource or server without providing an address or full name. Generally associated with Active Directory, which provides a locator service.

Logical drive

A volume created within an extended partition on a basic disk. You can format and assign a drive letter to a logical drive. Only basic disks can contain logical drives. A logical drive cannot span multiple disks.

See also *basic disk*; *basic volume*; *extended partition.*

Logical volume

A volume created within an extended partition on a basic disk. You can format and assign a drive letter to a logical drive. Only basic disks can contain logical drives. A logical drive cannot span multiple disks.

See also *basic disk*; *basic volume*; *extended partition.*

Logon script

Files that can be assigned to user accounts. Typically a batch file, a logon script runs automatically every time the user logs on. It can be used to configure a user's working environment at every logon, and it allows an administrator to influence a user's environment without managing all aspects of it. A logon script can be assigned to one or more user accounts.

See also *batch program.*

Long file name (LFN)

A folder name or file name on the FAT file system that is longer than the 8.3 file name standard (up to eight characters followed by a period and an extension of up to three characters). Windows 2000 supports long file names up to the file-name limit of 255 characters. Macintosh users can assign long names to files and folders on the server and, using Services for Macintosh, long names to Macintosh-accessible volumes can be assigned when created. Windows 2000 automatically translates long names of files and folders to 8.3 names for MS-DOS and Windows 3.*x* users.

See also *name mapping*.

Loopback address

The address of the local computer used for routing outgoing packets back to the source computer. This address is used primarily for testing.

M

MAC

See *media access control.*

Magazine

A collection of storage locations, also called "slots," for cartridges in a library managed by Removable Storage. Magazines are usually removable.

Magneto-optic (MO) disk

A high-capacity, erasable storage medium which uses laser beams to heat the disk and magnetically arrange the data.

Magnifier

A screen enlarger that magnifies a portion of the screen in a separate window for users with low vision and for those who require occasional screen magnification for such tasks as editing art.

Manual caching

A method of manually designating network files and folders so they are stored on a user's hard disk and accessible when the user is not connected to the network.

Master Boot Record (MBR)

The first sector on a hard disk, this data structure starts the process of booting the computer. It is the most important area on a hard disk. The MBR contains the partition table for the disk and a small amount of executable code called the master boot code.

Master file table (MFT)

The database that tracks the contents of an NTFS volume. The MFT is a table whose rows correspond to files on the volume and whose columns correspond to the attributes of each file.

Maximum password age

The period of time a password can be used before the system requires the user to change it.

Media

The physical material on which information is recorded and stored.

Media access control

A sublayer of the IEEE 802 specifications that defines network access methods and framing.

Media label library

A dynamic-link library (DLL) that can interpret the format of a media label written by a Removable Storage application.

Media pool

Logical collections of removable media that have the same management policies. Media pools are used by applications to control access to specific tapes or discs within libraries managed by Removable Storage. There are four media pools: Unrecognized, Import, Free, and application-specific. Each media pool can only hold either media or other media pools.

See also *Removable Storage*.

Media states

Descriptions of conditions in which Removable Storage has placed a cartridge that it is managing. The states include Idle, In Use, Mounted, Loaded, and Unloaded.

Memory leak

A condition that occurs when applications allocate memory for use but do not free allocated memory when finished.

Metric

A number used to indicate the cost of a route in the IP routing table to enable the selection of the best route among possible multiple routes to the same destination.

MFP

See *multi-function peripherals*.

Microsoft Challenge Handshake Authentication Protocol version 1 (MS-CHAP v1)

An encrypted authentication mechanism for PPP connections similar to CHAP. The remote access server sends a challenge to the remote access client that consists of a session ID and an arbitrary challenge string. The remote access client must return the user name and a Message Digest 4 (MD4) hash of the challenge string, the session ID, and the MD4-hashed password.

Microsoft Challenge Handshake Authentication Protocol version 2 (MS-CHAP v2)

An encrypted authentication mechanism for PPP connections that provides stronger security than CHAP and MS-CHAP v1. MS-CHAP v2 provides mutual authentication and asymmetric encryption keys.

Microsoft Indexing Service

Software that provides search functions for documents stored on disk, allowing users to search for specific document text or properties.

Microsoft Internet Directory

A Web site provided and maintained by Microsoft used by applications such as NetMeeting to locate people to call on the Internet. The Microsoft Internet Directory is operated through an ILS server.

Microsoft Management Console (MMC)

A framework for hosting administrative consoles. A console is defined by the items on its console tree, which might include folders or other containers, World Wide Web pages, and other administrative items. A console has one or more windows that can provide views of the console tree and the administrative properties, services, and events that are acted on by the items in the console tree. The main MMC window provides commands and tools for authoring consoles. The authoring features of MMC and the console tree might be hidden when a console is in User Mode.

See also *console tree*.

Microsoft Point-to-Point Encryption (MPPE)

A 128/40-bit encryption algorithm using RSA RC4. MPPE provides for packet security between the client and the tunnel server and is useful where IPSec is not available. The 40-bit version addresses localization issues based on current export restrictions. MPPE is compatible with Network Address Translation.

See also *IPSec*.

Microsoft Tape Format (MTF)

The data format used for tapes supported by the Backup application in Windows 2000. There are three major components to MTF: a Tape Data Block (Tape DBLK), otherwise known as the tape header; one or more Data Sets; and On Tape Catalog Information (On Tape Catalog Inf).

Minidrivers

Relatively small, simple drivers or files that contain additional instructions needed by a specific hardware device, to interface with the universal driver for a class of devices.

Minimum TTL

A default Time To Live (TTL) value set in seconds for use with all resource records in a zone. This value is set in the start of authority (SOA) resource record for each zone. By default, the DNS server includes this value in query answers to inform recipients how long it can store and use resource records provided in the query answer before they must expire the stored records data. When TTL values are set for individual resource records, those values will override the minimum TTL.
See also *Time To Live*.

Mirrored volume

A fault-tolerant volume that duplicates data on two physical disks. The mirror is always located on a different disk. If one of the physical disks fails, the data on the failed disk becomes unavailable, but the system continues to operate by using the unaffected disk. A mirrored volume is slower than a RAID-5 volume in read operations but faster in write operations. Mirrored volumes can only be created on dynamic disks. In Windows NT 4.0, a mirrored volume was known as a mirror set.
See also *dynamic disk*; *dynamic volume*; *fault tolerance*; *redundant array of independent disks*; *volume*.

Mixed mode

The default mode setting for domains on Windows 2000 domain controllers. Mixed mode allows Windows 2000 domain controllers and Windows NT backup domain controllers to co-exist in a domain. Mixed mode does not support the universal and nested group enhancements of Windows 2000. You can change the domain mode setting to Windows 2000 native mode after all Windows NT domain controllers are either removed from the domain or upgraded to Windows 2000.
See also *native mode*.

Mode Pruning

A Windows 2000 feature that can be used to remove display modes that the monitor cannot support.

Mount

To place a removable tape or disc into a drive.

See also *library*.

MouseKeys

A feature in Microsoft Windows that allows use of the numeric keyboard to move the mouse pointer.

MP3

Audio compressed in the MPEG1 Layer 3 format

MPEG-2

A standard of video compression and file format developed by the Moving Pictures Experts Group. MPEG-2 offers video resolutions of 720 x 480 and 128 x 720 at 60 frames per second, with full CD-quality audio.

MS-CHAPv2

See *Microsoft Challenge Handshake Authentication Protocol version 2.*

Multicast IP

IP packets sent from a single destination IP address but received and processed by multiple IP hosts, regardless of their location on an IP internetwork.

Multicasting

The process of sending a message simultaneously to more than one destination on a network.

Multihomed computer

A computer that has multiple network adapters or that has been configured with multiple IP addresses for a single network adapter.

Multiple boot

A computer configuration that runs two or more operating systems. For example, Windows 98, MS-DOS, and Windows 2000 operating systems can be installed on the same computer. When the computer is started, any one of the operating systems can be selected.

See also *dual boot*.

N

Name devolution

A process by which a DNS resolver appends one or more domain names to an unqualified domain name, making it a fully qualified domain name, and then submits the fully qualified domain name to a DNS server.

Namespace

A set of unique names for resources or items used in a shared computing environment. The names in a namespace can be resolved to the objects they represent. For Microsoft Management Console (MMC), the namespace is represented by the console tree, which displays all of the snap-ins and resources that are accessible to a console. For Domain Name System (DNS), namespace is the vertical or hierarchical structure of the domain name tree. For example, each domain label, such as "host1" or "example," used in a fully qualified domain name, such as "host1.example.microsoft.com," indicates a branch in the domain namespace tree. For Active Directory, namespace corresponds to the DNS namespace in structure, but resolves Active Directory object names.

Naming service

A service, such as that provided by WINS or DNS, that allows friendly names to be resolved to an address or other specially defined resource data that is used to locate network resources of various types and purposes.

Narrator

A synthesized text-to-speech utility for users who have low vision. Narrator reads aloud most of what the screen displays.

Native mode

The condition in which all domain controllers within a domain are Windows 2000 domain controllers and an administrator has enabled native mode operation (through Active Directory Users and Computers).

See also *mixed mode*.

NDIS miniport drivers

A type of minidriver that interfaces network class devices to NDIS.

Nested groups

A Windows 2000 capability available only in native mode that allows the creation of groups within groups. See also domain local group; forest; global group; trusted forest; universal group.

NetBEUI

See *NetBIOS Extended User Interface*.

NetBIOS Extended User Interface (NetBEUI)

A network protocol native to Microsoft Networking that is usually used in local area networks of one to 200 clients. NetBEUI uses Token Ring source routing as its only method of routing. It is the Microsoft implementation of the NetBIOS standard.

NetBIOS over TCP/IP (NetBT)

A feature that provides the NetBIOS programming interface over the TCP/IP protocol. It is used for monitoring routed servers that use NetBIOS name resolution.

NetWare

Novell's network operating system.

Network adapter

Software or a hardware plug-in board that connects a node or host to a local area network.

Network basic input/output system (NetBIOS)

An application programming interface (API) that can be used by applications on a local area network or computers running MS-DOS, OS/2, or some version of UNIX. NetBIOS provides a uniform set of commands for requesting lower level network services.

Network Control Protocol (NCP)

A protocol within the PPP protocol suite that negotiates the parameters of an individual LAN protocol such as TCP/IP or IPX.

Network Driver Interface Specification (NDIS)

A software component that provides Windows 2000 network protocols a common interface for communications with network adapters. NDIS allows more than one transport protocol to be bound and operate simultaneously over a single network adapter card.

Network file system (NFS)

A service for distributed computing systems that provides a distributed file system, eliminating the need for keeping multiple copies of files on separate computers.

Network Information Service (NIS)

Formerly known as Yellow Pages, NIS is a distributed database service that allows for a shared set of system configuration files on UNIX-based systems, including password, hosts, and group files.

Network News Transfer Protocol (NNTP)

A member of the TCP/IP suite of protocols, used to distribute network news messages to NNTP servers and clients, or newsreaders, on the Internet. NNTP is designed so that news articles are stored on a server in a central database, and the user selects specific items to read.

See also *Transmission Control Protocol/Internet Protocol.*

Network security administrators

Users who manage network and information security. Network security administrators should implement a security plan that addresses network security threats.

Node

In tree structures, a location on the tree that can have links to one or more items below it. In local area networks (LANs), a device that is connected to the network and is capable of communicating with other network devices. In a server cluster, a server that has Cluster service software installed and is a member of the cluster.

See also *local area network.*

Noncontainer object

An object that cannot logically contain other objects. A file is a noncontainer object.

See also *container object*; *object.*

Nonrepudiation

A basic security function of cryptography. Nonrepudiation provides assurance that a party in a communication cannot falsely deny that a part of the communication occurred. Without nonrepudiation, someone can communicate and then later deny the communication or claim that the communication occurred at a different time.

See also *cryptography*; *authentication*; *confidentiality*; *integrity.*

Nonresident attribute

A file attribute whose value is contained in one or more runs, or extents, outside the master file table (MFT) record and separate from the MFT.

Nontransitive trust relationship

A type of trust relationship that is bounded by the two domains in the relationship. For example, if domain A trusts domain B and domain B trusts domain C, there is no trust relationship between domain A and domain C. A nontransitive trust relationship can be a one-way or two-way relationship. It is the only type of trust relationship that can exist between a Windows 2000 domain and a Windows NT domain or between Windows 2000 domains in different forests.

See also *trust relationship*; *transitive trust relationship*.

Normal backup

A backup that copies all selected files and marks each file as backed up (that is, the archive bit is set). With normal backups, only the most recent copy of the backup file or tape is needed to restore all of the files. A normal backup is usually performed the first time a backup set is created.

See also *copy backup*; *daily backup*; *differential backup*; *incremental backup*.

Novell Directory Services (NDS)

On networks running Novell NetWare 4.*x* and NetWare 5.*x*, a distributed database that maintains information about every resource on the network and provides access to these resources.

NT-1 (Network Terminator 1)

A device that terminates an ISDN line at the connection location, commonly through a connection port.

NTFS file system

A recoverable file system designed for use specifically with Windows NT and Windows 2000. NTFS uses database, transaction-processing, and object paradigms to provide data security, file system reliability, and other advanced features. It supports file system recovery, large storage media, and various features for the POSIX subsystem. It also supports object-oriented applications by treating all files as objects with user-defined and system-defined attributes.

NTLM

A security package that provides authentication between clients and servers.
See also *NTLM authentication protocol.*

NTLM authentication protocol

A challenge/response authentication protocol. The NTLM authentication protocol was the default for network authentication in Windows NT version 4.0 and earlier. The protocol continues to be supported in Windows 2000 but no longer is the default.
See also *authentication.*

NWLink

An implementation of the Internetwork Packet Exchange (IPX), Sequenced Packet Exchange (SPX), and NetBIOS protocols used in Novell networks. NWLink is a standard network protocol that supports routing and can support NetWare client/server applications, where NetWare-aware Sockets-based applications communicate with IPX/SPX Sockets-based applications.
See also *Internetwork Packet Exchange*; *network basic input/output system.*

O

Object

An entity, such as a file, folder, shared folder, printer, or Active Directory object, described by a distinct, named set of attributes. For example, the attributes of a File object include its name, location, and size; the attributes of an Active Directory User object might include the user's first name, last name, and e-mail address. For OLE and ActiveX objects, an object can also be any piece of information that can be linked to, or embedded into, another object.

See also *attribute*; *child object*; *container object*; *noncontainer object*; *parent object*.

Object linking and embedding (OLE)

A method for sharing information among applications. Linking an object, such as a graphic, from one document to another inserts a reference to the object into the second document. Any changes you make in the object in the first document will also be made in the second document. Embedding an object inserts a copy of an object from one document into another document. Changes you make in the object in the first document will not be updated in the second unless the embedded object is explicitly updated.

See also *ActiveX*.

Offline media

Media that are not connected to the computer and require external assistance to be accessed.

On-media identifier (OMID)

A label that is electronically recorded on each medium in a Removable Storage system. Removable Storage uses on-media identifiers to track media in the Removable Storage database. An application on-media identifier is a subset of the media label.

On-screen keyboard

A utility that displays a virtual keyboard on a computer screen and allows users with mobility impairments to type using a pointing device or joystick.

OnNow

See *Advanced Configuration and Power Interface*.

Open database connectivity (ODBC)

An application programming interface (API) that enables database applications to access data from a variety of existing data sources.

Open Host Controller Interface (OHCI)

Part of the IEEE 1394 standard. In Windows 2000 Professional, only OHCI-compliant host adapters are supported.

OpenType fonts

Outline fonts that are rendered from line and curve commands, and can be scaled and rotated. OpenType fonts are clear and readable in all sizes and on all output devices supported by Windows 2000. OpenType is an extension of TrueType font technology.

See also *font*; *TrueType fonts*.

Operator request

A request for the operator to perform a task. This request can be issued by an application or by Removable Storage.

Original equipment manufacturer (OEM)

The maker of a piece of equipment. In making computers and computer-related equipment, manufacturers of original equipment typically purchase components from other manufacturers of original equipment and then integrate them into their own products.

Overclocking

Setting a microprocessor to run at speeds above the rated specification.

P

Package

An icon that represents embedded or linked information. That information can consist of a complete file, such as a Paint bitmap, or part of a file, such as a spreadsheet cell. When a package is chosen, the application used to create the object either plays the object (if it is a sound file, for example) or opens and displays the object. If the original information is changed, linked information is then updated. However, embedded information needs to be manually updated. In Systems Management Server, an object that contains the files and instructions for distributing software to a distribution point.

See also *embedded object*; *linked object*; *object linking and embedding*.

Packet

A transmission unit of fixed maximum size that consists of binary information. This information represents both data and a header containing an ID number, source and destination addresses, and error-control data.

Packet assembler/disassembler (PAD)

A connection used in X.25 networks. X.25 PAD boards can be used in place of modems when provided with a compatible COM driver.

PAD

See *packet assembler/disassembler*.

Page fault

An error that occurs when the requested code or data cannot be located in the physical memory that is available to the requesting process.

Page-description language (PDL)

A computer language that describes the arrangement of text and graphics on a printed page.

See also *printer control language*; *PostScript*.

Paging

The process of moving virtual memory back and forth between physical memory and the disk. Paging occurs when physical memory limitations are reached and only occurs for data that is not already "backed" by disk space. For example, file data is not paged out because it already has allocated disk space within a file system.

See also *virtual memory*.

paging file

A hidden file on the hard disk that Windows 2000 uses to hold parts of programs and data files that do not fit in memory. The paging file and physical memory, or RAM, comprise virtual memory. Windows 2000 moves data from the paging file to memory as needed and moves data from memory to the paging file to make room for new data. Also called a swap file.

See also *random access memory*; *virtual memory*.

PAP

See *Password Authentication Protocol*.

Parallel connection

A connection that simultaneously transmits both data and control bits over wires connected in parallel. In general, a parallel connection can move data between devices faster than a serial connection.

Parallel device

A device that uses a parallel connection.

Parallel ports

The input/output connector for a parallel interface device. Printers are generally plugged into a parallel port.

Parent object

The object that is the immediate superior of another object in a hierarchy. A parent object can have multiple subordinate, or child, objects. In Active Directory, the schema determines what objects can be parent objects of what other objects. Depending on its class, a parent object can be the child of another object.

See also *child object*; *object*.

Partition

A logical division of a hard disk. Partitions make it easier to organize information. Each partition can be formatted for a different file system. A partition must be completely contained on one physical disk, and the partition table in the Master Boot Record for a physical disk can contain up to four entries for partitions.

Password authentication protocol (PAP)

A simple, plaintext authentication scheme for authenticating PPP connections. The user name and password are requested by the remote access server and returned by the remote access client in plaintext.

Path

A sequence of directory (or folder) names that specifies the location of a directory, file, or folder within the Windows directory tree. Each directory name and file name within the path must be preceded by a backslash (\). For example, to specify the path of a file named Readme.doc located in the Windows directory on drive C, type C:\Windows\Readme.doc.

PC Card

A removable device, approximately the size of a credit card, that can be plugged into a PCMCIA (Personal Computer Memory Card International Association) slot in a portable computer. PCMCIA devices can include modems, network adapters, and hard disk drives.

PCI

See *Peripheral Component Interconnect.*

PCNFS Daemon (PCNFSD)

A program that receives requests from PC-NFS clients for authentication on remote machines.

Peer-to-peer network

See *workgroup.*

Performance counter

In System Monitor, a data item associated with a performance object. For each counter selected, System Monitor presents a value corresponding to a particular aspect of the performance that is defined for the performance object.

See also *performance object.*

Performance object

In System Monitor, a logical collection of counters that is associated with a resource or service that can be monitored. See also performance counter.

Peripheral

A device, such as a disk drive, printer, modem, or joystick, that is connected to a computer and is controlled by the computer's microprocessor.

Peripheral component interconnect (PCI)

A specification introduced by Intel Corporation that defines a local bus system that allows up to 10 PCI-compliant expansion cards to be installed in the computer.

Permission

A rule associated with an object to regulate which users can gain access to the object and in what manner. Permissions are granted or denied by the object's owner.
See also *access control list*; *object*; *privilege*; *user rights*.

Physical location

The location designation assigned to media managed by Removable Storage. The two classes of physical locations include libraries and offline media physical locations. The offline media physical location is where Removable Storage lists the cartridges that are not in a library. The physical location of cartridges in an online library is the library in which it resides.

Physical media

A storage object that data can be written to, such as a disk or magnetic tape. A physical medium is referenced by its physical media ID (PMID).

Physical object

An object, such as an ATM card or smart card used in conjunction with a piece of information, such as a PIN number, to authenticate users. In two-factor authentication, physical objects are used in conjunction with another secret piece of identification, such as a password, to authenticate users. In two-factor authentication, the physical object might be an ATM card that is used in combination with a PIN to authenticate the user.

Ping

A tool that verifies connections to one or more remote hosts. The ping command uses the ICMP Echo Request and Echo Reply packets to determine whether a particular IP system on a network is functional. Ping is useful for diagnosing IP network or router failures.

See also *Internet Control Message Protocol.*

Pinning

To make a network file or folder available for offline use.

Plaintext

Data that is not encrypted. Sometimes also called clear text.

See also *ciphertext*; *encryption*; *decryption*.

Plug and Play

A set of specifications developed by Intel that allows a computer to automatically detect and configure a device and install the appropriate device drivers.

Point and Print

A way of installing network printers on a user's local computer. Point and Print allows users to initiate a connection to a network printer and loads any required drivers onto the client's computer. When users know which network printer they want to use, Point and Print greatly simplifies the installation process.

Point of presence (POP)

The local access point for a network provider. Each POP provides a telephone number that allows users to make a local call for access to online services.

Point-to-Point Protocol (PPP)

An industry standard suite of protocols for the use of point-to-point links to transport multiprotocol datagrams. PPP is documented in RFC 1661.

Point-to-Point Tunneling Protocol (PPTP)

A tunneling protocol that encapsulates Point-to-Point Protocol (PPP) frames into IP datagrams for transmission over an IP-based internetwork, such as the Internet or a private intranet.

Portable Operating System Interface for UNIX (POSIX)

An IEEE (Institute of Electrical and Electronics Engineers) standard that defines a set of operating-system services. Programs that adhere to the POSIX standard can be easily ported from one system to another. POSIX was based on UNIX system services, but it was created in a way that allows it to be implemented by other operating systems.

POST

See *power-on self test*.

PostScript

A page-description language (PDL) developed by Adobe Systems for printing with laser printers. PostScript offers flexible font capability and high-quality graphics. It is the standard for desktop publishing because it is supported by image setters, the high-resolution printers used by printing services for commercial typesetting.

See also *printer control language*; *page-description language*.

Power-on self test (POST)

A set of routines stored in read-only memory (ROM) that tests various system components such as RAM, the disk drives, and the keyboard, to see if they are properly connected and operating. If problems are found, these routines alert the user with a series of beeps or a message, often accompanied by a diagnostic numeric value. If the POST is successful, it passes control to the bootstrap loader.

PPTP

See *Point-to-Point Tunneling Protocol*.

Primary partition

A volume created using unallocated space on a basic disk. Windows 2000 and other operating systems can start from a primary partition. As many as four primary partitions can be created on a basic disk, or three primary partitions and an extended partition. Primary partitions can be created only on basic disks and cannot be subpartitioned.

See also *basic disk*; *dynamic volume*; *extended partition*; *partition*.

Printer control language (PCL)

The page-description language (PDL) developed by Hewlett Packard for their laser and inkjet printers. Because of the widespread use of laser printers, this command language has become a standard in many printers.

See also *page-description language*; *PostScript*.

Priority

A precedence ranking that determines the order in which the threads of a process are scheduled for the processor.

Priority inversion

The mechanism that allows low-priority threads to run and complete execution rather than being preempted and locking up a resource such as an I/O device.

Private branch exchange (PBX)

An automatic telephone switching system that enables users within an organization to place calls to each other without going through the public telephone network. Users can also place calls to outside numbers.

Private key

The secret half of a cryptographic key pair that is used with a public key algorithm. Private keys are typically used to digitally sign data and to decrypt data that has been encrypted with the corresponding public key.

See also *public key*.

Privilege

A user's right to perform a specific task, usually one that affects an entire computer system rather than a particular object. Administrators assign privileges to individual users or groups of users as part of the security settings for the computer.

See also *access token*; *permission*; *user rights*.

Privileged mode

Also known as kernel mode, the processing mode that allows code to have direct access to all hardware and memory in the system.

Process throttling

A method of restricting the amount of processor time a process consumes, for example, using job object functions.

Processor queue

An instantaneous count of the threads that are ready to run on the system but are waiting because the processor is running other threads.

Protocol

A set of rules and conventions by which two computers pass messages across a network. Networking software usually implements multiple levels of protocols layered one on top of another. Windows NT and Windows 2000 include NetBEUI, TCP/IP, and IPX/SPX-compatible protocols.

Proxy server

A firewall component that manages Internet traffic to and from a local area network and can provide other features, such as document caching and access control. A proxy server can improve performance by supplying frequently requested data, such as a popular Web page, and can filter and discard requests that the owner does not consider appropriate, such as requests for unauthorized access to proprietary files.
See also *firewall*.

Public key

The non-secret half of a cryptographic key pair that is used with a public key algorithm. Public keys are typically used to verify digital signatures or decrypt data that has been encrypted with the corresponding private key.
See also *private key*.

Public key cryptography

A method of cryptography in which two different but complimentary keys are used: a public key and a private key for providing security functions. Public key cryptography is also called asymmetric key cryptography.
See also *cryptography*; *public key*; *private key*.

Public switched telephone network (PSTN)

Standard analog telephone lines, available worldwide.

Q

QoS

See *Quality of Service*.

QoS Admission Control Service

A software service that controls bandwidth and network resources on the subnet to which it is assigned. Important applications can be given more bandwidth, less important applications less bandwidth. The QoS Admission Control Service can be installed on any network-enabled computer running Windows 2000.

Quality of Service (QoS)

A set of quality assurance standards and mechanisms for data transmission, implemented in Windows 2000.

Quantum

Also known as a time slice, the maximum amount of time a thread can run before the system checks for another ready thread of the same priority to run.

Quarter-inch cartridge (QIC)

An older storage technology used with tape backup drives and cartridges. A means of backing up data on computer systems, QIC represents a set of standards devised to enable tapes to be used with drives from different manufacturers. The QIC standards specify the length of tape, the number of recording tracks, and the magnetic strength of the tape coating, all of which determine the amount of information that can be written to the tape. Older QIC-80 drives can hold up to 340 MB of compressed data. Newer versions can hold more than 1 GB of information.

R

RAID-5 volume

A fault-tolerant volume with data and parity striped intermittently across three or more physical disks. Parity is a calculated value that is used to reconstruct data after a failure. If a portion of a physical disk fails, you can recreate the data that was on the failed portion from the remaining data and parity. Also known as a striped volume with parity.

Raster fonts

Fonts that are stored as bitmaps; also called bit-mapped fonts. Raster fonts are designed with a specific size and resolution for a specific printer and cannot be scaled or rotated. If a printer does not support raster fonts, it will not print them.

Rate counter

Similar to an averaging counter, a counter type that samples an increasing count of events over time; the change in the count is divided by the change in time to display a rate of activity.

Read-only memory (ROM)

A semiconductor circuit that contains information that cannot be modified.

Recoverable file system

A file system that ensures that if a power outage or other catastrophic system failure occurs, the file system will not be corrupted and disk modifications will not be left incomplete. The structure of the disk volume is restored to a consistent state when the system restarts.

Recovery Console

A startable, text-mode command interpreter environment separate from the Windows 2000 command prompt that allows the system administrator access to the hard disk of a computer running Windows 2000, regardless of the file format used, for basic troubleshooting and system maintenance tasks.

Redundant array of independent disks (RAID)

A method used to standardize and categorize fault-tolerant disk systems. Six levels gauge various mixes of performance, reliability, and cost. Windows 2000 provides three of the RAID levels: Level 0 (striping) which is not fault-tolerant, Level 1 (mirroring), and Level 5 (striped volume with parity).

See also *fault tolerance*; *mirrored volume*; *RAID-5 volume*; *striped volume*.

Registry

In Windows 2000, Windows NT, Windows 98, and Windows 95, a database of information about a computer's configuration. The registry is organized in a hierarchical structure and consists of subtrees and their keys, hives, and entries.

Relative ID (RID)

The part of a security ID (SID) that uniquely identifies an account or group within a domain.

See also *security ID*.

Remote access server

A Windows 2000 Server-based computer running the Routing and Remote Access service and configured to provide remote access.

Remote procedure call (RPC)

A message-passing facility that allows a distributed application to call services that are available on various computers in a network. Used during remote administration of computers.

Removable Storage

A service used for managing removable media (such as tapes and discs) and storage devices (libraries). Removable Storage allows applications to access and share the same media resources.

See also *library*.

Reparse points

New NTFS file system objects that have a definable attribute containing user-controlled data and are used to extend functionality in the input/output (I/O) subsystem.

Repeat Keys

A feature that allows users with mobility impairments to adjust the repeat rate or to disable the key-repeat function on the keyboard.

See also *FilterKeys*.

Request for Comments (RFC)

A document that defines a standard. RFCs are published by the Internet Engineering Task Force (IETF) and other working groups.

Resident attribute

A file attribute whose value is wholly contained in the file's file record in the master file table (MFT).

Resolver

DNS client programs used to look up DNS name information. Resolvers can be either a small "stub" (a limited set of programming routines that provide basic query functionality) or larger programs that provide additional lookup DNS client functions, such as caching.

See also *caching*; *caching resolver*.

Resource publishing

The process of making an object visible and accessible to users in a Windows 2000 domain. For example, a shared printer resource is published by creating a reference to the printer object in Active Directory.

Resource record (RR)

Information in the DNS database that can be used to process client queries. Each DNS server contains the resource records it needs to answer queries for the portion of the DNS namespace for which it is authoritative.

Response time

The amount of time required to do work from start to finish. In a client/server environment, this is typically measured on the client side.

RGB

The initials of red, green, blue. Used to describe a color monitor or color value.

Roaming user profile

A server-based user profile that is downloaded to the local computer when a user logs on and is updated both locally and on the server when the user logs off. A roaming user profile is available from the server when logging on to any computer that is running Windows 2000 Professional or Windows 2000 Server.

ROM

See *read-only memory*.

Route table

See *routing table*.

Router

A network device that helps LANs and WANs achieve interoperability and connectivity and that can link LANs that have different network topologies, such as Ethernet and Token Ring.

Routing

The process of forwarding a packet through an internetwork from a source host to a destination host.

Routing Information Protocol (RIP)

An industry standard distance vector routing protocol used in small to medium sized IP and IPX internetworks.

Routing table

A database of routes containing information on network IDs, forwarding addresses, and metrics for reachable network segments on an internetwork.

RPC

See *Remote Procedure Call*.

Rules

An IPSec policy mechanism that governs how and when an IPSec policy protects communication. A rule provides the ability to trigger and control secure communication based on the source, destination, and type of IP traffic. Each rule contains a list of IP filters and a collection of security actions that take place upon a match with that filter list.

S

Safe Mode

A method of starting Windows 2000 using basic files and drivers only, without networking. Safe Mode is available by pressing the F8 key when prompted during startup. This allows the computer to start when a problem prevents it from starting normally.

Screen-enlargement utility

A utility that allows the user to magnify a portion of the screen for greater visibility. (Also called a screen magnifier or large-print program.)

Script

A type of program consisting of a set of instructions to an application or utility program. A script usually expresses instructions by using the application's or utility's rules and syntax, combined with simple control structures such as loops and if/then expressions. "Batch program" is often used interchangeably with "script" in the Windows environment.

SCSI

See *Small Computer System Interface*.

SCSI connection

A standard high-speed parallel interface defined by the X3T9.2 committee of the American National Standards Institute (ANSI). A SCSI interface is used to connect microcomputers to SCSI peripheral devices, such as many hard disks and printers, and to other computers and local area networks.

Search filter

An argument in an LDAP search that allows certain entries in the subtree and excludes others. Filters allow you to define search criteria and give you better control to achieve more effective and efficient searches.

Secure Sockets Layer (SSL)

A proposed open standard developed by Netscape Communications for establishing a secure communications channel to prevent the interception of critical information, such as credit card numbers. Primarily, it enables secure electronic financial transactions on the World Wide Web, although it is designed to work on other Internet services as well.

Security Accounts Manager (SAM)

A protected subsystem that manages user and group account information. In Windows NT 4.0, both local and domain security principals are stored by SAM in the registry. In Windows 2000, workstation security accounts are stored by SAM in the local computer registry, and domain controller security accounts are stored in Active Directory.

Security association (SA)

A set of parameters that define the services and mechanisms necessary to protect Internet Protocol security communications.

See also *Internet Protocol security.*

Security descriptor

A data structure that contains security information associated with a protected object. Security descriptors include information about who owns the object, who may access it and in what way, and what types of access will be audited.

See also *access control list*; *object.*

Security event types

Different categories of events about which Windows 2000 can create auditing events. Account logon or object access are examples of security event types.

Security ID (SID)

A data structure of variable length that uniquely identifies user, group, service, and computer accounts within an enterprise. Every account is issued a SID when the account is first created. Access control mechanisms in Windows 2000 identify security principals by SID rather than by name.

See also *relative ID*; *security principal.*

Security method

A process that determines the Internet Protocol security services, key settings, and algorithms that will be used to protect the data during the communication.

Security Parameters Index (SPI)

A unique, identifying value in the SA used to distinguish among multiple security associations existing at the receiving computer.

Security principal

An account-holder, such as a user, computer, or service. Each security principal within a Windows 2000 domain is identified by a unique security ID (SID). When a security principal logs on to a computer running Windows 2000, the Local Security Authority (LSA) authenticates the security principal's account name and password. If the logon is successful, the system creates an access token. Every process executed on behalf of this security principal will have a copy of its access token.

See also *access token*; *security ID*; *security principal name*.

Security principal name

A name that uniquely identifies a user, group, or computer within a single domain. This name is not guaranteed to be unique across domains.

See also *security principal*.

Seek time

The amount of time required for a disk head to position itself at the right disk cylinder to access requested data.

Serial Bus Protocol (SBP-2)

A standard for storage devices, printers, and scanners that is a supplement to the IEEE 1394 specification.

Serial connection

A connection that exchanges information between computers or between computers and peripheral devices one bit at a time over a single channel. Serial communications can be synchronous or asynchronous. Both sender and receiver must use the same baud rate, parity, and control information.

Serial device

A device that uses a serial connection.

SerialKeys

A Windows feature that uses a communications aid interface device to allow keystrokes and mouse controls to be accepted through a computer's serial port.

Server

A computer that provides shared resources to network users.

Server Message Block (SMB)

A file-sharing protocol designed to allow networked computers to transparently access files that reside on remote systems over a variety of networks. The SMB protocol defines a series of commands that pass information between computers. SMB uses four message types: session control, file, printer, and message.

Service access point

A logical address that allows a system to route data between a remote device and the appropriate communications support.

Service Pack

A software upgrade to an existing software distribution that contains updated files consisting of patches and fixes.

Service Profile Identifier (SPID)

A 14-digit number that identifies a specific ISDN line. When establishing ISDN service, your telephone company assigns a SPID to your line.
See also *ISDN*.

Service provider

In TAPI, a dynamic link library (DLL) that provides an interface between an application requesting services and the controlling hardware device. TAPI supports two classes of service providers, media service providers and telephony service providers.

Session key

A key used primarily for encryption and decryption. Session keys are typically used with symmetric encryption algorithms where the same key is used for both encryption and decryption. For this reason, session and symmetric keys usually refer to the same type of key.
See also *symmetric key encryption*.

Sfmmon

A port monitor that is used to send jobs over the AppleTalk protocol to printers such as LaserWriters or those configured with AppleTalk or any AppleTalk spoolers.

Shared folder permissions

Permissions that restrict a shared resource's availability over the network to certain users.

See also *permission*.

Shiva Password Authentication Protocol (SPAP)

A two-way, reversible encryption mechanism for authenticating PPP connections employed by Shiva remote access servers.

Shortcut key navigation indicators

Underlined letters on a menu or control. (Also called access keys or quick-access letters.)

ShowSounds

A global flag that instructs programs to display captions for speech and system sounds to alert users with hearing impairments or people who work in a noisy location such as a factory floor.

Simple Mail Transfer Protocol (SMTP)

A protocol used on the Internet to transfer mail. SMTP is independent of the particular transmission subsystem and requires only a reliable, ordered, data stream channel.

Simple Network Management Protocol (SNMP)

A network management protocol installed with TCP/IP and widely used on TCP/IP and Internet Package Exchange (IPX) networks. SNMP transports management information and commands between a management program run by an administrator and the network management agent running on a host. The SNMP agent sends status information to one or more hosts when the host requests it or when a significant event occurs.

Single-switch device

An alternative input device, such as a voice activation program, that allows a user to scan or select using a single switch.

Slot

Storage locations for cartridges in a library managed by Removable Storage.

SlowKeys

A Windows feature that instructs the computer to disregard keystrokes that are not held down for a minimum period of time, which allows the user to brush against keys without any effect.

See also *FilterKeys*.

Small Computer System Interface (SCSI)

A standard high-speed parallel interface defined by the X3T9.2 committee of the American National Standards Institute (ANSI). A SCSI interface is used for connecting microcomputers to peripheral devices, such as hard disks and printers, and to other computers and local area networks.

Small Office/Home Office (SOHO)

An office with a few computers that can be considered a small business or part of a larger network.

Smart card

A credit card-sized device that is used with a PIN number to enable certificate-based authentication and single sign-on to the enterprise. Smart cards securely store certificates, public and private keys, passwords, and other types of personal information. A smart card reader attached to the computer reads the smart card.

See also *authentication*; *certificate*; *nonrepudiation*.

SNMP

See *Simple Network Management Protocol*.

Software trap

In programming, an event that occurs when a microprocessor detects a problem with executing an instruction, which causes it to stop.

SoundSentry

A Windows feature that produces a visual cue, such as a screen flash or a blinking title bar instead of system sounds.

Source directory

The folder that contains the file or files to be copied or moved.

See also *destination directory*.

SPAP

See *Shiva Password Authentication Protocol.*

Sparse file

A file that is handled in a way that requires less disk space than would otherwise be needed by allocating only meaningful non-zero data. Sparse support allows an application to create very large files without committing disk space for every byte.

Speech synthesizer

An assistive device that produces spoken words, either by splicing together prerecorded words or by programming the computer to produce the sounds that make up spoken words.

Stand-alone drive

An online drive that is not part of a library unit. Removable Storage treats stand-alone drives as online libraries with one drive and a port.

Status area

The area on the taskbar to the right of the taskbar buttons. The status area displays the time and can also contain icons that provide quick access to programs, such as Volume Control and Power Options. Other icons can appear temporarily, providing information about the status of activities. For example, the printer icon appears after a document has been sent to the printer and disappears when printing is complete.

StickyKeys

An accessibility feature built into Windows that causes modifier keys such as SHIFT, CTRL, WINDOWS LOGO, or ALT to stay on after they are pressed, eliminating the need to press multiple keys simultaneously. This feature facilitates the use of modifier keys for users who are unable to hold down one key while pressing another.

Stop error

A serious error that affects the operating system and that could place data at risk. The operating system generates an obvious message, a screen with the Stop message, rather than continuing on, and possibly corrupting data. Also known as a fatal system error.

See also *Stop message*.

Stop message

A character-based, full-screen error message displayed on a blue background. A Stop message indicates that the Windows 2000 kernel detected a condition from which it cannot recover. Each message is uniquely identified by a Stop error code (a hexadecimal number) and a string indicating the error's symbolic name. Stop messages are usually followed by up to four additional hexadecimal numbers, enclosed in parentheses, which identify developer-defined error parameters. A driver or device may be identified as the cause of the error. A series of troubleshooting tips are also displayed, along with an indication that, if the system was configured to do so, a memory dump file was saved for later use by a kernel debugger.

See also *Stop error*.

Streaming media servers

Software (such as Microsoft Media Technologies) that provides multimedia support, allowing you to deliver content by using Advanced Streaming Format over an intranet or the Internet.

Streams

A sequence of bits, bytes, or other small structurally uniform units.

Striped volume

A volume that stores data in stripes on two or more physical disks. Data in a striped volume is allocated alternately and evenly (in stripes) to these disks. Striped volumes offer the best performance of all volumes available in Windows 2000, but they do not provide fault tolerance. If a disk in a striped volume fails, the data in the entire volume is lost. You can create striped volumes only on dynamic disks. Striped volumes cannot be mirrored or extended. In Windows NT 4.0, a striped volume was known as a stripe set.

See also *dynamic disk*; *dynamic volume*; *fault tolerance*; *volume*.

Subkey

In the registry, a key within a key. Subkeys are analogous to subdirectories in the registry hierarchy. Keys and subkeys are similar to the section header in .ini files; however, subkeys can carry out functions.

See also *key*.

Subnet

A subdivision of an IP network. Each subnet has its own unique subnetted network ID.

Subnet mask

A 32-bit value expressed as four decimal numbers from 0 to 255, separated by periods (for example, 255.255.0.0). This number allows TCP/IP to determine the network ID portion of an IP address.

Subnet prioritization

The ordering of multiple IP address mappings from a DNS server so that the resolver orders local resource records first. This reduces network traffic across subnets by forcing computers to connect to network resources that are closer to them.

Subpicture

A data stream contained within a DVD. The Subpicture stream delivers the subtitles and any other add-on data, such as system help or director's comments, which can be displayed while playing multimedia.

Symmetric key

A single key that is used with symmetric encryption algorithms for both encryption and decryption.

See also *bulk encryption*; *encryption*; *decryption*; *session key*.

Symmetric key encryption

An encryption algorithm that requires the same secret key to be used for both encryption and decryption. This is often called secret key encryption. Because of its speed, symmetric encryption is typically used rather than public key encryption when a message sender needs to encrypt large amounts of data.

Synchronization Manager

In Windows 2000, the tool used to ensure that a file or directory on a client computer contains the same data as a matching file or directory on a server.

Syntax

The order in which a command must be typed and the elements that follow the command.

System access control list (SACL)

The part of an object's security descriptor that specifies which events are to be audited per user or group. Examples of auditing events are file access, logon attempts, and system shutdowns.

See also *access control entry*; *discretionary access control list*; *object*; *security descriptor*.

System administrator

A person that administers a computer system or network, including administering user accounts, security, storage space, and backing up data.

System files

Files that are used by Windows to load, configure, and run the operating system. Generally, system files must never be deleted or moved.

System media pool

A pool used to hold cartridges that are not in use. The free pool holds unused cartridges that are available to applications, and the unrecognized and import pools are temporary holding places for cartridges that have been newly placed in a library.

System policy

In network administration, the part of Group Policy that is concerned with the current user and local computer settings in the registry. In Windows 2000, system policy is sometimes called software policy and is one of several services provided by Group Policy, a Microsoft Management Console (MMC) snap-in. The Windows NT 4.0 System Policy Editor, Poledit.exe, is included with Windows 2000 for backward compatibility. That is, administrators need it to set system policy on Windows NT 4.0 and Windows 95 computers.

See also *Microsoft Management Console*; *registry*.

System Policy Editor

The utility Poledit.exe, used by administrators to set system policy on Windows NT 4.0 and Windows 95 computers.

System state data

A collection of system-specific data that can be backed up and restored. For all Windows 2000 operating systems, the System State data includes the registry, the class registration database, and the system boot files.

System volume

The volume that contains the hardware-specific files needed to load Windows 2000. The system volume can be (but does not have to be) the same volume as the boot volume.

See also *volume*.

Systemroot

The path and folder name where the Windows 2000 system files are located. Typically, this is C:\Winnt, although a different drive or folder can be designated when Windows 2000 is installed. The value %systemroot% can be used to replace the actual location of the folder that contains the Windows 2000 system files. To identify your systemroot folder, click Start, click Run, and then type %systemroot%.

T

Taskbar

The bar that contains the Start button and appears by default at the bottom of the desktop. You can use the taskbar buttons to switch between the programs you are running. The taskbar can be hidden, moved to the sides or top of the desktop, or customized in other ways.

See also *desktop*; *taskbar button*; *status area.*

Taskbar button

A button that appears on the taskbar when an application is running.

See also *taskbar.*

TCP/IP

See *Transmission Control Protocol/Internet Protocol.*

Tcpmon.ini

The file that specifies whether a device supports multiple ports. If the Tcpmon.ini file indicates that a device can support multiple ports, users a prompted to pick which port should be used during device installation.

Telephony API (TAPI)

An application programming interface (API) used by communications programs to communicate with telephony and network services.

See also *Internet Protocol.*

Terabyte

Approximately one trillion bytes, or one million million bytes.

Terminal Services

Software services that allow client applications to be run on a server so that client computers can function as terminals rather than independent systems. The server provides a multisession environment and runs the Windows-based programs being used on the clients.

See also *client.*

Thread

A type of object within a process that runs program instructions. Using multiple threads allows concurrent operations within a process and enables one process to run different parts of its program on different processors simultaneously. A thread has its own set of registers, its own kernel stack, a thread environment block, and a user stack in the address space of its process.

Thread state

A numeric value indicating the execution state of the thread. Numbered 0 through 5, the states seen most often are 1 for ready, 2 for running, and 5 for waiting.

Throughput

For disks, the transfer capacity of the disk system.

Time To Live (TTL)

A timer value included in packets sent over TCP/IP-based networks that tells the recipients how long to hold or use the packet or any of its included data before expiring and discarding the packet or data.

For DNS, TTL values are used in resource records within a zone to determine how long requesting clients should cache and use this information when it appears in a query response answered by a DNS server for the zone.

Timer bar

The colored bar that moves across the screen according to the frequency of the data-collection update interval.

ToggleKeys

A Windows feature that beeps when one of the locking keys (CAPS LOCK, NUM LOCK, or SCROLL LOCK) is turned on or off.

Token Ring

A type of network media that connects clients in a closed ring and uses token passing to allow clients to use the network.

See also *Fiber Distributed Data Interface*.

Total instance

A unique instance that contains the performance counters that represent the sum of all active instances of an object.

Transitive trust relationship

The trust relationship that inherently exists between Windows 2000 domains in a domain tree or forest, or between trees in a forest, or between forests. When a domain joins an existing forest or domain tree, a transitive trust is automatically established. In Windows 2000 transitive trusts are always two-way relationships.

See also *domain tree*; *forest*; *nontransitive trust relationship*.

Transmission Control Protocol / Internet Protocol (TCP/IP)

A set of software networking protocols widely used on the Internet that provide communications across interconnected networks of computers with diverse hardware architectures and operating systems. TCP/IP includes standards for how computers communicate and conventions for connecting networks and routing traffic.

Transmitting Station ID string (TSID)

A string that specifies the Transmitter Subscriber ID sent by the fax machine when sending a fax to a receiving machine. This string is usually a combination of the fax or telephone number and the name of the business. It is often the same as the Called Subscriber ID.

Transport Layer Security (TLS)

A standard protocol that is used to provide secure Web communications on the Internet or intranets. It enables clients to authenticate servers or, optionally, servers to authenticate clients. It also provides a secure channel by encrypting communications.

Transport protocol

A protocol that defines how data should be presented to the next receiving layer in the Windows NT and Windows 2000 networking model and packages the data accordingly. The transport protocol passes data to the network adapter driver through the network driver interface specification (NDIS) interface and to the redirector through the Transport Driver Interface (TDI).

TrueType fonts

Fonts that are scalable and sometimes generated as bitmaps or soft fonts, depending on the capabilities of your printer. TrueType fonts are device-independent fonts that are stored as outlines. They can be sized to any height, and they can be printed exactly as they appear on the screen.

See also *font*.

Trust relationship

A logical relationship established between domains that allows pass-through authentication in which a trusting domain honors the logon authentications of a trusted domain. User accounts and global groups defined in a trusted domain can be granted rights and permissions in a trusting domain, even though the user accounts or groups do not exist in the trusting domain's directory.

See also *authentication*; *domain*; *two-way trust relationship*.

Trusted forest

A forest that is connected to another forest by explicit or transitive trust.

See also *explicit trust relationship*; *forest*; *transitive trust relationship*.

TSID

See *Transmitting Station ID string*.

Tunnel

The logical path by which the encapsulated packets travel through the transit internetwork.

TWAIN

An acronym for Technology Without An Interesting Name. An industry-standard software protocol and API that provides easy integration of image data between input devices, such as scanners and still image digital cameras, and software applications.

Two-way trust relationship

A link between domains in which each domain trusts user accounts in the other domain to use its resources. Users can log on from computers in either domain to the domain that contains their account.

See also *trust relationship*.

Type 1 fonts

Scalable fonts designed to work with PostScript devices.

See also *font*; *PostScript*.

U

UART

See *Universal Asynchronous Receiver/Transmitter.*

Unallocated space

Available disk space that is not allocated to any partition, logical drive, or volume. The type of object created on unallocated space depends on the disk type (basic or dynamic). For basic disks, unallocated space outside partitions can be used to create primary or extended partitions. Free space inside an extended partition can be used to create a logical drive. For dynamic disks, unallocated space can be used to create dynamic volumes. Unlike basic disks, the exact disk region used is not selected to create the volume.

See also *basic disk*; *dynamic disk*; *extended partition*; *logical drive*; *partition*; *primary partition*; *volume.*

Unicode

A fixed-width, 16-bit character-encoding standard capable of representing the letters and characters of the majority of the world's languages. A consortium of U.S. computer companies developed Unicode.

UniDriver

The UniDriver (or Universal Print Driver) carries out requests (such as printing text, rendering bitmaps, or advancing a page) on most types of printers. The UniDriver accepts information from a printer specific minidriver and uses this information to complete tasks.

Uniform Resource Locator (URL)

An address that uniquely identifies a location on the Internet. A URL for a World Wide Web site is preceded with http://, as in the fictitious URL http://www.example.microsoft.com/ A URL can contain more detail, such as the name of a page of hypertext, usually identified by the file name extension .html or .htm.

See also *HTML*; *HTTP*; *IP address.*

Universal Asynchronous Receiver/Transmitter (UART)

An integrated circuit (silicon chip) that is commonly used in microcomputers to provide asynchronous communications. The UART does parallel-to-serial conversion of data to be transmitted and serial-to-parallel conversion of data received.

See also *asynchronous communication*.

Universal Disk Format (UDF)

A file system defined by the Optical Storage Technology Association (OSTA) that is the successor to the CD-ROM file system (CDFS). UDF is targeted for removable disk media like DVD, CD, and Magneto-Optical (MO) discs.

Universal group

A Windows 2000 group only available in native mode that is valid anywhere in the forest. A universal group appears in the Global Catalog but contains primarily global groups from domains in the forest. This is the simplest form of group and can contain other universal groups, global groups, and users from anywhere in the forest.

See also *domain local group*; *forest*; *Global Catalog*.

Universal Naming Convention (UNC)

A convention for naming files and other resources beginning with two backslashes (\), indicating that the resource exists on a network computer. UNC names conform to the \\SERVERNAME\SHARENAME syntax, where SERVERNAME is the server's name and SHARENAME is the name of the shared resource. The UNC name of a directory or file can also include the directory path after the share name, with the following syntax: \\SERVERNAME\SHARENAME\DIRECTORY\FILENAME.

Universal Serial Bus (USB)

A serial bus with a bandwidth of 1.5 megabits per second (Mbps) for connecting peripherals to a microcomputer. USB can connect up to 127 peripherals, such as external CD-ROM drives, printers, modems, mice, and keyboards, to the system through a single, general-purpose port. This is accomplished by daisy chaining peripherals together. USB supports hot plugging and multiple data streams.

UNIX

A powerful, multi-user, multitasking operating system initially developed at AT&T Bell Laboratories in 1969 for use on minicomputers. UNIX is considered more portable—that is, less computer-specific—than other operating systems because it is written in C language. Newer versions of UNIX have been developed at the University of California at Berkeley and by AT&T.

Unrecognized pool

A repository for blank media and media that are not recognized by Removable Storage.

Upgrade

When referring to software, to update existing program files, folders, and registry entries to a more recent version. Upgrading, unlike performing a new installation, leaves existing settings and files in place.

URL

See *Uniform Resource Locator.*

USB

See *Universal Serial Bus.*

User account

A record that consists of all the information that defines a user to Windows 2000. This includes the user name and password required for the user to log on, the groups in which the user account has membership, and the rights and permissions the user has for using the computer and network and accessing their resources. For Windows 2000 Professional and member servers, user accounts are managed by using Local Users and Groups. For Windows 2000 Server domain controllers, user accounts are managed by using Microsoft Active Directory Users and Computers.

See also *domain controller*; *group*; *user name.*

User Identification (UID)

A user identifier that uniquely identifies a user. UNIX-bases systems use the UID to identify the owner of files and processes, and to determine access permissions.

User mode

The processing mode in which applications run.

User name

A unique name identifying a user account to Windows 2000. An account's user name must be unique among the other group names and user names within its own domain or workgroup.

User principal name (UPN)

A friendly name assigned to security principals (users and groups) that is shorter than the distinguished name and easier to remember. The default user principal name is composed of the security principal name for the user and the DNS name of the root domain where the user object resides. The user principal name is the preferred logon name for Windows 2000 users and is independent of the distinguished name, so a User object can be moved or renamed without affecting the user's logon name.
See also *distinguished name*.

User profile

A file that contains configuration information for a specific user, such as desktop settings, persistent network connections, and application settings. Each user's preferences are saved to a user profile that Windows NT and Windows 2000 use to configure the desktop each time a user logs on.

User rights

Tasks a user is permitted to perform on a computer system or domain. There are two types of user rights: privileges and logon rights. An example of a privilege is the right to shut down the system. An example of a logon right is the right to log on to a computer locally (at the keyboard). Administrators assign both types to individual users or groups as part of the security settings for the computer.
See also *permission*; *privilege*.

User rights policy

Security settings that manage the assignment of rights to groups and user accounts.

Utility Manager

A function of Windows 2000 that allows administrators to review the status of applications and tools and to customize features and add tools more easily.

V

Value bar

The area of the System Monitor graph or histogram display that shows last, average, minimum and maximum statistics for the selected counter.

Vector fonts

Fonts rendered from a mathematical model, in which each character is defined as a set of lines drawn between points. Vector fonts can be cleanly scaled to any size or aspect ratio.

Video for Windows (VfW)

A format developed by Microsoft for storing video and audio information. Files in this format have an .avi extension. AVI files are limited to 320 x 240 resolution at 30 frames per second, neither of which is adequate for full-screen, full-motion video.

Video Port Extensions (VPE)

A DirectDraw extension to support direct hardware connections from a video decoder and autoflipping in the graphics frame buffer. VPE allows the client to negotiate the connection between the MPEG or NTSC decoder and the video port. VPE also allows the client to control effects in the video stream, such as cropping, scaling, and so on.

Virtual Device Driver (VxD)

Software for Windows that manages a hardware or software system resource. The middle letter in the abbreviation indicates the type of device; x is used where the type of device is not under discussion.

Virtual memory

The space on the hard disk that Windows 2000 uses as memory. Because of virtual memory, the amount of memory taken from the perspective of a process can be much greater than the actual physical memory in the computer. The operating system does this in a way that is transparent to the application, by paging data that does not fit in physical memory to and from the disk at any given instant.

Virtual private network (VPN)

The extension of a private network that encompasses links across shared or public networks, such as the Internet.

Virus scanner

Software used to scan for and eradicate computer viruses, worms, and Trojan horses.

Volume

A portion of a physical disk that functions as though it were a physically separate disk. In My Computer and Windows Explorer, volumes appear as local disks, such as drive C or drive D.

Volume mount points

New system objects in the version of NTFS included with Windows 2000 that represent storage volumes in a persistent, robust manner. Volume mount points allow the operating system to graft the root of a volume onto a directory.

W

WDM Streaming class

The means by which Windows 2000 Professional supports digital video and audio. Enables support for such components as DVD decoders, MPEG decoders, video decoders, tuners, and audio codecs.

Wide area network (WAN)

A communications network connecting geographically separated computers, printers, and other devices. A WAN allows any connected device to interact with any other on the network.

See also *local area network.*

Windows 2000 Multilanguage Version

A version of Windows 2000 that extends the native language support in Windows 2000 by allowing user interface languages to be changed on a per user basis. This version also minimizes the number of language versions you need to deploy across the network.

Windows File Protection (WFP)

A Windows 2000 feature that runs in the background and protects your system files from being overwritten. When a file in a protected folder is modified, WFP determines if the new file is the correct Microsoft version or if the file is digitally signed. If not, the modified file is replaced with a valid version.

Windows Internet Name Service (WINS)

A software service that dynamically maps IP addresses to computer names (NetBIOS names). This allows users to access resources by name instead of requiring them to use IP addresses that are difficult to recognize and remember. WINS servers support clients running Windows NT 4.0 and earlier versions of Windows operating systems.

See also *Domain Name System.*

Windows Update

A Microsoft-owned Web site from which Windows 98 and Windows 2000 users can install or update device drivers. By using an ActiveX control, Windows Update compares the available drivers with those on the user's system and offers to install new or updated versions.

WINS

See *Windows Internet Name Service.*

Winsock

An application programming interface standard for software that provides TCP/IP interface under Windows. Short for Windows Sockets.

See also *TCP/IP.*

Work queue item

A job request of an existing library, made by an application that supports Removable Storage, which is placed in a queue and processed when the library resource becomes available.

Workgroup

A simple grouping of computers intended only to help users find such things as printers and shared folders within that group. Workgroups in Windows 2000 do not offer the centralized user accounts and authentication offered by domains.

Working set

For a process, the amount of physical memory assigned to a process by the operating system.

X

X.25

X.25 is a standard that defines the communications protocol for access to packet-switched networks.

X.400

What is an ISO and ITU standard for addressing and transporting e-mail messages. It conforms to layer 7 of the OSI model and supports several types of transport mechanisms, including Ethernet, X.25, TCP/IP, and dial-up lines.

X.500

The X.500 is the standard for defining a distributed directory service standard and was developed by the International Standards Organization (ISO). This ISO and ITU standard defines how global directories should be structured. X.500 directories are hierarchical, which means that they have different levels for each category of information, such as country, state, and city. X.500 supports X.400 systems.

X Window System

X Windows is a standard set of display-handling routines developed at MIT for UNIX workstations. These routines are used to create hardware-independent graphical user interfaces for UNIX systems.

Y

Ymodem

Ymodem is a variation of the Xmodem file transfer protocol that includes the following enhancements:

1. The ability to transfer information in 1-kilobyte (1,024-byte) blocks
2. The ability to send multiple files (batch file transmission)
3. Cyclical redundancy checking (CRC)
4. The ability to abort transfer by transmitting two CAN (cancel) characters in a row.

Z

ZIPI

A MIDI-like serial data format for musical instruments. ZIPI provides a hierarchical method for addressing instruments and uses an extensible command set.

Zero Wait State

The condition of random access memory (RAM) that is fast enough to respond to the processor without requiring a wait states.

Z axis (X axis)

Used in defining specific graphical display locations. The optical axis that is perpendicular to X and Y axes

Index

TotalRecall Gives You *Four* Levels of Computer Certification Practice Exams, Books, and eBooks

- Study formats and prices vary so you can choose one that best fits your level of knowledge and skills.
- Each format offers you either free or discounted access to our popular BeachFront Quizzer test engine. See description below.
- ALL come with our exclusive Money-Back Guarantee—pass the exam your first time or get money back!

1. InsideScoop Certification Success Series

Paperback books in the InsideScoop series offer a package of comprehensive study manual and CD-ROM of the BeachFront Quizzer test engine with answers/ explanations linked to relevant chapters in an integrated eBook. The study manual includes detailed information about each core exam topic with pre/post assessment quizzes; an abundance of figures, diagrams and photos; chapter summaries; helpful tips and time management techniques for test taking; lists of useful websites, articles and other learning resources; and an extensive glossary of 600 computer, IT, and telecommunications terms. **Books are $89.99**

2. InsidersChoice Certification Success Series

Paperback books in the InsidersChoice series offer a package of comprehensive study manual and FREE download of the BeachFront Quizzer test engine with answers/ explanations linked to relevant chapters in an integrated eBook. The study manual includes detailed information about each core exam topic with pre/post assessment quizzes; an abundance of figures, diagrams and photos; chapter summaries; helpful tips and time management techniques for test taking; lists of useful websites, articles and other learning resources; and an extensive glossary of 600 computer, IT, and telecommunications terms.

Paperbacks are $59.99 and eBooks are $44.99

3. ExamInsight IT Certification System Series

Paperback books and eBooks in the ExamInsight series offer a package of compact study guide and 50% discount to purchase a download of the BeachFront Quizzer test engine with answers/ explanations linked to relevant chapters in an integrated eBook. The study guide includes compact information about each core exam topic with pre/post assessment quizzes; an abundance of figures, diagrams and photos; chapter summaries; helpful tips and time management techniques for test taking; and lists of useful websites, articles and other learning resources

Paperbacks are $39.99 and eBooks are $29.99

4. ExamWise IT Question Book Series

Paperback books and eBooks in the ExamWise series offer a package of Q&A workbook and 30-Day FREE access to a BeachFront Quizzer online practice exam. Each ExamWise Q&A workbook offers you approximately 300 practice questions organized by core exam topic. Questions are arranged in a unique format of two questions per right and page, with answers and brief explanations on the reverse page.

Paperbacks are $39.99 and eBooks are $29.99

The BeachFront Quizzer Test Engine Makes Passing Certification Exams as Easy as a Day at the Beach...

The BeachFront Quizzer test engine was pioneered in 1995 by Bruce Moran, an ex-NASA IT professional turned vocational computer instructor and certification trainer before launching his own book publishing operation in 2002. This popular test engine introduced interactive and adaptive features that other publishers have since tried to imitate, but never duplicate. It offers you four helpful study formats:

1) Adaptive technology generates 15-25 questions in 30-minute sessions to help you identify your strengths and weaknesses for each exam topic.

2) Study sessions help strengthen your weakest exam topics by generating up to 250 questions per topic until you can answer each correctly. Explanations for each question are linked to relevant chapters in an eBook study manual and often to web sites to help you develop a complete understanding of why an answer is correct. By focusing on your rough spots, we'll get you certified fast—guaranteed or get money back!

3) Simulated exams generate randomized questions about core exam topics in 60-90 minute sessions and then provide a score summary by topic. Taking multiple practice exams will build your confidence and ability to concentrate during the real deal!

4) Flash card drills present questions to answer mentally and then allow you to click F4 to display the correct answer.

Visit our web sites for more information:

www.TotalRecallPress.com / www.bfq.com

TotalRecall Certification Publications Microsoft

InsideScoop: TotalRecall's Complete Certification System Series:

InsideScoop to MCP / MCSE Certification: **Exam 70-210**
Managing Microsoft Windows 2000 Professional

InsideScoop to MCP / MCSE Certification: **Exam 70-216**
Implementing and Administering a Microsoft Windows 2000 Network Infrastructure

InsideScoop to MCP / MCSE Certification: **Exam 70-217**
Managing a Microsoft Directory Services Infrastructure

InsideScoop to MCP / MCSE Certification: **Exam 70-219**
Designing a Windows 2000 Directory Services Infrastructure

InsideScoop to MCP / MCSE Certification: **Exam 70-220**
Designing Security for a Microsoft Windows 2000 Network

InsideScoop to MCP / MCSE Certification: **Exam 70-221**
Designing a Microsoft Windows 2000 Network Infrastructure

InsideScoop to MCP / MCSE Certification: **Exam 70-227**
Installing, Configuring, and Administering Microsoft Internet Security
and Acceleration (ISA) Server 2000, Enterprise Edition

InsideScoop to MCP / MCSE Certification: **Exam 70-270**
Installing, Configuring, and Administering Microsoft Windows XP Professional

InsideScoop to MCP / MCSE Certification: **Exam 70-290**
Managing and Maintaining a Microsoft Windows Server 2003 Environment

InsideScoop to MCP / MCSE Certification: **Exam 70-291**
Managing, and Maintaining a Microsoft Windows Server 2003 Network Infrastructure

InsideScoop to MCP / MCSE Certification: **Exam 70-292**
Managing and Maintaining a Microsoft Windows Server 2003
Environment for an MCSA Certified on Windows 2000

InsideScoop to MCP / MCSE Certification: **Exam 70-293**
Planning and Maintaining a Microsoft Windows Server 2003 Network Infrastructure

InsideScoop to MCP / MCSE Certification: **Exam 70-294**
Plan and Maintain a Microsoft Windows Server 2003 Active Directory Infrastructure

InsideScoop to MCP / MCSE Certification: **Exam 70-296**
Planning, Implementing, and Maintaining a Microsoft Windows Server 2003
Environment for an MCSE Certified on Windows

InsideScoop to MCP / MCSE Certification: **Exam 70-297**
Designing Microsoft Windows Server 2003 Active Directory and Network Infrastructure

InsideScoop to MCP / MCSE Certification: **Exam 70-298**
Designing Security for a Microsoft Server 2003 Network

InsideScoop to MCP / MCSE Certification: **Exam 70-299**
Implementing and Administering Security in a Microsoft Windows Server 2003 Network

ExamInsight: TotalRecall IT Insight Certification Book Series:

ExamInsight For MCP / MCSE Certification: **Exam 70-210**
Managing Microsoft Windows 2000 Professional

ExamInsight For MCP / MCSE Certification: **Exam 70-216**
Implementing and Administering a Microsoft Windows 2000 Network Infrastructure

ExamInsight For MCP / MCSE Certification: **Exam 70-217**
Managing a Microsoft Directory Services Infrastructure

ExamInsight For MCP / MCSE Certification: **Exam 70-219**
Designing a Windows 2000 Directory Services Infrastructure

ExamInsight For MCP / MCSE Certification: **Exam 70-220**
Designing Security for a Microsoft Windows 2000 Network

ExamInsight For MCP / MCSE Certification: **Exam 70-221**
Designing a Microsoft Windows 2000 Network Infrastructure

ExamInsight For MCP / MCSE Certification: **Exam 70-227**
Installing, Configuring, and Administering Microsoft Internet Security and Acceleration (ISA) Server 2000, Enterprise Edition

ExamInsight For MCP / MCSE Certification: **Exam 70-270**
Installing, Configuring, and Administering Microsoft Windows XP Professional

ExamInsight For MCP / MCSE Certification: **Exam 70-290**
Managing and Maintaining a Microsoft Windows Server 2003 Environment

ExamInsight For MCP / MCSE Certification: **Exam 70-291**
Managing, and Maintaining a Microsoft Windows Server 2003 Network Infrastructure

ExamInsight For MCP / MCSE Certification: **Exam 70-292**
Managing and Maintaining a Microsoft Windows Server 2003 Environment for an MCSA Certified on Windows 2000

ExamInsight For MCP / MCSE Certification: **Exam 70-293**
Planning and Maintaining a Microsoft Windows Server 2003 Network Infrastructure

ExamInsight For MCP / MCSE Certification: **Exam 70-294**
Plan and Maintain a Microsoft Windows Server 2003 Active Directory Infrastructure

InsidersChoice to MCP / MCSE Certification: **Exam 70-296**
Planning, Implementing, and Maintaining a Microsoft Windows Server 2003 Environment for an MCSE Certified on Windows

ExamInsight For MCP / MCSE Certification: **Exam 70-297**
Designing Microsoft Windows Server 2003 Active Directory and Network Infrastructure

ExamInsight For MCP / MCSE Certification: **Exam 70-298**
Designing Security for a Microsoft Server 2003 Network:

InsidersChoice to MCP / MCSE Certification: **Exam 70-299**
Implementing and Administering Security in a Microsoft Windows Server 2003 Network

InsidersChoice: TotalRecall's Insiders Certification System Series:

InsidersChoice to MCP / MCSE Certification: Exam 70-270
Installing, Configuring, and Administering Microsoft Windows XP Professional

InsidersChoice to MCP / MCSE Certification: Exam 70-290
Managing and Maintaining a Microsoft Windows Server 2003 Environment

InsidersChoice to MCP / MCSE Certification: Exam 70-291
Managing, and Maintaining a Microsoft Windows Server 2003 Network Infrastructure

InsidersChoice to MCP / MCSE Certification: Exam 70-292
Managing and Maintaining a Microsoft Windows Server 2003
Environment for an MCSA Certified on Windows 2000

InsidersChoice to MCP / MCSE Certification: Exam 70-293
Planning and Maintaining a Microsoft Windows Server 2003 Network Infrastructure

InsidersChoice to MCP / MCSE Certification: Exam 70-294
Plan and Maintain a Microsoft Windows Server 2003 Active Directory Infrastructure

InsidersChoice to MCP / MCSE Certification: Exam 70-296
Planning, Implementing, and Maintaining a Microsoft Windows Server 2003
Environment for an MCSE Certified on Windows

InsidersChoice to MCP / MCSE Certification: Exam 70-297
Designing Microsoft Windows Server 2003 Active Directory and Network Infrastructure

InsidersChoice to MCP / MCSE Certification: Exam 70-298
Designing Security for a Microsoft Server 2003 Network

InsidersChoice to MCP / MCSE Certification: Exam 70-299
Implementing and Administering Security in a Microsoft Windows Server 2003 Network

ExamWise: TotalRecall IT Insight Certification Book Series:

ExamWise For MCP / MCSE Certification: Exam 70-210
Managing Microsoft Windows 2000 Professional

ExamWise For MCP / MCSE Certification: Exam 70-216
Implementing and Administering a Microsoft Windows 2000 Network Infrastructure

ExamWise For MCP / MCSE Certification: Exam 70-217
Managing a Microsoft Directory Services Infrastructure

ExamWise For MCP / MCSE Certification: Exam 70-219
Designing a Windows 2000 Directory Services Infrastructure

ExamWise For MCP / MCSE Certification: Exam 70-220
Designing Security for a Microsoft Windows 2000 Network

ExamWise For MCP / MCSE Certification: Exam 70-221
Designing a Microsoft Windows 2000 Network Infrastructure

ExamWise For MCP / MCSE Certification: Exam 70-227
Installing, Configuring, and Administering Microsoft Internet Security and Acceleration (ISA) Server 2000, Enterprise Edition

ExamWise For MCP / MCSE Certification: Exam 70-270
Installing, Configuring, and Administering Microsoft Windows XP Professional

ExamWise For MCP / MCSE Certification: Exam 70-290
Managing and Maintaining a Microsoft Windows Server 2003 Environment

ExamWise For MCP / MCSE Certification: Exam 70-291
Managing, and Maintaining a Microsoft Windows Server 2003 Network Infrastructure

ExamWise For MCP / MCSE Certification: Exam 70-292
Managing and Maintaining a Microsoft Windows Server 2003 Environment for an MCSA Certified on Windows 2000

ExamWise For MCP / MCSE Certification: Exam 70-293
Planning and Maintaining a Microsoft Windows Server 2003 Network Infrastructure

ExamWise For MCP / MCSE Certification: Exam 70-294
Plan and Maintain a Microsoft Windows Server 2003 Active Directory Infrastructure

ExamWise For MCP / MCSE Certification: Exam 70-296
Planning, Implementing, and Maintaining a Microsoft Windows Server 2003 Environment for an MCSE Certified on Windows

ExamWise For MCP / MCSE Certification: Exam 70-297
Designing Microsoft Windows Server 2003 Active Directory and Network Infrastructure

ExamWise For MCP / MCSE Certification: Exam 70-298
Designing Security for a Microsoft Server 2003 Network

ExamWise For MCP / MCSE Certification: Exam 70-299
Implementing and Administering Security in a Microsoft Windows Server 2003 Network

TotalRecall Certification Publications
CompTIA Titles

InsideScoop: TotalRecall's Complete Certification System Series:

InsideScoop to CompTIA A+ Hardware:	Exam 220-301
InsideScoop to CompTIA A+ OS:	Exam 220-302
InsideScoop to CompTIA Network+:	Exam N10-001
InsideScoop to CompTIA Security+ (Second Edition):	Exam SY0-101

InsidersChoice: TotalRecall IT Insight Certification Book Series:

InsidersChoice to CompTIA A+ Hardware:	Exam 220-301
InsidersChoice to CompTIA A+ OS:	Exam 220-302
InsidersChoice to CompTIA Network+:	Exam N10-001
InsidersChoice to CompTIA Security+: (Second Edition):	Exam SY0-001

ExamInsight: TotalRecall IT Insight Certification Book Series:

ExamInsight For CompTIA A+ Hardware:	Exam 220-301
ExamInsight For CompTIA A+ OS:	Exam 220-302
ExamInsight For CompTIA Network+:	Exam N10-001
ExamInsight For CompTIA Security+: (Second Edition):	Exam SY0-001

ExamWise: The TotalRecall Question Book Series:

ExamWise For CompTIA A+ Hardware:	Exam 220-301
ExamWise For CompTIA A+ OS:	Exam 220-302
ExamWise For CompTIA Network+:	Exam N10-001
ExamWise For CompTIA Security+ (Second Edition):	Exam SY0-101
ExamWise For CompTIA I-Net+ Certification:	Exam IK0-002
ExamWise For CompTIA Server+ Certification:	Exam SK0-001

Money Back Book Guarantee

This guarantee applies only to books published by TotalRecall Publications, Inc.! We are so confident in our products that we are prepared to offer the following guarantee to YOU, our valued customer: If you do not pass your certification exam after two attempts, we will give money back!

Visit http://www.totalrecallpress.com/
Select "Money Back Book Guarantee" for details.
Registered book purchasers who qualify will receive:

1. 50% cash refund of purchase price
2. free TotalRecall book of equal value

NOTE: You must pay for shipping and handling.

To qualify for this TotalRecall Guarantee
you must meet these requirements and perform the following tasks:

1. Register your purchase at the TotalRecall web site
   http://www.totalrecallpress.com/
2. Fail the corresponding exam twice (No time Limit)
3. Contact TotalRecall for the RMA # and to claim this guarantee
   Send email to **mailto:Guarantee@totalrecallpress.com**
   Subject must contain your Membership # or Registration #

Ship the following to claim your refund:
1. RMA # from returned email
2. Documents of exam scores for both failed attempts
3. Return the Book to the following address:

TotalRecall Publications, Inc.
Attn: Corby Tate
1103 Middlecreek
Friendswood, TX 77546
888-992-3131 **bfquiz@swbell.net**
281-992-3131
281-482-5390 Fax http://www.bfq.com/ or http://www.bfqd.com

It's a Passing day here at the BeachFront.
Thank you for using the TotalRecall Certification Success Program.
Bruce Moran, President

70-270 Download Instructions

BeachFront Quizzer (BFQ) version 4.0

System Requirements: Windows 95 & 98, Windows NT, XP Windows 2000 and Server 2003 with a minimum of 6 MB hard disk space and 16 MB RAM

The Center For Technology Certification, Inc. will help you accomplish your Microsoft Certifications. This state of art software program is designed to cut your study time in half, and get you to a passing level in the easiest and shortest amount of time possible. The program will adapt to you personally, and then lay out a prioritized study plan that will visually show you your progress on a day to day basis. When the software has recognized that you are at a passing level in each objective category, you're ready to sit for the exam! It's really that easy!!

Installation Instructions:

70-270 Practice Exam with eBook and Engine Download

1. Go to http://snipurl.com/EC70-270 and download the Special Edition practice exam ZIP file to a folder on your hard drive.
2. Open the WinZip file and Execute Quiz32.exe OR Execute SetupBFQ.bat to install the practice exam

This will install all softwre files:

4. Open the LicenseKey.txt file Copy and Insert the 12 digit number **License Key** when requested or type in the following License Key Numbers when requested.

Download Exam: http://snipurl.com/EC70-270

BFQ Microsoft Windows XP Professional Special Edition = **286274647880**

The software is very user friendly.

After the program is installed Click on the Help button menu

Select contents for the on-screen manual. (You may want to print the Help File)

We are here to support you all the way. If you have any technical questions on the content, make sure you contact us. We are very proud of our pass rate, and we want you to contribute.

Please let me know that the download and installation worked properly.

Thank you for purchasing our product and

Good Luck with your exam!

Sales: 877-654-2265 or 727-450-0476

Technical Support: bruce@financialexams.com

888-992-3131 or 281-992-3131

281-482-5390 Fax

Good Luck with your certification!

THIS IS BOOK IS GUARANTEED:See details at www.totalrecallpress.com

Made in United States
Orlando, FL
04 November 2026

90208240R00374